Commemoration Book
Chelm (Poland)

Translation of
Yisker-bukh Chelm

Original Book Edited by:

M. Bakalczuk

Originally published in Johannesburg, 1954

A Publication of JewishGen, INC
Edmond J. Safra Plaza, 36 Battery Place, New York, NY 10280
646.494.5972 | info@JewishGen.org | www.jewishgen.org

©JewishGen, Inc. 2021. All Rights Reserved
An affiliate of New York's Museum of Jewish Heritage – A Living Memorial to the Holocaust

Commemoration Book Chelm (Poland)
Translation of *Yisker-bukh Chelm*

Copyright © 2021 by JewishGen, INC All rights reserved.
First Printing: December 2021, Tevet 5782

Editor of Original Yizkor Book: M. Bakalczuk
Project Coordinator: Leah Z. Davidson
Layout and Name Indexing: Jonathan Wind
Reproduction of Photographs: Sondra Ettlinger
Cover Design: Rachel Kolokoff Hopper

This book may not be reproduced, in whole or in part, including illustrations in any form (beyond that copying permitted by Sections 107 and 108 of the U.S. Copyright Law and except by reviewers for public press), without written permission from the publisher.

JewishGen INC. is not responsible for inaccuracies or omissions in the original work and makes no representations regarding the accuracy of this translation. Digital images of the original book's contents can be seen online at the New York Public Library website or the Yiddish Book Center website.

Printed in the United States of America by Lightning Source, Inc.

Library of Congress Control Number (LCCN): 2021949983

ISBN: 978-1-954176-23-2 (hard cover: 628 pages, alk. paper)

About JewishGen.org

JewishGen, an affiliate of the Museum of Jewish Heritage - A Living Memorial to the Holocaust, serves as the global home for Jewish genealogy.

Featuring unparalleled access to 30+ million records, it offers unique search tools, along with opportunities for researchers to connect with others who share similar interests. Award winning resources such as the Family Finder, Discussion Groups, and ViewMate, are relied upon by thousands each day.

In addition, JewishGen's extensive informational, educational and historical offerings, such as the Jewish Communities Database, Yizkor Book translations, InfoFiles, Family Tree of the Jewish People, and KehilaLinks, provide critical insights, first-hand accounts, and context about Jewish communal and familial life throughout the world.

Offered as a free resource, JewishGen.org has facilitated thousands of family connections and success stories, and is currently engaged in an intensive expansion effort that will bring many more records, tools, and resources to its collections.

Please visit https://www.jewishgen.org/ to learn more.

Executive Director: Avraham Groll

About the JewishGen Yizkor Book Project

Yizkor Books (Memorial Books) were traditionally written to memorialize the names of departed family and martyrs during holiday services in the synagogue (a practice that still exists in many synagogues today).

Over the centuries, as a result of countless persecutions and horrific atrocities committed against the Jews, Yizkor Books (Sefer Zikaron in Hebrew) were expanded to include more historical information, such as biographical sketches of famous personalities and descriptions of daily town life.

Following the Holocaust, the idea of remembrance and learning took on an urgent and crucial importance. Survivors of the Holocaust sought out other surviving residents of their former towns to memorialize and document the names and way of life of those who were ruthlessly murdered by the Nazis. These remembrances were documented in Yizkor Books, hundreds of which were published in the first decades after the Holocaust.

Most of these books were published privately, or through landsmanshaftn (social organizations comprised of members originating from the same European town or region) that still existed, and were often distributed free of charge. Sadly, the languages used to document these crucial histories and links to our past, Yiddish and Hebrew, are no longer commonly understood by a significant percentage of Jews today. As a result, JewishGen has undertaken the sacred responsibility of translating these books into English so that the culture and way of life of these communities will be preserved and transmitted to future generations.

In 1986, a group of farsighted JewishGenners started a project to pool their efforts together in groups based upon their ancestors from each town and donate money to get the Yizkor books of their ancestral towns translated into English. As the translated material became available, it was made accessible for free at www.JewishGen.org/Yizkor. Hardcover copies can be purchased by visiting www.JewishGen.org/Press (see below).

It is our hope that the translation of these books into English (and other languages) will assist the countless Jewish family researchers who are so desperately seeking to forge a connection with their heritage.

Director of JewishGen Yizkor Book Project: Lance Ackerfeld

About the JewishGen Press

JewishGen Press (formerly the Yizkor Books-in-Print Project) is the publishing division of JewishGen.org and provides a venue for the publication of non-fiction books pertaining to Jewish genealogy, history, culture, and heritage.

In addition to the Yizkor Book category, publications in the Other Non-Fiction category include Shoah memoirs and research, genealogical research, collections of genealogical and historical materials, biographies, diaries and letters, studies of Jewish experience and cultural life in the past, academic theses, and other books of interest to the Jewish community.

Please visit https://www.jewishgen.org/press/ to learn more.

Director of JewishGen Press: Joel Alpert
Managing Editor - Jessica Feinstein
Publications Manager - Susan Rosin

Notes to the Reader

The images in the original book were reproduced from photographs from the time of the first edition. These reproductions were already of poor quality, being pre-war and at least 30 or more years old. As a result the images in the book are not very good and the best achievable.

A reader can view the original scans of the book on the websites listed below.

The original book can be seen online at the New York Public Library site:

https://digitalcollections.nypl.org/items/dc2d9bf0-6498-0133-0d33-00505686d14e

or

at the Yiddish Book Center web site:

https://www.yiddishbookcenter.org/collections/yizkor-books/yzk-nybc313722/bakalczuk-felin-meilech-yizker-bukh-khelm

To obtain a list of all Shoah victims from Chelm, the reader should access the Yad Vashem web site listed below; one can also search for specific family names using family name option. These lists are continually updated by Yad Vashem, so it is worthwhile to periodically search these lists.

There is more valuable information (including the Pages of Testimony, etc.) available on this website: http://yvng.yadvashem.org

A list of all books available from JewishGen Press along with prices is available at: https://www.jewishgen.org/press/

Acknowledgements

We, who are members of the Chelmer Organization of Israel, are mostly second and third generations after the Holocaust.

We were not born in Chelm, but our parents and grandparents, who survived the war and came to Israel and other countries in the world, told us with nostalgia, warmth and longing stories about their former life in Chelm.

The stories were vivid and detailed, so when we arrived in Chelm we, the second and third generations, felt as if we were at home. We were "infected with the Chelm bug" and together with a local Polish group, we work to revive the "Phoenix" of the Jewish community of Chelm, which was so brutally erased and did not survive after World War II.

This book is an important and central part of this activity of commemorating the heritage of the Jewish community of Chelm.

We would like to thank all those involved in this important commemoration project.

Ben-Zion Levkovitz

Chairperson of the Chelmer Organization of Israel

November 2021

Credits for Book Cover

Front Cover Photo:
Fajga and Mordechai Rozenknopf, residents of Chelm who were murdered in Chelm at the beginning of the war, photo courtesy of Shlomit Beck.

Front Cover Background Photo:
The eastern wall of the magnificent Chelm synagogue, page 66 [101]

Front and Back Cover Background Color and Texture: Rachel Kolokoff Hopper

Back Cover Photographs (top to bottom):
Charming Jewish children, Sulka and Leibl Nisenbaum, who were annihilated by the Hitler murderers, page 56 (88);
Musical band at the Lines HaTsedek in Chelm, page 76 [112];
Wolf and Chaya Ruchl Waserman,
parents of Manasha, Shlomo and Shneier Waserman, page 59 [94].

Back Cover Background Photo: *Fall Grass* by Rachel Kolokoff Hopper

Back Cover Poem: *Spring in the Old Country,* by Hilel Szagel, page 304 [405, 406]

GeoPolitical Information

Chełm, Poland is located at 51°08' N 23°30' E and 132 miles SE of Warszawa

	Town	District	Province	Country
Before WWI (c. 1900):	Chełm	Chełm	Lublin	Russian Empire
Between the wars (c. 1930):	Chełm	Chełm	Lublin	Poland
After WWII (c. 1950):	Chełm			Poland
Today (c. 2000):	Chełm			Poland

Alternate Names for the Town:
Chełm [Pol], Chelm [Yid], Khelm [Rus], Kholm [Ukr], Chelem, Khelem, Chołm

Nearby Jewish Communities:

Sielec 7 miles S
Sawin 10 miles NNW
Rejowiec 10 miles WSW
Świerże 12 miles ENE
Opalin, Ukraine 14 miles NE
Kraśniczyn 15 miles SSW
Wojsławice 15 miles S
Siedliszcze 15 miles WNW
Uchanie 17 miles SSE
Krasnystaw 17 miles SW
Dubienka 18 miles ESE
Cyców 19 miles NW
Osowa 20 miles N
Skryhiczyn 20 miles ESE
Skierbieszów 20 miles SSW

Dubeczno 21 miles N
Grabowiec 21 miles S
Łopiennik Górny 21 miles WSW
Trawniki 22 miles W
Izbica 23 miles SW
Tarnogóra 24 miles SW
Biskupice 24 miles W
Lyuboml, Ukraine 24 miles ENE
Gorzków 25 miles WSW
Sobibór 25 miles NNE
Piaski Luterskie 27 miles W
Włodawka 28 miles N
Włodawa 29 miles N
Horodło 29 miles SE
Łęczna 29 miles WNW
Hrubieszów 29 miles SE

Jewish Population: 7,226 in 1900

Map of Poland with **Chelm** indicated

TABLE OF CONTENTS

Article	Author	Page
Preface	Mellech Bakalczuk-Felin	2

HISTORY OF THE JEWS IN CHELM

Article	Author	Page
The Beginning and the History of a Yiddish Community	Dr. P. Friedman	6
The History of the Jews of Chelm	Dr. S. Milner	21
The Myth of Chelm in Jewish Literature	I. Janasowicz	23
The Chelm Stories Are Not So Foolish	Joseph Gotfarsztajn	28
Chelm	S. Wasserman	33
My Home Town	Hersh Sziszler	64
"Bund" and its Social Revolutionistic Work	K. Winik	95
How Chelm Was Saved From a Pogrom in 1905	S. Winer	109
The History of the Jewish Workers Party Poalei-Zion (Left) in Chelm	Shmuel Szargel	111
Jewish Life and Work in Chelm	K. Winik	129
Chelmer Jewish Gymnasie	Chava Biderman-Biale	150
The Fate of the Chelm "Tarbut" School	J. Floimenbolm	154
Concerning the "Zeirei-Zion" Party	S. Beker	155
The Revisionist Party	J. Zilber	158
Chelm Help Zbonsziner Refugees	B. Aminodov	161
The Scouts Association	W. Gotlib	162
Chelm, An Old Beautiful Jewish Town	B. Binsztok	165
How the Peretz Library was established in Chelm	I. Achtman	168

Jewish Theatre	I. Achtman	172
About Posters in Yiddish at the First Anniversary of the Death of Sholem Aleichem	Berl Naturman	177
The Poalei Zion Party in in the Chelm City Council	J. Beker	178
The Artisans Union	H. Handelsman	189
Chelemer Cultural Life	D. Goldreich	195
Skhus Oves un Skhus Katoves [Ancestral Merits and in the Merit of a Jest]	Yisroel Aszendorf	197

MEN OF FAME, PERSONALITIES, TYPES AND CHARACTERS

Men of Fame and Personalities	J. Milner	201
Shmuel Mordekhai (Arthur) Zigelboim	R. Henes	216
Al Kiddush HaShem [In the sanctification of God's name]	R. Zygielboim	222
Dr. Yitzhak Sziper – Deputy from Chelm in the Polish Sejm	K. Winik	227
A Poem About a Chelemer Malamed, a Customs House and Shabbos Shire	Yakov Frydman	232
Moshe Lerer	A. Ajzen	233
About Moshe Lerer: Extracts of the "Lexicon of Yiddish Literature"	S. Kaczergyynski	236
A Jewish Wedding in Chelm in the Old Days	Moshe Lerer	237
About Joseph Milner	N. Gris	239
The Sixty Years of Joseph Milner	H. Herz	240
Samuel Winer	Ch. Wilner-Winer	241
Personalities and Types Who Are No More	H. Shishler	243
The Rebbe, Reb Note	M. Unger	255
Famous Rabbis	J. Kornblit	258
Shlomo Samet	R. Richtszrajber	260

The Fighting Girl of Chelm – Chava Szafran	K. Wasserman	262
Sholom Goldhar	J. Nunison	264
Captain S. Winer – A Brave Fighter against the Enemies of our people	S. Winner	265
Motel Baliar	Baliar (Stoler)	269
Teachers of Chelm	Ben-Aaron	271
Motl Tovya's	J. Linherz	272
Moshe Zamler		273
Feiwl Fryd	H. Sh.	273
K. Waserman and A. Y. Dubelman		275
Leibele Stol, Mendl Stam, and Dr. Yisroel Oks	M. Tenenboim	275
Yisroel Yitzhak Nankin	Y. Ceber	277
The Uncle from Chelm	Sh. Tenenboim	278
Moonlit Nights	Alkwit-Blum	280

MEMOIRS AND NOTES

Chelm A Poem	Hilel Szargel	283
Those I Remember	Pinye Lerer	286
Why Y.L. Peretz Did Not Deliver his Lecture in Chelm, Shavous, 1912	Shmuel Winer	293
Spring in the Old Country	Hilel Szagel	304
Kalayev, the Great Russian Revolutionary – A Chelemer…	I. Milner	305
Hrubiewszower Street	Shloyme Wasserman	314
The Shtibl of the Belzer Hasidim	Moyshe Grinberg	325
A Poem	Chelm	328
A Page of Memories	B. Binshtok	329

Chelm and its Environs	B. Orensztajn	336
Apolin	Khaim Furman	341
Chelm in the Years 1924 to 1931	Chaim Worzoger	344
Chelm As I Remember It	F. Zygielboim	348
Some Memories	B. Alkvit	353
Woislowicz	Y. Kelner	355
Reminiscences	T. Ayzen	356
Jews of My Town	R. Szrojt	358
Light and Shadow	R. Tseber	360
A Day in Chelm	E. Shindler	362
Mayn Shvester Perl	Y. T. Shargel	363

DESTRUCTION OF CHELM

The Slaughter of the Jews in Chelm	L. Kahan	369
The Death March – Chelm-Hrubieshow-Sokal	B. Bruker	374
The Death March	J. Herz	381
Lipa the Butcher from Chelm (Poem)	Schneur Wasserman	388
Whose Am I, Who Is Left for Me?		390
Chelm at the Time of the Hitler Occupation	J.Groskop	392
About the Two Last Actions in Chelm	J. Grinszpan	399
Eyewitness Testimony	I. Iser Zilber	400
Eye Witness Account	G. Libhober	405
Not a City, but a True Cemetery	G. Libhober	408
Eye Witness Account	Yoel Ponsczak	409
Eye Witness Accounts	Manis Zitrin	411

Eye Witness Accounts	Shloime Brustman	413
Between Life and Death	H. Akhtman	414
In the Chelm Work Camp	Yoshe Akhtman	422
Revenge! Revenge!		425
In Those Days	J. G.	427
Habeit Mishamayim U'Reeh		428
Eyewitness Tesimony of Moshe Hochman	M. Hochman	430
A Bottle of Ashes	Avrohom Lew	436
A Conference on Social Self Help		437
During the Days of the Destruction	Khaim Sobol	452
Chelm	Shlomo Wahrzorger	454
The Last Action	M. Milchteich-Lorber	456
Jewish Heroism	K. Binsztok	459
A Gruesome Summation	Y. Fainsztok	460
The Avenger, Esther Terner	A.Y. Kornblit	463
Jewish Avengers		463
On the Tenth Yortsayt of the Slaughter in Chelm	Y. Yoykenen	466
The Miracle of the Last Jews in Chelm	B. Mitzfliker	466
The Suffering, Death and Heroism of Chelemer Landslayt	A. Goldman	468
The Great Catastrophe	S. Brayer	471
Chelm during the Ghetto Rising	B. Alkwit	472
Chelm After the Liberation	Moishe Gantz	475
That Which I Lost Will Never Return		477
When Chelm Fell	Yankev Tsvi Szargel	478
Eyewitness Account	Bela Szargel	481

Chelm	I.I. Sigal	482
Witness Testimony	R. Engiender	484
Poems	Sholem Shtern	485
The End of a Jewish City	H. Sziszler	487

CHELEMER LANDSMANSCHAFTEN

The Chelemer Landsmanschaften in South Africa	H. J. Monty	492
Chelm in America	B. Binsztok	504
The First 26 Years of the Chelemer Branch of the Workman's Circle in New York	S. Winer	513
A Chelemer Story in an American Way	B. Alkwit	516
The Chelemer Landsmanschaften in Paris	Dr. B. Orlean	518
Chelm and Surrounding Areas Society for Mutual Aid in Argentina	J. Eplboim	521
Chelm Landsmanschaften in Australia	R. Zeber	523
Chelmer Jews in Montreal, Canada	I. Achtman	526
Chelmer Jews in Cuba	I. Achtman	528
Chelmer Jews in Brazil	M. Jakobowicz	529
Chelemer Relief in Mexico	L. R.	530
We Plant Trees in the Forest of the Martyrs		532

YIZKOR

Memorial Dedications	536
Necrology - Index to Memorial Dedications	587

NAME INDEX 597

Commemoration Book Chelm
(Poland)

51°08' / 23°30'

Translation of *Yisker-bukh Chelm*

Edited by: M. Bakalczuk

Published in Johannesburg, 1954

In honour of
Aliza Kolker
By Liliane Nisenbaum

In honour of
Frajdla Nisenbaum nee Zygielbau
By Liliane Nisenbaum

Acknowledgments:

Project Coordinator

Leah Z. Davidson

Our sincere appreciation to Avraham Beker, of the Chelm Organization in Israel for permission to put this material on the JewishGen web site.

Our sincere appreciation to Yad Vashem for the submission of the necrology for placement on the JewishGen web site.

Our grateful thanks to Gerald Simon for obtaining the pictures to be included in this translation.

This is from *Yisker-bukh Chelm* (Commemoration book Chelm)
Editors: M. Bakalczuk-Felin, Johannesburg, Former Residents of Chelm, 1954 (Y, 731 pages).

Note: The original book can be seen online at the NY Public Library site: Chelm (1954)

This material is made available by JewishGen, Inc. and the Yizkor Book Project for the purpose of fulfilling our mission of disseminating information about the Holocaust and destroyed Jewish communities. This material may not be copied, sold or bartered without JewishGen, Inc.'s permission. Rights may be reserved by the copyright holder.

JewishGen, Inc. makes no representations regarding the accuracy of the translation. The reader may wish to refer to the original material for verification. JewishGen is not responsible for inaccuracies or omissions in the original work and cannot rewrite or edit the text to correct inaccuracies and/or omissions. Our mission is to produce a translation of the original work and we cannot verify the accuracy of statements or alter facts cited.

Preface

by Meilech Bakalczuk-Felin

This historic monograph *"Chelm"* is issued as a result of the initiative of a very small colony of Chelemer in far-off South Africa, with the help of Landsleit in the Diaspora and in Israel. Surviving Chelemer Jews, spared by fate and providence from the gas-chambers in Sobibor and Maidanek and other extermination centres, and the wonderful intuition which inspired them to go abroad to distant continents, before and during the Hitler period, took upon themselves the duty of immortalizing their home-town in a memorial work. To be sure this book is by no means complete and does not tell of many periods and generations of the Chelemer Jewish community, which existed for roughly 700 years. This book has not been written under normal circumstances of historiography, and the published material about the destruction is mostly the work of untrained and inexperienced writers. The various memoirs, descriptions and notes, evidence and documents were sent in by persons scattered over many countries. It was therefore difficult to synchronize the dates and names and clearly establish the facts and happenings with any exactitude.

There was also no possibility of making any direct contact with Chelemer Jews, who could have supplied important material. Chelm is annihilated and gone. The houses are empty, without a Jewish soul, and the very streets have become a Jewish cemetery, saturated with the blood of Jewish martyrs, who have bequeathed a silent Will: "When we are led to the slaughter, may our souls remain!"

On account of all this it was difficult to collect all the necessary materials. Yet, with great effort, it has been possible to bring together a valuable collection of sources and documents, material and descriptions which unfold before us Jewish life in Chelm - its institutions and Societies, its schools and educational systems, organizations and political parties. There have also been published scientific tracts about its literary works and folk-lore. A very important contribution to the book is the material dealing with the destruction of Chelm, which was the main stimulus to issuing this historical monograph.

In the book are published valuable first-hand evidence and documents about the holocaust in Chelm. How the Nazi monster displayed his bestial cruelty in the first few months of the Blitzkrieg on the 1st December, 1939, in the bloody onslaught and death-march of Chelm, Hrubieszow and Sokol. The physiognomy of Hitlerism, red in tooth and claw, came to the fore - the real nature of Hitler, Streicher and Reinhardt Heidrich, Hans Frank and the S.S. General Globoznik, who was the supervisor over the Lublin reservation and established the death camps of Maidanek and Treblinki.

There was no room for self-deception or illusion that the Jews would survive the Nazi regime. The first Chelm slaughter should have served as sufficient warning, not only to the Chelemer Jews, but to Jews throughout the world that one could not take the German torments and murders as merely a sporadic incidental phenomenon of war.

II

The **death-march in Chelm was** in fact the beginning - the first part of the great Jewish catastrophe.

Already in the olden days, Chelm was a place of renown and many historic writings speak with praise of the work of the Jewish community of Chelm, which occupied a central position amongst Jewish communities in Poland. Together with the famous Jewish centres such as Krakow, Posen and Lemberg, it was deeply rooted in the proud and creative Jewish settlement in Poland where there was Torah and learning, Chassidism, Messianic romanticism, deeply rooted Jewish tradition and active work in the world of the mind. In the field of Jewish industry, commerce and handicraft, as well as in the world of culture, Chelm played its great part.

There is a legend that when the Jews migrated from the West, an epistle fell from heaven, stating:- "Go to Poland! There you will find rest." But in the land of promised rest, Jews have suffered many torments and tribulations, attacks and persecutions.

In various documents we find a catalogue of persecutions and pogroms of Jews in Chelm; including the barbaric holocaust of the Chelemer Cossacks under Chmelnitzki: In the years 1655/1656, was the Jewish population reduced by two-thirds, and in the walls of the ancient synagogue were the graves of a bride and bride-groom who were killed close to the synagogue, during their marriage ceremony.

Danger hovered over Jews in Poland for many generations and I. L. Peretz has commemorated this danger in his Chelemer story: "The Shabbas Goy Struck Jankele - a father of a large family - in the teeth, and took away from him the bread which he was carrying for his family." Then a meeting of all the Chelemer people were called by the Rabbi, because they realized that the danger was great.

In the various periods between one danger and another, Jews in Poland, including those of Chelm, found great moral strength to overcome their torture and troubles and struck anew deep roots in the Polish earth. The Chelm community evolved its own individuality, yet reflected in miniature, the most important qualities of the Polish Jewish community.

On the broad highways of Jewish history in Poland, Chelm occupies an important place. Even though little has remained of its pristine glory, we can see from that little the pulsating and creative forces which have during generations given rise to great names, Rabbis and learned men and modern thinkers. Institutions of all sorts grew. Political parties came into being - parties who fought for political and social liberties and kept vigilance to the very last day when the cataclysm raged over the streets of Chelm. Even under the German occupation, -active social work did not stop. Even between one "action" and another it continued. Proof of this can be found in the Minutes of the *"Conference of Social Self-Help"*, which took place in 1942. At that Conference representatives of Chelm district participated. The Minutes of the Conference which we publish in this Book are the best witness of the high quality and inexhaustible energy of Chelm. The Conference ranged over a wide held such as the fight against the epidemic of typhoid fever, the feeding of the starving, particularly children etc. Chaie Roze Ochs, delegate at the Conference spoke with great responsibility and deep concern about the fate of Jewish children, fearing that they would not survive the horror conditions of the time.

Definite reports about the Resistance Movement in Chelm have not survived. We only know of heroic revolts on the part of individuals.

III

In the course of the death-march, the Germans wanted to exempt Dr. Ochs and send him home, but with great dignity he rejected that offer stating: "Where the Chelm Jews, my brethren are, there I shall be!" He was shot during the death-march. Near the old synagogue, there lived the Lax family. When Mrs. Lax saw in 1940 how the Germans set fire to the Synagogue, she cried out aloud and uttered her protest against their action. As a punishment, the S.S. beat her nearly to death, and while she was still living, threw her into the burning Synagogue.

There has also been published *"The Martyrology of Zalmele the Beker"*, who was thrown by the Hitler murderers into boiling tar and was later crucified. He was under suspicion of having hidden some Jews in his bakery.

It is difficult to decipher and properly to interpret the evidence of Joel Ponsczak about the action at Wlodawa on the 26th October, 1942, he writes as follows:- It was twilight. No shooting was heard. Patrols marched up and down the streets. The hiding place was small and there were more than 20 people crowded into it. The heat was overpowering. At last dawn came. The murderers ran amok through the Jewish streets. All the time shots and the explosion of grenades were heard. The "action" lasted the whole day. Towards evening somebody knocked at our door.

We thought that they were patrols, but it was Mr. Mandel of the Judenrat, who gave us the frightful news of the two days of the "action." 800 people were killed and 3,000 were taken away on foot to Wlodawa. About the last "action" in Chelm on the 6th November 1942, the same Joel Ponsczak writes: "Towards evening my family and I, including my sister and brother-in-law and children, as well as two Slovak Jews, and a certain Samuel Szwarz and his wife, went to the school-house. We had a room to ourselves. There were also Jews in other rooms. They were all my friends and acquaintances. We visited each other during the night. When day broke, the murderers started their butchery. There was an absolute battle in the streets. The firing of machine-guns and explosion of grenades did not cease until evening, when it became calmer.

The above experience of Joel Ponsczak testifies to the existence of a Resistance Movement amongst the Jews of Chelm. He actually speaks of battles in the streets. There were certain individual cases of heroism, like the resistance of Mietek, son of Hersh Velcher, who fought with a Nazi during the death-march and fled to the forest.

It is a fact that the social activity never stopped in Chelm and the passive resistance was strong amongst the Jews of Chelm as is to be seen also from the Minutes of the Conference.

Hope and optimism were always the characteristic traits of the Jewish community in Chelm. This is evidenced in the treasury of folklore which has made the name of Chelm famous. Even though it is now **established that Chelm was in the nature of a fictitious creation of Jewish** humour, there is no doubt that Chelm contributed much to Jewish folklore, always a way of consoling the despair and resignation which might have overwhelmed the Jewish mind oppressed by the hardships of Jewish life.

Now Jewish Chelm has been transformed into a mountain of skeletons. As already mentioned the death sentence was passed on the town on the 1st December 1939. The defenseless Jews were driven from their homes at dawn to the market-square surrounded by S.S. formations and local satellites. The community of Chelemer Jews stood overwhelmed in sorrow and dumb despondency, facing the multitude of murderers and executioners who viewed with hatred and murderous intent the helpless mass. The Jewish old men turned their eyes heavenwards, waiting for a miracle. Perhaps something would happen as is told of former times of woe. But no miracle occurred. The sky was dull and cloudy and they were sealed hermetically in a circle of Nazi and Fascist bayonets and **machine-guns. Nor later was there a miracle** when the Jews perished from hunger and cold, from epidemic and disease. No salvation appeared and when the deportation came, the children's "action" and, at last, the complete annihilation in November 1942, the Germans had done their job thoroughly and had completely liquidated the Jewish population of Chelm.

IV

The published material in this book will demonstrate every stage of the Nazi tactics. The last line had now been written to the chapter of the Jews who had lived in Poland and had been rooted there for hundreds of years.

Over the Jewish ruins, gaunt spectres move in the night; martyred Jews call upon us to remember their tragic end and their glorious past. Until the official historiography is compiled, these Yiskor books with vivid, first-hand information, descriptions and documents will serve the purpose of unfolding the great tragedy of Jewish martyrdom and heroism in the years of the Nazi war against the Jewish people.

With every day and every hour of Jewish life in the clamp of Nazism, they showed the greatest human endurance. After the barbaric holocaust of 1655/1656, the Resolution of the Council of the Four Countries was as follows:- "May God take revenge for the innocent blood which was spilled like water, for the bodies which lay in the fields without burial. Everyone, who has but a spark of honesty must mourn for ages to come!"

This Resolution of the Council of Four Countries should be recalled at the present time. May the *Yiskor Book of Chelm,* together with the other Yiskor books which have appeared and will yet appear, remain an imperishable *"Book of Life"* and an eternal tomb-stone in memory of the six million Jews who were annihilated in our greatest national holocaust.

The History of the Jews in Chelm

The Beginning and the History of a Yiddish Community

Dr. Philip Frydman, America

Translated by Rae Meltzer

About 40 miles from Lublin in the southeasterly direction is Khelm [Chelm]. In Russian the name of the shtetl is "Kholm". The Hebrew origin of the name is Helm, Him, Hel"ma,

The date of the founding of Khelm is not certain. Apparently, a community existed here in the time of the "Ruthenian" [Little-Russian] Duke Roman Mstyslavysh who died in 1205. During his reign he often resided in his official residence in Khelm. Twenty years later during the reign of his son, Danilo Romanovitsh, the town became an official ducal residence, about 1235. He also built a fortress around 1240. When the Tartars invaded Poland they tried to capture Khelm, but the fortress held fast against the Tartars. Because of the security of the fortress and the nature of the terrain, which helped to defend the town, Danilo decided to make Khelm his capital city. In a second Tartar attack in 1261, the town and the fortress were partly destroyed.

In 1377, Khelm and the entire duchy were incorporated into Poland. This was an important event in the development of the state and of Khelm. At that time Poland was a leading power in the economic and political affairs of Eastern Europe. The separation from the static Little Russian regime to the advanced and large Polish state meant new economic opportunities and development for Khelm.

Khelm was situated on the big international commercial routes from the Black Sea to the Baltic Sea into middle Europe. The international trade route brought the first Jews to Khelm. At that time there was intensive colonization in Khelm. From the East came "Ruthenians" and from the West, Polish colonizers.

Since we do not have direct data to tell us when the first Jews settled in Khelm, let us look at the data from the neighboring Jewish communities. We have documents from nearby Lubomil [by the Bug] that a Jewish community existed there from 1370-1382. This, of course, does not confirm that Jews first came there in those years; but it does confirm that during those years Jews were certainly there.

[Page 13]

It is possible to imagine that the Jews had already lived in Lubomil for some time prior to the first recording in a legal document of Jews living in Lubomil. In a neighboring town to the east is Ludmir [Vladimir Volinski] where the Jews are noted around 1171-1180. [This data is questioned by some historians who believe that the reference is not to Ludmir, but to Valdemar in Meklenburg, in northern Germany]. Thus it would appear that in the 13th and 14th Century several Jewish communities existed. We have not yet found any direct documentation for the date when Jews came to Khelm. We will have to appeal to the Talmud for enlightenment on that question.

Among the Jews of Khelm there was a traditional legend, and the elders of the community told this legend around 1900. According to the legend, the oldest Jewish gravestone in the Khelm cemetery is dated 700 years earlier. The local Jewish tradition held that the Jewish community in Khelm was already organized by 1300 when it established its own cemetery. Another, not entirely reliable hypothesis, is based on a quote from "Original Seed" [a publication written around 1200] which refers to the Jews of Khelm and Vladimir. The author of this article was not able to see this rare publication, and he simply reports this unverified data.

Nevertheless a Jewish community existed in Khelm in the 15th century. Around 1900 it was still possible to decipher the dates on the old gravestones in the Jewish cemetery in Khelm. The worthy researcher and first historian of the Jews of Khelm discusses his findings in his work (1,2). According to his findings, the following dates were still legible on the gravestones in 1900.

1 gravestone marked	1442
L gravestone marked	1483
2 gravestones marked	1484
1 gravestone marked	1496

[Page 14]

[2]

It appears that the Jewish community of Khelm was well established and had some rich merchants. In 1492 a Pole mentions a Khelmer Jew, named Yekov, a tax lessee of the Polish King. In that time, a tax lessee was a business that required a lot of capital and brought in a huge profit.

In the 16th century, more facts emerged about the economic life of the Khelmer Jews and the life of the Jewish community.

According to the Polish tax registry of that time [about 1518], the first place in commerce was held by the southeastern part of Poland where the Jews of Lemberg, Khelm, Pshemysh, and Belzer lived. The Jewish merchants played a big role in the commerce of "Red Russia" [Rustshervana].

According to other information from the year 1530, the majority of goods that came through the Lublin tollbooth to the famous Lublin markets belonged to the Belzer, Khelmer and Lemberger merchants. The important Belzer and Khelmer merchants traded [about 1569] in leather, flour, oxen, textiles, wool, and merchandise from the Black Sea.

In that time there were big Jewish capitalists in Khelm. One of them, R'Yehudeh Ahrun from Khelm was appointed by the King to the position of tax collector for the entire district of Khelm [in 1520]. Two years later he was elected to head up the organization of Jewish communities from Lublin, Khelm, and Belzer districts. This was a very important position, which led to Jewish autonomy in Poland and to the significant role played by Khelm in the life of Polish Jews. Documents from 1520 indicate that R'Yehudeh Ahrun was given the title of "Doctor of Jewish Law" [legis mosaicae]. It is possible that he was a Rabbi.

There is information that in that period Jews were farmers. There are documents from the 16th century that show that Jews from Khelm paid the local priest tithes for their fields. The Christian farmers were excused from paying this tithe. The priests would complain whenever a Jew bought a piece of land that the church should not bear the loss from such a transaction and again collected the tithe from the new buyer.

[Page 15]

[3]

The Khelm community at that time belonged to the larger Jewish community in Poland. The first official census of the Jewish population in Poland was held in 1550 with the following census data for Khelm: 371 Jewish souls who lived in 40 houses. A comparison with the census of other larger Jewish communities in Poland were: Cracow, the capital, had a census count of 1800 souls; Posen had 83 Jewish houses, Lemberg 71; Lublin 42; Lubomil 39, Ludmir 30, Belz 22. On the average one can estimate 9-10 souls per Jewish house. In the larger towns and cities, where there were two-and three storied houses, as for example in Posen, there were more than twice as many souls per household.

In that time the Jewish community in Khelm was in debt to the Polish King for 171 florins. Another document of that time gave evidence of the important role the Khelm Jewish community played in the life of Polish Jews. In 1557, King Zygmunt August issued a decree that Jews from Cracow, Posen, Lublin, Lvov [Lemberg], and Khelm were forbidden to involve themselves in matters concerning other Jewish communities. According to the King's decree, Jews could act only on matters involving the community in which they lived and should not get involved in the affairs of another community.

[Page 16]

[4]

It appears that some influential Jews from the aforementioned five communities, or perhaps official community representatives from the "big five" wanted to take the power over all Jewish matters into their own hands and the King issued his decree to protect the smaller communities from usurpation [illegal seizure of power].

From the second half of the 16th century there are a series of archival materials from which we can deduce the pattern of various financial enterprises of the Jews of Khelm. This information was limited and restricted. We learn of local credit operations that were apparently not from the very large financial enterprises of the Khelmer Jews. The information about the income and charitable activities of the largest Jewish banking institutions is missing. In the archival materials that exist, there is reference to financial dealings with the priests. In the years 1577- 1594, many financial transactions between the Russian-Orthodox Bishop of Khelm and the Jews of Khelm are in the archival records. [In Russian the Bishop is called "Vladyke"] This "Vladyke" took out loans from Jews for various amounts ranging from 40 zlotys to as much as 170 zlotys. They were short-term loans for up to 6 months to one year. For that time the amounts were significant. For a loan of 170 zlotys [in 1580] the Bishop had to give, as a guarantee, his entire estate, which was not "small potatoes"; it included several villages and also their houses. In general, "Vladyke" conducted business with the Jews. In 1582, the contract is extended for another 4 years. The Bishop is not only a "borrower", he is also a "lender'. In 1594 he makes a loan of 78 zlotys [plus interest] to a Jew of Khelm.

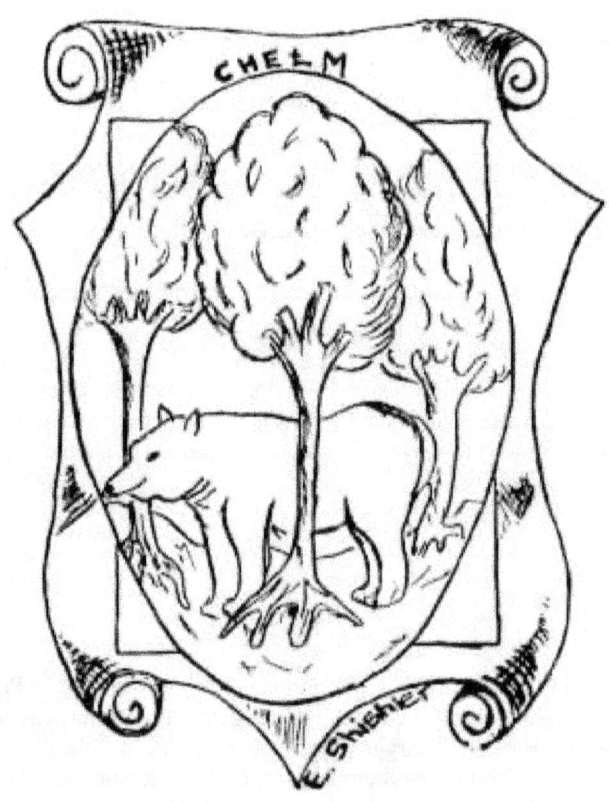

Drawing by E. Shishier of the "Crest & Coat - of - Arms" of Chelm

[Page 17]

[5]

The close economic ties are already evidence that the mutual relations between Jew and non-Jews were not bad. A curious light on these relations comes from another archival source of that time.

Through a mysterious chance, a judicial complaint is reported in the year 1550. The Christian woman "Marushya" files a complaint that the "Jewish Doctor" [which refers to the rabbi "Reb" Yuda], where she was employed as a servant, raped her and she bore him a child. He promised her to provide for the child and he has not kept his word. The priests of Khelm began circling around this "spicy" matter. The Khelmer "Vladyke" [Bishop] Vasily Baka wrote to his superior a report that "the Hebrew [Jewish] Rabbi had a child, a son, with "Marushya" and the child had already been baptized by the priest Sylvester.

The correspondence ends with this report. No Jewish sources about this whole matter were found, and it is therefore difficult to research this affair and decide whether there was any concrete evidence to support the accusations or was it just a frame-up. In general, Jewish sources do not know anything about Reb Yuda and it is almost unbelievable that this event had any connection to R'Yhudh Ahrun, referred to above. In 1522, he was already a man of advanced age. Jewish Law was very strict about acts of prostitution, especially involving a respected representative of the Jewish community and moreover a rabbi.

[Page 18]

[6]

It is possible that this was a process conducted by the priests to pursue a certain Polish cause. In that time the church agitated fiercely for Jewish households to employ Christian domestics, until 1565 when the legislature passed a new law forbidding Jews to employ Christian domestics. The scandal of the Khelmer Rabbi may have been factor in the turn-around of the decree.

It is interesting and characteristic that the opposite attitude prevailed in the judicial complaints about fights between Jews and gentiles. These fights did not have the character of anti-Jewish pogroms. The attackers were not always the gentiles. In one instance the Jews started the assault. In the year 1559 a Jew filed a complaint that he was beaten by the servant of the Bishop. In 1514, a complaint was filed by an employee of the Khelmer "Vladyke" that some Jews severely injured him. In the same year a Jew filed a complaint to the effect that a servant in the Greek Orthodox Church physically attacked him. A third complaint in that same year was from a gentile, claiming that a group of Jews bloodied his nose and destroyed his clothes.

A serious case was reported in the year 1580. The synagogue sexton, Shmeun, declared to the court that "citizen Timosh" with a group of his friends, "armed with bombs, clubs and stones", entered the synagogue on the holy Passover during prayer time. They threw stones and fired their weapons, destroying the roof and 11 doors. They smashed the pulpit and lectern and wounded 4 Jews. They stole various silver and gold ritual objects from the synagogue. The cost of the damage and destruction was estimated by the leaders of the community to be 2,000 zlotys.

[7]

The wounded Jews: Avrum Zakhnovytsh [Avrum Ben Shkhna?], Mashko Yoviovitsh (Moyshe Ben Yual], Yekov Zyv, and the sexton ["Shkolnik" in the original text]. Bysko also brought a complaint to the court. Both complaints were confirmed and supported by the leaders of the community. For the first time we learn the names of the Khelmer community leaders. They were: Pinhas, Shaul, Avrum Festytsh, and Kalmen. Also the sexton, Shmeun, and the "Shkolnik" Bysko were not officers of the synagogue, as we understand it in our day. The sexton Shmeun steps forward as an official representative of the Synagogue. Also Byska the "Shkolnik" is apparently an important officer of the community. The office of "Shkolnik" or "syndicate" [?] in that time meant a judicial or legal consultant and lobbyist for the government posts, church and royal court affairs.

A second less serious event happened two years later. In April, 1582, five Khelmer Jews, including Shaul Novokovytsh, Shloymeh Yakubovitsh, Marek, "Yakubk Doktor" [apparently the Rabbi] and the "Shkolnik" Byska brought a complaint against the director of the local Christian school. The complaint was that the director was drunk and with one of his students came into the Synagogue during prayer time and began to mock the prayer service. They punched the cantor in the face and tore his clothes. They stole some candelabras and went away. During the night at 3:00 a.m., the director returned with some of his students with clubs and burning torches. The Synagogue was locked for the night, and the drunken adventurer -director ran to the house of an officer of the Jewish community screaming, "Get up you robber, you Shkolnik! Your Synagogue is burning!

[Page 19]

[8]

Whether the director really intended to set fire to the synagogue, or he was just threatening, cannot be confirmed from his actions.

The names of the Jews who filed a complaint were the elite leaders of the community. The five who filed the complaint included 2 who held high office in the community [the Rabbi and the "Shkolnik"]; perhaps the other 3 who were involved in filing the complaint were not private citizens.

Almost all the above mentioned rogues and adventurers were from the circles that were directly connected to the church. This was not an accident. There were other similar accidents. Often students from Christian schools attacked Jews, as the Jews walked past the church, cathedrals and Christian schools. These types of attacks upon Jews occurred in many Polish towns. Often the goal was to arouse anti-Semitic baiting or a pogrom. Sometimes the purpose was to force Jews to pay a bribe to the students and to the church. Perhaps, these attacks on Jews were more common and severe in the Khelm district than elsewhere. In the 18th century, a special assessment for the church workers in the Lubliner and Khelmer district was instituted where none had previously been levied.

But all these events pale in comparison to the catastrophe that befell the Jews of Khelm and all the Jews of southeastern Poland when the Cossacks and Tartars attacked from the Ukraine.

[Page 20]

[9]

In Khelm, where at that time about 400 Jews lived, The Cossacks beleaguered the Castle in November 1648. The Cossacks burned the Castle and the entire town. In this fire many Jews were killed. Reb Nison Hanover, the classic chronicler, does not mention the massacre by the Cossacks in Khelm. Other sources say this explicitly. A book published in Cracow in 1650 by an author who came from a neighboring town [Zamoshtsh or Shebreshin] refers to the massacre of 1648 in his book. In the "prayer for the dead" contemporaneous with the massacre, the martyrs of Khelm are mentioned. It appears that the pogroms were repeated once again in 1655-1656, when the Cossacks together with the Moskoviter assaulted Poland and the area of Lublin and Khelm. The chronicle of Shmual Fybysh describes the evil government decrees in the years 1655-1656 when almost all the Khelmer Jews were slaughtered! It is difficult to ascertain how much of this information is supported by the facts, and how much of it is exaggerated. In spite of these events, the Jewish community in Khelm quite quickly revived.

The Christian citizens were apparently astonished by the speedy recovery of the Jewish community in Khelm. They used their political clout in 1659 to organize an economic action against the Jews demanding that officials should prohibit Jews from making and selling liquor. This business was the major source of income for Jews during that time.

[10]

The "Dominicans" also wanted to use the political situation for their own purposes. They filed a lawsuit demanding land that had belonged to the Jews of Khelm. This land was taken from the Jews by the Dominicans during the pogroms by the Cossacks. When the Jews were able to return to Khelm and claim their land, the priests insisted that the land belonged to them. Similar situations happened in other Polish towns, during and after pogroms. Attempts were made by gentiles to steal or confiscate Jewish inheritances. The provisional legislature of the Bratslaver province, which included Khelm, supported the demands of the Dominicans and insisted that their deputies in the central parliament in Warsaw do the same [1666]

In general, the situation of the Jews of Khelm got worse. All the Jewish communities, including Khelm, had heavy expenses after the Cossacks onslaught and destruction. In 1684, we find the first record of a huge loan that the Jews were forced to take from the priests. In that year, the leaders of the Jewish community of Khelm, Itska Aronovytsh, Haym Shmeunovitsh, Itska Levkovitsh and Zusman Levkovitsh took a loan of 1 000 Polish zlotys from the priest of Dubno. On this sum they had to pay annually, on St. Bartholomew's holy day, interest of 10%. After the death of the priest, the interest would be reduced to 8% forever. Of the 8%, half would go to the Catholic Church of Khelm and the other half to the magistrate of Khelm. The contract does not say anything about paying back the principal investment; but stipulates that the interest must be paid forever. These conditions make the contract very dubious. In this time there were many instances of extortion from Jews. This was a dark and dreadful time for the Jews because the Catholic anti-Semitism was very strong and they constantly incited ritual-murder and other frame-ups.

[Page 21]

Often the churches or the priests threatened to extort huge sums of money from the Jews. They "prettied up" the extortion in various ways. The Jewish community paid a bribe over and above the sum of the loan, which loan they never received. They often obligated themselves to pay a high interest rate on a loan, which was actually a bribe for a fictitious loan. Perhaps, the Khelmer Jew's loan was also a bribe to avoid a fateful sentence. Whether the loan was real or fictitious, the important point is that this is evidence that the situation of the Jewish community in Khelm was not as good as in previous times.

The Jewish community in Khelm slowly pulled out of the severe crises of the 17th century. Jewish commerce began to thrive again, particularly the export of leather to Prussia and Silesia. In the export of leather, the Jews of Warsaw and Khelm played a major role. The leather trade with Breslau and Silesia was brisk. In 1722 several Jewish families settled in Breslau. Among the 159 Polish Jews who settled in Breslau, it was recorded that 9 were from Khelm. In the years 1763-1764, reference was made to the famous trading fairs in Breslau, which attracted many merchants, among them Jews from Khelm. The horse trade for export and domestic commerce, in both Poland and Lithuania, was controlled by Jews. A Polish writer, using a pseudonym "khelmer", complained bitterly in a Polish-Warsaw newspaper [end of the 18th century] about the Jewish trade in horses. He recalled that in 1554 Jews were forbidden to trade in horses. Luckily, his complaints had no practical effect. However, a new tax on leather merchants aroused great concern and confusion among the Jewish leather merchants.

[12]

In 1789 the Polish legislature decided to levy a new tax. The butchers had to pay the tax on every head of cattle, and they also had to pay a stamp tax on every calf, sheep and goat. At the same time the Polish legislature passed a law forbidding the export of raw leather, thus banning and outlawing the participation of Jews in the leather business. This new law was a serious blow to Jewish merchants, leather tanners, and artisans. It started consternation in the Jewish community, which prepared for speculation and a big rise in prices. The Jewish leather merchants, to avoid severe financial losses, hid their leather and pelts. The Polish government punished the Jewish tanners and artisans in the Khelmer and Krasnostaver region, confiscating their leather reserves, and distributing this leather among the gentile tanners and shoemakers.

Meanwhile, the Jewish community in Khelm once again pulled together after the discriminations and great hardships of the second half of the 1700s. The Khelmer community once again achieved prominence in the Jewish community of Poland, but she never regained the great status she once held.

In the census of 1765, the Jewish community of Khelm reached 1,418 souls, and in the whole Khelm region, the Jewish population was 9,787. The census did not count children less than one year of age because they were not taxed, and so the government was not interested in including them in the census. A more factual count would add about 82 children less than one year of age, bringing the total population to about 1,500. Even this figure is an undercount because the Jewish community hid the very poor Children and orphans over age one [an additional 20-30%] to reduce their head-tax.

[Page 22]

[13]

However, during that time Khelm no longer belonged to the larger Jewish communities in the land. According to the census of 1765, twelve large Jewish communities had populations of over 2,000. They were:

| Brod | 7,200 |
| Lemberg | 61,160 |

| Clita [Leshno] | 51,000 |
| Cracow | 3,500 |

Communities that were close neighbors of Khelm had census counts as follows:

| Lublin | 1,460 |
| Ludmir | 1,400 |

In the above census data, the children under one year of age are included. The "hidden" population is not included in this census.

The Khelmer community regained an honorable place in the activities and commitments of the autonomous organization of Poland. The Council of Four Lands, an autonomous Jewish governing body in Eastern Europe in the 16th-18th century, became the responsibility of several smaller autonomous provinces. One of these was the Council of the Khelmer-Belzer Land, which had their meetings most of the time in Lubomil. Deputies from Khelm were active in both the Khelmer-Belzer Land Council and the Council of Four Lands. In 1739, the Deputy from Khelm, R' Hershl, was the Head of the Council of Four Lands. [Reliable information about the Khelm deputies is presented in the following chapter.]

[Page 23]

[14]

In the years of the great reform organization in Poland, and in the time of the great Four-Year Assembly [1788-1792] when open discussions were held about the question of reform in behalf of the Jews and the Jewish community, one of the spokesman was the Khelmer Rabbi R'Hyrsh Br' Yusyf. Generally, few writers participated in this discussion; mostly the active participants were adherents of the "Enlightenment" movement, and fervent supporters of reform, The only Rabbi among them was Hershko Yazefovytsh, and he was the only one who had the energy and courage to represent the national - conservative Jewish position. His pamphlet, which was published in Polish in 1789, was called "Passing Thoughts About the Way to Make Polish Jews Productive Citizens for the Nation." An answer to Yazefovytsh's pamphlet was published by the Polish deputy Mateaus Butrymovytsh, a great friend of the Jews and passionate adherent of radical reform of Jewish life in the spirit of the Enlightenment and assimilation. Hersh Yazefovytsh pointed out that such reforms limit the function of Jewish autonomy and abolish separate Jewish clothing, create general secular schools for Jewish children; altogether, this can result in the disturbance of Jewish traditions and religion. There is the hypothesis that Hersh Yazefovytsh was a member of the commission that the Four-Year Assembly created in order to prepare a project for a new Jewish Law. The exact details supporting this hypothesis are lacking.

[Page 24]

[15]

The reform laws affecting the Jews did not pass, because Poland was wiped off the map of the independent countries of Europe and divided among her 3 powerful neighbors. Khelm belonged to Austria from 1795-1807, and from 1807-1812 to the Great Duchy of Warsaw. From 1812-1915, it was ruled by Russia, and a portion by the Congress of Poland.

During the division of Poland, the old trade roads were disturbed and abandoned. These old routes had a huge influence on the development of Jewish commerce in Khelm. The new economic situation and the new roads and routes were not as favorable for Khelm, which was located in a relegated corner of southeast Congress-Poland. The political situation in Khelm became very tense. The Russian government began a strong political Russification program, especially after the failure of the Polish Uprising of 1863. In the Khelm region lived many peasants who belonged to the "Uniate Church of Little Russia", and were Greek Catholics.

The Russians put a great deal of pressure on them to leave their Church and join the Greek-Orthodox Church. In 1875, the Greek Catholic Church was outlawed, which initiated a bitter 30-year struggle on the part of the Greek Catholics [Ruthenians] against the Russian government. There were bloody demonstrations, strikes, arrests, bitter press campaigns, etc. In order to strengthen the Russification program, the Russian government circles began, at the end of 1880, to consider a plan to create a separate Khelmer region and unite this region with Russia. Just short of the start of WW I, the Russian Duma [Parliament] on January l, 1913, made a decision to create a new region from parts of the Lublin and Shedlets region.

[Page 24]

[16]

The Duma's decision aroused a storm of protests in the Polish population world-wide. Understandably, the political tension did not help the economic stability and development of Khelm. To the old anti-Semitic population was added the reactionary Russian officials and clergy. Their attitude toward the Jews had a spokesman who was a highly placed Russian priest. During his visit to Khelm in 1889, his travel book was published in an influential Russian newspaper. The priest, Gorodetsky, writes in the newspaper that the Jews of Khelm made a very negative impression upon him. He refers to the Jews as "parasites in the guise of human beings", and writes further that in "the major part of town, the small Jewish houses with tiny shops, where the dirty Jewesses and Jews are pushing from every door." The statistics indicate that the Jewish population in Khelm had sharply decreased from what it was in 1900.

The Jewish households began to grow and by 1920, had increased three-fold; the Jewish population in the past 40 years increased only two-fold. However, trade and commerce were once again in Jewish hands. According to Dr. Shyper's data, in 1921, 88.3% of commerce and trade in Khelm was in Jewish hands, and in 1926, 82% was in Jewish hands.

Year	Total Population of Khelm	Jewish Population	% of Jews
1827	21,793	1,902	1%
1856	3,662	2,493	68.0%
1893	11,887	6,356	53.5%
1910	17,555	7,814	44.5%
1921	23,221	12,064	51.1%
1931	29,074	13,537	46.5%

[Page 25]

[17]

At the outbreak of World War II there were between 15,000 and 18,000 Jews living in Khelm. This number probably does not take into account the refugees who ran east and south during the "September Panic"; in their flight, they got stuck in Khelm. "The town [Khelm] is beleaguered by "wanderers " writes one of the "refugees" in his memoirs .... they wait outside the bakeries and food shops ...... thousands of "wanderers" with starving faces and dry, cracked lips."

The true Hell started when the Germans entered the town. Robberies, torture and murder according to the familiar Nazi pattern raged in Khelm. At the end of 1939, in November or December, the Nazi S.S. conducted their first "Aktzion " of dreadful tortures. They forced between 1700-2000 Jews to the marketplace and then drove them brutally toward Sokol and Belzshets and the Russian border [eastern Galicia was occupied at that time by Russia.] During the forced march of the Jews, the Nazi SS used savage and ruthless attacks upon them and shot them to death. The unfortunate Jews on the march died on the way of exhaustion, hunger, and disease.

The barbaric "liquidation-aktzion" happened in Khelm in December, 1942. A Polish woman, connected to the underground movement, made a report immediately after the "liquidation-aktzion". She lived among Jews and experienced the horror and brutality of the aktzion Briefly, the most important points in her report are:

In Khelm the Nazis did not organize a ghetto. Jews, until the end lived together with Polish neighbors, in the same streets and their own houses. In Khelm, from 1940 until October, 1942, people were anxiously silent.

[Page 26]

Perhaps in the quieter moments of life in Khelm, under the Nazis, when feeling frightened, they sang the peculiar song "Habt Mshmym Vrah." (Hebrew). This song was published by Sh. Kaczergynsky in his collection, *Songs of the Ghettos and Camps [Lagers]*, (New York, 1948), p. 120-121. This song was carried by a Khelmer Jew, Yual Pontshak. The song is very original and expresses strong feelings. The SS "aktsye" [aktzion] began in the night of the 5th-6th December, 1942. The "aktsye" was to end on the 15th of December, but the date was moved to December 25th. The Jewish population of Khelm, at that time, was about 11,000. The rest, one may conclude, perished from persecution, forced labor in the camps, hunger and illness. The region around Khelm, Vlodave and Hrubyeshov, as well as the rest of the Lublyner region, had many work camps in 1940-1941. In these work camps, Jews were subjected to inhuman conditions and forced to do very hard labor, A partial list of 20 work-camps in the region around Khelm, Vkodave, and Hrubyeshov is shown below:

Name of Camp	Number of Workers
Vytkov	[more than 350 Jewish workers]
Verashyn	11,060
Oshtshov	1,500
Dolhobitshov	number unknown
Myrtsh	750
Varenzsh	number unknown
Maryshyn	number unknown
Obrovyets	200
Turkovyts	250

[Page 27]

[19]

Name of Camp	Number of Jewish Workers
Bushne	100
Aukhrynov	?
Sovyn	140
Luteh	200
Osov	200
Rude Bay Opalyn	650
Krykhov	?
Dorohusk	150
Shelyshtshe-Baym-Vyepsh	146
Kamyen	115
Zshmudzsh	200

Of the more than 5,700 Jewish workers recorded on the list, about 1,700 were from Warsaw, the rest from Khelm and the surrounding shtetlach. Research data collected after the war by the Polish State Commission Researching German Crimes produced the following lists from the forced labor camps.

Tshernyeyov	200 Yiddish Workers
Konyn	150

Additional information for those mentioned previously:

Myrtshe	3,000
Osov	{illegible number}
{illegible name}	300
Krykhov	2,500

[20]

The long-lived work camp in Krykhov was liquidated in March 1944.

11,000 Jews survived in Khelm [in spite of constant persecution] until the end in 1942. During the December "aktsyeh" [aktion] 7,000-8,000 Jews were murdered or sent to the Sobibor death camp.

"About 3,000 Jews hid, or ran away and later joined various partisan groups." From the report of the Polish woman referred to earlier. Her report continues, "The liquidation was carried out by the Nazi SS. The Germans were heavily armed. They had revolvers, hand grenades, and machine guns. In order to liquidate the thousands of Jews they were forced to assemble in front of the church. The Nazi SS used machine guns to kill individual men and women. Those who tried to run away were killed with revolvers and hand grenades. Civilian Germans also participated in these murders of Jews. The German burgermeister, for example, killed a Jewish woman."

In a historical study by T. Brustyn-Bernshtayn: "Stages in the process of expulsion and banishment in the German politics of destruction and annihilation of the Jewish population: *Leaves for History*, Warsaw, Volume 3, [1950], Section 1-2, p. 51-78. The following data is given about the Jews of Khelm during the Nazi period.

Date & Year	Number of Jews in Khelm
1939	{illegible number, probably 15,000}
1940	10,000
June, 1941	11,500
April, 1942	10,815
June, 1942	7,000

[Page 28]

[21]

The number of Jews in Khelm in 1940-1941 increased because of the refugees from Cracow [June, 1940). Later [May, 1942], about 2,000 Jewish refugees from Slovakia came to Khelm. In the year 1942 there were four big "aktsyes" [aktions] in which the majority of Khelmer Jews were deported to the Sobibor death camp. A small number of Jewish skilled workers were left in Khelm until the Nazis shot and killed them on March 31st, 1943.

As everywhere else, many Jews in Khelm worked for German industries and factories that did not want to lose this skilled slave labor force. The Jews were forced to work "dirt-cheap" until their last drop of blood. The bureaucracy wanted to hold onto the Jewish slave labor for commercial profit. On May 12th, 1942, the head man of the Nazis in Khelm appealed to the SS leader of the Lublyner district to let the Jewish slave labor pool remain in Khelm because they were essential. The German industrial bureaucracy insisted that they needed several thousand replacements for the Jewish workers who were deported from Khelm. In a report from the German Labor Office: "The deportation of Jewish workers seriously affected the number of qualified metal workers for military production and for the railroad workshops in Khelm, which currently employ 158 Jewish specialists. Stop their deportation, unless they can be replaced." The reply from the SS in accordance with the agreement with Berlin, was that their political goal [annihilation of the Jews] was their primary goal and could not be altered by practical arguments. Thus the fate of the remaining Jews in Khelm, who were skilled specialists, was doomed.

[22]

In the Lublyner area, not far from Khelm, various partisan groups were active. The Jews who were in the National Polish section of the Partisans were later traitorously murdered by their Polish colleagues, who belonged to "Armia Krajowa" and "Narodowe Sily Zbrojne". The situation for the Jews was more favorable and secure in the "Armia Ludowa" organized and armed by the Left . The best situation for the Jews was in their own partisan group. The number of Khelmer Jews in their own partisan groups is not known.

A woman from Khelm, Ester Bas-Meltzer, who was saved in Warsaw, writes in her memoir: *In the Nails of Death*, (Montreal, 1950), what she found when she returned to Khelm after the 1945 Liberation. "There were just a few Jews who had returned to Khelm. They were met with open hatred by their Polish neighbors". The whole shtetl, the empty Jewish streets, were in her eyes like a "virtual cemetery " [p. 47-48].

Torah and Learning in Chelm [Khelm]

In the 16th century, Khelm was already an important cultural center. The old men talked about the synagogue [shul] and said she was 800 years old. That means that she was built in 1100. The legend exaggerates somewhat; but the "shul" was in truth, exceptional and not an every day type. It was an edifice with birds painted on two walls. The edifice was modeled after the old Crackow shule. The Khelmer "shule" was built in the 17th century. Reference to the Khelmer "shule" appears in an article by Rohel Vyshnytser " *Eastern-Western Buildings in the Shule" Architecture From the 12th to 18th Century.*" YIVO, v29, (1947) p.40-41.

[Page 29]

[23]

The Jewish community of Khelm was already renowned in the 16th century. From the 16th to the 19th century, Khelm had a long line of prominent rabbis who were celebrated for their torah learning and wisdom. They held the most respected positions and were the leaders of the Yeshiva in Khelm. The reputation of the rabbis and teachers of Khelm was imposing, even though it was not yet complete. In this long chain of Rabbis, which began in the 16th century, a few links are missing. Some of the less renowned rabbis are not noted in the historical sources, in the agreements, or in other works and documents that are the source of our information.

The first reference to the Khelmer Rabbis stemmed from the official Polish documents: R'Yhudh Ahrun (1520-1522], R'Yuda [1550], R'Yekov (1582). These documents tell us very little. Information about the character and personality of these rabbis does not exist in the Jewish sources. The first identified rabbi, and head of the Yeshiva that was mentioned in the Jewish sources, was R'Shmeun Auyerbakh, [he lived in Khelm from about 1510-1513]. R'Shmeun was descended from a highly esteemed rabbinic family. His brother, R'Dovid Tebele, was the father of R'Shmeun Volf Auyerbakh, who was the Rabbi of Pozen and Prague. After him, was the Khelmer R' Shmeun Zalmen, a wise disciple. He is praised by Ben Dovid from "Mahrsh"l" in his books. In the 2nd half of the 16th century, the renowned R' Alyh Bel-Shem, lived in Khelm. R'Alyhu Br'Yhudh Ahrun was a student of "Mahrsh"l.

[Page 30]

[24]

Together with "Mahrsh"l", Alyhu Br'Yhudu Ahrun was involved in certain matters concerning verdicts and judgments. He was a brilliant Talmudist and is referred to in the writings of Mahrsh"l [si' m"b] and is also referred to in the "Calculations Emphasized" by R'Yual Syrkes [si' e"z]. Alyhu Br'Yhudu Ahrun, was also highly regarded as a cabalist and mystic and a man who worked miracles. His grandson, R'Yhudu Lyb Hkhahn, tells of a miracle performed by his grandfather Yhudu Ahrun, in his introduction to the book [written by R' Lyb Khhan's father R'Afrym of Vilna]. The famous miracle of R' Alyhu Bel-Shem was his creation of the Golem. The renowned R' Hkham Tsvy Ashkhanazy was a grandchild of R' Alyhu Bel-Shem. Hkham Tsvy's son, the celebrated R' Yekov Emdyn, writes in his biographical work, "Megyleth Sefer" [published by A. Khhna, Warsaw, 1896] about the story of the Golem in the following words: "From R' Alyhu Bel-Shem, our great grandfather [as told to me by my father]. The Bel - Shem made the Golem so that he would serve the Bel-Shem, but the Golem could not speak," Later the stories about the personality of the famous Bel-Shem were embellished and other legends were added.

The Bel-Shem from Khelm died in 1583 in his home-town. According to a legend told by R'Yusef Levenshtyn from Seratsk, the Bel-Shem forbade the placement of a gravestone on his grave. He requested that only a mound of stones be thrown on his grave. Another legend contradicts this one. It was told by a Hungarian Jewish officer, Dr. *{illegible name}* Sonto, who was stationed in Khelm during World War I. He claimed that he saw the grave of the Bel-Shem and that it had a gravestone; however, the name was worn away and illegible. Nevertheless, the Bel-Shem left a gravestone forever in the memories of his people.

[25]

A second well-known Rabbi in Khelm was the Mahrish"A, R'Shmual Alyezr Br. Yuda Halevy, or Shmual Aydelsh, who was one of the most renowned Talmudic scholars in Poland. First he was the Head of the Jewish community in Pozen, where his mother-in-law, Mrs. Aydelsh, organized and supported his Yeshiva. After she died, the Yeshiva fell apart and Mahrish"A became the Rabbi in Khelm in the years 1605-1615. He moved to Lublin and Astrog [Austrah] where he died in 1632. He was succeeded by R' Alyezr Perles.

In the beginning of the 17th century, the Rabbi of Khelm was R' Ytshak Br. Shmual Halevy. He was the brother of the famous Lemberger Rabbi R'Dovid Halevy, who was called "T"Z" after his famous book "Tury-Zhb". R'Ytshak was first the Rabbi in Ludmyr, then in Khelm. From Khelm he went in 1627 to head up the Yeshiva in Pozen. In the thirties and forties of the 17th century, the Rabbi in Khelm was R'Moyshe Ben Mayr Katsenelboygen. First he was the Rabbi in Lubomi, then in Khelm, and later in Mohylev and Belarussia. The rabbinical position was then occupied by his son R'Shaul Katsenelboygen. R'Shaul did not remain long in Khelm. He took a Rabbinical post in Brod, then in Pyntshev, and later in Krakow. For a time, R'Mordkhy Br' Bnymyn Volf Gyntsburg, was the Khelmer Rabbi. Later he went to Brysk in Lithuania.

It appears that in the second half of the 17th century there was frequent turnover in the rabbinical positions and heads of the Yeshiva in Khelm. Perhaps this was due to the difficult times in Poland after the wars of 1648-1656.

[Page 31]

[26]

Toward the end of the 17thcentury, we hear new names occupying the rabbinical positions. First was R'Ykusyal Br' Hushe Hkhhan from Lublin, who later became the Rabbi in Ludmyr. After him, the Khelmer Rabbi was R'HII Br.'Yuneh Halevy. Later he became the Rabbi in Vilna until he died in 1706. He was the grandson of R'Alyezer Ashkhnazy, and the author of the book, "Meleh H".

In order to be as accurate as possible, we note a hypothesis that is offered, but not substantiated by other sources. This hypothesis holds that the well-known R' Yual Bel Shm who lived in Zomoshtsh around the end of the 17th century and the beginning of the 18th century, was a Khelmer. About Yual Bel Shm, there are only legends and stories. About his miracles there is very little verified historical material, so one has to approach all the specifics of his biography with great caution

In the beginning of the 18th century, the Rabbi in Khelm was R'Mayr Br' Benymyn Volf from Lublin. Later he left Khelm to become the Rabbi in Opt and Lublin. And the new Khelmer Rabbi was R' Shmual Shmelke BHG"G Mordkhy Marglyus. R'Shmual Shmelke was the leader of a school movement in Krakow before he became the Rabbi of Khelm. He was also the representative of the Province of Khelm to the Council of Four Lands, an autonomous Jewish governing body in Eastern Europe from the 16th to the 18th century. In the Protocols of the meetings of this Council in 1718, his signature confirms that he was a member of the executive. In the period from 1721-1722, there was reference to other Rabbis and men of great erudition in the Torah who lived in Khelm. They were: R'Shlemeh Br'Shmhh, Hakhan Rapoport and R'Yhushue Hershi Br' Mayr. Mentioned at the same time was R'Tsvi Hyrsh Br' Pynhas Zelig. He also represented the Province at the Council.

[Page 32]

[27]

The Life of the Jews in Chelm [Khelm]

Accurate particulars about the participation of the Khelmer Jews in the Council of Four Lands [the autonomous Jewish governing body] can be found in the book by Ishral Haylperyn "Pynkus Ved Arbe Artsus" published in Jerusalem. Haylperyn documents in his book, [see index p. 617] more than 60 different positions where the Jewish community or the Rabbis of Khelm and the elected officials from Khelm to the Council are mentioned

A prominent scholar was chosen for the honored position of Rabbi of Khelm in the last half of the 18th century. His name was R'Shloymeh Ben Moyshe. He is known in the history of Hebrew Literature as R'Shlaymeh Khelma or as the author of the book "Mrkhves H'Myshna". He was born in Zamoshtsh. R'Shlaymeh was the Rabbi of Khelm for many long years. Then he became the Rabbi of Zamoshtsh and the surrounding region. He was an active member and participant of the Council in Brod.

After the death of the Lemberger Rabbi, R'Rappoport, the vacancy was filled by R' Shlaymeh in 1771, who remained for 6 years. Then he decided to go to Israel. On the way he stopped in Salonika where he finished and published the second and third volume of "Mrkhves H'Myshna", as well as other books. He died in Salonika in 1778. He was a prolific author of disputations about the Myshna. He published major works in 1751, 1777, and 1782. He was also the author of a book "Shery Neymah" about Hebrew grammar and vocal music. Apparently his intellect and knowledge ranged over many areas.

R'Shlaymeh Khelma was one of the first exponents of rationalism and the enlightenment among Polish Jews. From his earliest years he was a student and follower of "Rambam", which led to his intensive study of logic, astronomy, and mathematics.

[Page 33]

[28]

R'Shlaymeh Khelma's most beloved discipline was mathematics. He fought with passion for general education to enlighten everyone. He maintained that the grammar of the language is essential for understanding all knowledge.

It is therefore no wonder that the leaders of the Enlightenment had high regard and respect for R'Shlaymeh Khelma. He was considered a pioneer of the enlightenment in Jewish life. One of the most famous Galician scholars, Yhudh Leyb Myzes, in his book "Knas Hames" [Vienna, 1828] makes R'Shlaymeh Khelma a major figure. This book was written in the form of a dialogue between the Rambam and his devoted pupil, the expert on the "Myshna", R' Shlaymeh Khelma.

About 1760, the Rabbi in Khelm was R'Haym Br'Yekov. According to Sh. Mylner, he was the author of a book: "Khukhby-Itshak" We were unable to locate this book in the scientific or bibliographic literature. We could not find any specifics about R'Hayim or his work.

In the 1770's, the Rabbi in Khelm was the scion of a famous rabbinic family of respected scholars of the Torah. His name was Ytshak Br' Mordkhy Hloy(?) from Lemberg. He was the nephew of the Holy R'Yhushue Raytses from Lemberg. As is well known, the brothers Haym and Yhushue Raytses were tortured and died "el kydush hshem" [martyrdom for being a Jew] in Lemberg in 1728. R'Ytshak was first a Rabbi in Leshno; then he came to Khelm. Later he became the Rabbi in Krakow and the surrounding region.

We referred to R' Hyrsh Br' Yusef [Hyrsh Yozepovitsh, in an earlier section.

[29]

One of the last very prominent Rabbis in Khelm in the 18th century was R'Shaul Br' Mayr Marglyus. First he was the rabbi in Komarno, then in Lublyn, and toward the end of the 18th century he came to Khelm.

R' Ytshak Br'Yusef was the Khelmer Rabbi for a short time when he was young. He was from Zamoshtsh, where his father held the position of Rabbi for 35years. His name was R'Yusef Br'Yekov Ytshak and he was greatly respected for his Talmudic scholarship and wisdom. His major work was "Myshness Hakmym" [1792]. Subsequently, R'Yusef published two other books. It was evident from his writing that, like R'Slaymeh Khelma, he was drawn to rationalist thinking and was influenced by the work of the Rambam. After his death, his son R'Ytshak left Khelm to take over his father's rabbinical position in Zamoshtsh.

Shmeun Mylner reminds us that in the 19th century the Rabbis of Khelm were R'Yusef Kezys [later Rabbi in Yanov] and R' Aryh Leyb Nayhoyz.

Khelm was indeed a town that respected and nourished the study of Torah. It was also a significant cultural center in the 16th, 17th, and 18th centuries. The list of prominent scholars of the Torah who came to Khelm speaks for itself. The Rabbis of Khelm and the Heads of the Khelm Yeshives came from the most important and largest communities in Poland, or left Khelm to take honored and impressive positions elsewhere. It is evident that the rabbinate and the Yeshiva of Khelm had an honorable name in the Jewish world. In modern education, Khelm led the way. Prominent leadership from Khelm encouraged the growth of the Enlightenment [Haskalah] movement among the Jews of Poland, by the end of the 18th century.

[30]

Unfortunately, we have very little information about the history and culture of the Khelmer Jews in the 19th century. Regrettably, the history of the Khelmer Jewish community in independent Poland was like virgin soil. The cultural life in Khelm, between the two world wars went on different tracks than in the old Polish state. Modern schools and a Polish-Hebrew "gymnasium" were established. Weekly Jewish newspapers were published. A young Khelmer philologist, Moyshe Lerer [lyter], from the YIVO archives in Vilna, began studying the language of Khelmer Yiddish and the folklore of Khelm. He also researched some of the scientific work done in Khelm. He perished in a German concentration camp in Norveh, Estonia.

Khelmer Jews in Jewish Folklore

In Jewish folklore, Khelm acquired a reputation as a "town of fools". Khelmer stories were a beloved part of Jewish folk humor and there are many versions of Khelmer stories published in numerous books. How did it happen that a town, which had a name and reputation for scholarship and honorable rabbinical studies of Torah, became the target of mockery and folk humor? Thus far it has not been established how this came about. One thing is certain: the Khem stories have no basis in reality or historical fact. The Khelm stories about fools are wonderful "merchandise"; an international treasure of folklore that is transferred from folk to folk and place to place, from ancient times going back to the earliest centuries. All that is changed are the geographic names, the personal names and the institutions. Thus, for example, the famous story about the Khelmer "shule", and how it was built, can be found much earlier in "fool's town" in England [Gotham Belmont] or in Germany [Shilda] with the only change being the church or state-house, instead of the "shule".

[Page 35]

[31]

"Foolish Towns" were beloved objects of folk humor. We find them in various lands, cultures and historical periods. Let us cite one of the more familiar examples. In old Greece "Abdera" was called a "town of fools". "Beothie" was named the "land of fools". It is superfluous to say that there was no factual basis for this judgment. The famous Greek philosopher, Democritus, came from "Abdera".

In England in the 15th century, Gotham, a village in Nottingham was called "The City of Fools". In the 16th century, a book was published bearing the title "Gotham Tales". There were other English towns that were called "fool's towns" such as : Belmont, Kogeshall in Essex, Ustwick in Yorkshire, Suffolk, and Norfolk. In Holland, Compen was called "town of fools".

Germany had the largest number of towns that were called "towns of fools". It also had the greatest number of stories about fools. We will mention only the most important ones: Shildo [or Shildburg] by Targau; Teterov in Mecklemburg; Shefenshtedt in Brunshveig; Bukstehude by Hamburg; Pirna in Saxon, and Iglav in Mehren, Austria. etc. The German tales about fools very likely were the source of the Jewish folk tales about fools. Already in 1558, the well-known German "Shoemaker and also Poet", Hans Zaks, wrote a funny play ["Shvank"] about "lapenhoyzer peasants". In this play, Zaks tells various stories, which were later told by Jews about the fools of Khelm. In the same era, the German book of folk tales was published. The book was about the "Lalenburger" a fictitious name for the actual town of Shildburg]. The book immediately became very popular in middle and eastern Europe. In 1597, the first translation into Yiddish was published, under the title "Shildburg, a Short History".

[32]

"The Stories of the Fools" entered into Yiddish folklore under the name of "Shildburger Stories". When did they become "Khelmer Stories"? Thus far the research on this question has not yielded a single answer. It is known that in the 19th century, other Jewish communities were called "towns of fools". Thus, for example, the Jewish community in Posen was called a "town of fools". Over time, the whole matter of the stories about the "towns of fools" was concentrated around Khelm. For the first time, in 1867, several Khelmer stories by an anonymous author came out in Vilna. [The publisher was Avrohm Ytshak Dvorzshetsky]. It was a small book of 32 pages, called "Lightening Jokes and Laughter". One chapter of the book is called "The Wisdom and Witticism of a Certain Town H." According to the editor, Noah Prilutsky, all the evidence points to Ayzk Mayr Dyk, as the author of the small anonymous book.

In the 20th century, the literature of "Khelmer Stories" grew immensely. To present an idea of this expansion a bibliography is available. It is on page 37 at the end of this chapter.

[Page 36]

Footnotes:

1. From the historic work of Shimon Milner "The Jews of Khelm" St. Petersburg, [1902], p.154-160.
2. Shimon Milner, "The Jews of Khelm", quotes on p.156 from the Hebrew inscription on the oldest gravestone in the Khelm cemetery.

[Page 39]

The History of the Jews of Chelm (from Lublin)

by Dr. Shimon Milner

Translated by Gloria Berkenstat Freund

He was born in the year 1882 and died in New York in the year 1952. It can be said – and this will not be an exaggeration – that he was, in the intellectual sense, the greatest achiever in Chelm. He was the first and the only one who wrote (in Hebrew) the history of our city and he was then not even 20 years old. This was his very interesting work (that was later cited in various encyclopedias): *The History of the Jews of Chelm*, published in 1902 in the collection of the Petersburg *Ha–Meliz*, under the editor Leon Rabinowitz.

It is easy to say set down the history of the Jews in Chelm. Monographs in this field like Dembicer's about Krakow, Shlomo Duber's about Lemberg existed in this area and Shlomo Borukh Nisenbaum's book, *The History of the Jews of Lublin*, was published at the same time as Dr. Shimon Milner's work about Chelm. However, there were opportunities in all of the cities to create such works about them; they had previously been written about and studied and there was material. As for Chelm, everything was needed and had to be investigated. There was not even a *Pinkas* ["notebook" usually containing historic and demographic information about a city or town] in Chelm. Dr. Shimon Milner, while still young, would spend entire days at the Chelm cemetery, digging up old headstones, tapping the almost erased letters with his fingers and in such a manner he put together a series of headstones that served for a historic orientation about the city of Chelm. Perhaps he then did not know himself the kind of contribution he had made of the knowledge of "epitaphs" (from headstones) that occupies such a large place in the research of the history [of Chelm] and that his Chelm headstone research even would later be cited by the English–Jewish Encyclopedia.

Dr. Shimon Milner was the first Chelemer who left to study abroad and he was a student in the famous Bern University from which graduated such a great Pleiades of Jewish writers, learned poets, communal workers, among them, the well–known builder of Israel and of the revived Hebrew language. Dr. Shimon Milner published articles without number in *Ha–Meliz*, later, in other Hebrew newspapers. He was the chief editor of the daily newspaper, *Undzer Lebn* [*Our LIfe*] in Warsaw in 1910 and 1911. In 1913, he published a brochure dedicated to the 11th Zionist Congress in Vienna. Here we wish to add that he was a delegate to the sixth Basel Congress, to the Uganda Congress and he belonged to 177 "naysayers" about whom Ahad Ha'am [Asher Zvi Hirsch Ginsberg – essayist and Zionist intellectual] wrote his well–known: *HaBokhim* [*Those Who Weep*].

Dr. Shimon Milner later dedicated himself to the Amsterdam philosopher, our Baruch Spinoza. It can be said that Spinoza was a main focus in his life and that he took the place of Dr. Shlomo Rubin who so popularized Spinoza. Dr. Milner published and himself wrote large and interesting works about Baruch Spinoza (in English) and in America he was considered one of the greatest experts of the subject. He was the founder of the Spinoza Foundation, which was an international institution and had braches all over the world. He was the president of the Spinoza Museum in The Hague and Rijnsburg (both in Holland) and was appointed to the post by the government and he was the editor of a philosophical journal.

It is truly a remarkable phenomenon. Our Shimon Milner from Chelm – and Baruch Spinoza from Amsterdam – met on the great and long road of Jewish thought.

***

Since the book, *The History of the Jews of Chelm*, by Dr. Shimon Milner is a historic work of great significance, we publish it and print it in its original, in the Hebrew language, just as it was written by the author.

דר. שמעון מילנער

ער איז געבארן אין יאר 1882 און איז נפטר געווארן אין ניו־יארק, אין יאר 1952. מען קאן זאגן — און דאס וועט ניט זיין איבערגעטריבן — דאס ער האט, אין אינטעלעקטועלן זין, די גרעסטע פארדינסטן פאר כעלם. דען ער איז געווען דער ערשטער און דער איינציקער, וואס האט אנגעשריבן (אין העברעאיש) די געשיכטע פון אונדזער שטאט און ער איז דאן בסך־הכל אלט געווען נישט גאנצע 20 יאר. דאס איז געווען זיין זייער אינטערעסאנטע ארבעט (וואס איז שפעטער ציטירט געווארן דורך פארשידענע ענציקלאפעדיעס): "לקורות היהודים בחעלם" (דערשינען אין יאר 1902 אין "המאסף" פון פעטערבורגער "המליץ", אונטער דער רעדאקציע פון ליאן ראבינאוויטש).

ס׳איז לייכט צו זאגן אנשרייבן די געשיכטע פון די יידן אין כעלם. אויף דעם געביט האבן דאן עקסיסטירט אזעלכע מאנאגראפיעס ווי דעמציצער׳ס וועגן קראקע, שלמה דובערנ׳ס וועגן לעמבערג און אין דער זעלבער צייט, ווי דר. שמעון מילנער׳ס ארבעט וועגן כעלם, איז דערשינען שלמה ברוך ניסענבוימס בוך "לקורות היהודים בלובלין". אבער אין די אלע שטעט זיינען געווען פריער גענויער אויסגעשריבן, דך, אר- בעטן, וועגן וואס זיי האבן שוין פריער געשריבן און שטודירט גע־ האדען, ס׳איז געווען מאטעריאל. בנוגע כעלם האט מען אלץ געדארפט זוכן און גריבלען אליין. ס׳איז אפילו אין כעלם נישט געווען קיין פינקס. דר. שמעון מילנער, אלס א יונגער יינגל נאך, פלעגט פארברענגען גאנצע טעג אויף דעם כעלמער בית־עולם, אויסגראבן אלטע מצבות, טאפן מיט די פינגער זיינע די כמעט אפגעריבענע אותיות, און אויף אזא אופן האט ער צונויפגעשטעלט א גאנצע ריי מצבות, וואס האבן געדינט צו דער היסטארישן אויינטאציע וועגן דער שטאט כעלם. ער האט דאן עפשר אליין נישט געווסט וואס פאר א בייטרעג ער׳ט דורך אים גענאכט פאר דער הוסטאצט פון "עפיאטאפיעס" (פון מצבות), וואס פארגעמט אוא גרויסן פלאץ אין די פארשונגען פון די געשיכטע און אז זיינע כעלמער מצבות־פארשונגען וועלן שפעטער ציטירט ווערן אפילו דורך דער ענגליש־יידישער ענציקלאפעדיע.

דר. שמעון מילנער איז געווען דער ערשטער כעלמער, וואס איז אדעק לערנען אין אויסלאנד, און ער איז געווען סטודענט אין דעם בארימטן בערנער־אוניווערסיטעט, פון וואנ־ נען ס׳איז ארויס אוא גרויסע פלעיאדע פון יידישע שריפטשטעלער, דיכטער, געלערנטע, געזעלשאפטלעכע טוער, צוישן זיי די באקאנטסטע ביערן פון ישראל און פון דער אויפגע־ לעבטער העברעאישער שפראך. דר. שמעון מילנער האט פאר- עפנטלעכט אן א צאל ארטיקלען אין "המליץ", שפעטער — אין אנדערע העברעאישע צייטונגען. ער איז געווען אין די יארן 1910 און 1911 דער הויפט־רעדאקטער פון דער טעג- לעכער צייטונג "אונזער לעבן" אין ווארשע. אין 1913 איז דערשינען זיין ברשור געווידמעט דעם עלפטן ציוניסטישן קאנגרעס אין וויען. און דאס חיל מיר צוגעבן, אז ער איז גע־ ווען נאך א דעלעגאט אויף דעם זעקסטן באזעלער־קאנגרעס אויף דעם אוגאנדא־קאנגרעס, און ער האט געהערט צו די 177 "ניין־זאגערס" וועגן וועלכע אחד־העם האט אנגעשריבן זיין בארימטן : "הבוכים".

דר. שמעון מילנער האט זיך שפעטער געווידמעט דעם גרויסן אמסטערדאמער פילאסאף, אונדזער ברוך שפינאזא. מען קאן זאגן אז שפינאזא איז געווארן א הויפט־ציל אין זיין לעבן און אז ער האט פארנומען דעם פלאץ פון דר. שלמה רובין, וואס האט אזוי פאפולאריזירט שפינאזא׳ן. דר. שמעון מילנער האט ארויסגעגעבן ער אליין געשריבן גרויסע און אינטערעסאנטע ווערק וועגן ברוך שפינאזא (אין ענגליש) און ער האט זיך געלעבנט אין אמעריקע פאר איינעם פון די בעסטע קענער פון דער פראבלעם. ער איז געווען דער גרינדער פון "שפינאזא־פאנדיישן", וואס איז געווארן אן אינטערנאציאנאלע אינסטיטוציע און האט אירע אפטיילונגען אין דער גארער וועלט ; ער איז געווען דער פרעזידענט פון "שפינאזא־ מוזייאום" אין דעם האאג און רייזנבורג (ביידע אין האלאנד) און איז גערופן געווארן צו דעם פאסטן דורך דער רעגירונג, און ער איז געווען רעדאקטער פון פילאסאפישן ושורנאל.

ס׳איז באמת א מערקווערדיקע דערשיינונג. אונדזער שמעון מילנער פון כעלם — און ברוך שפינאזא פון אמס- טערדאם — האבן זיך געטראפן אויף דעם גרויסן און לאנגן וועג פון דעם יידישן געדאנק.

• • •

היות דער ספר "לקורות היהודים בחעלם" פון ד"ר שמעון מילנער איז א היסטאריש ווערק פון א גרויסן באטייט, דערי בער פארעפנטלעכן מיר און דרוקן עס אין זיין אריגינאל, אין דער העברעאישער שפראך, אזוי ווי עס איז געשריבן געווארן דורכן מחבר.

[Page 45]

The Myth of Chelm in Jewish Literature

Translated by Gloria Berkenstat Freund

Without a doubt, the "Chelm myth" is a product of many generations of anonymous oral inventions found in the deep memory of the people.

The "Chelm myth" in its present form is a result of the long transformation from the people's mouths to the people's ears. The generations and the years roll on their way and like a childish snowball the myth changes its shape and grows larger through rolling. Dozens of motifs, Jewish and non-Jewish, are adapted and made accessible, with the help of variations, so that they pass into the area of humor. Alien themes are localized, stabilized and made Jewish through a more familiar colorization and even through an accessible literary bridge. Over the years, systematic, collective, creative activity occurs, from which will come the expression of a rare "epic of humor" entitled "The Wisdom of Chelm." We think of the "Chelm myth" as a collective anonymous folk creation which immediately raises the question: why did Chelm happen to have the honor of becoming the object for the humorous folk fantasy?

[Page 46]

And although the question is posed, we must, however, leave it for scholars and folklore specialists. Perhaps, when it is left for them, they will discover the concealed laws of the whimsical muse.

We, for our part, will simply draw the reader's attention at this moment to a mistaken idea, namely, that contrary to what some people believe – that this saintly community, Chelm, is well known primarily because of the "Chelm myth" – in fact, Chelm must have been known enough in the past so that it could become the traditional object of Jewish folk humor.

Even if we accepted the idea that the first folk story about Chelm was created by chance (in other words, was connected to Chelm by chance), we must then recognize that chance would not have succeeded in reinforcing the folk invention if the name Chelm had not been known well enough to the Jews, at least, within the borders of Diaspora Poland

And even if there were not any other historical evidence, in other words, if the city of Chelm did not have any other documentary evidence about the past, the sole fact that the Chelm stories exist in Yiddish folklore is evidence that this city was once a definite influence in Jewish life – an influence that made its name known far and wide, an influence that, perhaps, ended as a result of its rivalry with another, larger city within the borders of the Kingdom of Poland. And incidentally: in the rivalry between the other city and the city of Chelm, we must look for the likely origin of the Chelm story.

[Page 47]

Naturally it occurs to us to say that there is now not even one kernel of authenticity in the Chelm story and even if there is, it is of meager importance. The Chelm that we have known in the course of the last dozen years, of course, has no connection.

If however we look for the "historical" cause for connecting the Chelm myth with the city of Chelm, it is clear that by this we mean to learn a very interesting and deeply concealed quality of folk invention, in other words, a secret from its laboratory, because we believe that in the outward causality is present a definite resolution.

However, until this quality is revealed, until it is exactly defined, for us it is beyond doubt that Chelm was not created through the folk story. In the past it already had grown in Yiddish life and its name must have had a well known ring if it could be gradually used as a synonym for a Jewish popular look at certain actions in human life.

* * *

The collection of "Chelm Stories" in Jewish folklore tells not only about Chelm, about her experience in Jewish life, but simultaneously tells us about the deep-rootedness of this life in Polish soil. Without this feeling of being rooted in the Polish soil, of the sense of deep roots having been planted, the folk creation could not have woven its grotesque web around a concrete geographical idea, around a city.

It is therefore true that in later times the "Chelm Story" reached places where the name Chelm sounded fictitious. Even to this day someone can be heard saying: "It is just like Chelm" and the one saying it does not have to explain the geographical reality of Chelm. Because of the folk myth, Chelm has become a synonym, for example, like Sodom. The strength of the created folk synonym extends further than the original "reality" that was invented and thanks to its strength remains the creation in folk memories. This is its great worth, which takes it out of the narrow limit of the folklore specialist and makes it the living property of people of culture, of artists and writers. It is however more than certain that when speaking about Chelm humor in Yiddish folk invention, along with its actual living significance, there is also in mind its cultural historical worth. We are interested in the fruit as an object that can quench our joy as well as in the tree on which the fruit has grown. When it comes to the Chelm humor-fruit, the folkloric tree is, of course, important for us and particularly the climate in which it ripened and in the course of years matured. Therefore it is important for us to assert that the humorous work arose by being rooted in the land, where all protagonists figure in an actual city.

[Page 48]

From the Chelm myth we must make an inference: if every folklore inventor is bound to a well known common theme, is it not all the more so for the creator who bases his work on an actual geographic idea? Most certainly we must therefore have a feeling of an unchanging creation.

Making a city the protagonist in a work that was "written" over the course of generations could only be done when the lives of the people in that city are seen as unchanging over the years. And not only this city, but Yiddish also had to be secure in the land in which the city is found, because, if not, they would never have indulged in the luxury of completely entrusting their humorous creative energy to such a city.

The French could indulge in such luxury with "Tarascon" in France. The Jews in Poland could indulge in such luxury in regard to Chelm.

According to the discourse of Reb Pinkhas Koricer, the Jewish exile was easier in Poland. Jews in Poland lived not only with their own customs and old practices, but also with a sense of home. Only with this sense could the Chelm myth be born.

Here are two anecdotes that characterize the most vivid sense of home of the Jews in Poland. One of them is told this way:

Jews travel on the train. They converse. "What is your city called?" – One of the Jews asks the other.

– My city? Answers the one who is asked – The gentiles call it Medziboz, but the world knows it as Mysliborzyce.

(There is no telling what comes to the minds of the gentiles. But "the world" that is the Jews knows the correct name).

And the second anecdote:

A Jew from a small *shtetl* comes into an office in a larger city. The clerk rummages in his papers and asks;

– Who does your city follow?

– Earlier it belonged to the followers of the Aleksanderer [*Rebbe*] – the Jew answers – but now we have expelled them from their *shtibl* (small prayer house) and the city chiefly follows the Ger [*Rebbe*].

(That the city belongs to a prince, too, or is part of a *voivode* (province) does not occur to the Jew. For him, it is clear, that the city belongs to one *rebbe* or to another).

[Page 49]

The Chelm stories, as in the cited anecdotes, arose in a world of Jewish stability, in a world where the concept of home is concrete and real.

In another story, this reality of home is in our final incident transformed into "a Chelm story," with the typical moral of Chelm wisdom.

* * *

In the "Chelm stories," the folk inventiveness shows a distinct tendency to concentrate the subject matter in one geographic area, in one concrete area of Jewish settlement. Such a tendency is generally familiar in the folk story.

There are all kinds of stories in Jewish folk fantasy bound to the "*ergetz hinter di Hore-khoyshek*" (somewhere behind the legendary mountain of darkness) – stories of wonder that are framed in the geographic novelty of wonderland. While it is clear that actions of fantasy can occur only in a place of fantasy that does not let reality control its every moment, this land on the other side of the Sambation,[1] this place "under the seven mountains" or "under the seven rivers" where every step is imbibed with the miraculous, is also highly suitable. And it once happened that when the nameless teller of folk stories wanted to approach the boundaries of our geographic reality, he just brought with him from "under the legendary mountain of darkness" a piece of its miracle-imbibed atmosphere, a piece of its mystical climate. The "flowers and fauna" in such stories were, of course, familiar, homey, one's own, but the impreciseness of the area of action still remained. Such a story teller never risked using a specific geographic name, unless it appeared to be very far away.

The people had other designations for the extraordinariness of a smaller subject of wonder: "somewhere in Goshen" or "somewhere in Bobryk." First in the Hasidic story we begin to meet the well-known city or *shtetl*, concrete places and names that one can see, believe can be touched by the hand. In the newness of *Hasidism*, the people stopped going up to heaven and began to bring heaven down to earth. *Hasidism* revolted against the mysticism that lies outside the earthly life and proved that only the earthly life is full of mysticism. Therefore, it is clear that the Hasidic storyteller did not need to carry away his fantasy somewhere to a wonderland. Wonders, according to their world view, can happen in and really do happen here on earth, in one's own small space. They did not need a specific climate, no special atmosphere, no imagined area, no likely conditions that would make them believe. All of these attributes were created only through one magical strength, the strength of rapturous belief.

The Chelm story is in one respect comparable to the Hasidic story. It is, also, in its action not far from our reality. The stage on which it appears is in the very middle of our life. Contrary to the *Hore-khoyshek* story, it wants to lead to belief so it states the concrete place of its occurrence. It buys our trust with the illusion of nearness and, therefore, probability, because without this it would mainly lose its humor.

[Page 50]

The Chelm story is a crooked mirror. In order that the comedy of the warped lines properly impact, the reflections must always by found near the objects that become deformed in it. Only in confrontation with reality can the proper comedic effect by summoned.

* * *

A Chelm story can be recognized from a mile away. It contains a definite established nucleus around which moves the comedy and situation.

The comedy of the Chelm story is built upon a kind of principle of humor. It is literally a golden treasure for a certain theory of laughter.

The comedy of Chelm achieves its result automatically as a human effect.

This automatic result is a consequence of not noticing and not comprehending the consequences of an action.

The comedy of the actions of the heroes of the Chelm stories consists in their inventing for themselves a certain fiction and carrying it out, not seeing what follows in the end.

The comic effect becomes clear because the actions of the Chelmers lack the natural logical connection between cause and result.

It is automatically one-dimensional and perfunctory; this is the stumbling point of Chelm's good will.

When Chelm buys an extinguisher in order to fight fires in the city, this is actually a logical wish realized in fiction. This fiction becomes comical only when a second cause and another fiction (the walling in of the extinguisher with a thick brick wall, in order that thieves would not be able to steal it), makes void the first effort. The mechanism, the way the fiction is automatically carried out, not taking into account its effect, brings out laughter among those with normal human judgment.

The Chelm story is an example of good intentions, which in the reality of life, become transformed into their opposite with laughter guarding the person against the routine in life; and with laughter over the Chelmer actions, we guard against the routine that transforms our fiction into the opposite of that which we wanted. In this manner, the folk experience wanted to underline that good will is not enough; this good will must be recognized; that means one must take from the understanding and consider the attendant phenomena of each fiction and bind it with the understanding of the intention.

When Chelm wants the fallen snow to remain fresh and unwalked upon, this is certainly a good wish. (The snow can be thought of as an allegorical indication of a definite ethical quality in our life). However, the fathers who are equal to realizing this wish are unnatural and, therefore, comedic. They are unnatural because of the chain of logic among them. The Chelm storyteller asks: Who disturbs the snow? The answer is: The *shamas* (the synagogue beadle), who is the first to go out into the street, in order to wake the residents for religious services. The answer is logical and correct. However, this logical truth misleads the Chelmer on a detour to illogic. Because if the *shamas* disturbs the snow, we must find a way that he will not do it. (As for myself, a correct conclusion.). The solution that four people should carry the *shamas* is in itself again logical. However, it becomes illogical in connection with the first impulse for the first action – the wish that the snow should be entirely undisturbed.

[Page 51]

We see, therefore, that the joke about the Chelm heroes admits that they, the heroes, have good will. Their actions in carrying out their will is comic, because the Chelmers act automatically, they look to remove a certain condition through an action that strengthens the earlier condition tenfold.

When the *shamas* becomes old and cannot go around the *shtetl* rapping on the shutters looking to summon the Chelmers, how will the *shamas* be able to carry out his functions without exerting himself? This is not a bit comic and, in fact, logical. However, on the way from inclination to realization, the Chelmers lose the connection to the expression and the reality of life.

All of the shutters are brought to the *shamas* at home in order for him to be able to rap on them and, thereby, not needing to go around the *shtetl*. The importance of the actual activity is lost. The *shtetl* both will not hear the rapping and exactly like the extinguisher, the entire effort and energy is wasted because there was no thought given to the link between the two actions and the result.

The same automatic reaction to the action, the same omission of an essential connecting link between the action and the result is seen, too, in the story about the water mill that is built, not near the water, but on a mountain and in many other Chelm stories.

* * *

The same Chelm story is a rich source of material for literary-artistic forms.

In essence, this great humor epic is taken as the great artistic revitalizer of the popular, anonymously created works of artistic consciousness and artistic permanence.

[Page 52]

The Chelm story contains those allegorical moments that can be applied in connection with general human events and actions that fill our lives.

Until now we have very rarely elected to use the Chelm story material in our literature.

We know the comedy, *"Chelmer Khakhomim"* ("The Wise Men of Chelm") of Aaron Zeitlin that was successfully presented on the Yiddish stage, but it is not available in book form.

Gershonson, the young Yiddish writer from Soviet Russia who perished tragically, also wrote a similar comedy. The comedy is found in the work of the popular artists Sh. Dzehigon and Y. Shumakher.

The stories of Chelm were recorded at that time by M. Kipnis. He finished a folkloric work. It is not known if the text will be published in book form.

Shlomoh Simon published a book in New York under the name, "The Heroes of Chelm." An accurate adaptation of the Chelm stories for children.

The book *"Chelmer Khakhomim"* by Y.Y. Trunk, artistically fashioned from Chelm story material, is worthy of a separate discourse.

Yiddish writers have used the Chelm story material, carrying it over to their towns and places. (For example: Leib Kwitko in his children's song, "Leml's Present.") Others again have given the style of Chelm to their things; the stories themselves, however, have no connection with Chelm material. (For example: Y. L. Peretz, *Der Chelmer Malamed* ["The Chelm Teacher"].) It is certain that other Chelm stories wait for their great genius who will do justice to the Chelmer literary material. And until this happens, it is our duty again and again to record all the nuances, all the variations of the Chelm story, as it travels among Jews all around the world.

It would be a great accomplishment if the Chelm *landmanschaftn*, which are spread all over the earth, could stimulate and even organize both the renewed collection of the Chelm stories and their artistic revision. The latter is not a restraint on the organization, but an appropriate bonus, for a book of Chelm story material would perhaps stimulate Yiddish writers and artists and even without this, the interest in the theme is great enough. Only a little bit of initiative is required for it to be realized.

Translator's footnote:

1. The legendary, impassable river of rocks, on the other side of which the ten lost Tribes of Israel may be found.

[Page 53]

The Chelm Stories Are Not So Foolish
(A sort of historiosophy [philosophy of history] to the Chelm stories)

by Joseph Gotfarsztajn, Paris

Translated by Gloria Berkenstat Freund

Joseph Gotfarsztajn is a Jew from Lithuania and well known essayist and pedagogue in France. His last book: *L'Ecole du Meurtre* (*The School of Murder*) made a great impression in the French literary world; it is a great understanding of the German pedagogical politics that educated a generation for murder.

Gotfarsztajn wrote a thesis for the university about "humor" as he was an expert in the subject. He is the former director of the Jewish Teachers Seminar at the Federation of Jewish Societies in France and the manager of Jewish People's University in Paris.

A difficult question: what kind of wonderful strength is inherent after all in the Jewish people that they were able to resist and preserve themselves for a period of 2,000 years from physical and spiritual conversion, not possessing any characteristic of a national organism while many nations in their own territories were really ground into dust under the wheels of history, as expressed in modern, flowery language. Or in time, took on a completely different body and a completely different soul? After all, how could the persecuted Jewish people, the "sheep scattered among 70 nations," endure while disregarding the most basic principles of sociology and national psychology.

To explain this remarkable phenomena we have had to look to a verse from the chapter *Vaetchanan* ["And I pleaded..."] from *Deuteronomy*: "…Surely a wise and discerning people is this great nation."

However, a time came (also in the ostensibly naïve city of Chelm) when they stopped leaving it to verses from *Tanakh* [Hebrew bible] and from the *Midrash* [commentaries] because "modern citations" came into vogue – and the above mentioned question was posed again with fervor and sarcasm, so to say. Understand? And how? The "iron one" [the hard question] – both that already examined and that still hidden to this day – flowing from history demands an answer, a quick one, because our historians and historical philosophers push themselves to the fore. Can they not see? They do not believe in miracles. *Moshe Rabbenu* [Moses our teacher] is a figure of legend to them. They consider *Mosheikh* [the redeemer] a utopia and their own existence an anachronism. And here it seems to them that the survival of the Jewish faith hangs by a thread, despite explicit assurances that the Jews were given in ancient times that "the Eternal One of Israel does not lie…" [1 Samuel 15:29], an assurance with which they also were disillusioned. They began to create a new historical scaffolding; this time an "iron" law. However, these structures also did not endure for long. The unique Jewish fate simply laughed at all of the theories.

[Page 54]

To be truthful, I must admit that, although I do believe in miracles from heaven (because I also essentially bear, stubborn Litvak that I am, a Chelemer soul), the mystery of Jewish existence tormented and preyed upon me for many years. True, at the time I was still involved with other problems too, not necessarily purely Jewish problems, as, for example, the knowledge of the theatrical side of humor. I endeavored to learn the mechanism of the comic that is inherent in the joke. This is not something I remember for no reason but because this observation is a precondition to the understanding of the conclusions that I will make in this article.

2.

One day I learned that my good friend, the well-known Jewish historian, Josef Milner, was involved with gathering material for the Chelm Yizkor Book [memorial book]. I was not lazy and I went to Milner. We had a conversation that (because several months have already passed since that day and I cannot remember this dialogue word by word) probably [consisted of] these words:

– I have known for a long time that you were born in Chelm, but I have just learned today that you are an avowed Chelemer; you are a Chelm patriot despite the unwise call to you of the Chelm stories.

– If you are such a great sage already – Milner said to me, too, as a joke – then write an article for me for the Yizkor Book and show the foolishness of the Chelm stories.

– No, dear friend – I protested – I will not show the foolishness in my article, but, the opposite, I will attempt to show with the brightest glow the deep wisdom that is attached to these thoughtful, naïve fables. As the Chelm stories are fables without parables, they are stories of an absurd world that some ingenious dialectic has driven into an impasse and cannot find a way out of it. They are commentaries about the old Jewish way of life in which the pleasure has died; they are an illustration, a sketch of the exiled underground life that the Jewish people led for so long, helping out here with rigorous but unworldly logic and here with spiritual manna. Logic led the city of Chelm – and our entire exile – to the absurd and to our last terrible destruction. However, the spiritual manna in the end had its last remnants brought here where the oranges bloom, where a familiar Jewish folklore sings. The Chelm stories in a certain sense are really a sort of commentary on the Jewish philosophy of history. I mean that they enable us to describe the key that unlocks one of the blocked and hidden cells where lies amassed a certain part of Jewish spirituality and of Jewish historical energy.

[Page 55]

3.

Jewish spirituality? The energy of Jewish history? What does this have to do with anything? What kind of logical connection could be possible between both phenomena: Jewish humor – Chelm stories, for example – and Jewish history?

I think there is present a certain logical connection between both of these phenomena which has enraged so many logicians, rationalists, historical philosophers and even theologians, mystics and metaphysicians.

And as follows:

Before anything, let us first talk a little about humor in general. Let us record in a few lines the route that a joke takes in the entangled labyrinth of human thought.

There is probably no significant philosopher who in the frame of his own subject has not lingered on the role that humor plays in the spiritual life of this or another civilized community of people. Several names: Aristotle, Kant, Schopenhauer, Moses Mendelssohn, these four great philosophers have given humor an important place in their systems. However, they did not write special studies on the theme. Therefore, such thinkers such as Theodor Fischer, Kuno Fischer, Harold Hedfings, Spenser, [Elohah] Heker, Theodor Lipps and, above all, Sigmund Freud and Henri Bergson strongly immersed themselves in the problems of humor, of the comic, of the joke. As for the special Jewish joke, Felix Weltsch researched it not only in length and width, but so to say, in depth.

Because of the lack of space, we will not even be able in this article to list by name all of the faces in which the humor was clad, all of its aspects and genres. I also cannot pause for the controversies that arose between one joke researcher and another, both with regard to the reasons they evoke laughter and with regard to the intent, the "meaning," the moral of this or that category of jokes. However, here I must absolutely not brush off the dissident opinion.

According to all of them, it appears that humor is a very important ingredient of several truly spiritual, creative activities. In a certain sense, humor is even a means of control against bias in thought; it sometimes goes hand and hand with the creative fantasy; it is a kind of yeast for the dialectic method in ideas. According to Bergson, the joke is a remedy against the mechanization and the automation of human actions and human tasks, a good remedy against all that shows a tendency to become stiff and dulled.

In our present time, when the majority of people have stopped thinking with their own brains and they constantly desire to become either "leaders," political leaders or minuscule screws in a machine "mass," humor has really become, unfortunately – in some Jewish circles – a very rare article. Therefore, the terror of the various slogans, the demagogic *shlogverter* [literally "words of beating" – catchphrases] increased everywhere and as their name indicates – they "*shlogn*" [beat] in the empty void of the minds and they "*shlogn*" [beat] out every crumb of critical thought, every feeling for responsibility and, as a result, also the drive for freedom. Because with responsibility, freedom is not available.

[Page 56]

And truly so: a good joke criticizes; a good joke liberates the thought; a good joke teaches thinking. Therefore, dictatorship and humor are not an equivalent pair; therefore, it should be understood, humor has no *raison d'être* in the legends where those in power are afraid of criticism, except for the "commonplace" criticism, so called "self-criticism." For this is pseudo-criticism that teases the appetite but does not satisfy it and is a mockery of itself.

Laughter is – once again according to Bergson – not only a social phenomenon, but also a sort of social corrective. Everything that cannot conform to life is ridiculed, the laziness, the automatic, the rigidity, the pedantry.

Felix Weltsch believes that this definition does not apply to every kind of humor because there is also present a good-natured laughter, a light-hearted one that does not intend to punish and to scold. Just now the play element in Jewish humor is strongly represented. It is enough to remember our illustrious Sholem Aleichem, who dines on Jewish folklore and borrows his stories from Jewish jokes and anecdotes in order to understand the truth of Weltch's observations of the Chelm stories. There is already agreement about the Chelm stories. They actually are nothing more than illustrations, moreover absurd, but we no longer hold on to them.

It is also worthwhile to take note of Sigmund Freud's view of humor. Freud strongly emphasizes in his book, *Jokes and their Relation to the Unconscious*, the liberating character for the joke. The founder of the psychoanalytic doctrine teaches us that thanks to the joke a person can be freed from a mass internal disruption. For instance, the aggressive joke permits one person to attack another and the other will not take any offense. Still more: one can even joke on one's own account and, at the same time, there is no need to be ashamed of oneself and feel the shame from others.

4.

Many Jewish jokes show this tendency. The Jew laughs about himself; he laughs about his troubles; he laughs partly, as Sholem Aleichem says, through tears, but thus he weighs the merits and demerits of his dark fate and indirectly, of his enemies with good courage, without anger.

Felix Weltch says in his very interesting study that was published in the *Yidishn Almanakh* [*Yiddish Almanac*] (of the year 5706 [1946], published in German), the joke is the most important literary medium of an oppressed people. The joke is the weapon of the physically weak and spiritually strong person. In the last era of Jewish misfortune – during the gruesome persecutions against Jews in Germany under Hilter's regime – the joke played an enormous role that will be rightly revealed later by future historians. The voice of the tortured, tormented and spit-upon folk could be heard through the whispering, murmuring joke. However these jokes penetrated through all crevices and through all openings of society. No one could stop it. It could not be defeated by any concentration camp.

[Page 57]

An important contribution to the acquisition of the joke (spiritual property gained against our will through a river of blood and a sea of tears), which survivors of the concentration camps acquired in the various death camps was gathered by Y[isroel] Kaplan in Munich in 1949 in a published brochure, *Dos Folks-Moyl in Natsi-Klem* [*Voice of the People in the Nazi Vice*]. This collection of local dialects in the ghettos and Nazi concentration camps shows that even on the threshold of death the Jewish people were not done with the enjoyment of humor. Who knows how many Jews it saved from despair and from suicide! As one of the extracts from life, Y. Kaplan remarked in his forward that what almost everyone reveled in was the eternal "voice of Jacob." Sayings, jokes, anecdotes, wishes, various contemplations and inventions – this was the good balm for the concealed hearts and dejected moods.

5.

Voice of Jakob? Then can the Jewish joke also be considered a "voice of Jakob" in the biblical sense, with a biblical origin, so to say? Usually we believe humor came later and was alien to the Israelites, and that the "witticism," the small laugh, the invention, the aphorisms were a later invention from the Talmud and from the legends.

I do not really know how to thank the French-Jewish writer Emmanuel Berl for opening my eyes through his extremely interesting and instructive article in *Revue de la Pensée Juive* [*Review of Jewish Thought*] of January 1951.

In addition to many other truths and values, Emmanuel Berl "uncovered" – no, he accented the smile that "floats" on the faces of our ancestors. The "smile of the 90-year old Sarah when she learns that she will have a child. Rebecca's smile when she took Laban's *teraphim*.[1] Jakob's triumphal smile after he defeated the angel who wrestled with him. Joseph's smile when he quietly asked that his golden cup be placed in Benjamin's sack."

This *Halakah* [Jewish law] is certainly not yet true humor and this surely does not have anything to do with jokes. However, the climate in which humor can arise and thrive was created through these smiles. Later the Torah relates the uproar when God appeared to Elijah the Prophet; we read that this happened not in a storm but actually in "complete silence." Slowly, calmly, thoughtfully and we find again in the area of calm, good-hearted humor.

[Page 58]
6.

I said "area" just now and I meant to say "sphere" because humor is completely not dependent upon the area in the geographical sense, but it is dependent on the spiritual outlook from which it draws its inspiration. The sphere of Jewish spirituality was first rooted in the idea that every person, even men of perfect saintliness, sin in regard to God, in regard to people and in regard to themselves. A sort of feeling of compassion developed toward people who transgress and at the same time a sense of degree and of nuance.

Both concepts were dictated by King Solomon to be written in the Book of Proverbs and – centuries later – drove us Jews to tell jokes and anecdotes.

In the Jewish joke, it is worthwhile to laugh at simple, arrogant people, ignorant people, idlers, impractical people, loafers, fools, misers, rich men achieving wealth, skinflints, wicked people, foolish heretics, hypocrites, hypocritical Jews, disguised people, magicians of all sorts and more and more ridiculous people who are taken to task. However, as I already have said, a joke can just entertain and play a game without any designated intention and without a moral lesson, but even such a joke also "jabs" and sometimes hits the mark. This is the tragic-comic joke. This is the tragic-comic joke of Charlie Chaplin and the tragic anecdote of Franz Kafka.

It vexes me that I cannot linger here on the tragic comedy of Chaplin's performances, of that genial, Jewish mimic and acrobat[2] who is – in the area of film – a brother of our Menakhem-Mendel, the tragic optimist, a brother also of Mendele's [Mendele Mocher Sforim] Benjamin the Third.

I must briefly explain to the reader how Franz Kafka is pertinent because his fate is closely connected to the fate of the Chelm idlers, although as seen above, they belonged to two different worlds.

Much has already been written (in the German language) about Franz Kafka, who died young. He was considered a classic and a founder of existential modern world literature. It is accepted by the world that Franz Kafka undertook – and also in great measure succeeded – to be the artistic community spokesman of humanity that finds itself at the crossroads of the absurd and the tragic and at the crossroads of madness and ruin.

As the community also the individual! From this, all of Kafka's heroes take the impulse "to leave their own skin," to become an animal, a dog, a tortoise. The human existence has lost its meaning for them, after the clay Golem [being magically created from clay] like a machine without the ineffable name of God on its forehead fought the slaughter of people, after human relations became so entangled that no one knows any longer what is good and what is bad, after some stranger has brought a lawsuit against every individual for nothing and yet again for nothing, after the "great anonymous one" has confounded one thing with another and no one knows any longer what is what.

[Page 59]

We know that Kafka was a pessimist who did not see any sense in his own suffering, not in the suffering of everyone else who was just like him, riveted to the heavy "wheelbarrow" that is called life. Ask yourself: how do we compare the eternally optimistic Chelemer "sages" who find an exit from all calamities yet again after a seven-day meeting? But Franz Kafka basically had a hidden pessimism. Just like the naïve ones in Chelm, he also meant that the human could be saved through believing in God's unity (and necessarily also in the unity of the world) despite all the obstacles on the way that leads to God, despite dualism, that is, our idol-worshipping civilization. Marthe Robert cites in her article about "Franz Kafka's Humor" (published in the above-mentioned *Review of Jewish Thought*) one of his aphorisms which is evidence of this real-Jewish reasoning. "Believing" writes Kafka, "means the release of the indestructible itself, or more correctly: be indestructible, or more correctly: be."

Felix Weltsch was correct. In his study, "Religious Humor in Franz Kafka" (published in German together with Max Brod's study, "Franz Kafka's Beliefs") he emphasized the Jewish tone of the poet's shout. Weltsch writes that the humor, Kafka's humor comes from the "superiority that sees the duality in false unity, but without losing sight of unity as the goal."

7.

In different ways, but with the same intention – and probably also in the same direction – go both the protagonist Kafka and the hero of Chelm toward the indestructible unity of God's world. They go through many metamorphoses, many transformations, but we must hope that the absurd will be vanquished.

No, *Mosheikh* [the redeemer] is no utopia and the world runs simply according to a certain Godly plan, although we do not see it because life has divided us and we fell – particularly we Jews were divided – between <u>being</u> and <u>not being</u>, between the requirement to remain what we once were and the enticing call from outside that draws us to another world.

The *Gemara* says that by changing a place of residence and by taking another name one can often change bad luck to good luck. This is what Chelm did! This real Jewish city disguised itself; it put a mask on its face; it disguised itself as a fool, just as Kafka disguised himself as a pessimist. The "smart and sensible" in Chelm – it is hard to determine whose advice this was and why at first glance the entire normal city suffered such a fate – began to speak of optimistic foolishness and to search for the secret of its extraordinary existence through a contrary logic whose result was that the rabbi lost his mind, the cat was victorious over an entire community of Jews, all of Chelm disappeared in fire and then the city was rebuilt and the city reached the point where it lacked 10 men for a *minyon* [prayer group]. Enlightenment, trains and … Chelm.

[Page 60]

This "disguising" logic penetrated into all of the Chelm stories. Even the answer to the question that we first posed about how the foolishness of the world was distributed over Chelm is found in this story:

After the six days of creation, the Most High sent out into the world one of his ministering angels and gave him two sacks to take with him. One sack was full of the intelligent and astute and the second with the foolish and naïve souls. The angel flew over Brisk *gubernia* [county] and, flying slowly, released from both sacks an intelligent soul here and a foolish soul here.

However, when he flew by the high Chelemer mountain, the sack in which the foolish souls lay got caught on the mountaintop and thus the foolish souls fell out all at once through the hole in the sack and they all fell in Chelm.

From then on developed in Chelm, the utter fools who won fame all over the world.

This genre of humor also is present among gentiles. The Germans, for example, also possess their foolish stories. However, a great distance separates their stories of fools from the Chelemer stories. The Schildberger stories simply are clownish routines whose function is to amuse the "simple people." While the Chelemer stories are according to both their theme and their tone wry examples that tell of a wry and absurd life.

Chelm, one can say, was chosen as a capital city for Jewish thought whose outwitted sage begins to hurt. The short, Jewish joke, as sharp and burning as it may be, is sometimes unable "to scorch" the bitterness that has gathered in the folds of Jewish life.

The Chelm story is a protest against the tragic fate of a people that sank in mud, in poverty, in need, although it needed to carry out a very important mission in the world: saving it from decline and freeing it from the contradictions that gnaw at it and make it a ruin.

The Chelemer stories come to teach us that formal logic will not save us all from ruin, not the stagnation and maintenance of the old and also not so-called progress that does not know where and for what it progresses, so to say. Only that human progress whose purpose is "to repair the world of the kingdom of the Almighty" [knows its purpose].

This is, ultimately, the sense, the meaning of the Chelemer stories that are highly prized as stories of fools, however they are saturated with wisdom.

By all means, read them again – you will see for yourself.

Translator's footnotes:

1. Genesis 31:19 states: "Laban had gone to shear his sheep, and Rachel stole the *teraphim* [household idols] that belonged to her father." Gotfarsztajn's text translated here states it was "Rebecca." Emmanuel Berl's French text, quoted by Gotfarsztajn, speaks about Rachel and the *teraphim*. Berl also gives Sarah's age at 100 (not 90)
2. The widely reported rumors that Charlie Chaplin was Jewish have been refuted many times.

[Page 61]

Chelm

by Shneier Wasserman, Argentina

Translated by Gloria Berkenstat Freund

Shneyer Wasserman

Many cities and *shtetlekh* [towns] of devastated Europe had the sad privilege of having their devastation written about with more or less accuracy. The Holocaust literature takes the place of honor in the Jewish post war creativity. It is a natural impulse to console both those who have personal testimony from the greatest destruction in Jewish history (and in this case most of the Holocaust writers usually were not writers) and from the writers who did not see the destruction with their own eyes, but with their hearts. The recent efforts try to do justice artistically to great destruction and this is one of the most difficult tasks for the artists of our generation, whose horrified mood perhaps can shout the pain, but succeeds very little in giving it artistic form.

Some of this kind of literature expresses itself in providing the chronicle of the destroyed homes. In this case very important scrolls of destruction were written about the larger cities: Warsaw, Lodz, Vilna and so on. Historically, very important bloody documents, whose authors were surviving writers – witnesses of the great tragedy.

On the contrary, I have reservations about the descriptions from people who picked up a few episodes from someone returning from a camp or ghetto and about those (from quickly told episodes) who seek to create literature in books of hundreds of pages. In several cases it appears that the sort of book that was published had only a scarce connection with the narrator himself.

In order not to err in the manner of making literature of the Holocaust, I have fulfilled the desire of many *landsleit* from my city Chelm, as well as from the publisher of books that I should write memoirs about the city of Chelm, so well-known in Yiddish folklore.

I already have spent a quarter of a century far from Chelm. During this time important events have taken place in the city of which only a few reached me. In addition, it is not possible to write only about the pre-war [events] and omit the most important [occurrences] in which everyone is interested: the terrible days of the Hitler occupation. I waited. Perhaps one of the survivors would unfurl the bloody scroll of Chelm or would at least search for authentic evidence of the horrible events that would provide a report about what took place. In time, I received such evidence.

[Page 62]

The first survivor who came to Argentina was a childhood acquaintance of mine, Noakh Szucmacher.

He survived the first months of the Nazi occupation and was in the group of Jews who were led out of Chelm to the Bug [River]. Therefore, his testimony about the first bloody mass-drama is believable.

Tankhn Nisenbaum is the second witness on whom the largest part of my chronicle is based. This man belonged to the "fortunate" 15 Jews who survived in Chelm itself. I met him in Sao Paulo, Brazil at [the home of] his brother-in-law, Moshe Klerer – well-known in Chelm and a resident of Brazil for many years.

However, the information that Tankhn Nisenbaum possessed was incomplete because of the isolation in which he found himself, as we will later explain.

Thus, the chronicle of destruction must be limited to this scant information that I have collected up to now.

If other survivors are able to complete this bloody chronicle with more information, it would be very important for the history of the destruction of Chelm and for the history of the destruction of the Jews in general.

If no one else does this, with my notes I will save at least a part of the available information about our tragedy from forgetfulness.

And before this – a little about the former life in Chelm.

* * *

At this moment, 25 years have passed as I begin to write my reminiscences of a vibrant Chelm, which means of the past when there was a lively Jewish community.

However, I lived in Chelm for more than 20 years; first under the Czarist yoke and later under the Polish aristocratic enslaver … in those "happy times," when the Jewish community in my city along with all Polish-Jewish communities wrestled for survival, for their own culture and language – for the right to their own life as a national minority.

The 20 years that I lived in Chelm beginning with my early childhood years provide me with the ability to be able to record the more important episodes that remain in my memory. Let this be a poor *matzeyvah* [headstone] for my city, which occupied an important place in Jewish folklore, in Yiddish literature and, particularly, in communal-cultural life.

It must have been during the years 1904-1905, during the period of the stormy years in Czarist Russia – when after a fire in our wooden shared barracks in the village of Adolfin, nine kilometers from Chelm, that we moved into the city.

[Page 63]

One peasant wagon was enough for all our "bags and baggage" and all our household effects. The wagon stopped at the first house on Hrubieszow Street – this became our city home.

I was then four or five years old.

From then on began my acquaintance with Chelm. Chelm, like the entire, great Russian Empire, was then full of revolutionary turmoil and revolutionary events and the first impressions that I absorbed as a child were connected to them. Impressions that provoked my curiosity imposed fear at the same time.

An unframed paper portrait of the last Russian czar and the czarina hung on the wall of our narrow, wooden room. My father – a believer in the czar's mercy and in the czarina's good-heartedness – had brought the portrait home from an annual fair when we still were living in the village. The portrait of the imperial couple was saved from the fire along with the inherited brass candlesticks and the broken sewing machine.

My mother's nephew, Solomon Sztajnworcl, or as we called him, "the Nikolayever," because he lived in Nikolayev [Mykolaiv, Ukraine] for a long time, suddenly arrived on a Friday night, when my mother already had put the food in a warm oven for *Shabbos* [Sabbath]. He arrived with a comrade. Both were hungry, in rags and with daggers in their chest pockets – in the revolutionary style of the time. The comrade pointed to the pitiful czarist portrait and the scoundrel, like one of the family, tore our portrait off the wall. He tore it to pieces with his fingers and both revolutionaries stepped on him with their feet.

My father was concerned about the desecration of the czar and was ready to argue with the rebels, but my mother, who was concerned with her own problems and not with those of the czar and czarina, quickly gathered the torn pieces of the paper portrait, threw them into the burning oven in order to erase any trace of the "crime." To still the argument between the two sides, she took down two fresh round crackers that she would bake every Friday from the "café" and gave them to both rebels – here and let there be peace.

The "strikers" or "cyclists" – as these people then were called – had perhaps not anticipated such a high reward for their efforts. However, it came of good use for them; this was seen with the appetite with which they devoured the crackers.

My mother was ashamed of her nephew and despised him no less than did my father. The family would have been less ashamed of a thief. This, on average, was the view of the older generation of Jews toward the revolutionaries of that time, who were the lighters of the bonfire for the later great October fire…

[Page 64]

Shortly after this the Chelm streets witnessed a bloody spectacle about which I first read many years later and learned the sense, or the nonsense of it:

I sat at the window, looking at the events outside and cried. Only we children were in the house. Our parents were at the city fair and therefore I maintain that this was on a Tuesday because the fairs in Chelm were always on Tuesdays.

But here were our parents on a peasant wagon coming from the fair, quickly taking the little bit of old clothes into the house. The street was lively, peasants, too, quickly left the fair, whipping their exhausted horses. Young people with great "pompadours" in black blouses – the traditional dress of the revolutionaries then – walked around the streets and searched for underworld people, such as a thief, an "author" – that is what the one taking the stolen goods was called – or another sort of member of the underworld. He was dragged out of his hiding place, received broken bones both dry and "wet" and, beaten he was thrown onto a peasant wagon and taken to the hospital.

The building in which we lived immediately became full with the "strikers." They were suspicious of our Christian boss, Szundecki, not only him, but his wife. She was a strange person: a mixture of a swindler, thief, rich woman and "mother" of all the beggars and the neglected. All kinds of clothing, furs, sofas, that she would buy from the thieves or get through fraud was found in her attic. She would use them or sell them. She herself was in rags and tatters. The group learned of this and went up to the attic and took away two full wagons to the police along with her husband with whom they had earlier carried out a sentence. The innocent hard working Szundecki – a giant, a gentile – perhaps did not know at all of his wife's illegal commerce, but he caught the blows.

And during the disturbance, when everyone was busy with the treasure in the attic, a "striker" hastily entered our room. He took a shiny dagger out of his chest pocket and quickly asked, as if he were dealing with a gravely sick person: "Where is the eastern wall?"

He stood [there] and recited the afternoon prayers…

Meanwhile, a pale Jew, a pious man, immersed in a good pedigree from his *payos* [side curls] to the tip of his long coat was led out of the neighbor's house. But piety does not lead to an income; because of his bitter income, he did business with a small amount of stolen objects to earn an income. The pious Jew was led by the hand and one of the "best men" was our Solomon. He truly felt like an in-law at a wedding and he called out self-confidently to my mother, who was standing on the porch and watching: "Aunt, do you see? This is your God's Cossacks!" My mother was ashamed and went back into the house. I still hear how the Jew being taken pleaded with each "punch" he received from his "best man": "I am the father of small children. Have pity. You are still Jews…"

[Page 65]

This event in which I became interested in later years took place not only in Chelm.

The reason for such strange events was that the underworld for many years had supplied sorts of gangsters who would mix into conflicts among workers and bosses and always on behalf of the latter. Every sort of request from the worker for his improvement would be rejected by these people with strident voices. For many years, somewhere in a tavern, these people with shiny cap visors, their hats [worn] impudently on the side and with knives in their bootlegs were the distributors of justice between workers and bosses.

With the awakened consciousness of the workers in the great contest to free themselves from the czar, it was necessary to first free themselves from the little "*tsareles*" [Yiddish diminutive of czar] – the despotism of the manufacturers and bosses, for whom the procurers stood in service. This feeling of revenge of the workers against all kinds of people from the underworld, therefore, was self-evident. And it was not simply revenge – but neutralizing them.

As I was informed many years later, the czarist police gave permission that day across the entire country for the workers to settle accounts with the underworld, and the revolutionary organizations, it appears, agreed to this.

This was a provocation from the police to expose active revolutionary elements that was successful. The police, who were passive on this day, immediately in the morning, put out its nets not for the intelligentsia, but for the rebels against the czar.

While one can understand this strange act in the larger cities like Warsaw and Lodz where the underworld was dense and harmful to the evolution of the worker organizations, as we saw earlier, it was not justified in Chelm. Here it was quickly a pious imitation of the large cities.

May demonstration of the progressive workers movement in Chelm in 1936

[Page 66]

The best known of the thieves was Kishl the thief. This was a short and agile Jew who became a partner with a large gentile and they divided the roles between them thus:

The large gentile, dressed in a wide fur coat, would come to a place, push himself in where it was crowded to make it even more crowded and the small Kishl would move through unnoticed moving his fingers into the pockets of the naïve, toiling peasants and disappear. His partner remained as if nothing had happened here and would order something from the tailor. The peasant who had been robbed would tear his hair in surprise; but no one had been here!

Meanwhile, Kishl would slip part of the stolen items into someone's hands and divide the remainder with his partner…

After the yearly fair, before traveling home, Kishl would drop into the Jewish restaurant, eat at the same table as all of the fair merchants and often buy the recitation of grace for himself, as a thank you to the Most High for the good "transactions" that he had made…

Mentshn and Workers

The Jewish population in Chelm consisted of artisans and workers, but it is appropriate to refer to these workers with Sholem Aleichem's term: "*mentshn*" [people]. These are the "people" hired for the term of a year, from *khol hamoed* [intervening days of a holiday] to *khol hamoed* with food, drinks and a place to sleep.[1] Bosses mainly were as poor as their "people," who had their beds in the workshop itself, where the meager meals were distributed. There were no larger industries in Chelm as there were in other Polish Jewish cities. No Jewish workers were employed in the only foundry located there. Jews only worked in the two mills along with non-Jews. The tailors, shoemakers, cabinetmakers and house painters were small enterprises with few workers. The "inherited trades," too: watchmaker, hatmaker and bootleg maker worked in similar conditions. The same unhygienic, crowded workshops in the residences of the 'heirs" as with the "simple" artisans.

The remaining part of the Jewish population consisted of small traders, brokers and undetermined pursuits.

Great poverty kept the Chelemer Jews in its grip and the poverty was particularly noticeable in the area that was called (I do not know why) the *Neye Tsal* [new number]. This street stretched parallel with the main street, the Lubelsker (Lubliner) only a little below. Chelm is a hilly city and one part of the city lies lower, the other – higher.

The *Neye Tsal* actually was the oldest area of the city and its houses were more ruins than houses.

[Page 67]

From this deep poverty an organized working class, in the modern sense of the word, began to spread out at the end of the First World War with its professional and cultural organizations.

Chelemer Panorama

Certainly, the cities and *shtetlekh* all over Poland were similar to each other and, each city described, possessed the main characteristics of another. Yet, I will try to show the face of Chelm, as it is preserved in my memories.

Perhaps, the only thing that distinguishes Chelm from a number of other cities is its hilliness. I am not talking about such mountains that entice the interest of tourists, but there are enough hills to make the panorama of the city interesting. There are steps in some places that lead down or up from one street to another. They are present from the Lubliner Street to the *Neye Tsal*. However, in most places one went down and up without steps. There were ideal ice-skating spots during the winter for rascals, *kheder* [religious primary school] boys in comradeship with the gentile boys.

The church (the Greek Catholic church) occupied the highest spot in the city. The church gazed down very unexpectedly from the highest point with its brass cupola and its bronze crosses, like gilded epaulets on a Czarist general. At the side of the church was the aristocratic Greek Orthodox cemetery. There rested the aristocrats: the religious hierarchy and their allies, the military. The spot was considered as the most beautiful place to stroll in the city. However, no Jewish strollers were permitted there. This place was too sacred for Jewish steps. Young Jews made their first walking excursions in this beautiful spot after the First World War at the rebirth of Polish independence.[a][2]

The church was converted into a Polish Catholic Church. According to the premise of the Poles, the Russians had once expropriated this church for their ways of God, the Poles took it back after the liberation and, since, Poland's rebirth was a "democratic" one, the Jews were free to go everywhere. However, all sorts of hooligans also had the freedom to do what they wanted to do to the Jews. This beautiful strolling spot was the place of daily attacks by the hooligans on the Jews. Yet the Jewish young people continued to stroll there and the hooligans did not cease "amusing" themselves on the Jews.

A little further, but also on Lubliner Street, was the old and blackened church, as if blackened like Poland's fate under the Czarist rule. As was said, the Russian-Czarist regime did not permit the renovation of the Catholic Church in order to discredit it in the eyes of its believers.

[Page 68]

According to legend, the synagogue building had been given to the Jewish *kehile* years earlier by a Polish prince, a friend of the Jews.

The synagogue and houses of study were located in the center of the city and, therefore, the street was called *Szkolna* (*Shul* – School Street).

The Jews believed that the remains of the Prague golem [creature believed to have been created by magic by Rabbi Judah Loew in Prague to defend the city's Jews] lay in the attic of the old synagogue and, therefore, one should not enter it. How did the *golem* from Prague happen to be in Chelm? – But, one does not ask such a question.

The repairs for the Jewish *kehile* took place when a rich widow, Gitele, [Chana's daughter] (Arnsztajn) died in the city. From the money that she left according to a will or what was taken from her heirs, a fence was erected around the cemetery, a new roof was placed on the house of prayer, the synagogue was renovated and a *Talmud-Torah* [school for poor young boys] was built.

Paintings of Jewish historical locations – the Western Wall, Rachel's Tomb and other sacred places – appeared on the wall of the synagogue, whose color was unrecognizable from age.

Painters were brought all the way from Lublin for this refined work. The entire renovation occurred when Anshel Biderman was the head of the *kehile*.

The forest near Hrubieszower Street, or as it was called in Yiddish, Rubishover Street, also belonged to the city panorama. This was a forest of over a *viorst* in length [a little over one kilometer] at an end of the city on the road to Rubishov. An entire week, the forest that stretched in two straight lines on both sides of the highway served as a wood reservoir for Jewish as well as non-Jewish paupers. Ignoring the usual ban and Gajawa and his unmanageable aids who guarded the forest, they gathered the thin branches that had been broken off by the wind or the thin branches that they themselves broke with the help of long scoops and placed them together in bundles. There, they would also gather blackberries and mushrooms during the ripe summer months, some for their own use and others to sell. This was during the week. But, from *Shabbos* morning into the late night, this forest was made *Shabbosdik* [in the spirit of *Shabbos*]. They did not gather any more [branches] and came there for a "May picnic." The forest's *Shabbosim* began with the arrival of spring and it ended with the arrival of autumn. The *Shabbos* dawns began with the singing of Jewish young people who strolled into the forest in groups. On the way, they knocked on the windows of friends, woke them up and took them along. Thus, the group grew larger along the way. There was hunger, a lack of hope for a large number of the young, but it was life and especially Jewish life.

[Page 69]

During the years 1904-1905 secret gatherings were held in the shadows of those trees and many revolutionary acts were planned there. More than one death sentence against a local czarist political henchman or a traitor was carried out there.

In time the city began to become more of a large city and a cultivated area for strolling was created at the other end of the city. A park like Saxon Garden [in Warsaw] was created with an artistic brook and with a music hall over it. During the day on *Shabbosim* and Sundays, this garden would be full of those strolling.

There were baracks from czarist times. There also were two *pulks* [regiments] of soldiers from before Polish independence: an artillery regiment and an infantry regiment. The military hospital, which was among the largest in the country, was a particular pride of the city middleclass.

Jewish Way of Life

However, the Jewish way of life did not become more urbane. The education of the Jewish child lay in the old Sephardic *khederim* and *Talmud–Torahs* [religious primary schools for poor boys]. There was no communal library. At that time there was one private library that lent books for "rent" for those readers who were no longer satisfied with the books for a *kopek* from the itinerant bookseller. I do not know how long this library had existed. I knew of this library from when I became a reader in 1914–1915. Its owner was named Bibkowski. This was a "Russian" Jew who had done his military service in Chelm and had married here. The library was in his private residence. He also had the only Jewish newspaper kiosk on the main street at Lubelski that at that time was the only modern corner of culture in the city.

The Jewish religious life at that time in Chelm, as in all Jewish communities in Poland, was strongly rooted. It appeared that modern winds never would have any influence on the local Middle Ages way of life.

In addition to the synagogue and house of prayer already mentioned, there was a large number of Hasidic *shtiblekh* [one–room houses of prayer] where the old and young Hasidim from various sects studied and prayed. These were the Hasidim – mainly followers of pious, good Jews. At that time, as I remember, Chelm did not have its own esteemed Hasidic rebbe. The only rebbe, who drew his chain of descendents from several generations of Chelm rebbes, was Reb Nutala.

He was a quiet, modest Jew. He did not maintain a large court and did not preside over a large table.[3] He did not create a sensation with miracles.

[Page 70]

A group of the Chelm Jewish intelligentsia and culture workers
The deceased poet, L. Malach [Leib Malach, pseudonym of Leib Salzman] is in the center

During the summer one would find him sitting in his small garden before the house he inherited on Lubliner Street, where he enjoyed the pleasures of this world with a glass of tea. He sat on a soft chair with a hand hanging from a white cloth that was tied around his neck. His hand was in the mentioned position for his entire life. Whether this was the result of something that occurred at his birth or from an accident I do not know. Reb Nutala was the last of the Chelm rebbes. He did not have any children and after his death, his [rabbinical] seat was inherited by Reb Pinkhasl, a distant relative from a different city.

In the same courtyard, where the Rebbe, Reb Nutala lived, his brother, a grain merchant, also lived. The latter's children left on their worldly way and his oldest son, Moishe Lerer was the last chairman of YIVO [*Yidisher Visnshaftlekher Institut* – Yiddish Scientific Institute] in Vilna under the Soviet regime.

Moishe Lerer was a man with a deep Jewish and worldly education. During his early years, he studied in "distant Odessa" as a teacher. Jewish folklore was his beloved field of knowledge.

When the Jewish *folks–shul* [people's school] was founded after the First World War, Moshe became its teacher [and remained there] for many years.

In 1939, when the Soviets occupied the bordering nations, Moishe Lerer, as mentioned, was the chairman of the Vilna YIVO. He remained in this cultural office until the Nazi invasion and he shared the tragic fate of the all of the Vilna Jews.

Chelm Stories and Anecdotes

When people learn of my Chelm lineage, hundreds of people ask:

"From where do all of these stories and anecdotes about Chelm come?"

Others simply ask:

"Must there not be something in the fact that those from Chelm are called "fools?"

There are also soft–hearted people who do not want to shame anyone or want to comfort me and say:

[Page 71]

" There also can be exceptions in Chelm."

Indeed, there is no lack of those from Chelm who deny their origins. They are ashamed to admit their Chelm background. They say they are from Lublin. They save their prestige and it is not a big lie because Chelm belonged to and still belongs to Lublin *gubernia* [county].

Yet the further question is: why was such a "strong" defamation of fools thrown down on Chelm, or the opposite: why do they ascribe such smart stories, the most beautiful anecdotes to Chelm?

The answer is that there is no scientific–historical reason or that no one arrived at this explanation. There is no lack of hypotheses and some of them also sound very witty.

In the old home, every city and *shtetl*, just like every person, also had a nickname in addition to their own name. For example:

Pinsker *khazeyrim* [pigs], Warszawer *freser* [Warsaw gluttonous eater], Lemberger *fifkes* [sly ones], Piasker *ganovim* [thieves], and so on. Among others, the nickname "fools" had yet to fall on one. This name fell on Chelm for the same unknown reasons as the nicknames of other cities. However, if this is so, if fools, let this be woven into the material with a witticism somewhere, a story, an anecdote, as it happens, for example with Hershele Ostropoler [a prominent character in Yiddish humor], in whose name witticisms were written of which he had no idea. Chelm was a sort of collective Hershele Ostropoler.

I scarcely believe that there are such readers who would consider these lines as an attempt to defend Chelm. There is no reason to justify the city. The opposite, Chelm entered Yiddish literature and folklore as no other city has.

Rare stories and anecdotes were created around Chelm and thereby enriched Yiddish literature. It is enough to remember the two stories by Y. L. Peretz: *Der Chelemer Melamed* [*The Chelemer Teacher*] and the *Der Shabbos Goy* [*The Sabbath Gentile*]. And not only Peretz. A large number of Yiddish writers drew full buckets from this well. The anecdotes are particularly a blessing for children's literature. Sh. Bostamki, the editor of the first Yiddish children's journal in Vilna, *Grininke Beymelekh* [*Little Green Trees*], won the small readers with his "Chelemer fools." This material is being republished today in all children's publications in the entire Yiddish world. The poet, Aaron Zeitlin, published a comedy, *Chelemer Khokhim* [*Chelemer Fools*], a few years ago. And quite a curious case was with their beloved folk–singer, [Menakhem] Kipnis, who in 1923 or 1924 published a collection of Chelemer stories.

Kipnis came to Chelm with a concert of songs and it is said about it that he and his female singing partner, Zeligfeld, strolled along the Chelm streets on the eve of the concert. Seeing the two unfamiliar guests passing the black market that had blossomed then, the merchants thought that they were Americans with dollars. They did not lose any time and asked: "How much?"

[Page 72]

The guests understood what they meant and answered with a joke:

Zeligfeld said: "80 he."

And Kipnis answered: "70 she."[4]

They threw this refrain from the famous folksong at the merchants, instead of dollars. The Chelemer merchants understood the joke and were insulted that they were taken "for granted" and decided to boycott the concert.

They were not satisfied with just not going to the concert, but they also placed a guard at the concert hall and did not let the audience in. Not long ago, I met a *landsman* [person from the same town] who was one of the guards at the theater – and best of all, who today, 30 years after the event, is still incensed by this "insult"…

Is this not itself a fine Chelemer anecdote?

Kipnis took "revenge" on Chelm for this failure with a fine collection of Chelemer stories.

If the failed concert really led to this or it was more because of his inclination to folklore, Chelm created such a hypothesis because Kipnis published the stories immediately after the failed concert. It also can be that Chelm, with its version of the failed concert, took revenge on Kipnis.

Revenge for revenge…

And Kipnis did try to give an explanation of where the name "Chelemer fools" originates.

He tells in one of his stories:

The angel who distributes souls to those who are being born flew with two sacks of souls across Chelm. On one side he carried a sack of smart souls, on the other side, a sack of foolish souls. Just when he had to pass the Chelm mountain, the sack of foolish souls got entangled in the mountain and all of the souls were scattered in Chelm…

As mentioned, the wellspring of the Chelemer fools is not yet exhausted. Writers and painters have available a treasure of inspiration for a long time, although Chelm, as a Jewish community, is no longer here.

A Great Fire

The church bells suddenly started [ringing] with all of their bronze strength on a *Shabbos* morning. Sleep in the city was interrupted. Everyone got out of bed and began running to the place of the fire.

The *Neye Tsal* [street name] was burning.

The old, wooden, dried up little houses surrendered to the flames without any resistance. The shingled roofs and the wooden walls burst into flames one after another. Men stood helpless and women rang their hands. The *pozarne komande* (firemen) with their barrels of water and hoses did their duty.

[Page 73]

However, their work gave the impression of children at play or of ridicule. After every spray of water from the hoses, the flames answered with wanton "screeches" and knocks and proudly spread further. The few tin roofs on which the naïve observers of the tragic spectacle lay their hopes that they would stop the spreading of the flames, these roofs began to spring up and roll like *megilus* [scrolls] of fire and surrendered with crackling.

After the fire, half of the Jewish population remained without a roof over their heads. My two Torah [study] rooms also disappeared in the fire. The first, at Itshe Szepel's [house] and, the second, at Pesakh the teacher's [house]. Both were crowded, wooden cellar rooms, where the beds, kitchen, the table with wooden benches for teaching and the chickens with which the rabbi's wife traded in the market, lived peacefully together.

Half a room at Itshe Szepel's was fenced off with a "folding screen" and rented to a young couple for a "golden temple." That was then when I studied, just after the wedding.

Various rumors circulated in the city about the fire. One of them stubbornly blamed the regime. The czarist administration with the regional police superintendent at the head – a box–shaped, fat swine, an angry little dictator – a kind of mini–czar –

had set fire to the poor part of the city as a means to remove Jewish poverty. It is possible that the rumors were not groundless because at the time the czarist regime intended to convert the Polish city into a Russian *gubernia* [province].

Chelm – A Russian Province

Chelm belonged to the Lublin *gubernia* for all the years, but there was a long conflict about its authentic Polishness.

The population in Chelm and mainly around Chelm was a mix of Poles and Ukrainians. The surrounding villages had mainly Ukrainian–speaking peasants who spoke Ukrainian or as they called it, *khakhlatske*. Every Polish–speaking peasant was thought of by the other peasants as an aristocratic maniac, a poser, a boaster. However, the population in the city, in the surrounding *shtetlekh*, mainly spoke Polish and the official language was Russian during the Czarist times.

It mattered even less to Czarist Russia that it was the ruler of the 10 Polish *gubernias*, but it crawled out completely from its bearskin to Russify Chelm. Indeed, it used the pretext that the majority of the population there was not Polish. Naturally, they did not ask the population. Power was in the hands of those who had won the conflict.

According to a Czarist *ukaz* (decree), Chelm or, as the city was called in Russian, Kholm, was designated in 1913, as I remember, as an independent Russian *gubernia*.

[Page 74]

The former Siedlce *gubernia* with a governor with his own personal retinue was moved to Chelm.

The Russians celebrated their "victory." The Poles walked around with lowered mustaches and the Jews really were at wit's end.

Rumors about various acts of terror ran ahead of each other.

[They] learned of the Shedlitz [Siedlce] pogrom on the Jews during the time of this governor who was now the absolute ruler of Chelm. And more rumors from which the hairs on the head stood up. Thus, in the national political fight about where Chelm belonged between the Russians and the Poles (I do not say Poland because an independent Poland did not then exist) there also was a third side – the Jewish one.

In truth, to the average Jew, the concern about the entire struggle about Chelm was whether it was good for the Jews or not good for the Jews. The Jews thought of every change in political life in Czarist Russia as a new evil that would fall on their heads. The Jews remembered the Cossack whips very well. Therefore, the choice between the two led to the question: which of them is worse…

The *gubernia* was created and the Russification machine for the Chelm population started with all of the power of the czarist functionaries. Poles were punished with jail for speaking Polish in public places.

The excesses were not anything new for the Jews. In truth, they did not have to wait for pogroms until Chelm became a Russian *gubernia*. Jews did not have to wait until then to hide in the cellars, in the attics and in the neighboring *shtetlekh* and villages.

However, this Russification did not last long. In 1915, German–Austrian troops occupied Chelm as all of Poland. The national status of Chelm went through its last convulsion at a separate peace that *Junkerist* [junkers – German word meaning country squires who had great political power in Germany during this period] Germany made with the White Guard Ukrainian Hetman [Pavlo] Skoro Padskyi in 1917 when Germany generously assigned Chelm to Ukraine.

*A group of male and female friends from Poalei–Zion
[Workers of Zion – a Marxist–Zionist group] in Chelm*

[Page 75]

After the German–Austrian Occupation

Chelm, along with all of Poland and a large part of Europe, was under the military boot of Germany and its partner Austria for three years (from 1915 to 1918).

The population experienced a difficult life under this occupation. The honeymoon – the hope that the Jews then associated with a German victory over the Czarist Army – quickly dissipated. They simply had changed the czarist whip for the German riding crop, exchanged one evil for another. The oppression of the occupying armies was quickly felt. Forced labor, hunger and epidemics became a dark specter in every house.

In 1915, cholera, which made the Chelm population sparser and the number of victims in the old cemetery larger, already had appeared. Cholera retreated with the coming of winter and in its place typhus arrived, which raged the entire winter and completed what the cholera had begun…

The population experienced a bitter life.

Yet among all the horrors, young people grew up who yearned for life. Military service was not a problem for the Polish youth, so the young remained physically and spiritually thirsty for a more beautiful and better life, for a revived life.

And suddenly – such an unprecedented will for a new life! The October Revolution.

The glow of revolutionary fire in Russia lit many corners of the world. The revolutionary waves were carried across Poland as across other European lands. The Jewish youth in Poland broke with the way of life of the Middle Ages. A war broke out between parents and children, not as if there was a difference in one generation, but in tens of generations.

The narrow, stifling Chelemer houses also opened their shutters to the new events. The young sharpened their ears for the sound of the new times. They began to create organizations, professional, cultural. First of all, they thirstily turned to self-education. They wanted to make up for the lost years when their entry to the world was closed.

[Page 76]

They began to read modern books. And a communal Jewish library was founded in the city still under the German-Austrian occupation.

Feywl Frid was the initiator of the communal Jewish library in Chelm.

After long years of absence, he suddenly reappeared in the city. Where had Feywl Frid been? Where did he come from? – No one could answer this [question] for sure. Some said that he escaped from czarist exile in Siberia; others said that he came from abroad. And he himself? – He was silent about this.

Yet he was not such a quiet one.

At the initiative of the energetic, intelligent Feywl Frid, the first Jewish People's Library was founded in Chelm at the end of the First World War.

And Feywl Frid was not only the founder of the library. He should be considered the father of modern communal and spiritual life in general.

He was a man who boiled over with initiatives and he had the strength to influence people to accomplish the initiatives. His contribution was invaluable to the Jewish population during the first years of the Jewish renaissance in Chelm.

At first, he was busy with private lessons. Later, [he was occupied] with the founding of the *Folkshul* [people's school – secular public school]; he became one of its teachers. He also was one of the first lecturers of cultural history for the adults.

During the days of the Nazi invasion, he and several hundred Chelemer Jews together evacuated to the Soviet Union. After the war, he returned to Chelm. But he did not remain there for long. His wife (née Fiszer), a medical doctor, had perished with their daughter.

A little later a man who became heartrendingly famous during our tragic time, began to influence Chelemer communal life, although in another direction. This was the Bundist worker, Shmuel (Arthur) Zigelboim.

A workers club was founded then in the city for the first time. Lectures, readings, etc. would be given. Workers and people who simply loved culture came to the workers club. Almost no political hue of any kind was known at that time. They would come mainly on *Shabbos*. But the premises also were not empty on weekday evenings. It was the primary communal meeting spot and, therefore, a pleasure for the culturally thirsty young people. A beautiful library was quickly created and the young people just swallowed the books. It cannot be known who read with an explicit interest in [acquiring knowledge] and who took books because it was the fashion, but everyone carried around books. It is said that if only today, in the American nations, there was a trend for Yiddish books… That the trend to read would be so great that non-readers would be ashamed and at least learn a few of the names of books and writers so as not to remain embarrassed in a society…

[Page 77]

From the beginning, the library and the club were non-partisan and were not named after any personalities that would give the institutions a certain political coloration.

But on a certain *Shabbos*, the club was disturbed by the first political arguments:

"Someone" had nailed a political label over the library. It was given the name of the deceased Bundist leader, [Bronislaw] Grosser.

From then on it was not just a library, but [it was] the "Grosser Library."

This was the first public party work of the young Shmuel Zigelboim.

The harmony of the non–partisan club disappeared because of this and sharp quarrels took its place.

Group meetings began in private locations. Political differences began to emerge, pecking out of its hard shell of previous indifference [of] workers or "people hired on an annual basis."

The first political grouping among the Jewish workers in Chelm was the Bundist under Zigelboim's leadership.

A little later the *Poalei–Zion* [Workers of Zion – Marxist–Zionists] party was founded. Feywl Frid again played a leading role. These two groupings were the only two political workers groupings in Chelm for several years. In time, *Poalei–Zion* became the main power for the Chelm Jewish workers, taking over even more from the Bund. The communist party first became a significant strength in the Jewish neighborhood in the later years.

Meanwhile, both the Bund and *Poalei–Zion* were housed under one roof in the [earlier] created club that still was considered non–partisan. The cultural work still was done jointly. Evening courses were given for adults through which many later leading male and female comrades received their first elementary education.

Cultural communal workers breaking the ground for a new building for the Jewish Folkshul in Chelm

[page 78]

In time *Poalei–Zion* separated and rented its own premises on Lubliner Street at Koper's in "Komenice," which I think was then the most beautiful house in the city.

Inheritance from the Austrian Occupation

Several Austrian–Jewish officers, who contributed to the shaping of worldly Jewish life in the city, remained in Chelm immediately after the German–Austrian armies were defeated and the Austrian Empire fell apart.

Dr. Kanfer, an Austrian first lieutenant, was a man of wider culture. As soon as he threw off his military uniform with the collar covered with stars, he began to speak a very charming eastern Galician Yiddish and became active in Chelm Jewish society. He would appear with instructive Yiddish lectures and quickly became the manager of the *Folkshul* that already was in existence.

His speech was calm and his actions were not hasty, laden with knowledge, of his own time; his speech was eagerly listened to and his views were respected by various groups even though Dr. Kanfer was counted as a right *Poalei–Zionist*. However, his beloved area was literature, although he was occupied with communal and pedagogical activities. Therefore, he also worked with Polish–Yiddish publications in his free time.

I once entered his *Folkshul* director's office and saw a new Yiddish book on his desk. Dr. Kanfer was sitting inspired, his gaze warmly caressed the book that had a personal inscription from the author and he spoke enthusiastically:

"What a distance the author has covered from his *A Roman fun a Ferd–Goniv* [*A Romance of a Horse Thief*] to now!"

This book was Y[osef]. Opatoshu's just published *In di Polishe Welder* [*In the Polish Woods*].

Dr. Kanfer and his family were in Chelm for several years. He occupied the post of director of the *Folkshul* without interruption. His wife was the teacher of Polish at the same school. Later, he left for Krakow and, according to arriving news, edited a Polish newspaper. There were rumors before the [Second World] war that Dr. Kanfer died in Krakow.

A second colorful figure was the Bundist communal worker, Dr. Fensterblau, an inheritance from the Austrian occupation.

I think he also came from eastern Galicia, from Krakow or near Krakow. His Yiddish was a very familiar one, like he would never have worn an Austrian officer's uniform. In addition, he was a very temperamental speaker and communal worker.

[Page 79]

At that time, the two political parties – Bund and *Poalei–Zion* – were most active in the Jewish neighborhood. Later, after the split in *Poalei–Zion*, the left *Poalei–Zion* remained the most important.

Workers Struggles

The "people" or "the people hired on an annual basis" who were tormented in the crowded workshop rooms of the Chelemer artisans where they worked, "ate" and "slept" together, these "people" truly became encouraged. The "idyll" between the worker and owner disappeared. The workers from the various trades began to organize in their trade unions, too, with the rise of modern organized Jewish communal life.

Professional communal workers and leaders emerged from among the workers themselves. Collective demands began to be presented and strikes became a frequent occurrence. Despite the fact that there were no large industries in the city, a strike involved hundreds of workers. They would last for weeks and thanks to the patience and stubbornness of the workers, the results almost always were in their favor.

It happened that I took part in several such trade strikes and because of their importance, in my opinion, I will spend some time on them:

It was during the first post–war [First World War] years, when the Polish currency fell so low that printing small banknotes was not worthwhile to the state. Paper, ink and printing would have cost more than the value of the banknote. They would tear one banknote into four even parts and each part had the value of a fourth of the torn banknote.

There were cases in which someone sold their house for a designated sum and by the time the house had formally been registered and the agreed upon sum was received, he could buy a pair of shoes for the sum or just a herring.

The wages for which we began working on Sunday lost half their value or more when we were paid on Friday.

I speak about it deliberately do that today's reader can have an idea about the character of the economic struggle at that time.

Therefore, all of the agreements between the owners and workers using Polish money were groundless. They had to look for a solution.

This example was given by the government itself: it designated a sliding scale wage–price list for the state and municipal employees.

The wages were designated according to a firm foreign currency – according to the American dollar. In paying the wages they would take into account the price of the dollar and pay the equivalent in marks, or later, in Polish *zlotes*.

[Page 80]

Such a program already existed in the larger cities and was a common occurrence in private undertakings but was still new in Chelm.

Naturally, the owners opposed such a demand. Strange, too, is that a number of workers fought this demand with the pretext that it was not achievable. In truth, this demand was fought by those workers who had other political beliefs than those in whose hands lay the leadership of the strike. This was "natural" in the inter–party struggle of the time.

In truth, the strike was a hard one, long drawn out; it lasted five weeks. However, the workers won completely. This was a strike by the tailors of men's clothing.

In addition, it was typical that although the trade unions already were well organized in other cities as in the entire country and the workers already had graduated from a school of struggle, the kinship between the owner and the worker had not completely disappeared.

According to the agreement that was reached after the strike in the first floor premises in Kuper's "Komienice" of the Artisans Union, my brother who is now in Buenos Aires signed for the Artisans Union and I in the name of the Workers Union.

At that time we, the representatives of the two fighting sides, both still lived in our parents' house…

This was not an exceptional case at that time.

Naturally, the victory of the workers in that complicated strike immediately found a reverberation in other trades. The tailors of women's clothing struck a short time after this. There were no strikebreakers because the place was small enough; everyone knew everyone and was ashamed for one another. But efforts by the workers themselves continued because of political party opposition to their actions.

This strike also was won. Although the win must be credited to the good organization of the strike, a man, actually from the opposition, contributed something here.

Berl Kelberman was then the leader of the women's clothing owners. Later, he was one of the 15 Jews who remained alive in Chelm itself, working in a Gestapo workshop.

A slender man, neatly dressed and just as tidy in character, he felt in his conscience that the strike was dragging on and he rushed his owner colleagues to end the strike in behalf of the workers.

As already mentioned Berl Kelberman was one of the 15 artisans who survived the Nazi hell in Chelm. He is now in the United States.

[Page 81]

The strikes that broke out were not the only ones in Chelm. If I spend time on them it is because these [strikes] are known by me. I also believe that mentioning all of the strikes would be an unnecessary repetition of similar struggles.

Cultural Flowering

The workers and the young in general were not very satisfied with just economic wins. The thirst for "spiritual nourishment" was never stilled even [when those then working in] the cultural field were called naïve. Some of the young in Poland, in Lithuania and in other eastern European lands are the creators and users of culture today in the most varied American nations, as well as in the compact and small, secluded American communities. These are the present buyers as well as readers of the Yiddish book, the listeners to Yiddish literary lectures. You can recognize them by the flame of enthusiasm in their eyes. When they speak of Yiddish literature, when they quote a Yiddish poet, whose poetry they would hear sung or recited at various literary–oral evenings, as they then would call the Friday night evenings. Whoever speaks, when they quote a writer, whom they have heard or seen themselves – and this was a frequent phenomenon – there is no greater joy to equal this.

I do not remember any one empty *Shabbos* in Chelm, not one *Shabbos* without a reading, without a lecture throughout the years. Lecturers, party leaders and writers would come from Warsaw with various lectures. I remember the martyr Yisroel Shtern [a poet and journalist deported to his death at Treblinka in 1942], singing out a complicated lecture; Uri Zvi Grinberg, the blond who then was beloved by the young with his just published *Mefisto*; the tall, thin, quiet Z[usman] Segalowicz, Yisroel Mastbaum, Peretz Markish and so on. Party lectures were self–evident. Each of the parties brought in its speakers and there was no lack of an audience. Not only the Chelm young people stormed the premises where the lectures were given, but young people came together from the surrounding *shtetlekh*: from Rawicz, Wojslawice and Grabowiec and others. Some came on foot, some in wagons, but they tried not to miss a lecture and at the same time to spend a little time in the large city.

However, the city tasted not only "imported" culture. Its cultural life did not remain backward in comparison to larger cities in Poland.

I already have mentioned the Chelm *folkshul*, which maintained its existence until the Holocaust and even progressed despite obstacles and all of the material and political difficulties caused by the Polish government. A Hebrew *gymnazie* [secondary school] also existed for many years until the Holocaust. The Bakalar family among others occupied the posts of teachers and director of this *gymnazie*. This was an intelligent family and one of them was a better reader than the next. I think this family was not from Chelm, but were in Chelm for years and influenced the cultural growth of the society.

[Page 82]

On a higher lever were those, almost systematic lectures on cultural history that contributed significantly to the worldly ideas of the Chelm young people. The first one who gave these lectures was the previously mentioned Feywl Frid. This was right after the German–Austrian occupation or during its last months. Shmuel Zigelboim [taught] the same course at the Bundist premises a short time after this. During the winter of 1921, I directed this course in the premises of *P.Z.* [*Poalei–Zion*] on Lubleski, three times a week. The course was attended for a certain cost by the young people of all [political] leanings, even by guests from the surrounding *shtetlekh* for a certain cost.

However, I believe that the central place for self–development was the library. The city already had several community libraries that served the readers every evening. Yet readers had to wait in a line to receive a book to read. There were so many readers.

Literary circle at the Jewish gymnazie

Writing about my city that was tragically annihilated by Hitlerism as all other Jewish cities in Poland, I do not try to give any preference to any one communal movement. Yet I give more detailed attention to several organizations and less detail to others or none at all. I was close to the organizations described; I was an insider and a [participant]. However, it is difficult for me to speak about every movement from which I stood completely at a distance because of my beliefs. Speaking and writing only from memory, particularly after all of my own as well as not my own perished by the same terrible death, would be a disparagement of their work, life and death.

I only know of the existence of the Zionist movement with all of its branches, about the existence of a group of politicians with a certain influence in the artisans union. I remember the scout organization, but all of this I remember as just an on–looker and I am concerned with just recording their existence. Alas, I cannot provide more facts.

[Page 83]

The Dark Beginning

That which I am going to relate or record I heard from the mouth of Tankhn Nisenbaum as I already said in my introduction. I met him in Sao Paulo, Brazil, after his arrival here to [visit] his sister and brother–in–law, Moshe Klerer.

The storyteller was among the 15 Jewish artisans who worked for the Gestapo, isolated in the Chelm jail and thus escaped from death.

Here I will only present the storyteller, Tankhn Nisenbaum, who told me everything that he saw himself and that which he heard from others. His speech is simple without polishing and corrections like he himself, the young, strong carpentry worker, Tankhn Nisenbaum.

Tankhn Nisenbaum sat across from me, on a chair in the home of my *landsfroy* [woman from the same town], Sura Rywka, who was my neighbor in Chelm on Hrubieszow Street and spoke.

His story was – as [could be expected] – a lava eruption of personal remembrances and, against my will, I often had to restrain his rush of words in order to get facts and dates from his [story of a] general character:

The Nazis Army occupied Chelm on the 9th of October 1939.

They did not wait for long in Chelm to begin the terror that already horrified the world.

A group of Nazis immediately drove up to the well–known family [of] Moshe Pomeranc at Refomacka [at the] corner of Agrodowa [and] chased the entire family out of the house without permitting them to take with them the smallest thing from there. And they settled in the house. However, this would have been the mildest, the least [thing] that one would have expected from these beasts.

The Nazis were not satisfied with this alone:

The Pomeranc family, which was thrown out of its home, was forced to wash the bathrooms of its own house with their bare hands, wipe them, wash the toilets with their own shirts and then put them back on their bodies accompanied with the wild mockery of the Nazis and their local collaborators – the *Endekes* [members of the Polish National Party] hooligans.

The effect of those wild deeds by the Nazis on the frightened Jewish population in the city is easy to imagine. The tone was set and the Jews awaited in anguish further dark deeds by the Nazis and their Polish collaborators. And they did not have to wait long for the "further [actions]." Acts of individual torture and murder were daily events.

[Page 84]

The looted Pomeranc family residence had to be kept clean. The Germans were "civilized" people and believed in hygiene. So they caught 15 Jews in the street to clean the residence. After their work, these 15 Jews were forced to box under the command of a Gestapo officer. Yosef Stoliar's eye was knocked out during this "spectacle."

Most of the 15 Jews died after the boxing.

One [act of] vandalism chases another:

The Kuzmirer Rebbe's son, himself also a rebbe, was living in Chelm at that time. The beasts entered his residence, chased out the rebbe, ignoring the fact that he was paralyzed, took along the *shamas* [synagogue warden] and the Hasidim who were there at the time. They were all forced to wash the Nazi automobiles. This was not enough. They [the Germans] thought of various practical jokes to insult and humiliate the victims for the enjoyment of the torturers and the local Polish masses.

It was clear to the Jews in Chelm that their lives and possessions were [being treated] completely recklessly, as never before even during the dark moments of Jewish history. The words law and moral were a bloody mockery for them, the Hitler hordes, and together with their Polish and Ukrainian partners they were now the exclusive bosses over the lives of the Jews in Chelm. These hordes in Chelm, as all over Poland, did not even try to mask their dark deeds along with the ridicule of the Jews for their own pleasure, as well as for practical objectives, as they had done in other nations.

During the first days of the occupation they tore open the Jewish businesses and the occupier and their underworld members were let loose. Whoever wanted to, took.

An "exception" was made for the Jewish furniture businesses, which, instead of just looting them, they became the "legal" property of the Chelm Ukrainians.

The evil decrees immediately began to pour over the heads of Jews, one worse than the other:

The first decree was that the Jews in Chelm could not go outside into the streets later than six o'clock in the evening. Otherwise it was known: death!

After this came a contribution of 100,000 *zlotes* that only the Jews in Chelm had to pay immediately. The money was collected by the *kehile* among the Jews in the city and the occupier was paid what was demanded on time. As soon as the demanded sum was paid, a new [demand] was made of 40,000 *zlotes*. The Chelm Jews did the impossible and the sum was also provided. A little hope still shone among some Jews that perhaps they would get off with money – and in addition, Jews are accustomed… However, as soon as the second contribution was paid, the occupiers demanded a third – this time only 10,000 *zlotes*.

[Page 85]

As frightening and difficult as these material offerings were for the poor Chelemer *kehile* that was then completely looted, it was a "trifle" in comparison to the blood offerings, with Jewish lives that would soon be sacrificed in mass volume on the Nazi sacrificial alter.

The Bloody March to the Bug River

The arbitrariness began during the first minutes after the ravaging Nazi–boots set foot on the soil. An hour had not passed without looting, without persecutions and without Jewish blood. However, the first extermination took place on the 1st of December 1939. Seven weeks after the occupation of the city.

Noakh Szuchmacher, who also took part in the bloody march to the Bug and was one of the few fortunate ones who survived, told about this mass murder. As already mentioned, he also was the first Chelemer who arrived in Argentina after the war.

As he told it, this occurred in the following manner:

The Nazi chief, Fisher, gave an order to Anshl Biderman, the head of the community, that all Jews, aged 16 to 60, should come on the first day of December. This included only healthy men. Approximately 2,000 Jews came.

The head of the community ran around all night to Jewish houses and presented this dark order. However, he did not mention that this applied only to the healthy afraid that because he was afraid that everyone would say they were ill and he would not be able to provide the required number of Jews. Sick and healthy came to the marketplace as they were ordered. As soon as the number of Jews were at the spot, they were surrounded by the Gestapo and they began to lead them to the Hrubieszow highway on the way to the Bug River with the pretext that they were being taken to the Soviet side.

The first victim in this bloody march was Itshe, Shepele's son. I knew this man from my *kheder* years. He was a *melamed* and I studied *Khumish* [Torah] and Rashi with him. He lived in the *Neye Tsal* at that time. His father was a *Nikolajevkser* [one who had served in the army of Tsar Nikholai I] soldier. I knew his brother's son as a young communist and, I think, today he occupies an important office in the Polish government.

When Itshe Shepele's, found himself among everyone at the marketplace, he realized that he had made a mistake: they had demanded men from 16 to 60 and he already was older. He was already 63. He went to the Gestapo leader with his papers in his hand and showed him his mistake. The answer from the brown [shirted] murderer was – a shot from his revolver.

[Page 86]

Itshe, Shepele's son, was the first victim of the bloody march to the Bug. The second one annihilated was a son of a well–known family, Menasha the headstone engraver. The family was itself distinguished from others by this profession itself. But it was better known because of the sons who were considered as members of the Chelm intelligentsia. Their family name was Mendelbaum. Some brothers lived in Paris until the last war. The only son who remained in Chelm with his father was a cripple and this was the reason that he was shot at the marketplace before the march began. The baker, Yankl Brilant, also was shot there.

With [the events] before the start of the bloody march, it already was clear what the march itself would bring.

And the mass slaughter began one kilometer from the marketplace.

Two thousand Jews were being led on their last "stroll" through the Hrubieszow forest, in whose shade they had once spent their time reading, and in discussions and in arguments.

Twenty people were shot immediately at the entrance into the forest. Among those shot were:

Dr. Aks, Sekuler, the old well–known dentist, Benya Salan, Shimeon Zajdradem and Gecl Majer, Ahron Grinman, Yitzhak Goldman and his son, Avraham. The female Dr. Feldman, also was with them, although, it was said that there were only men in the group. It is possible that Mrs. Feldman went along herself or she accompanied someone in the group. The story–teller did not remember the remaining men who were shot.

Hrubieszow is located seven miles from Chelm and there was a highway between the two cities on which would stretch unending caravans of business owners. Day and night, heavily laden wagons harnessed three and four horses across would be pulled over the highway and the jabbering by wagon–drivers to the horses never stopped. This was the trade transport between Chelm and Hrubieszow.

Here, the peaceful highway was escorted by Jewish corpses on the 1st of December 1939.

Over half of the 1,200 Jews were left lying on the peaceful seven–mile highway between Chelm and Hrubieszow.

Frightened peasants from the surrounding villages came to Chelm another day and told about what they had seen: that hundreds of Jews who had been shot were lying on the road.

The remaining families of the group that had been sent out ran in despair to the Nazi authorities to seek justice, to ask for pity. The city steward was then a Chelemer *Volks–Deutsch* [ethnic German]. Szuchmacher said [they told him – the *Volks–Deutsch*] that he should go to the military commandant 'to inform' him about the injustices that were committed against the group of Jews sent out.

[Page 87]

The commandant listened to him and "calmed" his *Volks*–comrade with the words:

"Today we are taking the Jews for breakfast. Tomorrow if we need to, we will take the Poles for lunch. And you," the commandant answered – "go home and do not mix into our things."

The intervention of the *Volks–Deutsch* with the commandant rings a bit naïve to the reader, as naïve as it rang for me when I was told it, but I relate it as I heard it.

The Germans brought together 800 more Jews. They joined the remainder of the Chelm Jews and they were led to the Bug together. Not more than 400 Jews remained of the two groups, from the Chelemer and from those from Hrubieszow, [who were marched] to the Bug.

The Nazi commandant gave a speech to the remaining half–dead Jews before crossing the Bug River and promised them that none of those remaining would be killed. However, he warned them that after they crossed the Bug to the Soviet side, none of them could return. Anyone who returned would be shot immediately.

This time the Gestapo commandant kept his word; none of the remaining unfortunate ones were shot.

They chose a flat place in the river through which the several hundred unfortunate ones were driven across the river. Those driven, with guns pointed behind them, went into water up to their chests in the middle of a winter night, carrying the weakened ones who could not go by themselves.

Eight Jews died from exhaustion and cold crossing over to the Soviet side.

After a short time on the Soviet side, they [the Soviets] sent back those who had come over. They were placed on boats and sent back to the German side.

The Jews who were sent back did not all reach home. Of all those who returned to Chelm through various roundabout ways, there only remained 150. The remainder perished on the road from exhaustion. The only name that the storyteller remembered of those who perished on the road home was Chaim Itshe Szpader, a butcher with the nickname "Tshela." He died from injuries to his legs.

Szuchmacher returned to Chelm. As a returnee in fear, grasping the true nature of the Nazis and the consequences for [returning] moved him to a daring step:

He again crossed the Soviet border, leaving his wife and children and the remaining family in Chelm, whom he believed were not in as much danger as he was.

Later, he did his military service in Anders' Army. As already mentioned, after the war, he was the first Jew from Chelm who arrived in Argentina. A little later, he settled in Australia. His entire family perished in Chelm.

[Page 88]

Tankhn Nisenbaum, from whom I have taken most of the information about the destruction of Chelm, later worked in the Gestapo workshop and even saw the photographs that the Nazis took of the terrible slaughter in the Hrubieszow forest.

The Hospital for Mentally Ill

Chelm was not a very large city, but it always had the largest hospitals. The military hospital near the Hrubieszow forest that was inherited from tsarist times was one of them. The sick would be brought here from distant areas. A very large military cemetery, not very far from the hospital, arose there during the course of time, particularly at the time of the First World War. Straight wooden crosses over the graves told of the same fate and ancestry of those under them.

Another hospital arrived at Wygon [a village near Chelm] for the mentally ill. This place and the good forest air were appropriate for a healing institution. A city for the sick grew there with a great deal more comfort than for the healthy. The ill were sent to this hospital from throughout Poland.

There were 300 patients in each hospital when the German hordes occupied Chelm. The "superior" German race immediately showed its "superiority." Gestapo members broke in there [in the hospitals] and sent out all of those in the hospital. The sick, who had come there to heal found their graves at Wygun, where the hospitals stood.

Murder of Children

Tankhn Nisenbaum told of a case of the torture of a child that made the hair stand on end. No matter how much one is accustomed to hearing about the deeds of the Nazi scoundrels, I always shudder when I hear of the torture of children.
[Page 89]

In addition – this was not done at anyone's order, but for their own sadistic pleasure. Nisenbaum, the storyteller, who himself survived the frightful horror and told this story often, was moved by what he was saying and he controlled the tears that choked him.

Here is what he related:

Among the names of the S.S. murderers, one of the *schar–fuhrer* [squad leader], with the nickname of the "the blond" excelled the most. This was a scoundrel, a sadist who surpassed all of his colleagues with his cruelty.

In a terribly cold winter morning, this "blond" rode out on a bicycle. A 12–year old Jewish boy came towards him. The scoundrel sprang off his bicycle and gave it to the child to lead with his bare hands. Each time the child wanted to warm one hand and lead the bicycle with the other, the "blond," whipped him on his frozen hands with his riding crop. The child led the bicycle with his bare hands for a long time before the eyes of a helpless city; they could do nothing but cry and gnash their teeth, until the child's hands froze completely and the flesh peeled off the bone.

Later, the child's hands were cut off at the hospital.

*Charming Jewish children, Sulka and Leibl Nisenbaum,
who were annihilated by the Hitler murderers*

Jews at forced labor under the Hitler tyranny

The Gestapo in Chelm

The storyteller, Tankhn Nisenbaum, had been caught at that time with a number of Jews for work. The work, in the courtyard of the Gestapo, began with moral and physical torture of the workers by the Gestapo gang. The work consisted of cleaning the rooms and polishing the boots of the murderers. The Jews had to polish the boots, sort each pair and know to whose feet each pair of boots belonged and to place them in front of the door of their owners. In case of an error – and there were many such, because they were not shown earlier to whom the boots belonged – they received blows. From the highest floor where the gang was located, the boots were thrown down right at the heads of the Jews, with scorn and laughter. This was such a morning entertainment for the Nazi murderers.

[Page 90]

The Gestapo then consisted of these:

First chief – [Herman] Rohlfing; vice–chief – Fisher; aides – Schlesinger, Urban, [Rolf] Maurer, Steinert, Feldman, [Emanuel] Schafer, [Johannes] Krauz, Braunmiller, Ashendorf and [Rudolf] Theimer. The last two were especially for Jewish problems.

A larger number of Jews, caught in the streets, as was the way, worked serving the Gestapo at the beginning. In time, the young, strongest and most capable were chosen from among those gathered together.

The latter thought that because they worked for the murderers themselves, they were temporarily secure in their lives. However, something else occurred:

On a certain day the vice–chief of the Gestapo left on furlough for his bloody fatherland, to his thieving home. The Jew, who previously had served in his residence, remained there, as before. On the eve of the vice–chief's return to Chelm, the man who cleaned his room tried hard to have his work please the murderer and he asked a second Jewish worker at the Gestapo to help him with the work. As a wage for the help, the former treated him to a small glass [of whisky] from a bottle that was in the vice–chief's room.

When the murderer returned, he immediately noticed that there was not as much in the bottle as there had been when he left it at his departure.

The young man who had served in his room confessed his "crime" and told him under what conditions this had occurred.

The sentence from the Gestapo–murderer was carried out on the spot:

Still very young men, both the one who drank and the one who treated him, they were harnessed to a horse and a wagon, which they were forced under a whip to pull and to gallop through the entire city, to the train station. On their backs was pasted the tag:

"Thus are Jewish thieves punished."

When exhausted, half–dead, they pulled the wagon to the spot. They were shot by the vice–chief himself.

Jewish Police

However, it was not enough for the murderers to kill. For their sadistic pleasure, they determined that the annihilation of the Jews would also be carried out by Jewish hands – this was, by the way, the devilish tactic all over Poland and everywhere that their bloody paws reached. They created in Chelm as everywhere a Jewish police.

[Page 91]

This occurred right on the eve of the devilishly conceived total annihilation of the Chelm Jews. Along with the Polish, Ukrainian, Latvian and Lithuanian police that the Gestapo had at its service, they also created the Jewish one. The Jewish police recruits were communal scum just as those from the listed nationalities.

This was at the beginning of 1942.

Someone named Szwarcblat, from Libewna, three miles from Chelm was designated as the chief of the Jewish police. Vice–chief – a certain Genik. The latter previously was a guard at the Warsaw Jewish Hospital on Gęsia Street. I do not know if he was from Warsaw or if he only worked there.

The Jewish police immediately received their "responsible" work to carry out.

Creating the Ghetto

After the Jewish police [force] was created in Chelm, the driving of the Jews into the ghetto – the last isolation before their complete annihilation – was carried out with their help.

The following streets were designated for the ghetto:

Szerlecka, Pocztowa, Katowska and a little of Lwowska to a point opposite the Polish cemetery. There was an "exchange" of the non–Jews who lived in these streets that were designated for the ghetto and the Jews who lived outside the ghetto.

The Jews had to leave everything that they had in their previous residence in contract to the Christians who took everything up to the last feather from the residences they left.

The Jews came to the ghetto with empty hands. In the short time that they were given to live by the Germans, they had to begin to arrange [things for themselves] anew.

Even more painful was the fact that there were Jewish partners to the German robbery and murder of the Jews.

The class differences under the slaughtering knife of the slaughterer also did not cease. The community providers, the *bale–takses* [person responsible for collecting the government tax on meat] took the designated ghetto under their control and traded with it for as long as the trusteeship of the Jews was still under their authority.

The community leaders distributed the residences [in the ghetto] when the Jews were driven to the ghetto. However, the size of a family was not taken into consideration with the distribution of a larger or smaller apartment. The size of the sum of money that was given for receiving a better, more comfortable apartment was considered. The richer Jews also purchased more comfortable residences in the ghetto and the worst were distributed to the not well–to–do families.

The shameful trade went on in the clutches of the angel of death.

Alas, the date that the Jews were driven into the ghetto and the manner of their expulsion is unknown to me. It would be easy to allow my own fantasies, but I am not writing any kind of novella, but a bloody chronicle.

[Page 92]

The only "facility" in the ghetto that Nisenbaum knew to speak about was the special Jewish jail on Siedlecka Street.

The First Deportation Action

The first mass extermination of the Chelm Jews took place *erev Shavous* [the eve of the holiday celebrating the giving of the Torah], during the same year in which the ghetto was created, 1942.

Meanwhile, the first sent to the gas–ovens were those least capable of working:

The old, the weak, children and those who did not have any ransom money. This time, too, the Jewish community carried on a bloody trade and provided 3,000 Jews of both sexes from among the very poorest to the Gestapo. Meanwhile, the richer ones ransomed themselves.

Tankhn Nisenbaum, the storyteller, already was working then in the workshop at the Gestapo and the deportation did not affect him. But, he had left his wife, his mother and a brother at home. He could not rest knowing the danger that threatened those closest to him. Although he did not have permission to leave the workshop, he risked his life and left for the marketplace where the unlucky 3,000 Jews stood. He looked for them among [the 3,000 Jews]. He considered that in the worst case he would ask the Nazi commandant who was the same one for whom he had worked. His chief, who was occupied with the deportation, did notice him and was angry with him. He warned him that he could join them because he was not the head leader of the bloody deportation, but one who had arrived from Lublin especially because of it. Nisenbaum open–heartedly told him why he had come and why he was ready to risk his life.

Meanwhile, more and more new groups were brought to those already standing in the marketplace waiting for their dark end. Nisenbaum noticed his brother among a new group and succeeded in asking for his life for another bit of time…

The deportation had run its course: it began at a designated hour and was supposed to end at a designated hour. However a minute after its conclusion, a Chelm *Volks–Deutsch* brought the hiding Pinya the *shoykhet* [ritual slaughterer]. This *Volks–Deutsch* had beat the Jew with a stick the entire way from the Jew's hiding place to the collection point, shouting:

"*Yude, host gevolt krig. Nadir, krig!*" [Jew, you wanted a war. Now, have a war!]

When he brought the half–dejected victim to the commandant, the latter looked at the clock!

It was a minute after the designated hour and the commandant told the Jew to return home.

This is what is known as German punctuality!…

The 300[5] Jews all were packed into trucks and they were taken to Sobibor.

[Page 93]

The smaller children were placed in sacks like rags and thrown into the same trucks.

The devilishly devised gas–ovens surely did not have to be used for the children.

Nisenbaum could not relate anything about the fate of the remaining Chelm Jews after the deportation of *erev–Shavous* 1942.

Earlier, when he worked for the Gestapo in their residence proper, he still somehow had contact with the outside world. Later, the Gestapo workshop was isolated in the Chelm jail. The 15 Jews then in the workshop lost every possibility of maintaining a connection to the rest of the Chelm Jews.

Yet, as the several survivors in Chelm itself and the several hundred Chelm Jews, who evacuated to the Soviet lands, established at the congress in Silesia after the liberation, the last extermination of the Chelm Jews took place on the days of *Shavous* 1943.

Exactly to the day of the first deportation.

On this spring day and the day of *Matan Torah*, when the world was given the Torah, on this day the remaining Chelm Jews were taken away to the oven of Sobibor.

Shavous, 1943, is the day of mourning for their martyrs for all of the Chelm Jews throughout the world.

May the Chelm Jews, wherever they are, in whatever corner of the bloodied earth, sanctify this *yahrzeit* [anniversary of a death] for their own, for all Chelm Jewish martyrs!

15 Jews in the Gestapo Workshop

What happened to each of the Jews who survived is one of the thousands of wonders. I provide this wonder as Tankhn Nisenbaum, one of the 15 surviving Jews in Chelm, told it to me.

It is already known from previous sentences that 15 Jews were caught to work at the Gestapo. At first they did house work, served the murderers in their residences. Later they were allocated to a workshop. The workshop exclusively served the Gestapo gang and their families. The jail was allocated as a place for the workshop and various artisans worked there: tailors, hatmakers, shoemakers and carpenters. Tankhn Nisenbaum, himself, was a carpenter. Berl Kelberman was a tailor of women's clothing. One of my neighbors from the same street, a long time friend of our household, Chaim Sobel, a gaitermaker, also was there. My childhood friend, with the same trade, Manes Citrin, also was there. These were some of the 15 surviving Jews whom I knew.

These 15 Jews worked in the Gestapo's workshop for 22 months in the most frightening conditions. They were completely isolated from their families and from the world in general. And then at the beginning of Germany's end, at the victorious march of the Red Army and by the Allied armies, when the Jewish workshop that had worked for Germany a result of which they had delayed the hour of their death for a little while, then, when there was an order to take the Jews from the workshop on their last road, the Chelm Gestapo left the workshop whole. They hid it from the higher powers.

[Page 94]

Why did it [the Gestapo] do this?

There was no humanitarian spark in their action. The opposite, this was in blind self–interest.

The Chelm workshop did not work for the government, but privately for them, the Gestapo murderers and for their wives and concubines. They needed the looted goods to be altered to be taken with them when the sharp slaughtering knife of justice was on their chest and the never–stilled revenge by the tortured nations and even more by the Jewish people had brought out a "feeling of regret" from a number of Nazis.

On the eve of the [Jewish] New Year, on the eve of the complete dispersion of the German "undefeated" armies, one of the Chelm Gestapo chiefs, very intoxicated, acted out a scene of revenge in the jail where the workshop was located.

Dead drunk, he also forced the tortured Jews to drink with him, and drinking, he began to beat his chest, crying and swearing that he was not at all guilty for what the Nazis had done. Just the opposite, he was just a believer in equality for all people…

Oh, what a drunk Nazi is capable of!…

When the Red Army neared Chelm and the brown mice ran in panic, they did not have any time to liquidate the workshop with true German exactitude, but they did, after everything, think to shoot into the jail so as not to leave any living Jews.

With luck, however, the Jews lay hiding and the bullets being shot did not hit any Jews.

Wolf and Chaya Ruchl Waserman,
parents of Manasha, Shlomo and Shneier Waserman

[Page 95]

Tankhn Nisenbaum described the "miracle" that none of the bullets hit anyone with this interesting event:

Three nights before the arrival in Chelm of the Soviet Army, Soviet shrapnel ripped open a deep hole in the courtyard of the prison where the 15 Jews were located. The Jews were aware of what was happening outside and made use of this accident: they all entered the hole and covered it with a clothes closet that was located there.

When the suspicious stillness ceased outside, one of them tried to stick out his head to see what was happening.

To their joyful surprise a Ukrainian member of the Red Army stood near the jail.

The Red Army member grabbed for his gun and asked:

"Who are you?"

"We are Jews" – was the answer from the half–dead 15 happy Jews.

This was enough of a legitimization for the Red Army member.

He gave a whistle and a Soviet *rezvedka* [scout] immediately came riding. The officer jumped down from his horse, seeing a miracle before him – living Jews – he began to kiss everyone.

The officer also was a Jew.

With tears in his eyes, the Jewish officer told them that he was from Stalingrad and that he was searching for Jews and until them, he had not found one living Jew. They were the first living Jews he had found.

Still more Red Army Jews joined them. They tried to console and help the victims in any way they could at such a time and in such a place behind the front lines.

It was the eve of the Days of Awe. The surviving Chelm Jews, for the first time in years, again gathered freely somewhere in an improvised small synagogue together with a number Jewish members of the Red Army and poured out their hearts at the great crime that had happened to those closest to them and to a great number of the Jewish people and simultaneously rejoiced in the victory that then was certain over the Nazis.

After the Liberation

Tankhn Nisenbaum's story about those rescued ended here.

The additional [information] was taken from telegraphic news and from letters.

Chelm was the first larger Polish city the Red Army took in its advance on Germany. Therefore, the Polish Democratic People's Republic was proclaimed there with [Boleslaw] Bierut as its president. Later, the government moved to Lublin and with the further advance of the Red Army and the Polish *Armia Ludowa* (People's Army), the government later settled definitively in the permanent capital, Warsaw.

[Page 96]

According to the arriving news, in addition to the 15 surviving Jews, two women were hidden with Christians. Later, a number returned from the Polish and Soviet armies. Several hundred who had evacuated to the Soviet land also returned. All of these together perhaps would have founded a Jewish settlement in Chelm. But the life of the survivors again was threatened. This time not by the Germans who lay hiding in their lairs during the first phase of their great defeat. This time the danger came from "our" own liberated Poles.

The Chelm medical man, Dr. Evri, came with the first divisions of the Red Army. He was the son of the well–known wealthy baker, Shlomo Evri, who in his time lived a worldly life and permitted his children to study [secular subjects].

Dr. Evri was the oldest son and he received his medical diploma from the Russian–Tsarist University. He younger brother, Motka Evri, was a councilman in the Chelm city council, elected on the list of left *Poalei–Zion* [Marxist–Zionists] and was murdered at that time in an armed robbery in his house.

Dr. Evri, it seems, went along with the Red Army during the German invasion and worked there at his post as a medical man. At the liberation of Poland, he had the good fortune to be among those liberating the city of Chelm. As with every Jew, his joy at the liberation was mixed with sadness because of the Jewish annihilation and the death of his own family. And he also was destined to share the fate of his family and of all the annihilated Jews.

Dovid Goldrajch, who returned to Chelm from the Soviet Union, wrote in a letter:

"Dr. Evri and another Jewish colleague were also destined to find their grave on a hill outside the city."

In the evening, when Dr. Evri sat in his house with his friend, they were shot by a Polish pogromist.

They were not the only returning Chelm Jews who were murdered by Polish hooligans.

It was told of a Chelm butcher that when he returned to the city and approached his own house, a Pole, who had grabbed this house and its entire contents, came out opposite him and threatened:

"You should disappear, if you do not want to get a knife in your back".

The threatened one left for Italy.

Of the several hundred Jews who returned to Chelm after the liberation, I think that no one remained because of the pogroms during the first month of Poland's independence, with its bloody finale in Kielce. Several perished at the hands of hooligans and the remainder dispersed.

[Page 97]

In a second letter, the above–mentioned Dovid Goldrajch wrote to me:

"We are in Chelm with the children, the last 50 Jews; most of them not from Chelm. And, we, too, are on our way. We will all leave the city quickly."

And a short time later I received a letter from him from Silesia.

Dovid Goldrajch's wife, it seems, had hidden in Chelm itself as an "Aryan." Because in his letter there was the following two–line postscript:

"I have to play the tragic role and laugh when my heart bleeds."

Work card of Irena Szreder [Goldrajch]

Yankl Beker and his family, who returned to Chelm from the Soviet Union after the liberation, also quickly left for Lodz and he now lives in Israel.

Family Chronicle

A son of my brother with the same mother, Chaim Borukh Warzoger, and his family, who saved themselves in the Soviet Union, returned from there to Silesia. One of his younger sisters, Fraydl, temporarily remained in Lutsk with one of her uncles and she perished there [at the hands of] the Nazis.

My brother, Avraham Sholem Warzoger, or as he was known, the Chelemer baker, lived in Chelm for dozens of years. A number of his sons were active in the Polish revolutionary movement long before the Second World War and thanks to them the entire family was saved in the Soviet Union. The sons entered the Red Army there and a number of them distinguished themselves in the fight against the murderers.

Two daughters died during the evacuation.

Later, everyone returned to Poland and lived for a time in Silesia. Now, the family has settled in Israel. One son, Shlomo Warzoger, became known as poet in the [concentration] camp, who contributed to our Holocaust poetry.

[Page 98]

Yehuda Warzoger, another of my brothers, lived for many years in a village near Chelm. He was a good–natured blond giant with grey child–like eyes. He went through the Russian–Japanese War and the First World War and the revolution in Russia and came home healthy. He lived for dozens of years in the village, in the best of relationships with his non–Jewish neighbors. The same neighbors murdered him and his wife during the first days of the terror of the Nazi occupation. Their sons survived in the Soviet Union, joined the Red Army in the fight and a number of them remained there.

Three of my sisters with many branched families, with children and grandchildren, all perished. I do not even know the place, the time and manner in which they were murdered by the German killers.

One, Ester, a loving sister, and her husband, Yitzhak Gorn and their three children all perished.

Hinda, my sister with the same father, and her husband, Ahron Tuchsznajder and their children perished.

Eidl, a widow, in accordance with her husband's name and origin, perished with her children and grandchildren. Only one of her daughters, Czarna, and her child survived in a camp.

Other more distant relatives, too, whose number and names it is impossible for me to know. They all went on the road of the martyrs – the largest and bloodiest in our history.

These were all my own sisters and brothers remaining in Chelm who were a part of the 18,000 Chelm Jews who perished.

If the sad duty to record this bloody chronicle fell on me, to erect a stone at the head of the unknown mass grave of my 18,000 *landsleit* [people from the same town], I have taken permission from them, from the martyrs, to record the names of my own, the blood of my blood and the flesh of my flesh, [the memories of] whose shortened lives will follow me to my grave.

* * *

Not deviating from my established task to record only the chronicle of the destruction, I omit the names in this chapter, "Family Chronicle" of our family members and even of my own brothers who left Poland a long time before the war and are now located in various lands. I do not even mention those of them who achieved esteemed places in Jewish society.

I dedicate these few lines to avoid possible mistaken dissatisfaction by those who are not mentioned here.

If only there were even more survivors who were not mentioned…

Note:

    a. The Polish anti-Semitic authorities also forbid Jews to enter other places. An inscription at the entrance to the spacious steps said: "Forbidden for Jews here." The Polish hooligans made use of this to beat Jews when they found them there.

Translator's footnotes:

1. The holidays referred to are either Passover or *Sukkos* – the Feast of Tabernacles.
2. The article refers to the Greek Catholic church and to the Greek Orthodox cemetery. The article then indicates below that the Russians had expropriated the church. The article is referring to the Eastern Orthodox Church.
3. Hasidic rebbes presided over tables at which their followers gathered to hear the words of the rebbe, to sing songs and enjoy refreshments.
4. This exchange echoes the words of a popular Yiddish song, *Achtsik Er un Zibetsik Zi – Eighty He and Seventy She*. The words of the first verse are:
> "Today marks the fiftieth anniversary
> The old couple have been so happy together
> They have both gotten older.
> Eighty he, and seventy she."
5. The number previously was given as 3,000

[Page 99]

My Home City

by Hersh Sziszler

Translated by Gloria Berkenstat Freund

Hersh Sziszler

Although may years ago I left my home city with which I was bound and connected, I will not forget it – and even now it stands before my eyes with its characteristic Jewish way of life and with its beautiful landscape.

Chelm was an old Jewish city, a Jewish community of major importance, widely known across the entire Jewish world for her rabbis and sages, for her personalities and for the folklore – the fantastic stories, wise jokes and witticisms.

The Jewish population was approximately 60 percent of the general population. There were many Jewish artisans, merchants and shopkeepers. There were sawmills, alcohol trade, mills and various industrial undertakings that belonged to Jews.

The Chelemer Jews were a great predominant power in the municipal and surrounding trade, in the industry of the city. Jewish banks, such as the Merchants and Artisans Bank, charitable societies and institutions, a *Talmud-Torah* [religious school for poor boys], a school system [with instruction] in Yiddish, Hebrew and Polish.

There was an intensive communal Jewish life: various unions, clubs, dramatic circles, libraries and Jewish newspapers would be published.

The city had a Jewish face with its streets and neighborhoods in which lived naïve, pious Jews, honest artisans, merchants and shopkeepers, Jewish paupers and rich men, beaten down Jews – in the style of Sholem Aleichem's Menakhem-Mendl – and loafers – so-called *shtekl-dreyer* [stick-turners – Jews living with sporadic income], Jewish scholars who sat in the houses of study and the Hasidic *shtiblekh* [one-room synagogues] studying the Laws of Moses.

So the large house of study that was overcrowded with Jews in long *kapotes* [caftans] and with Jews in modern garments, Jews with beards and *peyos* [side curls] and Jews without beards and *peyos* is so clearly remembered as well as the neighboring large synagogue that told stories from hundreds of years ago.

Who does not remember the *Shabbosim* [Sabbaths] and the holidays when touching melodies and *Shabbos* songs resounded from Jewish windows; the *Shabbos* nights with *Havdalus* [ceremonies marking the end of *Shabbos* and the beginning of the week] and the evening meals ending *Shabbos* that had so much appeal, sanctity, sincerity, vision and tradition?

[Page 100]

And can we forget the *khederim* [religious elementary schools], *Talmud-Torahs* where young boys filled the narrow Chelemer, Jewish alleys with the sound of their voices; the pale Moshelekh and Shlomolekh [Moshes and Shlomos] from outside who studied in Chelm, *esn teg* in Jewish homes; the students in the Jewish public school, in the Hebrew schools and in the Jewish-Polish *gymnazie* [secondary school]; the prayer leaders and singers with their sweet praying and the choir boys with the sweet singing; the *melamdim* [teachers in religious schools] who could not draw an income from their teaching profession and had to search for a source of income from the various weapons they produced for their students: rifles for *Lag B'Omer*, swords for *Tisha b'Av*, flags for *Simkhas Torah*, *dreydlekh* [tops] for Chanukah and rattles and noisemakers for Purim?[1]

Lag B'Omer takes place on the 18th of Iyar, the 33rd day of the counting of the *Omer* – counting the 49 days between Passover and *Shavuos* – the holiday celebrating the receiving of the Torah at Mount Sinai – and it was customary for children to celebrate with bows and arrows. It may have been the custom in Chelm to use rifles.

Tisha b'Av – the ninth of Av – commemorates the destruction of the First and Second Temples in Jerusalem. The swords may be an illusion to a line in the prayer of consolation [*Nakhem* – comfort]: "They have put Israel to the sword…"

Simkhas Torah is the holiday that celebrates the conclusion of the annual cycle of Torah readings and the beginning of the new one. Children are given flags as part of the celebration.

On *Purim* – the commemoration of Esther and Mordechai saving the Jews from Haman – it is customary to make noise to drown out every mention of Haman's name.]

And who does not remember the pious women with their *sheytlekh* [wigs] in their long crinoline dresses going to the synagogue with the woman's *sidurim* [prayer books] and *makhzorim* [prayer books used on holidays], the Chelemer young people and the Chelemer "common people" – the wagon drivers, the porters, the coachmen who waited impatiently for their difficult income?

And who does not remember the Tuesday days when the fairs took place in Chelm and large crowds of peasants would travel to Chelm?

Or can we forget the First of May demonstrations by the Jewish unions and parties, by the Bund, *Paolei-Zion* [Workers of Zion – Marxist-Zionist movement], the communists and groupings from other ideologies that marched in the ranks with belief, earnestness and devotion, carrying their flags high and proud with hope for the future?

And can we forget the Jewish masses in Chelm who filled the halls of the clubs and unions, theaters and cinemas?

It is very difficult to make peace with the idea that the Jewish city Chelm was so savagely exterminated.

The Historical Chelm Synagogue

The Chelm synagogue was one of the oldest synagogues in Poland. It was said that it was built in the year 1100. According to the municipal archives at the Chelm city hall, the Chelm synagogue – under the name *chóralny* [choral] synagogue – was built in the year 1124.

There were engraved letters – the year 5657 [1897] – on one of the synagogue walls that led to Szkolna Street. It was said that this was the date when the synagogue was renovated.[a]

The building was rare and unique and it was a remarkable synagogue artistically and architecturally. It was famous among all of the synagogues in Poland for its paintings and artistic works, for its fine Torah reading desk and Torah ark, and hanging from the vaulted ceiling its giant copper lamps on massive chains that sparkled with beauty on the *Shabbosim* and holidays.

[Page 101]

There are many old legends and folk stories from hundreds of years ago about this Chelm synagogue that people would tell each other in the twilight in the corners of the synagogue with a sigh and confidence in God.

The eastern wall of the magnificent Chelm synagogue

We see in the picture from right to left: Feywl Fryd, Dovid Goldrajch, Yakov Beker and lawyer Gedalyah Bakalczuk on the empty spot where the famous Chelm synagogue stood, which the Hitler vandals destroyed

[Page 102]

The synagogue was sanctified over the course of generations. The most valuable objects of Jewish religious significance were found there, such as artistically adorned curtains over the Torah ark, Torah scrolls, etc.

A fine Elijah's chair[2] stood on the pulpit, with a copper menorah. Wine would be carried to the children on *Shabbos* and holidays in a silver pitcher and a silver cup.

There was a gallery above where the ordinary Jews sat. Legends arose about this gallery and about the women's synagogue.

The synagogue had giant, thick walls that created the appearance of a fortress. There truly were times when Jews found protection in the synagogue from the foes of Israel when edicts, repressions and pogroms threatened the Jewish population.[b]

The Hitlerist vandals used dynamite to blow up this historic house of prayer that stood on the street corner, standing in such historical majesty through the centuries and completely demolished the historical Chelm synagogue, leaving an empty spot that is a silent witness to the destruction of Chelm.

The *Kehile*

The *kehile* [organized Jewish community] in Chelm was organized at the end of the 18th century and is one of the oldest Jewish communities in Poland. During the earlier years the *dozores* [members of the community council] of the Chelm Jewish *kehile* were nominated. In 1905, after the first Russian revolution, the *dozores* were elected.

The tasks of the Jewish *kehile* were mainly to satisfy the religious needs and to provide assistance to the poorest Jews in the city.

In 1910 a loan office was opened by the *kehile* whose director was Yehuda Leib Milner, of blessed memory. Avraham Ornsztajn was an active worker at this loan office. The funds for the loan office were given by *IKO* (Jewish Colonization Organization) [in the amount] of 10 million *funt* [Tsarist currency], which the most generous donor, Baron Hirsch, had given on behalf of the needs of the world Jewish population.[c] Loan offices were organized in many Jewish cities and *shtetlekh* [towns], including Chelm, thanks to this considerable sum the Chelm loan office existed until August 1914. Then, it was liquidated when the First World War began.

The need among the Jewish population in Chelm, as in other Polish *shtetlekh*, was great, mainly during the First World War.

[Page 103]

The German-Austrian occupation regime introduced [ration] cards for bread, potatoes and for other foodstuff and the *kehile* was given the sensitive work of dividing the products. The head of the *kehile* then was Anshel Biderman.

Democratic elections for the *kehile* took place in 1919. Every man age 25 and older had *kehile* voting rights. Women did not have any voting rights. The first head of the *kehile* was Motl Goldsztajn and the above-mentioned Anshel Biderman was elected for a term in office. All societies, unions, institutions and Hasidic circles were represented in the *kehile*.

In addition to the *kehile* issuing marriage documents, birth documents, death notes, dividing help among the Chelm Jewish poor and giving subsidies to Jewish institutions and also to the educational and school institutions, it also organized matzo for the poor and gave medical help to poor patients as well as providing them with places in hospitals.

With the activity of Anshel Biderman, the *kehile* also helped build the large house of prayer, remodeling the large synagogue, and the bathhouse, slaughterhouse, the rabbinical court and the cemetery were under its leadership and supervision. The rabbis, *shoyketim* [ritual slaughterers] and all kinds of religious personnel were employed by the *kehile*.

The *kehile* placed taxes (*etat* [Jewish community tax]) on the population and covered its budget from this and other income.

The Chelm Jewish *kehile* represented a large Jewish population. Jews in Chelm numbered 12,064 (twelve thousand sixty-four), approximately 25 percent of the general population in the city according to the census of 1921. At that time the number of Jews in Poland was 2,845,364.

During the later years, according to the census in Poland in 1931, the Chelm Jewish population grew to 18,000. The Christian population also grew because the Radom train station was moved to Chelm. New neighborhoods with an exclusively Aryan population were built because of this.

The work of the Chelm Jewish *kehile* expanded greatly because of the increase of the Jewish population.

Anshel Biderman, long-time chairman of the kehile in Chelm

[Page 104]

During the last years until 1939 the *parnosim* [community or synagogue trustees] and the *dozores* of the *kehile* were the following people: Avraham Baumgold, E. Kratka, Moshe Jermus, Haim Hauzman, Berl Akslrad, Ahron Dovid Hipszman, Moshe Beker, Yisroel Bursztyn, F. Dreksler, M. Barg, N. Goldberg, Yisroel Borukh Kornblum, Yakov Kornblum, Ezriel Buchbleter, Avraham Frydman, Berish Finlsztajn, Berish Landa, Berish Drimler, Shlomo-Yitzhak Dinitc, Pinkhas Mandl, Avraham Baum, Yitzhak Szwarcman, Ben-Zion Lang, Hershl Fructgartn and so on.

The chairman of the *kehile* council was B. Finklsztajn. The chief secretary of the *kehile* for many years was Y. Zilbersztajn (son-in-law of A. Lipszic – the owner of the lamp business).

On the first day of its brutal rule the Nazi-Hitlerist regime in Chelm made the *kehile* community leaders responsible for the behavior of the Jews in the city and they were forced to collect the levy placed on the Jewish population.

When the Germans created the *Judenrat* [Jewish council], the *kehile* members were nominated as members of the *Judenrat*.

The *Judenrat* was liquidated after the persecutions, monetary extortions and deportations already had taken place. All of the members of the *Judenrat* were then thrown alive into pits outside the city and shot. Only Meir Frankl, one of the [members] of the *Judenrat*, Reb Dovid Lederman's son-in-law, survived the Hitler years. But he was murdered – by Polish Nazis – in his own mill on Lwowska Street (Parkrower) after the liberation.

For many years the premises of the *kehile* was in Fishl Lewnstajn's [house], at Pijarska 1, across from the Polish church and the administrative offices.

The Chelm House of Prayer

On the eve of the Second World War Chelm Jewry celebrated the 25th anniversary of the Chelm house of prayer that was built on the eve of the First World War. The building was completed *Shavous* [holiday celebrating the receiving of the Torah] 1914 and was a close neighbor to the large Chelm synagogue.

A corner of the Chelm house of prayer.
Mr. Anshel Biderman is near the Torah ark

[Page 105]

Various strata of the population, merchants, shopkeepers, artisans prayed in the house of prayer and it was a central point where Jews met and learned various news.

The house of prayer was built thanks to the initiative of the well-known communal worker, Anshel Biderman, who would give sermons from the pulpit for the congregation on the issues of the day.

Before the reading of the Torah during the 25th anniversary celebration Reb Anshel Biderman told interesting episodes connected with the house of prayer.

The anniversary celebration of the house of prayer was very impressive and no one could then imagine that the large congregation of the house of prayer's worshippers would perish so savagely.

Talmud Torah

A *Talmud Torah* existed in Chelm that was known by the name *Talmud Torah* and *Yeshiva* [religious secondary school] of the Chelm *Kehile* in which many hundreds of orphans and poor children were educated and raised in the religious spirit.

In 1938 the religious institution mentioned passed through a difficult crisis, was about to close when a group of middle class Jews numbering 114 under the name *Talmud Torah* and *Yeshiva* of the Chelm *Kehile* Society began to strongly undertake the support of this holy institution.

We read a call by the council of the *Talmud Torah* and *Yeshiva* of the Chelm *Kehile* in the *Chelemer Shtime* [*Chelm Voice*], no. 39 (764) of Friday the 30th of September 1938 in which there was an appeal for support, saying among other things:

Left: Hershl Helfman, chairman of the Khevre Kadisha [burial society]
Right: Reb Zalman Helfman, gabai [sexton] of the Hakhnoses Orkhim [Sabbath shelter for poor wanderers]

[Page 106]

"We expressed many important precepts. *A Golden Book* was announced in which everyone could be listed. The person who was listed would receive a page in the *Golden Book* in his name as an eternal souvenir for his help for our *Talmud Torah* and *Yeshiva* of the Chelm *Kehile*. The income should be the guarantee of its existence."

Lubavitcher *Yeshiva Achei HaTmimim*

In Chelm there existed *Achei HaTmimim* [Brothers of the Pure Ones], the Lubavitcher *yeshiva* that was founded thanks to the initiative of the Lubavitcher Rebbe, may he live a long life. This *yeshiva* taught in the house of prayer school on the eve of the First World War.

Reb Efraim Unger, son-on-law of the Rzeszow Rebbe, Reb Yehuda Zindl Rokeach, may the memory of the righteous be blessed, was the spiritual leader of the *yeshiva*.

Mealtime for Jewish soldiers in house of prayer during the days of Passover

During a large celebration at the Lubavitcher *yeshiva* Rabbi Unger, may he live a long life, appealed for the strengthening and guarantee of the existence of the *yeshiva* in Chelm that was the only Hasidic [provider of] ethical education in the entire area and it must especially be sanctified because it was founded by the Lubavitcher Rebbe.

Charitable Societies and Institutions

It has been established on the basis of historical sources that certain charitable societies and institutions existed in Chelm in the 18th century and even earlier. The *khevre kadishe* [burial society], *beis yesiymin* [orphanage], *Ahiezer* [help for my brother – a society for providing medical help], etc., were founded many, many years ago.

On the whole their number increased after the First World War. Jewish community life intensified and expanded with the rise of the Polish state and the number of different institutions that played a significant role also grew.

[Page 107]

The following societies and institutions carried on vigorous activity during the last years [before the Holocaust]:

Old Age Home

The *moyshev-skeynim* [old age home] was in a better financial condition than the above-mentioned societies and institutions.

A large building with all of the modern facilities was built.

The managing committee took care of the need for the hygiene and cleanliness of the old age home and for the health of the old men and women.

The Jewish community warmly supported this institution. The *kehile* subsidized it and Chelm *landsleit* [people from the same town] overseas sent financial help from time to time.

The last managing committee of the old age home consisted of the following people: Nukhem Goldberg, A. Hochgraf, A. Lew, M. Jermus, Kh. Feldman, Y. Huz, D. Korengeld. F. Nejdl, M. Micfliker, Y. Bergman, Y. Herszhorn and Sh. Lauwaser.

The old age home, the only Jewish institution in Chelm that was not destroyed by the Hitler murderers

[Page 108]

A celebration during the brick laying at the raising of story of the old age home in Chelm in 1918

During the last years, on the eve of the destruction in 1939, its chairman was Benyamin Blumensztraud. He was a dedicated communal worker, a Jew of stately appearance and a man of good character. He died on the eve of the Hitler tyranny.

The old age home building remained undamaged. This was the only Jewish communal building not destroyed by the Nazi vandals.

Beis Lekhem

The *Beis Lekhem* [house of bread – organization providing aid to the poor] assured that the poor Jews did not starve. The main task was that Jews would be able to celebrate the *Shabbosim* and holidays in a good frame of mind.

The *Beis Lekhem* collected *challahs* [breads for celebrating *Shabbos*] and other foods throughout the city, bringing it into gloomy, poor Jewish homes.

Old men and women from the Chelm old age home

[Page 109]

Gmiles Khesed

This was an important institution that was recognized by every strata of the Jewish population as a very useful one, thanks to its constructive help.

The *gmiles-khesed kase* [interest free loan fund] was supported by the Joint [Distribution Committee] in Warsaw. It would distribute interest-free loans among the shopkeepers and artisans. When shopkeepers needed to renew their licenses on the eve of the new year, they came to the *gmiles-khesed* for a loan and when a wagon driver or coach driver had a horse fall, he was helped by the loan institution.

Many Jews came to the *gmiles-khesed kase*. Thanks to the loans they received, Jews organized their matzo bakeries (*lodn*) before Passover and, during the summer, orchard keepers borrowed money to rent orchards. Many loans also were divided among impoverished men.

The managing committee worked hard to support this institution. The majority of borrowers did not exactly repay their loans simply because of the great poverty in the city and because of the heavy taxes imposed on the Jews by the Polish regime.

The income from the *gmiles-khesed* shrank and only with help from abroad and from the Joint did the *gmiles-khesed* exist until the Second World War.

The office of the *gmiles-khesed* was in the large house of prayer. Dr. Y. Aks was the chairman of this important institution and the secretary, N. Derman, was an important activist and a very gifted man showing great expertise in the work. Everyone who was employed worked at their position for many years.

[Page 110]

Hakhnoses Orkhim

Hakhnoses Orkhim [institution to help visitors, particularly for Sabbaths and holidays] occupied a respected place among the philanthropic institutions. This institution built its own premises.

Poor Jews from neighboring cities and from more distant locations were received in the *Hakhnoses Orkhim* house with great friendliness and were given a free meal and clean bed.

The community workers in this institution covered their budget through members' dues and from various undertakings.

Biker Khoylim

A *Biker Khoylim* [Society to Help the Sick Poor] that carried on aid work also existed in Chelm. In *Undzer Shtime* [*Our Voice*], no. (45) 5 of Friday the 29th of January 1929, there is an announcement that the *Biker Khoylim* Society asked all worshippers to consider the difficult situation in which the society finds itself and donate when they are called up to the Torah on *Shabbos Parshes* [weekly reading] *Beshalakh* [When he let go] and *Mishpatim* [Laws] on behalf of the *Biker Khoylim* as was the custom all through the years.

Lines HaTsedek

Lines HaTsedek [society to provide beds or overnight accommodations for the sick] was the most popular and most beloved institution in the city. It arose in the years of the First World War when various illnesses reigned in Chelm, such as typhus, cholera and the like. There was great need and poverty under the German occupation.

Lines HaTsedek management committee workers, doctors, nurses
At the bottom, M. Lewin

[Page 111]

Lines HaTsedek carried out an enormously useful work. It distributed medical help, engaged doctors to help the poor patients and organized tours of duty to visit the sick at night. Its premises were located in the center of the city on Lubliner Street in Reb Fishl Rojtman's building. Existing at *Lines HaTsedek* was the *Biker Khoylim* in which the Chelm intelligentsia was active.

Managing committee of Lines HaTsedek in 1917

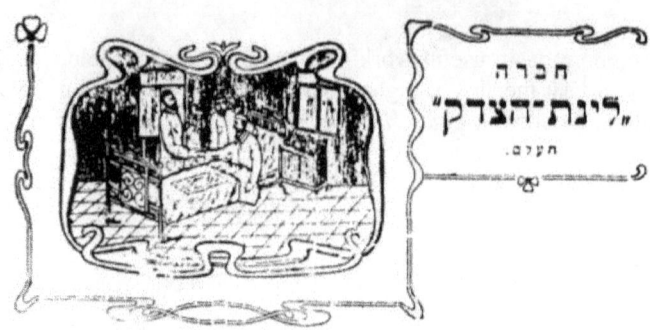

Fascimile of a traditional greeting that Lines HaTsedek Society would send to weddings and other celebrations

[Page 112]

Musical band at the Lines HaTsedek in Chelm

An active managing committee carried on the work of the *Lines HaTsedek*.

The first chairman of the *Lines HaTsedek* was the old-time physician, Matish Lewin. After his death, Yehoshaya Binsztok stood at the head.

In 1939, on the eve of the Hitler attack on Poland, the *Lines HaTsedek* Society found itself in a bad position because of its large deficits. It was forced to suspend its activities temporarily. This evoked great concern in the poor circles. A large aid campaign was undertaken then to be able to revive the activities of *Lines HaTsedek*. Money collections, social events and various events were organized for this purpose.

In 1939 the managing committee of *Lines HaTsedek* had the following composition: chairman – B. Felhendler; vice-chairmen – M. Lederman and G. Nelkenbaum; secretary – Y. Rozenblat; vice-secretary – Sh. Goldbaum; treasurer – A. Mincer; owner – Y. Huz.

Among the most commendable *Lines HaTsedek* volunteers also were: Avraham Winik, Yehoshua Beker, Yosef Grinman, Artshe Karp and others.

Malbish Arumim [Clothing for the Needy] Society in Chelm

[Page 113]

Malbish Arumim [Clothing for the Needy] Society in Chelm

Malbish Arumim

This charitable society was concerned with clothing the poor Jewish children and orphans and was located in the *Talmud Torah* building on Seminarski Street.

The income for this society came from flower [selling] days, from collecting levies and various opportunities were used to cover the budget.

Goods and leather were purchased and given that the largest number of community workers wee artisans – shoemakers and tailors – they sewed the clothing and shoes for the needy children at no cost.

The clothing and shoes were distributed to the children twice a year – *erev Pesakh* [on the eve of Passover] and *erev Sukkos* [on the eve of the Feast of the Tabernacles] in the small butcher's synagogue and in a room of the *Talmud Torah*. Approximately 200-300 children were clothed and given shoes by the *Malbish Arumim*.

Malbush Aromin [clothing the poor] workers during the clothing distribution

The Orphans' Home

The orphans' home was founded before the First World War.

Jewish orphans from Chelm and its surroundings were taken care of in the orphans' home.

[Page 114]

The Jewish population warmly supported the home for Jewish orphans.

Hakhnoses Kale

The task of the *Hakhnoses Kale* Society [society to help poor young brides] was to help poor Jewish girls get married, giving them a trousseau and money for marriage expenses.

This charitable body was very warmly supported by the Jews in Chelm.

The Bank System

Three Jewish banks functioned in Chelm. One of them did not have any longevity. The other two banks were luckier.

The Merchants Bank in which the merchants and shopkeepers had confidence had an eminent position.

The managing committee consisted of the following people: Y. M. Lederman (today in England), Leibl Rozen, Sh. Helfbajn, Y. Szildkraut, Sh. Dawidzon, K. Mendelbaum, Berl Akslrod, Meir Kalmanowicz, G. Warman (all perished in the time of Hitler) and Yosif Ralnik (now in Israel). The director of the bank was Ahron Shtal (perished).

Ahron Shtal, director of the Merchants Bank

The third was the Cooperative Bank. Its director was S. Rabinzon. In the city the bank was called "Rabinzon's Bank." There was great order in the bank. This actually was a bank for artisans, for the Jewish Handworker's Union whose delegates appropriately were on the council and the managing committee – representatives.

The following handworker-activists were the representatives on the managing committee of the Cooperative Bank: Wewtshe Handlsman, E. Kratka and Chaim Hausman. Represented on the council were: Sh. Bornsztajn and Moshe Yermus.

The Retailers Cooperative

The Retailers Cooperative was founded in Chelm in 1929. It numbered 41 members during its founding.

The few banks in the city were communal and had the purpose of alleviating the economic conditions of the Jewish retailers and artisans.

[Pages 115-116]

The *ORT vo Remeslenovo i. Zemieledecheskovo Trouda* – The Society for Handicrafts and Agricultural Labor] Society, whose task it was to spread crafts among the Jewish young, occupied a respected place among the various Jewish institutions in Chelm. The premises of the society were located at Pocztowa Street, no. 54.

Several sections for locksmith work, mechanics, tailors and others functioned at *ORT*.

Dozens of young Chelm Jews received theoretical knowledge and practical training in various crafts. Important personalities were active on the managing committee of *ORT*, active workers who devoted a great deal of time and effort on behalf of the *ORT* Society.

The Rozen Family*

The Prostak Family**

The Rozen Family*

*Not in original book. Courtesy of Ariella Levinger-Limor
**Not in original book. Courtesy of Shlomit Beck

Managing committee of the ORT Society in 1918

**From right to left, sitting: Dr. Y. Feldman, Dr. Mrs. Zajsn, Dr. A. Zajsn, teacher at ORT Avraham Berland
Top row, standing: Y. Tenenbaum, Meir Kalmanowicz, A. Szajn, Dr. A. Szebtl, Gershon Lustiger, Z, Kratka**

The TOZ

The *TOZ* [*Towarzystwo Ochrony Zdrowia Ludności Żydowskiej*] (Society to Protect the Health of the Jews) was founded in 1929. Among the first initiators of this society was D. Wilenka.

The society played a significant role, mainly with its care for the young generation. It organized summer colonies for the children and young people, healed the sick through quartz lamps and diathermy. It fed the poor children who lived in the poor neighborhoods – Pocztowa, Katowski and others.

The *TOZ* also held hygiene contests in the school and homes.

Many Jewish doctors were active in the work of *TOZ*. The following doctors helped in the activities of *TOZ*: Dr. Laya Frid, Dr. Dovid Walberger, Dr. Avraham Lipszic, Dr. Cygelman, M. Sakuler, Mrs. Tanya Evry, Dr. M. Lipkowcz, Dr. M. Lewin.

These and other doctors gave medical help both at *TOZ* and at the *Lines HaTzedek*. They also gave lectures about hygiene, medicine, about sexual questions, venereal and various other illnesses.

The managing committee of *TOZ* consisted of the following people: Dr. D. Walberger, Motya Lewin, S. Szajn, Nakhum Goldberg, N. Derman, Dr. Wilenka. The technical chief was Motl Goldman.

ORT Society in Chelm

Summer colony organized by the TOZ Society in 1933

[Page 117]

The Chess Club in Chelm

The Chess Club, or as it was called, Chess-mate Club, was a well-known society in Chelm. This was a great center for the Chelm Jewish intelligentsia as well as the assimilated strata and snobs.

The Chess Club was located in the house of Mr. Fishl Lewensztajn, a well-known Chelm landlord. It is interesting that despite the fact that the Chess Club included the strata of assimilated Jews, they devoted themselves to Jewish cultural work.

Incidentally, Yiddish plays were staged in one of the club's rooms, a spacious room, and the income was used for charitable purposes, for Jewish societies such as *Lines HaTsedek*, the Old Age Home, *Hakhnoses Kale* and others. *Motke Ganev* [*Motke the Thief*] by Sholem Asch was once performed at the Chess Club, which was a great success. Lectures on purely Yiddish literary themes were also held there.

In addition to the various cultural performances, dance evenings and the masquerade evenings famous in Chelm took place at the Chess Club. Particularly interesting and impressive were the Chanukah and Purim balls there. These once were successful attractions that drew great numbers of the Jewish intelligentsia.

As already said, all of those who were involved with the Chess Club were the "cream," many of them from a rich milieu.

The baking of free matzos for the poor was the initiative of the Chess Club.

The Chess Club in Chelm arose before the First World War and was then located in the Jewish *kehile* [organized Jewish community] building that also belonged to Mr. Lewensztajn. In about 1918, the club moved to Mr. Lewenstzatjn's large building at Lubliner 6 where it remained until the last days of its demise.

The School Choir in 1927, photographed with Cantor Yakov Brajtman (the first on the left) during a visit from America to Chelm, his home city

[Page 118]

The Yiddish Press in Chelm

The title, "Yiddish Press," can be misleading because in truth one can think that there were many Yiddish newspapers and journals in Chelm.

I know that there were only three Yiddish weekly newspapers: the *Chelemer Shtime* [*Chelm Voice*], *Chelemer Folksblat* [*Chelemer People's Newspaper*] and *Chelemer Wokhnblat* [*Chelemer Weekly Newspaper*]. Each of the three Yiddish newspapers had its followers and coworkers.

I, the writer of these lines, was connected with the *Chelemer Shtime* from its birth, being an active coworker until the eve of the Second World War. It began to publish in 1924 under the name *Undzer Shtime* [*Our Voice*] with the subheading "Independent-Democratic Weekly Newspaper for Literature, Communal and Economic Questions." Its first editor was Nakhum Goldberg and its publisher and [executive] editor was Yehoshua Wajnsztajn. A year later the newspaper changed its name to *Chelemer Shtime*.

For a time, until 1928, Feywl Frid edited the *Chelemer Shtime* and, later, the hardworking Fishl Lazar edited the newspaper. Gershon Lustiger was drawn to the editorial work in 1934 and was its editor until its last day.

The *Chelemer Shtime* was very popular in Chelm and in the area. It introduced a section, "Chelm and its Surroundings," where various episodes, notices, feature articles, announcements and writings about Jewish life in the Chelm province were published. Later, separate sections were introduced for the cities of Wladowa, Zamoszcz, Hrubieszow and others where their specific circumstances were highlighted.

Despite the fact that large Yiddish daily newspapers from Warsaw – the *Heynt* [*Today*], *Moment*, *Undzer Ekspres* [*Our Express*], *Folks Zeitung* [*People's Newspaper*] – and Warsaw afternoon newspapers and evening newspapers arrived in Chelm, the *Chelemer Shtime* that was read in every Jewish home was awaited with particular anticipation.

The *Chelemer Shtime* was an independent newspaper and was interested in all matters and dealt with various problems of Jewish life. It was a tribune for all strata and shades [of opinion], for Zionists, for leftist ideologies and for various movements. It widely illustrated each cultural undertaking in Chelm and its surrounding area and this stimulated the activity of the Jewish intelligentsia in the city. Precise reports about the meetings of the city council, the municipality, of the party gatherings and of the activities of the various charitable societies and institutions were published in the columns of the *Chelemer Shtime*.

Facsimiles of the mastheads of the newspapers Chelemer Shtime and Chelemer Woknblat

[Page 119]

Reproduction of the editorial member card for the Chelemer Woknblat issued in 1931 under the name Hersh Sziszler

Special editions of the *Chelemer Shtime* were published with the latest telegrams and news when important events occurred in the country, such as when Pilsudski seized power in 1920.

Two Polish newspapers were published in Chelm. The newspaper *Zwierciadło* [*Reflection*] was published by the anti-Semite Jan Czarnecki. The *Chelemer Shtime* would react sharply to its articles.

This anti-Semite Jan Czarnecki once carried to excess his contempt for the Jewish population and he was punished by the administrative regime with a sentence of seven days in the so-called Chelemer bourgeois jail. Jewish merchants and members of the middle class often were sentenced there for administrative offenses.

After leaving the prison he wrote in his anti-Semitic newspaper about the jailhouse in which Jewish merchants were being placed with serious criminals… His [statement] on behalf of the Jews surprised everyone and it was thought that he had become a repentant sinner.

The *Chelemer Shtime* reprinted this statement with the appropriate commentary.

[Page 120]

The coworkers and editors of the *Chelemer Shtime* were: Feywl Frid, Yosef Goldhaber, Dovid Goldrajkh, Fishl Lazar, Gershon Lustiger, Hersh Sziszler, Ben-Zion Bruker, A. Kornblit and others. No royalties were paid. The editors themselves received a minimal wage.

Various writers, cultural workers and artists took part in this newspaper. From time to time, a Chelemer *landsman* [person from the same town] in America, Canada, Australia, South Africa and *Eretz-Yisroel* sent articles.

The *Chelemer Shtime* provided a place for local young writers many of whom are known and well-recognized writers today.

The *Chelemer Shtime* was the tribune for Chelemer Jews during the most difficult times of anti-Semitic turmoil and harassment, allowing their words and protests to be heard against every edict and assault by the Polish regime, by the city council and tax office against the Jews, citizens with equal rights under the Polish Republic.

The *Chelemer Shtime* continued to exist with great stubbornness and power of endurance and with great financial difficulties until the 8th of September 1939 when Poland was already in ruins and half occupied by the brown-shirted Nazi murderers.

The second weekly newspaper, *Dos Chelemer Folksblat*, was the publication of the *Poalei-Zion* [Marxist Zionists] (left). It was published from 1928 until 1930 under the editorship of Feywl Frid and it was printed in Branfeld's printing shop.

Ahron Wolfson, typesetter for the Chelemer Shtime, who set the newspaper from its first issue until its demise. He perished at the hands of the Hitler murderers

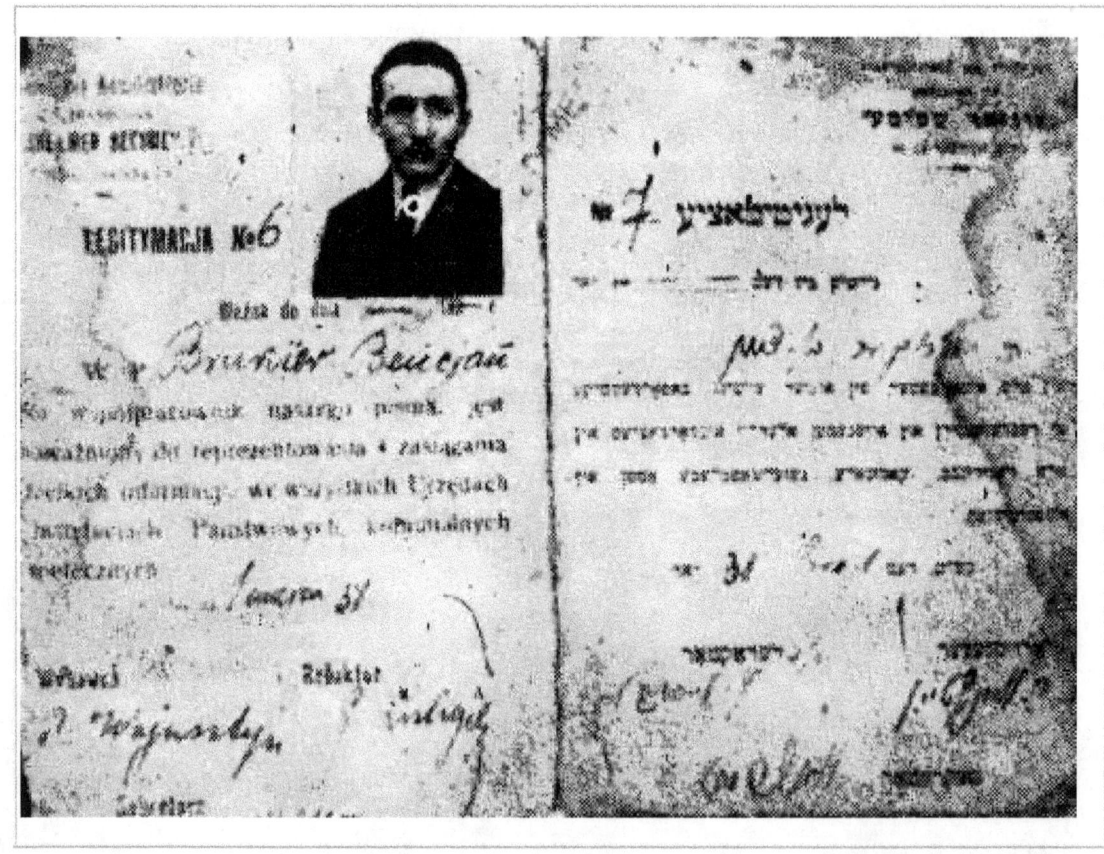

Facsimile of an identification card for the Chelemer Shtime (then called the Undzer Shtime) issued in the name of Ben-Zion Bruker

[Page 121]

Dos Chelemer Folksblat began to publish in 1930. Hersh Goldman, the owner of a printing business, was its editor and publisher. (He is now in Brazil.)

This newspaper was impartial and was published regularly every Friday from 1930 to 1933 in a smaller format than the *Chelemer Shtime*. It was well distributed and had a section on the life of artisans edited by Gershon Lustiger, secretary of the Artisans Union in Chelm.

There also was a sports section put together by Sh. Icykowicz and a humorous section put together by H. Sziszler.

Jewish Streets

Chelm had many streets and alleys. Each of them was made up of a world of its own. The main street was Lubliner Street, which was well known in the city as well as in the neighboring cities and *shtetlekh*.

Lubliner Street

Lubliner Street was the largest and most liked street in the city. It extended from one end to the other end of the city and possessed beautiful brick buildings and businesses. The majority of the residents and business owners were Jewish.

[Page 122]

Lubliner Street was known as a commercial street. Most of the businesses in the city were located here: the bank, the stock exchange and in past years even the market days took place here. It was the center for meeting people. Here were the cafes, cinemas, theaters and so on. The street was the street for strolling. Strolling began at the *Gurke* (cathedral) and extended all the way across the train line that cut through Lubliner Street, an area of several miles.

The post office, the Saxon gardens were located on Lubliner Street where the Jewish young were often attacked by Polish hooligans when they wanted to prevent Jews from getting a bit of fresh air there.

The *Polonia*, the theater building that the Germans had built during the time of their occupation during the First World War, was located on Lubliner Street, opposite the municipal garden. The *Polonia* was located on the property of M. Neihaus, the state-approved rabbi.

Rabbi Neihaus's *shtibl* [one room synagogue] was located at the same location neighboring the *Polonia*.

The famous ring of businesses that belonged to the municipal administration and was inhabited by Jews throughout who ran their businesses there for many years also was located on Lubliner Street.

Fragment of Lubliner Street in Chelm

[Page 123]

A group of Jews with canes at the trading market on Lubliner Street talking politics

The Polish regime brought to bear its "established policy," and then began to tear down the ring of businesses as a result of which hundreds of Jewish families remained without bread.

The *kehile* offices, the Yiddish newspaper businesses, the Jewish printers and Jewish editors were located on Lubliner Street. The entire Jewish political and communal life throbbed. The Bund, the Jewish Cultural House, *Poalei-Zion*, the Jewish Handworkers Union and many others had their premises on Lubliner Street.

But many other streets in Chelm also were saturated with Jewish life, among them the *Naye Tzal*, Siedlecka Street, Wesola Street, Szkolna, Reformacka and many other streets, and Jews also settled a part of Hrubieszowska Street.

Krzywa Street

It was called *Ulica* [street in Polish] *Adrianowska* before the First World War. However when Poland received its independence the name was changed to Krzywa [curved] Street. The street really was crooked, going zig zag, in other places wider and others narrow. It began nearby from behind the *gurka* [small hill] – the Russian cathedral that the Poles made Polish and sanctified as Catholic and when the Jewish young people wanted to stroll around its meadows, Polish hooligans attacked them bloodily. It cut through the spots and alleys where Jewish commerce was located. Its neighbors were the *shoykhetim* [ritual slaughterers] alley, the butchers' alley, the trade in meat and fish, of fruits and vegetables, of hot beans and *kvas* [a fermented yeast-based drink], of homemade cigarettes and other Jewish sources of income.

It was a typical Jewish street in Chelm. It extended parallel in a zig-zag from Lubliner Street. The religious life of Chelm was also found on this street, the old, historical synagogue, the fine house of prayer, the historical *shtiblekh* [small, one room houses of prayer] and the Jewish booksellers.

[Page 124]

The interest-free loan fund was located at Krzywa Street, in the house of prayer building. The committee that gave out food cards to Jews also was here at the same time as the interest-free loan fund. The small Jewish factories that would make raisin wine were located here. Gershon Lazar's oil factory whose smell of oil and the clanging of the electrical motor echoed around was also found here.

The Kuzmir *shtibl* of the Rabbi, Reb Moshe Leibele Twerski was located a little further along from the tumult of Gershon Lazar's oil factory. At that time this street and the surrounding streets were filled with Jews, young and old for the celebration of *tashlikh* by the Kuzmirer Rebbe and his *hakofes*.[3]

Hakofes is the circular procession with the Torah scrolls performed on *Simkhas Torah*, the holiday celebrating the completion of the yearly cycle of Torah readings and the start of the new cycle.]

Striding across a little further on Piarski Street where the Jewish *kehile* was located, on the right side of the *shtibl*, lived the city Rabbi, Reb Gamliel Hochman, who was widely known for his intelligent advice and instructions. The butcher's small synagogue was also located on this street. The butcher's small synagogue was a world unto itself. Here *kehile* matters were debated; here were heard the protests against every injustice that occurred in the city; here, on Passover and *Sukkous*, clothing was distributed to poor children and orphans.

Leibish Rajfer's soda-water shop was located here. After the *cholent* on *Shabbos*, the Jews came here to drink soda-water with syrup. This business was open on *Shabbos* and Leibish Rajfer gave everyone his sweet and cold drinks. He did not take any money from anyone. He knew everyone and had a good memory. He asked for the [payment] of the debts later in the week.

The *Naye Tzal*

The *Naye Tzal* was a purely Jewish street where no Christian residents were seen; no gentile neighbors existed here. The only gentiles who were noticed here were peasants who would drive into the Jewish courtyards on market days, [tie up] their horses and wagons and then they would go to the Jewish artisans to order a garment.

The "slippery steps" that led to the Naye Tzal, Pocztawa Street. The picture was taken after the liberation of Chelm by the Russian Army

[Page 125]

Chelm possessed about 100 streets and alleys and, since its emergence until its ruin, the *Naye Tzal* was the Jewish street in the city. The major part of the Chelm Jewish population was concentrated here, middle-class Jews, artisans, shopkeepers, toiling workers and also the poor people.

The *Naye Tzal* began at the corner of Lwowska Street and extended to Siedlecka and a series of adjacent alleys were enclosed in it such as *Naye Welt* [New World], Siedlecka, Iszczilutcka and other streets that were also well settled by Jews. However, the *Naye Tzal* still remained as the Jewish street of Jewish Chelm.

Hundreds and thousands of Jews were tightly packed in the above-mentioned street. Every courtyard, every house and room was packed, overcrowded with the young and old who struggled for their livelihood and their income and existence. Yet each one was full of faith, believing in the dream and hope of good times, of a more beautiful world.

There were Jewish shops, food and cheap sweets shops in almost every second or third house on the *Naye Tzal*. The majority of them were shrunken, meager with empty shelves and had a pitiful appearance. Their owners appeared preoccupied. They were constantly worried about where they would get the money to buy a little bit of fresh goods, a little bit of food, flour and sugar, to fill the empty shelves of their small shops.

The *Naye Tzal* was always moving, Jewish. It breathed and lived with all of the Jewish joys and sufferings. The journeymen here drowned out the street [noise] from the open windows with their singing. The echo of shoemakers hammering here could be heard – from the early morning to late into the evening. Carpenters, builders, locksmiths, painters, porters, wagon drivers and others also had their homes on the street; their children were born here; they had weddings for them [here].

Every Jewish holiday had its colossal and important reverberation on the *Naye Tzal*. The arrival of the holidays was taken note of here weeks before by the Jewish artisans, the shops, the *khederim* [religious primary schools] and the *kheder* boys from the entire area.

Pocztawa Street after the destruction. The ghetto where the Chelm Jews were imprisoned and tortured was located here.

[Page 126]

A group of Chelm Jewish coach drivers

Of all of the Jewish holidays, the holiday of Passover was the most strikingly noted. *Erev Pesakh* [on the eve of Passover] many of the Jewish bakeries that were located here were converted into matzo bakeries (*ladns*) that were a particular attraction for many of the young people in Chelm. Several members of the Chelm Jewish intelligentsia often helped the poor girls with the matzo as well as [helping] the men with the oven peels, rollers, kneaders who stood on their feet at the matzo bakery from six in the morning until late in the evening and [their presence] allowed them to catch their breath.

Baking the matzo was a great undertaking; it demanded a lot of money. However, the majority of the owners of such enterprises were poor Jews who waited for the matzo-baking season for the entire year. Others maintained rented orchards during the summer months and lost money very often when there was a bad harvest. These Jews came together before Purim to discuss and to set up their matzo bakeries. They often ran around looking for interest-free loans. The existing interest-free loan fund in the city often helped them out with loans, too.

Passover arrived and dressed up Jews could be seen leaving the *Naye Tzal* someone in a new jacket and new suit of clothes, someone with a remodeled garment. The young from the *Naye Tzal* were dressed up and left with pride to stroll on Lubliner Street or in the municipal garden. They met friends and acquaintances there.

Shabbos on the *Naye Tzal* could easily be observed: the closing of the shops on Friday night, the call to the synagogue by Reb Chaim *Haftacz* [embroiderer]– "*Shabbos, Shabbos Yidn.*" – he sealed the week and *Shabbos* emerged, as if from under one's feet… Jewish artisans, washed, hurried to the synagogue or the house of prayer; their *Shabbos* clothing gleamed. *Shabbos* morning, after the prayers, the pious women and children carried the ordered *cholent* [Sabbath stew cooked overnight] for the *Shabbos* meals.

[Page 127]

During the day on *Shabbos* Jewish speakers from various parties dropped in on the *Naye Tzal* and gave their speeches from the balconies. This occurred on the eves of voting for the parliament, city council or the Jewish *kehile*.

Particularly impressive were the Jewish weddings celebrated here. In the previous good years, the wedding events were carried out with all of the details and they were furnished with *klezmer* musicians, a *badkhn* [wedding entertainer who improvised rhymes about the bride and groom] who placed the bride on a symbolic velveteen throne before the wedding ceremony. Neighbors were invited and those who were not invited felt insulted. Others looked into the windows, pushed each other to catch a glimpse of the bride, to see the bride's charm, to see the groom and what kind of person he was and to see the in-laws. The *badkhn* got excited; Reb Motele the *klezmer* played a mournful, sorrowful melody. The women sobbed and there were tears in everyone's eyes.

And when pogromists, hooligans decided to have fun [at the expense of] the Jews, they went to the *Naye Tzal*. They chose here [the *Naye Tzal*] out of all of the other Jewish streets and began to break Jewish windowpanes and beat up Jews. It also happened that Jews from the *Naye Tzal* were not frightened and Jewish wagon drivers occasionally let the unruly hooligans have it with the stanchions from the wagons.

[Page 128]

These are short highlights about the Jewish street in Chelm – the *Naye Tzal* – that played a central role in Jewish life, mainly among the Jewish working masses and artisans.

The Jewish *gymnazie* [secondary school], the Widzolowski School, the Klara Morgenstern School and the Zionist organization were located at Budowski and Podwolna Streets. The Socialist Jewish group also had a location here for a time.

There were many more streets in Chelm that were purely Jewish and there were dozens of other streets in Chelm whose residents were mixed, Jews and Christians – and also there were streets in Chelm where Jews rarely lived.

Today all of the streets in Chelm stand empty and vacant. The pulsing Jewish life was ruthlessly exterminated. Sadly a dark wind blows through the streets of the *Naye Tzal*, Krzywa, Szkolna, Iszczilutcka and many others that were densely inhabited by Jews, by good Chelm Jews who were well-known in the large Jewish world.

The Jewish Chelm artisans and good students, the wagon drivers and the rabbis, the butchers and the teachers, the porters and the intelligentsia, the Hitler animals terrifyingly annihilated all of them; all of their bodies were burned in the gas ovens of Majdanek and Sobibor. Now a dark wind blows that carries the sacred dust of these martyrs through the empty and vacant Jewish streets of Chelm.

Notes:

    a. Feywl Fryd wrote an historical assessment of the Chelm synagogue in the *Chelemer Shtime* [*Chelm Voice*] concluding that it was around 800 years old and that a Dominican church had stood on its location and the Jews had bought it to build a synagogue.

    b. Dr. Meir Balaban remembers the Chelm synagogue in his work *Festung-Shuln fun der Poylisher Melukhe* [*Fortress Synagogues of the Polish State*], and in *YIVO Bleter* [*YIVO Pages*] of 1942 there is an interesting work about the synagogues in Poland by Ruchl Misznicer, which describes the architectural art of the Chelm synagogue.

    c. It is said that the Tsarist regime took a one million [*funt*] bribe for giving *IKO* permission to provide support to the Jewish population in Russia.

Translator's footnotes:

    1. *esn teg* was the custom by which religious students would be provided with meals in Jewish homes. They might eat with one family one day and another the next.

    2. A chair is set aside at circumcisions for Elijah the prophet who is said to witness all circumcisions.

    3. *tashlikh* – casting off – is a symbolic act of casting away one's sins by throwing small pieces of bread into a running natural body of water. *Tashlikh* takes place on the afternoon of the first day of Rosh Hashanah.

[Pages 129-130]

The "Bund" in Chelm and its Socialist-Revolutionary Work
(1904-1939)

by Nochum Winik

Translated by Howard Bergman

The Socialist-Revolutionary activity of the "Bund" in Chelm was widespread and it has a rich and great history. Regretfully, however, we are lacking historic sources for wide and detailed recounting. There has not been an adequate response from the landsmen Bundists to the requests by the Chelmer Landsmanschaft in Johannesburg to send in material about the labor movement in Chelm. The Bund archives in New York only sent some correspondence from the years 1905-1906, from 1916, and from 1923-1939. I therefore relied mostly on the published articles by Faivel Fried (one of the first socialist pioneers in the Jewish quarter in Chelm since the beginning of this century), on the letters from the Chelmer landsmen in Paris: Joseph {illegible name} Milner, Feige Rajn-Parobek, and Feige Shperling, and on my own recollections.

Certainly, my work now will not be exhaustive and for the periods up to the outbreak of World War II only an overview is given. Perhaps there will be some inaccuracies, but there will at least be a partial mirroring of the "Bund", a revolutionary mass party in the Jewish society of Chelm, calling on Jewish and non-Jewish workers to organize themselves into trade unions and to fight for freedom and socialism.

* * *

In 1934 in New York, Faivel Fried published in the edition of the Chelmer branch of the National Labor Association, *The Chelmer*, a dissertation entitled "Political Parties in the Chelmer Jewish Society", relating to the earliest years of national enlightenment and social activity in Chelm. Among others, he wrote the following:

"Until the year 1904 no political-social movement in the real sense of the word existed in Chelm. In 1904 the Zionist Organization in Chelm, under the influence of the late publisher of the Warsaw *Haint,* A. Goldberg - who at that time was a Hebrew teacher in Chelm - together with E. Dubkowski, began to conduct educational work among the Jewish masses and, at the same time fought with the elements of orthodoxy.

This work was, however, washed away quickly from the revolutionary wave that engulfed all of Russia and also spilled over into the sleepy town of Chelm.

Nochum Winik

Peretz Schiffer, a former Chelmer child prodigy, organized at that time in Chelm revolutionary circles among the Jewish and non-Jewish workers, but those circles did not have any determined party direction. At the end of 1904 the author of these lines (Faivel Fried) returned to Chelm from London and together with Niske Mandelbojm, Tsimerman, Chinke Yantche Foyas, and Joseph Milner, founded a Zionist-Socialist Circle, S-S, which grew into a mass movement within a short time. This S-S party was the first one in Chelm to organize economic strikes, first to lead political activities within the Jewish quarters, and from time to time organize open demonstrations in the area of the officers club. But as soon as there arrived in Chelm "professionals" from the "Bund", the S-S Zionist-Socialist movement receded into the shadows and the "Bund" assumed the hegemony over the Jewish working class.

In early 1905, the "Bund" organized outings in the surrounding forests, led all economic and political strikes, made contact with the non-Jewish revolutionary parties, and became the dominant political power in Jewish society. How strong the "Bund" was at that time can be deduced from the fact that the local police were simply afraid to enter the "teahouse" of Chaim Tuchman, the gathering place of the Bundists.

On the evening of October 12 the news spread in Chelm with lightning speed that the Czar had signed the Constitution. The "Bund" organized a mass meeting, and a speech was delivered by Ruevele Szocher's son, Meyer Tselnik, who was a baker. The historic 17th October was approaching. A general strike had been declared for several days throughout the country, and Chelm would not remain aloof.

The next day a joint demonstration of Jewish and non-Jewish workers, consisting of several thousand people, was organized by all parties. The banner bearer was a penitent from the "Chelmer Strong Men", a certain Abish "Gorb". Suddenly, a racket broke out, the mass of people began to stir, and Abish "Gorb" threw away the banner and was the first one to run off. In a stampede the crowd dispersed in various directions. The author, who was in the front rows, picked up the banner and together with several dozen unafraid comrades conscious of the cause, continued the demonstration.

As it later became clear, the disturbance was caused by several gendarmes who on seeing from a distance the enormous demonstration, became scared and started to run. A large number of the demonstrators thought that they were being chased, and therefore became confused.

Several days went by, but there was hardly time to enjoy the Czar's Constitution, and already foreboding messages began to arrive about slaughters of revolutionaries and Jews. Chelm also expected a pogrom, and the worker parties quickly created a well-armed self-defense. Fortunately, Chelm got by with only fear and a pathetic counter-demonstration by the local anti-Semites (the "black hundred").

At the end of October, a State of Emergency was declared, and a hail of repressions fell on the labor parties. The P.P.S. (Polish Socialist Party) responded with individual acts of terror. The "Bund" as well as the S-S could no longer conduct their work legally, and they were compelled to start underground activities. The outside professionals left town and the author of this article and other comrades in leadership positions were sought by the police. All this had a bad effect on our work. The "Bund" had therefore determined that at all costs a professional activist must be engaged. I had to travel to Lublin myself to see Comrade Samuel (Comrade Chanin) to demand from him that a "representative" be sent to Chelm to conduct the Bund activities there.

But by that time the "Bund" was no longer legal in Lublin. Comrades Dovid, Samuel, and Sara Szweber were already imprisoned in the Lublin Castle. After a great deal of searching, I reached Comrade Fishl Gelenter with whom I was later smuggled into Chelm.

But it was destined that Comrade Gelenter would spend only one night in Chelm. The next day, after we stole ourselves into my home, the police arrested us. From the prison I managed to send out a request that pressure should be put on my rich uncle, Fishl Lewensztajn; that he should come to the police station and free Comrade Gelenter under the pretext that the latter was one of his representatives in the hardware merchandise who happened to become acquainted with me in the store.

That idea succeeded, and Comrade Gelenter was released right away. I was taken to the Lublin prison, where I spent several years, and then I was sent out of Poland. Some time later it became known who the stool pigeon was."

(The above are excerpts from F. Fried's article which give us information about the initial activities of the "Bund".)

* * *

In his *Reminiscences,* Faivel Fried writes that from prison, he let it be known that a neighbor who lived in Fishl Berele's courtyard was the stool pigeon who "buried" him and who denounced everyone, and how the neighbor's brother, Szmul, who was also in the movement, took upon himself the task of removing the stool pigeon. Some time later that stool pigeon was shot and his body was thrown into the River Bug near the town of Wlodawa, about 30 kilometers from Chelm. The police traced their search of the perpetrator to Szmul Fried who was arrested in Warsaw and brought before a military court where he was sentenced to death. However, because of Szmul's young age, his death sentence was commuted to life imprisonment. His defender was the famous lawyer Landau.

Several notices about the revolutionary activities of the "Bund" in Chelm are found in the *Folks Tsaitung* editions of October 24 and November 6, 1906, published in Vilna. In the section dealing with political party life, the following correspondence from Chelm is published:

"In most recent times our party work in Chelm (Lublin Gubernia) started to be more normal. Regular circles, gatherings, organizational meetings, etc. are being conducted. With regard to cultural aspects, the achievement of the local workers is quite low. There is a lack of intellectual strength. We do not receive any support from the regional Lublin Committee, as if it did not exist".
Signed: Sholem

In one edition of the *Folks Tsaitung,* in the section "Professional Life", we read the following correspondence:

"Thanks to the "Bund" Organization, which already exists in Chelm for a long time, the economic condition of the local workers has greatly improved. Instead of earlier working between 16-18 hours a day, Jewish workers today only work 14 hours a day. At almost all trades workers have higher wages and better treatment."

"But because of the repressions and arrests which took place recently, the proprietors declared a lockout and made the following demands: 1) a 15-hour workday; 2) a reduction in the wages; 3) work on Saturday nights, 4) piece work, and 5) firing certain workers known to be seditious, and so on."

"The proprietors threatened to arrest the troublemakers, with the help of the police. But all of that did not frighten the workers. The proprietors, through their delegates, turned to the Organization, demanding that the long strike be ended. But the workers accomplished their objectives."

Signed: Sholem

In a letter, Faivel Fried writes the following:

"In 1904 I and Shmulke Winer (now in America) organized the first illegal meeting, which took place in the courtyard of Tsale Bereles. At that time the illegal library was also created. At the illegal meeting the speakers were Peretz and Efroim Shiyes, the latter appearing at various meetings of Jewish and even non-Jewish workers."

"When I returned from London in 1905 I was arrested, together with Joseph Milner (now in Paris), in an apartment of a midwife who was also a dentist. In that apartment revolutionary work was conducted. The midwife was in charge of political circles of the S-S and to her apartment would also come Russian revolutionaries. One of them, a certain Bielakov, was the leader of the political work among the Russian groups".

"In those days there appeared on the horizon a baker fellow, **Meyer Tselnik,** a Bundist, and quite an original type. He organized all maidservants in town. He also became the "mediator" between the housewives and the maidservants. He, Meyer Tselnik, took an active part in the political circles of the town."

The Jewish workers' exchange at that time was in the "teahouse" of Sheva and Chaim Tuchman, near the steps of the new customs house. **Yankele Dantsiker** was the leader of the S-S group. He spoke at various meetings and helped organize demonstrations of Jewish and non-Jewish workers. In those years, 1904-1906, the seamstress **Chinke Yantche Foyas,** or as her father was called, "Yantche of Soda-Water", was very active in the Bund Movement in Chelm. It is told that she was one of the most ardent activists among the Chelm Bundists. In 1906 she was deported and she never returned".

* * *

I, the writer of these pages, remember an illegal meeting which took place a Friday evening in the Kuznar (prayer) "House" number "Piervy" (there were two such houses, one was called "Piervy" and the other "Vtoroy", meaning "First" and "Second"- *translator*). I was 9 years old and I remember how an organized worker group arrived at the Piervy House as if to pray. The room was full of the faithful, and when the cantor stood at the pulpit to start the prayers, the workers declared that the meeting was starting. Nobody was allowed to leave. Speeches were made by Faivel Fried, Meyer Tselnik, and others. Right after the meeting, arrests were made.

While I was in Paris in 1952, I met with Joseph Milner. He informed me that, according to his recollections of the years 1904-1906, at a gathering organized by the group "Freiheit" (Freedom) in Chelm at the house of Tsale Berele (Faivel Fried's father), Nochum Brofman also appeared in the name of the "Bund". He spoke very well and the subject was the political situation in Russia and Poland. He became very popular and there was no Bund meeting or "celebration" at which Brofman would not be present and participate. His mother lived across from the barracks and throughout the years she made a living selling milk. The same Nochum Brofman was seen in Chelm in 1919-1920, was present at all Bund meetings, but no longer took any active part in the Bundist Movement, nor in any other movement.

Due to the arrests and repressions, as happened in many other towns, a standstill occurred among the workers in Chelm after the revolutionary years of 1904-1906. Because of the informers who appeared in the Jewish quarter in Chelm in the years 1906-1907, most members of the Bund Organization were arrested.

In 1911 there appeared on the Jewish workers exchange, at that time located in the Lublin quarter next to the Polish Church, Shiye (the Nose) Tenenboim. A house painter by profession, he was a devoted Bundist. He started to organize the Jewish painters and related trades. Later, with the outbreak of World War I, Tenenboim was drafted into the army and was never heard from again.

* * *

World War I broke out. The Germans occupied Chelm. They kept the population in fear and dread, not allowing any freedom of expression. The situation became somewhat better when the Austrians took over the occupation of Chelm. Young people took the liberty of gathering in various private homes and took walks until late into the night. The Lublin Jewish society was full of young couples taking walks between the Sobor and the Saxony Garden and farther. The occasion then arose to meet and to convey to one another information about a gathering or about an illegal meeting. On account of caution, almost no one knew, until an hour before the meeting, where the meeting would take place, what the agenda would be, who the speakers would be, etc.

The day before the Purim Holiday of 1916 it became known that a special Purim evening was in preparation. On Purim day, one told the other person about a get-together. The people making the announcements, responsible party activists, were then the following: Moshe Shimel (dressed in his black cape which still remained with him from the years 1905-1906; he seldom walked without it and without eye glasses), Yakov Shtekn, Szmul Mordkhe Zygielbojm, Mechal Lindenboim, Sara Lindenboim, Note Tom, Kaplan (the only Litvak and a very original person), and Motl Shechterzon (now in Australia).

Moshe Shimel

The first Purim evening which took place in the shared apartment of Moshe Shimel and Mechal and Sara Lindenboim left a great impression on the Chelmer Jewish workforce. A new spark of life entered the hearts of all assembled. Lectures were delivered and workers songs were sung and recited. Sara Shalit very beautifully recited I. L. Peretz's "*Mein Nit Az Di Velt Iz A Kretchme*" (Do Not Think The World Is A Tavern--*translator*.)

To the extent that I can remember, the following older Bundists were present at the Purim evening: Moshe Shimel, Sara and Mechal Lindenboim, Kaplan, Sara Shaht, Rueven Shechterzon, Aaron Dovid Hipshman, Dovid and Meyer Bojm, Henoch Flajszer, Mrs. Flajszer (now in Israel), Motl Shechterzon, Note Tom, and other comrades who already had some seniority in the activities of political organizations. Among the younger comrades, who had not yet been able to show participation in any movement or organization, were: Szmul (Artur) Zygielbojm, Yekl Dreksler, Isroel Dreksler, Vovke Gotlieb, Avrom Yakov Shnobel (now in Israel), Sheva Shnobel (died in Israel), Yakov Palman (now in South Africa), Yochevet Palman (died in Israel in 1947), Golde and Keyle Shperling, Feige Rajn (now in France), Szmul Parobek (died in Paris), Itsil Reif, and Rikel Rajchbind (in South Africa).

During the same evening the first administration was selected whose task it was to create a workers home. The committee included: Moshe Shimel, M. Lindenboim, Kaplan, Y. Shtekn, Szmul Zygielbojm, Aaron Dovid Hipshman, and Yudl Graber.

A youth commission was selected which was to carry on the work among the young people. This youth commission included: S. Parobik, A. Y. Shnobel, Feige Rajn, and N. Winik. It was not easy to find a suitable hall where we could meet. The first room rented was from the "grobn kop" (thick head) on the market square. After long searches, a house was finally rented on Ablanski Street (opposite the bath house). Several months later we celebrated the joyous occasion of the first gathering in the house which was named Workers Home. It did not take long before almost all Jewish workers in Chelm began to concentrate around the Workers Home. Active cultural work was being conducted.

The most important tasks for the Committee then were: a) to create a library at the Workers Home; b) to arrange meetings in the evenings in general, and particularly on the Sabbaths and holidays, with artistic programs, and c) to enlighten the populace in the political situation of the world.

In a very short time several hundred books were assembled and the Jewish workers began to read them with great eagerness. Saturday afternoons became very lively events when almost all Jewish workers gathered to listen to various lectures on social and political issues.

At that time the question arose--to which party direction should the "Workers Home" belong? On that issue party frictions and opinion variations began. The discussions were heated and the bickering went on till late in the nights.

A drama group was created and it included M. Shechterzon, Rueven Shechterzon, Meyer Bojm, Sara Shalit, Sheva Binsztok, Faivel Dreksler, and others.

The first performance took place in the theater "Syrena" on the market square. The play was "Zhan un Madlena" and it made a great impression on all people in town who had seen the performance. Especially effective was the mass scene when actors came on the stage with red banners and sang revolutionary and workers songs. The performance encouraged many workers, especially the young ones, to join the just created political parties. The second performance, also in the same theater, was "Beide Kune Lerffls", with the main parts played by M. and R. Shechterzon. In the courtyard of the Syrena theater was a sawmill where a group of Russian soldiers, war prisoners, worked at that time. Among that group were several Jewish workers, former Bundists from Lithuania and Russia. They had seen the performance and established a connection with the members of the Bund Committee. After that a "Bund Circle" was created among the imprisoned soldiers, and from time to time they also visited and participated in the general debates. Thanks to that Circle, and also due to the position taken by some members of the Committee, the majority of the Committee of the "Workers Home" adopted a pro Bund point of view. After dozens of committee meetings, after many hot discussions, the seal of the "Bund" was put on the "Workers Home"

There were frequent meetings. At one meeting the "bread" issue was considered, a very realistic issue during that time of hunger. Many people came to the meetings and the hall simply became too small. Discussions also took place outside. At one stormy meeting on a Saturday afternoon Austrian police showed up at the "Workers Home" and ordered all participants to disperse and they arrested the members of the presidium. It later turned out that the police came at the requests and demands of neighbors from the closest houses who could not sleep because of the screaming and rackets coming every night from the meetings at the "Home".

After the stormy meetings at which the "Workers Home" took on the Bundist ideology, certain members of the "Home", as well as the group of Poalei Zion, left the "Workers Home". At the head of the group that left was Aaron Dovid Hipshman.

After the comrades from the presidium were released under the condition of no more gathering in the street and creating rackets, it was decided to look for new and larger quarters. In 1917 the Committee of the "Workers Home" succeeded in appealing to the commandant of the city, an Austrian and a sympathetic and democratic person, concerning a larger building for the Workers. To the astonishment of many people in the city, the commandant transferred to the "Workers Home" a 3-story house at Lublin Street 13 in the center of town, not far from Sobor. In December, 1917, a Bundist convention took place in Lublin and the Bundist Organization in Chelm sent two delegates, Comrades Szmul (Artur) Zygielbojm and Szmul Parobik.

The Bund Committee became very active and right away selected a special commission to handle the renovation of the new building in a way to provide for all needs of the work and to satisfy the "Workers Home" in all respects. On one floor of the house a stage was installed where theater performances and concerts could be provided for the members. The library was enlarged and it was named "Groser Bibliotek". The first librarian was Moshe Shimel and his assistant was Michal Bankirer.

It was also decided to open a children's home, to provide evening courses for workers, to organize the workers according to separate trade, to open an inexpensive kitchen for the workers, to form a cooperative which would sell products for less, and to open our own bakery for all the members.

At that time a Press Commission was created which had the task of distributing the workers' press, particularly the Bund's *Folks Tsaitutig and Yugtit Veker*.

Members of the "Bund" Committee in Chelm in 1930

Standing (from right): --?, Avroml Shteinberg, Note Torn. Sitting (from right): --?, --?, Moshe Lustiger; Leibele Rajzman

Preparations were made to open the children's home. In accordance with the decisions, the first children to be accepted were full- or half orphans and later the children of workers and members.

The first floor was prepared for the children's home by purchasing special furniture and pictures, as the first temporary teacher, Rozhe Shafran from Warsaw, was invited. Later the kindergarten teachers Toshe and Zoshe were invited. To the festive opening of the children's home a special visit from Warsaw was made by B. Michalewicz. The esteem of the "Bund" grew in town. A special committee to administer all questions with regard to the children's home was selected and included Comrades S. M. Zygielbojm, Polye Fruchtgartn, Esther Tuchman, Note Tom, N. Winik, Yakov Shtekn, and Golde Shperling-Zygielbojm. Of course, it was not easy to provide the needed budget the children's home required, as the population was impoverished from the war years and there was also great unemployment.

Various enterprises were undertaken, including flower-days, in order to secure the needed funds to maintain the children's home. Then, when the American products began to arrive and the children's home received a certain quantity, the children experienced a piece of paradise receiving both food and beverages. At the end of 1919 the two teachers left and they were replaced by Chana Heftman, a sister of the well-known writer, and journalist Yosif Heftman (Israel). When financial conditions became more difficult - already under the Polish government - the children's home was transferred to a smaller place in the Bukler courtyard on the second floor, at the corner of Lubliner and Podwalna Streets. Although the TSISHO (Central Jewish School Organization--*translator*) sent in monthly support for the children's home, it still was not sufficient. The community subsidized the children's home for a long period of time. But in the end, in the year 1924, the children's home was closed.

A large number of young people enrolled in the workers courses. The subjects offered were: Yiddish, Jewish Literature, Accounting, and History. The teachers were Faivel Fried, Moshe Lerer, Dr. Nerlas, Dr. Kanfer, and others. A People's University was created where political economy was taught and lectures were given on political and cultural problems. Among the lecturers included were Dr. Fensterblau (also a brother of Dr. Mirlas), Kaminski, Director Y. Lipman, Shlomo Samet, and others. The Peoples University drew many people of the town; not only workers or members of the Workers Home, but anyone who yearned for knowledge came to hear the interesting lectures. Sometimes the hall was too small to hold all listeners.

The Committee of the "Bund" was also concerned about organizing the workers with regard to their trades. A special commission including Yakov Shtekn, S. Parobek, Itzler, Feige Rajn, Golde and Keyle Szperling, and others was appointed. In a short time they managed to organize almost all Jewish needle workers in Chelm. Separate commissions were also set up to organize other trades, such as construction workers, furniture-workers, leather-workers, and those who worked in the nutrition branches. Active in the Trades Commission were: Asher Grinbojm, Note Tom, N. Winik, and Motl Shechterzon.

From all the trade commissions a Trade Council was created which had control over the trade movement and was concerned about securing better wages for the workers, a large number of whom were under the influence of the "Bund".

* * *

In the same location, around the end of 1917 and beginning of 1918, a workers kitchen opened up. A large number of workers with their families came to eat and spend free time in their own worker environment. At the head of the workers kitchen stood Yakov Shtekn.

A special place in the Bund Movement was occupied by a cooperative. This cooperative was located next to the Kuznar House on Andrjanowska Street. The responsible leader was Henoch Flajszer.

Since bread was then distributed with ration cards and was of poor quality, it was decided to open our own bakery for the members. The bakery was established in the courtyard of Mr. Evry in a basement. Later, at the end of 1919-1920, during the Polish-Russian War when the Polish Government was looking for and trying to arrest all those political leaders it considered "non-kosher", and especially the active Jewish political and trade union leaders, the bakery served as a good hiding place for many comrades. Next to the big baking oven where there was always a large amount of firewood, the basement was dug a little deeper and where there always stood the big boiler with boiling water for the bagels, a special opening was made for a person to crawl into. The area between the oven and the wall of the building was filled in with a very thick brick wall. The opening under the boiler led to the hiding place which was small, but in need it could hold several persons. Needless to say, there always had to be a person present to put the boiler back in its place so that nothing could be detected. Often, during searches and also during wild outbursts by hooligans against the Jews, people had to hide there. Some people spent entire nights in that stifling place to avoid being caught by the Polish reactionaries.

The man in charge of the bakery was Yossif Bankirer, now in Israel.

In 191? {illegible date} a drama group of the youth was created under the leadership of Meyer Tom (Meyer Fentak). In this drama group ably participated H. Handelsman, Frenkel, Akerman, Sara Baigel, Feige Shperling, Faivel Zygielbojm, Pinye Zygielbojm (perished in the Warsaw Ghetto). The first performance took place in city hall. There was also a drama group of adults. That group included: Faivele Dreksler, "Black" Chaim (Sheva Binsztok's husband), Israel Zygielbojm, Feige Rajn (Parobek), Keyle Shperling, and others.

A lot of time and energy was then devoted to organizing the youth. A large youth meeting was called and a committee of young people was established which included the following: Feige Shperling, Moshe Zygielbojm (a brother of Artur's who later left for Russia with the Red Army), Guterman, S. Nachtman, Beirach Sher, Hersh Handelsman, Yosif Elye (now in America), Leibele Rajzman, Feige Rozenkop, and others. The Youth Committee worked very energetically.

A very successful and imposing May demonstration took place in 1918. Participants in the beautiful train included all labor parties, such as the "Bund", the Labor Zionists, the Polish Socialist Party, and a part of the Ukrainian workers. Among the speakers was S. M. Zygielbojm, representing the "Bund", who spoke in Yiddish and all Christian workers listened to him calmly and respectfully.

In general, the years 1917 and 1918 saw an increase in the Bund Movement in all areas. In the political as well as in the trade movements; in the cultural as well as in the economic areas in all branches of social life in Chelm.

When the Poles took over power in the city, a rumor spread that the peasants were preparing a pogrom. On the initiative of the "Bund" a general meeting of all Jewish parties was called, in order to form a self-defense. Announcements in Yiddish and Polish were hung throughout about a mass meeting to take place in the Big Synagogue. A special appeal was also made to the Polish population to condemn this wave of incitement, otherwise it would have to bear full responsibility. At the meeting of the parties it was decided to adopt energetic means of self protection against any attack. It was decided to post guards of young workers at the roads on which the peasants would usually come to town. To the call from the "Bund" almost the entire Jewish population assembled in the Synagogue during the daytime.

Workers Children's Home at the Bund in Chelm in 1922

Sitting in upper row from right to left: Mager, Esther Tuchman, an American delegate, N. Winik, Note Tom, Avrom Shteinberg, Polye Fruchtgartn, and {illegible name}
Sitting in the middle of the second row is the teacher Chana Heftman

On the Synagogue platform the first to speak was Dr. Nfirlas. Suddenly, a detachment of Polish policemen appeared in the street next to the Synagogue demanding that the crowd disperse. The Bund commander responsible for the meeting was then S. Guterman, and the person in charge of our weapons arsenal was Chaim Lang, who had just returned from Russia. When the police commandant turned to Guterman with the demand that he tell the crowd to disperse, and the policemen lined up in two rows with rifles in their hands, Chaim Lang walked up to the police commandant from the side and quietly, in a quick motion with a sharp knife, cut off the policeman's revolver and leather holster.

When the police commandant noticed that his revolver was taken from him, he asked that the revolver be returned to him and that everyone should quietly depart. He at the same time gave the guarantee that no excesses, no attacks on Jews would occur. There was no other choice but to disperse, because the police stood around the Synagogue with bayonets drawn, ready to attack. Not wanting to allow the spilling of blood, the joint committee decided to cancel the meeting and asked the people to return quietly to their homes. The special self-defense guards, however, walked around the Jewish sections of town, the houses of prayer, during the nights to make sure that no attacks on Jews took place. It should be stressed that the self-defense group was trained primarily and prepared some time earlier by Chaim Lang. The weapons arsenal was located in the home of Bashe Shneiderman (a seamstress).

Several days later, S. M. Zygielbojm was arrested and put in the Chelm prison (on LublinerStreet). The news about Zygielbojm's arrest spread quickly throughout town. The Bund Committee decided that under all circumstances and by all means necessary he must be freed.

The next day (Saturday), a large meeting was arranged next to the dwelling of the police commandant. Dr. Fensterblau then spoke to the assembled crowd in Polish and stated that if Zygielbojm was not released right away, the crowd would go to the prison and break the gate.

When the crowd arrived at the gates of the prison, after the police commandant received a delegation and the prison warden listened to the plea of the delegates, the two people in charge must have communicated by telephone about the consequences of such a collision, and they decided to release Zygielbojm. The crowd received him with such enthusiasm that the people simply carried him out of the prison courtyard on their hands.

The crowd dispersed very quickly. The freeing of Artur Zygielbojm made a colossal impression.

At the end of November 1918, the Bund Party celebrated the wedding of Szmul Mordkhe Zygielbojm to Golde Shperling who had been a member of the Bund Party all the time. The Family Shperling played a significant role in the Bund Movement in Chelm at that time. The father was a shoemaker and burdened with children; four girls and three boys. The main breadwinner was Golde. She was a seamstress who worked a lot. Still, she found time to occupy herself with Bund Party work. After her wedding to Zygielbojm, the couple lived in a basement apartment at Leibl Rozen's in the courtyard on Boykes Street.

After the wedding, she had to work more and harder than before because she had to help her widowed mother with the children, and in the free hours Golde helped Zygielbojm in the Movement. The Bundist youth saw in Golde a devoted wife and an active party member. Her tirelessness helped her husband Artur to acquire knowledge. In 1920 Zygielbojm was called to Warsaw by the Central Committee, where he was given a party position in the Bund Movement In 1922 Golde and her two children moved to Warsaw. She perished in the Warsaw Ghetto together with her daughter Rivke. Her son Yoske is now in America.

Keyle, Golde's sister, was a committee member in the needle-trade union and she also worked very intensively in the Bund Movement. She read a great deal and was interested in all issues of social life. Keyle was also a member of the choir in the Workers Home. Later, she married Yakov Shtekn. In the 1930's. after a long illness, her husband Yakov died. Today she lives in Argentina.

Their younger sister, Feige, joined the youth Bund "Tsukunft" (Future-*translator*) in Chelm. For a long time she was the leader of the "Yugnt-Bund". She has always participated in the issues of the trade union movement, and even in the political issues of the Party. In 1921 Feige joined the Bund Committee where she was active in all areas. Now she is in France.

Their youngest sister, Teme, married Avromtshe Zygielbojm. They are now in Los Angeles (USA).

Both their brothers, Yosif and Peretz Shperling, are now in Argentina (Buenos Aires). Peretz is the president of the Chelmer Landsmanschaft.

Dr. S. Fensterblau, leader of the "Bund", died in Treblinka

* * *

During the first democratic elections to city council in Chelm in 1919, the Bund Party made an enormous promotional effort, announcing at meetings, through leaflets and posters, the postulates of the Party. The oppositions, both Polish and Jewish, were frightened by the Bund's large election work. On the list of candidates for city council all trade unions were represented The first person on the list was S. M. Zygielbojm. To the great admiration of the whole Chelm population, 19 of 24 candidates to be elected came from the Bund list. The elections were then voided by the governor's office in Lublin. Not until 1921 were new elections held for city council, when the "Bund" received only one seat--for Hershl Fruchtgartn.

In 1920 a notice was received from the Chelm city clerk stating that the house occupied by the Workers Home since 1917, which was in the hands of the "Bund", must be returned to the heirs of the owners. No appeals had any effect; only 3 months were granted to vacate the building and find other quarters.

A house was rented on Budowska (Boykes) Street for the "Bund" and trade union work. But the work, however, began to suffer. A number of Party leaders had left Chelm: Artur Zygielbojm was already in Warsaw; Dr. Fensterblau also left Chelm; Flajsher settled in Falenica. Several other comrades also left and the Bund activities in Chelm were reduced significantly.

The trade union movement, especially the needle-trade union, continued its work through the leadership of S. Parobek-Mager, Feige Rajn-Parobek (now in France), Keyle Shperling, Yochevet Palman, Chana Bakalarz, and others. To the first needle-trade union convention, which took place in Warsaw, the Chelm delegates were Yakov Shtekn and Szmul Parobek. In 1921, at the national convention of the leather industry, the Bund delegate was H. Handelsman, the youngest delegate at that convention.

The Library, "Groser-Bibliotek" at the Workers Home, was also transferred to the new quarters on Budowska Street. The library leaders then were Leibele Rajzman and Michal Bankirer. The Bund Committee in 1920 included: Note Tom, Mager, Polye Fruchtgartn, Leibele Rajzman, N. Winik, Kaplan, Feige Rajn-Parobek, and Avrom Shteinberg.

In 1920, during the war between the Poles and the Soviets, on a certain night, arrests were made which did not avoid Chelm. By chance I did not stay overnight in my home. When the secret police came to arrest me as a representative of the "Bund", they in the meanwhile arrested my younger brother, Akiva, a Labor-Zionist. He spent about 14 weeks in the Chelm and Kielce prisons (together with others from Chelm placed under political arrest).

Dr. Dovid Mirlas, chairman of the worker Cooperative "Einikajt" in Chelm. He died in 1920

Also arrested then as a representative of the "Bund" was Dr. Mirlas, who spent 3-4 weeks in the Chelm prison and about 10 weeks in the Kielce prison. Originally from Warsaw, Dr. Mirlas was a teacher of physics and chemistry in the Yiddish/Polish

High School. In prison he caught a cold, which turned into an inflammation of the lungs. When he was released, he was bed-ridden for several weeks and died.

Huge masses of the Jewish population in Chelm accompanied him as he went to his eternal rest.

* * *

To the above-listed reasons for the weakening of the "Bund", we also have to mention the creation of the "Com-Bund". In 1921, during the well known negotiations between the "Bund" and the Third International about the 21 conditions of entry, the "Bund" accepted only 19 and a half points; a split occurred in the Bund Party and the "Com-Bund" Party arose in Poland.

From the Chelm Bund Party the following important members left: S. Guterman, Yosif Elye, Moshe Shimel, Feige Shperling, H. Shechterzon, and others.

For a long time the members who split off did not conduct any separate work or activity in Chelm. But they created the first cell for the later strong Communist movement in Chelm.

After the departure of Motl Shechterzon to Israel (now in Australia), R. Shechterzon to America, Yakov Shtekn to Warsaw, Dr. Fensterblau to Galicia-Szmul, Chana Parobek to Warsaw, Itzler and Yakov Palman to Israel, and Avrom Yakov Shnobel to Israel, the situation developed that only a few of the older Bundist leaders remained in Chelm, such as Hershel and Polye Fruchtgartn, N. Winik, Note Tom, Esther Tuchman, Mager and his wife Feige, Avroml Shteinberg and his wife Molye.

At that time a new member joined , S. Berger. Also, the teacher Avrom Wajnsztajn would from time to time come to Chelm during the school vacations and help with the cultural work. Active with the young people were: Hersh Handelsman, Leibele Rajzman, Michal Bankirer, I. Palman, Feivel Zygielbojm, Nosn Bojm, and others. However, there was a lack of strength to replace those comrades who left Chelm.

On November 7 1923, a bomb exploded in the Citadel in Warsaw, and during the same night arrests were made throughout Poland. Some of the arrested were from Chelm: Orensztajn from the Zionists and N. Winik from "Bund". The leader of the Chelm security, M. N. Wikusz, a drunkard, wanted to know during the investigation if we, the few Jewish representatives, had our own airplane and flew the night before to Warsaw to bomb the Citadel. After being detained for several days, and proving that that night we were in Chelm and not in Warsaw, we were released.

* * *

In 1924 the "Bund" moved over to Lubliner Street 15-17. The Groser Bibliotek opened again and the Bund work continued, albeit on a smaller scale but quite active. From time to time, certain instructors and lecturers arrived from Bund Central.

At that time the "Bund" established a union of artisans and home manufacturers, under the leadership of M, Mager, H. Handelsman, A. Shteinberg and Note Tom. The transport workers were also organized by the "Bund".

The committee of the Youth-"Bund", "Tsukunft", also conducted some work among the young people. The *Folks Tsaitzitig* and other Bund publications were widely distributed. The "Bund" also participated in all May meetings and celebrated the Bund holidays. In a modest way the "Bund" renewed the work of political enlightenment.

From 1936 until the outbreak of World War II we saw again active Bund activity in Chelm. For example, we read in the *Naye Folks Tsaitzitig* number 90 of March 29, 1937, that Chelm ordered an additional 1,000 copies of the *Naye Folks Tsaitzitig* of the first three issues, April 1-3.In a book, *The Jewish Working Class,* published in Lodz in 1937, we read on page 128 correspondence from Chelm describing a strike by Jewish workers and how it was joined by Christian workers, such as Polish and Ukrainian workers from the mills and sawmills. There was a demonstration in town by the striking workers (Perhaps a thousand people--Jews and Christians--participated in the demonstration) which made an enormous impression in town, (The strikes and demonstrations took place already after the pogrom in Przytyk).

In the February 4, 1938, edition of the *Naye Folks Tsaitzitig* we read about a jubilee celebration in Chelm: "Chelm, like all other towns, suffers greatly from the crisis, Working conditions are bad; the wages are small; working time is increased; the trade unions, for various reasons are not active and some are not even functioning". The correspondence continued:

"Representatives of the Chelm workers, bakers, leather workers, and tailors appealed to the National Council of the Trade Unions about organizing trade unions. Some workers are already organizing themselves, others are still waiting for help from the political parties or from the National Council".

With assistance from the Bund Central Committee, the Chelm Committee started again to conduct some systematic work. There started to arrive from Warsaw frequent speakers and lecturers who gave public lectures, mostly under the heading "The most important events in Poland in 1937".

For the 40th anniversary of the "Bund", a festive celebration took place under the chairmanship of Comrade A. Shteinberg, with participation by Comrade Friedman, who lectured on the various stages of the 40-year history of the "Bund". The youth organization entertained with readings and songs, which left a great impression on the audience.

In the Warsaw edition of the *Naye Folks Tsaitzitig* for May 5, 1938, we read in the correspondence from Chelm that the Chelm Bund Committee approached the P. P. S. (Polish Socialist Party) before May 1st about organizing a joint demonstration. The P.P.S. had agreed but the city manager forbade it. The correspondent, Avrom Shteinberg, further reported that a few weeks before May 1st, local agents of the Polish security came in and took away all the stamps (of the "Bund", the "Tsukunft", the "Kultur Lige", and others) and until the last day it was not known if the May meetings on the premises would even be permitted. As soon as the permit was received, two separate meetings were organized--one for the members of the Bund Party, and the other for the youth. The speakers were A. Shteinberg, Ajzenshtein and Friedman. Two new banners were displayed at the May meeting.

In the October 8th, 1938, edition of the *Naye Folks Tsaitzitig*, we find a notice that the Chelm Bund Party had ordered 700 copies of the newspaper. In the October 28th edition we find in the list of stock workers two names from Chelm: Shiye Ajzenshtein and Isaschar Palman, each of whom had sold 50 copies.

In the working log of 1920 we find interesting information from the "Bund" regarding the social work in Chelm, such as: In the Bund Party in Chelm were registered 100 members. The Central Bureau of the Trade Unions counts 620 members, divided according to the following professions:

The Needle Trade	200
Nutrition Trade	50
Leather Trade	120
Wood and Building Trade	200
Other smaller trades	50
Total	620

About the cultural institutions, we found in the log the following items: The "Groser Bibliotek" has 800 books and 200 readers; The Yiddish Public School has a joint committee of the Labor Zionists and the "Bund"; evening classes are being offered to workers; there is a workers children's home by the name of B. Groser; two cooperatives are functioning, one of the "Bund" with 260 members and the other one operated by the Left Labor Zionists. The cooperatives also run bakeries

Participants in a "flower-day" for the benefit of the "Groser Bibliotek in Chelm

In conclusion, I want to remark that the Central Authorities of the "Bund" had always been in contact with the Chelm "Bund". From 1916 onward, the following Bund leaders had visited Chelm: Beinish Mahalewicz, Hershl Erlich (the latter was the first candidate from the Lublin Region to the Polish Sejm - National Congress, *translator*.), Wiktor Alter, Yakov Pat (Wilner), Gershon Ziebert (city councilman from Warsaw. He died in South Africa in 1937. He came to South Africa as an emissary from TSISHO to raise funds for the Yiddish public schools in Poland. World War II broke out and he could no longer return to Poland), B. Shefn?r {illegible name}, Hershl M??farb {illegible name}, Berl Kamashenmacher, Comrade Dina, Dr. B. Eisurowicz, Arye, Mordkhe Feigenbojm, S. Gilinski, Zusman, and others.

Chelm belonged to the Lublin Region and very often comrades would come from Lublin to give lectures, speeches, or for general visits. Comrades such as Dr. Hershom, Bela Shapiro, Fishel Wajs, Fan, Arbuz, Hecman, Yechiel Najman, D. Celeminski. The Lublin Comrades would frequently come to consult about various political issues in the Region and just for friendly visits.

In general, a lively social activity was going on in Chelm where the "Bund", in its way and fashion, contributed a lot to the political maturity of the Jewish workers, to the trade union organizing, to the economic improvement of the Jewish masses in Chelm, and to the cultural development of the Jews in Chelm.

*[**Editor's note:** The following notes are in the translation, but there are no footnotes in the text to reference them.]*

Notes:

1. Meyer Tseblik was later sent to Siberia. He escaped and settled in New York, where he took an active part in the Bakers Union.
2. The Revolution of 1917 set Szmul Fried free from Siberian hard labor and he received the highest awards from the Revolutionary Government in Russia. But for unexplained reasons he tried to commit suicide. He did not succeed but remained a cripple without a leg. He was murdered by the Hitler beasts in Chelm.
3. I believe that was Sholem Zilberman, a house painter, Chaitche the baker's son, who escaped to Africa because of political persecutions.
4. By profession he was a bookbinder, but he was never seen at this kind of work. He always had time and he liked to associate with people younger than himself, and he was friendly to everyone.
5. {illegible name} he was for many years the chairman of the Central School Organization.
6. Dr. {illegible name} held the rank of captain in the Austrian Army. He was Vice Commandant and Governor of Chelm. Thanks to him, the "Bund" obtained the large premises on Lubliner Street 13 for the Workers Home.

[Page 149]

How Chelm Was Saved From a Pogrom in 1905

(A page of history)

By Shmuel Winer, New York

Translated by Gloria Berkenstat Freund

Right after the dawn of the 1905 revolution, just as the despotic tsarist regime again felt itself firm in the saddle, it did not lose a minute and immediately took to its old bloody deeds – but with more zest, with still more fury than earlier. He [the Tsar] had to even things with the people, for the small concessions that had been torn violently from him. The first scapegoat was, as always, the Jew. To divert the anger of the people against the tsarist regime, the corrupt tsarist satraps turned to their old tested technique – provoke the dark masses against the Jews, [claiming] that the Jews were the sources of all troubles.

Their furious roar carried from one corner of the land to the other: *Bey zhidov – spasay Rossiyu* – beat the Jews and save Russia. A wave of frightening pogroms in which tsarism sought to drown the revolution in Jewish blood, spilled over Jewish cities and *shtetlekh* [towns] the length and breath of the land. Jewish blood poured like water, our sisters defiled, shamed, Jewish possessions were reduced to nothing. All of the atrocities were carried out according to a designated prepared plan – following the pattern of the terrible Kishinev slaughter at the beginning of the present century [20th], Passover, 1903 – a pogrom that in time horrified the conscience of the world. The cynical answer to the sharp protests from all part of the world against the inhumane outrages is well known – that the Jews themselves had made the pogroms, the "classic" answer of all those who have made pogroms from the Middle Ages until now.

The sad fate of passing through this tragic road also fell on Chelm. All of the stubborn ones began to carry around rumors that the regime was preparing a pogrom on the city with all of the last details. There no longer was any doubt. Everyone walked around deeply worried and afraid – what can we do! Finally, our city fathers' thought of old ways – mediation! A delegation of prominent Jews was dispatched to the main ruling Provoslavner [Eastern Orthodox] church in Chelm – to Bishop Jevlogi, famous at that time throughout Russia. The delegation was admitted to the synod, stood before the bishop and prevailed upon him to intercede for us, to help us in this difficult hour of need. The delegation came out as if slapped in the face. Their tears and pleas had hit deaf ears. "Now you have come!" he ranted at them with rage. "Where were you earlier? Why did you not pay attention to the insolent, young Chelm Jews [and tell them] not to agitate against the *Tsar Batiushka* [Little Father]! You brought the misfortune on yourselves," was his sharp verdict. "I cannot help you." And with that [the meeting] ended. In sum, it was bitter.

[Page 150]

However, the Jewish young people and the Chelm worker organizations did not sit with idle hands. The self–defense of the Bund and of the *S.S.* (Socialist–Territorialists) began, each separately, to feverishly prepare to encounter the pogrom "heroes" with armed resistance. Several Christian students and workers joined the self–defense, ready to defend Jewish lives.

Through our connection with non–Jewish students who where revolutionary sons of tsarist functionaries and officers, we learned accurately the day when the pogrom would break out. We had our spies in the camp of the enemy. This was supposed to occur in the middle of November 1905. This friend of ours told us that the police had mobilized the trash, gangsters and "heroes" with knives of the city and surrounding villages for this purpose. Now they only were waiting for the signal to start the "work" under the leadership of policemen who had changed [into civilian clothing]. This practice by the tsarist pogromists was one and the same in all of the cities and shtetlekh that experienced pogroms. The position of self–defense everywhere, therefore, was doubly dangerous. Whereas the fight against the hooligans alone would be half of a calamity, they might be able to cope with them alone. The worst thing consisted of this, that not only did the police not protect them, but [the police themselves] led them.

The last night arrived. Tomorrow was the fatal day. The S.S. self–defense gathered in a deep cellar in Berish Kuper's brick building on Lubliner Street. Berish Kuper's oldest son, Yankele Kuper, a secret member of the S.S., had quietly led us all here in the darkness of the night along with our poor, little bit of weapons. Everyone prepared for the morning in a firmly resolved mood to meet the bloody enemy face–to–face. Meanwhile, the night was used to organize. They divided themselves into small groups. The unflinching Yoyer Mendlbaum was the first to arrive with a group. We were also given a group and among others I can remember now was Nakhman Szafran. A young worker, a butcher, tall, broadly built, powerful, a true hero stood out among the quickly organized self–defense group in the cellar; we called him Shlomo Kalb. He had still other young, strong butchers, all with shiny, sharp butcher–knives in the leg of their boots. Woe to those hooligans who would come into contact with them. I remember, too, Ben–Tzion Zemelman, a carpenter, with several of his carpenter comrades – they were armed with carpentry hatchets. In addition, we possessed more than ten revolvers with which the group learned to shoot at a target throughout the night.

[Page 151]

Day began to dawn. The designated moment neared. Everyone was in a serious mood and resolved, prepared to protect their fathers, mothers, sisters and brothers with their lives.

A small patrol was sent out of the cellar, quietly looked around to see if the sinister band was gathering together somewhere.

A bit of time thus passed – for us it seemed almost an eternity – until our spies returned. They entered the cellar very agitated and stirred up. Hearts were racing – Who knew what kind of news they carried with them?! Everyone perked up their ears when they began to speak:

They walked quietly during the entire time, searching to see if the hooligans already were gathering somewhere. However, they did not notice anything unusual. It was quiet, calm as usual. A little later, a distant echo of some sort of tumult that constantly grew clearer reached their ears. The muffled stamping of horse hooves and the cheerful rolling of the wheels of heavy wagons over pointy stones, with which Lubliner Street was paved, began to echo even more loudly. A real shiver caught them at first – who knew what misfortune awaited them?

It did not take long; they noticed a large wagon in the distance pulled by two strong horses, chased after by nasty dogs, coming closer to the center of the city. On a clear, sunny, frosty morning the familiar faces of young Jewish men emerged before their eyes on the bridge. Around two dozen young people placed themselves on the bridge, all well–armed, even with bombs, open for everyone to see, unafraid, without any dread of the tsarist police. This simply meant putting one's life at risk! Our spies were dumbfounded by this unusual, fantastic scene. This meant that our brothers had come to help us in our difficult hour.

It did not take long and we learned that the Lubliner Bund had sent a division of its self–defense [group] to Chelm to help us ward off the pogromists. They had rushed their horses the entire night to arrive in time.

[Page 152]

To make it short now – no pogrom took place that day in Chelm! A day of sadness became a day of joy.

* * *

How can we actually declare this, that Chelm avoided a pogrom then?

Surely first, that if it had come to a contest between the two strengths – on one side the armed–to–the–teeth police and on the other side the two dozen young men from Lublin – it would have been a terrible tragedy for our brothers who had come here to help us. However, this sudden, unexpected and unafraid invasion of the Lubliner self–defense [group], displaying weapons in their hands, had such a terrific psychological effect on the police that it simply paralyzed them. This manifestation of Jewish strength and self–sacrifice of the forerunners of the ghetto fighters against the bestial Hitlerists 40 years later so overwhelmed the police power that they simply were thrown into a panic.

And the fact that the waves of the 1905 revolution then beat high also had a great deal to say. Mainly, however, the fact was that we did not have to depend on any miracles, that we resolutely decided to stage an armed resistance no matter how large a price we would pay. They sensed that if blood must flow, this time it would not be only our blood, and also that we would not just withdraw. They lowered their hands and withdrew quickly from their positions.

In short, thanks to all of the listed reason, a mere half a century ago, Chelm was saved from a bloody pogrom with who knows how many victims, and the Jews suffered only from fear.

A group of young Jews from the Makabi* Sports Club in Chelm in 1933.)

* A Zionist sports organization that organizes sports competitions for Jewish athletes similar to the Olympics

[Page 153]

The History of the Jewish Workers Party
Poalei-Zion (Left) in Chelm

by Shmuel Szargel, Israel

Translated by Gloria Berkenstat Freund

In 1916, under the occupation of the German-Austrian regime, several comrades who were followers of pre-war *Poalei-Zion* Party [Marxist-Zionists] came together in complete secrecy and elected party leaders from among themselves, connected with the central agency in Poland and began to carry out their activity as a party. The above-mentioned central agency welcomed the newly arising organization with interest and sent the poet, Leib Malach, to Chelm and, a little later, Kopl Dua, the political activist. This provided courage and the party organization undertook a wide series of political and communal activities. At first the leadership of the party was in the hands of Wewke Gotlib, Shlomo Diment, Yankl Szroyt, Leibl Rozenblat, Ruchl Robkowska, Ahron Dovid Hipszman, Meir Baum, Yankl Dreksler, Nakhum Laks, Binsztok, Leyzer Feldman, Borukh Beker, Moshe Larber and others.

Of the intelligentsia remaining from the Austrian occupation army, which also benefited other parties, *Poalei-Zion* in Chelm drew great communal and cultural strength from Captain, Dr. Moshe Kanfer and his wife, Gezela.

At first the party work was limited to only purely economic help for the poor Jewish populations. The largest, finest house at Lubliner 27 was rented from Berish Kuper and a tea hall, which served as a workers' house, was arranged there. There, just as in the meeting places of other parties, those Jews in Chelm without income and unemployed found support in the form of receiving free lunches, distribution of food products and so on. The party founded a cooperative bakery to better be able to serve the needy Jewish population in the cellar of the meeting hall and a consumer's cooperative on Przechodnia Street.

In the evenings and on the *Shabbosim* [Sabbaths], the premises were used for widespread cultural work that brought vitality among the Jewish workers. The first Jewish *folkshul* [public school] and the Borochov Library were founded at that time.

When the Jewish parties were legalized with the rise of the Polish Republic, wide horizons opened for the activity of the *Poalei-Zion* party, which was later transformed into the largest and most esteemed workers party in the city. The work grew and expanded so much that in order to provide a faithful picture of all of the activity one must stop at many branches [of the activity]. The party was active in political life and in the professional movement, in the city council and in the Jewish community and in the field of Jewish worldly education and Jewish culture. A youth movement arose under the leadership of Shneur Waserman, Akiva Winik, the Szargel brothers, Ruwin Frucht, Dovidl Goldrajch, Manes Citrin, Yankl Zisberg, Yitzhak Kornzajer and others.

[Page 154]

The first group of political actions by *Poalei-Zion* in Chelm was the election campaign for the first Polish *Sejm* [parliment] in 1919.

At that time *Poalei-Zion* in Chelm was the only party in the Jewish street that took part in the elections. The Jewish bourgeoisie parities in Chelm and in the region did not present their own lists, not wanting to mix in the territorial conflicts between Poland and Soviet Ukraine that aspired to *Chelmszczyzna*.[1]

The *Poalei-Zion* party was successful in influencing large portions of the Jewish working class and poor on behalf of their election victory.

The result of the voting was: the election of Dr. Maks Rozenfeld as a deputy to the first Polish *Sejm*.

Dr. Maks Rozenfeld died on the way to taking up his mandate and Dr. Yitzhak Sziper, who then joined the right *Poaeli-Zion* and later moved entirely to the general Zionists, took his place.

Of the later *Sejm* election campaigns where the Chelm *Poaeli-Zion* played an important role it is worthwhile to remember the *Selrab* bloc.

The (left) *Poalei-Zion* in Poland joined a bloc with the Ukrainian Peasants Party – *Selrab* for the *Sejm* election in 1928, so that in two election districts thickly populated by the Jewish and Ukrainian masses they would appear with a joint list. Here an important and responsible task fell to the Chelemer *Poalei-Zion*: on one hand, the political education about the significance of such a bloc and on the other hand, the technical execution of such a large election campaign. This also required large sums of money.

The awakened interest in the city and in the region for *Poalei-Zion* and the victorious result of the first *Sejm* election campaign was discounted as usual. Normal party work was strengthened and established in the city and party organizations were created in the nearby *shtetlekh* [towns] so that at the first *Poalei-Zion* regional conference of Chelemer and Lublin provinces that took place on the 10th of October 1919 in Lublin, taking part from the Chelemer region were:

[Page 155]

Hrubieszów, Wojslawice, Tyszowce, Lyuboml, Dubienka, Włodawa and Rejowiec.

The 1st of May 1920 was celebrated by the *Poalei-Zion* to an extraordinary extent. The May meeting was opened in a fully packed hall. The *Yugnt* organization arrived in the middle with its own flag, which evoked great enthusiasm from the crowd. The room became too small and the meeting had to be moved to the courtyard. *Poalei-Zion* [members] standing in rows with flags and slogans, marched to the marketplace where they joined the general demonstrations of the *P.P.S.* [Polish Socialist Party] and the Bund.

For the first time in the history of Jewish Chelm, Jewish workers and young people demonstrated in the streets of the city with red flags while singing Yiddish revolutionary songs.

A joint meeting took place at the marketplace. (All of the speeches were given in the Polish language. These were the conditions that the *P.P.S.* had set at the negotiations for a joint May demonstration) and after this the general procession marched through the main streets of the city.

The impression made by the *pogroms* and the "*Hallerczikes*" [anti–Semitic followers of Polish General Jozef Haller], who chased after Jews with beards, was still very fresh in the minds of the international workers at the May demonstration.

However, the war that Poland fought with the Soviet Union began to take other forms: the Red Army took the initiative and moved deeper into the country. The Polish ruling circle answered with … increased anti-Semitic and cruel persecutions of the Jewish workers movement.

In July 1920, searches were carried out in all of the Jewish workers institutions and simultaneously in the homes of all Jewish communal workers, bourgeois as well as proletariat. The searches were carried out in a brutal way. All leading activists were arrested.

[Page 156]

The premises were requisitioned or sealed. The inventory was demolished.

Two weeks later, after the arrests, all state offices were evacuated from Chelm, also taking with them the arrested worker activists Ahron Dovid Hipszman and his brother Hirsh, Mosher Lorber, Nakhum Laks, Feder, Moshe Distler and Bluma Lewensztajn from *Poalei-Zion*.

A picture from before the voting for the first Sejm in Poland. Representatives of the Central Committee of Poalei-Zion: in the center Sh. Juris, [who] traveled to Chelm from Rejowiec for the election meeting

The *Poalei-Zion* Party transferred the work onto illegal rails. A meeting of the remaining, not arrested members of the party committee took place in a most secret manner in an attic where Leibl Rozenblit lay hidden. From this attic, the above-mentioned leaders had carried on the entire party work during this illegal era. (Several years later, Leibl Rozenblit went to Warsaw and later to France where he also was very active as a member of the central committee of the left *Poalei-Zion*.)

According to a decision at the deliberations held then, the Comrades Regina Distler and Roza Lewensztajn, who after long searching succeeded in learning that the Chelemer arrestees were in a Kielce jail, left. The *Yugnt* leader, Akiva Winik was delegated to the *Sejm* deputy Dr. Sziper, to inform him about the arrests and to ask for his intervention with the central government. After his return, he [Akiva Winik] was also arrested.

The discussion about the problems that stood on the agenda of the world congress and the Polish national conference began among those in the ranks of *Poalei-Zion*.

Taking part in the first national meeting of the *Poalei-Zion* councilmen in the city councils and *kehilus* [organized Jewish communities] in Poland that took place in Warsaw in the days of *Shavous* [spring holiday celebrating the receiving of the Torah], the 25th and 26th of May 1928, were the alderman Mordekhai Evri and the three councilmen, Ahron Dovid Hipszman, Moshe Beker and Shmuel Barg.

In 1930, after a break of 10 years, *Poalei-Zion* again succeeded in receiving permission to organize a May demonstration; such demonstrations already took place yearly. And with each year the marchers under the flags of *Poalei-Zion* grew more numerous and larger.

From the 7th to the 9th of October 1930, a regional conference of the *Poalei-Zion* parties of the Chelm region took place in Chelm. Delegates from Wojslawice, Nekhan [Miechy], Ruda-Opalin, Dubienka, Włodawa and Kovel took part.

The agenda of the conference was:

1. The political situation in the country and the guidelines for the *Sejm* election campaign;
2. Organization of the election campaign;
3. Election fund;
4. Report of the World Congress of Working *Eretz-Yisroel*, which took place in Berlin.

At the 25th anniversary of the *Poalei-Zion* Party and the 15th anniversary of the Chelemer organization in May 1931, a commemorative gathering was organized. In his opening speech, Yakov Beker gave an overview of the 15 years of *Poalei-Zion* activity in Chelm. Moshe Beker spoke in the name of the "society evening courses" and *Tsysho*[2]; Moshe Baum in the name of *Yungt*; Efriam Wadzager in the name of *Yungbor* [Young Borochovists – followers of Ber Borochov, a Marxist Zionist]; Comrade [Yakov] Zrubavel reported on the theme "From the Pioneers to the Masses." The choir sang workers' songs; the dramatic circle under the leadership of Hilel Szargel performed various numbers very successfully. At the end, 50 members of *Yungbor* rhythmically marched with red flags in their hands.

[Page 157]

In June 1931 the party carried out a campaign "Against Unemployment, Reductions and Fascism." A series of gatherings and mass meetings took place. A meeting was supposed to take place on Sunday, the 26th of June, which was banned by the *starosta* [village head] at the last minute. It was ordered that the hall be closed that evening. Therefore, a short meeting took place on Post Street the next night in an illegal manner.

In March 1932 *Poalei-Zion* took an active part in the campaign to help the heroic fight of the striking coal miners. At meetings of the city council and the *kehile* [organized Jewish community], *Poalei-Zion* factions proposed appropriate resolutions with a demand to support the striking coal miners. The *starosta* forbid the holding of a public meeting. On the 16th of March, the Chelemer *Poalei-Zion* called upon the Jewish workforce to strike in a day of solidarity with the general strike throughout Poland. The *Poalei-Zion* strike committee was wherever there was a workshop of workers. On that day the police were very energetic in arresting many comrades.

In December 1932 a public farewell gathering was supposed to take place for the departure to Brazil of Juliek Wajsman, a managing committee member of the *kehile*, and his wife Serka, a teacher at the Jewish *folkshul* [public school]. However, the *starosta* did not permit the gathering to take place. The *Poalei-Zion* Party said goodbye to one of its oldest comrades in secrecy.

In January 1934 the entire movement was active in the work of organizing a widespread communal campaign against the new social-protection laws. In all professional unions, in *Yugnt* and the sports club, educational meetings took place and secret protest resolutions were adopted.

[Page 158]

One the largest political campaigns carried out by *Poalei-Zion* was in May-June 1936 at the workers congress in the fight with anti-Semitism. Dozens of gatherings and political meetings of the members of the professional unions and other institutions were carried out. Meetings and house meetings of streets and regions took place. The joint election gathering was supposed to take place on the 6th of June in a series of large halls in the city. But at the last minute an order arrived from the *starosta* that as the interior minister had forbidden the congress, he would not permit the organization of election gatherings.

Yugnt organization of Poalei-Zion in a May procession in 1936

The municipal interparty election committee of the congress decided at its meeting that the Chelemer *Poalei-Zion* was authorized to send 16 delegates to the congress in the following manner:

	Delegates
For the distribution of ballots	5
The Needle Union (the largest in the city)	1
All remaining *Poalei- Zion* professional unions	1
The *Tsysho* Organization	2
The Borochov Library	1
The councilmen from the city council and the *kehile*	6
Total	**16**

After the pogroms in Przytyk and Brisk, anti-Semitic hooligans also began to rage in Chelm. The economic boycott and the anti-Semitic tax machine caused the ruin of a large part of the Jewish population. The strata of the jobless and needy grew greater and denser. The *Poalei-Zion* Party answered by fighting harder at the city council and the *kehile* for the rights and equal rights of the Jewish masses, for party aid for the jobless and needy and also worked to expand the professional [union] movement.

The 17th of December 1938. That year, just as every year, a large Borochov memorial was organized for the 21st *yahrzeit* [anniversary of the death] of the unforgettable leader and teacher B. Borochov. None of the attendees at the great celebration realized that this was the last celebration in Jewish Chelm.

Eretz-Yisroel Work

The problems of *Eretz-Yisroel* – the ideological and the daily pragmatic – occupied a respected place in the political and educational work of the Chelm *Poalei-Zion*. The party in Chelm actively took part in the collections for the "Palestine Workers Fund" and prepared groups for emigration to *Eretz-Yisroel*. In 1925 a successful book collection was carried out for the fraternal party in *Eretz-Yisroel*; several hundred Yiddish books were collected and sent.

A protest meeting took place with the participation of Dr. Borukh Eizensztat, against the Palestine office that did not consider the poverty and the emigration needs of the Jewish working class in distributing the certificates [issued by the British Mandate in Palestine allowing legal immigration to *Eretz-Yisroel*]. (The certificates were distributed among all Zionist groupings except for the left *Poalei-Zion*.)

[Page 159]

A protest meeting took place on the 10th of September 1928 in connection with the persecutions against Yiddish in *Eretz-Yisroel* and the attack on the *Poalei-Zion* club in Tel Aviv at which the speakers Mordekhai Evri, Yakov Beker, Dovid Goldrajch, Chaim Gutman and Feywl Frid appeared and spoke.

The bloody events in *Eretz-Yisroel* of 1929, just as everywhere, also evoked great agitation, bitterness and protest in Chelm. In connection with the events, the *Poalei-Zion* Party carried out a large publicity campaign with gatherings and mass meetings of all unions and cultural institutions.

A meeting about "the bloody events in *Eretz-Yisroel*" took place on the 31st of August 1929 with the participation of Yakov Beker and Juliek Wajsman.

Several weeks later a report by Comrade Zrubavel on the subject of "The Teaching of Palestinian Events" took place in the municipal cinema, *Wersal*. On that evening, Comrade Zrubavel reported about the development of Yiddish literature and culture in Palestine and the role of *Poalei-Zion* in the spread of the Yiddish printed word in *Eretz-Yisroel*. A large sum of money was collected on the spot on behalf of the aid fund for the *Eretz-Yisroel Poalei-Zion* Party.

Summer, 1930. Despite the great heat, a publicity campaign was carried out about the participation of *Poalei-Zion* in the World Congress for Working Israel that took place in Berlin. In September 1930, the party itself had passionate discussions about the agenda of the Congress and the declaration that was published only in Hebrew. The organizers of the Congress had barely agreed that a Yiddish translation of the official Hebrew declaration would be provided. At one of the party meetings at which the question was discussed, the porter, Motl Karp, called out during his appearance: "I am a porter. I can carry two sacks of flour even at one time, but I do not know if I will be able to carry two declarations at once…"

In 1936, during the unrest in *Eretz-Yisroel*, the party carried out widespread publicity work at meetings, mass meetings and gatherings.

In May 1938 a solemn appearance was arranged of Comrade Leibl Ben-Shmeuni, the representative of the *Eretz-Yisroel Poalei-Zion*.

The Chelemer *Poalei-Zion* took a very active part in the elections to the Zionist Congress of 1938, just before the Second World War. The party succeeded in persuading a large number of Jewish workers to take part in the voting under the flag of *Poalei-Zion*.

In June 1939 the last large public demonstration for *Eretz-Yisroel* took place with a lecture by Comrade Zrubavel. The call from Comrade Zrubavel still rings for me like an echo and as the last warning to save ourselves from the coming storm.

[Page 160]

The Professional Work

At the time when *Poalei-Zion* already had a good workers party and *Yugnt* and other important locations, such as the school, library and people's university and other institutions, the work began to infiltrate the professional movement. They had to convince the comrades that they had to become members of the professional unions then in existence, which were under the influence of the Bund and "reds." As a result, the general election meeting in October 1925 of the needle union (which was completely under the influence of the Jewish "reds") chose two *Poalei-Zion* comrades for their managing committee.

Executive of the Poalei-Zion in 1930
First row from the right: Chana Szargel, Yakov Feterzajl, Ester Szrojt–Warzager
and Metek Evri
Bottom row: Sh. Szargel, Y. Beker and H. Warzager

A great deal of effort and energy was placed in the organizing of each union and sections that had not yet been organized until then, such as the trade employees, printers, factory workers, gaiter and belt makers. The successes in the professional area can be summed up in the organization and founding of a "cultural office," a division of the central council of the local professional unions in Poland, which was under the influence of *Poalei-Zion*.

Vigorous work in the professional area was accompanied by strikes and fights for better wages, leaves and so on. Meanwhile, the economic crisis in the country sharpened and there was much unemployment among the Jewish working class in Chelm with the arrival of the winter of 1927-28. In addition there was the sudden bankruptcy of Shmuel Rubin and partners' mill and the number of unemployed families increased by several dozen people.

[Page 161]

The leadership of the transport union, to whom the last ones [employed by the mill] who were not then organized [into a union] turned, made attempts to receive compensation for the unemployed remaining mill workers, but nothing came of it. With the approach of spring, the work began on the [building for the] train management (in the context of the decision of the Polish government to move it from Radom to Chelm so as to create a secure Polish majority in the Chelm area where the majority of Jews and Ukrainians lived) and this brought a bit of a revival. The cultural office opened an office for worker rights where over 150 Jewish and 30 Polish unemployed workers registered. It is an example of how far the influence of *Poalei-Zion* had penetrated into the professional [union] movement and among the Polish workers so that the Polish workers who registered at the "office" declared that they did not trust the Polish office. And non-skilled Polish workers came to the cultural office and asked that they be permitted to join a professional union.

In September 1928, the mill workers asked to be organized in a separate mill-workers union. As soon as the union was legalized, it joined the action for higher wages. After a three-day strike, they won: 1) a wage raise of 25 to 35 percent; 2) the recognition of the union; 3) the hiring and dismissing of workers only through the union. The action involving all of the mills in the city was led by Councilman Moshe Beker, the secretary of the union. On the 18th of October a solemn gathering of all of the mill workers, Jewish and Polish together, took place in honor of the victory. Councilman Mordekhai Ervri, speaking for the *Poalei-Zion* faction in the city council, and Yitzhak Kornzajer, speaking for the Chelm Professional Class Unions, appeared with speeches of greeting.

In later years the professional union of mill workers carried out a series of wage actions. During one such action, the mill owner, Meir Frenkl, brought out a revolver and threatened to shoot the union representative, the Councilman Moshe Beker. But the resolute attitude of the above-mentioned comrade and of the workers near him forced the owner to give in to the declared demands. This had a colossal effect not only on the Jews but also on the Polish workers who during the city council elections agitated and partly supported the *Poalei-Zion* list. In March and April 1937 the sit-down strike in a mill by a group of mill workers lasted several weeks. The demands of the workers were: a modest wage increase that the owners did not want to give. The striking workers did not leave the mill during the course of the strike. The professional council proclaimed an action to collect [money] from all of the members of all of the professional unions for the strikers.

In 1929, the union of construction workers was organized and legalized. But a difficult struggle endured in defending the painters. The master craftsmen responded to their right to organize into a professional union with terror and harassment and even had several workers arrested, saying that they were communists.

[Page 162]

Because of political party disputes that took place in the clothing union, which had come under the influence of the "reds," the women's clothing division left them and joined the needle union of the left *Poalei-Zion* at Lubliner 10.

In the summer season of 1929 the above-mentioned women's clothing trade union carried out a wage action with success, which had a great influence on the further organizing of all of the needle workers. In later years, the needle union, under the leadership of *Poalei-Zion*, which already included nearly all of the Jewish needle workers in the city, distinguished itself with its active and [class] conscious activists and emerged as the avant-garde of the Jewish organized working class. There always was the warmest sympathy and support from the organized Jewish workers movement for the frequent actions for wage increases and against wage reductions carried out by the needle union.

Among the activists in the needle union were: Gruna Brik-Zilberman, Shasha Rozenblit-Rozenblum, Fayga Baum-Beker, Ester Szrojt-Warzager, Menakhem Kopelman, Chaim Borukh Warzager, Ruchl Apelcwajg, Liba Elzter, Moshe Stal, Bentshe Micflig and Yitzhak Apelcwajg.

A division for milliners also existed at the needle union for a short time.

The Trade and Office Employees Union, which was organized in 1925 with a small number of manufacturing employees, was the second largest by 1929 in size and scope among the professional unions and encompassed almost all of those employed in the city. Both the managing committee as a whole and the managing committee of the division of those making inexpensive clothing were very lively and active. The actions and strikes carried out by the union, which often became very embittered and sharp, helped the employees achieve wage increases and oppose wage reductions. Working for a percent was abolished and paid leaves were achieved and working on the night of *Shabbos* [Sabbath] was ended.

Among the activists in the Trade and Office Employees Union were: Mendl Winer, Hersh Edelsztajn, Daniel Feldman, Shmuel Szargel, Chaim Warzager, Chaim Bibel, Elyokim Elster, Moshe Bakalacz, Szechterzon, Yankl and Shmuel-Yosl Beker.

The Printers Union came to an agreement with the Polish print workers in the city in 1929 and they took them into their ranks. It was thus transformed into an international union. The managing committee that was elected that year on the 26th of June consisted of A.D. Hipszman, Feldman, Wolfson, Hersh Berman and Shlomo Szapira.

[Page 163]

In February 1935 a campaign was proclaimed [to require] every institution to employ at least one unemployed older worker. The campaign was crowned with success. Yankl Waserman, Meir Zonenszajn and others were among the leadership. The women in the candy factories also organized. Their earnings were very low, actually hunger wages. On the 28th of June 1929 the first demands were sent to the bosses for a 20 percent wage increase. A few immediately gave in to the demands and the rest only after they [the workers] went on strike.

On the 10th of August the organizing meeting of the bakery workers took place. At first they organized as a division of the food union and later they became a separate Bakers Union. The working conditions of the bakery workers were very difficult. The unhygienic, primitive facilities of the bakeries; working 12 hours and more daily and, mainly, that the work was night work. There was a bitter and difficult struggle for each small attempt to better the conditions for the bakery workers. Later, the plague of unemployment in the trade arose and it was established that each employed comrade give [his job for] one night a week to an unemployed comrade. In 1931 the master craftsmen began to seize the wages of the employed, cheap, unorganized workers. The union leadership established special controllers that checked the bakeries every night. On one such night, during the oversight at a bakery, they got into a sharp argument with the owner of the bakery. The latter called out the police and six bakery workers were arrested for several days. Several workers were terribly beaten at the police [headquarters]. However, this strengthened the union, which proceeded with its activities. Tuchsznajder, Elster, Mandelbaum, Globen and Licht were elected to the trade commission.

Organizing the porter workers was very slow and difficult. These were the older, weary men with tendencies and habits that were antithetical to class-conscious organizing and fraternally working together. However, the union was successfully organized thanks to the strenuous effort and work done by the porter Motl Karp. On the 12th of August 1929, he held the first organizing meeting with the porter workers. From then on, work started on gatherings and meetings, distribution of the workplaces [the locations each porter would have as solely his responsibility, such as at the train station] and economic actions. It was unanimously decided at one such gathering to criticize and condemn the ugly and bad habits of the porter workers who were abusive to each other and used ugly and coarse expressions to each other. Everyone who did not consent to this decision would pay a penalty to the union in the amount of one *zlote*.

[Page 164]

The union activists actually would explain that there were cases when the porter workers could not control themselves and, knowing that they would be punished, would call out: "And I give one *zlote* to the union and say to you again *in deyn tatns tatn areyn* [in your father's father – an insult to someone's ancestors]..."

After more than a year of professional work without coordinated management, the professional council of the city committee of *Poaeli-Zion* called a conference of the existing professional unions on the 7th of October 1929 in order to create a central municipal leadership of the professional unions.

Members of the following managing committees of the professional unions took part in the conference: needle-trade employees, printing, food, construction, transport, hairdressers and textiles: 54 delegates in total. Presentations were made by Yankl Beker, Yitzhak Kornzajer, Moshe Beker and Moshe Baum. In addition to the usual questions, there was discussion of the political situation in the country. One representative from each union was on the established organizing committee of the local central council of the professional unions in the city.

Horse-drawn carriages, an old, firmly established means of income for hard-working Jews in Chelm – men with healthy fists for answering hooligans when it was necessary – also realized that they needed to organize.

The first organizing meeting of the horse-drawn carriage drivers took place on the 21st of February 1930. Alas, they did not carry on much professional [union] activitiy...until the arrival of the bloody storm of anti-Semitism. Under the influence of rising Hitlerism in Germany, the Chelmer anti-Semites, among other rival trades that they brought to Chelm from Prussia, were Christian carriage drivers who grabbed the [main jobs] at the train station and forced the Jewish carriage drivers to stand in a side, back alley. Later, in 1938, the police ordered the Jewish carriage drivers to wear visible markings on their hats, "Jewish carriage driver" and the gentile carriage drivers should wear markings "Christian carriage drivers."

At the end of 1930 the textile trade was organized. Twenty female workers had been strongly exploited. They went on strike. The strike was particularly strong at the manufacturer Mernsztajn. The entire *Poalei-Zion* movement appeared to help the striking women, help them both in the strike committee and in the strike fund.

On the 23rd of January 1931, after six weeks of striking, the strike was completely won. Bluma Natlich and Ruchl Grinberg were among the most active in the division.

In the very midst of the fervor of the textile strike, the musicians sought organizational help. And when the textile strike was declared at an end, a strike was declared at the cinema, Korso. The ownersmade use of strike breakers. The professional movement answered with a call to the Jewish population to boycott the cinema. There were almost no Jewish visitors to the movie showings. The police stood on the side of the management and arrested the [union] security guards and the representatives who had issued the call [to boycott] and they [the management] instituted a lawsuit against them [the arrestees]. The presidium of all of the professional unions was called to the police commissariat and official reports were filed against them for taking part in the boycott activity. The work inspectors threatened the closing of the union. All of the means of terror did not frighten them off. The strike and the boycott continued until the management was forced to give in to about 60 percent of the demands that had been made.

[Page 165]

Shortly later, when sound film came in, the musicians union failed.

In February 1931 the workers at the egg exporting warehouses asked that they be organized into a union.

On the 10th of June that year the professional union of the egg workers received a notice about a 25 percent wage reduction. It was decided to reject the wage reduction at a specially called meeting and to issue a demand for paid leave. The egg merchants answered with a general dismissal of all of the workers. When the representatives of the union pointed out to them that the wage reduction was illegal because, according to an agreement with the workers they [the egg merchants] were obligated to pay the current salary until the new year, there was a cynical reply: "We keep our commitments when it benefits us." A sit-in strike was declared. The owners and the police removed the workers from the warehouses and put four prisoners from the jail in their place. The prisoners, under the guard of the prison police, worked for half a day and after the energetic intervention of the leaders of the professional unions, who pointed out that it was unacceptable to use prisoners as strike breakers, the work of the prisoners was halted in the afternoon. The strike was won after four days. The owners also had to pay [the wages] for the days of the strike. The secretary of the egg union was H. Y. Mantszarsz.

In October 1933 the hat makers organized as a division of the needle union. The first activity for an eight-hour workday and a wage increase of 25 percent to 40 percent was completely won.

The Metal Workers Union was organized in March 1937.

The photographic workers organized in April 1937 and created a Photographic Workers Union.

[Page 166]

At the same time, attempts were made to organize the Polish workers, which were not successful.

In July-August 1939, the leather workers sought organizational help. Gerszman, Hochman and Yankl Beker spoke at the founding meeting of the newly arising union.

Youth Activities

In the course of the up-hill progress of organizing and strengthening the professional unions, they did not forget the young people and the very youngest members of the proletariat who came to the workshops to learn a trade and were used in a disgraceful manner both by the owners and by the older workers. To solve the special youth problem, youth divisions of the largest unions, such as the Needle Workers Union and Hairdressers, were trained.

On the 14th of August 1929 the first large meeting of the Needle Youth Division took place. Ester Szrojt, Moshe Stal and others spoke. Questions about minimum wages, better treatment and so on were discussed. A managing committee and a cultural commission were chosen. The managing committee was warmly greeted by the representatives of the *Poalei-Zion* Party and *Yugnt*.

The union managing committee was therefore forced to lead a struggle for a supplementary wage for the youngest of 50 *groshn* a week. And in 1935 there even was a fight for a special holiday wage for the youngest hairdressers.

The *Poalei-Zion* activists in the professional unions did not only worry about the quantitative growth of the professional movement, about drawing in the most widespread masses in the ranks of the professional class unions, but also for deepening the class consciousness of everyone working and for the political education of the union leadership cadres.

Therefore, the professional unions under the leadership of *Poalei-Zion* really grew and the influence of *Poalei-Zion* also grew within the professional movement.

While there were worries that the professional unions were not drained of their political content and did not change into a mechanical tool of only economic struggle, they themselves changed through this, becoming powerful, fighting institutions for the widespread working classes.

It should also be understood from this why all political, financial and election activities of the *Poalei-Zion* Party were so warmly supported by the professional unions and their large membership and why the number of devoted votes for the list of *Poalei-Zion* would rise so greatly from one time to another at various elections.

[Page 167]

In addition, it is necessary to mention that both the moral and the material support of the members of the professional unions came from their good will, that there was no external or internal pressure.

There was a very loyal relationship with members in the unions who held different views! There was never any case in which someone was harassed or discriminated against because the members of the union had their own political-party ideology.

Kehile Council and Managing Committee

During the *kehile* [organized Jewish community] elections in 1924, *Poalei-Zion* received 126 votes and one seat (Ahron Dovid Hipszman). The term of office for the *kehile*, where Anshel Biderman was the chairman, lasted for seven years. At the meetings of the council the *Poalei-Zion* councilman, Hipszman, would appear sharply against the step-motherly relation to the interests of the Jewish worker and masses of the people. Dissatisfaction with the *kehile* council and managing committee grew among all parts of the Jewish population. The news about new voting was received with great satisfaction. The election was designated for the 20th of May 1931. Everything was prepared for this election contest. The *starosta* [village chief] prepared for it. Right at the start, on the 26th of March 1931, he arranged to seal the premises of *Poalei-Zion*, the premises for the Evening Courses Society that also served as the premises of the professional unions as well as the premises of the Borochov Library. Despite the persecutions *Poalei-Zion* carried out a widespread, mass campaign work with meeting, gatherings, house propaganda [campaigning door to door]. The results of the election were as follows:

Party	Votes	Councilmen
1) *Poalei-Zion*	363	3
2) *Agudas Yisroel*	292	3
3) List of the former chairman	243	2
4) Artisans	229	2
5) Philanthropic institutions	154	2
6) General Zionists	165	2
7) Kuzmirer Hasidim	101	1
8) *Mizrakhi*	86	1
9) Retailers	49	0
Totals	**1,682**	**16**

The results of the election were a surprise, especially because only men of 25 and older had the right to vote.

Poalei-Zion appointed three councilmen: Ahron Dovid Hipszman, Juliek Wajsman and Berl Akselrod, and when Wajsman and Akselrod were elected to the *kehile* managing committee, Fishl Kopelman and Yankl Szrojt took their places and when Szrojt left, Fishl Iliwicki [took his place].

The first meeting of the newly elected *kehile* council drew a large number of Jewish workers and ordinary people who filled the small *kehile* room and the corridor and they even stood on the stairs wanting to catch at least a word, a sound of what was being considered at the meeting. However, they left in disappointment because after the first item, the election of a managing committee, the meeting was adjourned.

The civil majority at the *kehile* were frightened by the great strength represented by the *Poalei-Zion* faction on the council and the managing committee and decided among themselves to continue to run the *kehile* economy themselves and in the old way. (This meant taking care of and serving only the religious interests of a certain part of the Jewish population.)

Many months passed and no meetings were called. However, the unemployment, poverty and need of the Jewish population kept growing and there was an urgent, daily demand for help. The *Poalei-Zion* faction then decided to oversee the *kehile* and every day, in the early morning hours, a minimum of two comrades from the faction were in the office of the *kehile* and requested, pressured and demanded of the official and of the chairman that they eliminate the accumulated charges and the like in all cases of need for support, for notes to doctors and to the hospitals.

The newly elected *kehile* chairman, Dr. Wilenka, completely stopped serving at the *kehile* offices. Therefore, one found Juliek Wajsman, the *Poalei-Zion* councilman sitting on the chair of the chairman at the *kehile* offices. The situation lasted several months until the *kehile* chairman in agreement with the *starosta* [village head] called a meeting of the council for the 24th of November 1931. A group of policemen, who only let into the gallery Jews with beards and long kaftans, stood at the entrance to the meeting. The *starosta* sat near the presidium. When the chairman opened the meeting in the Polish language, the *Poalei-Zion* councilmen shouted, "Yiddish, Yiddish!" The shouting stopped when the chairman began to speak Yiddish. The atmosphere at the meeting became heated when the *Poalei-Zion* councilmen protested against the bringing of the police to the meeting and demanded that they be removed. The *starosta* answered the leaders of the *kehile* that he brought the guards himself and he had absolutely forbidden allowing the *Poalei-Zion* councilmen speak. The latter insisted on their rights and demanded that they be able to speak. The *starosta* reached an agreement with the chairman that members of the managing committee did have to be allowed to speak.

[Page 169]

Juliek Wajsman, who received permission to speak, proposed that they urgently consider the questions: 1) the anti-Semitic excesses; 2) a census; 3) suspend members of the council for committing abuses. There again was turmoil. The *starosta* shouted that they should be quiet or he would begin arresting them. Wajsman answered him sharply and directed the *starosta* to arrest him. Wajsman, protesting against such arbitrariness, was led out by the police. Akselrod began to speak and declared in Polish that the entire *Poalei-Zion* faction was in solidarity with Juliek Wajsman and if the meeting was to continue everyone would have to be arrested or Wajsman had to be freed. The speeches and protests from the *Poalei-Zion* councilmen lasted less than an hour until the *starosta* ordered that [Wajsman] be freed. Right after the first item, as soon as the election of the chairman and vice-chairman, the meeting was quickly closed when they began to proceed with the agenda, so that they would not have to deal with the further points on the agenda. Many further meetings looked the same.

The meetings were very tempestuous at which small, paltry sums of only 1,000 *zlotes* for social aid and for the Jewish *folkshul* and the Children's Home were considered in a budget of 160,000 *zlotes* for the years 1932-33.

Many months passed and no meetings of the council or of the managing committee took place. At the beginning of 1933 there was a meeting of the council. Two questions were on the agenda: 1) an urgent proposal by the *Poalei-Zion* faction about an activity [to provide] coal; 2) an activity report by the managing committee. Before the agenda was considered, the chairman of the council made a proposal that a telegram of welcome be sent in honor of the new constitution and he added: "We do not yet know what the constitution will give us, but we need to applaud it." Hipszman, the councilman, spoke very sharply against the proposal to applaud the new constitution. He showed its dangers for the entire working class and particularly for the Jewish [workers] that lay in wait. He proposed not applauding it, but protesting against the new social protection laws. The coal campaign was then supported with 1,000 *zlotes*. After hearing the report, Councilman Akselrod, in his appearance [before the council], gave a very biting critique of the activities of the managing committee. He listed a series of questions about the need and poverty among Jewish workers and the ordinary Jewish people who were not being helped and he ended with a motion of mistrust of the managing committee that was adopted by a majority vote.

The last election to the Jewish *kehile* took place on the 5th of September 1936. *Poalei-Zion* received 389 votes and had three councilmen: Yakov Beker, Berl Akselrod and Ahron Dovid Hipszman. Later, when Beker and Akselrod were elected to the managing committee, Fishl Iliwicki and Yisroel Hercman were elected to their seats on the council.

[Page 170]

It was the time of the Przytyk and Brisk [pogroms]. We already felt the incoming storms. But alas, it must be noted that a large majority of representatives of Jewish Chelm did not see and did not understand what kind of time they were living in, and when a passionate discussion developed at the first meeting of the newly elected kehile council, when Y. Beker proposed as an item to be considered "the situation of the Jewish masses," the council chairman closed the meeting immediately after the choice of an election commission (to elect the managing committee). The *Poalei-Zion* councilmen and those gathered in the gallery did not leave the meeting hall, but listened to a report from Councilman Yakov Beker about the situation of the Jewish masses and the events in *Eretz-Yisroel*.

Yugnt and *Yungbor*

At the end of 1917 and the beginning of 1918, a society, *Matan Basayser* [anonymous giving], which set as its purpose to provide help to the impoverished, dejected Jewish masses, was founded by a group of young people, a number of them even *Yeshiva* [religious secondary school] students. Thanks to the initiative of the leading comrades of *Poalei-Zion* of that time, the young people's group in time was transformed into an organized group to create the *Poalei-Zion-Yugnt* [young people] in Chelm. The newly arisen *Yugnt* organization developed very rapidly and in a short time was transformed into the largest youth organization in the city. Akiva Winik, Shlomo and Yitzhak Fiszer, Cyrl Dubkowska, Mosher Kelerer, Motl Brand, Yosef Hendel, Shneur Waserman, Dobele Waserman and Yitzhak Kodnzajer were members of one of the first *Yugnt* committees.

One of the most important tasks that the *Yugnt* organization took upon itself at that time was eradicating illiteracy among the Jewish working young people. Thanks to the initiative of the youth committee, an evening school was founded in a room in the *Folkshul* [public school] where young workers came to learn to read and write after a hard workday.

In the election campaign to the first *Sejm* carried out by the *Poalei-Zion* Party, *Yugnt* worked very actively [with the party] and had a great part in the election victory.

[Page 171]

The *Yugnt* organization was a creative, exuberant source for the *Poalei-Zion* Party. For years dozens of *Yugnt* comrades were sent over to the ranks of the party. All of the best and most active volunteers from the party came from the *Yugnt* organization.

In 1919-1920 *Yugnt* had it own meeting place at Reformacka 6. A dramatic section for the young was also created there which later grew along with the dramatic society for the adults and for years had a respected place in the cultural work of the Party and *Yugnt*.

At the beginning of 1924, when a number of leading *Yugnt* comrades left Chelm, a *Yugnt* managing committee was called together under the leadership of Yankele Pinchesowicz where a new *Yugnt* committee was elected consisting of Hilel Szargel, Mendl Szulman, Beinush Gotlib, Yitzhak Ceber, Yisroelke Fiszbajn and Yankl Binsztok. The committee took to the work energetically. Standard young people's circles for culture and propaganda were established; *Shabbos* [Sabbath] day excursions to the Hrubieszow Woods; the spreading of the young people's press and the revival of the evening school. The *Yugnt* committee had to put in a great deal of work to gather the financial means to support the evening school.

Lipa Gotlib was arrested on the eve of the 1st of May 1924 for spreading the May appeal of the *Yugnt* Central Committee and the journal, *Di Yugnt Fan* [*The Yugnt Flag*]. He was kept in jail for seven months until his trial. He was brought to his trial, which took place on the 22nd of November, locked in chains. He was sentenced to a year of hard confinement.

On the 7th of February 1926, Yankl Pinchesowicz, the leader of *Yugnt* and one of the most active comrades of the *Poalei-Zion* Party, died at the age of 23. Over 1,000 people took part in his funeral. Ribbons and garlands were carried by the *Poalei-Zion* Committee, *Yugnt* Committee, *Tsysho* [Central Jewish School Organization] Board of Trustees and Pedagogic Council, the managing committee of the Evening Courses Society and others. In the center of the city, Wipusz, the leader of the secret police, shoved into the marching funeral procession and tore away the ribbons and arrested Chaim Bilen for shouting, "*Nie dawaj*" (do not give). The premature death of Y. Pinchesowicz was a heavy blow to the *Yugnt* organization and a great loss for the Chelm *Poalei-Zion*.

This was a time of tempestuous revival of the youth movement and through it of the entire *Poalei-Zion* movement. The activists began to penetrate the professional movement. Ester Szrojt, Ruchl Apelcwajg, Yochoved Brik and Chana Teper-Szargel gathered the young needle workers around themselves and thus transformed the needle union, which had been under the influence of the Jewish "left," into a strong opposition. Shmuel Szargel, Chaim Warzager and Chaim Bibel were active in organizing the union of workers employed in trade. Mendl Szulman organized the hairdressers union and other young activists helped with the founding of the remaining professional unions.

Ahron Dovid Hipszman

[Page 172]

The first lecture circle at *Yugnt*, which was created then, was led by Dovid'l Goldrajch. The circle would come together once a week in the Noakh and Miriam Krajdman family house. The above-mentioned young people belonged to the circle.

The active youth work also enlivened the region. Young activists went to the neighboring *shtetlekh* [towns] and also helped to build youth organizations. The Chelemer Regional Committee of *Yugnt*, which included the *shtetlekh* of Rubienka, Wojslawice, Tyszowce, Uchanie, Luboml, Wlodowa and Ruda-Opalin, was founded in 1928.

A regional meeting of the young people in the Ruda region lasting two days took place on the 24th of July 1928. One hundred and fifty young people from Chelm, Wojslawice, Tyszowce, Wlodowa and Ruda-Opalin took part.

A one-time publication, *10 Yahr* [*Ten Years*], was published for the 10th anniversary of the Chelm *Yugnt* organization, printed on two sides, with 1,000 copies, in a large format.

The move to Chelm of the teacher Chaim Gutman greatly benefitted the young workers. He was the spiritual patron of *Yugnt*. He took over the further leadership of the lecture circle and provided the initiative for the founding of *Yungbor*. The technical organizing work of erecting a beautiful children's organization that numbered around 120 children was led by Sholem Goldhar, who was very energetic and full of initiative. However, after a short amount of time he left for the *linke* [left] and the leadership was assumed by Chaim Warzager and, later, by Shayndl Warzager and Shlomo Rajn. In time, their own circle of *Yungbor* instructors was trained, such as Efroim Warzager, Fayga Niclich, Gesha Grinbaum, Rayzele Szklacz, Shlomo Warzager, Mirl Tenenbaum, Ester Magier, Shayndl Elcter, Sura Cimerman, Welwl Barg and many, many others.

The innumerable independent cultural-political activites, the magnificent *Yugnt* and *Yungbor* events; the May and Borochov commemorative gatherings; the anti-war days; International Youth Days and Women's Days and more and even more magnificent youth meetings; the excursions and daytime *Shabbos* [Sabbath] in the suburban forests; the hearty banquets that would often be organized when saying goodbye to comrades who were leaving or during the transfer [graduation] from *Yungbor* to *Yugnt* and from *Yugnt* to the party and so on. All of this was a great and significant contribution to the cultural life of the Jewish settlement in the city of Chelm.

[Page 173]

Evening Courses for Workers Society

With the creation of the *Poalei-Zion* Evening Courses for Workers Society in Poland, a division also was created in Chelm. The party premises at Lubliner 27 also were the location of the Evening Courses Society.

It was the time of the blossoming of Yiddish literature and culture in Poland and it can be said boldly that *Poalei-Zion* wrote a prominent page in the history of cultural creativity and educational work in that era in Jewish Chelm.

All of the Jewish literary figures, artists or cultural workers, who would travel through Poland, were invited by the Chelm division of the Evening Courses for Workers. [Yakov] Zrubavel and Dr. Josef Kruk, Peretz Markish and Dr. Rafal Mahler, Borukh Glazman and Alter Kacizne, Dr. Borukh Eizensztat and Nusan Buksbaum, and many, many others visited our city through the invitation of the society.

The literary events that would occur were very impressive and drew attention.

People's universities were organized at the above-mentioned society and lectures by Shneur Wasserman, Ruwin Frucht, Ytizhak Kornzajer, Akiva Winik and others on various cultural and scientific questions took place regularly. From the city's intelligentsia, Feywl Frid and his wife, Dr. Leah Frid, Dr. Oks, Dr. Skuler, Dr. Yosef Feldman and Moshe Lerer gave lectures along with Mendlzon, Kratke, Glincman, Bornsztajn and Kornblit from the young students. Kornblit's lectures drew a very large number of visitors and were given regularly for a very long time.

It is especially worthwhile to remember the dedicated and multifaceted activities of the well-known and talented teacher, Moshek (Moshe) Morgnsztern, who not only gave lectures at the People's University, but, in his time, was the most responsible secretary and leader of the Evening Courses Society. He led the evening school and he, himself, was the most active teacher who taught the young workers to write and to read without a *groshn* in payment. He also actively helped the *Poalei-Zion* Party in various other areas.

The Chelmer delegates took an active role in the Cultural Congress that was organized by the central managing committee of the Society of Evening Courses in Warsaw.

[Page 174]

The managing committee of the society would very often wrestle with great economic and financial difficulties and yet the cultural work was not interrupted. The harassments and persecutions by the regime and the frequent sealing of the premises would hinder and impede the vigorous spread of cultural and, also, sometimes stopped the cultural work for a time. But as soon as the disturbances were removed and the premises were reopened, the normal cultural activities were revived and renewed.

On the 14th of September 1933, the activity of the Evening Courses Society across the entire nation was stopped according to an order from the Interior Ministry. An intensive search was carried out of the Evening Courses for Workers Society and the cultural center for the Jewish working class in Chelm was locked and sealed.

Borochov Library

The Jewish Workers Library named for Ber Borochov was founded by *Poalei-Zion* during the first years of Polish independence in the center of the city at Lubliner Street number 51. There was among its 400 readers during the first years of its founding an outstanding number from the Polish worker intelligentsia. The number of books reached around 8,000 Yiddish and Polish [books]. All campaigns and undertakings on behalf of the library would take place with great success. Among its leaders during the course of its existence were Dr. Moshe Konfer, Feywl Frid, Moshe Lerer, Akiva Winik, Moshe Beker, Yakov Zwi Szargel, Dovid Goldrajch, Doba Waserman, Yitzhak Kornzajer, Yakov Beker, Yehosha Kratke and Shmuel-Yosl Beker. The latter dedicated almost 10 years to the library until the outbreak of the horrible [Second] World War.

The library managing committee, which would be elected at party meetings, took care of buying the new books, repairing and binding the old books and for the cultural-esthetic appearance of the rooms.

The reading room that was active at the library with short interruptions contained newspapers and journals from almost the entire Jewish world.

The party and *Jugnt* would also use the library room for cultural and professional work. Therefore, the library also "benefitted" from the persecutions endured by the *Poalei-Zion* Party. The *starosta* [village head] sealed it many times and it [the library] had to wander from place to place and this disrupted its full development and expansion.

Dramatic Circle and Choir

At the time of illegality, when political work was very inhibited, the comrades of *Poalei-Zion* created the first dramatic circle in the city, which served simultaneously as a source of income for the party organization.

[Page 175]

Among those taking part in the dramatic circles during the years 1918-1919 were the following comrades: Itshe Achtman, Meir Baum, Yosef Dreksler, Ruchl Dubkowska, Rywka Herc and Noakh Goldhaber. The directors of the circle were Sholem Goldbaum and Shmuel Szimel [and] after him Feywl Dreksler, who remained the leader and director of the circle for many years and transformed it in time into a municipal theater that also served the neighboring *shtetlekh*.

The work of the first dramatic circle was very earnest and faced a great challenge. The dramas and tableaus that would be presented in the largest theater rooms of the city would draw large groups of the Jewish population.

The dramatic circle did not transform itself into a professional theater group, although many of those who took part later led dramatic circles and some of them, such as the Ziglboim brothers, Piniele and Feywl, completed their theatrical training in Dr. M. Wajchert's theater school in Warsaw and they took part in the well-known experimental Warsaw Youth Theater.

For a long time comrades Rayzele Kelberman, Ber Feldman, Perele Laks, Serke Zisberg, Moshe Klerer, Ruwin Frucht, Rukhtshe Sobol, Itmar Wajc, Avraham Berenfeld, Feywl Zigelboim, Rukhtshe Lazar, Gershon Nisen, Avraham Cikl. Sara Szalit, Yankl Zisberg, Dovid Czechowicz, Yakov Szargel, Shimeon Mandlbaum, Motek Diker, Yehezkiel Milsztajn and Moshe'le Dreksler took part in the success of the dramatic circle.

When Feywl Dreksler left Chelm, others took his place and at various times took upon themselves the difficult and responsible role of putting together, organizing and leading the dramatic circle. The most capable came forward, such as: Avraham Cikl, Motek Diker, Hilel Szargel (he adapted the dramatic material, painted the scenery, directed and also acted), Mikhal Ribeizn and Zaynwl Zalctreger.

[Page 176]

The vocal evenings, which would be carried out with the participation of Serke Zisberg, Moshe Klerer, Avraham Bernfeld, Itmar Wajc, Shimeon Mandlbaum, Nota Kuper and Bentshe Torn, must also be mentioned.

During the short time Yakov Zwi Szargel spent in the city when he came to Chelm as a guest in 1934, he put together an original evening of stage adaptations and song.

The appearances of the choir, under the leadership of Chaim Gutman, a teacher from the Jewish *Folk-Shul* [public school], which were new in Jewish cultural Chelm and would draw many hundreds of listeners, need to be recorded. The accomplishment of building up a choir of workers' children, which was carried out by Bentshe Torn after Gutman's departure, was one of the most important and remained so until the end of days [the destruction of Chelm].

Musical and dramatic circles of the Poalei-Zion organization at Lubliner 27
This photograph was taken in 1928

Sports and Physical Culture

bhere always were *Poalei-Zion* groups that were involved with sports and physical culture, but an official sports club that was a member of the worker sports central, *Gwiazda* (*Stern*) ["star" in Polish and Yiddish], was organized in 1930. In a short time, four divisions were established: 1) ping-pong; 2) light athletics; 3) gymnastics; 4) football (soccer). The latter two developed particularly well. A special sports corner with the appropriate equipment was organized where gymnastic exercises with the participation of many dozens of young people and older workers would take place at designated hours. The beautiful displays of gymnastics and pyramids were used later at evening [events] and gatherings. The football division developed very rapidly and very quickly appeared publicly in football competitions with the strongest and oldest sports clubs in the city. In one such competition with the football team of the 7th *Pulk* [regiment] at their field, the young sports club, *Stern*, played so well and with such supremacy that it so frustrated the Polish players and they began to play brutally and one of their players intentionally gave a sharp blow to the goalkeeper, Manashe Atlas, and broke his leg. Play was interrupted and Comrade Atlas was taken to the hospital. After this, many football competitions took place with great success.

In 1932 sports competitions between the *Stern* clubs in Chelm and Lublin took place for the *Stern* Central cup.

The fifth division, the swim section, was created for the summer season of 1932. And a swim stadium was created – the only one in the city.

A larger number of athletes, in special uniforms and under their flags, took part in an all-Poland *Stern* competition that took place in Warsaw in 1933.

[Page 177]

A large sports commemoration took place on the 9th of December 1933 in the Rosursa Hall with the participation of a representative from *Stern* Central to celebrate the beautiful successes of the sports club and its divisions.

At the head of the leadership of the club stood: Yehosha Kratke, Shmuel Yosl Beker, Manashe Atlas, Altr Galik, Shmuel Zajdfodim, Mordekhai Elcter and Zishe Kornfeld.

Chelemer Folks-Blat

The sympathies and good feelings that the *Poalei-Zion* Party awoke for itself among a significant number of Jews [led to] a search for an opportunity for constant direct contact with the masses and this could be attained only through a public forum. And in the second half of 1928, the party started to publish its own newspaper.

The prospectus for this organ, which indicated the maturity of the party and its devotion to the masses, was published on the 7th of September 1928. The name – *Chelemer Folks-Blat* [*Chelm People's Newspaper*] – and the editorial colleagues then consisted of the comrades: Yitzhak Kornblit (chief editor), Chaim Gutman (proof reader) and Mordekhai Evri, Sholem Goldbaum and Moshe Beker (colleagues) were the expression of what the newspaper would be.

[Page 178]

The *Chelemer Folks-Blat*, which served as a non-rigid party weekly newspaper about culture, political and communal questions, brought joy and enthusiasm among friends and respect and recognition among opponents. The articles and the stories, the poems and the belle-letters always stood on an appropriately high level. Friends and comrades from abroad also participated: Shneur Waserman from Argentina and Avraham Brik from Jerusalem, Yakov Zwi Szargel from Tel Aviv and Hersh Sziszler from South Africa. The editorship, which later went to Feywl Frid, Yakov Beker and Hershl Lerer, with the participation of previous comrades, tried to improve the newspaper from week to week.

Alas, because of the well-known economic difficulties in which Jewish Chelm then found itself, the newspaper had to close, not lasting for a full two years.

Translator's footnotes:

1. *Chelmszczyzna* – Chelm Land – an historical region during the First Polish Republic. It was part of the Ruthenian Province.
2. *Tsysho* – *Tsentrale Yidishe Shul Organizatsye* – Central Yiddish School Organization – was a network of Yiddish schools created by Socialist and Yiddishist activists in Poland in the 1920s.

A May demonstration in Chelm in 1930

[Pages 179-202]

Jewish Life and Work in Chelm

by Akiva Winik

Translated by Howard Bergman

Chelm, my hometown, at the outbreak of World War II had a Jewish population of around 18 thousand. Only a remnant of a few hundred Chelmer Jews remain, escaping the Nazi sword in the last days before Hitler's occupation of the town. Very few Jews saved themselves from the Chelmer Ghetto.

For 700 years a Jewish community existed in Chelm, which experienced a variety of difficult times in its history.

The historian, Dr. Raphael Mahler, in his book *The Jews in Old-Time Poland*, writes about the blood accusations the Chelmer Community and the surrounding area have endured. He stresses the fact that in 1761 several Jews in the small town of Wojslawice (Chelmer area) were executed at the hands of the hangmen, among the victims two rabbis and two elected heads of the community, because of blood accusations. And in the 17th century, the bishops of the Eastern Dioceses - Chelm, Luck and Kiev - made life very bitter for the Jews through harsh edicts and persecutions.

In his book *The Jews In The Ukraine From The Oldest Times*, I. S. Hertz writes that, "During the Christian Easter Procession in 1580, a part of the mob broke into the Chelm Synagogue and created a devastation just when the Jews were praying. A number of worshippers were wounded." Hertz cites the fact that "while marching on Zamosc-Wolin, the Cossack-Tatar mobs destroyed a row of settlements and killed people in the region of Chelm and Hrubieszow. Jews were killed in Dubienka and Korytnica, and Hrubieszow was destroyed. Several hundred Jews were murdered and a large number of Unitarian (?) Ukrainians."

In the same book, I. S. Hertz writes:

"Chelm was a town that developed and grew very well. In November 1648, the Cossacks burned the town. The Chelm population, including the Jews, put up a resistance but could not resist the pressure from the enemy. The town and the castle fell victims to the flames. Around 400 Jews perished in Chelm. In Uchanic, near Chelm, a successful resistance was made and the enemy could not take the fortifications. However, many people died of starvation and pestilence. In Wlodawa, at the River Bug, a huge massacre was then perpetrated. The number of Jews killed was estimated at around ten thousand."

There is a document from the 17th century by the *Vaad Arba Arotses*[1] concerning great internal feuds in Chelm and in Galil (Galicia? Galilee?). In September 1671, steps were taken against those feuds, at a session of the V.A. A. in Jaroslaw. That document was found by Professor Szymon Dubnow, in the town of Dubno:

(A copy of the document is printed in this space, in Old Yiddish with some Hebrew and in Old Russian. Not translated here. – Translator).

Besides the internal feuding among the Jewish Community Officials and rabbinical and Jews in general, fractions existed among the diverse national groups and sections of the population which consisted of Ruthenians, Unitarian peasants, Greek Catholics, Ukrainians, Russians, Poles, and Jews.

Akiva Winik

Between the years 1795 and 1807, Chelm belonged to Austria. Since then colonists of Austrian-German origin lived in Chelm and surrounding villages until the recent time, and during the latest German occupation they helped the Hitler hordes to exterminate the Jews.

From 1807 till 1812 Chelm belonged to the Warsaw Grand Duchy; from 1812 till 1915 Chelm was under Russian authority. To all these political circumstances the Jewish population in Chelm had to make adjustments and had to endure many persecutions.

The town lived through a very difficult time when World War I broke out. Chelm was shelled by the Germans and the Russian Army.

Life under the first German occupation was hard and bitter. Bread was made from a mixture of pulp and flour and distributed on ration cards. The population was starving and the mortality was growing from day to day. Epidemics broke out. The Jewish community decided to conduct a wedding at the cemetery, believing that this deed would stop the epidemic. This was actually carried out: An old maid and a widower were found and the wedding took place on the grounds of the cemetery. After that, the plague did indeed diminish and the Jews interpreted the change as having been helped by the superstitious ritual.

The Germans introduced forced labor. Working conditions were terrible and punishment for every trivial thing was very severe.

In 1916 the Austrians took over the town and in many respects the situation became easier. In the Austrian garrison there were Jewish officers who showed a great interest in the Jewish population. In particular, much was done for the Chelmer Jews by: Major Kalrnis (he was city mayor), Dr. Fensterblau (vice mayor), and Dr. Kanfer. In the years 1916-1918 help arrived from the Jews in America. It should be noted, however, that during the difficult occupation years, active social help and activities were conducted, especially under the Austrian authorities. Workers Cooperatives, important institutions, cultural establishments, and children's homes were opened.

The Jewish working masses in Chelm were then the most dominant and active social force in Jewish life.

With the emergence of the independent Polish Republic, the economic and the cultural-social life changed a great deal.

The city of Chelm, within a short time, spread out and a new district was created on the northeast and new streets emerged, such as: Wesola, Pijarska, Podwalna, Kopemika, Budowska, and others. Near the marketplace, new streets developed. Jews divided lots on the "New World" and Kotawska Street. The streets Czarna, Pieracki, Oblonska, Narutowicza were created. To the left of Lubelska Street stretched a new street, Palestynska. Many Jewish dwellings were built below the hill, on the south side. The "New Cal" became densely populated.

Commercial activity developed on a large scale. On the Lubliner (Lubelska) Street a marketplace was built containing 80 shops, all of which were in Jewish hands. Opposite the Polish Church, large buildings went up with fine shops and hotels. A new and handsome movie house was built, as was the Theater "Polonia", where performances, meetings, and lectures were often held. The Polonia Theater was owned by the rabbinical family Najhojz.

The grain business developed very strongly and new mills were built. Before World War 11 the following motor- and rolling-mills existed: *Michalenko Mill* (the owners were: the Christian Grzegorz Nfichalenko, Yakov Sztul, I. M. Lederman, Eliezer Lederman, and Yosif Rolnik); *Boguszewski Mill* (the property of the Christian Boguszewski; but administered by Jews); *Lemberger Mill* (owners: Zalman Lemberger, Berisz Handelsman, Mates Klajner, and Yakov Yitzhak Goldrelch); *Grozinski Mill* (owned by Christian Grozinski) *Pola???ywka Mill* (owners: Avrom Dovid Lederman, I. M. Lederman, M. Frenkel, and A. Bojmgold) *S. Rubins Mill; Wierzbicki Mill.* There were also about a dozen Jewish bakeries. Most administrators and managers of the mills, merchants and shopkeepers were exclusively Jews. The workers were also Jews.

In the area of heavy industry where the Jews were pioneers during the last years before the War, the ownership was almost exclusively in the hands of Christians of German origin.

The Jews acquired new sources of income, as well as new trades. The Jews even created a metal workers union.

Until the Polish boycott movement started under the slogan "Swoj do swego" ("To each his own") the Jews did not live too badly, economically. But when the anti-Semitism in Poland became stronger and the Owszem Policy[2] penetrated to all levels of the Polish population, the economic situation of the Jews became continually worse throughout the country and it also affected the Jews in Chelm.

Religious Life

The religious way of life was dominant in Poland, even up to the last years. Also Chelm was a religious Jewish town with famous rabbis, such as Rabbi Shloyme ben Moyshe Chelmo who was a brilliant man and expert in the Middle Ages philosophy; The {unintelligible word} who was the Rabbi in Chelm at the beginning of the 17th century, and who authored a profound commentary on the Talmud. Also, up to the last years, there were many houses of prayer including Hasidic houses, such as the Kotzker House, the Kuzmer House, the Radziner House, the Belzer House, and the several hundred-year-old Synagogue which had a square shaped courtyard. Many tales and legends surround the name of the Great Synagogue. It was a massive and handsome structure, the walls covered with oil paint, with an almemar *(reading desk - Editor)* under a baldachin *(canopy - Editor)*. The windows were tall; almost up to the ceiling, from which heavy brass fixtures were hanging. The Synagogue also had a balcony on which a separate minyan used to be arranged during holidays. The entrance to the balcony was by a staircase on the right side of the anteroom.

One had the feeling of great holiness upon entering the Synagogue. Jews who used to pass through town would make a special stop to visit the lovely, majestic Synagogue.

In the courtyard opposite the door of the Chelmer Synagogue there was an entrance on the left side to the Beit Hamidrash (House of Study). On the right side was a small "house" of the society to assist "poor brides" with a dowry, and other "houses" for other charitable societies.

In the 1920's the Beit Hamidrash was rebuilt. The walls were repainted with oil paint and adorned with artistic paintings of Eretz Israel.

Chelm was a significant center of Hasidism. In Chelm resided the Trisker Magid (Preacher), a student of the saintly Magid, Reb Ber Mezeritscher.

In the 1920's settled in Chelm the Kuzmir Rabbi, Reb Motele, who had a great voice. At every prayer service his coloratura voice rang out with great sweetness. Therefore, the prayer services on Saturdays would not end until about two o'clock in the afternoon.

The Kuzmir Rabbi had very many adherents. Hundreds of Hasidim used to arrive from all corners of Poland to the Rabbi who would set the table for a large crowd and celebrate until it became totally dark.

During the High Holidays large groups of Hasidim would come together among whom there were prayer leaders. Their melodies penetrated the whole body. Hundreds of Chelmer Jews would come to the House of Prayer to listen to the melodies, occupying all windows, to catch every gesture, every tune and song. Later, the Hasidic artisans would repeat the melodies at work in their workshops.

Simcha Torah Holiday was a joyful celebration at the Kuzmir Rabbi's house. The Rabbi, who was lame, would dance during the "hakofes" (the circular procession with the Torah) with his own small Torah, which had golden trees of life. The Hasidim would make a circle around him and the Rabbi, covering his head with the talit, danced holding his little Torah above his head.

The Kuzmir Court brought unusual rapture and joy to Jewish life in Chelm.

Before World War I the "kheder" (religious school) was practically the only institution of learning for Jewish children in Chelm. The studying went on till late in the evening and, because of the fear of demons, one would hold the tsitsit or the Gemara in one's hands while walking home from kheder. That served as a protector against all wild devils and demons.

On the right side of Seminarska Street there was a house of Torah Study where children from the large Jewish poverty stratum studied. The children received meals several times a day.

Higher up to the left on the same Seminarska Street was a yeshiva (a school of higher Talmudic learning) where one would find students also from the surrounding area.

Many legends were spread among the students in the kheders and the yeshiva.

Very popular were the legends and the stories about the Rabbi Elijah Ba'al Shem who, it was said, created the golem (an artificial man) in Chelm.

I heard the story in the following version:

"No one was allowed to enter the attic of the Old Synagogue. No one even knew where the key to the attic could be found. One person whispered to another the secret that in the attic there lies the golem of the famous Rabbi Elijah Ba'al Shem.

It was said that Elijah Ba'al Shem created from clay a golem who would stand on market days with an ax in his hand, and as soon as he saw that a peasant was going to beat up a Jew, the golem killed the peasant.

An entire week the golem served the Rabbi, the Rabbi's wife, and he performed the manual labor in the Beit Harnidrash.

When the local landowner found out about the golem's might, the Ba'al Shem led the golem to the attic, withdrew from him the ineffable name of God, and converted the golem into a heap of clay. The Ba'al Shem locked the door, took with him the key, and since then the attic remained bolted."

There were many miracle stories about Rabbi Elijah Ba'al Shem. It is told that before his death he left a will that after his demise when his coffin would be led past the Russian Church (apparently there was no other road to the cemetery), and Christian hooligans started throwing stones - as is their habit for many years - no one should run away but they should stop with the coffin and not move.

As a continuation, it is told that when Rabbi Elijah Ba'al Shem expired, his will was honored. When his funeral procession approached the Church, gentile hooligans ran out of the Church and began to throw stones at the coffin and at the Jews who accompanied the saintly man. Nobody ran away. Rabbi Elijah sat up and looked into the Torah scroll that was in the coffin, and a few minutes later the Church sank together with the hooligans. Right after that the Ba'al Shem Tov stretched out in the coffin like a corpse. The frightened Jews looked at one another in astonishment and the funeral procession continued.

It was said that since that miracle the hooligans no longer threw stones during Jewish funerals.

About the church that sank, boys who studied in the kheder of the teacher Leib Paks would say that when one goes down to the cellar and starts jumping on the wooden floor, one can hear a kind of echo of a bell sound which is the reverberation of the sunken church.

This version went around among the children. It was also said that the Leib Paks house was built on the same place of the sunken church.

At the Chelm cemetery on a certain spot there were bricks thrown in the shape of the Hebrew letter "B". On some of the bricks letters were carved. It was said that on the anniversary of Rabbi Elijah Ba'al Shem's death an angel would appear and carve a letter on a brick. Therefore, everyone was afraid to touch the bricks.

That was the grave of Rabbi Elijah Ba'al Shem. There was no tombstone on the grave.

In the "Oytser Israel", page 137, part three, in New York, the following information is to be found:

(Ba'al Shem -Text in Hebrew, not translated in these pages.)

School Matters

The Jewish Public School was the first modern educational institution in Chelm. The school was established in 1918, thanks to the initiative of the Labor Zionist Party with the help of the "Bund" and a number of impartial persons. The instruction language was Yiddish. The Hebrew language and the study of Eretz Israel was obligatory. The students in the school came from the poorest strata of the Jewish population in Chelm. Many of the parents could not even pay the minimum tuition. The school budget was mostly covered from various enterprises and flower days, and from occasional supports by relief committees and Chelmer people overseas. In the first several years, subsidies for the school were sent by the Medem-Dinezon-Reichman Committee and later by the TSISHO (Central Yiddish School Organization) in Poland. The teaching personnel belonged mostly to the Labor Zionist Party. Dr. M. Kanfer was the School Administrator. Later, the administrator was his wife, Gazela Kanfer, who also taught Polish in the School. The teaching staff included: ??irkin, Faivel Fried, Moyshe Lerer, Blume Bojm, and Alter Bakaliar (Hebrew teacher).

The School developed very nicely and the number of students grew. In 1920 there were 200 students in the Jewish Public School.

Tishe Bov at the Chelm Cemetery

Thanks to the strong demand by the Labor Zionist faction in the Jewish Community, especially by the Councilman, Aaron David Hipshman, the Community Administration, in 1923, decided to give a small subsidy to the (Jewish) Public School.

In 1923-1924 Yakov Alster of Cracow was engaged as School Administrator. He created a circle of youth who helped with the school work, including teaching. To that student circle belonged: Zalman and Avrom Kratki, Mendelson, Sister and Brother Bash, Neryam Koyfman, (later the wife of Yakov Alster), Nfirke Atlas, Royze Shwartsman-Gutman, Glintsman, Yenkl Bornshtein, Komblit, and others.

After the School Secretary, Michal Ribayzn, left for Warsaw, I, the writer of these pages, took over as Secretary. During my tenure a group of graduates from the Jewish Middle School in Chelm was organized. This group traveled to Warsaw to participate in pedagogical courses set up by the TSISHO. These graduates later became teachers and worked in the TSISHO schools. Several of them taught at the Chelm Public School.

After Alster resigned, Akiva Bakszt of Zhetl became the administrator. In 1924, when I left for Warsaw to attend the teacher seminar run by TSISHO, the School Secretary became Sholem Goldbojm, and the administration was led by Chaim Bibel (now in Israel).

There were frequent changes in the teaching personnel of the School. In 1926-1927, after completing my seminar, I worked as a teacher at the Chelm Public School. The teachers at that time were: Genye Levy, Chantshe Helfenbein, Avrom Kratki, Michal Balyar, Pesl Goldfeld, Sheva Kruk, Yosele Rozenblat, and the writer of these pages.

For the school year 1928-1929 the School Administrator became Chaim Gutman who also was a good musician. He introduced a lot of joy into the school. He initiated into the school program the studies of music and singing. Also, there were created a student club, a drama group, a school choir, and a sports section. Their successes - both morally and financially - were the organized student-evenings, which became renowned in Chelm.

Teachers Council of Public School in Chelm

The School at that time was partially subsidized by the city administration, thanks to the victory of the Labor Zionist faction in the election to the City Council. A subsidy was also provided by the Jewish Community, but at the beginning of school year 1929-1930 the situation became very difficult. The new political atmosphere in the country had a strong influence on the Chelm City Administration, and even on the Jewish Community Council, which further reduced the subsidy to the Jewish Public School. The School found itself in a critical situation.

At the beginning of 1930 the TSISHO assigned a representative, Yakov Peterzayl, to Chelm who became in charge of the rescue action for the School. A series of meetings took place, a conference of the trade unions with the participation of the Labor Zionists and the "Bund", and money collections were carried out from house to house. This school action was concluded with an imposing school celebration.

The teacher personnel at that point included: Chaim Gutman, Sheva Kruk, Motele Shener, Royze Shwartsman, and Serke Wajsman.

For the school year 1930-1931 the administrator of the Public School was Berl Akselrad, and his wife Neche had a position in the Children's Home.

In 1932 the owner of the building of the Public School, the well known assimilated Jew, Dr. Lipkowicz, obtained a warrant to evict the School. During the most severe winter time, in the month of February, the eviction took place. The appeals and efforts of various people, the heartrending cries of the small children to wait with the eviction at least two months until spring, had no effect. The city hall official was touched and willing to wait, but the heartlessness of the owners won out. The news about the eviction very quickly spread throughout the whole town. The school officials made desperate efforts to rent new quarters for the School but did not succeed; first, because there were no suitable locations for a school in general and, second, the thought had matured that it was time to build our own school building.

Unsuccessful efforts were made to obtain from city hall a free lot for the School. There was no other choice but to buy a lot with our own money. In 1932 a building site was purchased on Katowski Street (opposite Siedlecki Street) in the very center of the hardworking Jewish population. The purchase of the building site was registered under the names of Aaron Dovid Hipshman, Moyshe Beker, and Julek Weissman. (The first two perished under the Germans, the third one now lives with his wife and son in Sao Paulo, Brazil).

The selected building committee immediately started the work on the school building, and that created great enthusiasm among comrades and friends, as well as among many people in general, who volunteered to work without pay, thus saving the building committee a good deal of money.

The celebration of laying down the cornerstone of the school building took place on July 3, 1934.

Over a thousand people assembled. In the name of the building committee, the celebration was opened by Councilman Moyshe Beker. Speeches and greetings were delivered by: Yenkl Beker, in the name of the Poalei Zion Party Committee; City President, Stanislaw Gut, on behalf of City Hall; Vice Chairman, City Council, I. M. Lederman; Chaim Bibel, in the name of the Trade Unions; Feige Nitslach, on behalf of the "Youth" Organization; Berl Akselrad, on behalf of the cultural institutions and the teachers who were waiting for the School; N. Buksboim of the TSISHO Office in Warsaw

---

Jewish School Organization - Division Chelm

INVITATION

We have the honor to invite you to participate in
THE CELEBRATION OF LAYING THE
CORNERSTONE OF OUR OWN SCHOOL

The celebration takes place on Sunday, July 3, at 11:30 A.M. with the participation of the Delegate from TSISHO, Comrade N. Buksboim, at our own site in the open air at Katowska 40 (end of Siedlecka)

Program:

1) Greetings
2) Speeches
3) Laying of Cornerstone

Respectfully

The Administration

איינלאדונג

מיר האבן דעם כבוד אייך איינצולאדען אנטייל צו נעמען אין
דער פייערונג ביים ריינו דעם גרונדשטיין פון או
אייגענעם שור בני.

די פייערונג קומט פאר זונטיק דעם 3 טן יולי 11:30 פ. מ. מיטן
אנטייל פון דעלעגאט פון צ. י. ש. א. ח' נתן בוקסבוים אויף
אינדזער אייגענעם פלאץ אונטערן פרייען הימעל קאטאוסקא 40
(סוף שפרדזנסקא)

אין פראגראם: 1) באגריסונגען 2) רעדעס 3) לייגן דעם גרונדשטיין

מיט כבוד
די קארח אלמונג

דאטע: דעם 28.__.1934

Facsimile

The ceremony of laying the cornerstone took place. The first stone was laid by Nathan Buksboim, then the City President. Later, other representatives of the city and invited guests spoke. In the evening a conference was held by the administrations of the Trade Unions and cultural institutions, at which the Building Committee presented its plans for collecting the money for the school structure. The collection actions were carried out quite energetically, but they still did not succeed in procuring a large enough amount of money required to erect the building.

In June, 1935, premises were rented on Lubliner (Lubelska) St. 78 for a children's home named for Mordche Evri. It was in the middle of summer, during a great heat, at a time when children abandoned their school benches. Still, there were more than 20 children attending. In order to obtain the financial means to operate the children's home, the entire party activity became involved in conducting enterprises, renting cinema halls for special showings, and the members themselves walked around selling tickets. During the first month an income of over 200 Zloty was realized, from three movie showings (Azef, Tsheluskin Expedition, Memories from Dead House). Some time elapsed and the financial difficulties became so great that the children's home had to be closed.

In January, 1938, Dr. Leah Fried approached the Labor Zionist Committee stating that she was prepared to help open the children's home under the name of Mordche Evri, and that she herself would conduct the fund raising in town

In only a number of days, the above mentioned, with the help of Dr. (Mrs.) Witenka, collected over 400 zloty.

The laying of the cornerstone of our own school building in Chelm, 1934.
The speaker is N. Buksboim, delegate of TSISHO in Poland.

An extensive committee was created for the children's home which included: Dr. Leah Fried, Faivel Fried, Dora Dubkowska, Bashke Tsimennan, Za??l Zaltstreger, Blume Gomulka, Chana Szargel, Shmuel Szargel, Yankl Beker, Dovid Goldreich, and Berl Akselrad. A 3-room apartment was rented on Lubliner Street 80, all necessary installations were made, including a kitchen to provide two warm meals daily for the little children. Neche Akselrad was appointed administrator. After more than 40 children were accepted, assistants were hired; first Esther Solman, and later Ruzhke Gertner.

To the festive opening of the Children's Home over 60 persons came, such as representatives of various organizations and institutions. Festive speeches were delivered.

Children's Home at the Jewish Public School in Chelm.
To the left is the teacher, Neche Akselrad-Bakalczuk.

Once the Children's Home was secured, planning was started to create afternoon- and evening schools, and we began to realize the renewal of building our own school. That school was to serve as a house of culture encompassing the Children's Home, the Library, the Peoples University, and other cultural institutions. At that point S. Szargel was sent to Warsaw where he conferred with the representatives of TSISHO. Without delay the TSISHO paid out a certain subsidy for the Children's Home, and promised a larger amount for renting temporary quarters for the School, until the building was completed.

The erecting of the school structure started. Building materials were purchased. Carpenters and construction workers began to work on the lumber. Unexpectedly, everything went well. The structure was already provisionally erected (on the site of the Goldreichs, at Seminarska 19). It was waiting to be to be taken to its school site, to be attached to the previously prepared foundation, where it was destined to be converted into the dreamed of House of Culture for the Jewish working families in the hard working Jewish Chelm. But September 1, 1939, approached quickly, and all goals and dreams were shattered with the coming of the gruesome times.

Jewish-Polish Schools

We all are familiar with the striving among Jews to send their children to gymnasiums. Parents looked forward to practical purposes and careers for their children. Our beloved Jewish classical writer, Sholem Aleichem, in a humorous and brilliant story, "The Gymnasium", describes this chase to the gymnasiums.

Also in this respect, Chelm did not lag behind. Already at the beginning of the 20th century, a Russian gymnasium opened in the center of town, next to the Polish Church. Jews already then tried to register their children in that gymnasium. But there was a quota percentage and, in addition, there was a condition that a Jewish student had to pay tuition for two students. Such luxury only the well-to-do parents could afford.

A classroom of the Jewish Gymnasium.
In center: Director, Dr. A. Shifman, A. Bakalar

In 1918 the Jewish Gymnasium was opened with Polish as the language of instruction. The School was well established and the graduates from that Gymnasium were a pride for the Jewish population in Chelm.

The Wadzilawski School

For several years there existed a private school established by Mr. Wadzilawski named the "Hebrew-Polish School". That meant that the main subjects were taught in the Polish language and in some instances in Hebrew. The school had few students because the tuition was too high for students with modest means.

There existed a school run by the teacher, A. Sobol. It was a secular/religious school. Later was founded:

The Klara Morgenshtern School

There was in Chelm an intelligent family, the Morgenshterns, who distinguished themselves with their pedagogical abilities. The oldest daughter, Klara, established a school with Polish as the language of instruction, in accordance with the program of all Polish Government schools but with the difference that no classes were held on the Sabbath. Most of the students were Jewish children. The School was located on Budowska Street and it was maintained by the Polish Government.

At the beginning, some Jewish religion was taught. The school was indeed called "Klara Morgenshtern School". Only later, in 1928, did the school authorities change the name of the School to "Kazimierz Wielki" (Kazimierz the Great).

A group of the Jewish Gymnasium students.
From right to left: Itzik Fisher, Hirsh Hertz, B. Meyer,
A. Shreibman, Yechiel Wasserman.
(Part of the group now lives in America and Israel)

The Religious Hebrew School "Tarbut"

Of all the various types of schools that existed in Chelm, the "Tarbut" School was the youngest, it opened in 1922.

In the paper *Chelmer Shtinie* of Friday, July 8, 1927 (?), we read an article by the "Tarbut" School Director, N. Bloch, entitled "With Joint Efforts Toward A Common Goal", stating the following:

"Six years ago the "Tarbut" School in Chelm was a dream, a fantasy of a few individuals today the School is a reality. Six years ago it was barely a beginning - today it is a center which includes almost 200 students … Six years ago it was necessary to look for students intensively, talk to every father separately, influence him in a variety of ways to enroll his child. Today, regretfully, we cannot comply with the requests from parents who want us to accept their children. Together with the enormous development, the thought matured to build or to buy our own building for the School. The more the realities of life worsen, the more we need spirituality which gives us strength and courage to endure everything. We believe in the good will and the willingness to make sacrifices on the part of the Jewish masses in Chelm. That belief gives us the courage and assurance to begin with carrying out this daring action of establishing a home for the "Tarbut". With joint efforts toward the common goal."

The Hitler hordes already started to knock on the gates of Poland when our teachers and school activists made plans to erect our own buildings for the Jewish children.

The "Klara Morgenshtern School, maintained by the Polish Government

Social and Cultural Life

With the establishment of the Polish Republic a great revival began among the Jews in Poland. Organizations and societies were created and also in Chelm important social activity took place. Very active work was conducted by the Left Labor Zionists and the "Bund". Visible were the activities of the Revisionists "toward the common goal".

I will only describe, albeit briefly, the following organizations which are not mentioned in this book by other writers:

The Zionist Organizations

The General Zionist Organization was mostly occupied with collecting money for Zionist Funds by selling Shekels. The Organization distributed certificates for immigration to Eretz Israel to devote oneself to the Hebrew revival movement. Only during elections to the Sejm (Polish Parliament), to City Council, or to the Jewish Community Council, did the Organization become politically active. In the same situation was the Organization "Mizrachi" which was affiliated with the Zionist Organization. The leader of the "Mizrachi" was Mr. Berish Finkelshtein. Later he became chairman of the Community Council.

The spiritual leader of the Zionist Organization was Shloyme Samet.

Hechalutz (Pioneers)

In 1930 the "Hechalutz" was founded in Chelm. The Organization developed very well; it already counted several hundred comrades who were young people. Many of the members went through the "hachsharah" (the training for agricultural emigrants) and prepared to travel to Israel. Funds were available for members without means.

The leaders were: Hipsh, Bojm, Yankl Edelshtein, Tshesner, and others.

"Klara Morgenshtern School - in center, the teacher, Klara Morgenshtern

Hashomer Hatzair

The seat of the Hashomer Hatzair was on Siedlecki Street, in the house of the teacher Sobol. The members were also young people. They lived a kibbutz life and performed physical work, such as chopping wood, guarding halls. The girls were governesses, seamstresses. Some members gave Hebrew lessons.

The Hashomer Hatzair was praised and respected and it had many admirers and sympathizers. It also had a drama section, which often gave performances, such as: "Bar Kochba", "Al Naharut Babel", "Isha Ra'a", and others. The amateur ensemble included: Y. Borenshtein, V. Glintsman, M. Torn, Blume Orgun, Tsipe Boyarski, Y. Wasserman, A. Lipshitz, H. Hertz, B. Tseichn, Dovid Kornblum, Z. Shwartzber, S. Sobol, S. Meches, and others. The plays were performed under the direction of F. Dreksler, M. Tom, and others.

A Purim Show, performed by the children of "Gan Yaldim" in Chelm in 1925.
The teacher (in center) and two children are now in Israel. All others perished.

The Left (Communist) Party

The Communist Organization, created in 1920, at the beginning had a great influence on the Jewish working masses, having had the support of a large number of trade unions, which also conducted certain cultural activities. They had their own library, a reading room, and often they arranged lectures with the help of lecturers from the Center.

The Communist Party conducted intensive political activities and organized party cells among the military and in the villages. The Party's center was in Lemberg (Lwow). But the Polish reactionary government would not long tolerate the Communist activities and repressions against the Communists began nationwide, as well as in Chelm.

However, the Communist activity was not interrupted; it was carried out in a conspiratorial manner. One of the Communist activists in Chelm was Shimel who used to walk around town in a black cape.

Some Chelmer students of the Vilna University - Mendelson, Zalman Kratko - were active members in the Vilna Communist Party. They were arrested and sentenced to several years in prison. Zalman Kratko, I was informed, now lives in

Poland and holds a responsible position in the Government. The Communist activist Chantshe Helfenbein is also in Poland now. She was sentenced to 8 years in prison before World War II.

The leadership of the Left Trade Unions in Chelm included Yosif Grinberg, Ruven Furer, Hersh Shechterzon, and others.

Purim Show, performed by the children of the "Tarbut" School in 1939

A Chalutz group on excursion in 1933

Hechalutz Organization in Chelm
Part of the group lives in Israel, others in America.
In center - Moyshe Lang

The above and other organizations in Chelm created institutions., established evening classes for adults, people's universities, drama circles, and libraries. Very often, requests were made to Warsaw to send artists, writers, poets, lecturers, and party leaders, who infused exhilaration among the Jewish masses; among people who yearned for a new word, new thoughts, a new book and literary creations.

Polish Security used to trail every newly arrived lecturer. I remember that during the lecture by Meyer Her, secret police interrupted his lecture, and took him to the police station. The reason given was that his passport was not a legitimate one. Between 7 and 8 months he sat in prison until his trial, then was sentenced to another 6 months and deportation to Russia An impartial commission of several persons was organized who supplied him with clean laundry and, twice a week, with food, and that maintained his health.

In the 1930's I found out that the same Meyer Her became the editor of the Moscow *Emes,* replacing Moyshe Litvakov.

Meyer Her was a lecturer of great depth, and he was very knowledgeable in Yiddish and Hebrew literature.

Countless lectures and symposia were given in Chelm, both by our own local people and with the help of writers and lecturers from Warsaw.

Photo has no caption but on the photo itself is indicated that it is a group of Chalutzim. The date is 1934.

The Drama Circle

The Drama Circle in Chelm was created in 1916 when the city was occupied by the Austrians during World War I. The founders of the first Drama Circle were: Itshe Achtman, Berl Naturman, Berl Luksenburg (in Durban, S. Africa), Itshe Luksenburg, Yekl Rozenblat, Shloyme Greber, Noyech Goldhaber, Israel Zygielboim (in Johannesburg). The directors were Fishl Ilewitski and Meyer Boim. The women in the Drama Circle were Tobe Hertz, Sure Helfer (now Mrs. Lerman in Israel), Tsharne Bukler, Rivke Hertz (in Israel), the sisters Chantshe and Neshe Boyarski (in America). The meetings took place in a house on Budowska Street. The plays were performed in the hall of the "Syrena" (on Lwowska Street). Later, when the "Syrena" burned down, performances were given in the hall of the "Polonia", almost every month.

The plays were by Peretz Hirshbein, Yakov Gordin, Sholem Aleichem, and other fine playwrights. The Chelm Drama Circle performed the play "Yoel" even before it was performed by the "Vilner Trupe". It is interesting to note that the amateurs took their work of acting quite seriously and responsibly. Once, when the play "Di Puste Kretshme" by P. Hirshbein was being performed in Lublin, B. Luksenburg was delegated to go and see the performance. Later, the play was performed in Chelm.

When the Drama Circle performed the play "Chasye Di Yisoyme" in the "Syrena" hall in 1916-7 with the participation of Fishl Ilewitski, Meyer Boim, A. Achtman, Tobe Hertz, Surke Helfer, and others, that very day the Mother of the Yiddish Theater, Ester Rochl Kaminska, was in Chelm and she came to see the performance. She was so pleased and enthused with the acting that she walked up to Tobe Hertz and Surke Helfer and kissed them for the fine performance.

*Social workers at the Zionist Organization in Chelm.
In center, Shloyme Samet.*

*Jewish Progressive Workers demonstrate May 1, 1936, against war and Fascism.
Many of them were arrested by Polish authorities and sent to prison.*

*A group of Labor Zionists in Rejwitz (Rejowiec?), vicinity of Chelm.
In the center is the then Communist Leader, H. Dua, who was killed by
Polish hooligans, after the liberation from the Hitler hordes.*

After a few performances, the Drama Circle was joined by the so called, town's "aristocracy" and "intelligentsia". Several rich Jewish girls and some ladies - wives of doctors who were indeed striving to perform in the Yiddish Theater and also to help the poorer classes of Jews. The new members were Dr. Tsicrelman's wife, Manie Shneider, the sisters Sarah and Shure Lewin (daughters of Feldsher - old time "surgeon" - Matye Lewin), Ruzhe Morgenshtern, Miss Blumenschtrauch, Dentist Minkus, Dentist Lishchen (who wrote plays himself), the Evris and brothers Rozenblat, Avrom Zayde-Zigel, Regina Lewitska, and others.

In accordance with a decision by all members, a portion of the profit from the performances was given to "Linat Hatsedek" but the main part was spent on a "store", a matzo bakery, created by the Drama Circle. For a period of four weeks (between Purim and Pesach) all members of the Drama Circle worked 14 hours a day (of course, without pay) in the matzo bakery. They themselves purchased the flour, carried the water from the pump (quite a distance, uphill); kneaded the dough, baked the matzos, then distributed them to hundreds of poor Jewish families for Pesach. Those free matzos were a great help for many families. The "bakers" in the "store" were B. Luksenburg, Itshe Luksenburg (Z"L),and Yekl Rozenblat (Z"L).

This free "store" existed for several years and all the expenses were taken from the various theater performances.

Also arranged were "flower days" in the streets, in which the members of the Drama Circle actively participated and obtained funds for the free "store". In general, all participants in the theater performances, and in the other financial enterprises, felt that it was not just a question of distributing charity, but a moral duty of reciprocal help.

The Musical Section

Almost at the same time as the Drama Circle was created, a Musical Section was founded by the following persons: three brothers Luksenburg (Itshe E"H, Berl - now in Durban, and Chaim - now in Johannesburg), Bentshe Feldman, Bentshe Meyer, and Dovid Wolberger.

Later, many new participants joined, people who could play a variety of instruments. In time, the Section increased to 25 members and included: The Brothers Morgenshtern, the Brothers Rozenblat, Nochum Goldberg, Brothers Orenshtein, Yosif Dreksler. Shlivke, Yoske Goldhaber, Shloyme Greber (he married Miss B. Orgun; they are in America) Avrom Helfer, Sholem Meyer Getsl, Shmul Shimel-Kitei E"H, Gedalye Hertz, and the women: Zlate Blumenshtrauch, Chantshe Boyarski, the Sisters Dubkowski, Tobe Hertz, H. Bukler, and others.

The Musical Section arranged frequent concerts, sometimes with the help of the Drama Circle. The income was for the same goal as that of the free "store": to distribute free matzos to all poor families in town.

Every evening, walking by the house on Budowska Street one could hear various rehearsals from the windows: music from one, theatrical dialogues from another, etc. It was very lively and interesting for the Jewish youth in Chelm; they could live in their own environment and also take advantage of their talents and certain abilities.

Years later, almost every organization tried to create its own drama section among its own members, in order to derive some income from the theatrical performances.

The director of the Drama Circle of the Workers Home, which often performed for the benefit of the Yiddish Folkshul, was Faivele Dreksler. The main performers were Reyzl Kelberman, Moyshele Klerer, Sister and Brother Bernfeld, and others.

The repertory was quite varied: melodramas with song and dance, operettas, and similar.

For the most part, the performances were financially successful. In such cases the director received payment for his work of directing and acting, if his acting became necessary.

Theater "POLONIA"

SENSATION   A Guest   SENSATION

Monday, June 14 of this year, exactly at 9 in the evening
The Famous Artist and Poetry Reader

Avrom MOREWSKI

Will appear only once with an unusually rich program
1) **THEATER and JEWS**
List of ten subjects
2) **RECITATIONS:**
Shakespeare: from **"HAMLET"**
"SHYLOCK"
Popular Stories

Y.L. Peretz Dybuk, 3rd Act
S. Anski Der Dukos, Second Act
A. Katsizne

Poster about an artistic evening
(Partial translation)

From time to time, artists would come from Warsaw and other cities to play theater in Chelm. There used to come individual artists looking for good local amateur talent to help them put on a play, or, sometimes, entire ensembles would arrive with plays ready to perform.

One can remember many fine performances by the cast under the leadership of Zygmund Turkow and Ida Kaminska; the troupe of the artist Lipman, and also Dovid Sherman's group, etc.

Also the great Director, Avrom Morewski favored Chelm with an artistic evening.

Libraries

With the revival of the political parties in 1918-1919 Jewish libraries were also established at the organizations, such as the "Groser Library" at the "Bund"; a Library at the Trade Unions of the Jewish Communists, the "Peretz Library" at the Zionist Organization, and the "Borochow Library" at the Left Labor Zionists.

The "Peretz Library" had an energetic librarian, Chishele Roznfeld, who literally devoted her entire life to the "Library". The "Peretz Library" developed normally, the readership reached around 500 and the number of books - Yiddish, Polish, and also Hebrew - about 5,000. The librarian shared her fate with all Chelmer Jews and they perished together in the annihilation of the readers and the books by the "brown (shirted) Fascist bearers of the new Hitler culture".

Chelm in the Jewish Literature

The Jewish Community of Chelm is eternalized in the Jewish Literature, in the classical national prose as well as in the poetry.

Although Dr. P. Friedman in his article *On the History of the Jews in Chelm* included a bibliography of books on Chelm; it is, however, worthwhile to add the following list of authors about Chelm: L. Olickij, Y. Batashansky, Naftali Gros, F. Halperin, Shniur Wasserman, Shloyme Wasserman, S. Worzoger, Chaim Worzoger, Y. Trunk, Dr. Shimon Milner, Yosif Neiner, Moyshe Lerer, Dr. R. Mahler, L. Nitslach (reports), Y.L. Peretz *(Der Chelenier Melamed, Der Shabes Goy),* Dovid Frishman, Friedman, Faivel Fried, Aaron Zeitlin (comedy, *Chelemer Chachomim),* Y. Kipnis *(Chelenier Stories),* Michele Ribayzn, Ber Shnaper, Yakov Tsvi Szargel, Hilel Szargel, Hersh Shishier, and others.

It is to be hoped that now, with the publication of the *Yizkor Book Chelm* the interest will be called forth among our writers, as well as among the Jewish historians, to continue the literary and research work around the famous Jewish Community in Chelm.

Translator's footnotes:

1. The Council of Four Lands - an autonomous Jewish governing body in Eastern Europe in the 16th to 18th centuries
2. The official government sanctioning of boycotting Jewish businesses. Owszem is a polite way of saying "yes, certainly". In other words, no bodily harm but to boycott the Jews was "owszem"

[Page 203]

Chelmer Jewish *Gymnasie*

Chava Biderman-Biale

Translated by Gloria Berkenstat Freund

Chava Biderman-Bialya

The Chelm Jewish *gymnasie* (European middle school or high school) that was called "the Humanistic *Gymnasie* of the Jewish Community" was founded in September 1918. Poland had received its independence and the situation was uncertain and uneasy. The Jews in the cities and *shtetlekh* felt uncertain and nervous, not knowing whether the Jews would be treated with a liberal or anti-Semitic spirit by the Polish government.

Ignoring this uncertainty, the Jewish parents worried about the future of their children, about giving them an education and learning and a good upbringing. It was not yet known how the Polish government would solve the question of education for the young Jews who during all of the years of the Czarist regime were denied their rights, as it imposed restrictions and a quota.

Prominent parents from the city came together and conferred about how to better the position of education and thus provide better training and a better future for the young.

After great deliberation, a parents' committee was created that together with the Jewish *kehile* (community organization) decided to found a national middle school that would take in male and female students not only from Chelm, but also from the surrounding areas.

There was much discussion until the decision was realized. At the beginning the *gymnasie* opened with 3 classes and 2 preparation classes. The number of students exceeded 400. There was great enthusiasm in the city when the *gymnasie* opened. Each of the builders and founders of the *gymnasie* lived to see an historic moment.

All of the necessary accommodations were arranged in the *gymnasie*. A physics laboratory was provided, with all of the necessary instruments for physics and chemistry, a reading room with many books in Polish and Hebrew. The language of instruction was Polish, but Hebrew, Jewish history, *Khumish* (Five Books of Moses) and *Tanakh* (Bible) were taught.

The first head teachers of the *gymnasie* were: Dr. W. Lipman (Director) and Dr. Mirlas. They established the classes on a very healthy pedagogical basis.

Dr. Mirlas was a magnificent mathematician, an extraordinary pedagogue and lover of children. He also had a wonderful way of illuminating all mathematical problems, and the students, who generally did not make an effort with mathematics, waited for his lectures with curiosity and interest. It was the same with his lectures in chemistry and physics. For hours he would illustrate the matter in the laboratory with experiments and exercises. The children would make thermometers and other instruments. The lectures of Dr. Mirlas reached a very high level of achievement.

[Page 204]

Regrettably, he was not destined to take pleasure in his students for long. After a few years of work, he became ill and died. The grief among the students was great and, to this day, we remember him with great reverence.

Bakaliar, the Hebrew teacher, who taught us *Khumish* and *Tanak*, is etched deep in my memory, as is his son, Asherke Bakaliar, who soon became the teacher of the class and who studied Hebrew and Hebrew literature with us.

He put much love into his work. He planted in us this love. We achieved a great deal of learning in Hebrew, which for us was like a foreign language. We achieved so much that we were able to write compositions about the prophets Isaiah and Jeremiah and about leaders and classics of Hebrew literature and also of Jewish history. Reports and performances by the students in Hebrew were often arranged.

Later there were other Hebrew teachers, Dr. Lauer and Dr. Liber, who were magnificent Hebraists at that time.

There were no limits to our achievements in Hebrew. We ourselves didn't believe how great were our accomplishments in Hebrew, both in speaking and in writing.

The Polish language was the language of communication among us children in the *gymnasie*. This curriculum was very well established. The administrators in Lublin determined during their visitations that the best Polishists in Congress Poland graduated from our *gymnasie*. We knew the literature and the language thoroughly. We knew well the works of Mickiewicz, Slowacki, Kraszinski, Zheromski, Eliza Orzeszkowa, Reymont and of Boleslaw Prus.

To this day, after long living in Africa, Polish literature is for me an open book in my memory, living and fresh, as if I had just left the school bench in the Chelm Jewish *gymnasie*.

Our *gymnasie* graduated very good teachers of Polish, such as Roze Szwarcman, Miss Huberman, Miss Elboim and many others, who after finishing *gymnasie* were distinguished teachers in the Polish public schools in various towns and, also, in the vicinity of Vilna.

[Page 205]

Bernsztein became director of the *gymnasie* after A. Lipman's departure from Chelm. And the last director was Yakubowski, who was also a teacher of Latin. He was a person of much culture and education and was a great expert on classical world literature. He fought the contention that Latin is an archaic language that cannot be of use in life. He taught the language and made it interesting and alive, teaching it in a classical-modern manner.

Director Yakubowski rendered great service to the *gymnasie*. He himself would give interesting lectures at the student gatherings a few times a week. The lectures were held all year long. This was a sort of people's university for the *gymnasie* students (male and female). He developed in us a feeling for learning and for art, a thirst for learning and for understanding problems and creativity in many areas of learning.

To this day, students (male and female) of the Jewish *gymnasie* all over the world hold dear the memory of the director Yakubowski and have an eternal gratitude to him. We considered him a superman, who with heart and soul instilled the idea and the aspiration to live ethically and compassionately and value highly the worth of culture and art and their significance for the future.

The teacher, Dr. Anisfeld, the mathematics teacher in the higher classes, also put instruction on a higher level. Although he was somewhat conservative, he was very devoted to his work and he became very beloved as a guardian and teacher by we in the class. Even when he later left for Lublin, he was interested in the course of studies and progress of the *gymnasie*, returning often to visit us.

The teacher of general history for all classes was Mr. Heler. Although history was always interesting for students, his lectures doubled the interest. He made the more difficult chapters of history and the problems of the past era so clear, universal and accessible.

[Page 206]

His wife, Heler the teacher, was a distinguished natural science teacher. So, too, Mrs. Cuker, Mrs. Meirson, Miss Blumenfeld and Miss Bund were great professional pedagogical strengths in the field of Polish studies and in the subjects of geography and natural science.

The Jewish *gymnasie* had great success from the first day of its existence. There was a friendly cooperation among the parents, students and teaching personnel. Every administrative body carried out its mission in a magnificent manner.

The after-school work was established on a higher level. There existed a student organization named "Self Help." All of the *gymnasie* students belonged to this organization. Funds were gathered to support the poor students with tuition and to buy textbooks. Many events were held for this purpose, such as a Chanukah ball, a Purim play and also concerts and entertainments in the city gardens.

Our school society worked very intensively; when one event ended, a second event was organized. There was initiative and creative energy, both in the scope of our *gymnasie* activity and also in the general areas of society. Our society took an active part during the elections to the *Seim*, to the city government and to the *kehile* (Jewish communal organization).

The "Self Help" society also organized excursions to other cities, such as Lemberg, to Kazimierisz and to other historical places in Poland.

A literary circle also existed at the *gymnasie* that was comprised of students of other institutions of learning and others in the city who were supportive.

The literary circle dealt with works of modern literature, economic and social problems, and periods of general and Jewish history.

A group of students and several teachers from the Jewish gymnasie

From the right (sitting): - ?; Dr. Lauer, Anisfeld; Dir. Yakubowski; ?; ?: Mrs. Heller and Dr. Heler

* * *

I recall many memories and pictures of the school years in the Jewish *gymnasie*. I am happy that I have expressed some of my memories in my short article. These were the best years of creative work by the Chelm young people.

Horrible cruel fate brutally annihilated many of my fellow *gymnasie* student comrades, as well as the teachers who taught us with devotion and love to aspire to a more beautiful world in an ethical humane society.

The heart is torn with grief and pain by these remembrances.

However, may these lines in the Yizkor Book be the holy, holiest memorial to all those who perished - my comrades, my teachers, our beloved and dear home CHELM!

[Page 207]

The Fate of the Chelm "Tarbut" School

Yehushua Floimenboim (Israel)

Translated by Gloria Berkenstat Freund

The "*Tarbut*"[1] School in Chelm was founded in 1931 by a group of social activists with Josif Rolnik at the head. It was incorporated into the network of "*Tarbut*" schools in Poland whose center was in Warsaw. Like all new "*Tarbut*" schools, the Chelm school also received government approval.

There was great interest in the "*Tarbut*" School. The number of school children increased significantly. Financial resources were beginning to be found to spread Hebrew education in Chelm.

Accomplishing all of the school plans was not an easy task. The greatest difficulty was finding premises that would meet the requirements of the school authorities.

After a series of money collections, the school moved to Josif Janowski's two-story building on Narutowiczer Street, no. 14.

The names of the school's community workers were as follows: Josif Rolnik (chairman), Eng. Yakov Tenenboim, Shmuel Friszman, Shmuel Plus, Shimkhah Payas, Yekheil Gutfraynd, Benimin Blumensztrof, Dr. A. Zeifin, Mrs. Dr. Wilenka and Gershon Lustiker.

The teacherscouncil consisted of: N. Bialablacki, Naftali Blok, Moishe Halpern, Mrs. Blok, Nakhama Kuliner, Miriam Arnsztejn and others.

The language of instruction was Hebrew. The *Tanak* and the *Mishnah* were studied in the higher grades. There were frequent visits by school authorities and from the "*Tarbut*" officials in Warsaw. The level of achievement was at a very high grade.

On the eve of the war the construction of the school's own building was planned and, for this purpose, a collection of money was organized which met with great success. The decision was made to buy Yashia Barenholc's unfinished two-story building located on Szedlecka Street.
However, the arrival of the German occupying government disrupted the school plans.

* * *

It was a cloudy rainy autumn day when the German troops occupied Chelm. The weather was dreary and ugly as was the mood of the Jews.

From early in the morning, horrible rumors were spread that the Germans were torturing the Jewish population.

The panic lasted several days. The bolder people crept out of their houses. There also were Jews who thought that the devil was not as frightening as he was painted to be.

Finally it began. A host of military men let themselves loose in the city and caught for work only Jews, who would return battered.

[Page 208]

Leibele's son, Reb Moishe the Kuzimer *Rebbe*'s [Hasidic rabbi] grandson, was severely beaten during this forced labor.

Once, Jews were caught in the center of the city on Lubliner Street and, like sheep and cattle, put into trucks accompanied by abuse and blows.

The Jews who were caught were taken away to dig the "*Prokhownia Berg* [Gunpowder Mountain]."

Afterward, a series of taxes began that caused desperation and a great disquiet among the Jews.

On that "tax-day" posters appeared in the city announcing that the German government had given permission for the opening of the elementary schools. The "*Tarbut*" school received a decree that it should open, too.

The school manager then turned to the school secretary to help organize the school; the technical facilities and equipment had been demolished.

The school opened in the course of several days and was occupied by a much larger number of children than before the war. The eagerness of the students was so great that even the average children showed surprising achievements. All the children behaved calmly and they went home without noise and without uproar.

A good faculty was assembled. The director of the Pulower "*Tarbut*" School, H. Rabinowicz and his wife who were refugees, also came to work. The spirit in the school was elevated both for the teachers and for the students. This was the only satisfaction in the day-to-day anxiety. Although there was special permission that made the school legal, shadows and dangers hovered.

On the 20th of November, 1939, the teachers and children were already in class. The mood of both the teachers and the students was more oppressive than usual, as if they felt that this was the last day of school.

Around 10 o'clock in the morning the doors of the class were thrown open. Two members of the Gestapo came in who dispersed the children with screaming and curses.

The Gestapo gathered the faculty in the school office. First there were coarse youthful expressions and brutal questions and, later, all of the teachers were brought to the Gestapo. There the school manager, who was blamed for wanting to organize Jewry, was murderously beaten. Afterward, he was hurled into a detention cell.

The teachers were released late in the evening on condition that they leave the city within 24 hours, or else they would be murdered.

That is how the "*Tarbut*" School was "liquidated."

Translator's footnote:

1. The *Tarbut* schools were secular Zionist Hebrew language schools that prepared their students for life in Palestine.

[Page 209]

Concerning the "*Zeirei-Zion*" Party
(Notes)

Sh. Beker, Israel

Translated by Gloria Berkenstat Freund

The Zionist movement in Chelm is strongly bound to my memory of Aryeih Milner's house at the edge of the city, where the first seeds of Zionist-Hebrew activity were sown.

In 1907-1908, when the elections to the Russian Duma [Parliament] were to occur, Chelm had to choose a delegation to Lublin. A quarrelsome dispute arose around these delegate elections between the Russians and the Poles, with each side wanting to underscore its domineering influence.

There was also a division among the various orientations of the Jewish community. There was a group of the young, among them Avraham Arnsztayn and Aryeih Milner, who stood out in the forefront of revolutionary-national thought, declaring that we should designate an independent Jewish delegation to Lublin and not rely again on the Russians nor on the Poles.

The election took place on a Tuesday in January. It was damp and raining outside. Coming into the school, we, the bearers of Zionist thought, turned to every Jew in whom there beat a heart, urging them to send an independent Jewish delegation.

Our satisfaction and joy was great when the voting reflected the national consciousness [Zionism] of the Chelm Jews, who did not surprise us. The delegation that was elected consisted of three Jews.

We labeled the victory a national action and an acknowledgment of us, although it cost us a great deal and the writer of these lines was arrested, accused of leading a revolutionary agitation. Yet the event stimulated the spread of national-Zionist thought in the city.

[Page 210]

A year later when Josif Milner, the student in Toulouse, returned to Chelm from France, we turned to him for help in creating a branch of the Zionist movement in Chelm. Two decisions were made at the first meeting, which took place in a house on Brisker Street: a) to start a collection of money on behalf of *Keren-Kayemet* (Jewish National Fund); b) to found a library. The founding of a library was especially difficult because the Zionist movement was illegal and, for this reason, it was difficult to find a location for the library. Only one Jew, Eli Haim Klajner (now in Israel), was not afraid of the consequences and gave us a room for the library.

Thanks to the library and the availability of Hebrew books, we became popular among the varied layers of the Jewish population. However, the religious fanatical Jews, knowing of our heretical library, denounced us to the government. Fearing a search, we were forced to close the library and our activity was restricted to collecting money on behalf of *Keren-Kayemet*.

We succeeded in achieving an important accomplishment when the income from a masked ball was designated to help the Hebrew library in *Eretz-Yisroel* named after Dr. Kuznowicz. We attracted to this undertaking all of the assimilated circles in the city, who through this, incidentally, were drawn nearer to the illegal Zionist movement.

At that time, we also began to spread Zionist ideas among the school youth, who would come from the neighboring villages to study in Chelm. In this way Zionist thought infiltrated into the *shtetlekh* surrounding Chelm.

During the First World War we were forced to interrupt our activities because of the strict decrees of the occupying government and because of various other dangers connected to the continuation of our Zionist work. During that period, our activity was not suspended and was mainly concentrated in the area of helping the Polish war refugees who flooded the city. The young men were then mobilized for the army, or they left the city due to various circumstances. Because of this, no memories remain of the widespread Zionist activity that, until the war, we carried on with great success.

After Chelm's liberation from the German occupation, many young people returned from Russia and other places and they spread the "*Zeirei-Zion*" ideals.

[Page 211]

The first area conference in Poland was organized with the participation of the leader of *Zeirei-Zion*. The conference lasted 10 days and nights at which a plan of activity was worked out. Abraham Grabaski (now in America), Kalman

Lubartowski, of blessed memory, Zeev Eizenberg (Barzeli) who perished in the waters of Yarkun near Tel Aviv and others were delegates to the *Zeirei-Zion* conference.

District Conference of "Zeirei-Zion" in Chelm in 1919

The first *Zeirei-Zion* organization in Poland was then created in Chelm. It is worth mentioning that the best known worker in *Zeirei-Zion* was the Chelemer Tomaszower Rebbe's daughter, Tziporah Najchaus, of blessed memory, who distinguished herself with ebullient initiative and theoretical knowledge.

After the *Zeirei-Zion* conference, we devoted all our energy to doing tangible work for *Eretz Yisroel* and to bettering the condition of Jews wherever they lived. We founded a Hebrew school system, which graduated hundreds of students, *folk-shuln*, kindergarten, cooperatives and other institutions. The *Zeirei-Zion* party planted roots in all the layers of Chelm society.

[Page 212]

With the start of the third *aleiyah* [immigration to Palestine], professional construction workers who were much needed in [*Eretz*] Yisroel] immigrated from Chelm. The Chelm immigrants the first construction workers in the country and dedicated their greatest strength and abilities in this area. The writer of these lines immigrated to Israel from Chelm with the first Chelemer *halutzim* [pioneers] group.

The *Zeirei-Zion* movement in Chelm devoted its greatest strength to the building up of the land and made a contribution on behalf of the national awakening of the people.

Managing Committee of the Zionist organization in Chelm – this photograph was taken on the occasion of the celebration of the Balfour Declaration

First row, sitting from right to left: Y. Wadzalowski (Hebrew teacher), Josef Beker Aryeih Milner, A. Arnsztajn and Yeshaya Arnsztajn
Second row, standing: M. Lang, M. Evri, Itshe Meir Lederman, Feiwel Alias, A. Halperin, A. Szener and A. Wajnsztajn

[Page 213]

The Revisionist Party

by Yehoshya Zilber, Tel Aviv

Translated by Gloria Berkenstat Freund

I took part in the Revisionist Party from 1932 until my departure for Israel, that is, until 1939. In 1939, the Revisionist Party had its greatest momentum.

The Chairman of the Party was then the advocate (lawyer) Rogak and the commander of *Betar* (*Brit-Trumpeldor*) was Sender Davidson, who is now in Israel.

The reason for the great momentum of the party in Chelm was understandable and natural because the young and the masses had already begun to understand that the Jews would not build a nation with the slogan, "not with soldiers and not with force, but through the spirit of labor," but "the state of Judea was felled by fire and blood and it will be resurrected by fire and blood." In this spirit, *Betar* began to give the young people military training, and *Betar* organized military courses for the liberation of the land.

The Chelemer *Betar* also created a *hachsharah* settlement on the estate of the landowners, Podczacki, under the direction of Commander Shlomoh Hercberg, who, together with Borukh Davidson, went to Israel in 1937 with a general *aleyah* from *Betar*. The same Shlomoh took part in the struggle against the Hitlerist beasts during the Second World War and today is an officer in the Israeli army. Borukh Davidson is now the instructor of the Israeli police.

The Chelemer *Betar* under my leadership, also in 1933, organized and carried out the boycott action against the movie theater owners for showing German films. The boycott action had the greatest results because the owners stopped showing German films and as a sign of remorse they gave a few hundred *zlotys* to the Passover collection for the poor.

The Revisionist Party, *Betar* and *Brit Hahayal* [Revisionist Party paramilitary organization], which we had just created, twice in the years 1933 and 1936, brought the great Revisionist leader, Ze'ev Jabotinsky, of blessed memory, to Chelm for two great political lectures. The city was transformed into one great demonstration for Zionist ideas during the days of his arrival and stay in Chelm. The days will always remain in the memories of the surviving Chelemer Jews around the world.

The Chelemer *Betar* also took part in the work of sending weapons to Israel, and three of the Chelemer *Betar* members were caught in such activities and were arrested. The three arrestees were the following: Moshe Szufl, Pinkhas Kolodny and I, the writer of these lines. The anti-Semitic organ, *Gonietz Warszawski*, published an incitement and my photograph during my trial, presenting me as the Jewish marshal in Poland and demanded a severe punishment for me.

Under my leadership, the Chelemer *Betar* also organized a self-defense [organization] that had to be ready in the event of a pogrom that the anti-Semites wanted to make on the Polish religious holiday of *Bosza Ciala* [Corpus Christi]. For three days and nights, *Betar* and *Brit Hahayal*, under my leadership, were armed and based in the Jewish clubs. The societies and *Makabi* club on Lubliner Street were ready to react to each attack. The Polish village chief, Woronowicz, learning of this, summoned me to him and said "I am very pleased that you are ready to protect yourself from sudden attack and I also ask you to join with the police, whom I have ordered to be in contact with you and to give their help if it is needed."

[Page 214]

After a conference between me and the police commander, I sent out patrols over all of the streets and alleys of the city. An armed *Betarist* or *Brit Hahayal* went with each policeman and thus the city was guarded against a pogrom.

In 1937, the Revisionist Party also published a weekly under my editorship with the name, *Der Nacionaler Wokhnblat* [*The National Weekly*].

How great the activity of the Revisionist Party was in Chelm is shown by the City Council elections in 1937. Out of a total of eight Jewish city councilmen, the Revisionist Party had four, and the only Jewish alderman – Abraham Szein; the left *Poale-Zion* – and the Zionist organization – one.

[Page 215]

In March 1939, when a secret military mobilization was decreed in Poland, I called together a meeting of the community workers in the auditorium of the Jewish community, warning them of the volcanic eruption, that we were up against and calling on the Chelemer Jews to take part in the great plan of the Revisionist Party: immediately, we were sending 100 thousand Jews to Israel against the wishes of England.

Alas, the volcanic eruption came before we expected and at the end of July, I and a ship of 875 people, organized by the *Irgun*, left Poland, and after six weeks of wandering from port to port, at the beginning of the war we arrived in Israel, where I and others were arrested immediately by the English. And after sitting in a concentration camp, Sarafend, for a short time, we were freed.

The national education of the *Betar*, *Brit Hayahal* and the Revisionist Party saw its first fruit in Israel.

The former commander of *Betar* in Chelm, Sender Davidson, who was already in the country in 1933, was the commander of the old city of Jerusalem during the unrest in the land in 1936-1939, where he and his *Betar* members protected the Jews from Arab ambushes.

In 1939 he also brought a ship of illegal Jews to Israel and was arrested. By 1944 he had served four years in the country and in South Africa for taking part in the underground work of *Irgun*, *Etzel* [acronym: *Irgun Tsvai Leumi* – National Military Organization].

I, the writer of these lines, was also arrested by the English for taking part in the struggle for the land of Israel and served in all of the Israeli prisons and also in all of the South African jails, where I was sent for about four years.

Top: – Revisionist movement in Chelm.
Reception for Ze'ev Jabotinsky [in center, left – Dr. Sakular]
Bottom: Jewish Betar members in uniform with weapons during a parade.

Y. Zilber at a mass meeting in Chelm in 1933 against the Hitlerist beasts

[Page 215]

Chelm for the Zbonsziner [Zbaszyner] Refugees

by B. Amindov

Translated by Gloria Berkenstat Freund

One night at the beginning of the winter of 1938, Hitler Germany expelled twenty thousand naked and barefoot Jews to Poland, to the *shtetl* Zbaszyn that was on the Polish[-German] border, because the Jews were of Polish origin.

Jewish society was struck by fear by the savagery and they organized widespread aid for the benefit of these refugees. A "Central Aid Committee for the Zbaszyner Refugees" was established.

Jewish Chelm joined this aid work, too. A conference took place in the meeting hall of the Chelm *kehile* at which representatives of all of the Jewish parties and organizations were present. A committee was elected consisting of the following: Dr. Josef Feldman (chairman), Yitzhak Szwarcman (secretary), Dr. Izrael Aks (treasurer), Friszman, Moshe Beker, Berl Liberman, Ben-Zion Bruker, Shlomohle Bursztajn, Shimeon Sajkowicz, Abrahamle Sztajnberg, Motl Goldman, Gershon Lustiker, Anshel Biderman, Hirszfeder, the attorney, Rabinowicz, the attorney, Mrs. Dr. Willenka, Mrs. Aks, Mrs. Feldman, Engineer Tenenboim and Councilman Goldberg.

An appeal went out to all religious Jews that was edited by Councilman Goldberg and Ben-Zion Bruker. This appeal had a warm response from all circles of the Jewish population in the city.

[Page 216]

Immediately, special meetings took place in the synagogues, organizations and parties that called on members to give extensive assistance to the Zbaszyner refugees.

The money collections in Chelm surpassed all expectations. Never before in Chelm had campaigns brought in as much income as the aid campaigns for the Zbabszyner refugees. Many Christians also contributed donations to the campaign.

The clothing campaigns that were headed by Mrs. Dr. Feldman[1] were particularly successful. Several women and female *gymnazie* students, working girls and students at *Beis Yakov* schools [religious school for girls] went together to collect clothing that was packed in boxes that were prepared by Basha Lerber's grandson. The boxes of clothing were sent very quickly to the Zbaszyn refugees.

The Chelemer *starost* [village chief] was not pleased that the Chelemer Jews had given such a large sum to the aid campaign and he tried to prevent the transfer of the money. However, an appropriate agency of the central committee of the government authorities prevailed so that the amount could be sent undisturbed.

The amount of money and clothing that Chelm sent for Zbonszin was substantial aid for the Zbaszyn refugees.

Translator's footnotes:

1. The use of Mrs. Dr. indicates that Mrs. Feldman was married to Dr. Feldman.

[Page 217]

The Scouts Organization

by W. Gotlib, Australia

Translated by Gloria Berkenstat Freund

It was the time of the First World War. The Austrians occupied Chelm. The committee of the recently organized Scouts organization consisted of the following people: J. Mandelboim, B. Luksenburg, M. Morgnsztern, J. Dreksler, M. Ebri, Herc Fiszlson, Sh. Beker, the writer of these lines and a few others, whom I no longer remember.

I was invited because I has been a member of *Hashomer* [Socialist-Zionist youth movement] in *Eretz-Yisroel* and it was calculated that I had work experience and I could help with the organizing of the Scouts organization in Chelm.

Young boys and girls of age nine or older were registered as Scouts with the permission of their parents and several groups were created. They held physical exercises, marches and outings. In addition, they were taught Jewish history, books were read to them and they learned Yiddish and Hebrew songs. Educational discussions were led with them and there was close contact with the parents who would be invited for consultations with the administration of the Scouts organization.

The children quickly learned the rules of sports discipline. They had special uniforms which delighted the children. They took great pleasure in singing songs and marching while singing.

The Scouts organization had a great influence on the Jewish population in Chelm.

The first public parade took place during a "Herzl celebration." The Scouts marched through Lubliner Street to the old historic synagogue in the finest order with resounding Yiddish and Hebrew songs, drawing the attention of Kolmus, the president of the Austrian City Hall, who sent out a patrol of Austrian soldiers to clear the way for the marching Scouts.

The Jewish population stood closely packed on the sidewalk, heartily and warmly greeting the marching children, accompanying them with long lasting applause and admiring how they went, so perfect and proud.

The streets and alleys next door to the old historic synagogue were overflowing with people. The doors of the synagogue opened and great streams of Jews pushed inside, occupying the women's section and the remaining synagogue rooms and entrance hall.

The memorial prayer for Dr. Theodore Herzl was eloquently given and the speakers were heard with the greatest attention… The Scouts and their leaders were passionately thanked by the crowd with expressions of appreciation to the young Scouts and the committee for their part in this memorial evening.

This event is also remembered:

Winter, after midnight. I hurried to go to a sick person who was under the medical supervision of the *Linas haTzedekh* [an organization to help the sick]. A thick wet snow was falling. On the way, I was stopped by an Austrian soldier and he led me away to the City Hall, where I had to wait until the morning. When Kolmus, president of the City Council, came and recognized me immediately, he strongly reproached the soldier, asking why he had detained me, the commandant of the Scouts.

Jewish Scouts division in Chelm in 1915
From the left in front is found W. Gotlib, commandant of the Scouts movement

[Page 219]

* * *

The outings with the Scouts were a substantial part of our program of activities.

The outings would regularly last from early in the morning until the evening and took place in the Hrubieszower or in the Rejowiecer Woods. Sometimes the outings would last a full two days. Our goal was to harden the young children to various circumstances and make them independent of their parents, although for a short time.

At first, mainly the mothers were uneasy that their children were being taken and they were being led to the woods and fields. The leaders would have an answer for such troubled mothers, explaining that we should be relied on and that they should believe in the good results of the methods of the Scouts organization.

The young Scouts would come together very early at dawn, at 5 o'clock. All were happily playful and the children marched with firm and sure steps through the streets of Chelm that were still enveloped in early morning fog and empty of people. Everywhere, we noticed craftsmen going to work, still with sleep on their eyelashes, and women and children looked out of the windows. The singing of the children and the orders of the leaders: "One, two, three, four" – echoed in the quiet morning…

We stopped outside the city, in the lap of the meadows and fields, in order to eat breakfast. Each little Scout had a stick and during a rest they would be stood together in the same way that soldiers stand their guns.

The path through the aromatic fields and through the trees in the forest was leisurely, and we went along carefree until we came to the appointed spot.

The Scouts worked industriously like bees setting up the tents with the greatest precision. Fires were lit and kettles of water were set up to boil. The ruck-sacks were opened wide to take out the food that was brought along.

Each day that we were on the outings with the children was unforgettable. The birds warbled and flew from tree to tree. The children did the same thing, with their songs echoing in the woods. They moved freely and played football [soccer].

When they became tired from various games and sports exercises, they lay on the soft grass. Several of the children fell asleep and several were drawn to sweet melodies and listened to the stories of Sholem Aleichem and Y.L. Peretz that we read aloud for them.

When twilight fell and the evening and night came, we sat by the fire. The children told each other

[Page 220]

all kinds of episodes and stories, about various events and developments. In the night shadows of the forest, one child huddled against another and they connected in an intimate closeness and strong friendship.

The young Scouts stood watch during the night just as in military situations and this song echoed here and there in the surrounding quiet:

> Go to sleep my dear son,
> Listen to the song (that I will sing to you)
> In distant places many years ago
> There was a city…

The night disappears. The morning stars appear and the blue bright light shoots up. The sun appears and it becomes lighter and lighter.

A signal from the leaders is heard: *Kumu, kumu*. A movement, like disciplined soldiers; the children run out of their tents and we go to the crystal-clear well water to wash ourselves.

According to the daily plan, seven o'clock was the time for breakfast and the work continued until night.

It also happened that the sky would be enveloped with clouds and a pouring rain would descend. However, the leaders' plan would not change because our motto was to harden ourselves in the worst weather and in the most difficult situations.

* * *

Our Scouts organization developed quickly and was well appreciated in the neighboring cities. Reciprocal visits by the Scouts organizations would take place very often.

A conference of the Jewish Scouts organizations took place in Warsaw. I was sent to the conference on behalf of our Scouts organization. Since the First World War had not yet ended, I needed an illegal pass to Warsaw, which was under German occupation.

Several hundred representatives came to this gathering that was opened with our national hymn, *Hatikvah*. And when the chairman announced the agenda of the conference, the Wilhelm German occupiers entered and dissolved the conference.

Then consultations were held and a central administration was chosen.

I then left the Chelemer Scouts organization for ideological reasons. As thanks, the Scout gave me the following gift: a Scout knife with a bone handle and the knife case was silver. On the case was sewn the emblem of the Scouts and the inscription: strength and truth.

This gift was very dear to me and in 1920, when I left for *Eretz-Yisroel*, my leave taking with the Chelemer Scouts was very touching.

[Page 221]

Chelm, An Old, Beautiful Jewish Town

by B. Binsztok, New York

Translated by Gloria Berkenstat Freund

Chelm is an old Jewish city.

Chelm is well known in all Jewish communities. The name "Chelm" brings a smile or hearty laughter to Jews everywhere.

Chelm is a magnificent, beautiful city, built in the bosom of an amazing, beautiful high mountain. The Bug River, where the Curzon Line became famous as the boundary between the Soviet Union and Poland, lies a 20 minute train ride from the eastern side of the mountain.

Hundreds of thousands of genuine Russian and Ukrainian peasants and their wives and children would travel together (the czar provided free trains) to a three-day holiday every year at the end of summer, in order to drink the water from the "holy wells" on the mountain. They would also drink tea and snack on rolls at the Jewish *tishlek* [small tables] that were put out in the hundreds in all of the streets in the city. The last czar, Nikolai [Nicholas II], was present at these ceremonies in Chelm several times.

The overseer of the mountain with its "holy wells" and over all of the holy *pravoslawne* [Russian orthodox] learning institutions was the mournful, well known *pravoslawner*, Jepiskop [Father] Jewlogi, Rasputin's right hand. He was very much concerned with the Russification of the Chelemer area. Chelm and the entire area were supposed to become a pure Russian *gubernia* [province]. However, the First World War undid the plan, from which remained government buildings that had been begun or completed; the Jews renovated these into housing.

The *pravoslawner*, Father Jewlogi, or as the Jews of Chelm would call him, "*Zawali Drogi* [*zawalidrogi* – idler or loafer in Polish]," made a very great effort to lead the Jewish population onto the "right path," too, and, particularly the young Jews during the stormy years of 1905-1906. He would call quiet meetings with city businessmen, demanding that the Jews keep an eye on the young people who need to go on the "right path and, chiefly, to esteem and love the czar. The businessmen would promise him. And when they went with the wide steps down from the mountain, they would hear the thundering voice of Meir, son of Raub'ele Szakher, a baker, then a Bundist. (Today he is in New York. His name is Meir Celnik; he is no longer a Bundist, but a very sympathetic class conscious bakery worker.) His voice rose, called and damned "the bloody animal with its bloody nails." This was the title of the last Czar Nikolai. Later, Meir Chelemer left Chelm to the relief of the well-to-do in the city.

Ben Binsztok

[Page 222]

The "mountain" provided many Jews in the city with income. Ten thousand blond *pravoslawner* clerical students, male and female, lived in Chelm at the expense of the Czarist government. The Jews in Chelm provided food and clothing – the most beautiful and best.

The father of a *khazan* [cantor] in New York had a "contract" to repair and make new boots for the students. He was named Reb Melekh Hersh. He was Jew – a stately person, trustee of the *khevre kadishe* [burial society] and very respected in the city. If a poor man, may this never happen to you, lay ill for weeks and months, his neighbors would "call in" Reb Melekh Hersh. They would wait near the door, wringing their hands and with their eyes turned toward heaven, they would wish: "*Oy*, may he be the good angel!" Reb Melekh Hersh, a very reticent person, would try to save the poor man with his own remedies. First, he brushed his throat with his usual brush, a thick hard twig from a broom with a piece of cotton from an old jacket, bound to the tip with cobbler's thread and dipped in vitriol. Afterward, he took the temperature with his thermometer and then, right after this, placed a feather under the nose…

Tailors had the contract to repair and make new, beautiful fitted uniforms. Butchers provided good, fat, unroasted forequarters. And other Jews in the city provided all other needed products and food.

In Chelm, *l'havdil* [word used to separate the religious from the secular, the Jewish from the non-Jewish] there were *pravoslawner* churchs with holy wells, houses of prayer, Hasidic *shtiblekh* [houses of prayer], where young men enthusiastically studied.

The walls of the Chelemer synagogue, with the hidden grave of the bride and groom who perished while standing under the *khupah* [wedding canopy] in the synagogue courtyard at the hands of Chmelnitski's Haidamacks [rebelling Ukrainian peasants who massacred Jews in 1648], describe the sad Jewish history of hundreds of years.

Culturally, Chelm was on a high level. Two weekly Yiddish newspapers were published, a Zionist and a populist. There was a Yiddish and a Hebrew library, later, also an eight-grade Hebrew school that Moshe Fiszelson (died four years ago in New York) ardently helped build and then fought for its support by the Chelemer *landsleit* in America.

There were parties, secret and open, in Chelm Jewish circles, where all Zionist and Socialist opinions were enrolled and presented. Chelm had a distinguished Jewish working class that took an active part in the liberation struggle against the Russian Czar and later against the fascist forces in the Polish government. The Chelemer Jewish intellectuals and class conscious workers were always found in the first ranks of the struggle. Many of them today occupy responsible positions in the Soviet Union and in *Eretz-Yisroel*. Many fell on the battlefield in the struggle for freedom.

[Page 223]

Shlomoh Elboim, the 23-year old son of a bread baker in Chelm, whom the Polish anti-Semitic government held and tortured, together with many, many thousands of other Jewish workers in the Polish concentration camps and jails, escaped to Paris where he joined the "Botwin" Company and went to Spain to fight against Hitler, Franco and Mussolini. He threw a fear into the fascist bands in Spain with his fearlessness. He received the rank of an officer for his heroism. As the chief of a machine gun division, he would always maneuver to have his position behind the enemy lines. He fell on the battlefield just two days before the "Botwin" Company returned from the front to be dissolved.

In 1920 when the Red Army entered the city, Berl Zeidenberg, a watchmaker in Chelm, joined them to struggle against the Polish "ladies" who first declared war against young and weak Bolshevik Russia with the lying pretext of "saving Western civilization."

Berl Zeidenberg fell on the battlefield in Kiev.

Shmuel Zigelboim (Arthur), whom the Bund in New York sent as a representative to the Polish government in exile in London and who so tragically perished, committing suicide, took his first steps at the very beginning of his *Bundist* party work in 1916 in Chelm. He was born and raised in a village near Krasnystaw, not far from Chelm. As a result, he knew the Polish language very well, which he polished still more in Warsaw, where he worked before the First World War as a cane maker.

In 1916 the Bund founded the "workers' home" in Chelm and Sh. Zigelboim was appointed as the economic manager. Jewish workers would come there in the evening – to read a newspaper, a book, to hear lectures, attend concerts, entertainments and similar undertakings.

The impression remains in my memory of a *Bundist* mass meeting in Chelm that took place at the very end of the First World War.

The Austrian monarchy had collapsed and the Austrian occupation regime ran away and left Chelm abandoned. The Germans were still in Warsaw and in the surrounding cities and *shtetlekh* to Demblin – the border between Austria and the German area of occupation.

Chelm became a world unto its own: the telegraph, the telephone, railroad traffic ceased. Disquieting rumors spread: one heard and then saw… Jews in Chelm in fear of death… Suddenly, there appears on the street of Chelm an appeal: the *Bund* calls all of the Jews in Chelm to a mass meeting in the great Chelm synagogue.

[Page 224]

The frightened Jews stood head to head in the synagogue, one pressed to the other, like herring in a barrel. The synagogue has a high ceiling around 50 feet high – this helped with breathing a little.

A crack of a special "rattle" that was on the reading stand was heard. It became dead silent…

The *Bundist* leaders spoke, one after the other, about the crash of the Austrian-Hungarian monarchy and about the winds of freedom. Shmuel Zigelboim spoke last. His voice was then more beautiful, clearer than the last time when I heard him speak, several years ago, at the forum of the International Garment Workers Union in New York. Here, in the great Chelemer synagogue, he called out, pointing with his left hand to the western side of the synagogue: "There, there, there the sun is rising!"… Jews looked at each other and asked: "What does he mean?"

In the morning, after the mass meeting, the Chelemer Jews found out what Zigelboim meant: the first Polish independent government was founded in Lublin which is located to the west of Chelm. [Jedrzej] Moraczewski, the *pepesowetz* (Polish Socialist), stood at the head of the government.

Then came other governments: reactionary, anti-Semitic. [Wladislaw] Grabski came and brought ruin to a large part of the Jewish population.

The Jews of Chelm, as in all of Poland, had to accept one Polish cabinet and *Sejm* [Polish parliament] after another and the next was always worse than the last. The famous Jewish historian, Dr. Yitzhak Sziper, may he rest in peace, who perished *Al Kiddush HaShem* [In the sanctification of God's name] at the hands of Hitler's beasts, was chosen as the deputy in the *Sejm* from Chelm.

Jewish Chelm, in the years before the Polish fascist rule, fought with tooth and nail to repel the hard attacks, the bitter edicts and decrees from the government that aimed to weaken and to exhaust the Jews in Chelm and their institutions that were built with so much self sacrifice and devotion.

The Chelemer *landsleit* in America and Canada, the majority of whom were concentrated in New York, Chicago and Montreal, helped with sums of money in order to alleviate the need and poverty that increased particularly in the years 1936-1939 because of the policies of the anti-Semitic fascist Polish government.

The difficult economic life of the Jews in Chelm lasted until 1939. The war brought still more suffering. Hitler attacked Poland and the Polish government with Josef Bek at the head escaped to Romania. The Red Army came to Chelm. However it was only there 11 days. The Soviet commandant received an order to withdraw to the eastern side of the Bug River, about a 20 minute journey by train from Chelm. There days earlier, before the Red Army left Chelm, it turned in particular to the Jewish population with a call: "Jews take your wives and children, take your old men, take your bedding, take everything that you can and come to us. We will give you trains, trucks, wagons and horses; we will help you – come with us because the Nazis are murdering all of the Jews everywhere and they are coming!

[Page 225]

The Jews in the city, with Biderman, the head of the *kehile*, in the lead, held a meeting and decided that: "We are not going, we are not traveling" because "our great grandfathers and we all were born here, lived our entire lives here – where will we go now?"

There were Jews who did not agree with the decision of the meeting and went to Russia with the Red Army. The vast majority, however, remained in Chelm and were murdered by Hitler's beasts. Only a few, miraculously, survived.

[Page 226]

Chelm, the old, beautiful Jewish city was totally destroyed.

Hitler installed the Sobibor death camp near Chelm, where the last remaining Jews in the camp rose in revolt against the executioners. Several hundred Jews saved themselves. The city of Chelm was given the honor that on the same day that the Red Army drove out the accursed Nazis from Chelm, the "Polish Committee of National Liberation" proclaimed from Chelm, "Democratic freedom and equality for all citizens, without distinction as to race, religion or national origin," and that "Jews must receive legal and actual equality in the new Poland."

[Page 225]

How the "Peretz Library" Was Created

by Itshe Akhtman, Montreal, Canada

Translated by Gloria Berkenstat Freund

When I saw the book, "A Thousand Years of Pinsk" and other *yizkor* [memorial] books, I thought, is there someone who will publish a *yizkor* book dedicated to our city, Chelm. To immortalize the memory of the nearly 20,000 Jews who lived there.

There is not another city in the world that was as well known as Jewish Chelm. Let it be celebrated. A world of literature was written about it. Why should this city, after its great destruction, become silent?

However, when I noticed the appeal in the Jewish press of the Chelemer Aid Union in Johannesburg about publishing a *yizkor* book dedicated to Chelm, various remembrances about the city began to swim up. The closest to me and the most beloved of all of the memories was the cultural life in Chelm from the First World War, 1914. I want to record several facts and information here about one cultural body in our city, the Peretz Library, with which I had close contact.

It was in the summer of 1914, right after the outbreak of the war. At that time, the German and Austrian troops were chasing the czar's army. The Russians had already left Zamoscz (Peretz's birthplace) that lies not far from Chelm. We were a small group of young men from a *shtibl* [small house of prayer] who sat in the *shtibl* and looked out at the Germans impatiently. Naïve small *shtetl* fantasies soared with us, that each German is a Goethe, a Nietzsche or a Thomas Mann.

[Page 226]

At that time, while the artillery shells still resounded, the group of naïve *shtibl* youth only thought about establishing a Jewish library, fantasies of Jewish youth in Polish *shtetlekh* that became reality.

It was summer, 1915, the Germans grabbed civilians on the streets for work. We were a group of young friends who hid in an uncompleted building on Szedecka Street. Lying in that hiding place in great fear, the idea to establish the Peretz Library was born in us.

Itshe Akhtman

Receipt from a collection that was carried out on behalf of the Peretz Library in Chelm, in 1927

[Page 227]

It was decided that each of the group would give 10 rubles. We collected 250 rubles and immediately contacted two publishers in Warsaw that sent catalogues and wished us luck.

At that time, Warsaw was separated from Chelm by a border. Chelm belonged to Austria and Warsaw to the Germans; we had to smuggle the books from Warsaw to Chelm. There was no civilian train traffic then. Smugglers traveled in wagons and carried goods from Chelm to Warsaw and back. We gave such a smuggler the collected 250 rubles with a list to buy a number of Yiddish books. The "trip" to Warsaw then took 10-12 days and after great difficulties and hardships, we received the books. There was unlimited joy.

We rented a small room and each shareholder had to give one evening a week to serve as a librarian. The books had to have literary worth. Subscriptions began to increase. We had more readers than books. The room became crowded; new readers came every day, and simply, one needed influential intervention to become a reader.

We began to look for a larger meeting place for the library because of the growing number of readers, and for money to buy new books. At that time an old house stood empty on Badowska Street. The owner, Josele, was away in Russia and, at that time, he and his entire family perished at the hands of the Ukrainians during the pogroms. We moved the library to this house.

[Page 228

Because the expenses were greater and money was needed, the Peretz Library decided to create a musical and dramatic section that from time to time arranged performances, concerts and other social events that helped the growth of the library.

The Peretz Library was of great importance in the city at that time. Many of the young Chelemer Jews received a cultural education thanks to it.

However, the vast Holocaust destroyed everything including the Peretz Library that was created by the young Chelmer Jews, ambitious young fanatics with great hopes and belief

№ 3

„פרץ ביבליאטעק"

כערם.

ה׳

האט בעצאהלט זיין מיטגליערס

אבצאהר

כערם, דעם ___ 191

פארזיצענדער

סעקרעטאר

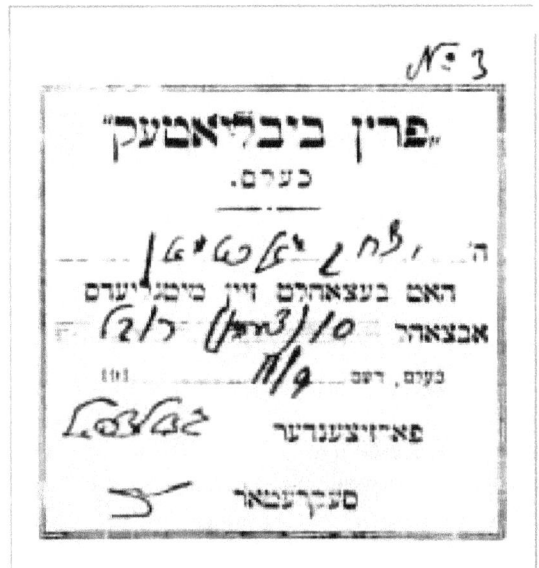

Receipt for member dues for the Peretz Library

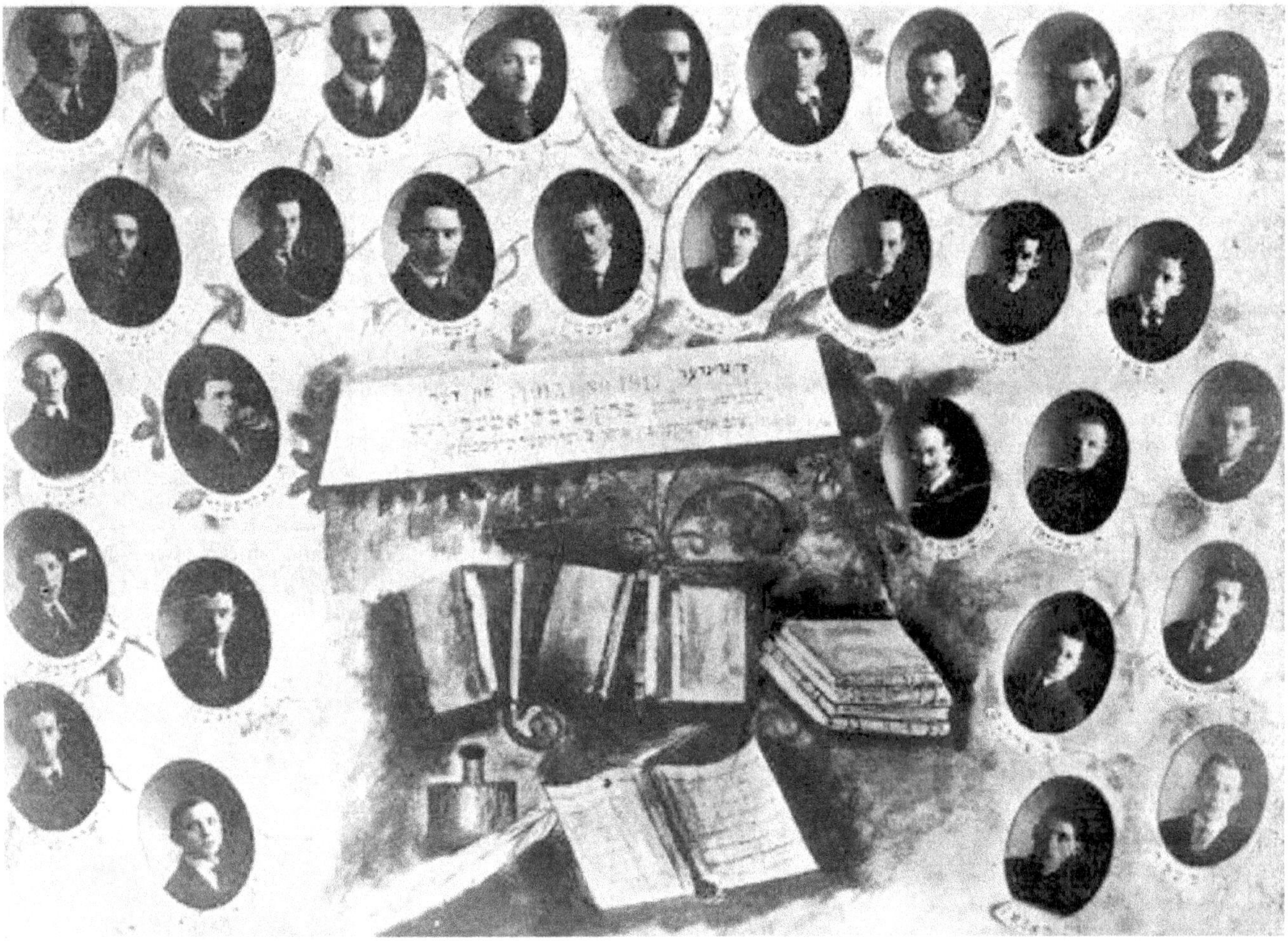

The founders of the Peretz Library in Chelm (1915-1917)

[Page 229]

Yiddish Theater

by Itshe Akhtman, Canada

Translated by Gloria Berkenstat Freund

In about 1910-1914, amateurs began to perform Yiddish theater. At first, they produced J. Gordon's plays. In as much as the amateur ensemble at first consisted principally of those who had been captured by tendencies toward assimilation and spoke more Russian than Yiddish at home, the first performances were weak. There were amateurs who did not even understand the text of the plays. Later, these circles were enlarged by the general public and workers.

At this opportunity, it also must be remembered that in 1909-1910 a young man from Chelm named Abraham Diker (Fitshke's son) who had musical and theatrical abilities gathered children 10-15 years of age and presented Goldfaden's *Akeydes Yitzhak* [*The Sacrifice of Isaac*].

The performance with the children and with amateurs under the direction of Abraham Diker had great success and was performed in Chelm's largest theater, *Sirena*, and, also in Zamocsz, Hrubieszow and in other cities.

In 1915, after the occupation by the German-Austrian powers, a musical-dramatic section was created of young men and girls, who had the insight and taste for music and literature. Those families with musical abilities were: Luksenburg, Ilywicki; the Herc family had artistic abilities.

The above mentioned section presented the plays of Sholom Alecheim, Peretz Hirshbein, Dovid Pinski, Fishl Bimko, A. Gordon and so on.

Conditions were difficult for Yiddish theater under the German-Austrian occupation. It was necessary to apply great energy in negotiating the receipt of permission from the occupying forces to present theater. In addition, there was fear, in general, of gathering in one place or walking the streets, people fearing that they would be taken for forced labor.

[Page 230]

But risks were taken and Yiddish theater was presented. All of the seats in the large galleries of the *Sirena Theater* were occupied when a Yiddish theater presentation or a musical-artistic evening took place.

* * *

The Yiddish theater developed robustly after the war. Artistic vitality in Chelm increased and famous Jewish artists from abroad and from larger Polish cities would visit Chelm very often.

Dramatic Circle in Chelm

Text of Poster:

Program:

Tuesday, on the 20th of the month, one performance presented by local art lovers will take place under the title

Sholom Aleichem Evening
with the following program:

1) A memorial service presented by the choir

2) *Tsezeht Un Tseshpreht* [*Scattered Far and Wide*]
Comical picture in three acts by Sholom Aleichém

Cast

Meir Szalant	Mr. M. Boim
Talcha his wife	Miss R. Herc
Flora	Miss M. Feder
Motvej	Mr. B. Naturman
Haim	Mr. Sh. Brekher
Valadji	Mr. D. Herc
Hana	Miss Sh. Alergand
Moshka	B. Herc
Moshe Zajensztater – Szalanter's in-law	Mr. A. Cikel
Itela his wife	Miss T. Herc
Pesela, poor relative	Miss Sh. Helfer
Dowid'le, Matvei's friend	Mr. G Herc
Beni with a parasol	Mr. Y. Akhtman
Masha, a maid	Miss T. Herc

3) *Agenten* [*Agents*]
A comedy in one act of Sholom Aleichem

Cast

Menakhem Mendil, seller of *Shabbos* candles and wine	Mr. A. Cikel
Mark Lamternisher	B. Naturman
Akim Bakfisz	Y. Akhtman
Lazar Terkeltoib	M. Boim

and 4) The Poet's Own Songs
Prompter Kh. Feder Arranger Y. Akhtman
Printer M. Wajnsztajn, Chelm

Facsimile of a Poster

[Pages 231-232]

Facsimiles of various programs from the Yiddish theater, performed by amateur efforts in Chelm

Facsimile of a Poster

A play performed by the local amateurs in the years 1920-1921

Theater hall, "Polanya," one of the local theater halls where Yiddish theater and Yiddish lectures were often presented. The building was built by the German occupying government during the years 1916-1917.

[Page 233]

About Posters in Yiddish at the First Anniversary of the Death of Sholem Aleichem

by Berl Naturman, Canada

Translated by Gloria Berkenstat Freund

In 1916, *Poalei Zion* [Marxist Zionists] already had its own choir, orchestra and a dramatic society.

When it was learned that the great Yiddish classical writer and brilliant humorist, Sholem Aliechem, had died, we, the dramatic society, decided to stage his play, *Tsezeyt un Tseshpreyt* [*Scattered and Dispersed*] at the *shloshim* [30th day after a person's death] of his death. We rehearsed intensely then at the Toybele Herc's house from 10 o'clock in the morning until the start of the evening because we were not supposed to be in the street at night.

We ordered posters from Wajnsztajn's print shop several days before the 16th of May, when the memorial evening for Sholem Aleichem was to take place.

Every public advertisement or announcement had to be shown to the county commandant according to the law of the occupying regime to receive approval from the commandant before it could be published.

Suddenly Mr. Wajnsztajn out of breath came running from the commandant to us with the news that they would not let us publish the posters unless we remove the Yiddish text.

However, we could not permit ourselves to dishonor Sholem Aleichem's name and not use any Yiddish text.

I, the writer of these lines, Itshe Actman and Avraham Honig went to Anshl Biderman to help us in some way. We gave Biderman a complete lecture about Sholem Aleichem's creations for the masses. However, he stood up and said: "Gentlemen, do not use any "foreign words" with me. I cannot persuade anyone because a law is a law."

We remained puzzled as if bathed in a cold shower. There remained for us only to say good night and leave.

When we reached the street we again began to think about what to do. One of us said that maybe we should go to the commandant ourselves and try to explain to him the significance of the evening and so on. We three all looked and without spelling out things immediately agreed that we would do this and we really did go straight to the commandant.

The commandant's headquarters was near the Russian cathedral where we had to pass a separate guard and identify ourselves. Two private secretaries sat in the entry-room to the commandant's office, who did not permit entry to both those with special, important assignments or with high recommendations as to their political legitimacy. In addition, they had to show precisely what it was a question of, so that. God forbid, the master would not be disturbed with superfluous matters.

Hearing why we had come, the other one entered a terrible fury, understand that such rascals as we dared to disturb the commandant with such an unimportant trifle. The commandant to complete such important matters, such as supervising the royal and imperial city matters and do we not know that his majesty is involved in a bloody war with Russia on so on and so on. With luck one of the secretaries also was an amateur actor who had appeared several times with Polish amateur societies, and had really excelled in the role of the father in a play by [Stanisław] Przybyszewski. He interceded for us and said that he himself would enter the office of the commandant and if he found him in a good mood would ask him to welcome us.

We waited and the few minutes seemed to us like an eternity. We were afraid that he would send up away to forced labor or even worse, that we would be honored with a portion of blows from which we already felt the pain as well as the shame. While we stood so despondent and already having regret for the entire matter, the office door suddenly opened and no other than the commandant himself appeared, taller, thinner, clean shaven, the Count Pan Żaba and with an almost unfortunate helpfulness invited us into his office and he turned to us and he asked the secretary to have us state what this was about.

Understand that we did not take long to answer and we stated what this was about, that we were leading a gathering for the great Sholem Aleichem who had died not long ago and as he was a great Yiddish poet who always wrote for the Jewish people, it would be a great dishonor for him if the poster was not printed in the language in which he created. And we brought him proof and citations from Heine, Geothe and Börne and others and looking over everything with the secretary who shook his head in agreement at what we said. He suddenly turned to us in an affable tone he said: "You have permission. I will be at the performance myself."

We remained standing in bewilderment, as if forged to the earth, no being able to understand what had happened here. However, the secretary came to our aid and as if we had awakened from sleep let us know that the audience was over and we had permission to print the poster in Yiddish, too. Thus did we, young men, unconsciously and unknowing that we were Yiddishists in the present sense of the world, winning a great victory for Yiddish.[1]

Translator's footnote:

1. A Yiddishist is a person who advocates for the use of Yiddish and for Yiddish culture.

[Page 235]

The *Poalei-Zion* Faction in the Chelm City Council

by Yakov Beker, Israel

Translated by Gloria Berkenstat Freund

The City Council was a communal platform in the true sense of the word. There were representatives in the City Council representing all political parties and communal groupings from Jewish and Polish society. The struggle of the opposing interests of these groupings was mirrored on the dais of the City Council.

Poalei-Zion was represented with a large faction from 1927 until the devastation of Chelm in 1939. During this period, elections took place three times and each time they came out stronger and with more support. The first City Council election took place in 1919. Because, Chelm had a Jewish majority, there was a "danger" that the City Council would have a Jewish majority. This caused great aggravation for the anti-Semitic supervisory regime. In the first City Council, *Poalei-Zion* was represented by Dr. Moshe Kanfer. The threat of a Jewish majority was avoided by a simple means: it was decided to annex the surrounding villages, such as Bazylany, Majdan, Wygun and Nowiny (a little village five km from Chelm). Thus, Chelm became a "real Polish city."

Nevertheless the peasants from the little villages complained that they had to pay more taxes. However, it was clarified for them that they were fulfilling "an important national mission."

An exceptionally intensive election campaign was carried out during the voting for the City Council on the 11th of November 1927.

Scores of gatherings, meetings and rallies were organized in the city's largest ballrooms on the part of *Poalei-Zion*. Representatives of the parties, the unions and the most active workers from *Tz. K.* [*Tzukunft* – Future] would appear at the rallies.

Poster from the Bund and Poalei-Zion painted on a wall during an election campaign for the Chelm City Council

[Page 236]

The day of the election was a true mobilization of the entire *Poalei-Zion* multitudes, of the "youth," "jamborees of scouts" and the *P.Z.* comrades from the surrounding *shtetlekh*. The election brought a victory for *Poalei-Zion*, having received 1,054 votes and electing three Councilmen: Mordekhai Erwi, Moshe Beker and Ahron Hipszman. Shmuel Szimel took the place of Erwi when he was chosen as an alderman and, later, he was replaced by Shmuel Barg.

The general results of the election were as follows:

Poalei-Zion (Left)	1,054 votes	3 seats
(M. Erwi, A.D. Hipszman and M. Beker)		
Tzeri-Zion	319 votes	1 seat
(Lazar Lederman)		
Bund	307 votes	1 seat
(Hershl Fructgartn)		
The Jewish "Red"	287 votes	1 seat
(The list was invalidated)		
Artisans	585 votes	1 seat
(Israel Bursztin)		
Jewish National Bloc	1,349 votes	4 seats
(Yakov Sztul, Y. M. Lederman, Yitzhak Bukhna and Finkelsztajn)		
Total Jewish Vote	3,901 votes	10 seats
Polish Civil Bloc	1,777 votes	6 seats
P.P.S.	2,559 votes	8 seats
Total	**8,237 votes**	**24 seats**

From the results shown above, it can be seen that the Polish workers in Chelm, the *P.P.S.* [Polish Socialist Party], scored a victory, too, receiving eight councilmen as opposed to six Civil. There was an ability to create a socialist city council and to run the city economy in the interest of the working masses from both populations [Jewish and Polish]. However, the Jewish and Polish workers received no satisfaction from the socialism of the *P.P.S.* The *P.P.S.* faction often joined the rightist Polish reactionary bloc.

At the first session of the newly elected City Council, the Town Council of five men was chosen: President – St. Gut; Vice President – Terfitz (both from *P.P.S.*); Alderman – Mordekhai Erwi and Feiwl Rozenblat (both proposed by *Poalei-Zion*) and one Alderman from the Polish Civil Club. Due to the protest of the rightist Polish Club, with the support of the Jewish Nat. Club, the election of the aldermen was invalidated. And at the second session of the City Council, it was shown that, in such a short time, the *P.P.S.* had gained complete control of the bloc, and with their votes, the Polish right received two aldermen and Jewish Chelm remained with one Alderman – *Poalei-Zion* representative, M. Erwi.

[Page 237]

The *Poalei-Zion* councilmen were presented with a very difficult test; in order to take a position on all of the city council business they had to have knowledge of the questions of the city economy, budget and other very complicated problems.

However, the three *Poalei-Zion* councilmen were simple workers, had never even visited a middle school and had not properly mastered the Polish language. At first, professors, teachers, high officials from the rightist Polish bloc would look with mockery at the three men who did not fit at all into their group. The Polish anti-Semitic intelligencia would scoff because our councilmen spoke a Polish full of errors. In time this attitude changed. They were quickly persuaded that they had before them serious and uncompromising men; mockery against them did not help, nor flattery and they could not be frightened by threats.

It can be asserted with full reliability that there was no field that concerned the life of Jewish workers or any of the painful problems of Jewish national and social life that the *P.Z.* councilmen did not bring to the forum of the City Council. The *P.Z.* learned about the needs of the Jewish people in daily life. They described this need with their entire power on the dais of the City Council.

The former mockers noticed with amazement how the *P.Z.* councilmen began to show proficiency and insight about the most entangled questions of city economics, finances, the school and hospital systems, and so on.

The first clash came at the first solemn session (after the election for the City Council). At this session the representatives of various factions read their ideological declarations that were heard by everyone present. The representative of the *P.Z.* faction had just begun to read their declaration. At first, he read in the Polish language and then immediately changed to Yiddish. The Polish rightist councilmen began a dejected uproar. They would not permit such a "desecration." The chairman, the *peposovyetz* [word derived from initials of the Polish Socialist Party – *P.P.S.*] Gut, interrupted the speaker, demanding that he leave the podium. He did not move from his place and ended his reading to the accompaniment of screams. He demonstrated in the open the struggle that *P.Z.* carried out for the rights of the Jewish masses; for the right of the Yiddish language. This was the first, but not the last stormy session of the Chelemer City Council.

The "ardent" sessions would take place when the yearly budgets would be dealt with for the city. During the discussion of finances and taxes, the *P.Z.* councilmen would demand that everyone living in only one room with a kitchen be freed from housing taxes; that the shopkeepers and artisans, who had licenses in the 4th and 8th categories, be freed from business taxes. They publicly came out against taxing cultural undertakings. Conversely, they would make motions to in- crease the taxes of the well-to-do, of the owners of large enterprises and large houses and to increase luxury taxes and so on.

[Page 238]

In dealing with the medical and hospital systems, the *P.Z.* councilmen demanded full free care for the poor population. The *P.Z.* sharply protested against the particularly warm relations with the privileged neighborhoods in which the rich lived and against the step-motherly relations with the poor quarters in questions concerning the development of the city. Speaking about the Jewish institutions like the Jewish public school, libraries, *TOZ* [Society for the Protection of Health], *Linas HaTzedek* [institution for assisting the sick], and so on, the *P.Z.* councilmen would just indicate that the existence of the institutions was a witness to the depravations of the Jews because as citizens of the country they, of necessity, carried the burden of all of the expenses in the country. Therefore, it was the obligation of the state to take upon itself the full support of all of the institutions. Thus, they would make motions that the City Council should turn to the government about taking over the expenditures of all of the institutions and until this happened, the City Council must properly subsidize all of the institutions.

The motions did not always have the same fate. The greater number would be rejected by the majority. Certain motions would be accepted. In the course of the first term of the City Council, the Town Council carried out a series of measures that were accepted positively by the surrounding population. The *P.P.S.* found themselves under strong pressure by the *P.Z.* councilmen and the *Poalei-Zion* alderman. Polish workers were frequent visitors in the gallery of the City Council and would listen attentively to the utterances of the *P.Z.*, and the *P.P.S.* often found themselves in an uncomfortable position. During the first term there was a successful fight for a series of grants for the Jewish institutions.

The *P.Z.* faction was in constant contact with its voters. There was an active faction office. The councilmen and Alderman Erwi would receive clients three times a week. The office was overflowing with Jewish artisans, poor shopkeepers, workers and women during the reception hours. They would submit pleas about taxes, about support; complaining about injustices against them on the part of certain officials. In great part, workers who had certain matters to discuss and not having any patience to wait until they would be received in the office would search for the councilmen at their workplaces or simply in the middle of the street and give their requests or complaints…

The *Poalei-Zion* faction would take positions from the podium of the City Council not only on local matters, but also regarding all events of general political life in the world and in the country.

When the bloody unrest broke out in 1929 in *Eretz-Yisroel* – provoked by the English – *Poalei-Zion* demanded that the City Council protest against English imperialism and grant 500 *gildn* to the Jewish victims. On 10/11/1929 a solemn session of the City Council took place dedicated to the 10th anniversary of Poland's independence. The presidium of the City Council wanted only to utilize the celebration for a ceremony and endeavored that no separate faction could express itself. However, *Poalei-Zion* would not yield its right. They read a declaration in which, among other things, they declared: "At every opportunity, the Jews of Poland contributed to the struggle that the Polish people carried out for their liberation.

[Page 239]

"Today the Polish landowners and capitalists have the power and not the Polish workers and peasants; the Jewish masses are without rights. Therefore, we will carry the struggle further until the final goal of socialism." *P.Z.* would read similar declarations at every appropriate opportunity. These "demonstrations" would create a great deal of bitter blood among the reactionary councilmen.

P.Z. would call frequent meetings at which reports would be given about their activities and all of the city's economic business would be discussed. There were enough stormy sessions, both of the City Council and the Town Council, and intense work was carried out. Scores and scores of motions were proposed by the *Poalei-Zion* councilmen and the *Poalei-Zion* alderman, and they courageously fought for them.

The Work of *Poalei-Zion* Alderman Erwi in the Chelemer Town Council

Mordekhai Erwi joined the *P.Z.* Party in 1927. He was in his blossoming years and demostrated energy and initiative as well as intelligence and education, and was thus accepted by *P.Z.* with great satisfaction because such people were much needed at that time. Therefore, it is understandable that when *P.Z.* had the possibility of having a representative in the Chelemer Town Council, they believed that Erwi would be the most suitable candidate for the office. At the first session of the newly elected city government, Erwi was given control of the finance department. It is hard to know if this was by chance or with a purpose. It is a fact that he was given the most difficult department with the most responsibility. He had to take care of the finances of the city while simultaneously representing the poorest section of the population.

M. Erwi actively began to study his new assignment in order to be able to use each paragraph for the benefit of the poor population. Possessing an extraordinarily sincere relationship with people, Motek Erwi very quickly became beloved by the widest strata in the city. Up to 10 Jewish officials and employees were employed by Alderman Erwi's department. This fact greatly pleased the Jewish population. The behavior toward the clients was also very different from the other departments – straightforward, non-bureaucratic. He would speak Yiddish to the Jewish clients.

[Page 240]

Alderman Erwi supported the struggle of the *P.Z.* faction in the City Council to free the poor population from taxes in a concrete manner. Thanks to the support of Alderman Erwi as finance director, hundreds and hundreds of requests asking to be freed from taxes would be forwarded to the province. Many of them would be dealt with positively and those that were returned with a refusal would again be sent with a new rationale. Alderman Erwi took an active part in the sessions of the Town Council and, returning to the dais of the Town Council, took a stand on the conduct of other departments with which he did not agree. This provoked opposition to him by the remaining members of the Town Council. They began a quiet, but stubborn struggle in opposition to him. This made him more popular and beloved by the Jewish population.

In one of the first sessions of the Town Council, an intense conflict broke out between Alderman Erwi and the rest of the Town Council members when he was dealing with a budget proposal calling for the Town Council to appropriate 15,000 *zlotes* for the unemployed; 15,000 *zl*. for the poor for heating: 5,000 *zlotes* for clothing Jewish children; 1,500 *zlotes* to open a trade course for the young Jewish unemployed trade workers; for the Jewish public school and children's home – 3,000 *zl.*; night school – 2,000 *zl.*; for the two Jewish libraries, for *TOZ* [the Society for the Protection of Health], *Linat HaTzedek*[organization caring for the sick] and the old age home – appropriate subsidies. Alderman Erwi strongly declared that he came to the City Council to defend the interests of the poor Jewish masses and, therefore, he would demand that the Town Council support the Jewish institutions just as it supported the Polish.

In connection with the census that was to take place on the 26th of February 1928, with a view toward apportioning the Chelm districts for the *Sejmik* [county legislature], the Town Council, at the initiative of Alderman Erwi, decided to send out an application in Yiddish to the Jewish population and thus Jewish registration commissars were employed.

The application in Yiddish was very warmly received by the Jewish population. Therefore, all of the Jews' enemies strongly resented it. The *Endekes* [Polish anti-Semitic nationalist party] and *Kadekes* [extremely religious anti-Semitic party] newspapers published the entire Yiddish application on the first pages of their newspapers with the appropriate aggressive, ludicrous invective toward the Polish middleclass of the city who had permitted it.

At the City Council meeting in October 1928, after the results of the census were used to increase the area that constituted Chelm in the *Sejmik*, a president was chosen for the City Council. The *P.P.S.*, faithful to the lines drawn, then also joined the *Endekes-Senatorial* Club – creating a Polish majority and enabled the election of an *Endeke* chairman and a *P.P.S.* vice chairman. The *Poalei-Zion* faction delivered a sharp statement and left the session; later, the remaining Jewish councilmen did the same.

[Page 241]

The following report was published in the organ of the Left *Poalei-Zion* in Poland, *Arbeter Zeitung* [*Workers Newspaper*], No. 3 of 1/1929 under the title, "One Year of the *Poalei-Zion* Fight in the Chelm City Council." Because of the characterizations of the report we print it here without any changes: -

"Proposals that had as their goals to satisfy the needs of the local poor and the Jewish masses without means were filed by the *Poalei-Zion* faction:

    1. [Proposal] to entirely free all of those living in one room with a kitchen from the payment of old and out of date taxes, enacted and sent to the budget commission.
    2. An urgent proposal that the City Council turn to the government to free those living in one room dwellings from taxes.
    3. [Proposal] to free all those living in one room dwellings, the owners of 4th category patents and 8th category work patents from the payment of new city taxes for building roads and health purposes. (Passed.)
    4. An urgent proposal to repair the steps on the Post Street. (Passed.)
    5. An urgent proposal to appropriate 15 thousand *zl.* for coal for the poor. (Sent to budget commission and passed there.)
    6. An urgent proposal that the City Council turn to the government to undertake steps to prevent an increase in the rent for one room residences. (Passed.)
    7. An urgent proposal to undertake steps that evictions would not be carried out during the winter. (Passed.)
    8. Proposal to subsidize the Jewish institutions.

Figures Reflecting the Activities of the Faction:

Interventions carried out in the tax department	902
Of these, freed from paying the state-local taxes	702
Of these, freed from paying the city taxes	200
In the department of communal protection and aid	127
Received the ability to travel to the Warsaw and Lublin hospitals	63
Received support for unemployment	53
Freed of paying penalties for arrests	11
Interventions with the Town Council Secretariat	87
Interventions with the Town Council Presidium	37
Total	**1,153**

[Page 242]

Alderman Erwi in his presentation against the budget at one of the sessions of the budget commission, demonstrated that Chelm is a city with a 60 percent Jewish population and that they benefit from the support and subsidies the least. According to the statistics, during the past year, from 1/4/28 to 31/3/29, 391 people benefited from the support given out; of these, only 28 were Jews. A child in the *powszechna* school [Polish primary school] cost the City Council 26.42 *zl.* for the past year. At the same time, a child in the Jewish school cost only 7.50 *zl.* His bold presentation, with his pointed exhibits, strengthened the hatred toward him on the part of his Polish opponents on the City Council and Town Council. However, this made him more popular with and more beloved by the Jewish population. However, his young effervescent life was cut short…

On the night of the 28th going into the 29th of July, 1930, he was murdered in his own apartment at the age of 31. The news about his murder spread lightning fast over the entire city in the dusky darkness of daybreak. The entire Jewish population of the city and also a portion of Polish labor were certain that this was a political murder and that a political opponent and courageous fighter for the interests of labor and the Jewish poor had been eliminated. Later, it was shown that this was just an assumption.

Over 10 thousand people took part in the funeral that was arranged by the *Paolei-Zion* party committee. Almost all of the businesses and workshops were closed until the end of the funeral. The city was enveloped in sorrow.

[Page 243]

The funeral procession stopped at the City Hall building. Eulogists spoke from the balcony: the city president [mayor] Gut, and, in the name of *Poalei-Zion*, Yankl Beker.

The representatives of the professional unions, the *kehile* and other Jewish institutions and Nator Wasynczuk, of the Ukrainian Peasants party – *Selrab* [Peasant Worker Party, part of the Communist Party in the Western Ukraine] – spoke at the cemetery.

At the conclusion of *shlishim* [the 30 days of mourning] a sad assembly took place in the city movie hall with the participation of President Gut; Zerubavel; Yakov Feterzeil of [the Central Committee of] *Poalei-Zion* in Poland;. Hershl Frukhtgartn – party committee of the *Bund* in Chelm; Izbicer of the *Poalei-Zion* in Brisk; Moshe Yermus – of the artisans – and Yakov Beker in the name of the Chelemer *Poalei-Zion*.

With the death of M. Erwi, the *Poalei-Zion* Party lost one of its most capable people.

The funeral of M. Erwi

The City Council, the first in which *Poalei-Zion* played such a role, was dissolved in 1933 after the audits of the city economy were carried out in the City Hall and in various departments. The president, vice president and two aldermen were dismissed from their offices. Only Alderman Frokopiak was left for a short time to lead the City Hall and, later, he was replaced by the state commissar, Gorszalkowski.

The new city council elections took place on the 20th of May 1934. It was at the time when the influence of Hitler began to penetrate the countries of Europe. Polish reactionaries and Fascism began to lift their heads. The persecution of labor intensified.

The *Poalei-Zion* Party ignored the arrests and provocations and carried out an extensive election campaign with meetings, assemblies and electioneering [from house to house].

On the day of the election, extraordinary provocations were made against the Jewish voters at the election offices in the poor Jewish quarters. A document with a photograph was demanded of everyone who came to vote. [A document with a photograph] was not then common among large parts of the Jewish population. The work in the voting offices was intentionally prolonged and voters had to stand for hours before they had a chance to go into the voting office. When night fell, large groups of of hooligans came and chased off those waiting in line and succeeded in closing the voting offices. In such a manner, many hundreds of Jewish worker-voters were not permitted to cast their votes. However, *Poalei-Zion* received 1,140 votes, 100 votes more that in the earlier voting and elected three city councilmen. It was said that if not for the extraordinary chicanery, *Poalei-Zion* would have had five city councilmen. The general election results:

The headstone of Mordekhai Erwi who perished tragically. The Hitler murderers demolished his grave and headstone along with hundreds of thousands of graves and headstones in the Jewish cemetery in Chelm.

[Page 244]

Poalei-Zion	3 city councilmen
Jewish National Bloc	9 city councilmen
P.P.S.	2 city councilmen
Polish Civil Bloc *B.B.W.R.* [*Bezpartykny Blok Wspolpracy z Rzadem* – Non-Party Bloc for Collaboration with the Government)	18 city councilmen
Total	**32**

Just as in the earlier election, at the call from *Poalei-Zion*, a multitude appeared; this time scores of meetings, assemblies and electioneering [from house to house] was carried out with complete enthusiasm. The results of the voting showed that *P.Z.* was not only not weakened, but the opposite; it received an increase of almost 100 votes.

Elected were Moshe Beker, Yakov Beker and Ahron Dovid Hipszman. Because the *P.P.S.* had a significant defeat and received only two councilmen, the City Council had an absolute rightist majority.

Therefore, the role of the *P.Z.* faction carried an exclusively oppositional character. Councilman Yakov Beker resigned from his office immediately after the first session, and was replaced by Berl Akslrod. Akslrod settled in Chelm in 1930, with his wife, Nekha, who also was a teacher with pedagogic training. He was the manager of the Jewish *Folks-Shul* [public school] and as a comrade of Stasz in the party, a man with education and knowledge of foreign languages; he quickly took a leading position in the *P.Z.* movement. He excelled in mastery of the Polish language and it was also his fate to take part in the difficult oppositional struggle that was carried out by the *P.Z.* both in the city council and in the *Kehile*. He was a courageous fighter. For a time, he was an alderman.

[Page 245]

The first session of the newly elected city council looked like a military parade. Taking part in it were the *staroste* [provisional governor] and vice president, the oldest priest, the president of the court and high military officials. (This was a hint that the communal institutions also were being created to serve the military leaders of the country.)

At the election of the Town Council, the candidacy of the lawyer, Tomaszewski, as president was made known by the Polish Civil Bloc. The Jewish National Bloc asked for a recess of 10 minutes and afterward declared that although they were not asked for their votes, they would, however, give their votes for the above-mentioned candidate. The *Poalei-Zion* faction announced an ostensible candidate, Comrade Yakov Peterzeil of Warsaw. The councilmen of the Jewish National Bloc also gave their votes to the candidacy of Pawliak, as vice president, although each of them knew very well that Pawliak was a public anti-Semite. Two weeks earlier as vice commissar, during a celebration by the city firemen, he ordered that one of them dress as a Hasidic Jew and that he should lay down with his bottom up on a cask of water and tremble and that this should be a part of the general march past the entire city. Understand that the excited Polish population was amused and ridiculed the Jews who tremble [from fear] of a fire…

Poalei-Zion Committee
First row sitting [from the right]: Yakov Beker, Yisroel Moshe Beker, Ahron Dovid Hipszman, Berl.
Akslrod and Yakov Szrojt (America)
Second row: Fishl Iliwicki, Fishl Kopelman, Moshe Bojm, Zisha Kornfeld (Israel), Shmuel Szargel
(Israel), Haim Bibl (Israel), Moshe Strojl

It was necessary to have six votes to elect an alderman. The Jewish National Bloc had, with six votes, elected Abraham Szajn as Alderman. *Poalei-Zion* had their three votes and the two votes of the *P.P.S.* They received a refusal to their request that the Jewish National Bloc give them one vote so that there would be another Jewish alderman. And so, instead of another Jewish alderman being chosen, there was another Polish *Endek*.

The reactionaries grew bolder and cockier. A wave of anti-Jewish excesses began – pogroms in Brisk and in Pshitek, edicts against kosher slaughtering, separate benches for Jewish students, beatings by student hooligans in Warsaw streets, official anti-Jewish boycotts, supported by the government. (*Owshem*boycotts [Our Own, government policy of a general boycott of Jewish products and workers] were declared by the then Interior Minister Skladkowski.) Each day brought new edicts and oppressions.

On the dais of the City Council, the *P.Z.* councilmen expressed the accumulated cry of protest and rage of the Jewish masses. However, the Polish Civil councilmen were impertinent. They would heckle, interrupt in the middle of the speeches. There was even a case when a councilman, Rikhter Uminski, was threatened with prison. The *P.Z.* councilmen did not let themselves be terrorized, but continued their fight.

[Page 246]

The edicts that began to be strewn over the heads of the Jewish population in the country did not steer clear of our city. Many Jewish families were ruined by the edict against kosher slaughter. The boycott also was strongly felt. On market days, anti-Semitic young people would distribute slips of paper to the peasants urging them not to buy from Jews. There were even cases where hooligans would picket the Jewish businesses and not allow any Christian customers to enter. In addition to all of this came a new edict with the name "Urbanistic." Under the cover of ostensibly beautifying the city, various ruses were invented to bring harm to the Jewish population.

This "Urbanistic" policy completely ruined several hundred Jewish families in our city.

Fifty or 60 businesses were found on the so-called *rynek* [market] in the center of the city (on Lubliner Street), from which hundreds of Jewish merchants, retailers, artisans and workers drew their livelihood. Our local anti-Semites were conspicuous at this *rynek* and they decided to lay off workers because of "urbanistic and strategic motives..." The *P.Z.* councilmen immediately realized the danger, knowing precisely the political results expected by the rulers of the country. They understood that here no pleas and interventions would have any effect. Therefore, they proposed that the remaining Jewish councilmen immediately undertake a series of measures, such as threatening to leave the City Council and not voting for the budgets. (In order to support the extraordinary budgets, as well as in order to receive loans, it was necessary to have the votes of several Jewish councilmen.) The Civil Jewish councilmen did not accept the *Poalei-Zion* proposals. They hoped to repeal the edict in other ways, with other means. However, the edict was not repealed; all of the owners received papers asking them to leave their businesses. The owners of the stores and workshops did not want to voluntarily leave their spots, from which they had drawn their income for many years.

[Page 247]

Then firemen came and shattered the *rynek* with axes and hammers. This was a frightening and unforgettable picture: thousands of Jews stood with teeth pressed together and clenched fists and it was as if a pogrom had been staged against their possessions and the lives of several hundred families were ruined.

At one of the last sessions of the City Council, Berl Akslrod, the *Poalei-Zion* councilman, came out publicly with a very strong speech against the hypocritical politics of the city landlords concerning the Jewish population, with their speedy rush to tear down the *rynek*. Akslrod's presentation made a strong impression; as a result, the representative of the Jewish National Bloc, Yankl Sztul, delivered a statement that the stand of *Poalei-Zion* was correct and that they would support it. Moreover, he reported that the president had fooled and misled them (the Jewish National Bloc).

The session of the second City Council had ended long ago. However, no new elections had yet been set. The rulers of the country knew very well how much wrath had been gathered against them, particularly among the Jewish population. Therefore, they had to insure their leadership by entirely changing the voting methods.

New elections were set for the 20th of May, 1939 by the supervisory regime on the basis of the new voting edict, according to which proportional voting was created. The city was divided into six regions and was cut up so that the regions that were populated by the Polish population would provide the largest number of councilmen. Everything had been prepared so that the leftist Jewish councilmen would no longer have access to the city council.

The election month was during the month of May. In as much as it was a very beautiful and warm spring, all of the meetings took place under the open sky. The *P.Z.* meetings took place on the *Neier Welt* [New World] (Katowski Street), near Szwarcman's Square. On *Shabbos*, thousands of Jews would assemble on the Square and would listen with tension to the speeches of the *P.Z.* councilmen and other leading comrades. On the part of *P.Z.* this time, the best speakers were sent from Left *P.Z.* (Zerubavel, Mietek from Lodz and so on).

Teachers and school social workers during a reception for Zerubavel, who is sitting in the center

* * *

[Page 248]

On the day of the elections, the Jewish voters ran into unending difficulties. Old Jews, men and women, would stand in line for hours and then not leave until they were able to give their vote. The results of the elections brought a great surprise: of the 3,907 Jewish votes submitted, the Left *P.Z.* and the Prof. Union received 3,031 and brought in 8 councilmen (a ninth was short a few votes). The Jewish Civil [Bloc] – 2; the *P.P.S.* – 8: the Polish Civil Bloc – 14 (this time 32 councilmen were elected). The workers again received the majority. The Jewish population expressed their appreciation to the *P.Z.* Party for their courageous and worthy struggle, which they carried on in the Chelm City Hall during the course of 10 years. Moshe Beker, Berl Akslrod, Ahron Dovid Hopszman, Israel Goldrajkh, Sh. Szener and Israel Berman (a shoemaker) were elected for the *P.Z.*

The matter of the elections hit the ruling clique like a thunderbolt. The elections were not certified for months. At the end, the supervisory regime announced that the voting was declared void in two regions (those in which the Jews received five councilmen – four *P.Z*).

The new elections for the regions were set for the month of … September. This picture is deeply etched in the memory of the writer of these lines: the 3rd of September, 1939, the first three days of the war pass. However, Hitler's battalions have already succeeded in penetrating deep into the country… The streets of Chelm are blocked by luxury taxis. Polish nobility, capitalists, high officials are rushing to the borders in order to leave the country quickly… On the symbolic spot on which the *rynek* earlier had been found, I meet Mr. Akslrod, who is going around and collecting signatures from the Jews, while notices on the walls of the Chelm streets shout out that the elections for the two regions have been declared void and that new elections will take place in two weeks… Mr. Akslrod does his work, although he immediately knew, as I and many others, that now no elections would take place.

Occupied with "beautifying" the cities, saving the "Polishness" of Chelm and other cities, they lost Poland…! The ruling clique that administered Poland until 1939 received its punishment. How horrible it is, however, that the innocent victims – almost all of Polish Jewry and among them, approximately 18,000 Jews from our hometown, Chelm – paid for their crimes and for the crimes of their former partners…

Flower sale arranged by Poalei-Zion in Chelm in 1920

[Page 249]

The Artisans Union

by Hersh Handelsman

Translated by Gloria Berkenstat Freund

The Jewish Artisans Union in Chelm wrote an important page in communal life. It was founded in 1919, several years later than in other cities in former Czarist Russia, where a movement to organize Jewish artisans had begun in 1912. The idea of organizing the Jewish craftsmen arose because of the impoverished condition of the Jewish artisans in the Pale of Settlement. The invisible communal role of the Jewish craftsmen also provoked their striving to free themselves from their servility in facing the Jewish leaders in *kehile* life, who looked at the artisan as if he belonged to a lower layer of the Jewish population.

From the information I received from Josef Szperling, the Chelemer artisan-advocate, we know how the Chelemer Artisans Union was organized and about the first phase of its activities.

The first organizational conference was held in the house of Haim Atlas. This was after the First World War and the rise of the Polish state, which introduced democratic ordinances and gave equal rights to the Jews. The Jewish *kehile* began to organize on a more democratic basis; the so-called rich people no longer had an exclusive monopoly in *kehile* matters.

Immediately after the First World War, the architects of the founding of an artisans union began to recruit members within the walls of the synagogue and then the recruiting was taken to the houses, going from one artisan to the next. The registration of members took place at a fast tempo. Craftsmen from every corner of the city enrolled as members of the founding artisans' administrative body. Artisans from neighboring *shtetlekh*, who were driven from their residences to Chelm by the war, registered as members.

Hersh Handelsman

A general meeting was then called that among other points on the agenda proposed the election of a managing committee. In fact, a managing committee was elected at this conference with the following people: Israel-Yitzhak Nankin (chairman); Welwele Milsztajn; Berl Kelberman; Lev Sztekn; Shlomoh Brustman; Josef Szperling; Josef Cymerman and still others.

[Page 250]

At the first meeting of the managing committee, a plan of activities was presented and a motion by W. Cymerman to found a parts and work tools cooperative was unanimously accepted. The same W. Cymerman offered his shop as the place where the cooperative would open, emphasizing that he would not accept rent money.

This cooperative was quickly opened. In truth it was an enormous and important help for the poor artisans, who, before the development of the cooperative, had to pay high prices for all of the necessary parts and materials because of the instability of the exchange rate and the everyday rise in prices for all of the goods and of the tools and articles that were needed by the artisans. Because of the developing speculation and price instability, the artisan could not buy any goods and, as a matter of course, could not earn enough even for his poor way of life.

Simultaneously, cultural activities began among the artisans.

In 1921, the Artisans Union created a dramatic section and, although all of the members were family people, they took on the production of two shows from poems by J. Gordin: *Khasye di yesoyme* [*Khasya the Orphan*] and *Der Gebrukhene Hertzer* [*The Broken Heart*]. Both productions were a great success. The theater, Sirena, overflowed with a large audience that was eager to see how artisans act.

There was a court of arbitration even in the first phase of the Artisans Union and various internal disputes were taken care of in the best way. However, the Artisans Union went through many crises at various times. There was a shortage of money and there were times when there was not enough in the treasury to pay rent to the owner, Berish Kuper, in whose house the artisans' meeting hall was located.

The artisans' meeting hall was in Berish Kuper's house from the time of the founding of the union until September 1939. This house at Lubliner 27 was well known in Chelm. Lubliner Street was the main street in Chelm and Berish Kuper's building with the number 27 was also well known. The meeting hall for Left *Poalei-Zion* was also there and various social events and entertainments, splendid evenings and lively meetings took place there.

* * *

Israel-Yitzhak Nankin

[Page 251]

The artisans' meeting hall that was the home of the Chelemer Jewish artisans was located on the second floor and many craftsmen had their apartments there. Jewish life pulsed day and night in this house. Lubliner Street was a neighbor of *Neie Tzal* Street and *Neie Welt* Street that were thickly populated by Jews.

The artisans' union was an important economic-communal force that consisted of about 1,200 members. All trades were incorporated into the union such as furriers, tailors of women's and men's clothing, makers of ready-to-wear men's and women's clothing, construction workers, masons, house painters, furniture and cabinet makers, tinsmiths, copper and brass workers, locksmiths, shoemakers and gaiter makers, harness makers, butchers, watchmakers, goldsmiths, decorative painters and others.

Later, the following sections were divided according to the guild law: tailors of men's clothing, makers of inexpensive ready-to-wear clothing, tailors of women's clothing, seamstresses, hatmakers, furriers, a leather section, gaiter makers, shoemakers of ready-to-wear shoes, harness makers, tinsmiths, locksmiths, painters, glaziers, construction section, knitwear makers, carpetmakers, smiths, hairdressers, bakers, watchmakers, headstone carvers, metal workers and others.

The artisans organized for mutual aid and widows and orphans of artisans were provided with support. Loans would be made. When a cooperative bank was founded, the Artisans Union was represented in the bank by six or seven representatives. These were the artisan activists who were representatives in the bank: Shimshon Bursztyn (vice chairman of the bank), Wewtshe Handelsman (who was chairman of the shoemaker section), Moshe Yermus, Shlomoh Brustman, Berl Kelberman and M. Rubinson.

[Page 252]

The Artisans Union had representatives in all of the philanthropic institutions and in societies, such as: the interest-free loan fund, clothing for the poor, old age home, in *TOZ* [Society for the Protection of Health] and in other institutions.

The following artisan activisits were elected to the *kehile*: Haim Houzman, Moshe Yermus, Wewtshe Handelsman, Ezrial Kratka, Shlomoh Brustman. Ezrial Kratka and Haim Housman were on the *kehile* managing committee. Haim Houzman and Karp were also wardens. And when Nankin, for many years the chairman of the Artisans Union, died, Izrael Bornsztajn was elected chairman in his place. He was also elected as a councilman to City Hall.

The Artisans Union was active in all of the above mentioned institutions and reacted to unfair trade by various community activists.

The public meeting report in the January 15th, 1926 *Chelemer Undzer Shtime* [*Chelm's Our Voice*] (independent democratic weekly covering literary-communal and economic questions) can serve as a historic document about the artisans, as follows:

"Sunday, that is the 10th, a meeting of artisan managers took place in the Artisans Union meeting hall under the chairmanship of Mr. Nankin. In short talks, the managers, Housman, Kratka and Karp, pointed out the actions of the Orthodox councilmen, with the presidium at the head, who determined from their report that they had done everything wanted by the poor artisans. However, the times were already different and the Jewish artisans would take every means to oppose the will of those who take advantage of the economic situation of the Jewish artisans.

"The councilmen also pointed out the various vexations they had to endure both on the part of the Orthodox who spoke with one voice more than the other groupings and on the part of the Zionists, who, ignoring the understanding about mutual aid, constantly betrayed the artisans on every important question dealt with by the *gmina* [community].

"Councilman Karp pointed out the ridiculousness of the plan to build a Jewish hospital that would cost a colossal sum in such difficult times that the city would in no circumstance give and only because Mr. Biderman wanted it. On the contrary, one did not want to oppose the demand of the artisans for an artisan's school that could be achieved with a small sum of money.

A banquet in honor of laying the foundation of the new old age home in Chelm
In the center: Anshel Biderman and on the sides, the Chelemer rabbis, editor Fishl Lazar and other Chelemer Jews

"Mr. Nankin spoke afterward, pointing out that despite the fact that today we have an elected *kehile*, actions are still being carried out without the knowledge of the councilmen. People are taking responsibility on their own, making various decisions that are causing great harm to the Jewish population. And the speaker further said that it is unacceptable to participate in the production of city hall's city budget, as was done by the Messrs Biderman and Janovski who participated at a time when the Jews needed to avoid giving aid to the unjust existence of a city hall government whose term ended long ago. However, thanks to the indirect assistance of the Bidermans, the city hall regime continues to exist.

[Page 253]

"The meeting was closed with a read through and unanimous acceptance of the following resolution.

"In the report of the meeting called together by the Artisans Councilmen, Sunday, the 10 of January in the meeting hall of the Artisans Union, under the chairmanship of Chairman H. Nankin, the following resolutions carried:

"Learning of the activities of the *gemina* by our comrade councilmen after 16 months of work

1. We condemn the injurious actions by a number of the councilmen with the presidium at the head, for their independent action, not asking and not considering the ideas of the councilmen working with them in the managing committee and in talks bringing with it shame on the Jewish population in Chelm.

2. The assembly issues its strongest protest against that group of councilmen who impede through various class conscious means the ability to work in common with the workers and to implement our just proposals – working against the desire of the Jewish population to resolve all of our national, cultural and religious social demands;

3. The assembly stands firm that the actions of the other group of councilmen shattered and ruined every wish for democratic councilmen to be able to carry out rational and reformed direct taxation and to apply its entire energy to struggle against the indirect taxes that fall principally on the poor and working sections of the Jewish population.

4. The assembly accepts the actions of the artisan's councilmen in opposing the other group of councilmen who wish to be lawless and independent in their *gemina* work – and we challenge you to continue to fulfill your struggle for all of our absolutely just requests and to be entirely firm in your support of the democratic majority of the Chelemer Jewish population.

5. The assembly demands that the artisan's Councilmen remain watchful in its further work and demand a grant that would provide for the existence of an artisan's school; that this is an absolute necessity to be able to increase our productivity and strengthen our old material position that is being taken away from us by various means, and to support the subsidies that are justified – and already exist."

From this report, we see how the artisans' representatives — Nankin, Houzman, Kratka and Karp — strongly defended the respect and dignity of the Jewish artisans and reacted to unjust actions by the *kehile* in challenging a just tax system and a subsidy for an artisans' school.

[Page 254]

A very complicated condition resulted when the Guild Law of 1927 was enacted in Poland. This law reestablished a series of old qualifications from the past with the aim of limiting Jewish entry into crafts. A difficult struggle was carried out to repeal this edict, but nothing was of help.

During the course of the years 1925-1927, preparations took place to issue these Guild Laws that threw fear among the Jewish craftsmen who imagined that they would not be able to legalize their workshops.

However, according to the Guild Law, all previous craftsmen were free of the substantial procedure of examinations. They only needed to go through a small examination of practical work, not any theoretical examination. The examining commission consisted of representatives of the administrative regime, of representatives of the Christian artisans and of the Jewish Artisans Union.

A socialistic artisans union was organized in connection with the Guild Law. Artisans – home manufacturers, who took work home from craftsmen or from enterprises – were members of the administrative body.

Thanks to the activity of the *Bund*, the home artisan enterprises were successfully freed from the Guild Law. This was a great relief for these artisans.

This socialist Artisans Union had approximately 50 members. The managing committee of the union consisted of the following people: Hersh Fruchtgartn, (chairman); Abraham Sztajnberg; Y. Mager; Hersh Handelsman.

In 1929 the Jewish Artisans Union organized evening courses for their members, wanting to give them a little education and professional knowledge in order for them to be able to receive permission to run their workshops legally.

[Page 255]

Many groups of artisans became guilds after their legalization and each guild had its own management. The chairman of the metal trade was Josef Fiszboim. A. Kornfeld and Kh. Goldgevikht were active advocates in this trade; W. Kornfeld and P. Grynberg were trustees.

Such guilds were established for other lines of work.

The most meritorious artisan advocates were: Berl Kelberman, Shlomoh Brustman, Moshe Jermus, Gershon Lustiger, Dovid Nisnboim, Haim Hoizman, Ezrial Kratko, Shimshon Bursztajn, Wewtshe Handelman, Yisroel Bursztajn, Ahron Sziszler, Motl Goldman, Khona Kamanszteper from Szelest, Y. Nankin, Icykowicz, Nodelman, Nusenkorn, Hercberg, Dumkop, Szteper, Figlosz, Gojwaser, Mager, Wetsztajn, B. Feldhendler, Abraham Berland, b. Grynwald.

Jewish Artisans Union with flags during a celebration

[Page 256]

In 1931 a convention encompassing three *poviats* [counties] — Chelm, Zamoszcz and Hrubieszow — took place in the artisans' resource room. Approximately 150 delegates attended the convention.

The Jewish toiler, the Jewish artisan went through great difficulties in Poland. The enacted guild laws disrupted the development of Jewish crafts and, in addition, the abrupt higher taxes completely impoverished the Jewish artisan.

However, the artisans union eased the situation through the difficult times. It joined the populist Artisan Central in Warsaw that was under the chairmanship of Rasner and Noakh Prilucki. The artisan representatives from Chelm often would participate in the country-wide conference of Jewish artisans in Poland and they also were a contact with the general artisan cells in Poland.

The Jewish Artisan Union occupied a distinguished position in public Jewish life in Chelm and was an important communal organization that was of great use to the craftworker, defending his interests and inculcating in him the love and responsibility for the communal interests of the Jewish people.

Lev Sztekn, artisan advocate in Chelm

[Page 255]

From Chelm's Cultural Life

Translated by Gloria Berkenstat Freund

It can be said that Chelm played its role in Jewish life equally with all of the Jewish cities in Poland.

It is a shame that no statistical material remains that could tell about the cultural, school and library systems. However, that which is preserved in my memory will give witness and give the following details:

* * *

There was no library in Chelm until the outbreak of the First World War. The simple reader was exposed to the story books of Josef Itshe, Hinde's son (many of the survivors must remember him).

The best readers would be delighted with Peretz's *Yom-tov Bletlekh* [*Holiday Pages*] and other publications from the Yiddish library that were received by Mordekhai Dubkovski, Hebrew and literature of the Enlightenment from Yehuda Milner, may he rest in peace (incidentally, the latter, was one of the most beautiful personalities that Chelm possessed).

Starting in 1916 a Yiddish-Hebrew library arose from which developed the Hebrew-Yiddish library named after Y. L Peretz and the worker library named after Ber Borokhov.

[Page 256]

For a time the *Bund* and the prof. unions also had libraries that were under Communist influence. The *Bundist* library closed because of *Bundist* inactivity in Chelm. The Communist library – as a result of persecution.

The Peretz Library, with 500 readers and almost 6,000 books, and the Borokhov Library, with its 300 readers and almost 3,000 books, lasted right up to the last minute. There were a large number of Polish books in both libraries.

It should be remembered that Khishele Rozenfeld, a daughter of the "Horodler teacher," continually led the Peretz Library. It was one of the best Jewish libraries in Poland as a result of her effort and energy.

There remains a fact which has not been clarified:

In 1945 thousands of Yiddish and Hebrew books from the Peretz Library were dug up from a chamber on Szienkewicz Street; who hid them is still not known after all efforts [to find out].

The dug out books were sent to Lodz by the writer of these lines and in 1946 they became the foundation of a *P.Z.* [*Poale-Zion*] Yiddish-Hebrew library in Lodz.

[Page 257]

The cultural work in Chelm between the First and Second World Wars was carried out in general by all of the parties and youth organizations that existed in Chelm. Reports on various problems were arranged. However, in the main, *P.Z.*, whose literary judgments and other literary undertakings were renowned and were truly a respected contribution to the cultural work in the city, excelled during the entire period.

* * *

Chelm was one of the few cities in Poland that possessed a weekly newspaper. Even before the publication of the *Chelemer Shtime* [*Chelm Voice*], three issues of *Aygns* [*Property; Possessions*] (written) were published that took up 24 closely written sides and which dealt with real problems of that time.

Later, in 1924, at the initiative of Nakhem Goldberg, and with the assistance of Sheike Wajnsztajn (publisher-owner), the publication of the *Chelemer Shtime* began; it was published without interruption until the outbreak of war. Feiwl Fryd and Fishl Lazar were editors for a time. For such a city as Chelm, the publication of a weekly newspaper was clearly of great importance and if someone among the Chelemers abroad preserved the 16 years of publication of the *Chelemer Shtime*, it would be a terrific contribution to the research about the life of the Jews of Chelm during the course of the years 1924-1939.

One year, a newspaper was published in Chelm through the *P.Z.* under the name, *Chelemer Folksblat* [*Chelemer People's Newspaper*]. However, it was not able to exist for more than a year.

In general, both newspapers were important contributors to the Yiddish press in Poland.

For nearly two years, Hersh Goldman also published the *Chelemer Woknblat* [*Chelemer Weekly Newspaper*] with advertisements and a section about the life of artisans in a smaller format than the *Chelemer Shtime*.

* * *

After the First World War, the question of a "Jewish secular school system" was placed in the foreground.

In Chelm, too, a kindergarten and Jewish school was created. It was inter-party at the beginning. It remained this way until 1927. Later it was led by *Poale-Zion*. Children from the poorer environment continually studied in the school. The Messrs. Hershl Frukhtgartn and A.D. Hopszman made important contributions to the school.

In 1939, the construction of its own building was started. However, the Hitlerist murderers destroyed everything.

A Jewish *gymnazie* in the Polish language also existed in Chelm from 1918 to 1931 that struggled continually for its survival.

[Page 258]

A "finishing school" also existed in Chelm that also had started to construct a building just before the outbreak of the war.

It still can be said that the competition in the field of education in Chelm was first class.

* * *

A dramatic section at the Jewish intellectual club and at other community institutions was active in Chelm between the two wars.

Feiwl Dreksler (perished), under whose leadership the dramatic section stood for a time, must be remembered. The sections principally gave and staged plays from the Yiddish repertoire. In addition, from time to time they produced things from unfamiliar repertoires. There were many associates in the development of the dramatic sections during the first years of their existence: Moshe Klerer (now in Brazil); Reizele Kelberman; Serka Citrin-Ziskind (perished); Abraham Bernfeld (living).

There were also musical sections led by Dr. Walberger, Josef Goldhaber, Tuvya Klajner (all perished) that assisted the dramatic circles, and from time to time, appeared in concerts.

Our singer, Dora Dubkowski, appeared in concerts all over Poland before the war (perished);

Ida Hendl, the famous violinist, is one of ours.

Literary reading circle in Chelm in 1926
In the center, F. Zigelboim

From these notes, it can be seen that Chelm gave worthy contributions to Jewish life in Poland. There are no more Jews in Chelm. The Jewish community has disappeared forever, just as it disappeared from the other communities in Poland.

However, during the time that Jewish Chelm lived, there is nothing to complain about – it was one of the most beautiful Jewish communities in Poland.

[Page 259]

Skhus Oves un Skhus Katoves
[Ancestral Merits and in the Merit of a Jest]

by Yisroel Aszendorf, Buenos Aires

Translated by Gloria Berkenstat Freund

There was a Chelm with *skhus oves* [ancestral merits invoked in the interest of descendents.] A Chelm underground. This was the Chelm that had pulsed for many years with a strong Jewish communal life, with political parties, with cultural institutions, with a rich reserve of cultural people who did not only provide for their own needs, but provided for other Jewish settlements, even my *shtetl* [town] that was far away near the Russian-Romanian border to which came a Hebrew teacher from Chelm (Moshe Lazar). He taught me *Tanakh* [Hebrew Bible] and modern Hebrew literature and stimulated me into making my first poetic attempts.

I know, too, about the widespread activity of the various Chelm *landmanschaftn* [organizations of people from the same town] around the world, but I will now dwell on another Chelm, the Chelm that lives crying [through the] jokes – about Chelm's merits.

Every Jew liked to *hear* a joke every once in a while. Others liked to *tell* jokes, but there were many Jews who also liked to *create* jokes. Almost ever *shtetl* had its own clown or creator of witticisms. However, the majority of them did not cross the boundaries of their *shtetl*. Only a few did cross and also took their towns with them, such as Hershele Ostropolier and Efraim Grajdinger. However, the *shtetlekh* did not play any particular role in their stories. The heroes were Hershele and Efraim, the people, the individuals. The only city that remains in the history of Jewish folk-humor is Chelm. Chelm alone was the hero and not an individual, but as a community at large.

A number of stories and anecdotes were assembled over the course of many years. Did they really happen in Chelm and not in other Jewish communities? – This is not very important. What is important is that they exist. Are some of them rooted in the humor of another people? – What is important is they were made Jewish by Chelm. Those that are told about Chelm are these stories and no other.

The foolishness of the Chelemer [person or people from Chelm] is not foolishness that comes from maliciousness, although there can be a maliciousness in such foolishness that goes with goodness, with naivety. The Chelemer are not people who make fools of others; they fall victim of their attacks. Thus the Chelemer became similar to the Don Quixotes who always were ready to help other people and thus catch many blows from fate and from people.

The Jewish joke is in general a joke that bites, that jabs, that burns – pepper and salt. Chelm humor is a naïve one, mild, not a joke of deceiving and swindling, but of the deceived and swindled. And this is the main thing: the Chelemer is not satisfied with the skeleton of the joke, but clothes it in flesh, fills him with the blood of the story.

[Page 260]

Let us take the first story:

The first snow fell in Chelm, covered the autumn muds and the moldy roofs of the houses. What a light for the eyes! Then what? When the *shamas* [sexton] goes to wake the Jews for prayer, he will disturb the beautiful, white and fresh snow, make it dirty. The Chelemer worried and sought a solution for how to avoid this. The end of the story is not important. The Chelemer decided to put the *shamas* on a table and four Jews would carry him. This anecdote is important because the Chelemer strive for purity, for beauty.

The second story:
The Chelemer *shamas* became old and weak. The Chelemer thought about what they could do so that he would not have to go every morning to knock on the shutters and drag himself on his sick feet through the wet, muddy alleys.

They decided to bring the shutters to the synagogue. The *shamas* would knock on them there and not have to drag himself and lose his strength. What kind of characteristic trait is revealed here for us in the character of the Chelemer? – Pity.

Story number three:
A Chelemer bought a sack of feathers at a fair and dragged it through a field to Chelm. On the way he suddenly had an idea: the wind was blowing now in the direction of Chelm, so why should he carry the load on his back. He would let them go with the wind. The wind would bring them home to him.
Here we see how the Chelemer even trusts the wind with his property. The Chelemer <u>believes</u>.

I will mention the famous stories in which the Chelemer go through the world to find justice.

The various stories reveal for us the soul of the Chelemer, the soul that longs for beauty, that is full of mercy, that possesses belief and that searches for virtue. Oh what positive character traits the Chelemer possess!

True, the Chelemer seldom attains his goal; he constantly suffers defeat in his quests, caves in, but that is the fate of the honest and just in this world most of the time.

Various Jewish writers have tried to make artistic improvements to the Chelm stories, each in their own way. Did not Sholem Aleichem use Chelm as a pattern when he created Kasrilevke? Did he not see the Chelemer when he made the small people stately with great ideas?

Hundreds of Jewish cities and *shtetlekh* [towns] in Poland disappeared. But the heavenly Chelm was not annihilated. Chelm was created from the Jewish nation and it will continue to live like the nation. With our departure from Poland we took with us so much pain and misfortune. Of course, without a doubt, we need a little joy. Therefore, let us tell the stories about the good- natured, naïve Chelemer Jews again and again.

[Page 265]

Men of Fame, Personalities, Types and Characters

The Men of Renown and Personalities

by Josif Milner, Paris

Translated by Gloria Berkenstat Freund

Chelm was always an important Jewish cultural and population center and was world famous not only for the stories with which she so enriched our Yiddish folklore. Chelm is one of the oldest Jewish communities in Poland.

Jews were already living in Chelm almost 500 years ago. In the course of the seventeenth century, they even excelled materially. In 1529 a Jew, Reb Eidl, lived there. He would be referred to in Polish as "Doctor Yudka" and the Polish emperor appointed him rabbi for three areas: Chelm, Lublin and Belzyce. His power was great and his moral influence was even greater.

There was an old *shul* [synagogue] in Chelm where the shutters were on the roof…there would be laughter and it would be said: Chelm fools!... However, the truth is that this dated from 1582, when an enemy of Israel, Tomosz, wanted to kill the Jews and they barricaded themselves in the attic of the *shul*. And they had to save themselves that way for many generations. In the sorrowful well known period of the Chmielnicki massacres, 1648 to 1669, more than four hundred Chelm Jews perished to sanctify the name of God.

The list of the famous Chelm rabbis is very large. We will note only a few of them: Rabbi Elihu *bel-Shem* [miracle worker], the grandfather of *Hokhem Tzvi* (the latter was the father of Mr. Yakov Emdin). He was born in Chelm in 1550. The "*Hokhem Tzvi*" wrote that Reb Elihu *bel-Shem* created a *golem* [a clay figure of a human, often with superhuman powers]. In Chelm, many legends were woven around him. For example: he did not permit a headstone to be erected after his death. There was a hill in the Chelm cemetery and it was always pointed out that this is the grave of the Reb Elihu *bel-Shem*!...

The *MaHarSha* was rabbi in Chelm for ten years. This was, in fact, his first rabbinate. From Chelm, this well-known expert on Hebrew grammar, the author of *Markvat haMishnah*, became the rabbi in Salonika.

In 1789, in the year of the French revolution, a Chelm Jew, Hershke Yosefowicz, wrote a booklet in Polish: "Thoughts on How to Make a Jew into a True Polish Citizen."

As mentioned, the list of remarkable Jews from Chelm and its surroundings is large and it is too long to be able to dwell upon each one separately. Therefore I will be satisfied with the following persons:

Reb Elihu *bel-Shem*

The Chelm *khevra kiddishe* [burial society] was proud of two things: they would show everyone the headstone from the year "*khes*" and the little hill under which was the grave of Reb Elihu *bel-Shem* [miracle worker]. I knew both things well. I myself saw the headstone with the "*khes*," that is, for the year of the massacres of Bogdan Chmielnicki.[1] My brother, Dr. Shimon Milner, in his "History of the Jews of Chelm," even transcribed and published the contents of the headstone. However, we all, in my father's house, had great discussions about this. We were sure about that letter "*khes*" but in time it disappeared.

However, the little hill, where Reb Elihu *bel-Shem* was buried, is a fact. There lived in Chelm a legend about Reb Elihu *bel-Shem*. It was told that on the day of his funeral all of the "impurities" sank down… And before his death, Reb Elihu *bel-Shem* had asked the heads of the community that there be no headstone placed on his grave. And thus was created the little hill.

And who was Reb Elihu *bel-Shem*?...

He was born in 1550 – that is 400 years ago – in Chelm proper. He studied *Torah* in Lublin, with Reb Shlomoh Luria, and was later the rabbi in Chelm. He wrote a famous *sefer* [religious book], *Poski-Dinim* and he created a legal code for *agunes* [deserted wives].

Reb Tzvi Hirsh Ashkenazi, the famous "*Khokhem Tzvi*," was his grandson. We must remember the great influence of Reb Tzvi Ashkenazi on the Jewry of his century. His grandson was Reb Yakov Emdin himself, one of the greatest rabbis of his generation and the great opponent of Shabbatai Tzvi.

So, as we Chelemers perhaps can say, and with justice, Reb Yakov Emdin also had origins in Chelm. The little hill in our old cemetery is a witness.

The *MaHarSha*

The *MaHarSha* was the rabbi in Chelm, which actually was his first rabbinate. He arrived in Chelm in 1610. There are biographies of the *MaHarSha* that say he was rabbi in Chelm for ten years; others – that he remained in the position only until 1614, and from there he went to Lublin, where he was placed at the head of his large and famous *yeshiva*, to which were drawn young Jews from all corners of the world, even from France and from Italy. The *MaharSha* was the most popular among all the rabbis of that time.

He was born in 1555 and, it is said, in Chelm. He died in 1631 in the *shtetl* Ostrog, and his name was Reb Shlomoh Eliezer son of Yehuda Eidels. His epoch was the "*Tor Hazahav*" [golden age] of the rabbinical literature. The *MaHarSha* refreshed it and added a beautiful style of scholarship that was started in Chelm.

[Page 267]

The *bel Markvat haMishnah*
(Reb Shlomoh of Chelm)

His name would be written in our old *seforim* [prayer books]: Reb Shlomoh of Chelm. The entire Jewish world would refer to him as "*bel* [author of]*Markvat haMishnah*" because his famous book of commentaries on Rambam carried the name: "*Markvat haMishnah*." This book was published in 1751 in Frankfurt-on-Oder.

Everywhere he is called Reb "Shlomoh Chelemer" but he was born in Zamosc. He was only the rabbi in Chelm and there he wrote his famous *seforim*. In addition to *Markvat haMishnah*, Reb Shlomoh of Chelm wrote a *Shulkhan Orekh* [guide to observance of religious laws used in daily life] and a *sefer* [religious book]: *Shaarei Neima, Hug Haaretz*.

Reb Shlomoh of Chelm was a famous grammarian and geographer (his *Eretz-Yisroel* biography is entitled *Hug Haaretz* and he wrote many *responsa* [published religious opinions]. Reb Shneur Zalman considered Reb Shlomoh of Chelm a great authority on *Halakah* [legal portions of the Talmud] and of religious laws.

– And do you know where Reb Shlomoh of Chelm died? In Saloniki!... He died as rabbi of Saloniki. At that time, we see the road from Chelm to Saloniki was not very long. Rabbis were even traded.

And today?... The two old *kehiles* [Jewish communities] of Saloniki and Chelm no longer exist. The same Nazis made a ruin of them. Is this not the same path and fate?

Reb Abraham *ben* Yosef of Chelm

Thus he is referred to, and under this name, he is found in many encyclopedias. A famous writer of liturgical poems. The French Jews – chiefly from southern France – always exulted that the poems were created on French soil because the blue sky of France influenced the spirits and stirred the poetry… As you see we cannot be ashamed of our Chelm sky.

Reb Abraham *ben* [son of] Yosef of Chelm was not in Chelm by accident. He is a Chelemer by birth. He was born in Chelm and we know the date of his death (1650). That means he was born and lived in Chelm more than three hundred years ago and he was the rabbi in Chelm.

A book of poems by our Reb Abraham *ben* Yosef was published in two volumes in Krakow in 1607. The famous Zuntz dedicated an honored place to him praising his great talent. The historian Shteinschneider holds that he was one of the greatest religious poets of his time. His book, which was published in Krakow, is no longer here in the world. In the passage of so many centuries it was lost.

[Page 268]

Tuesday, January 18, 2005There is only one example in the British Museum. This is the only example in the world and Zender registered this book in his famous catalogue from the "British Museum." The name of Reb Abraham *ben* Yosef of Chelm is also remembered as a great poet in "*Or haChaim*" [commentary on the Torah by Reb Chaim *ben* Attar].

Reb Yitzhak *ben* Yosef Hochgelernter

Was one of the most famous Talmudists in Poland, a scholar whose father was a scholar. His father was already well known in the Jewish world as the rabbi in Zamosc and Reb Yitzhak *ben* Yosef was the rabbi in Chelm (after the death of his father he left Chelm and took up the rabbinate in Zamosc, where he died in 1825). Others gave him the family name, the nickname, "Hochgelernter" [highly educated] because of his great skill and great knowledge. He himself was a modest man, a modest and shy person and would always sign his name simply as "Reb Yitzhak *ben* Yosef." At that time he already spoke several languages, French, Dutch and Polish. Jews exulted over him. Later, his children scattered widely in many other lands and in general the family "Hochgelernter" was well known everywhere. However, its cradle was with us in Chelm.

His well known book, *Zikhron Yitzhak*" in two parts appeared in 1800 in Lemberg The first part consisted of various analyses of answers to question on *Halakah*, showing a mastery of all of *Halakes* [legal parts of the Talmud] and they were sympathetically adapted for a wider public. In the second part were his explanations of the *Khumish* [Torah or Five Book of Moses] and of the five *megiles* [scrolls].[2] In the explanations of the last he showed a great talent as a "popularizer" because he understood that the *megiles* can become the basis for popular access for the Jewish masses and open for them the gates of our great treasures. He wrote a *Hut ha-Meshullash – Devri Torah* [Words from the Torah] and also a supplement to his father's book *Mishnais ha Khokmim*.

* * *

The "*Tosafot Yom-Tov*" in Ludmar and in Luboml

Reb Yom-Tov Lipman Heller, known to the entire Jewish world as "*Tosafot Yom-Tov*," was born in 1579 in Waldenstein, a small Bavarian village. He was not only a famous rabbi, but the greatest scholar of his generation with the greatest authority (his judgments were considered "law" by Jews). Reb Yom-Tov Lipman was also a great community worker who described both the economic condition of Jewry of his era as well as the moral condition in the ghettos of that era. He fought for improvements and this evoked strong opposition to him. There were zealots who denounced him as a… revolutionary!

Reb Yom-Tov Lipman Heller was the chief rabbi of all of the Czechs and he even had a rabbinical chair in Vienna itself. And the denunciation consisted of this, that one should read "between the lines" of his books. It was shown that in his *Melekh-Ma'adaneim* [*Delicacies for the King*] he criticized Christendom. At that time there was no greater offense that could be found for a Jewish rabbi, and on the 26th of June 1629 he was thrown into prison.

[Page 269]

His trial aroused all of the Jewish communities. Reb Yom-Tov Lipman defended himself with pride. He answered all of the attacks, even those that were misleading, such as that he had criticized Jesus… He told the judge that as a rabbi and as a Jew he would always defend his faith, even when he was threatened with death.

And the verdict of the judge was the following: although he deserved the death penalty, the Austrian Kaiser (*Yorem-Hoy'd*,[3] in Austria, Jews would in fact call him "*Kire*" [nickname of the Kaiser]), pardoned him and converted his punishment to a fine (twelve thousand dollars).

Jewish communities collected the sum that was later lowered to ten thousand dollars. *Tosafat Yom-Tov* had a narrow escape. However he left the country for Wolin. He became the rabbi in Ludmar (Vladimir-Volynsk), and also for a longer time, the rabbi in Luboml. And the *Tosafat Yom-Tov* also was involved with community work in Wolin. There he organized a "*vaad*" [council], a committee of Woliner Jews who reformed the structure of the Jewish *kehile* and its institutions. At that time, for instance, in Wolin, rabbinical sites were mostly left to themselves. He uprooted these customs. He even arranged that rabbis did not have to receive any salary, in order to have freedom in their community functions.

* * *

His temperament also brought out opposition to him here, mainly, among the rich men and the community "big wigs." He left Wolin and became the rabbi in Krakow. This was the highest reward at that time, standing on the threshold of the Chmielnicki massacres, 1648 to 1669....

Reb Abraham Sztern of Hrubieszow, the Famous Mathematician and Inventor

Reb Abraham Yakov Sztern was born in our neighboring town, Hrubieszow, in 1762. Imagine the *shtetl* that was founded before 1400, two hundred years ago.... It is known that in 1765 there were 1,023 Jews in Hrubieszow!... And that as interesting a personality as Reb Abraham Sztern grew up there. As we talk about him, we can never forget to add the "Mister." He was a very *frumer* [pious] Jew, with a long beard, always with a *yarmulke* [skullcap] on his head, and in a long *kapote* [black coat worn by pious Jewish men]. That is how he appears in the remaining photograph of him which is printed in every Jewish and even non-Jewish encyclopedia. He would appear in this costume before emperors and before the most important people of his time.

[Page 270]

He began his "career" in Hrubieszow as a watchmaker. And then he perfected the mechanism of the watches. This interested the famous Staszic who was the proprietor of all of Hrubieszow. The Pole, Stanislaw Staszic, was a strange person. He believed that all of the Polish Jews needed to be placed in a new ghetto, in order to reeducate them there and to make them worthy citizens. Staszic became acquainted with Reb Abraham Sztern and was amazed by the Jew... How did such great experimentation come to a Hrubieszow Jew?... He gave him the opportunity to settle in Warsaw and to study, particularly mathematics. He made great progress, learned several foreign languages. And in 1812 he succeeded in creating a calculating machine and this excited the entire world. He was chosen as a member of the Polish Academy (it was called the "Imperial Society for Friends of the Sciences"). He sat at the table with the greatest aristocrats of his time in his *kapote* and in his *yarmulke*. He was voted a yearly salary of 200 dollars. He was twice presented to the Russian Tsar Aleksander the First and he would be Radziwill's frequent and familiar guest. It is characteristic that Reb Abraham Sztern was so *frum* that when he was proposed to rise to the head of the Warsaw rabbinical seminary, he refused because it was against his religious beliefs... The Hrubieszow mathematician and inventor was a conservative!...

A great literature in Polish, Russian and Hebrew was created around Reb Abraham Sztern. The mathematician was also a poet. He wrote a book of poems, and he had a great influence on the Bialystoker Haim Zelig Slonimski, the "*Astronom*" who was so beloved through Aleksander Humboldin, and who founded *Hatzfire* [Hebrew periodical published in Warsaw from about 1862 to 1931]. Reb Abraham Sztern died in Warsaw in 1842.

The Tomaszower Reb Shimkhah Pinsker and His Son Dr. Leon Pinsker, the Author of "Auto-Emancipation"

There is an error committed in many of our almanacs. It is written that Reb Shimkhah s was born in Tarnopol and Dr. Leon Pinsker – in Tomaszow. The truth is that the father and the son were born in Tomaszow, which is in the vicinity of Chelm. Reb Shimkhah Pinsker was born in 1801 and Dr. Leon Pinsker in 1821 (they died in Odessa in 1864 and 1891).

Reb Shimkhah Pinsker was a famous archeologist and, in general, well educated. His father was a great *maskhil* [follower of the Enlightenment] and was in constant contact with the well known *Galicianer* scholars. Reb Shimkhah Pinsker became world famous because of his explorations of the Karaites [sect which rejects the Talmud]. The tsarist government awarded him two gold medals. The Odessa Jewish *kehile* voted a yearly salary for him, so that he could work quietly in his field. His *Likkute Kadmoniyyat* [*Collection of Antiquities*] is considered one of the greatest works to throw a light on many historical facts. In general, he wrote dozens of great historical-archeological works in the course of his life, even in reference to the development of the Hebrew language. His death brought out a great sorrow among Jews at that time.

[Page 271]

Do we have to write specifically about his son, Dr. Leon Pinsker?

As is known, he was the author of *Auto-Emancipation*, which was the preamble for Herzl's *Jewish State*, and one of the founders of the *Hibbat-Zion* [Lovers of Zion] movement (with the other Zamoscer, Aleksander Zederboim) and he also organized the famous "Katowice Assembly" that was the "antechamber" for the Zionist Congress.

There were many old Jews in Tomaszow (around 1905) who remember the father and the son. I myself was shown a little house in Tomaszow where Reb Shimkhah lived and where Dr. Leon was born. In 1916, I wrote about this in the Moscow *Yevreyskaya Zhizn* [Jewish Life](that was published instead – because of a censor-closure in Petersburg – in *Razsvet*) and I had the honor that A. Droyanov, in his work, cited this effort of mine.

Y.L. Peretz and His Birthplace, Zamosc

Zamosc was always considered an … "intelligent" city in the Lublin area, and Zamosc would be talked about with great respect:

"With us, in a secluded corner … if only you would see Zamosc!... What a city, what people!..."
Zamosc was the city of Dr. Ettinger, the pioneer of the *haskhalah* [Enlightenment], the popular author of *Serkele*, the witty Krilov of Yiddish literature. And also of Yakov Eichenboim of Zamosc – in 1840 he published (in addition to many other things) his famous Hebrew *haKerav [The War]* in which a chess game is described in beautiful songs; his father was named Moshe Gelber. Aleksander Zederboim, one of the most famous journalists and community workers of his era, was born in Zamosc (in 1816). He founded *Hamelitz* [Hebrew periodical] and his correspondent in Zamosc was Reb Dovid Szifman, who once sent a report about the Zamosc *mikhvah* [ritual bath]… And Zederboim published a special article: "It is a scandal that in my birthplace, the *mikhvah* is dirty…"

And Yitzhak Leib Peretz was born in Zamosc.

Peretz's father was a wood merchant and a contractor to the military. He would come to the *beis-midrash* every *Shabbos* dressed in a top-hat. This was the *beis-midrash* of the "Germans." An entire group of our own people in Zamosc were referred to in this manner for generations because they would be dressed in short jackets, with a "hat" on their head[4] and even shaved. Among the "*apikorsim*" ["heretics"] was our Peretz's father, Dr. Geliber and the Margulius brothers. They founded a "Talmud group" and they studied a page of *gemara* with their rabbi, Reb Shabtai… The *beis-midrash* was, *lehavdl* [a word to separate the sacred from the profane], a sort of "club." There only the "aristocrats" of the city were welcomed and they were referred to as such.

[Page 272]

–Peretz?... This is then an "aristocrat!"…
Moshke Peretz, an uncle of Yitzhak Leib, had a great influence in the *beis-midrash*; and his brother-in-law was Reb Shmuel Leibush Lewi, one of the most original and one of the nicest Zamoscer Jews. He was a great philanthropist. He would send Zamosc Jews to the Belczer *Rebbe* before Purim at his expense. They would remain there until after Passover. During that time, Reb Shmuel Leibush Lewi would support their wives and children. His "adjutant" (today one would say "secretary") was Reb Dovid Montag, a popular figure in Jewish Zamosc. He was a famous *mohel* [ritual circumciser].
–Reb Dovid?... He was the *mohel* for all of our middle class children.
Peretz's father, his brother Moshe and Reb Shmuel Leibush Lewi were the greatest donors in Zamosc. The best donations were received from them and Dovid Montag would be the specialist in giving "bribes." If it was necessary to save an impoverished man and not shame him, Dovid Montag would be sent. He had great tact and a dear heart. He would "shove in" the few rubles so that no one was insulted. And he had great influence on Yehoshua and Yitzhak Leib, on both Peretz brothers. Yitzhak Leib would talk about him with the greatest love. Dovid Montag would often give praise: "Yitzhak Leibush?... He is, as you know, mine!...."

Yehoshua Peretz would handle freight. As is known, there was no train to Zamosc and all goods were shipped to Rawicz (the Germans built a railway during the First World War). From Rawicz they were brought on wagons. And goods would get lost in Rawicz. Yehoshua Peretz would buy the freight and collected the monies (and it was a very good business).

Yitzhak Leib Peretz loved his Zamosc. He would laugh heartily when he would explain that the Zamoscers were called the "*kugel-fresers*" [pudding eaters]. The people of Zamosc were fond of food. And in the surrounding pious *shtetlekh*, they were held as "debauched." In Szczebrzeszyn, for example, one did not want to become connected to Zamoscers by marriage… Yitzhak Leib Peretz would remember with great pleasure the time when he was a lawyer in Zamosc. His "petitions" were renowned. Once, in a narrow circle of his acquaintances, he explained that as a lawyer he needed to travel quickly to Szczebrzeszyn. The only contact was the wagon driver, a blond Jew, with two dripping eyes and with two dead horses. He would arrive in Zamosc every day with ten women and fifty children.

Peretz called him near and said:

"Shlomoh, you get three rubles, do not wait for other people and leave at once!..."

"Sit inside!"

As soon as he moved, a woman sprang out of a shop: Shlomoh, you are leaving already!... Shlomoh stopped and the woman carried out a small package and sat inside. Upon leaving Zamosc, the driver had a *minyon* [ten men needed for prayer] of men and women. He understood that this did not please Peretz and he said to him:

– *Pan* [Mister] Peretz, if I would arrive in Szczebrzeszyn with only one passenger, it would be said that Shlomoh has become crazy!...

[Page 273]

Reb Yakov Reifman of Szczebrzeszyn

Szczebrzeszyn, a small holy community. Mud, so that one could drown in it in the summer; in all, a thousand Jewish families at the beginning of our century [20th]. It is true that Bogdan Chmielnicki was there in 1648 and exterminated all of the Jews. And, as is known, in this Szczebrzeszyn there lived such a personality as Reb Yakov Reifman, who studied and wrote his literally transforming work for the entire Jewish world. I knew people who would walk from Zamosc to Szczebrzeszyn in order to see and to speak with Reb Yakov Reifman and, among them my father, who was in constant correspondence with him.

He was actually born (in 1818) in a small village near Opatow. However, at age seventeen he married in Szczebrzeszyn and spent his entire life there, until 1895, when he died. He actually belonged to the great constellation of famous Jewish scholars, the creators of "Jewish Studies," such as Sh. Y. Rapaport, the Tarnopol rabbi, Abraham Geiger, the historian Yost, the Italian Shmuel Dovid Lutzato, Senor Zaks, the Lithuanian Jew from Paris, the Christian, Franz Delitzsch, etc. He would correspond with all of them. As a matter of fact, they would write to him, asking him for explanations of texts that they had badly understood and his opinion was for them a true scholarly judgment. The great poet, Yehuda Leib Gordon, dedicated songs to him and raised him to heaven. From London, Reb Moshe Montefiori sent to him in Szczebrzeszyn as a gift a gold cup engraved with Hebrew words.

Reb Yakov Reifman wrote monographs (such as, for example, *Toledot Rabbenu Zerahaya* [biography of Zerahiah ha-Lewi of Prague] and his *Hut ha-Meshullash* caused an upheaval. In it he closely examined the knowledge of Hebrew possessed by the creators of the *Talmud*. There were cases in which he skeptically referred to their knowledge of Hebrew grammar. He wrote dozens of books and hundreds of articles. He immersed himself in Jewish philosophy.

A great literature was created about Reb Yakov Reifman and not only in Sokolow's *haAsif* [a literary collection] or in Shafer's *Knesset Yisroel* [*The Jewish People*] and in other Hebrew publications. He was written about in all languages, in German, in English, in Russian and French… The question really arises: from which treasury did Reb Yakov Reifman draw his great erudition in the small and secluded Szczebrzeszyn?...

[Page 274]

Reb Shlomoh Yehuda Lederer – Student of Chelm –

He died in Chelm in 1894. I remember his death and his funeral. This means 56 years ago. He was then already an old man of approximately seventy-nine. So we calculate that he was born in Chelm in 1816; "Franz-Josef himself was not yet in the world," a Galicianer would say. Reb Shlomoh Yehuda Lederer, who was born in Chelm 135 years ago, knew Polish like a Pole. His Polish style was "first class" and his articles in the Polish-Jewish *Israelita* were famous. They were even cited in the Polish literature. It is true that Reb Shlomoh Yehuda Lederer was not the first Jew in Chelm who knew the Polish language so well. In 1789, the year of the French Revolution, a Jew, Hirsh ber [son of] Josef (Herszko Jòsefowicz), lived in Chelm; he was then under the influence of Jean Jacques Rousseau and published a Polish book: "Thoughts On How to Make the Polish Jew a Good Citizen of the Land." (Mysli stosowne do sposobu uformowania Zydòw polskich w pozytecznych Krajowi obywatelów [1789]).

However, Reb Shlomoh Yehuda Lederer was also a Hebrew poet. When he died, *Hamelitz* published an obituary notice, signed by my brother Shimeon Milner (who was then 13 years old), and N.S. (the pseudonym of Nahum Sokolow) dedicated a large article in a black frame to him in *Hatzfire*. Nahum Sokolow loved him a great deal and in his *Memorial Book* even published his biography, because under the pseudonym "the Student of Chelm," Reb Shlomoh Yehuda Lederer published a poem in almost every *Shabbos* edition of *Hatzfire*. There were also literary collections under the name *haNitzanim* [*The Buds*]; the editor was also a *Hatzfire*-man – H.N. Neimanowitz (the famous *haNatz*, who would write a feature article every Friday about everything that happened in the world, and he was, according to my understanding, the literary "father" of Yusznow). In *haNitzanim*, one could read poems by our Chelm "student."

He had two sons. I will only dwell upon one son, Mordekhai Lederer, an extraordinary type. He was very popular among the Jewish workers in Warsaw in the first years of the Zionist movement. He would organize Jewish "workers' associations." Once he led a demonstration of Jewish workers to the Czarist general governor, Prince Imeretinsky. The latter called out the Cossacks who chased and hit the Jewish demonstrators with murderous blows. Later, he left for *Eretz-Yisroel*. Around 1909, I met him in Jaffa (because Tel-Aviv did not yet exist). He would inspire everyone with his dynamic enthusiasm.

[Page 275]

Shalom Lederer

Chelm is world famous. Y. L. Peretz, himself, wrote about the "Chelemer *malamed*" [religious teacher] and he was not the only one. In German, English and French there are books dedicated to Chelm and they are popular under the name, "Chelm Stories." A French author wrote that the "Chelm Stories" have no author. Since very ancient times, they have been a portion of Jewish folklore and have been told among Jews.

Sixty years ago, in New York (and perhaps even more) a book about Chelm was published in Yiddish. Its author was Shalom Lederer, the brother of Reb Shlomoh Yehuda Lederer. I have not seen the book, but I heard much about it during my childhood. This book was very much talked about in Chelm. It was a sort of a "novel," where all kinds of Chelm stories were brought together and facts were added about the real Chelm. Shalom Lederer presented all kinds of types of living Chelm Jews who were instantly recognizable and he made them heroes of the Chelm stories. Chelemers in New York would need to look for this book by Shalom Lederer in a central library, which would bring a great deal to the studies about our city.

Reb Josef Mincer

He was already an old man when he arrived in Chelm around 1890, and he remained there until nearly 1903. A beautiful white beard, a *yarmulke* [skull cap] on his head, a face from a Reb Haim Zelig Slonimski – the *Astronomer* of Bialystok, the founder of *Hatzfire*.

Reb Josef Mincer was born in Zamosc and he was of a type of Zamoscer Jewish intellectual. Pious and at the same time infected with Nakhman Krokhmal's ideas, he boasted that he was a friend of Aleksander Zederboim's since childhood. He, himself, wrote "poems" in Gotlober's *The Morning Light*, paying careful attention to the "rhyme," and in addition to this journal (that was no less famous among Jews than Smolenski's *The Dawn* and one was in an ideological struggle with the other) he published "epigrams" in all kinds of other publications. There was a style of "epigrams" that was more "charades" than jokes.

–From where did Reb Josef Mincer come to Chelm?
There was a *gymnazie* in Chelm and according to Czarist law only 10 percent of Jews were accepted. Since Chelm Jews did not go to the *gymnazie* at that time – where one became a *goy* [non-Jew] – there were empty spots. This was sensed by Jews from Kowel to Oracze and even further near the Dnieper, and children were brought and they were delivered for studying at the "Chelm *gymnazie*." There was then a question from the parents about a Jewish "boarding house" (dormitory) for their children who would remain in the unfamiliar place. And Mincer came from Zamosc with his entire family and he opened such a "children's house," according to the current style.

[Page 276]

His son was the teacher of the "boarding house" and would do the lessons with the *gymnazie* students. It was truly well organized. The son was for those times a "sportsman" in Chelm and this consisted of him walking dozens of times from the mountain to the barracks every day at a set hour.

Once I accompanied him and we made our way together. And just at that point we noticed a "watchman" beating a poor Jew with murderous blows. The young Mincer went over to the "watchman" and gave him such a blow to his face that he let go of the Jew who quickly ran away. However, Mincer, I and the "watchman" remained. A crowd gathered. A report was made against us for preventing an official from "fulfilling his functions" (that is, beating a Jew!...). The "examining magistrate" quickly made me a witness because I was in all twelve years old. Mincer was placed before the "district court," the lawyer, Warman, was specially brought from Lublin. It was transformed into a political trial. There was turmoil. I gave my testimony and this was, perhaps my first political speech. My testimony was used by the lawyer. Mincer was freed.

However, the director of the *gymnazie* decreed that the boarding house be closed and the Mincer family left Chelm for Lodz.

Abish Lewensztein

In the past it was enough to print only one article in *Hamelitz* or in *Hatzfire*, so that all readers, all the enlightened, could read the author in even the most secluded corners. So it was with our Chelemer, Abish Lewensztein, Fishel Lewensztein's son, who wrote a great "tract" in *Hamelitz* (I do not remember the content) in about 1898. He did not forget to add his birthplace to his name ("Chelm, district Lublin") and when you would come to Biala or to Brisk or to another city, you would always find a young man who would ask:

"Are you from Chelm?... Perhaps you know Abish Lewensztein?..."
Abish Lewensztein was one of the first Zionists in Chelm and he had a very beautiful Hebrew library. He died very young of cancer.

Fishel Lewensztein, his father, was a sage. However, he had a brother in whom he could literally exult. This was Reb Josef Lewensztein, the Serotzker Rebbe. Serock was a *shtetl* near Pultusk in the Warsaw area and there were barely three thousand Jews living there. However, their rebbe, Josef Lewensztein, was famous in the world as one of the greatest historians of Polish Jewry. This was a biographer who should not have had a place in Serock, but a chair in a famous university. He wrote a lexicon and many historical works. It was enough to inquire of him about an historical date or event in Polish-Jewish history and, in no time, receive a response from him, written with a goose feather, and it had all of the particulars. Thus when my brother, Shimeon Milner, working on his *Likkute HaYhudim baKhelm* [*Collection of the Jews of Chelm*] turned to Reb Josef Lewensztein and asked him for particulars about Chelm rabbis, he immediately received several large sheets of paper with a list of the Chelm rabbis, from the first to the last rabbi. From where did he have all of this?... A file?... Or all registered in his memory?... And because of the list, a great debate took place. My brother embraced the idea of Reb Josef Lewensztein that the first rabbi in Chelm was Reb Shimeon Auerbak and the Russian-Jewish historian Wishnicer did not agree with this and, according to his understanding, the first Chelm rabbi was Reb Yehuda Ahron and the Polish king made him (in 1522) the chief rabbi of Lublin, Chelm and Belc.

[Page 277]

Abish Lewenstztein's brother-in-law was Betzaleil Frid, also one of the first Chelm Zionists. His son is Feiwel Frid, my student. Feiwel Frid was the editor of the weekly newspaper, *Der Chelemer Shtime* [*The Chelm Voice*], and my joy was great when I received the news that he survived the great catastrophe of Chelm and the entire Polish Jewry and that he lives in Lublin and works in its *kehile*.

Reb Moshe Palewski

In my birthplace, Chelm, there lived a Jew for whom the entire city had great respect. He was named Reb Moshe Palewski. No one dared to call him by his name, without added the title "Rabbi." He was not actually a Chelemer, but a Kobryner. And Kobryn already smelled of Lithuania, not far from Brisk… And then no one in Kelme presumed to call him "the Litvak," disregarding the fact that he did not speak Polish Yiddish, and a *"kometz"* [vowel sound representing the letter 'o' – here indicating Yiddish dialect spoken which emphasizes the 'o' sound] was… *"kometz."*

Reb Moshe Palewski was a *misnagid* [opponent of Hasidism] and no Hasidic *shtibl* could draw him to it. He would pray in the old Chelm *shul* that, as it was said, was about eight hundred years old (in Chelm, there was a headstone in the cemetery from 1248; just this year it would be seven hundred years old, has the Germans not made sidewalks from the headstones). He would, however, wear a *kapote* [long black coat] with a *gartl* [rope belt worn by religious men], a Jewish hat, a long patriarchal beard and *peyos* [side locks]. As a small child, my heart would strongly beat when I would be taken to Reb Moshe Palewski, to be questioned…

In Chelm, everything was known. There were no secrets for the Chelemers. And Jews would discuss until late afternoon in the same *shul* that Reb Moshe Palewski had a brother who was a "heretic," who became "depraved," going away to Paris and there became completely… French! This was talked about very quietly in order not, God forbid, to cause heartache for such a fine and good Jew. This was sixty years ago.

[Page 278]

You know, however, that the right hand and closest co-worker of General de Gaulle is named Gaston Palewski?

Gaston Palewski was one of the closest co-workers of Marshall Liotei in Morocco. He was Cabinet-Chief for Paul Renault in the catastrophic days of June 1940 and we would hear his voice on "Radio London" as the director of de Gaulle's cabinet. He remains in that post today. He was never spoken of as a "Jew." Perhaps he is not in the sense we understand the concept.

But anti-Semites forget nothing. Recently, anti-Semites in Paris spread a "tract" about him in which the act of naturalization of his father, Abraham Palewski, born in Kobryn, was published. This act is from 1891. Is Gaston Palewski our Chelemer Reb Moshe Palewski's brother's son?

Chelemer Family

– Do you know that such a Jewish family existed?...

Yes, there was a distinguished, an aristocratic Jewish family with the name "Chelemer" – a rich family of rebbes and rabbis. And the members of the family were grandchildren of Reb Lev Yitzhak of Berdychiv and they lived in Lyubar, Volyn *gubernia* and Kremenets *poviat*, and there were about five thousand Jews in the *shtetl* before the First World War.

The "Chelemer" family was related to the family of the righteous ones of Chernobyl and to the well known family from Tverecius. They had a great influence between Lyubar and Proskurov [Khmelnytskyy] and were famous as merchants, great forest merchants, and as intellectuals.

– Did they once emigrate from Chelm to Volyn and then took their name from their city of origin?

It is possible. I met them very often because the Chelemer family was related to my family and we are relatives by marriage (that is how fate wanted it that we should have a connection to everything that is bound with Chelm). In 1915, Shoshona Chelemer from Lyubar married a well known Warsaw journalist, Moshe Leizerowicz, who was my cousin. They both perished in 1944 in Trawniki, near Chelm. The S.S. annihilated all of the Jews in the camp a few hours before the arrival of the Russian army.

Shoshana Chelemer had a brother, Josef Chelemer, who was famous in the era of the first Zionist Congresses. He was a delegate to the congresses and was devoted, heart and soul, to Dr. Herzl, who also had great fondness for him. He lived abroad and one would always meet him in the literary cafes where the Jewish life of writers, correspondents and community leaders sparkled before 1914. The main headquarters was the Café Metropol in Berlin, about which we even wrote in our literature. Josef Chelemer was highly thought of. He knew everyone and everyone knew him (his son lives now in Israel and he changed his name "Chelemer" to Helkhemi [the Hebrew version]).

[Page 279]

I let myself end with a fact that sounds like an anecdote: Josef Chelemer arrived in Warsaw once and he telephoned his friend Nahum Sokolow, who did not know that he had arrived and he answered the telephone:

"Chelemer!"
Nahum Sokolow got angry and answered:
"Are you a *khokhom* [sage, wise man]!"
And he hung up the telephone receiver.

Reb Yehuda Leib Milner

Permit me – in a book dedicated to our city Chelm – to write about my own father. And why not?… Does not a son need to say *kadish* [prayer for the dead] on the grave of his father?…

His name was well known in Chelm and throughout the entire area. He was always surrounded by the young of the city, who simply followed his every word and loved him very much. He was a guide.

Actually he was not even a Chelemer, but a Litvak, born in a small *shtetele*, Nemoksht [Nemaksciai], Kovner *gubernia*. As a small child, he studied in a *kheder* and his teacher was a Jew, Reb Tzvi Hirsh. Later, this teacher was the mathematics professor at Heidelberg University, Herman Shapiro, the founder of *Keren Kayemet L'Yisroel* [Jewish National Fund]. Then, he taught in the Lithuanian *yeshiva* in Toyrogen [Tawrik] on the Prussian border. However, there winds blew from Lik; (*Der haMagid*) at the time of *haMe'assef* of Yitzhak Eichel, and with the entire *Pleiad* [group of seven learned or prominent figures, named after the constellation of seven stars].

Reb Yehuda Leib Milner

Thus my father stopped thinking of a "rabbinical position" and began to study languages.

The Lithuanian *shtetlekh* Zagare and Keidan [Kedainiai], where Benyamin Mandelstam (*Der Chazon Lemoed* [*The Timely Vision*]) and Schneier Zaks, Yehuda Leib Gordon and, Moshe Leib Lilenblum lived, had an influence on him. And he became a *maskil* [member of the Enlightenment] and remained as such for his entire life.

[Page 280]

He left Lithuania and arrived in Brisk. He married in Siedlec and as a "son-in-law *oif kest* [supported by his in-laws]," he studied for several years with the Siedlecer rabbi, Reb Borukh Mordekhai Libszic, the father-in-law of Reb Elihu Klatzkin, the Lubliner Rabbi, the grandfather of our great philosopher, Dr. Jakov Klatzkin. He remained a close friend of the entire family. And when Reb Borukh Mordekhai died, my father published a long obituary notice in Sokolow's *ha-Asif* [*The Harvest* – Hebrew yearbook] (of 5648/1887). He left Siedlec and came on business to Chelm, where he settled.

His appearance in Chelm was a sensation. He was basically followed in the streets. He was the first Jew in Chelm who wore a hat [rather than a traditional cap]!

–A German!...

And that is how it remained for many years. Chelm was a city of darkness. At that time an event happened in the city of which only select individuals knew. It is a story from more than 65 years ago. Do the remaining Chelemers remember an old, God fearing person who was called Reb Borukh Lukower? He had a son, Alter, who was "caught in the act" of reading a secular book. He read them surreptitiously in the attic. Reb Borukh, his father, detected it. He caught him in the attic and became very angry and furious. He grabbed a stick of wood that lay in the attic – and hit his son over the head, and Alter fell dead. At that time in Chelm, funerals were held quickly and the police did not know of the entire occurrence... In such an environment, my father published. He was immediately proclaimed an *apikoyres* [heretic]. Indeed, one had to possess deep moral worth in order to reach such a level that an entire city would give him the greatest respect, make allowances for his opinions and want to see him at the head of all the institutions of the *kehile* [organized Jewish community].

Little by little, other "Germans" arrived in Chelm and settled there. Other hats appeared and the "*Deitchishe shul* [German synagogue] (thus had the Jews called it), famous in that era, was founded, where my father was the *gabay*. It was not a simple *shul*. It fought its way into existence through great effort; it became a club. The zealots were outraged, and, in addition, there was the fact that my father had a library. This was a wonderful Hebrew library, where one would find unique copies. The youths from the Hasidic *shtiblekh* [prayer houses] were raised on the books from the library. My father would explain each book, its contents and tell about the author. More than one *auto-da-fe* occurred in the *shtiblekh* and the "captured books" of "Reb Leibl Milner" were burned. The youths had to work out a strategy in order to come to our house and take a book to read, because they would be "spied on..." They would come at night, in the dark, and they would hide. Are these not episodes from Smolenskin's "bereaved" in his *The Joy of the Godless*...?

[Page 281]

The rise of Zionism was a real revolution. It shocked Jewish society. This was the beginning of a communal transformation of our *shtetlekh*. My father would write reports from Chelm for *haMelitz* and would chastise the Chelemers who were so sunk in darkness. The "German *shul*" became the center. My father would give fiery sermons there every *Shabbos*. "*Shekels*"[5] began to be sold, later, by the Colonial Bank itself. Brochures were distributed. Old Jasinowski, who was named Herzl's *namyestnik* [viceroy] in Poland in around 1895, came to Chelm especially to see my father in order to organize the work. Speakers would come and little by little they entered the *shuls* and *beis-hamedrish*. The leader of the fanatics was Reb Efrayim Yehoshua and he, himself, would be an example and threw stones at the windows of the *beis-hamedrish* on the day of *shabbos*, when my father or a Zionist speaker was standing and giving a talk...

Here I present a story: It was a few weeks before *Pesakh* [Passover]... It was cold with snow on the streets. Travel was still by sleigh. And one evening such a sleigh came to our house; a couple of young people came into our house (among them Abraham Goldberg, the future editor of *Heint*) and said to my father: "Come immediately, the leaders of the city are assembled in the *beis-hamedrish* in order to excommunicate you!..." My father immediately got into the sleigh and I, a small boy, was taken along. As we entered the *beis-hamedrish*, which was packed with people, it became quiet. The buzz of a fly could have been heard... My father took off his heavy fur and turned to the Krilower Rabbi who was sitting in the front:

– You have, probably assembled here because *Pesakh* is coming, in order to think about how to have *matzoh* for the poor Jews?

Several words passed like a flash of lightning. The Jews were struck with fear. And the shoemaker, Hersh Nisel's son who did not have hands but "paws" cried: "Reb Leibl is right!..." And the "Reb Leibl is right" went from mouth to mouth and it echoed like a storm. A vote of revolt was created. A window was opened and the Krilower rabbi, along with Reb Mordekhai Lung and several respected business owners lifted the skirts of their *kapotes* [long black coats] and jumped out in fear…

There is another interesting story from the later years – 1911 – to record. The elections took place for the fourth *Duma*. *Vyborczkes* [electors] would come together in Lublin and elect the deputy for the *gubernia*. Chelm was a large provincial center. The bishop was Jewlog, himself. And the bishop forgot that there were more than 13 thousand Jews in Chelm. Who reckons with Jews?… And not asking anyone for advice, he presented his candidate. However, the Jews, going to vote, voted in the thousands for my father and Jewlogi[6] received only 800 votes. My father was elected as a *vyborczik* [elector]. It was a scandal. Jewlog's newspaper, *Rus Kholmsaya*, called for a boycott of the Jews, according to Roman Dmowski's version…

[Page 282]

I could make this chapter longer. It is a page of our community life over the course of 50 years. I will end by explaining that in 1913 Chelm sent only my father as a delegate to the Zionist Congress in Vienna. Before his departure, a banquet was held for him and all of the young people and the intelligencia of the city took part. It was no longer the same Chelm as when my father arrived there from Siedlec. Jewish Chelm produced children who were doctors, lawyers, writers and community workers. The city was transformed thanks to the courage and hard work of several personalities such as my late father. The mountain moved from its spot; it was pushed back from its place in order that the darkness would disappear…

***

This is a Hebrew article by Reb Yehuda Leib Milner that was published 67 years ago in *haAsif* [*The Harvest*].

(Hebrew text)

[Page 283]

The Mandelboims

Reb Chaim Nuta Mandelboim was the headstone engraver in Chelm. Headstone engraving was once considered a "good trade" among Jews. In Vilna, for example, there was the well know Hilel Noach Maged (he recorded the history of *Yerushalayim dLita* [Jerusalem of Lithuania – Vilna]), who was employed in the same trade. He changed his named to "*maged* [preacher]" and became a "*shteinshneider* [stonecutter]." It had the scent of sculpture, art…

Reb Chaim Nuta Mandelboim had seven sons. The first born was Beshka (Benyamin), the second Yair and the third Yakov. It was the era of the first Russian Revolution of 1905. Beshka and Yair were arrested in Lublin and spent almost a year there in prison. When they were freed, Yair left for Paris. He learned a trade, began to work, and little by little 'filled out papers" for his brothers remaining in Poland. The first to arrive was Beshka. He was a young man with fine taste and with talent, but a very modest person. He quickly learned French and acquired an interesting French library. But not ordinary books. Each book was a splendid edition and there were many rarities. He was known in French student circles in that era and his opinion was valued. He became the Paris correspondent for the Warsaw *Heint* [*Today*] and his "Paris Letter" was a great success. He would introduce the Jewish reading public – before the First World War in 1914 – to political life in France, as well as the great literary phenomena in French literature.

Right after the First World War, Yair Mandelboim came to Chelm. His father was already in the *oylem-hoemoes* [World of the Truth – i.e. dead]; his aged mother was still alive with five sons, among them Yakov who was at that time an efficient community worker in Chelm. He "took" them all to Paris. They settled in the French capital. All learned and spoke perfect French. All got married, had children and lived middle class lives. However, in 1942, they were "taken" for the second time, but this was the Gestapo. They were taken to Auschwitz, where all seven of the brothers perished with their wives and children. I believe 21 people. And of them no memory remains and no stonecutter or headstone engraver could engrave the names of the entire Jewish family that perished in the ovens…

[Page 284]

[Simon/Szymon] Mondszain, the Artist – A Chelemer

Right after the First World War, the artist [Simon/Szymon] Mondszain gained great name recognition in Paris. All of the French newspapers dedicated large articles of praise to him. It was immediately after the restoration of Poland as a nation and no one forgot to underscore that Mondszain was a Pole. It was also after Germany's first defeat and it was added that Mondszain came out of the trenches as a "volunteer" and also as a gentleman from the "Legion of Honor."

A splendid monograph was recently published in Paris about Mondszain, with a large and substantial description of his life and his artistic creations. It is a picture of Montparnasse before the First War. It is a description of the great artistic world, how he finds himself in the "cathedral'" and in the "rotunda" with Modigliani, Dikran, Pascin, Max Jacob, Vlaminck, Lahner and many others. Mondszain is there, too. Derain, Picasso, Matisse, Othon Friesz, Diego Rivera, the Mexican, the sculptors: Kokoine, Lipschitz, Zadkine, and writers like Gustav Kahn and Blaise Cendrars go by as in a kaleidoscope. The Chelemer Jewish young man, Mondszain, takes a very pleasing spot among them.

Manashe Dovid Mandelboim, well known headstone engraver in Chelm, the father of the Mandelboim artists

[Page 285]

Yes, Mondszain is a Chelemer. I, myself, still remember his parents. I still remember Mondszain as a small child. Charles Kinstler also is an example of the Chelemer era of artists. He was born in 1890. He describes how his artistic talent was revealed to him. I presume to say that he had that defining moment of influence in my father's house. He came there for essential books to read and became acquainted with the outside world. He was helped in leaving Chelm for Warsaw and later for Krakow. His talent enchanted the professors. Mondszain became known, and occupied the position of a great artist. Charles Kinstler tells us about the phases of Mondszain's development. The magnificiant reproductions confirm that we are in the presence of a first class master.

The monograph can be a jewel in every library and for we Jews a source of pride, as it shows us the ways in which a Jewish child passed through Chelm to reach the artistic world in Paris.

Our townsman, the well known Jewish-French artist, Mondszain, photographed during a large exhibition of his paintings in Paris

The Artist Sh. Shreier

Shmaryahu Shreier was born in 1899 in old Jewish Chelm. When the headstone was unearthed on the 20th of June and the historic headstone of the *kehile* that perished with its twenty thousand Jews [massacred by Bogdon Chmielnicki] was discovered, on this same day, his coffin was borne. In this way he was the first Chelemer Jew buried on the symbolic territory in a Parisian caisson.

Shmaryahu Shreier remained true to his birthplace in his art works. His types were Chelemer Jews, and as you look at the sky in his paintings you recognize at once the landscape of his city and of our Jewish *shtetlekh*. His last picture was – the Chelm market: there is a fair in the city!… Everything happens under the "Chelm mountain" that is famous in our Jewish culture and historical folklore, about which it is told that the Chelemers wanted to push it from its place. There is a fair in the city!… Male and female peasants from the surrounding villages are at the market; police move around and pay attention to order. The Jews on the thresholds of their poor shops wait for customers!… Their faces are terribly sad. Did they then already feel that on the cold day of the 30th of December 1939, at this same market, covered with snow, the Germans would come and undress them naked and lead them to the slaughter?…

[Page 286]

"Chelm" [The Chelm market], a study made in 1947 by our townsman, the deceased great artist Shmaryahu Shreier

* * *

In addition to his birthplace, the city of the world, Paris, had a great influence on Shreier, just as it had an influence on other artists. He was charmed by Paris. He got drunk with its atmosphere of freedom… He left his long studies in Germany and his soul was penetrated by the spirit of Paris. He immersed himself in the artistic circle as well as in its cultural ideals. He depicts Paris, the surrounding landscape, the fragments of its exquisitely beautiful gardens. Thus a Chelemer Jewish young man, a great Jewish talent, found the synthesis and created a bridge from his city to the River Seine.

Translator's footnotes:

1. The letter "*khes*" has a numerical value of 8 and indicates the date of the massacres.
2. There are five scrolls (*megiles*] in the Writings of the *Tanakh* or complete Bible: The Song of Songs read on Passover, the Book of Ruth read on *Shavous*, Lamentations read on *Tisha b'Av*, Ecclesiastes read on *Sukkous* and the Book of Esther, the only one referred to as "the" *Megilah*, read on Purim.
3. "May his glory increase" – said when referring to a kaiser or king.
4. The "Germans wore short jackets instead of the long *kapotes*, coats worn by Eastern European Jews.
5. "tax" paid before each Zionist Congress.
6. The name is spelled two different ways in this paragraph.

[Page 287]

Shmuel Mordekhai (Arthur) Zigelboim

by R. Henes

Translated by Gloria Berkenstat Freund

Shmuel (Arthur) Zigelboim

Shmuel Mordekhai Zigelboim was born on the 21st of February 1895 in Poland in the village of Borowice, Chelm *poviat*, Lublin *gubernia*. He spent only the first four years of his life in his birthplace. In 1899, his family moved to a neighboring town, Krasnystaw, where Shmuel Mordekhai spent a further eight difficult years of hunger. His father, Josef, or Joska the teacher, as he was called in the *shtetl*, was a tall Jew, thin and sickly. A cough never left him alone. He would teach the children in the *shtetl* how to write and read. Although Joska the teacher was a pious Jew, he was thought of as enlightened, a bit of a *maskil*. He would read newspapers and books. The burden of making a living fell entirely on Shmuel Mordekhai's mother, Hena, an energetic wide shouldered woman, the daughter of Reb Jankl the *shoykhet* [ritual slaughterer], a respected Jew, who in addition to being a *shoykhet*, was the *moyel*[circumciser] in the *shtetl* and the *khazen* [cantor] in the *shul*. The ailing Joska the teacher could not, with his small earnings, support his large family that consisted of 10 children. The mother, Hena, raised in a learned family, was a *shneiderin* [woman tailor] and was always surrounded by tiny children. She sewed small clothing and small pants on a "Singer" machine and therefore she received the name, Hena *der shneiderin*, in the *shtetl*.

[Page 289]

There was not enough to live on from both incomes – teaching and sewing. Therefore, Shmuel Mordekhai's childhood years in Krasnystaw were accompanied by hunger. Eating to satiation was a dream, but not the only dream of the small Shmuel Mordekhai. The family lived on the River Wiepsz in the area of the Trisker Hasidic *shtibl* [small prayer house]. The small Shmuel Mordekhai would wonder for long, long hours at the beauty and secrecy of the Trisker Hasidim. Perhaps here, at the edge of the Wiepsz River, was the original source of Zigelboim's later spirit and of his strong love of the Jewish people. Perhaps here, in Krasnystaw, his strong sentiments for the Polish people were born.

The owner of the apartment was a Christian and with their meager earnings, there was barely enough to eat and no rent money. However, the Christian owner did not throw them out of the apartment and let them live rent free.

At the age of 10, Shmuel Mordekhai had to give up his childhood, the dreams at the river of going to *kheder* and he went to work in the first large factory in the *shtetl*, which made apothecary boxes. Young Zigelboim had his first harsh experiences in the factory as the angel of death waved over him. Cutting the strips for the cartons, he once cut his own flesh and bone, two finger tips from his hand. (Zigelboim later described his experiences in the factory in a story entitled *Der Fabrik* ["The Factory"]). At 12, in 1907, Shmuel Mordekhai left home for the large city of Warsaw, without the warmth of his parents, at a turbulent time and in a raging sea of people. He worked at various trades in the large city: at a handkerchief factory, with women's purses, not sleeping, not eating, sleeping in strange beds and even in a garden on a bench. In his free time, the maturing Shmuel Mordekhai began to write songs. And on *shabbos* when he would meet Krasnystaw young men of his acquaintance, he would read them his songs, listen to their criticism, their praise. However, he never brought them to editors. With the outbreak of the First World War, he came back home to Krasnystaw and, with his family, he left the *shtetl* and moved to Chelm. At that time, he began his communal activities in Chelm into which he threw himself with all of his senses and, in the end, to which he sacrificed himself.

Zigelboim, already a young man of 20, threw himself with fervor into the practical day-to-day work of the Jewish workers' movement that strongly flourished. In December 1917, the first convention of the Bundist movement in Poland took place in Lublin. The Chelemer organization sent Zigelboim as its delegate. From the beginning, the young worker met the most important leaders of the movement at the convention and this brought with it a radical change in his life. He made a very good impression on the leaders of the movement with the report he gave. In 1920, the Central Committee in Warsaw remembered the young, capable provincial worker and called Zigelboim to Warsaw and gave him two responsible positions. He became the secretary of the Professional Union of Jewish Metal Workers and a member of the Warsaw Committee of the Bund and from that moment began his great communal rise. In the large Jewish workers' center, he had the opportunity to learn how to use his great energy and to develop his organizational and writing abilities. He was very beloved by the Warsaw Jewish workers and his pen name Comrade Arthur became very well known. In 1924, Zigelboim was elected to the highest division of the Central Committee of the Bund and remained a member until the end of his life. Arthur tested his strength in several fields. He was a political worker and professional worker; he was also a good speaker and writer, traits that are not often combined in one person. Zigelboim crossed the valley of need and loneliness during his childhood; in his youth, he always dreamed of raising himself. He set serious goals for himself and strove to reach them. And although he achieved a great deal during a short time and grew to the level of a central workers' leader, he did not have any self-satisfaction. The opposite, a certain dissatisfaction accompanied him; not a morbidity found with embittered people, but the feeling that comes from striving higher. During the difficult day-to-day communal work, he always had the feeling that he had not yet reached the height, the pinnacle, that he, the leader, still needed to show his readiness, his self-sacrifice. Arthur was a strange synthesis of a sober political worker, a realist and a romantic, a dreamer. And how strangely natural and organic it was for Arthur, who I still recall with the words he said when I once came into his room and was very frightened to find him sick in bed. He answered me with his wise smile on his lips: "Don't be afraid, I will not die a natural death." In 1939, Arthur was sent to Lodz, the second largest city in Poland, by the Central Committee in Warsaw to become the leader of the Jewish workers' movement.

At the International Socialist meeting in London (1942), organized by the English Labor Party. The leaders of a range of socialist parties are seated…Sh. M. Zigelboim [standing at the microphone] speaks about the annihilation of the Jews of Europe.

Shmuel Arthur Zigelboim in the center (in civilian clothes) with Russian prisoners, during the German occupation of Chelm in 1915-1916, during a meeting about political work)

[Page 291]

He remained in his responsible posts until the outbreak of the storms of war in 1939. Arthur came from Lodz to Warsaw by foot five days after the outbreak of the war, in order to be of service during the difficult fateful days. He was a member of the Warsaw defense committee at the time of the siege and defense of the capital. He edited the *Folks Zeitung* [*People's Newspaper*], found himself in all the demanding positions in the capital surrounded by the German army. After the fall of the capital, immediately at the entry of the Germans, the enemy demanded 12 representatives of the population as hostages, who would bear the responsibility for order in the city. The City President, Stefan Starzynski, proposed that the Jewish worker population provide one and this should be Ester Ivinska. Arthur categorically opposed a woman being a hostage and suggested himself as a candidate. And thus Zigelboim became the German hostage for the Jewish population. At the same time, another function was imposed on him; he represented the Bund in the new *Judenrat* that was created by order of the German occupation regime.

Hena Zigelboim, the mother of the "Bund" (as she was called in Chelm)

[Page 292]

One of his performances at a meeting of the *kehile*-council will remain unforgettable; what this was in general was the first bold opposition to a German decree on the part of a Jewish representative. The *kehile*-council dealt with the question of carrying out the German order to create a Jewish ghetto. They demanded that the Jews carry this out voluntarily themselves. When the question was discussed, Shmuel Mordekhai Zigelboim decisively fought against it. The majority decided to carry out the decree out of fear that not carrying out the order from the Gestapo would bring new trouble for the Jewish population. When the decision was taken, Zigelboim made the following declaration:

"An historic decision has taken place here. I was, it seems, too weak to communicate that we must not do this. I feel, however, that I do not have enough moral strength to be able to take part in this. I feel that I would not have the right to continue living, if the ghetto is carried through and my conscience should remain clear. I declare, therefore, that I resign my appointment. I know that it will be the duty of the chairman to report my resignation to the Gestapo at once and I consider the consequences that this will have for me personally. I can, however, not act differently."

Sitting from the left: Chana'tsha (in Poland), Yisroel, Pinya (perished in the Vilna Ghetto), Feiwel (in South Africa), Shmuel Mordekhai (Arthur), of blessed memory, Chava (died in Russia)
Sitting, second row: Fanya, may she rest in peace, (Yisroel's wife), the mother Hena, of blessed memory (perished in Chelm), Golda (Arthur's wife, perished in Warsaw Ghetto)
Third row, bottom: Ruwin (in South Africa), Josef, Arthur's son (in America), Abraham (in America)

[Page 293]

Zigelboim spoke again later before an audience of over 10 thousand assembled Jews who came to the building of the Warsaw *kehile*, having learned of the decree. He called for the Jews not to go voluntarily to the ghetto, not to lose courage and to remain in their homes until they were violently thrown out. The declaration at the meeting of the *kehile*-council, as well as the talk in the street did not remain a secret from the Germans. Zigelboim received a notice to come to the Gestapo to discuss important matters. What the invitation meant was clear. He did not go to the Gestapo and began to hide himself. The underground committee of the Bund decided that Zigelboim must escape from Poland. In particular, a special mission was part of this – to bring before the world the news about the atrocities that the Nazis were carrying out in relation to the Jewish population. The road was extraordinarily difficult and hazardous. He reached Holland and Belgium through Germany with a Dutch passport. Before an international forum in Brussels, Zigelboim described what the Nazis were doing in Poland. His report made a tremendous impression. For the first time, the free world heard authentic news of the torture and murder camp into which the Nazis had transformed an isolated Poland. Later, Zigelboim came to America, traveled around the country and made the American public aware of the scandalous deeds done by the Nazis in Poland. He created a *megilah* [scroll] of pain and insults for thousands of listeners.

Golda Zigelboim, wife of Arthur Zigelboim, perished with her daughter Rywka (right) in the Warsaw Ghetto. (Left) Josef Zigelboim, survived, lives in America

In Spring 1942, Zigelboim was sent to London as the representative of Polish Jewry in the Polish Parliament in Exile (national council). He held this difficult and responsible post for a year. His entire being was aflame for the fate of his people who were being annihilated and he, their messenger, could do nothing to help. Well informed by the Jewish underground movement about what was happening in Poland, he tirelessly did not stop demanding and challenging the Polish government, the leaders of the great powers, Churchill and Roosevelt, to do everything to stop the systematic annihilation of an entire people, the Jewish people. Nothing helped.

[Page 294]

A messenger who came to London from the Polish underground gave Zigelboim a demand from the Jewish representatives to the Jewish leaders in the free world: "They should go to the English and American offices; they should not leave until they received a guarantee that a decision had been made to save the Jews. The Jewish representatives in the free world should not eat or drink, they should slowly pass away face to face with the indifference of the world. They should die. Perhaps this would shock the conscience of the world."

Zigelboim received the challenges, the demands from his murdered Jews.

For a year in London, he tried everything to save the millions of victims and could not save even one lone Jew. The messenger of the murdered Jews took the new "way," the demand of the murdered: "Die yourself, perhaps that would help."

Shmuel Mordekhai Zigelboim was the one and only one, who carried out the order of the Jewish leaders in the Ghetto to the Jewish leaders in the free world – to make the highest sacrifice. On the night of the 11th and the 12th of May he ended his life by suicide.

He gave the most dear: his life, for that which was most dear in his life – for the Jewish people.

Children's home of the Bund in Chelm. We see Shmuel (Arthur) Zigelboim in the center.

[Page 295]

Al Kiddush HaShem
[In the sanctification of God's name]

by Ruwin Zigelboim

Dedicated to the Illustrious Memory of my brother, Shmuel Mordekhai (Arthur) Zigelboim

Translated by Gloria Berkenstat Freund

The speaker suddenly became quiet, interrupting his speech. A dead silence reigned in the hall. The several hundred people, who had come to the International Socialist meeting of the English Labor Party, earnest and moved, were listening to the Jewish representative of the Polish National Council, the leader of the Bund, Shmuel (Arthur) Zigelboim. He described the gruesome deeds that the Germans were doing in Poland, read reports from the underground in Warsaw, told about the revolts in the ghetto… about the heroic struggle and tragic death of the remnant of Jews. He had already been speaking for two hours to the non-Jews about the tragedy of a people who were being murdered systematically. Was he finished? The quiet lasted a minute. Zigelboim heard the quiet. He knew that he must speak further. He had lost the bond with those who were listening to him for only one minute, carried away by thoughts of the way people were living and seeing everything he was talking about and describing. He felt a meaninglessness in his speech, in searching for words, in giving speeches and making appearances in the light of the savage realities. This only lasted for a minute. He immediately brought himself back into the room; this was his duty, the only remedy – to speak to them, to make them believe what was happening there, being struck by fear and calling forth a response of protest in the world. He started speaking again: "Today, you have heard the frightening news from Poland; these are facts that make blood curdle in the veins. I have in my hand an excerpt from a letter that a Jewish woman in one ghetto wrote to her sister in another ghetto in Poland. The letter is a shocking call to the world. The woman writes:

[Page 296]

"My hand shakes. I cannot write, our minutes are numbered; only God knows if we will see each other again. I write and I cry; my children lament. They want so much to live… We all say goodbye to you." [Zigelboim continues,] "Thus is the atmosphere in which the Jews live in the ghetto of Poland. Try to imagine the people who see their nearest being dragged away to their death every day and each one knows that their turn must come. Imagine the thousands of Jewish mothers, the mothers who look at their children and know that their death is inevitable. Imagine the mothers from whom the children are torn from their hands with one smash into the wall. The little head of the child spatters in small pieces in front of the mothers.

Ruwin Zigelboim

Imagine the great crime of methodically massacring an entire people. Each of us who understands the cruelty of the crime must be grabbed by the feeling of shame that we find ourselves among the living, to belong to the human genus, if means are not found to stop the greatest crime in human history. The conscience of everyone must be shaken; the serenity must be exploded for those who ignore the facts, with their self-deception that makes them skeptical. Each of us who does not do everything possible to stop the mass slaughter will take upon themselves moral co-responsibility for [the dead]. In the name of the hopeless innocent people sentenced to death in the ghettos of Poland, whose hands stretched out to the world cannot be seen, I call to all people, to all nations, whose conscience is still weak, wipe off the burning shame that is thrown on the human race, force the Nazi murderers to stop the systematic massacre of a people."

Zigelboim left the hall alone; the people who congratulated him disturbed him, shaking his hand for his beautiful speech. He ran from them. He again had the feeling of despair and helplessness. It was a year's time that he was the representative of Polish Jewry in the Polish Government in Exile. He wrote, spoke, warned, pressed, did not let pass any opportunities to enlighten, to persuade, to call and to beg for help and everything struck a deaf wall of disbelief and indifference. He was the representative of a people that was being killed cold-bloodedly. If only he was seen to save one single soul. Yes, people come to hear him. What he has to say affects the people. However, it is a superficial effect; afterward they return to their daily lives. A few do not believe him. It is said that this is characteristic Jewish hysteria and, if there is a little truth, it is far away and, meanwhile we are alive. Yes, he knows that many of his Jewish and non-Jewish friends have begun to avoid him. He poisons their lives; they feel uncomfortable in his company. He knows what they think: "How can such a person always and constantly live only with one thought; he takes this too seriously, this Zigelboim." Well, yes, of course, one can be a representative, give public speeches, send telegrams of alarm to the world and then sit at home or in the company of friends, moaning, crying and have a little joy from life, do what everyone else does. His eyes flashed with anger. He pressed his hands into a fist and with anger, even a little brutally pushed through strolling Sunday crowds, almost running. He saw an empty spot on a bench in the square and suddenly felt so tired that he could not take another step; he sat down heavily. It was a beautiful spring day, one of the rare sunny days in foggy London. Here the trees were in bloom and spread an intoxicating aroma. Everything here was so normal.

[Page 297]

True, London was living through difficult days, was being bombed by German airplanes. And then such calmness, security. Between one bombardment and the second, one went out into the street, strolled. Zigelboim watched two children playing in the square: a young boy of seven and a young girl of the same age. He looked at their radiant little faces; looked at the two mothers who looked at them with such pride. He was transported by the sunshine and bright joy of the children and a smile, such a rare guest in recent times, played on his face. The ball with which the children played rolled over to his feet. He took it in his hand, wanting to throw it back. The children stood waiting with little outstretched hands and bright open eyes. Zigelboim looked at them for a time; his hand remained hanging in the air. He face twisted in a grimace and his eyes became bloodshot. He saw the last report from Poland; saw the outstretched little hands and the eyes of thousands and thousands of children open in childish astonishment and fear, in wagons, autos and on foot driven to their death, to the ovens. He tore himself from the spot and again began going fast, running. He again stopped at a square and here again heard the sound of childish laughter. How would it be, he thought, if these mothers of the beloved children were taken and they were sent there to look and see what the Germans are doing to the children of his people. How would they react? Would they shudder, scream, hit the murderers with their fist; or perhaps they would watch nonchalantly, and perhaps help. This is what the greatest number of the Polish people is doing. Throughout his life, he believed deeply in the people. With optimism, he went step by step in the strength of this belief. And what is socialism, if not the deep belief in the ascent of man. At age twelve, he left his poor home full of hungry children in Chelm, to go to the large strange city, full of belief in people, and saw for himself socialism, the Jewish workers' movement, the Bund, sensed in them the beauty, the exaltation of throwing oneself into the stormy, salty sea of human suffering and tears, fighting for justice and nobility. He walked with the masses and moved ahead; he became their leader. His optimism and belief in people helped him persuade them. They listened to him; the Jewish workers believed him. He was always ready for them, during the weekdays of communal work and on holidays, in struggle, in danger. Ready for the highest sacrifice for them, for the Jewish workers' movement, for the Jewish people. And now, when his people were perishing in blood, they presented him as their messenger to the world, a messenger to the world from a people who are being murdered and he cannot help. He cannot break down the wall of indifference and near-sightedness.

[Page 298]

Somewhere a clock chimed. Zigelboim listened to the monotone of the tick-tock that poured a coolness on his heated head. He looked around: the sun had set long ago, it was dark, the city began to be enveloped in a damp cold fog. The coolness refreshed him. His brain again began to think logically. One is not allowed to feel doubt. He must do everything possible, take advantage of every opportunity; he must fulfill his duty. He comes to his room, sits again at the writing desk. Looks again over the proposal worked out against anti-Semitism in the post-war liberated Poland. Tomorrow morning, he has to propose the draft at the session of the National Council. Yes, he is also convinced of the victory of the Allies; a liberated Poland will arise. However, will there be Jews? He hastily lays down the draft. No! He will not get tired of demanding that first of all, everything must be done so that Jews remain alive. This must be before the law against anti-Semitism. He wrote three proposals that he would bring to the session in the morning:

"1) The National Council demands of the government that it ask all of the Allied nations, particularly America and England, to immediately devise a plan of special acts against Germany that will force an end to the slaughter of Jews.

2) The dropping of precise descriptions of the slaughter of Jews in the German language in large numbers from airplanes over Germany.

3) The government should take steps for a special conference of all of the Allied governments to be called quickly to publish a blazing protest and a strong warning in the name of all the fighting nations to the German people and their government.

Zigelboim stood up from his place and began walking around the room. Doubt again bored into his brain. He already had brought in proposals twice about undertaking sanctions against the Germans. He had sent the proposals to Churchill and Roosevelt. The responses were diplomatically evasive. No! I will not tire of demanding my due, he shouted. And on the same day, he sent an appeal to President Roosevelt and Prime Minister Churchill.

"As the plenipotentiary representative of the Jewish workers' movement in Poland and in the name of the Jews who are being murdered in vast numbers behind the gates of the ghetto, I turn to your governments with this last desperate appeal.

[Page 299]

Here is an excerpt from the last report that has again come from Warsaw: a fierce storm is raging on the heads of Polish Jewry and the terrible storm gets stronger with each day. The entire Jewish population is being exterminated, the men, the women and the children. Of the three and a half million Jews from before the war, there now remain alive no more than a few thousand and the mass murder continues further. The surviving Jews in Poland beg you to find the means to save the remnant of Polish Jews who remain alive. As a man who represents the unfortunate Jewish population of Poland, I give you their last appeal for rescue.

He ended the letter and, tired, let his hand fall on the table. His eyes looked steadily in the distance. This time, would it move them, the leaders of the civilized world?

Jan Korski, the emissary from the Polish underground movement who came to London, also had a mission for the Jewish representative. He asked Zigelboim to wait for him at 5 o'clock. He was a little late. Zigelboim was already waiting for him. They heartily greeted each other and sat down. Korski asked, "What do you want to hear?" About the Jews, I am a Jew; tell me what you know about the Jews in Poland.

Korski calmly and matter-of-factly began to describe everything he knew about the Jews, everything he had seen. He told about the "hunting" of Jews in the street, about the "*aktsias*" [round-ups] in the ghetto, about the hundreds and thousands of wagons full of Jews which go away in indefinite, but then *definite* directions. He told of his talk with the Jewish representative before his departure. Zigelboim sat stiffly, with his body shoved forward. He heard, absorbing the horrors, his eyes wide open, looking far behind the speaker; he did not blink, his face was frozen, just a nervous twitch went back and forth on his countenance. Korski, speaking, studied his face. He looked very tired. His eyes protruded from their sockets and the twitch on his face appeared more frequently. Zigelboim suddenly began to ask questions. Tell me exactly how the Jews in the ghetto appear? How do the children's faces you have seen look? What did the women say who watched the "hunting" in the ghetto with you? How do the bodies of the dead Jews on the streets of the ghetto look? Do you remember the last words of a child who you saw die on the street? Oh, I forgot, you do not understand any Yiddish. Korski began to be irritated by all of the unimportant questions and details. He was also tired of the experiences, conversations.

"Herr Zigelboim," he interrupted, a bit nervously – "all of this is not important. In general, the conditions are terrible and savage. The population in the ghetto lives in a state of death, in a constant threat of death. I have delivered the instructions that the Jewish leaders in the ghetto gave me to the representatives of the English government, who answered me that this is not feasible for political and tactical reasons."

[Page 300]

Zigelboim jumped from his place and moved nearer to Korski, his eyes flaring with anger and contempt. "Listen," he screamed, "I beg you not to tell me what has happened here, what is said here, what is done here… This I know better than you, I want to hear what is happening *there*, what they want *there*, what they are saying *there*!" He yelled out his words and nervously began to pace across the room. "Nu, good," Korski answered with brutal simplicity and matter-of-factly. "I will deliver to you what your representatives in the ghetto want from their leaders in the free nations of the world. Here, this is what they have told me to say: "They [the Jewish representatives outside Poland] should go to the most important English and American offices and agents, they should not budge until they receive a guarantee that a decision has been made to do everything to save the Jews. They should not eat and not drink; they should die face to face with the world's indifference; they should die. Perhaps this will shock the conscience of the world."

Korski stopped. Zigelboim stood opposite him reconciled, with wide open eyes and looked at him. His face was a little clear and a smile had almost lightly moved his lips. But in his eyes there was something that had not been noticed earlier, such a strange fire that it frightened him a little. Zigelboim stuck out his hand, Korski gave it a firm press. "Herr Korski, I will do everything I can to help them, everything! I will do everything they demand; you do not believe me?" Korski left the room, closed the door behind him and remained standing. Something did not let him leave. The eyes with which Zigelboim had looked at him! And perhaps he need not have reported everything [he had seen and been told in Poland]; he turned around and knocked on the door. No one answered. From behind the door could be heard a nervous pacing across the room. Korski went down the stairs, tired and heavy.

* * *

Half the night passed. Through the open window, a thick, damp fog crept in that dissolved in the darkness of the room. Zigelboim stood near the open window, looking at the darkness. All his senses were on edge. He had already decided, finished… For a long time he had felt his physical existence was immoral as death and annihilation reigned around him. Earlier, he had not permitted the thought to come to him, while they there, in whose name he spoke, needed him to remain vigilant. They believed that he could somehow help. However, now they, too, do not believe in this and ask of him to try this last thing; perhaps that would help? Perhaps the world would hear? Why is he still standing; why is he dawdling? Zigelboim, the sober, logical idealist, had always accompanied Zigelboim the dreamer, accompanied and competed and demanded perfection. Now they both screamed at him, tore him: "It is nonsense." the logical one screamed at him. "You need to remain on the watch, fulfill your duty, do everything that can be done. You have become frightened, tired and this is for a showman, melodramatic. Commit suicide? Every lovesick boy, every weakling can do this. And what will be accomplished with your death? Will such a generous gesture change the course of your enemy? They will only be happy with it; they will rub their hands with joy. The opposite – just one more "martyr" – and they will be able to do everything that they wish, undisturbed. And those you will affect with your action –cause to shudder – nonsense, they will at most shed a tear, lay a few flowers on your grave and continue their cold diplomatic calculations. Futilely give away your life for what? Consider the logic?

[Page 301]

Zigelboim torn himself away from the window and began pacing across the room.

Stop. Cynic, the second one shouted at him. Everything is not yet lost; the world will have to hear.

What is logic? Write an appeal to statesmen, confer with them, make the effort to be logical and to the point, persuade them, when everything tears in me and they examine everything logically, with calm faces. They diplomatically make the calculations; it does not pay; it cannot be done and, meanwhile, the people perish. No, no, perish with them; this is the only way that remains to me, the envoy of a hopeless people.

I will not accomplish anything here. I bang my head on a hard, deaf wall. Those who hear the banging have already become accustomed to this; it no longer has any effect. It is necessary to throw oneself at the wall with momentum, spray it with one's own brains. Perhaps this will have an effect? They, there, believe in the "perhaps." And the "perhaps" began to grow with him, took on a real form.

[Page 302]

He stopped his pacing back and forth, went to the table, sat down and began writing, stopped momentarily, reflected and again wrote. He ended; his hands remained laying on the table. He lifted his head a little, took notice of all of the small things on the writing table and his gaze stopped at the *three red roses*. The owner, an old working woman who had looked after him with care, had placed the roses on the table, deeply moved by his speech at the meeting the night before. They stood, the roses, opposite him in bloom as with open mouths. Their beauty, literally, screamed; he gave one of them a caress. The velvet smoothness burned his hand. He drew it back, stood up and with quick steps went to the dark background of the room where the bed stood. The lamp on the table remained on and lit the last written words:

"I cannot remain quiet, I cannot live when the remnant of the Jewish people in Poland, whose representative I am, are being killed. My comrades in the Warsaw Ghetto perished with weapons in their hands in the last heroic struggle. I was not destined to die like them, together with them. However, I belong to them and to their mass graves.

"Now comes the last act of the tragedy behind the walls of the ghetto that has no equal in history. The responsibility for the crime of the annihilation of the entire Jewish population in Poland falls in the first instance on the murderers themselves. However, indirectly the responsibility also falls upon all of humanity, the people and the governments of the allied nations that have not made any effort up until now with concrete action for ending the killing. These nations became partners of the murders by passively watching the murder of unprotected millions of tortured children, women and men.

"With my death I will express the strongest protest against the passivity with which the world looks at and permits the extermination of the Jewish people.

"I know how little a human life is worth today. However, while I could not do anything during my life, perhaps with my death, I will help to break the indifference of they, who have the ability to save now, perhaps, at the last moment the still living Polish Jews.

"My life belongs to the Jewish people in Poland and, therefore, I give it away."

Shmuel Zigelboim
London, 12th of May, 1943

[Page 303]

Dr. Yitzhak Sziper – Deputy from Chelm in the Polish *Sejm*

by Akiva Winik

Translated by Gloria Berkenstat Freund

In 1916, in the middle of the First World War, when Chelm was under Austrian occupation, Professor Meir Balaban and Dr. Y. Sziper arrived in Chelm. Both were dressed in Austrian army officers' uniforms. They were looking for the *pinkhusim* [vital record books] of the Chelemer *kehile* [organized Jewish community], took photographic shots of the large old synagogue and of the very old headstones in the cemetery.

Dr. Yitzhak Sziper

Dr. Y. Sziper had already been in contact with the Chelemer group, *Poalei-Zion*. The Jewish officer in the Austrian army was a great historian and scientist, who later, by chance, was chosen by the Jews in the Chelemer *poviat* [district] as deputy in the Polish *Sejm* [parliament].

A mixed population of various nationalities lived in Chelm – in the southeast corner of Congress Poland – Ruthenians, Uniate peasants, Greek Catholics, Ukrainians, Poles and Jews. A quiet, but stubborn struggle took place among the various peoples, mainly between the Ukrainians and Poles in regard to making Chelm more Polish.

The Jews were in a vice, not knowing on which side to orient themselves. They did not reveal their choice in relation to one side of the other, not being sure which of the sides would triumph in the territorial disputes. The civil Jewish parties declared their "neutrality," not wanting to come out with a separate voting list for the *Sejm* elections in Chelm.

The Central Committee of the Bund then decided not to take part in the *Sejm* election throughout Poland.

The *Poalei-Zion* in Poland decided to take part in the election and thus the only Jewish candidate list in Chelm was for the *Poalei-Zion* party.

The election ordinances were then genuinely democratic. The *Poalei-Zion* party sent out propagandists through the province to make the population aware of the positions of *P.Z.* in the *Sejm* elections. Although a few campaigning comrades were then beaten in several villages, they enthusiastically and energetically continued their work.

[Page 304]

It is very interesting to highlight the following reason that brought a few hundred voters to the *P.Z.* list: a number of Ukrainian peasants – during the Czarist regime - were in a Kiev jail with B. Borokhow. There in the jail they became familiar with the socialist ideas that the leading theoretician, Borokhow, taught them. When the Ukrainians heard that the *P.Z.* list had a connection with Borokhow's ideas, they all voted for the *Poalei-Zionist* list.

The Krakow lawyer, Dr. Max Rozenfeld, who died traveling from Vienna to Warsaw before the opening of the Polish *Sejm*, stood first on the *P.Z.* list no. 2. Since, Dr. Y. Sziper was the second candidate on the list, he automatically became the deputy from the Chelemer *poviat* (district) in the Polish *Sejm*. This was on the 19th of March 1919, when Dr. Y. Sziper became *Sejm* deputy.

As a deputy, Dr. Y. Sziper would come very often to Chelm to give lectures, reports and the like. He also often intervened with the authorities when a Chelemer Jew turned to him.

My young friend, Shneiur Wasserman, the well known writer and poet from Chelm, states in his memoirs about the destruction of Chelm in *Morgn Freiheit* [*Morning Freedom*] the following important episode: - During the Polish-Bolshevik War, when the Polish *Halertchikes* [soldiers under the command of General Jozek Haller during and after the First World War, who were widely reported to be anti-Semitic and perpetrators of violence against Jews], arrived in Chelm, they would often attack the Jews and rip their beards. A pogrom against the Jews in Chelm also broke out at that time in which approximately 100 Jews were wounded and one Jew was killed. Many houses and shops had a pogrom against them.

The Chelemer Jews, in their deadly fear, turned to Warsaw and to their deputy, Dr. Y. Sziper, who immediately came to Chelm.

All of the Chelemer city fathers and the police officials reacted indifferently to the excesses against the Jews, but in Sziper's presence they took steps to calm the infuriated crowd; perhaps, they, themselves, had incited the mob.

Dr. Y. Sziper remained in Chelm for several days and conducted a meticulous investigation of the excesses that had occurred and he put together a list of those suffering and the value of the material damages.

[Page 305]

At the next sitting of the *Sejm*, Sziper gave a speech about the pogrom in Chelm and about the Polish pogroms in general. The speech made a great impression all over Poland. He often repeated that the Polish government was responsible for all of the troubles and excesses against the Jews, that: "Pogroms are swords with two edges; they harm the murderer just as much as the victim." He proclaimed: "Make a clear account, my gentlemen, whose losses are greater, the material and physical damage that the Jews suffered through the pogroms, or your moral ruin that you plant among the young Polish generation through incitement and pogroms against the Jews."

Turning to the gallery of the *Sejm*, he asked the Polish wives, mothers and sisters, how do they react to the rowdy deeds of their sons and brothers who invade the women's *mikhvah* [ritual bath] (such incidents happened then in Chelm) and bully the deathly frightened, ashamed, naked women.

Although his speech did not stop the waves of pogroms in the country, there was a certain compensation for the Chelemer Jews and for the Jews in Poland in general in that there was someone to openly and loudly protest in the *Sejm*.

Dr. Sziper, as a *Sejm* deputy, was never intimidated and he did not stop protecting Jewish respect and Jewish life with pride and honor.

Arrests of communal political activists (the majority Jewish...) occurred in Poland in 1920, and in Chelm, too, the arrestees were Jewish political activists from all factions. Several arrestees were ordinary, impartial Jews, even several young students in the Chelemer Jewish *gymnazie*.

Among the arrestees were Dr. Mirlas (chemistry teacher in the Jewish *gymnazie*); Distler (from Galicia, bookkeeper of the *P.Z.* cooperative at the "worker's home"); Moshe Larber; A.D. Hipszman (a print worker, chairman of the *P.Z.* org.); Haim (a water carrier, a Bundist); N. Laks, etc.

[Page 306]

Also, Miss Bluma Loszojnsztejn (the only woman among the arrestees, she was imprisoned with the female criminals).

I received a note from Mr. Rozenblum (a tailor, he was then treasurer of the *P.Z.* org.) a few days after the arrest asking that I come to see him. Rozenblum was then in hiding in an attic somewhere on Lubliner Street. L. Rozenblum instructed me to go to Warsaw to Dep. Dr. Y. Sziper [to ask him] to intercede with the Polish government about freeing the arrestees.

I then (a 17-year old young man, leader of the *Poalei-Zion* youth organization) went to Warsaw. It was, in general, the first time that I traveled by train and suddenly I was in such a seething city as Warsaw.

I remembered the address of the *P.Z.* worker's house in Warsaw, Karmelicka 23. There I learned that Sziper lived with his father-in-law – the Zionist leader and lawyer, Yitzhak Grynboim – on Tlomackie 6, opposite the Tlomackie synagogue.

Dr. Sziper received me with great comradely friendship and he told me that he could not go to the minister to intercede on behalf of the Chelm arrestees because, "Arrests took place all over Poland." His school friend, Dr. Szreiber, was arrested, too, and he could not help him because he first had to learn from the minister the reasons and intentions in general of the government toward the arrestees. He would then be able to intercede and see that the innocent Jews were released. He advised me to go home and to see that all of the arrestees' families were assured that everyone would be released quickly. Arriving home in Chelm, I calmed everyone with the certainty that now the arrestees would be released.

On the fourth day after returning to Chelm, five policemen came to our house at night for a search. The house, the books and papers were ransacked and I was taken to the police station, and after several days, to the Chelemer jail where the Polish activists were imprisoned.

[Page 307]

My information from Warsaw and the assurances from Dr. Sziper that we would all be quickly freed brought great reassurance. On a dark night, three days after the arrests in Chelm, we, the "great criminals," were lead out of jail and taken away under heavy guard to the train, everyone was placed in special prisoner cars and taken to the Kielcer prison.

I was among the 12 communal activists. I was the youngest of all of the arrestees in the Kielcer prison.

After three months sitting, the communal activists from Chelm were released from the Kielcer prison without a trial, thanks to the intervention of Deputy Dr. Y. Sziper. Because the formalities about me still had not been taken care of, I sat for several more days.

Three days after the Chelemer communal activists were freed, I saw my brother Nukhem walking on the other side of the fence of the prison. At my signal, he called up to me that I would soon be freed. An hour later, I was called to the prison office and given notice that I was free!

On the street, my brother informed me that Dr. Y. Sziper had specially traveled to the Lublin district for information and clarifications about my arrest; and thanks to Dr. Sziper's intervention, after four months – I saw the free world.

Several days after my homecoming, Dr. Mirlas, may he rest in peace, who became sick in prison, died.

Poalei-Zion group in Chelm. Dr. Yitzhak Sziper is found in the center of the photo.

Meanwhile, during my arrest, the *Poalei-Zion* conference took place in Danzig and the organization spilt into the right and left. Dr. Y. Sziper remained with the right wing of the party. A few weeks later, after the split, Dr. Sziper came to Chelm for a meeting that then took place in the auditorium of the Jewish community under the chairmanship of chairman Anshel Biderman, and Dep. Dr. Y. Sziper asked those assembled if they had continued confidence in him as deputy.

Besides a group of comrades from *P.Z.*, the assembled crowd shouted: "We are devoted to Dr. Sziper as deputy! Long live Dr. Sziper!" During the second *Sejm* elections, Dr. Sziper was chosen as the deputy of the Zionist organization in Poland.

* * *

When the writer of these lines studied in Warsaw at the Jewish teachers seminar run by TSISHO [*tsentrale yidishe shul organizatsye* – Central Jewish School Organization; a system of schools organized by the Bund] in 1923-1925, Dr. Y. Sziper taught us the subject, "Jewish History," consisting of the following cycles: a) "The History of the Jews in Poland; b) "The History of the Old Yiddish Literature and c) "The History of Yiddish Theater Art and Drama."

[Page 308]

Then, in 1923, Dr. Y. Sziper entrusted to me his manuscript: "The History of Yiddish Theater Art and Drama," in order to transcribe it for the Cultural League publishing house. I, then, had the opportunity to see the utterly masterful scholarly work of Dr. Y. Sziper: Tens and, perhaps, hundreds of old Purim songs, texts of various Purim plays that the historian, Dr. Sziper, had collected for his work. I tried to do the transcriptions without errors, with the greatest precision. When the book was published, I received a copy as a gift from Dr. Y. Sziper, which I safeguard with the greatest love.

While transcribing the manuscript, I had the occasion to be at Dr. Y. Sziper's house often and I also accompanied him home to Tlomackie Street, after his seminar lectures. I had the opportunity to speak with him. I was enriched with much news and profound thoughts after every conversation.

In May 1935, the day before my departure from Warsaw to South Africa, I went to say goodbye to my kindly teacher and friend, Dr. Yitzhak Sziper. After a long conversation, Dr. Y. Sziper said to me: "It is already 37 years that I have been a Zionist. *Nu*, in around three years it will already be 40 years, just as many as the Jews were in the desert and entered *Eretz-Yisroel*. I hope to emigrate to *Eretz-Yisroel* in a few years and settle there. And I will give lectures at Jerusalem University in Yiddish about the new history of the Jews in the world, stressing that Yiddish is not an obstacle to Hebrew."

When the war broke out in 1939. Dr. Sziper was still in Warsaw and shared the savage, torturous fate of the Jewish people. He consoled and called on the Jews not to lose their courage, advising that whoever was able to should go over to the Aryan side, to do it because there were more opportunities to remain alive there. However, he, himself, remained in the ghetto. He appeared publicly with reports and lectures in the ghetto; he awakened and called for resistance.

Dr. Y. Sziper, who was devoted to his historical mission, who lived with and was energized by Polish Jewry, perished with the historic old Jewish settlement in Poland.

In the forward of the book, "The Economic History of the Jews in Poland During the Middle Ages" that was published in 1911, Dr. Sziper writes: "We already know the *Shabbosdike* Jew [Jew celebrating Shabbos] with his *neshome yeseyre* [additional soul that possesses a Jew on Shabbos]. There is still time to become acquainted with the history of the weekdays and the weekday thoughts; there is still time to search for the light in the history of simple Jewish work."

Dr. Sziper searched for and found the warmth of the simple Jew, from his dreary day-to-day individual and collective existence. First, he breathed a new communal, national and democratic spirit into the science of Jewish history. Dr. Yitzhak greatly modernized Jewish historiography in Poland.

The Zionistic Socialism that united both the Jewish national ideal and the general progressive thought; the struggle for worker rights and social justice on one side and the awakening Yiddish cultural renaissance; the deep love of the Yiddish popular language and popular literature, were the chief basis of Sziper's synthesis and harmonious world view. Dr. Y. Sziper gave his time, his erudition, his great knowledge, energy and his life for his wonderful and important ideas.

[Page 309]

Y. Sziper takes a primary place in Jewish historiography along with the great historical and famous personalities such as: Prof. Sz. Dubnow, Prof. M. Schor, Prof. M. Balaban. These Jewish people, the Polish Jews will never forget Sziper, one of the most outstanding sons of Polish Jewry in the last decade.

The *Hazan* [cantor] Yakov Likhterman (former *hazan* of the Noyzk synagogue in Warsaw), who now lives in Capetown, wrote in the Rosh Hashanah edition of the "*Africaner Yidishe Zeitung*" [*African Jewish Newspaper*] dated, Friday, the 12th of September 1947 in an article entitled, "How Dr. Yitzhak Sziper Perished": That when he, Likhterman arrived with the last transport of Jews that were sent out from the Warsaw Ghetto to Majdanek on the 5th of October 1943, he met Dr. Yitzhak Sziper, sitting hunchbacked in a corner near the wall holding a little knife in his hand and peeling potatoes in the large hall among the 300 male potato peelers.

[Page 310]

During a check, there was an S.S. member who controlled a number of prisoners, making sure that their identification numbers were hung in the correct place and Dr. Y. Sziper had just then worn the tin number a little lower on his chest; the S.S. bandit harshly beat him over the head with a rubber stick until Sziper fainted to the ground, unconscious. He lay this way until noon; then he was carried into the camp.

From then on, Sziper's feet became swollen, so that every day, the *Hazan*, Y. Likhterman, along with Sziper's son-in-law, had to carry him to work – to peel potatoes.

On a certain day, in July 1943, the great Jewish historian breathed out his soul.

Unable to endure the hardship, hunger, blows, illnesses, the exhausted "detained refugee," Dr. Y. Sziper, died in the extermination camp, in the historic, mournful place – in Majdanek, Chelemer *poviat* [district].

He always lived and struggled for the Jewish masses; even in death he was the great Jewish tribune among the Jewish masses who he comforted and loved.

[Page 309]

A Poem About a Chelemer Malamed, a Customs House and *Shabbos Shire*
[the *shabbos* on which the "Song of Moses" is sung]

by Yakov Frydman, Israel

Translated by Gloria Berkenstat Freund

The Chelemer *malamed* [religious teacher] unfurls his handkerchief with a trembling hand
Takes out a small tobacco box and takes a sniff
Then he wipes his spectacles and strides
Off the ship to the Haifa shore.

The cat comes … and among Jewish sacks and packs
The Chelemer *malamed* lays down on his bundle:
It is said, a Jewish lord comes to the shore
To look through the packs of sisters and brothers…

Well, it probably has to be like this, probably.
And here indeed, the Jewish lord approaches:
Nu, Reb Yid, what kinds of things do you have in your sack
He asks with a *gemara* melody.

– Plenty of good things, says the Chelemer with quiet joy,
His eyes dropped modestly:
I carry, carry a humble cage,
A humble cage, with humble birds.

It must be, laughs the lord, a bird with a piercing whistle.
He unties the sack with damaged eyes,
In the sack – a cage, and in it – festive whistling,
Birds hop as on branches of trees…

Now, the lord opens his eyes in amazement:
Uncle, what can we learn from the birds?

[Page 310]

– I, says the Chelemer, brought them from Chelm.
The birds are really Chelemer [from Chelm].

The story is simple, do you want to listen?
(Wonder of wonder, the creation…)
A day before I left for Palestine
It was *Shabbos Shire*.

I stand on my stoop in the middle of the market
(the Jewish market, but without Jews…) Father!
Suddenly I see from the white mountain
A flock of birds flying…

Oy father, birds, birds…
And *raboysay* [gentleman] I ask you a question:

As Jewish children no longer share the snow
On *Shabbos Shire* there is no cereal for birds,

That Jewish children are in Chelm no longer,
What will the birds do without Jewish children?...
Nu, I did what I did... *nu*,
Ha, now you understand?...

The Jewish lord opens his eyes, like a common Jew,
And the Chelemer opens the cages:
Fly birds, fly to Jewish children...
And the birds obeyed and flew...

And the Chelemer *malamed* saw through his spectacles
The way in which the lord wiped his eyes...

[Page 311]

Moshe Lerer

(A Bundle of Memories)

by A. Ajzen

Translated by Gloria Berkenstat Freund

A

In January 1937, I arrived at the *Yidishe Visnshaflekhn Institut* [Yiddish Scientific Institute; YIVO] in Vilna as a research student in its literary-philological section. This was shortly after my departure from my hometown, Hrubieszow. A longing for the gentle manner of the colorful *shtetlekh* in the area of Lublin and Wolyn still lived in my heart and by no means could I become accustomed to the neatly executed lifestyle of the Litvaks with their self assurance, harshness and outward severity. Even the appearance of their large peeling walls suggested something secret, aristocratic that absolutely did not encourage me, but the opposite: it scared and repulsed me. Although I made acquaintance with a series Vilna of residents – I then quietly, literally longed for a "familiar" face, picture or reminder of my Polish homeland and landscape.

These were my feelings when I arrived at YIVO. I need not say that my new work and research spot did not create a remedy for my wound, at first... The leaders of the Institute – Z. Kalmanovitch, M. Weinreich, Z. Reizen – as well as the research students, were all pronounced Lithuanian types, who with their expression and clear scholarly bearing, simply threw a fear into my Polish Jewish sentimental soul. On the first day I wandered around the building on Vivulska Street 18 as if stupefied by the splendor of the treasures that opened before my eyes, and I continuously thought, what do I have to do to fit into the surrounding order of authority, erudition and industry?

During one of those days, a person who I met working in the YIVO library and to whom I turned for several books helped me make sense of my confusion. He looked at me with a sharp, inquisitive, pointed look and said to me in my own Lublin accent:

– I think you are from my region...
At that moment, these few words sounded like music... Is it possible? In the distant and strange Vilna, a Jew was talking to me in my familiar manner and with tenderness and feeling that only my manner of speech could generate.
–Who are you? Where are your from? I murmured, delighted.

–Moshe Lerer from Chelm...

This is how I made my acquaintance with Lerer. I had no inkling then that fate would later often bring me together with him and I would need to be a witness to his enormous suffering and torments. For the present, however, it was as if a burden was removed from me, that is, there was a close neighbor here in YIVO, not just pure Litvaks and there would be someone to speak to in my own Lublin dialect…

[Page 312]

B

Moshe Lerer – the expert in the Yiddish language, one of the first scholarly collectors and founders of the Institute – was not just a technical leader of the library. At that time he had, in miniature, typified the Polish sector of Yiddish philology. Although the Institute, as a research institution, did not make a distinction between Polish, Lithuanian and Ukrainian Yiddish in its work, the Lithuanian accent dominated the mentality and disposition of its leaders. Therefore, Lerer felt it was his duty to defend his Polish dialect. It was a real pleasure to hear him speak at Vivulski 18 with the same intonation, nuance and vocabulary as the average Hasidim around Lublin. And it was a greater pleasure to meet Lerer disheveled, and on edge, ready to berate and to make ashes of his opponents. Then at times his vocabulary was absorbed like a sponge and from his mouth began to pour the pearls that the Jews around Chelm, Hrubieszow and Zamosz had created during the course of hundreds of years.

Lerer also diverged from the YIVO representatives on the question of language. In this sense, he considered himself a student of Noakh Prilucki, who did not have any fear of making certain old *Deitchmerizmen* more Yiddish.[1] Such words as: *alzo* [therefore/then], *gelungen* [succeed], *farzictik* [assured], *endgiltik* [final/definite/ultimate], etc, were rejected by Kalmanovitch, Weinreich and Reizen and they suggested that *bekheyn, geratn opgehitn letstgiltik* be substituted… However, Noakh Prilicki and his follower, M. Lerer, said: What? You want, *alzo* [therefore], to make our Yiddish bloodless? You will not *gelungen* [succeed] in this. Be *farzictik* [assured] with your surgical knife; the *endgiltiker* [final] judgment will belong to the people!

[Page 313]

Both the teacher and his student derived their vocabulary and concepts from the original sources of the common folk. However, each of them gave a different, a separate meaning to the concept of "folk." Noakh Prilicki – the community leader and communal man – considered himself an heir of Dubnow's scholarship about Jewish universality and striving for full cultural autonomy.[2] Moshe Lerer, on the contrary, spiritedly defended the Soviet-Jewish theory about separate Jewish territories that have only weak common bonds. Each regional group yearned for its designated area for their own specific cultural expression. Lerer's assigned task in his narrow field at YIVO was to continue to fully understand the peculiarities of the Jews of Congress Poland. Only in this way can we partially explain the friction between him and the YIVO leadership. And the bitterness of M. Lerer now becomes entirely understandable to me. He was convinced that I – his *landsman* and neighbor – did not share his view on a series of questions. He always helped me find the necessary materials for my research theme, "Yiddish Prose in Poland." Therefore, he would very often reproach me and even be angry:

– You have almost become a Litvak with your speech. This is the way a Jew from Rabiechow speaks?

C

In 1940 – in the second year of the war – a great change took place in Lerer. This person, with his always restless, nervous work energy, became sedate and thoughtful. First of all, he was affected by the sad news that reached Vilna about the dreadful mass murder of thousands of Chelemer Jews, who were in those days forced by the Hitlerist murderers to the Bug River, to the Russian border. Chalk white, without a trace of blood in his face, he told this to me and wanted to hear my opinion about this unbelievable event. I could only answer him with my news about the hundreds of Hrubieshowers who were then being tortured together with the Chelemer Jews and together shot like sheep. He stood before me confused, pale and was in no way able to understand such a tragedy.

–How is it possible? How is it possible? He pleaded with a shaking voice.

Little by little, Lerer became accustomed to the dark truth of that slaughter. However, there remained a constant mark on his soul from then on. This mark was not washed away by all of the later encouraging events in his life from 1940 to 1941: not the fact that Noakh Prilicki became an official professor at the Lithuanian University in Vilna and lecturer of Yiddish philology; and not even the fact that the Soviets chose him as the responsible caretaker and conserver of the YIVO treasures. On this historical day, when the fate of Vilna weighed on the scale, Lerer, it seems, had taken spiritual stock of himself, once and for all. In his quiet, self searching glance, a penetrating eye could read the difficult, unstated question:

– What kind of significance does this all have compared to the slaughter of so many thousands of innocent people from my hometown?

D

[Page 314]

During the years 1941 and 1942, Lerer and I worked together in the Zatrocze concentration camp near Landwarow [Lentvaris, Lithuania]. Here, I clearly sensed that inwardly he had made up his mind about everything and ultimately had made peace with death. Barely fifty and some years old, he looked like an old man who was already critically ill, with his bent body, extinguished eyes and deep, sunken cheeks. His resignation, it seems, was noticed by the rowdy element in the camp and they bullied him. Tears get stuck in my throat when I remember the heavy work that was intentionally placed on his bent shoulders. We all tried to make it easier for him and to take upon ourselves some of his duties; if this work was with peat or in unloading goods – the younger ones among us tried to make it easier for him everywhere and to take his place. He appreciated this very much and a sort of tender feeling to all of us was planted in him along with his resignation and he wanted to comfort and cheer us up.

This love for us caused a series of changes in him and his character and ideology. A communist according to belief, he became tolerant of belief and took part in all religious meetings in the camp. As if by a magic wand, his former nervousness vanished and there appeared in him instead distinct signs of understanding, of fatherly devotion to his camp comrades and even hope. I still remember his enthusiasm when, due to my endeavors, Tiszka, the Troker priest, (later shot by the Germans) became a friend of the camp workers, warned about the dangers that threatened us and came to us in his free moments to study Hebrew. At first he [Lerer] was afraid that here the priest was somewhat of an outsider. Later, when everyone became convinced of Tiszka's pure, humanitarian intentions, Lerer seemed to have been revived. "There are still, it seems," he said, "virtuous non-Jews here in the land. If this is so, everything is not yet lost!!.."

Moshe Lerer

E

In 1942, when those in our camp were sent back to Vilna, Lerer became Heiki Lunski's co-worker in the ghetto library. Here, among Jews, in his family and with his beloved work, he felt stronger and exhilarated. He began to take an interest in cultural work in the ghetto and took part in communal life. Just before the liquidation of the ghetto, he took an active part in the initiative of several groupings to expand the activities of the United Partisan Organization (P.P.O.) and to place it on a wider popular footing.

[Page 315]

This initiative did not succeed. Lerer, the office man, ignoring his weak health, wanted to serve the underground structure in some way. He withdrew into himself immediately after this and again returned to his same quiet cultural service.

Several months later after the attempted expansion of the resistance, the liquidation of the ghetto began and the transportation of the Vilna Jews to the Estonian camps. Moshe Lerer was in one of the transports. Z. Kalmanovitch was sent away almost immediately after him. Both YIVO co-workers met in the same concentration camp, Kivioli. Their joint suffering and the dreadful fate of the people united these former opponents who were now in the same boat. Face to face with death, they helped and supported one another. Lerer died, weary, his life sucked out by the difficult camp torture rack, in Zelig Kalmanovitch's arms.

Translator's footnote:

    1. *Deitchmerizmen* are words and phrases that "cultivated" Yiddish speakers considered too much like German and frowned upon their use.
    2. Simon Dubnow, the author of "History of the Jews in Poland and Russia," stressed that the survival of the Jewish people depended on spiritual and cultural strength and their autonomy.

About Moshe Lerer

From Zalman Reizner's Lexicon of Yiddish Literature, Second volume, Vilna, 1927

Moshe Lerer (1895)

Born in Chelm, Lubin area, in family of rabbis. Until age 14, he studied in *khederim* [religious schools] and *shtiblekh* [small houses of study]. Then devoted himself to self education. Went to Warsaw in 1912, where he gave lectures. 1913-1916 lived in Odessa, worked in an office, later returned to Chelm and became active as a teacher in a *P.Z.* [*Poalei-Zion*] Jewish public school; was engaged in collecting Yiddish folklore of all kinds, published several philological-folkloric articles and notes in *Moment, Literarishe Bleter*, (For example: about Peretz's Yiddish in no. 101) *Yidish Filololgie, Landoy Bukh* (*Material for an Idiotikon* (regionalisms) *of Chelm*). Lately in Warsaw, as the regular correspondent for the *Yidishe Vishshaflekhn Institut*.

[Page 316]

From the *YIVO Bleter*, Volume 26, num. 1, September-October, 1945, from the article, *Yiskor* [prayer for the dead].

Moshe Lerer

He turned up in Odessa as a young boy and in his enthusiasm for the great Yiddish writers, he saw himself in the image of Mendele [the Yiddish writer, Mendele Moykher Sforim]. He was the grandson of a rabbi; *kvitlekh*[1] were written in his house and the authenticity of his feeling for the language rarely had an equal. If he had had the opportunity to study systematically he would have certainly become a prominent philologist. Life made him into a devoted collector and protector of everything Yiddish: a word, a saying, a page and a book and witty Yiddish understatements, a letter or a manuscript from a writer. He began working for YIVO in his hometown, Chelm. Then he was employed by YIVO in Warsaw as a collector. Finally he moved to Vilna and worked at YIVO itself in the archive. In 1940 he was chosen by the new regime as commissar of YIVO and he opposed almost all of those who had been at YIVO from 1925 to 1940. However, that period must be written about at length when one speaks of the martyrs. Lerer was confined with all of the Vilna Jews in the Vilna ghetto and he was taken to Estonia during the liquidation of the ghetto. There he died of dysentery.

Moshe Lerer

From Sz. Kaczergyynski's book: *Khorban Vilna*, from the article, "Life and Death of Z. Kalmanovitch in Estonian concentration camp Narva, pages 109, 110. (The book *Khorban Vilna* was published by the United Vilner Aid Committee by the CIKO publishing house, New York, 1947).

…Zelig Kalmanovitch slept with Moshe Lerer on plank cot num. 17, on the third level of the third barracks. They would talk to each other, write and Lerer would tell me they had already written down a great deal. Lerer became sick with the widespread stomach illness [dysentery] before Chanukah. Kalmanovitch would watch over him, would take care of him. Lerer died at Chanukah time and Kalmanovitch said *kaddish* [the prayer for the dead] for him. Lerer's death greatly affected Kalmanovitch. He walked around sick, ate little and once, when I came from work (a few weeks after Lerer's death), I was told that Kalmanovitch had died in an ambulance. Their bodies, like the bodies of others who died and were murdered, were burned in a heating boiler at the manufacturing factory where our barracks were.

Told by Meir Slivkin, Vilna, lived on Vilner Street, no. 21. Received and recorded by Sz. Kaczergyynski, Vilna, 1 May, 1945.

Translator's footnotes:

1. Notes to a rabbi requesting a blessing. For example, barren women ask for a blessing to conceive a child.

[Page 317]

A Jewish Wedding in Chelm in the Old Days

by Moshe Lerer

Translated by Gloria Berkenstat Freund

We publish Moshe Lerer's philological work that was published in the periodical publication, "Jewish Philology" – bi-monthly pages of linguistics, literary research and ethnography, under the editorship of Max Weinreich, Noakh Prilucki and Zalman Reizen. Volume 1, 1249, Publisher "Culture League," Warsaw.

The groom was called up (to read from the Torah) on the last *Shabbos* before the wedding and the mothers-in-law and closely related women in the women's section would shower him with nuts, candies and raisins.

During the day, there were refreshments at the groom's home. In the evening, there was a prelude – a feast with *klezmorim* [musicians].

Again in the evening, there was a wedding reception on the eve of the wedding at the bride's home; the *klezmorim* would play all kinds of dances, and the bride's friends would dance and receive refreshments.

After, the *klezmorim* would go to play for the in-laws, relatives and good friends – separately to each one's home.

The night before the wedding day, the relatives, friends and acquaintances would be invited to a party that was called a *khosn-mol* [pre-wedding feast]. The majority also then made a feast for the poor (for the poor people) with a beautifully covered table with many good things, after which they were given money.

If the groom needed to travel to the bride's residence for the wedding, there was a doubling of the rejoicing in taking leave of him. There was also a daytime celebration, if there was a rush to depart – and accompaniment by *klezmer* out of the city.

The night before the wedding, when the bride would be taken for the emersion for purification, in addition to sharing cake at the bathhouse – with the bathhouse attendants, the ritual bathhouse attendants – she was accompanied by *klezmer*, playing in the street and a celebration began in the house, during which the *bodkin* ["jester" who created humorous rhyming improvisations at a wedding] made the bride tender with his moralizing rhymes.

There was a *klezmer* accompaniment for the groom's arrival at the bride's residence and they made a ceremonial procession around the city hall, the market ring seven times. They stopped about a few *verst* [Russian measurement equaling .66 miles] from the city and gave a forewarning by way of a herald, a rider, to the bride's side. Thus, no step was made without music almost from the call for an *aleiyah*, until the last of the seven benedictions during the party at the home of the newly married couple on the *Shabbos* after their wedding. The noisy music was proudly played the entire time.

In general, the wedding began 12 to 1 during the day.

[Page 318]

The reception of the groom at his lodgings on the main night before the veiling of the bride is called "*kaboles-ponem*" [welcome]. Then, the groom also had the ability to show his learning and originality with a hair-splitting argument before the invited relatives, associates and friends – good students of the *Talmud*.

The visit to the bride with presents – most of them rings – by the mother-in-law for the veiling of the bride [prior to the marriage ceremony] was called, "*s'ketzl kumt*" [the kitten comes] (*s'ketzl kumt!*, mother-in-law; she would be accompanied with great joy).

The next morning after the *khupah* [ceremony], when the *sheitl* [wig] had already been sent to the bride at home, the regal *siddur* [prayer book] in the golden cloth with a lock, a *shkot* (a mirror in a [wooden] frame), etc, according to one's financial ability, the groom's mother, often with all of the relatives went to see the *nakhas* [proud enjoyment], that is, if the *mitzvah* was done in the true Jewish way, and the bride was lifted from the bed. After undressing her, her hair was cut, during which the young, often 14 or 15 year old bride heartbreakingly would cry over her beautiful cut locks and braids. After the cutting, the bride would be veiled. Afterwards, as a dairy meal was eaten, such as coffee with butter cakes, etc., a joyous musical march was led, that is, the groom's mother invited the bride and all on her [side] to the station, accompanied the entire way by klezmer. The refreshments here were: beverages, fruit layered cakes, preserves and the like. Here the mother-in-law also gave the young wife a present – a bracelet, brooch, rings and the like that was called *shein*-gelt [literally, beautiful money] (inspection money for looking at the bride in her veil for the first time in the groom's house). Everyone who wanted to be treated to the honor of looking at the bride, who the excited in-laws were allegedly hiding, disguised – had to pay a fee.

For the feast, one would return to the bride's side: "for lunch."

During the *sheva yemei hamishte* [seven days of celebration], a feast was made almost every day, often with klezmer. A *sheva bruchos* [seven blessings recited under the wedding canopy] was made on the *shabbos* after the wedding and the young couple was taken to *shul* to pray. The bridesmaids invited the bride with each of those close to her.

A very proud and lively feast was made on the last day of the *sheva-bruchos* with celebrating late into the night.

The week up until the [groom was called up to the Torah] was called the silver week; the week after his being called up to the Torah until the wedding was the golden week (stemming from the golden broth that was given to the fasting groom and bride after the wedding; the crowd would grab the leftovers).

[Page 319]

We publish the two following works about Josef Milner that were written for his 60th birthday.

The first work was written – in the Parisian Oyfsney, in 1947 – by Noakh Gris, the well known writer and author of the book, Kinder Martyrologie and of the book, Tzvishn Freynd [Among Friends]. He was a skillful scholar and an active communal worker in the Central Yiddish Historical Committee in Poland.

The second work was written by Henri Hertz, one of the greatest French poets, descended from generations of French Jews. His father was even a colonel in the French army during the time of the Dreyfus trial.

Henri Hertz is an old man of 75 and is much esteemed in France in general and in Jewish circles in particular.

Noakh Gris, Paris
About Josef Milner

by Noakh Gris

Translated by Gloria Berkenstat Freund

It is difficult to meet people in France today, particularly in Paris, who do not know the name of Josef Milner. Over 40 years of literary activity in Yiddish, Hebrew, Russian and French; 40 years "communal work in the best sense of the word"; since 1933 a central figure in French *OZE* [The Society for the Protection of Jewish Health]; thousands of saved Jewish lives including in particular, 5,000 Jewish children in the Hitler era in France – this is a general picture of Milner's many-sided activities.

Based on the energy that the birthday man shows, it is unbelievable that he is already in his 60's; reading over his historical and literary works, memories from his "notebook," one must wonder about his skills and exclaim: "I am 70 years old, and look at him; he is full of vigor, if not older." Milner has united within himself the best Jewish traditions: scholarship and communal work. Today, after the terrible Holocaust, we meet few people of Milner's age who are bound to our best traditions of the past and simultaneously stand with both feet in the center of our communal and cultural work.

Therefore it is necessary to describe a few details about the celebrant whose birthday was celebrated here not long ago at several universities in Paris: Josef Milner was born in 1887 in Chelm. His father, Reb Yehuda Leib, was an enlightened Jew well known in Lubliner circles. A rich man, who was occupied with writing and communal work: he was a correspondent for *Ha-Asif* and for *HaMelitz* and a delegate to Zionist conferences. It is no wonder that two sons who were raised in a modern way in such a house followed in their father's path.

Josef Milner studied in a Russian *gymnazie*; however, his father simultaneously brought the best Yiddish instructors for him. One of his teachers was the enduring editor of *Heynt* of Warsaw, Abraham Goldberg. When the revolutionary wave of 1905 flooded the Czarist Empire, it did not bypass the middle-class child, Josef Milner, and as a result he had to leave Russia. He left for Switzerland, where he graduated from middle school in 1907. The same year he came to France from Switzerland (Bern) and remains here until today. He studied chemistry in France and received an engineering degree.

Josef Milner did not separate himself from Jewish life, as many immigrants before him and after him did. He attended meetings, appeared with reports, conducted interviews with famous personalities and he wrote about everything in Sokolow's *Ha-Olam* [*The World*], in Vilna's *Hed-Hazman* [*Echo of His Times*] and in the Petersburg *Razsoviet*. He befriended Max Nardou and was able to converse with Georg Brandes. Milner's active and probing nature and curiosity prevented him from limiting himself to political and communal correspondences. Despite his engineering degree, he showed a great interest in literature and history, seeking the *pintele yid* [the Jewish essence in every Jew] everywhere. In this way he acquainted the Jewish reader with the Jewish writer in French literature, such as Andrei Safir, Edmond Fleg and many others (he was the first to reveal to the Jewish public that the famous French humorist, France's national humorist, Tristan Bernard, is a Jew).

Milner rummages through archives, chronicles, books, speaks with archivists and museum directors from the entire country and collects a great amount of material about the history of the Jewish communities in France and the history of famous Jewish families. He published the results of his work in hundreds of journals during the course of many years. His interesting articles are reprinted in all Jewish newspapers over the entire world.

A second chapter of Josef Milner's pursuits is "*OZE*."

Right after the Hitler upheaval in Germany, "*OZE*" moved to France. Milner became general secretary for France. He remained in this post without any interruption in his activities during the years of occupation until the end of 1947 (when he was elected as vice president).

The children's school defines the best chapter in Milner's life history. It is useful to measure a man according to his relationship to children and also according to his ability to laugh. Milner passed both tests. The first and most difficult and terrible epoch of Gestapo persecution where he was saved simply by a miracle (arrested twice by Petain's militia and by the Gestapo and the latter released him because they did not recognize… that he is Jew!...) The second test is familiar to all people who have met Josef Milner at meetings and banquets. As well as a sincere and hearty laugh with an open face, he is also chock-full of historical and scholarly anecdotes and stories.

[Page 321]

Nothing more will be added about his personality, but consideration will be given to a few more institutions where he presided or is active and where he takes care of people in need who make no requests with secret gifts. However, wherever we meet him he brings good natured assurance and humor. Let my article be an expression of the appreciation of the Jewish public for the merits of Josef Milner and wish him another creative year.

[Page 322][page 321]

The 60 Years of Josef Milner

by Henri Herc

Translated by Gloria Berkenstat Freund

We must greet Josef Milner at his 60th birthday, ignoring the fact that he wishes to be a "modest and shy person." We must add that he does not look 60 years old. There are many communal workers in our Jewish world – active leaders – who are "sexagenarians," but they do not look their age. The reason is probably their combative nature. Josef Milner is among those who appear strong and young and who are mostly active and dynamic, inspiring others and drawing them into the work. In general, Josef Milner has the appearance of an American, but he is not and everyone knows that he originates from the Polish-Jewish city, Chelm, and he still boasts about this…

He has a great name as a writer (in Hebrew, Yiddish and French). His work about the history of the Jews of France is considered the best in the field. However, I will pause particularly on Josef Milner, the speaker. He has all of the abilities of a great speaker, his gestures and his accent; a rhythm is always felt in his phrasing. He entrances his audience and one feels with him "when the heart speaks." He speaks very often in Yiddish. I, alas, do not understand the language because French Jewry has spoken French for more than 150 years. However, I always understand Josef Milner's speeches because we understand what he wants to say because we feel the inspiration from his heart and we are penetrated by his great courage.

[Page 322]

Communally, Josef Milner is the embodiment of *OZE* [The Society for the Protection of Jewish Health]… He founded it in our France; he led it in the struggle for France. It would not please many if he and it perished together. He was always on the roads and in the valleys during the time of the occupation, offering rescue and courage everywhere for the dejected, moving through the threads of the Nazi-nets and he crawled out alive, thanks to simple miracles. And he led French *OZE* to a victory that was the victory of the Jewish child.

Today, Josef Milner is the vice president of *OZE*. He is a leader of a great experiment, full of significant initiatives and wherever he appears he brings in a ray of light that lets us believe that our enemies will never conquer the Jewish people.

[Page 321]

Samuel Winer

by Chana Wilder-Winer, New York

Translated by Gloria Berkenstat Freund

Samuel Winer was born on the seventh day of Passover, 1888, to a well-to-do commercial family in Chelm. He had a traditional education in *kheder* [religious school for young children] until his 10th year. His father, Hersh Leib Winer, an enlightened man, was not satisfied with that sort of learning and enrolled him in the only modern *kheder* then in Chelm – with the Brisker *malamed* [religious teacher], Haim Rozenblum, an educated person, a teacher rather than a *malamed*. He stressed *Tanakh* [*The Torah, The Prophets* and *The Writings*]. In his class, the children had to know *The Prophets* by heart. He also taught Hebrew, Hebrew grammar, as well as Russian and arithmetic. He studied with the *malamed* until his 13th year. Then his father wanted to prepare him to study.[1] His dream – the usual Jewish one – to make his son a doctor. At that time, his father's business began to decline. It did not take long until he lost everything. Bitter need reigned in the home. The frightening times heavily oppressed his mood and influenced his entire later life and eventually led him to the ideology of socialism, in which he believes to this day. Instead of studying medicine, he was given as an apprentice in Erlikh's printing shop to learn to be a typesetter. For a time, his grandfather, Reb Mendl Winer, came every evening to his home to study *gemara* [rabbinic commentaries] with him.

[Page 322]

In his own time he sought to satisfy his deep thirst for knowledge through intensive reading and studying the best of what is in Hebrew. He remains grateful for the generosity of the distinguished, enlightened Milner family that then opened wide their rich private Hebrew library. He became a fervent Zionist. He read the modern Yiddish literature, and much in Russian.

[Page 323]

Chana Winer-Wilder

During Passover, 1904, a group of young men founded a Jewish library; it had to be secret and illegal under the repressive Czarist regime. It was actually the first communal library in Chelm. He became the librarian and purchaser of the books. The library was located in his home and existed for a few years.

In the spring of 1905, he was one of the founders of the *S.S.* (Socialist-Territorialists) in Chelm. Between 1908-1912, he was active in the *S.S* Party in Warsaw and later in New York – until the party dissolution at the convention of 1916. Between 1907 and 1912, the Czarist guard in Warsaw arrested him a few times and he was exiled once.

S. Winer came to America at the end of December, 1912. At the beginning of 1914 he joined the Jewish Typesetter's Union in New York, of which he is still a member. He has been a member of the Chelmer branch of the *Arbeter Ring* since 1918.

He has been employed as a proofreader at *Der Tog* [*The Day*], the New York Yiddish newspaper, since the first day of its publication (November 5, 1914) to the present. He was a student of Dr. Haim Szitlowski, and at *Tog*, where Dr. H. Szitlowski was a constant co-worker, S. Winer came in constant contact with him, which lasted until the last day of his life, May 6, 1943. (S. Winer's article in the journal, *Yidishe Kultur* [*Yiddish Culture*], New York, 1943, about the last years of the unforgettable Dr. Haim Szitlowski is full of reverence and respect for his great teacher).

In the middle 1920's he was one of the first builders among the founders of the American division of *YIVO*. Until around 1933, he was a member of the head managing committee of American *YIVO* (Yiddish Scientific Institute).

At the end of the twenties he joined the Yiddish division of the Spinoza Institute in New York, where Spinoza's philosophy was studied under Dr. Yakov Szacki. He was co-editor of the *Spinoza Book* that the Spinoza Institute published on the 300th anniversary of Spinoza's birth (New York, 1932), a book with important works about Spinoza and his philosophy. It is the only one of its kind in Yiddish. He also took part in the translation for the *Spinoza Book* of an early work of Spinoza named, *Tractate About the Betterment of the Intellect*.[2]

[Page 324]

The Yiddish division of the Spinoza Institute immediately proposed a new, accurate translation of Spinoza's *Ethics* in Yiddish. In order to be able to translate directly from the original, he studied Latin. The work on the translation was delayed a few years. Then, after completing the translation, he first began to compare his translation with Dr. Y. Klackin's Hebrew translation and with two English, two German, a Russian and a Polish translation. Meanwhile, the Yiddish division of the Spinoza Institute closed down. The translation was not published and the manuscript remained with him (however, he hopes that his work was not in vain and that *Ethics* will still see the light).

In his free time, he was very active in the Biro-Bidjan movement. When it was decided in the summer of 1936 to send an American people's delegation to Biro-Bidjan, S. Winer was elected in New York as a member of the delegation (with over 22 thousand votes). When the delegation was ready to leave in the fall, the rumors increased that any day now Hitler would launch his war machine. It was impossible for the delegation to travel because of this.

During the summer of 1937, he was among the first founders of *ICOR* [International Jewish Cultural Union], and throughout his years in America he also was occupied with all of his heart with many communal activities. It would take too much space to enumerate all of his activities for all of his years in America.

In 1943 the *ICOR* publishing house published his translation of Fredrick Engel's classic work about Marxist philosophy with the title: *Ludwig Feuerbach and the End of Classical German Philosophy*. S. Winer added a supplement to the end of the book of 30 plus of his short essays about every intellectual and philosopher mentioned there so that the Yiddish reader would be better able to understand the important work. These essays acquaint the reader with a part of the history of philosophy.

Among his additional publications was a large theoretical work: *A Hundred Years of Marxism* in *Yidisher Kultur*, the monthly journal of *ICOR*, in the editions of April and May 1947 and February, March and April, 1948.

In *Yidisher Kultur* of March and April, 1951, a large and timely philosophical work entitled "Ethics – the Central Problem in the World Crisis" was published. Another of his works, "Freedom – Individual Psychological and Social" was also published in *Yidisher Kultur*, June edition, 1952. It was also published as a separate book with the title, *Individual and Social Freedom* (This work, as his others, stood in the spirit of socialist humanism).

Translator's footnotes:

1. Most likely in a *gymnazie*, a secular high school
2. possibly *Tractatus de Intellectus Emendatione* (*On the Improvement of the Understanding*)

[Page 325]

Personalities and Types Who Are No More

by Hersh Shishler

Translated by Gloria Berkenstat Freund

Rebbe Heshl Lajner, of blessed memory

Rebbe Heshl Lajner, of blessed memory, was very well known and beloved in Hasidic circles. He was from a great, proud rabbinic family and descended from the famous Radziner court, a brother of the Radziner rebbe, Reb Gershon Henekh, of blessed memory. Rebbe Heshl Lajner was the author of a religious book, *Luketei Devrei Torah* [collection of discourses on the *Torah*].

He settled in Chelm in 1892. His residence was located on Lubliner Street, on the road to the armories, not far from the railroad tracks that crossed Lubliner Street. An accident happened at these railroad tracks to Rebbe Heshl Lajner's son, Reb Yakov, when the train locomotive gathered speed when he was crossing the train line and it killed him.

A *shtibl* [small prayer house] was located near his apartment where prayers were said and *Torah* was studied. He, himself, sat day and night in the study of *Torah* and in the service of God.

His glorious appearance elicited great awe and respect from all, even from the Russian regime. His *Hasidim* were always at his table during the third meal on *Shabbos*, and during his reading of the *Torah*, and they had great spiritual pleasure in finding themselves face to face with the luminous personality of Rebbe Heshl Lajner, of blessed memory.

It is worthwhile to note a characteristic episode. Reb Pinya Meir Gelczer (Pinkhus Tenenboim), who was one of his Hasids, once came to Reb Heshl Lajner. He told Reb Heshl that he was about to rent an orchard from a lord, but that he did not have the money to make a down payment. Rebbe Heshl Lajner immediately went to a second room and took a golden chain from the *rebbitzen* [rabbi's wife] and gave it to Reb Pinya Meir Gelczer, so that he would have a down payment for the lord.

This episode is just one of many similar good deeds that can give us a complete picture of the goodness and virtuousness of Rabbi Heshl Lajner, of blessed memory.

The Rabbi, Reb Gamaliel Hokhman, of blessed memory

The Rabbi, Reb Gamaliel Hokhman, occupied a much respected place among the many rebbes and rabbis of the Jewish *kehile*. He was the successor of the Tomaszower Rabbi, the Rabbi, Reb Yehieil Najhojz, and the so-called *kazyonny* rabbi[1]

The Rabbi, Reb Gamaliel Hokhman, came to Chelm from a small neighboring *shtetl*. In the course of several years he became the official rabbi and spiritual leader. In general, he was a modern rabbi. He created several societies, studied and read a great deal, even the Yiddish press of every party.

[Page 326]

The Rabbi Gamaliel Hokhman, of blessed memory

He also looked into various debt disputes, and when Jews of various social standing had conflicts, differences of opinion, they came to Reb Gamaliel, who reconciled them in the best way, with a lightening fast understanding of all the muddled situations and social-psychological considerations.

In addition, he gave beautiful sermons. He often gave sermons in the Chelemer synagogue.

The Rabbi, Reb Gamaliel Hokhman, of blessed memory, perished with his entire family during the last *aktsie*[2] in Chelm in 1943.

The Reisher (Rzeszow) Rebbe, Reb Yehuda Zundl Rikkh,

May the Memory of a Righteous Person Be Blessed

The Reisher Rebbe, Reb Yehuda Zundl Rikkh, was descended from the Belzer Hasidic dynasty. He arrived in Chelm at the beginning of 1920 and quickly became well known in the city and in the surrounding *shtetlekh* [towns]. He was known as a miracle worker. He gave medicine to the sick.

However, for all these years, the Reisher Rebbe was known as a great pauper. He was supported by the Chelemer tradesmen and common people. He was much beloved. He became the rebbe of the poor craftsmen and working people.

His son was the famous Rabker [Rabka, Poland] Rabbi and his son-in-law was the Rabbi, Reb Efroim Unger, who was elected as rabbi in the nearby *shtetl*, Swiercze.

The Reisher Rebbe, Reb Yehuda Zundl Rikkh, perished at the hands of Hitler's murderers. He was dragged away to the gas ovens of Sobibor with thousands of Chelemer Jews.

The Reisher Rebbe, Reb Yehuda Zundl Rikkh

[Page 327]

Berl Akslrad

He was a well known person in Chelm, known as an active communal worker who was represented in most important communal organizations in Chelm. He was the synagogue warden of the *kehile* [religious governing body], councilman and alderman in the Chelm city council and was managing director of the Jewish public school.

He perished in Kovno in the Ninth Fort [originally an early 20th century defense fortress] in 1944.

Berl Akslrad with his two children, Dwoyra'le and Yosele, who perished in Auschwitz

Nekha Bakalczuk-Akslrad

She worked with her husband, Berl Akslrad, in the Jewish public school and was the manager of the children's home. She survived the cruel war, losing her husband and two children.

[Page 328]

Her health weakened in the concentration camps and she suffered from kidney disease.

After the liberation, she worked in Poland and in Lintz (Austria) in the school. She traveled from there on a visit to Israel with her second husband, M. Bakalczuk, and then emigrated to South Africa where was an active worker in the Johannesburg Yiddish *folks-shul* [secular school].

She died of severe kidney disease – an inheritance from the German concentration camp years – in 1953.

Nekha Bakalczuk-Akslrad

Dovid Kornblit

He was a capable student in the Jewish-Polish *gymnazie* [high school] in Chelm. Later, he graduated from the Polish University in Vilna. He was a teacher of mathematics in the Hebrew *Yavna gymnazie* in Vilna and in the Hebrew teacher's seminar.

When the war broke out, he was a teacher at the Polish government *gymnazie*. He perished tragically at the hands of the Germans.

Moshe Beker

He was one of the earliest of the young people to become absorbed in the workers movement. He was an active synagogue person and one of the leaders of the left *Paole-Zion* in Chelm. He joined many Jewish communal and cultural circles. He was the synagogue warden of the Jewish *kehile* and an official at city hall.

Benimin Blumensztok

He dedicated a great deal of his lifetime to work on behalf of being an active worker, in general, for the Chelemer Jewish philanthropic societies.

Melekh Hersh Brajtman

He was called Melekh Hersh. He was known in Jewish Chelm as the *gabay* [trustee] of the *khevra kadisha* [burial society].

He was a good Jew with a good Jewish heart; he gave his entire time and energy and dedication to *kehile* philanthropic work. He helped the poor Jews, tradesmen and others. He often visited poor Jewish homes, providing them with bread and clothing.

Melekh Hersh was the *gabay* of the burial society in Chelm for many years. He did a great deal in his post; he did not permit the desecration of or cause shame to the dead, careful that the funeral was carried out with appropriate care according to the Jewish religion.

Melekh Hersh was one of the first founders of the *biker-khoylim* [a primitive hospital] in Chelm and, later, of the *lines hatzedek* [organization that provides nightly necessities for the sick poor]. He visited many sick Jews, worried about their condition. From his own pocket he often paid a doctor for a visit and paid an apothecary for a medicine that the doctor had prescribed.

Melekh Hersh Brajtman was a great follower of the Reisher [Rzeszow] Rebbe, Reb Yehuda Zundl Rikkh. It is well known that the Reisher rabbi was very poor. The Chelemer Jewish *kehile* gave him little support. However, Hersh often supported the Reisher Rebbe.

His son, Jakov Brajtman, is a famous cantor in America; he once came to Chelm on a visit to his parents and he enchanted the Chelemer Jews with his *davenen* [praying]. He prayed in the large synagogue, evoking great enthusiasm and admiration with his touching voice, and the Chelemer Jews spoke for years in admiration of his vocal music, although the best cantors in Poland often came to Chelm. Chelemer Jews had a reputation as experts about cantors. Therefore, Jakov Brajtman's *davenen* remained deep in the memory of much of the Chelemer Jewish population, and his father, Reb Melekh Hersh, was proud of his son.

[Page 329]

Khazan Jakov Brajtman, son of Melekh Hersh, vice president of the Cantor's Union in the United States)

The Chelemer Synagogue *Khazan* [Cantor], Reb Berish Greber

The Chelemer Synagogue *khazan*, Reb Berish Greber, was known to almost every regular Jew in Chelm. He was the *khazan* of the large synagogue in Chelm for many years. He was a good and beloved *khazan*; he possessed a sweet voice and prayed with his own established choir. Two of his sons, Shlomoh and Shmuel, who emigrated to America, were also his principal choir boys. Reb Berish Greber was also a good violinist. He wrote music. However, his material situation was very strained.

Because he received small wages from the *Kehile*, he would go through Chelm to the property owners every Thursday for support. He would go with the prayer house *khazan*, Reb Benimin Zinger, because his wages were also small.

The funeral of the Chelemer synagogue khazan, Reb Dovid Berish Greber, of blessed memory, who died on the 22nd of April, 1936. Left – the synagogue khazan, Reb Berish Greber.

[Page 330]

During the *erev yom-tovim* [the evenings before a holiday], such as Rosh Hashanah, and also on *Rosh Khodesh* [the start of a new Hebrew month], Purim and the days of Chanukah, the synagogue *khazan*, Reb Berish Greber, walked separately with his *shamas* [synagogue caretaker], Reb Shmuel Globn; the *khazan* of the prayer house; Reb Benimin Zinger, on the other hand, walked with his *shamas*, Reb Leibish Beder. Thus were the wage conditions of the *khazanim* at that time.

Reb Berish's *davenen* as the synagogue *khazan* was very impressive. During the Days of Awe, when he said, "*beRosh Hashana yikatevun uveYom Tzom Kippur yechatemun*' ["On Rosh Hashanah it will be written, and on the fast of Yom Kippur it will be signed,"] it thrilled everyone. Women in the women's section sobbed with bitter tears and the entire synagogue and anteroom felt the awe of the Day of Judgment. Reb Berish's *Un'taneh Tokef*[3] that brought forth so much belief, emotions and tears, was very moving and sweet.

In his older years Reb Berish could not be the *khazan*. His old wife and the difficult, poor life of want lay heavily on his health.

For years, the Chelemer synagogue did not find a successor of the standing of Reb Berish the *khazan*.

A. Goldberg

He was a well known Jewish publicist and writer. After the First World War, he left Chelm for Warsaw, where he was the editor of *Heint* [*Today*] and also took part in other publications.

Nakhum Goldberg

He was the first editor and founder of the *Chelemer Shtime* [*Voice of Chelm*]. He wrote notices and short stories. He was a capable journalist.

Ben-Zion Goldgewikht

He was a bookkeeper by profession. He gave a great deal of time to communal and cultural work. He was well versed in Yiddish, Hebrew and world literature.

Josef Goldhaber

Josef Goldhaber was a lover of the people and heartfelt man of the people who had studied a great deal and knew how to write and read more than 10 languages. He was also a talented writer of fine short stories and novels. His creations were also published in foreign language journals. He also worked at the local Chelemer Yiddish newspaper and at the *Ilustrirter Vok* that was published in Warsaw under the editor, A. Grofman, and at other periodicals.

[Page 331]

J. Goldhaber was much beloved in Chelm and also in the surrounding area, because in addition to all of his great virtues, he was a good fiddler and was very proficient in other musical instruments. His fiddle playing and his fine humorous character brought him many friends during his life. A circle of young and old Jews, who came to hear his anecdotes and jokes, his fiddle melodies and, also, his new creations, was always found in his home. He always befriended young writers, teaching them how to polish their language, the laws of style and of poetry.

J. Goldhaber was a very modest person, a friend of the poor and toiling Jews, of workers, wagon drivers, porters, tailors, shoemakers, friendly to everyone and he fit in well.

In great pain and suffering, he breathed out his noble soul, together with the other Chelemer martyrs.

Dora Dubkowska[4]

She was a famous singer and distinguished by her beautiful lyrical voice. She would often appear in concerts in many cities in Poland, having great success.

Meir Dubkowski

He was the Chelemer news dealer. He was one of the first who spread the Yiddish word and the Yiddish book In Chelm. On the eve of the First World War of 1914, M. Dubkowski organized the first Yiddish reading library in his residence on Budowska Street. Yiddish intelligence and culture was concentrated at his newspaper kiosk.

Hersh Diker

When Yiddish theater in Chelm and its adherents are remembered, the name of Hersh Diker cannot be passed over and left out.

Hersh Diker was a great lover of the Yiddish word and from his earliest years he was tempted by the Yiddish theater. Although he was the son of Hasidic parents, he quietly gave into the sweet sin on the theater boards.

In addition to Diker's inclination toward the Yiddish stage, he also had a flair for music. He played the violin and often appeared in public at social events that were arranged to alleviate the need of the poor Jews in Chelm.

H. Diker had a circle of amateurs around him. Diker would appear without pay with his amateur colleagues at poor weddings, and he gave the money that he would receive for providing music for dancing as a wedding gift to the poor bride and groom.

The custom of playing at weddings for the poor and then giving the money that came in from playing for the dancing to the poor couple was first introduced in Chelm by the Luksenburg brothers, who at that time, also led a musical group in Chelm.

[Page 332]

In the last years before the Holocaust, H. Diker excelled at collecting money year after year for the Passover needs of the poor. Diker would gather his assistants and go with them to the rich property owners of the city and to the Purim banquets and entertain them with fine Jewish motifs and melodies that he had especially prepared and thoroughly learned months earlier.

These Purim attractions were repeated year after year. Hersh Diker maintained the right to do this and it was very successful for him both morally and materially. The collected money helped many poor Jews bring *Pesakh* [Passover] into their poor houses.

Diker was a man of the people throughout, far from a rich man. He earned his living as a purchasing agent (*komisioner*). He was always extremely busy and bustling far away from home, always on the go; in Warsaw and in Lublin – purchasing goods for retailers and tradesmen in Chelm. However, Diker devoted the few minutes he had free to communal work.

In his last years, Diker earned his reputation by carrying out aid activities. At that time he created a permanent music group in Chelm that numbered around 30 members.

Hersh Diker also suffered the fate of the millions of Jews who perished in Poland. In 1942 he perished at the hands of the Hitlerist assassins. He contributed much to the Yiddish theater in Chelm.

Feiwl Dreksler

He came from a poor environment, having a great predisposition for the Yiddish stage. He was known as a gifted artist and accomplished director. He contributed much to the Yiddish theater in Chelm.

Lipa Herc

Lipa Herc or, as he was called, Lipele the butcher, was an overseer in the *kehile* and a communal worker, participating in many Jewish institutions as a managing committee member and also as president.

He was also an *Opiekun Spoleczny* [public guardian] at city hall for the Jewish and non-Jewish population in his region.

Lipa Herc was a good natured person and he gave generously to charity for the benefit of various institutions and for individuals, too.

He was a great businessman, furnishing meat for the military that was stationed in Chelm and also for the hospital.

[Page 333]

In the days of the Hitler occupation in Chelm, Lipa Herc tried to alleviate the terrible conditions of the Jews, giving great sums of money in payments to the Germans.

He, his wife and children perished tragically. One of his sons, Yehoshua Herc, was a fighter in a partisan camp. He survived and is now in Montreal, Canada.

Ahron Wolfson

He was the typesetter and co-editor of the *Chelemer Shtime* [*Voice of Chelm*]. He was devoted to Jewish communal work with heart and soul.

Dr. Dovid Walberger

He also took part in all of the cultural communal institutions and was very beloved in Chelm. He gave free medical help to the poor Jewish population. He also created a dramatic and musical circle.

Gershon Lustiker

He was very beloved by the ordinary people of Chelm. He struggled for years for the rights of the Jewish tradesmen. When the guild laws were published that were proposed against the Jewish craftsmen, he threw himself with life and soul into the struggle to combat these laws that undermined the economic foundations of Jewish artisans.

He, also, was editor of the *Chelemer Shtime*. His articles and human interest stories were written with great understanding and were rich in content.

Fishl Lazar

Fishl Lazar

He was editor of *Chelemer Shtime* for a time. He provided a great deal of space in the newspaper for Zionism. He was an enthusiastic Zionist and a co-worker in the Palestine office.

He helped edit provincial newspapers in the Lublin area.

Y. Lewensztejn

Known as "Berele's Fishele," he was born into the rich, aristocratic Lewensztejn family. He left for Warsaw as a young man, where he studied. He then became an important journalist and critic, taking part in many Yiddish and Polish newspapers and journals.

[Page 334]

Abraham Cikl

Known as "Zeide" [grandfather], he was a capable and talented actor and cultural worker. He devoted many years to the Yiddish stage in Chelm. He greatly assisted the development of Yiddish theater in Chelm.

Itshe Luksenburg

He made significant gains for Jewish communal and cultural life in Chelm, working with the creators of a musical group and dramatic circle.

Shimeon Fryd

He was well known among the Chelemer intellectuals. He was a teacher and guide for many of the young, who in later years took a respected place in Jewish cultural life in Chelm. He died during the last war in Russia.

Dr. Leah Fryd

Dr. Leah Fryd was a gifted and extraordinarily capable woman.

She graduated from the Vilna University Medical Faculty in 1928. She practiced for a long time in Vienna. She acquired a very good reputation in Chelm. She gave free medical help to the poor and needy people. She worked for *TOZ* [Society for the Protection of Health] and *Linas haTzedek* [Society to care for the sick poor] for a time

[Page 335]

In addition to her medical activities, Dr. Leah Fryd contributed a great deal of time to communal work. She was active in Jewish communal life. She also published popular medical articles in the Yiddish press in the Polish provincial cities.

Thanks to the initiative of Dr. Leah Fryd, a children's home was founded in Chelm.

Mina, Leah Fryd's daughter, was in Lemberg at the outbreak of the German-Russian War, where she was studying. Leah Fryd brought her daughter to Chelm.

Under the Hitler occupation, Mina Fryd had Aryan documents and was able to survive. However, when her mother, Leah Fryd was led to her death, she presented herself to the Gestapo and she perished with her dearly beloved mother.

Shaya Kratka

He was one of the most prominent and most active members of the Chelemer *Paole-Zion* Party (Left).

In 1939 he evacuated to the Soviet Union. In 1941, he voluntarily joined the Red Army. In 1944, he joined the Polish Division and was on the victorious drive to the Vistula River. He visited Chelm.

Shaya Kratka fell in battle near the Vistual River, when the Soviet Army carried out its assault against Warsaw. He fell

as a hero in the battle with Hitler-Facism.

Dr. M. Kanfer

He came to Chelm with the Austrian army in 1916 with the rank of an Austrian officer. He was an attorney by profession.

In 1918 he became the manager of the Jewish public school. Dr. M. Kanfer later was engaged in the legal profession and worked with the Yiddish-Polish newspapers writing literary treatises about Yiddish literature.

After leaving Chelm, he settled in his birthplace, Krakow, where he edited the Polish-Yiddish newspaper named *Novi Dziennik* [*New Daily News*].

He perished at the hands of the Germans.

Mekhele Rybajzen

An interesting type, Mekhele Rybajzen was full of paradoxes. He burst into the capital city of Poland – Warsaw – from Chelm and became the auxiliary secretary of the Yiddish Literary Union.

Mekhele Rybajzen was born in Chelm. His father was a tinsmith and very poor. He became an orphan[5] at a very early age. He left his poor home during his very early years and went to the large city of Warsaw, where he studied and worked and became friends with Yiddish writers.

Once on *Erev Pesakh* [on the eve of Passover], when he came home to Chelm for the holiday, Mekhele Rybajzen already looked like someone from a big city and typified a poet. His round, girlish face with generous tufts of hair became serious. He wore a plush hat with a wide brim, with a black cape. Mekhele elicited special attention and people looked at him with quiet envy because of his attire and with his transformation that called to mind the personalities of famous Yiddish writers of that time in Poland.

[Page 336]

I do not know if Mekhele Rybajzen wrote very much. After the First World War, Mekhele once showed me two of his poems that were published in a literary collection of *Young Yiddish Poets in Poland*. Rybajzen's two poems spoke about rain and clouds. I could not then appreciate their literary value.

Mekhele Rybajzen rapidly became popular in literary circles. Mekhele quickly became acquainted with all of the Yiddish writers, from the oldest lion heads to the youngest upcoming talent who came to the Literary Union on Tlomacki. At that time one often found caricatures in the Warsaw Yiddish newspapers that would make fun of Mekhele Rybajzen as secretary and treasurer of the Literary Union because of his striving.

However, Mekhele went his way. He always was dreamy and pensive. Rybajzen never wrote a line that was published in the local newspaper in Chelm, apparently, because he felt himself too good to write for a provincial paper.

It is not known if Rybajzen wrote anything in his last years. Before the last war, we received news that Rybajzen was revising a larger work. However, it is not known if it was published.

Mekhele Rybajzen perished at the beginning of the Hitler occupation of Poland. He perished on the highway trying to escape from the Hitler devils.

Mekhele Rybajzen

Translator's footnotes:

1. A *kazyonny* or "crown" rabbi was appointed by the government and carried out civil as well as spiritual functions.
2. German word usually used to describe round-ups and deportations.
3. "Let us proclaim," prayer said on Rosh Hashanah and Yom Kippur about the Day of Judgment.
4. Residents of Chelm knew her as Dwoyra.
5. *yosim*, the Yiddish word for orphan, can mean a child who has lost one parent.

[Page 337]

The Rebbe, Reb Note

(The legend of who he was, and how he became the rebbe of thousands of Hasidim in Chelm)

by Manashe Unger, New York

Translated by Gloria Berkenstat Freund

Manashe Unger, the writer of this article, is a famous researcher of Hasides. He, himself, is the son of a well-known Hasidic rebbe in Galicia. He published the books *Hasides in Life*, *Pshiskhe* [Przysucha] *and Kotsk* [Kock], *Hasides in Poland and Galicia*. He also has two books in Hebrew.

* * *

Chelm, the city that is so famous in the Jewish world because such rich folklore was created around her, was also known in the Hasidic literature because of her people's rebbe, Reb Note Chelemer, who was considered a *lamed-vovnik*[1] and a hidden saint, who did not want to be revealed until the Rebbe, Reb Mordekhai Neszkhizer requested it of him.

The Rebbe, Reb Nusan Note was different from other rabbis of his generation in that his followers were not "elevated" Hasidim, only simple Jews and ordinary people. He was from those rabbis of the people who were already a rarity in his generation because at that time, when he began his tenure as a Hasidic rabbi, there was already an almost canonized *Hasides*. At that time an important student of a rebbe could no longer become a leader of Hasidim as would happen earlier – the office of Hasidic rabbi was transferred only through inheritance, from father to son. There were already rabbinic dynasties and rabbinical courts. In this sense, the Rebbe, Reb Note was an exception in that he was not the son of a rebbe and still became a Hasidic rebbe. However, he, himself, left a Hasidic dynasty after him that continued his path in Hasides until our generation when Chelm was destroyed along with hundreds of other old Jewish communities in Poland by the accursed Nazis, may their names and memories be erased.

It is not known exactly when the Rebbe, Reb Note was born. It must be approximately over 200 years ago. However, it is known when he died. The Rebbe, Reb Note died on the 1st of Shevat, 5572, 1812, exactly 140 years ago.

Many Hasidic stories are told about the Chelemer Rebbe, Reb Note; how he was often asked to pray for a sick person, but the rebbe told him that he should pray to the Creator of the World himself.

The Rebbe, Reb Note Chelemer had many tenant farmers and village Jews among his Hasidim. The Rebbe, Reb Note would often say that even when a Jew interprets a verse of the Bible differently from the literal meaning and his intention is honest it can help more than the prayers of a rabbi.

And here is what the Hasidim say about Rebbe, Reb Note, how he became a rebbe and how a village Jew helped Jews despite his bad interpretation of a verse:

[Page 338]

It is told in a Hasidic legend that as a young man, the Rebbe, Reb Note was a *malamed* [teacher] for an *arendarz* [lessee] in a village near Wlodawka. He taught Hebrew to the two grandsons of the lessee, who ran a tavern and was the overseer of the landowner's forest.

Reb Note the *malamed*, taught the children all day in a small room that was adjacent to the tavern and, at night, when the entire household was asleep, he had to go to the woods to make sure that the peasants did not steal any wood from the forest.

When the village peasants learned what kind of new watchman they had received, they laughed heartily and said: "With such a *zydlak* [Jew boy], we will manage."

Almost immediately, on the first night when the *malamed* began to act as a guard, the peasants came into the forest with their wagons and axes and wanted immediately to begin chopping the trees in the forest. To be more secure, they began to shout from one corner of the forest to the other corner of the forest to hear if the *zydlak*, Note, was on guard. However, there was no answer from Reb Note. Then they were really sure that the forest guard, Reb Note, was sleeping somewhere comfortable and they took to their work at once…

The Hasidic legends relate that as soon as they started to cut a tree they suddenly heard a mournful cry that carried through the entire forest. At the beginning they thought that this was how the forest animals howl at night. But as they chopped the tree, the cry became stronger and stronger as if it came from the tree itself. This mournful cry softened the hearts of the peasants and they could no longer bear to remain in their places and one of them said that they must learn the origin of the lament.

The peasants stopped chopping the tree and left to follow the sound of the crying. However, in each side to which they went, it seemed as if the voice came from another side and, in addition, still higher and stronger. The matter became more curious and they divided themselves into a few groups and went to all four sides of the forest.

[Page 339]

However, each group separately thought that the crying was coming from another side… And everything in the forest became dark and the lament came from all sides, as if hungry wolves filled the forest, no, as if hundreds of people were lamenting a great devastation… And suddenly, trudging in the deep darkness of the forest, they saw a small fire slipping out from afar between two trees. Separately each group left for the point from which the little fire had been revealed, and they went and went and still farther they crawled into the forest, farther and farther they moved from the little fire and reached closer to the crying. They wandered in the forest this way the entire night and only in the morning did they reach a spot where a cave was located and they saw a clear glow coming out from the cave and, from inside, from the deep deepness, came the crying that tore their hearts into pieces from pain and sorrow.

One of the peasants doubled himself up while turning and lowered himself down into the deserted cave, and what did he see? The *zydlak* Note was lying on the ground and murmuring some sort of prayer. There was ash on his head and tears poured out of his eyes and not only did his eyes cry, his entire body cried, too – every limb in him separately, and it seemed as if all of the trees in the forest were crying with him… And a clear fire shone around him, a glorious shine that wound like a shining pillar into heaven…

When the peasant came out of the cave and told them what he had seen, the peasants remained standing amazed and listened to the strange prayers from the little Jew, Note, to his recitation of the midnight prayers about the destruction of the Temple and they actually completely forgot why they had gone into the forest so late at night… And the peasants stood this way in front of the cave and cried with Reb Note's lament on the Exile until they suddenly saw that it had become day and they remembered that they immediately had to return to the village to work on the lord's estate.

And when it was morning and the peasants wanted to enter the interior of the cave, they saw that Reb Note was lying on the bare ground asleep and next to him lay the rusty gun… The peasants left him sleeping and quickly returned to the estate and could not forget the wonder that they had seen in the forest at night.

And thus passed a considerable time. The peasants were no longer able to steal any wood from the forest. Reb Note's cries did not permit them to do so. Reb Note himself, who toiled the entire day with the lessee's two children, learned from the drunk peasants, why they were not coming to the forest to steal, how he, Reb Note, enthralled the peasants with his heartfelt laments in the cave, from which a small fire shone out and how he "prayed" there with such laments and wails that a stone could be moved…

The wife of the lessee began to watch the ways of Reb Note until one Friday at night, when Reb Note did not go into the woods, she glimpsed a light shining out of the cubbyhole where Reb Note slept and a wonderful song was heard, a song that no human voice could sing so beautifully, but of the sort sung by angels…

[Page 340]

And although the lessee's two young boys had not yet learned the *komets-alef* [one of the first letters of the Hebrew alphabet], the lessee's wife did not permit the dismissal of the *melamed* from his position. She told her husband, the lessee, what the peasants in the village were saying about their *melamed*, and what she herself had seen on Friday at night.

The reputation that Reb Note was a *tzadek* [righteous man] spread throughout the entire area. Reb Note himself learned what was being said about him in the village and he went to the Rebbe, Reb Mordekhai Neshchizer, and he explained to him what had happened in the village, that his deeds were known and, therefore, he wanted to escape from there. However, the Neshchizer Rebbe told him to remain with the lessee and to continue to act as he had until now because his fate was decided providentially that he should be a leader and a good defender for Jews when needed.

Reb Note remained a *melamed* with the lessee and taught the boys during the day and sat occupied with study and prayer in the abandoned cave in the forest, rose at midnight for study and prayer and prayed…

Until he also became known in Wlodawka and then in Chelm and he became a rebbe with thousands of Hasidim.

Once, the Hasidic legends further state, the lessee decided to travel to Chelm to Rebbe, Reb Note on *Yom-Kippur*.

All through *Yom-Kippur* the *rebbe* prayed himself in front of the pulpit and he did make himself known to the lessee. Rebbe, Reb Note's weeping and crying was without limit. None of the Hasidim could understand that the rebbe was crying more this year than every other year and they were afraid that the rebbe probably saw a difficult edict in heaven that he had to annul.

And when during *Ne'ilah* [concluding prayer on *Yom-Kippur*] the prayer: *Av yedaakha mi-noar* "Our father, Avraham, knew You from his youth on," arrived, the rebbe burst into powerful tears, which strongly moved the simple lessee who had stood sentimentally during the entire *Yom-Kippur* and did not understand why the rebbe and the Hasidim were crying so intensely and he began crying bitter tears. However, suddenly, the rebbe's face became radiant and he began to sing and dance with joy and the *Ne'ilah* praying ended with bliss and joyfulness.

The Hasidim stood amazed and they did not know what had happened.

At night, at the close of *Yom-Kippur*, when the Rebbe led a *seudah* [meal] with the Hasidim, he called the lessee to the table and asked him why he had cried so strongly this night at the prayer: *Av yedaakha mi-noar*.

"I will tell you the truth" – the lessee had begun to speak in his village way – "I had thought highly of you. However, as I saw how you relate to me, how you completely forgot me, it wrenched my heart and I burst into tears. In particular with the prayer, *Av yedaakha mi-noar*, it occurred to me, why must the patriarchs constantly be remembered in the prayers? The pretext is that when we remember the patriarchs in the *Yom-Kippur* praying, Satan comes and says: A trick that the patriarchs thought highly of God when he showed so many miracles? Everyone would have then believed in God. *Ne'ilah* begins and the prayer, *Av yedaakha mi-noar*, our father, Avraham, recognized You, *God, You were still young* and, therefore, God had to help. I burst into tears when I remembered that, I, too, recognized you, Rebbe when you were still young and taught my children and no one knew you, and now you have completely forgotten me."

[Page 341][Page 342]

Later, the Rebbe, Reb Note, explained to the Hasidim that a great edict against the Jews had been written down that day in heaven and he knew that he alone would not be able to annul it. However, with the help of the village Jew, who, although, he had interpreted the verse, *Av yedaakha mi-noar*, badly, his intention was pure and the edict was annulled and, therefore, the rebbe had then ended the *Nei'lah* prayer with joy.

And the Rebbe took out a little sack of money and gave it to the lessee and said: "Here, have a small fee from the Hasidim for what you did with me, when I was with you in the village and you will be able to make the payment to the Lord with this and show them that you have saved all Jews from the harsh edict this year simply with your interpretation of the verse, *Av yedaakha mi-noar*, and made a greater noise in heaven than all of the righteous of the generation."

Translator's footnote:

1. *Lamed-vov* has the numerical value of 36 in the Hebrew alphabet. A *Lamed Vovnik* is, by tradition, one of the 36 righteous people produced in each generation.

[Pages 341- 342]

Famous Rabbis

by J. Kornblit

Translated by Howard Bergman

In the last several years before the great destruction, Chelm was a large center of Torah studies. There existed a number of Yeshivot and religious educational institutions. Three years before World War II, in 1936, the Lubavich Yeshiva was founded; one year later, the Radzyner Yeshiva was established. The Lubavich Yeshiva grew very quickly, becoming one of the loveliest in the region, but the Radzyner Yeshiva also became a distinguished seat of Torah learning.

There were forty houses of study where Torah learning took place day and night. Every one of us remembers the nights in the Belzer, Kotsker, Radzyner, and Gerer (Gora Kalwaria) small Hasidic houses of prayer. When one entered the houses of the Kuzmir Rabbi, Reb Pinchas, and the Reisher (Rzeszow in Polish) Rabbi, one became carried away with the saintliness of the Torah and Hasidism, and one forgot the entire ordinary world.

Friday evenings, from every Jewish home, Sabbath melodies were heard and Sabbath candles twinkled. An air of holiness floated in every corner.

On Saturday mornings the streets were full of worshippers who were either going to or returning from the prayers. During the Sabbath day the streets were filled with promenading Jews. Lublin Street was overflowing with Sabbath Jews.

Jews in Chelm brought up their children with the Torah. The city could pride itself when compared with other towns.

The **Agudat Israel** (Israel Association) founded The Beit Yakov School where many students were learning. Parents would also send their children to study in other towns. Students from Chelm were enrolled in the Lubavich Yeshiva in Otwock; in Yeshivot and religious educational institutions in Kleck, Radzyn, Ludniir, Brisk (Brest), Baranowicz, and others.

The Agudat Israel maintained a large youth organization named "Tsairi Agudat Israel". The chairmen of A. I. were Hersz Grodzicki and Heszl Fasz. The influence of A. I. on the Jewish communal life was markedly strong.

There was also in Chelm an organization of **Mizrahi.** Its chairman was Reb Nosn Mandel. The organization also maintained the youth division "Tsairi Hamizrahi" and "Hapoel Hamizrahi".

Chelm had famous rabbis and teachers who were very influential in strengthening the faith.

To the extent that my memory serves me, I will recall the following Rabbis:

The Kuzmirer Rabbi, Reb Nukhem'che Twerski, HY"D[1]

The Kuzmirer Rabbi, Reb Nukhem'che, was the son of Reb Moyshe Leybele and grandson of Reb Nukhem'che who was the son of the Trisker Magid (Preacher). Rabbi Nukhem'che took over the leadership of the Kuzmirer Hasidim after the demise of his father. There were several thousand Kuzmirer Hasidim. Most of them lived in the Kielce region and when World War II broke out; the Rabbi was visiting his Hasidim in the town of Pinczow, where he probably died a martyred death together with all other local Jews. The Rabbi also had two brothers-in-law, one of whom was the son of the old Rabbi of Komarno. During the war he succeeded in traveling to the Soviet side, arriving in his home town of Komarno, near Lemberg (Lwow), where he perished when the Germans began the invasion of the Soviet Union. The second brother-in-law was Fishl Lazar, the longtime publisher of the ***Chelemer Shtime.*** In the last years, Fishl Lazar lived in Warsaw, where he was an instructor at Keren Hayesod. He perished in the first days of the war when German planes bombed Warsaw.

The Reyvitz (Rejowiec?) Rabbi, Yehoshue Avrom Alter Sochaczewski, HY"D

The Reyvitz Rabbi was greatly loved in town. Day and night his house was a place of study. The Rabbi and his sons would sit at the Torah and work, demanding the same from his Hasidim and those who were paying tribute. The Rabbi, together with his children and son-in-law, Rabbi Gershon Henech Leiner, were killed by the Nazi murderers in a gruesome way.

Rabbi Pinkhas'l Lerer, ZTs"L[2]

Rabbi Pinkhas'l was a descendant of Rabbis Tudrus and Notele of Chelm. He passed away several years before WW II during an election in the nearby town of Selc. Rabbi Pinkhas'l had very few Hasidim, and the poverty in his home could literally be seen on the walls. He often traveled to the Gerer Rabbi. Rabbi Pinkhas'l was a sincere and devoted Jew.

Rabbi Israel Najhojz, HY"D

Rabbi Israel Najhojz was the son of Rabbi Meyer Najhojz, ZTs"L, the Rabbi of Tomaszow, the last rabbi of Chelm. Rabbi Israel Najhojz was the brother-in-law of the Bayaner Rabbi of Lemberg, and assumed the leadership of the Tomaszow Hasidim. Up to the last days of the war, Rabbi Najhojz tried to obtain the rabbinical position after his father, but opposing Hasidim did not allow that to happen. During the Hitler occupation in Chelm, Rabbi Najhojz was tortured by the Nazis as "Der Rabbiner" of the town. He perished under most tragic conditions.

Rabbi Gedalye Leiner, HY"D

Rabbi Gedalye was the son of Rabbi Heshl, ZTs"L, who was a brother of the Radzyner Rabbi Gershon Henech, ZTs"L. Rabbi Gedalye was known as the author of the book *Arkhut Khaim*. Rabbi Heshl was the son of the Radzyner Rabbi, who was called the "Beit Yakov" and was highly respected for his honesty and righteousness. He perished together with all the martyrs of Chelm. To the consolation of all of us, his brother Rabbi Yerukhem Leiner, the current Rabbi of Radzyn who lived during the time of WW II in London, survived and now lives in the USA.

Rabbi Moyshe Hacohen Adamchyk of Chelm (The Rabbi of Krilow)

Rabbi Moyshe Hacohen Adamchyk, the Rabbi of Krilow, occupied the position of trustee to the religious community of Chelm for several decades. As an objective judge he would not deviate one iota from the "Shulkhan Arukh" (the Orthodox Religious Laws). He was the oldest Rabbi in town. He was known in the entire rabbinical world as a great Talmudic scholar and an honest man. His son published the well-known book "Gan Ruva", a commentary on "Pri Mgadim". In the book one will find an interesting introduction of his father, the Rabbi of Krilow.

The Krilower Rabbi passed away in the first year of the German occupation. After many long efforts, the Nazi authorities gave permission to bury him in a Jewish cemetery.

Rabbi Yehuda Hacohen Mendelson, HY"D

Rabbi Mendelson was one of the most outstanding Kuzrmirer Hasidim, a scholar and a great student of the Torah. The Kuzmirer Hasidim tried to have Rabbi Mendelson accepted as a member of the Chelmer Rabbinate, but there was opposition. In spite of this situation, Rabbi Mendelson performed the rabbinic functions privately. He would render rabbinical judgments and people came to him with (ritual) questions. He died together with the whole Chelmer Jewish Community a martyr's death.

Jews of Chelm!

Wherever you may now be, wherever fate of Providence has dispersed you, remember what the German Amalekim (murderers) have done to you.

YIZKOR, Remember the beautiful, flowering Chelmer Jewish Community so atrociously annihilated.

Although our lament is very great and it is difficult to find any consolation, yet we must have confidence in the eternity of our people. But we will never forget our fathers; our mothers; our brothers and sisters; friends and acquaintances; our neighbors, and all other Jews of the Chelmer Community, who, along with the other millions of our people, were burned and slaughtered. We will forever mourn our great devastation.

Let our pains and the feelings in our hearts, together with this Yizkor Book, remain an eternal memorial for you Jewish Kedoshim, to whom we pledge never to forget.

Translator's footnotes:

1. HY"D - "Hashem Inkoym Domoy" (May the Lord Avenge His Blood)
2. ZTs"L - "Zikhroyne Tsadik Livrokbe" (Of Blessed Righteous Memory)

[Pages 345-346]

Shlomo Samet, of blessed memory

by R. Rikhszrajber, Australia

Translated by Gloria Berkenstat Freund

Almost everyone in Chelm knew the intelligent communal worker Shlomo Samet, who would often stroll on Lubliner Street with slow steps, tapping with his cane on which he leaned, trailing his rubber foot.

Sh. Samet

Shlomo Samet was born to rich, middclass and Hasidic parents. As an only son, he was raised in great luxury and comfort. His father, the Hasid, Motya Samet, a significant wood merchant, was concerned about his only son's education and wanting him to be religious, he taught his son *Yidishkeit* and *Torah*. However, this was not enough for his son; he had a great desire to study worldly subjects. Disputes arose between father and son because of this desire. Shlomo, who was unaccustomed to having his wishes refused and not being given into, could not bear the injustice. He went outside the city and threw himself under a speeding train that cut off his foot. Shlomo was a cripple for his entire life.

In 1929 Shlomo Samet married my sister. We never spoke about his tragedy in order not to awaken his wound. Shlomo did not get on well with his father. After his mother's death, he retained an extraordinary reverence for her. However, he remained a great enemy of his father.

[Page 346]

This tragedy had a bad effect on Shlomo Samet's outward appearance. He always went around with an embittered face. However, Shlomo was not bad by nature. His house was open to poor and rich. One came to him, as to a good Jew, as to a rabbi for advice and instructions. He knew all of the laws of the land and could give advice, often better than a lawyer. Therefore, one came to him with various problems.

Shlomo Samet was known in the city as a well educated person; he knew our national language and foreign languages, too. He knew Latin perfectly. He was known as one of the greatest intellectuals of the city.

He was a great Zionist and follower of Yitzhak Gruenbaum [Polish Zionist leader]. He was an active worker in the Zionist movement. He was a member of the Zionist Central Committee in Warsaw for a time. He was also the representative to the Central Zionist Committee of Berlin, which delegated him to attend the inauguration of Hebrew University in Jerusalem. Shlomo Samet spent a year in *Eretz-Yisroel* and when he returned, he again worked actively in the Zionist movement in Chelm. He often gave lectures and led instructional work among the Jewish young people in Chelm, participating in all election campaigns. He also directed the department of the Palestine office in Chelm; everyone who traveled to *Eretz-Yisroel* had their papers approved by Mr. Samet.

Chelemer cultural workers in 1912

First row, sitting from right to left: – Avram'l Orensztajn, Josef Milner
Second row, standing: – Mondelboim, Josef Beker and Haim Zemelman

Once, because of various frictions with comrades, Shlomo Samet withdrew from his active work for the Zionist party. However, he maintained his longtime contract with the *Yidishe Vishshaflekhn Institut* [Yiddish Scientific Institute -YIVO] in Vilna. He often corresponded with Moshe Lerer, who was the secretary of YIVO in Vilna.

Shlomo Samet also often "sinned a little" with his pen. He wrote for foreign newspapers; from time to time, he also took part in the publication of the *Chelemer Shtime* [*The Voice of Chelm*].

He was also a constant co-worker with *HaTzefira* [*The Siren* – a Hebrew language daily newspaper]. In his home, Sh. Samet possessed a valuable library of treasures of old and the newest works and *seforim* [religious books].

During his last years, Samet was occupied with publishing a collection of Jewish folklore. He arranged this book in two volumes. In order to accumulate the finances for this, he rented out his rooms and this helped him in making a template and publishing the first volume of his collected folklore. The second volume did not live to see publication. Shlomo Samet's life was annihilated by the Hitler regime, this energetic, intellectual man. Shlomo Samet perished as a martyr together with all of the other Chelemer martyrs in the Hitlerist extermination *aktsie*[1] of the Chelemer Jewish community in 1942.

Translator's footnote:

1. The assembly, deportation and annihilation of Jewish populations by the Germans.

[Page 347]

The Fighting Girl of Chelm – Chava Szafran

by Karl (Yeheil) Wasserman, New York, NY

Translated by Gloria Berkenstat Freund

On the 23rd of December 1944, the Chelemer *landsleit* in America learned the sad news that Chava Szafran, *landsmeydl* [girl from one's town], was killed by a trolley car in Los Angeles, California. Her sudden death brought great sorrow and sadness to her friends and *landsleit* and many Jewish progressive workers and ordinary people also grieved for her.

Chava Szafran lived in Los Angeles for the eight years before her death, where she was the director of the Workers' School (a progressive English worker's school). She was also an active worker in the movement to fight Fascism and anti-Semitism in America. Despite her occupation as director of the Workers' School, she still found time to be the secretary of the *Morgn Freiheit* Association in Los Angeles[1], an organization that carried out political-communal activities in the Jewish neighborhood: the struggle against anti-Semitism, the distribution of the progressive worker newspaper, *Morgn Freiheit*, and, in general, the broadening of the Yiddish cultural world among the Jews in Los Angeles. Chava Szafran's personal appearances before the broad mass of Jewish people were all received with great success.

On the 24th of November, the *Morgn Freiheit* had an editorial dedicated to the memory of Chava Szafran with the following headline:

"Honor the Memory of Chava Szafran." "…an accident prematurely brought the end to a beautiful personality, to a creative life – to Chava Szafran – who was completely devoted to the brightest ideals, hopes and strivings of humanity. A devoted Communist, who distinguished herself in leadership positions, Chava Szafran was as one with the working class, as one with the Jewish people. …she devoted her strengths and capabilities to the struggle for Jewish anti-Fascist unity… Her untimely death is a great loss for the progressive movement and a personal loss for her numerous friends."

We knew her in Chelm as Chava, Ajdele *der fisherkes takhter* [the fish seller's daughter]. She was still a very young girl when she left Chelm. She graduated from the Chelm public school and later began being seen in the *Poale-Zion* youth movement that was located in Kuper's house. There she began not only as a simple member, but she participated, took part in discussions in general; she began to take her first steps on her political-communal way.

[Page 348]

She came to New York with her family in around 1920, settled in Brooklyn, in the Williamsburg area, a compact Jewish quarter. She began to play a role in the labor club there. The young Chava appeared at street meetings and spoke with fervor to the Brooklyn Jews about friendship and brotherhood among peoples and races; she spoke to them about creating a world of peace, freedom, equality and brotherhood.

When I came to America in 1926, after my wanderings from Europe to Havana, Cuba, and from there to New York, I met Chava Szafran, a leader of the Cap Maker's Union – professional union of the hat makers – Local 23. She was far different from the younger Chava in Chelm. Here, there stood before me a young girl, but also a union activist who had already led struggles for the interests of the workers.

It seems that Chava inherited something from her family and this was her progressiveness, her militancy. Her older brother, Fishl, was a *Bundist* in 1905, active in the movement; her second brother, Nakhman, was at that time an activist in the *S.S.* [Zionist Socialist] movement. In 1936, a brother's son, Jack Szafran, joined the American Lincoln Brigade as a volunteer to fight in Spain on the side of the Loyalists against Franco.

Yes, Chava Szafran was a beautiful personality. After her death, many prominent writers and activists wrote about her. It is interesting to hear what was said about her by the not long deceased labor leader and writer, A. Ged. In the *Freiheit* of the 26th of September, 1944, A. Ged wrote:

"…Among the militant fighters on both sides of the ocean she distinguished herself with her perfect honesty, humane simple good heartedness and spirit of sacrifice, ignoring any self-interest. She was always ready to help everyone and to be a flaming, holy believer in the justice of our ideals. She was most resolute in the struggle of all of us. She always offered encouragement and was an influence.

"Chava Szafran was an example of the proletarian fighter, a comrade who never had any enemies, only friends. She was the woman of our future. Therefore, the news of her premature and senseless death is so painful."

I met Chava at the end of the 1920's in faraway Denver, Colorado, where I was because of my health. Chava had come to Denver to recover after hired reactionary hooligan-gangsters had attacked her in Los Angeles and severely beaten her because she wanted to help the workers there.

Chava did not rest. She heard that the beet workers here in Colorado were strongly exploited because most were foreigners, Mexicans. She went to work organizing the heavily exploited beet workers, winning better conditions for them. However, she could not remain in Denver too long. As soon as she felt healthy, she traveled to New York. We heard of her creative activities, not only in the trade union area, but also in the cultural sphere. She studied until she became a teacher in the Workers' School (*Arbeter Shul*). She returned to Los Angeles where she became the director of the Workers' School there.

[Page 349]

In the *Morgn Freiheit* of December 1944, the famous Yiddish writer, Gershon Einbinder, known by the name *Chaver-Paver*, writes:

"…She, who previously was a student in the Workers' School in New York, was a teacher in the Workers' School in Los Angeles, the main teacher – her classes were always overflowing. I (*Chaver-Paver* – K.W.[2] was also a student in her class. I sat on the school bench and admired the Jewish shop-girl who now stood before my eyes in the role of an educated, fluent speaker of the language of the land. She also possessed so much wisdom, was devoted to her discipline and also possessed a magnetic strength to attract students and to inspire, to summon their ambition and their creativity.

"Yes, a girl, a student, a learned person, deeply versed in the doctrine of Marx and her classes were not only for beginners. Even writers in English, artists would come to study Marxism with her…"

[Page 350]

To this day, the Chelemers are proud that they had such a *landsmeydl* as she. It is a loss that she was torn away from our ranks so young. She stood at the battle front for years, taking part in terrible battles for the American and Jewish Workers' movement. She came out of many battles wounded. After she recovered, she again stood at the battle front. However, she was killed here on a peaceful night by a passing, speeding streetcar.

The *Morgn Freiheit* Los Angeles manager, A. Lekhowicki, writes, "Over 1,200 people came to her funeral; her funeral procession went on for a mile. People cried about the great loss as they passed her casket." The famous Yiddish-American writer, Samuel Ornitz, said in his eulogy: "'Our teacher' has left us."

This is how the girl who was brought up in the public school in Chelm lived and fought and ended as the director of the progressive *Arbeter Shul* in Los Angeles. Let the name of Chava Szafran be among the martyrs, those who fell for a more beautiful and better world.

Translator's footnotes:

1. *Morgn Freiheit* was a Yiddish language Communist daily newspaper.
2. Initials of the writer of this article.

[Page 349]

Sholom Goldhar

by Y. Nunison

Translated by Gloria Berkenstat Freund

Sholom Goldhar was one of the most courageous fighters for a socialist world order, one of the most passionate progressive socialist activists. He was born to poor parents in the summer of 1910 in the village of Strachoslaw, near Chelm. Sholom Goldhar's family later moved to Chelm.

He studied in a *kheder* [religious elementary school] and also graduated from a Polish public school (*powszechna*). After, he studied in a technical school, *Szkola Techniczna*, on Dr. Bieszower Street. He did not graduate from this school because of need and poverty and he became a gaiter maker.

He became interested in communal-political problems while still very young, when he was still in school. He joined the *Poale-Zion* Youth and because of his activities he very quickly was chosen for the committee of the *P.Z.* Youth.

He left to work in Kowel. Although he remained there a short time, he had time to clarify the ideology of the left *Poale-Zion* movement for the young people in Kowel.

When he returned to Chelm he became absorbed in the *Poale-Zion* movement with his head and body and was active in all areas. He led various groups and gave lectures. He organized the children's union, *Yungbar*, and edited a wall newspaper for children.

He was not happy with the gaiter maker's trade and became a bricklayer. He met Polish and Ukrainian workers at this work.

[Page 350]

In 1929, when Poland was overwhelmed with strikes and the political situation in the country became turbulent and tense, it became restrictive for him to be in the ranks of the left *Poale-Zion* and he joined the leftist workers' movement.

During the summer of 1930 he was arrested with Moshe Apelboim (Apelboim – a Chelemer young man who lived on Narjenczna Street; after spending two years in prison, he left for Spain to fight against Fascism and fell on the Spanish battlefield). Goldhar was accused by the "Chelemer train management" and in the surrounding villages, such as Ruda-Opalin, Plawanice, Okszow and Brzezno, of organizing and leading the strike of the train workers. He was sentenced to eight years of hard labor. He served in the jails of Chelm, Krasnystaw, Lublin, Sandomiersz, Placen (Plesno/Plössen) and Kochanowo.

His courage was not broken in prison. He was also part of the political organization there. He used the time that he spent in jail to enrich his education and knowledge. When the rights of the political arrestees were limited in 1937, Sholom Goldhar organized a hunger strike that lasted nine days.

He came out of jail physically broken; however, he was not morally shaken. He was full of belief in a better morning. However, it is unfortunate that his life was cut short. When the German army assaulted Warsaw, in the fall of 1939, he was killed by German shrapnel.

Honor his illustrious memory!

[Page 351]

Captain Binyamin Winer
– A Brave Fighter Against the Enemies of Our People
(Several Features from his Turbulent Life)

by Shmuel Winer, New York

Translated by Gloria Berkenstat Freund

Here, in the Yizkor Book for Chelm, I will try to draw several short features of the turbulent journey of one who represents Chelm in the socialist sector of the current divided world. One who excelled in the fight against the enemies who stood up to annihilate our people. One of the quiet heroes who again and again during the two World Wars and world crises, was found on the front lines of this terrible social concussion.

* * *

My brother Binyamin was born in Chelm, Passover 1891. His education was in the usual tradition in a *kheder* [religious elementary school]. He tasted the flavor of need when he was very young. He studied typesetting at age 13 at Erlikh's printing shop. A child of a poor generation, poverty drove him out of his parents' house at an early age. At 14, he left to find his luck among strangers. He returned home and then wandered again. At 17 he was already in Yekaterinoslav [Dnipropetrovs'k, Ukraine]. He also was intensively involved with self education. He married there a few years later.

In the autumn of 1912, he came home to enter the military. Although he was short sighted, he still had to present himself as a soldier so that a rich son could be freed from serving. He had no interest in serving in the Czar's army; going to America was all that remained for him. He waited until after the taking of the oath, so that his father would not have to pay a 300 ruble penalty for him. Immediately after the swearing in, he disappeared from the barracks. He hid for a few days before leaving the city.

It was the last night. Everything was ready; at dawn he needed to leave quietly with his wife for the border. His hiding place was attacked by the police and the military in the middle of the night and he was caught. A certain Chelemer informer and influential person had sensed something – he immediately brought the information where one does. The informer later explained that he thought it was actually me who was hiding there.

A military court sentenced him to a year in a military prison. The 300th anniversary of the reign of the Czarist Romanov dynasty occurred just then (beginning of 1913). Binyamin Winer was freed after over a month in prison thanks to the general amnesty declared by Czar Nikolai. He was immediately sent to serve in Penza [Russia]. It turned out that he was the only one in his company who knew how to read and write; they had no choice and they had to make him the company scribe. His service became easier.

August 1914. The First World War began. Among the long columns of those from the Russian military going by foot, Binyamin Winer marched to the western border in the burning heat on the dusty roads, with a heavy pack on his shoulders and a rifle in his hand.

[Page 352]

At the front, a new unusual career opened for him, for a Jewish soldier in the Czarist army. Because of corruption, theft and general chaos and treachery, Russian soldiers at the front very often went around with empty stomachs – simply suffering from hunger. He became known in his regiment for his administrative abilities. The commander had a bizarre idea for that time in the Czarist army, to appoint the Jewish soldier, Binyamin Winer, as the purchaser of provisions for the regiment. He carried out this responsible and difficult assignment in the best manner at a time when there was already a lack of foodstuffs. He won the trust of the peasants in the villages and they sold him as much food as he needed. His reputation spread far – he quickly became the purchaser for the entire division. He also did well with his increased responsibilities.

Luck did not protect him for very long.

And the day came that the Chief Commander of all the Russian Armies, the bitter anti-Semite, Nikolai Nikolaievitch, the Czar's uncle, came for an inspection of this part of the front, where he [Binyamin] was located. He [Nikolai Nikolaievitch] glimpsed the trouble. A *zhid* [1], a soldier in such a position! Heaven opens! So nothing more was needed. Several high officers, those guilty of this "crime" were demoted to lower ranks and he, Binyamin Winer, was, sent to the battle line in the trenches at his [Nikolai Nikolaievitch's] strict order.

It did not take long before he [Binyamin] was wounded. On his recovery, he was sent back to the trenches. In 1916 he was again wounded, this time so badly that he was no longer of use in the war and he was completely discharged.

The year 1917 stole in. The February Revolution broke out. This time the Czarist despot was not successful in saving himself as in 1905. The revolutionary surge gripped everyone in the entire country and put a quick end to czarism along with Czar Nikolai. Years of enormous social shocks followed. The struggle between the old order and the new that would take its place became more severe. His [Binyamin's] strongly developed sense of social justice led him to the ranks of the revolution.

1918. The civil war blazed. Various White Guard pogrom gangs spread death and devastation in hundreds of Jewish cities and *shtetlekh* across the length and width of Ukraine and White Russia. Jewish blood flowed like water. Binyamin Winer again voluntarily put on a military uniform and threw himself into the fight against the pogrom gangs. Every day he saw death in front of his eyes. Many times it appeared as if the end had come. There was no longer any escape – and each time his naked life was saved, literally as if by a miracle.

[Page 353]

It is worthwhile to note just one episode here – one of many. This was at the beginning, when the bands of murderers had the upper hand. December, 1918. A small riot of about 300 people's fighters, under the command of Binyamin Winer, started a battle with a horde of *Makhnovtses* [2] that went on a spree against the Jews in Yekaterinoslav. They massacred, raped, tortured and looted. This was an uneven fight from the start. On one side a few thousand wild cutthroats, well-armed by the Allies (America, England, France), with new, warm uniforms, well fed. On the other side – a bunch of several hundred poorly armed, poorly clothed, half hungry people's fighters. Yet, in this uneven fight the small army ranks inflicted heavy losses on the pogrom bands. Of the several hundred, few survived. Relegated to an attic, among a bunch of wounded soldiers also lay Binyamin Winer, passed out, boots filled with blood, without a drop of water, in a burning frost. It was on the third day in the middle of the night that he was quietly taken out in an unconscious condition with the others and saved.

As soon as he recovered a little, he was again back on the front lines. He excelled in battle and rose to the rank of captain. A gentle, easy-going person by nature, far from being heroic, he was a little shorter than average height. However, if one fell into his hands, pain and woe awaited this human riff-raff. He burned with revenge for our innocent spilled blood. A hundred and fifty thousand Jews were murdered at that time by the bloody hands of the *Petlurtses, Makhnovtses, Denikintses* [3] and the assorted other murderous bands that rampaged across the length and width of the country. They were virtually the forerunners of Hitler and provided an example that one could kill our sisters and brothers, tens of thousands of Jews without consequence and the "civilized" world would look on at the violence with indifference.

1921. The end of the Civil War neared and with it the dark end of all of the White Guard pogrom gangs. Such armies could show their "heroism" against unarmed, unprotected Jews, old people, women and children. They were not heroes against a people's army that fought for freedom.

[Page 354]

Captain Binyamin Winer also took off his military uniform and returned to civilian life. The country proceeded to recover after the fearful destruction, hunger and epidemics. As a capable administrator and organizer he now again laid his hand to rebuilding the disrupted state administration in a series of southern Ukrainian cities. He then returned to Dnipropetrovs'k (formerly Yekaterinoslav). Now he was occupied with organizing cooperatives.

Around 1930 he took advantage of the opportunity that the government gave to workers to qualify for a higher profession. Out of 5,000 applicants in his city, he was the only one to qualify to study as an engineer without prior academic education and he was sent to the Kiev Academy to study engineering.

Captain Binyamin Winer

Then his heart began to beat. A fear attacked him. Was it not too risky a step for him at this time? He was no longer a young man. He was approaching 40. His entire academic preparation for studying higher mathematics, he joked in a letter to me, consisted of the four elementary precepts in arithmetic: addition, subtraction, multiplication and division, which he had studied with the Lukaczen *melamed* [teacher in a religious elementary school] in his *kheder* [religious elementary school] as a child in Chelm.

Yet this did not impede him from receiving his diploma as an engineer in three years of study, instead of the normal four. His zeal, persistence and, chiefly, his sharp head was of help here. Naturally, he, his wife and daughter were supported by the state during the course of his studies.

He started to practice his new profession in 1933 with the hope that now finally his life would go smoothly and calmly. However, the beginning of his new career coincided with Hitler coming to power. Dark, threatening clouds began to creep over the world, particularly for our martyred nation [for the Jews]. With his great experience, he instinctively sensed what this meant. There was no more rest for him.

In September, 1939, Hitler's murderous army fired the first shot against Poland and ignited a conflagration. In a few days, Poland was finished. Jews escaped across the Soviet border in deadly panic. Several hundreds of thousands of Jews saved themselves in this way from the bloody hands of the Nazi assassins. They spread themselves across the cities and *shtetlekh* [towns] of the Soviet Union. Refugees from Poland also appeared in [Winer's] city. He had heard enough about the Hitlerist murders against our people. Every day the newspapers also were full of reports about the Nazi murders against the Jews – he did not skip even one line. The bestiality of the murder of Jews 20 years earlier again swam in front of his eyes. From then on, he no longer found any rest.

[Page 355]

On June 21, 1941, Hitler threw the entire power of his war machine against the Soviet Union. Binyamin Winer, immediately, on the same day, appeared voluntarily before the military commission in his city. However, he was totally rejected. That night he did not close his eyes. He personally had to take revenge against the Nazi beast for the spilling of innocent Jewish blood and also to defend his country against the barbarians.

He again appeared before the military commission in the morning. His plea could no longer be resisted and finally he was taken into the army with his old rank of captain.

With lightning speed, the frightening Nazi war machine cut deeper and deeper into Soviet territory and brought with it death and devastation. And right on the first day, the accursed monsters carried out their inhuman violence against the Jews they captured in the cities and *shtetlekh*. Hundreds of thousands of Jews, who because of the Nazi speed did not have time to save themselves by going deeper into the country, were tortured to death, buried alive, burned to ash by the beasts.

The world looked on with baited breath to the never before seen titanic struggle between two mighty forces. And when it appeared that it was already the end of the world, that the worst enemy of humanity was getting the upper hand – just then the wheel turned back. The terrible Nazi defeat at Stalingrad sealed the fate of Hitler. This was the beginning of his dark end. However, the road was still a long, superhumanly difficult one.

Our fellow townsman, Captain Binyamin Winer, marched in the ranks of the Soviet army. He found himself in the thick of gigantic battles the entire time. Earlier the Nazis inflicted heavy destructive blows. The losses on both sides were enormous – literally in the millions. Now that the Nazis had begun to receive the fitting blows, one right after the other up to their dark end, they could not recover. They were no longer given any rest. They were driven farther and farther. In the heat of the battles it seemed as if his end had come. This time our fellow townsman would not emerge alive. And, literally, through a miracle – again and again this naked life was saved. Or even worse – in a moment he fell into their paws alive. All roads were blocked. Unable to escape – he again escaped from captivity. Where did he get the power and endurance? He did not forget for even a minute the sacred will, the last cry of our saintly martyrs: *"Never to forget and never to forgive,"* when they were driven on their last road to the ovens and gas chambers. He drew courage and superhuman strength to throw himself into battle. To take revenge against the bestial murderers of the Jews.

Thus he crossed hundreds of cities and *shtetlekh*. He saw only death and destruction. He rarely met a surviving Jew. He came in close contact with Jewish partisans in the forests. He encouraged them and helped in any way he could.

In July, 1944, Captain Binyamin Winer marched into Chelm among the victorious Soviet armies. After 30 some years, he again walked on the earth where his little cradle had stood. One can imagine his deep emotional experience at this moment. He immediately went to look for Jews – and he did not find any. He went to the cemetery to look for his father's *matseyve* [headstone] – there is no headstone. Even the dead Jews were not allowed to rest in their graves. The cannibals paved roads and streets with Jewish headstones. A salty tear was shed – and one headed further on his way. It is not yet the end.

On the way to Lublin, the military division in which he found himself freed the remnant of surviving Jews. Skeletons, literally, from Majdanek, one of Hitler's death factories. He later took part in the difficult battle for Warsaw – among the most terrible in the war. The fighting was bitter. However, after heavy losses, the Nazis had to retreat from there. With a beating heart, Binyamin Winer first went to the former Warsaw Ghetto – where "a people in the midst of crashing walls" raised the flag of revolt against the accursed Nazis. He walked on the earth that had been burned to cinders, among the ruins where our heroes and martyrs covered themselves with eternal glory and saved the honor of our people. The enemy paid a heavy price in this uneven struggle. It took the murderers of the Jews as long to conquer the ghetto as to conquer all of Poland.

There were still a few big battles before the wild beast was brought to its knees. He went farther; took part in the battle on the accursed German ground. He lived long enough for the last battle and entered Hitler's snake's nest – Berlin – with the victorious Soviet troops and had the honor to see Hitler's desolate, dark end.

He fought for four long frightening years against our worst enemy with rare courage. He never complained. He went through the fiery deluge and came out alive. Now, that his mission had ended, his strength left him completely. He came home a shadow of a man. He had to have a few operations. His life hung by a hair. When he began to return a little to his old self, he was hit by another blow. He lost his beloved life-friend, his wife, Enya. It was difficult to console him.

Should he, perhaps, have been consoled that he now saw that the Nazis were already back in the saddle in Germany? Or that the danger from German rearmament under the same German generals who had drunk our blood – was coming nearer? He thought in his loneliness: Were six million annihilated Jews not enough? Was our terrible great destruction for nothing?

* * *

This is a short summary about the stormy, fertile life of our fellow townsman. A life that could have filled hundreds of pages of an exciting book. The colorful life of a brave, self-sacrificing fighter for his people.

Translator's footnotes:

1. Derogatory Russian word for Jew.
2. Followers of Nestor Makhno.
3. *Petlurtses* were followers of the Ukrainian politician, Symon Petlura; *Makhnovtses* were followers of the Ukrainian anarchist, Nestor Makhno and *Denikintses* were followers of Anton Ivanovich Denikin, a leading anti-Bolshevik White Russian general during the Civil War.

[Page 357]

Motl Baliar
(To the illustious memory of my brother)

by Chava Baliar (Stoler)

Translated by Gloria Berkenstat Freund

Who in Chelm did not know Motl Baliar, Gisha Lipele's son? He was known and respected by the young and old, the great and small!

He was a distinguished teacher in the *folkshul* [Jewish public school] in Chelm in the 1920's.

How did Motl become a teacher and then such a distinguished pedagogue – he was known in *folkshul* circles in Poland and also later in the Soviet Union – this is a mystery to me until this day.

Besides *kheder* [religious Jewish "primary" school], Motl did not attend any Jewish or general school. He never had a teacher. The bitter poverty at home, the simple hunger drove him from the house. He would sit for days in the field beyond the "*Nayer welt* [new world]" and read all kinds of borrowed books. I would bring him a piece of bread – as that was all there was in our house – with a drink of fresh, cold water from the deep well on the *Nayer welt*. If he received a few *groshn* coins from somewhere, this went for the purchase of books.

He became a teacher in the *folks-shul* where I studied at a very young age. When Motl entered a class, the children remained quiet and waited respectfully.

Everything about him summoned respect: his handsome, tall figure, wide shoulders, his high, deep forehead with large glasses, all suited him, made him more handsome and underlined his intelligence.

"Reading, learning, studying" – this was his advice, his counsel and order to each young person, boy and girl, his neighbors, relatives and acquaintances in Chelm.

I will never forget when Motl wanted to correspond with one of our brothers-in-law in America, who did not know any Yiddish. Motl obtained English instruction books and he went around the house the entire winter – back and forth – repeating loudly some kind of language that sounded so strange, so foreign. There was a clear path on the floor of the house from his constant pacing… The result was that immediately after Passover, Motl wrote and received English letters from our brother-in-law. He would not only read the letter to us, but would also show the grammatical root for every word. He stated, "You can never know how useful it would be if an English word stuck itself to you…"

[Page 358]

Oy! Was my brother correct! Today in America, we use many words that Motl explained to me and our mother at that time.

Motl was one of the builders and leaders of the Jewish *folkshul*. There was a time when the *folkshul* in Chelm did not have a home. The doctor, in whose home the school was located, needed the room for himself.

Motl then led the plan to build its own *folkshul* house. Money was spent in the city only for materials and to pay for the plot of land – the Jewish workers promised to do the building, the work for free.

Motl set down a world of effort for the plan that was never fulfilled because the Polish fascist government of that time withdrew permission immediately after the solemn ceremony of laying the foundation.

Motl Baliar with his wife; they perished at the hands of the Hitler murderers

It was very difficult to be a *folkshul* teacher under such extraordinarily bitter conditions.

Motl left for Vilna.

There, too, Motl, the *folkshul* teacher, was quickly discovered and recognized. He would write for the Chelm weekly newspapers and journals, as well as the *Grynike Beymelekh* [*Little Green Trees*] and other pedagogical journals.

When Hitler's murderers attacked Poland and the Soviets occupied Vilna, Motl wrote to us in America:

"We lack for nothing – I, my wife and our child – with the Soviet government. I am the superintendent for 110 Jewish schools – 60 day schools and 50 evening schools. I travel around in Vilna circles and organize the opening of new schools wherever they are needed. We have bitter compassion for our brothers, Yona and Yisroel, the dear and courageous fighters for a more beautiful and better world and humanity – who knows what has happened to them."

Alas, the sun did not shine in Motl's window for long… Hitler's hordes, which spread death and devastation in Europe, did not bypass Vilna.

Motl Baliar, the spirited *folkshul* teacher, poet and writer, was annihilated with his wife and child along with the famous Jewish community of Vilna.

They will always live in our hearts. Honor their memory!

[Page 359]

Teachers of Chelm

by Ben-Ahron

Translated by Gloria Berkenstat Freund

Almost all of the Chelm *khederim* [religious elementary schools] were located in the Jewish quarter, on the "*Naye Tzal*." The Hitler murderers created the ghetto here. *Khederim* were on Poczt Street and the surrounding alleys, where small and large half-collapsed *shteiblekh* [small one-room synagogues] and houses were located that were inhabited by tradesmen and toilers. The majority of Chelemer *khederim* were found there, where Jewish children, Moshele, Shlomele were educated in the traditional religious spirit.

Khederim were located on the *Naye Tzal*, where Jewish children began learning the *alef-beis* – and did not go beyond the *Khumish* [Torah or *The Five Books of Moses*] and Rashi [author of Torah commentaries]; there were *khederim* where more than the *Khumish* with Rashi was taught; there were *khederim* whose graduates were later able to enter *Talmud Torahs* [schools for boys from poor backgrounds] and *yeshivus* [school for the study of the Torah and Talmud].

The school of the *melamed* [teacher in a religious school], Abraham Yitzhak Grynberg – a teacher of the youngest children – was well known in Chelm. He was a sickly Jew who, when teaching children, appeared to be a "giant." The children were afraid of him, of his pointer and leather whip.

He began to teach the *alef-beis* to young children of age three and four and then led them to Rashi and the *gemara* [Talmudic commentaries on the *Mishnah*, the post biblical discussions of the Talmud]. He was popular in Chelm, as a very honest Jew and as a *melamed* who did not take money without a reason; he worked very hard from early in the morning until it was late.

His school consisted of one room in which his bedroom, kitchen and eating room were found. A long table with benches stood in a corner near the wall where he taught his students.

[Page 360]

Yankl was a second popular *melamed*. He had the habit of chasing after young mothers asking that they let him teach their children. The youngest children in the city were always found in his *kheder*. Great scholars did not emerge from his school.

There was a *melamed* in Chelm, whose *kheder* was also located on Poczt Street, just across from the "*glitsh-trep* [slippery steps]," whose name I do not remember. I think we called him "*Jagoda* [berry in Polish]." He was considered a good teacher. Older children were always in his school. "*Jagoda*" was known in the city as proficient in teaching. He taught *gemara*. The melodies of the Talmudic scholars Raba and Rav rang in the street.

There was also in Chelm the famous *melamed*, Binyamin Wolfson; he was a Litvak, who settled in Chelm after the First World War. The students in his *kheder* had sharp minds and they knew pages of the *gemara*. It was an honor to study with Binyamin Wolfson.

The Wlodower *melamed* was called Leibish Dovid *Melamed*. He was also one of the best teachers and had a good reputation as an honest Jew and good rebbe. The best students, who went on to the *yeshiva* [school for older boys where the Torah and Talmud are studied], graduated from his *kheder*.

Of the old *melamdim* at the end of the 19th century, Reb Yitzhak *Strazsnik* [scarecrow], the teacher of the youngest children, was well known in Chelm. No one in the city knew why he was called *strasznik*. Perhaps he was called this because he was a tall Jew and very strict with his students.

There was also a well known and famous *melamed*, Gedalia Hipszman; he was called Gedalia the fisherman. He was a very good teacher and his *kheder* had a good reputation in the city and in the surrounding *shtetlekh*.

There was also a melamed in Chelm that was called der krumer Avraham [the lame Avraham]. Gedalia Kritnicer was also a well known *melamed* in Chelm. He had six daughters. He was called Gedalia, the *melamed* with the daughters. The *melamedim*, Israel Dyn, Khona Yitzhakl, Josef Dovid Sznejderman, Reb Wowa Hershele Cykerman, Shlomoh Hirsh, Yehoshua "Cozzack," Itche Szepeles, Shmuel Hersh, and so on, were well known.

Every *melamed*, or as we called them, Rebbe, was very pious, and was careful to pray each day and not to commit the slightest sin.

One went to *kheder* six days a week. One left at eight in the morning and came home during the evening hours. One came to many *khederim* on *Shabbos* to study a chapter of the *Mishnah* or to interpret the weekly Torah portion.

A group of yeshiva boys, who in later years played a role in Jewish communal and cultural life in Chelm, at the Chelemer cemetery in 1913

[Page 361]

Motl Tovya's

Jakov Linherz, Rehovot

Translated by Gloria Berkenstat Freund

Motl Tovya's [Tovya's son, Motl], the synagogue *gabbai* [assistant to the rabbi], was a tall Jew, solidly built with a long, grey beard. He wore a tall satin hat on *Shabbos* and during the week and was always preoccupied, was always busy.

He was not absorbed by business matters; he was only engaged in *mitzvahs*[1] and good deeds. He was always happy, with a smile on his lips and he spoke words of faith to everyone: God will help! It will be good!

There was no Jew in Chelm, both young and old, who did not know *Motl Tovya's*.

He took care of the city's Jewish soldiers, seeing that they had somewhere to be on *Shabbos* and *yom-tov* [religious holidays]. When it happened that there were five or six soldiers left in the prayer house and everyone else had already left, he took them home with him on *Shabbos* and *yom-tov*. He would also provide Jewish prisoners with a *minyon* [10 men necessary for saying prayers] and with food.

He collected money to marry off orphaned or poor girls. One would often meet him carrying full baskets of cake and whiskey and everything necessary for the *bris* [ritual circumcision] or wedding of the poor.

His greatest *mitzvah* [good deed] was to entertain the bride and groom. He was the *bodkhen*[2], the *klezmer* [musician] and in-law at the wedding of the poor.

He was also the *gabbai* [usually an assistant to the rabbi] for the organization that distributed clothing to the needy, insuring that the poor children in the *Talmud Torah* [elementary school for poor children] had shoes and warm coats.

He also brought the *esrog and lulav*[3] to the homes of the sick. He did not forget to do the smallest thing on behalf of the needy. His did his aid work with complete commitment.

Translator's footnotes:

1. The Hebrew word for "commandments" is usually interpreted to mean acts of kindness.
2. Wedding entertainer who specializes in humorous and sentimental rhymes.
3. An *esrog* (*etrog* in Hebrew) is a citron; a *lulav* is composed of three kinds of branches, often a branch of myrtle, a branch of a willow tree and the frond of a date palm tree. They are waved during prayer services on *Sukkot*, the "Feast of Tabernacles" that usually takes place during late September or during the month of October.

Moshe Zamler

Moshe Zamler was a baker; he worked 15 hours, day and night. His eyes were red from not sleeping enough, but he had a strong will and strove in life. Even though he was not content with his appearance.

[Page 362]

I remember how he came to our home on a Friday afternoon, turning to my mother, may she rest in peace, saying that he needed to see me. At first, my mother wondered how it was possible that a Jew of more than 30 years of age had a need to see a 14-year old young man. I happened to be in the house and went over to him. He said the following to me: "I am ignorant; I can only read a little, but, unfortunately, I can not write. If have to sign my name, I place three crosses. I already have three children and they will certainly be ashamed of their ignorant father. Help me to become a person. I need your help. With God's help, I will compensate you. We are neighbors; when you have the time, and when you want to, come in and teach me to write.

I was very pleased by what he said. I began to fill my task in the best possible manner. In the course of eight months, Moshe Zalmer showed that he had learned to write in Yiddish, Polish and do a little arithmetic. His joy was without end.

Later, when I emigrated to *Eretz-Yisroel*, he accompanied me to say goodbye and he confided a secret to me that he was considering going to *Eretz-Yisroel* and he actually did.

When I met him in *Eretz-Yisroel*, he told me how he had sneaked across the border to Romania and how he worked at a saw-mill at a saw. He came to *Eretz-Yisroel* illegally using the name Leib Psubski.

He then asked his wife and children to come to *Eretz-Yisroel*. However, his fate was that on *erev Yom Kippur* [the eve of *Yom Kippur*] he fell at his defense post, hit with a bullet by an enemy – a follower of Hitler Germany.

We will never forget his memory!

[Page 363]
Feiwl Fryd

Feiwl Fryd was the nerve, the driving force in Jewish communal-cultural life in Chelm. With his erudition and political-communal consciousness, he brought clarity to the Jewish masses in Chelm.

I remember Feiwl Fryd from the year 1918 until I left Chelm in the year 1933. I heard news irregularly from him during the savage Hitler era. After the great bloody flood, I established a written bond with him.

Today, Feiwl Fryd is in Lublin, Poland. The fact that he survived and endured left a bitter stamp on him. He did not find a place in Chelm, no peace. The empty Jewish city where for many years he had occupied an esteemed place drove him to the neighboring city of Lublin. He is old, in pain, weak, often sick and with little energy for living.

Feiwl Fryd

I remember the radiant years of Feiwl Fryd; what colossal enterprising power and instinctive strength he possessed. He created and took part in the activities of many societies and organizations. He was the one who stood by the cradle of the workers movement, devoted to it with heart and soul.

My father, may he rest in peace, tried to make Feiwl Fryd loathsome to me; he once represented him to me in dark colors as a Bund member and revolutionary. He told me that in 1905, F. Fryd had caused great trouble with his "agitation" among the workers during the well-known strikes of that time. (He once came to our house in the *masterskaja* (factory) with a gun and threatened…)

Feiwl Fryd was the first one who took me into the Yiddish and literary world. As editor of the *Chelemer Shtime* [*Voice of Chelm*] in 1925, he encouraged me to write, made me a co-worker at his newspaper.

I remember the time when Feiwl Fryd was the librarian of the Borokhow Library in Chelm. He also was the founder of this library 30 years ago, when I first started to read Yiddish and Feiwl Fryd advised me about the first book I should read – Sholom Aleichem's *75,000*…

Feiwl Fryd was a good lecturer. His reports in the meeting room of left *Poalei-Zion* and in other auditoriums drew great masses.

It was said in Chelm that, under Czarist rule, Feiwl Fryd was exiled to Siberia for revolutionary actions. After the [First] World War, F. Fryd's activities became very visible. He was very active in the left *Poalei-Zion* Party; he was editor of the *Chelemer Folksblat* [*Chelm People's Newspaper*] for a time.

Feiwl Fryd was a child of the people. Therefore, he was beloved and respected by everyone. He was modest, did not consider himself better than anyone. He was acquainted with rich and poor, did not push himself to the front and to glory; was a dear and skillful cultural volunteer, a guide for many Jewish young people. He also was a teacher at the Jewish public school for many years.

At the end, it must be remembered that he was employed as a translator for the publisher, Sh. Jaczkowski in Warsaw, the publisher Goldfarb and others. He translated the works of Emil Ludwig, Zinkler, Zaszczekno, Dunkan and others.

Karl Waserman

During the years 1918-1922, before he emigrated to America, he traveled to Cuba – and years later, the intelligent and modest Waserman advanced greatly in his new home, America.

He graduated from a teacher's seminar and became a skillful cultural worker and a good teacher. He carried out his work as a teacher in many schools in America, in a series of cities, and became much beloved by hundreds and thousands of Jewish children, as well as by their parents.

Karl Waserman is by nature a dear person with a great love of people and, in particular, of children. He is a writer. One often meets him in the children's division of the *Morgn Freiheit* [*Morning Freedom*, a Yiddish newspaper], where he plays a large role among his co-workers, with children's games, jokes and riddles.

Waserman was also a co-worker at *Yungvarg* [*Youth*, a children's magazine]. It is thanks to the children's schools in New York that his book, *Shpiln un Retnishn* [*Games and Riddles*] was published. Waserman comes from Chelm from a poor family. His father was a tailor and died prematurely in America.

[Page 365]

A.Y. Dubelman

H. Sh.

Approximately 30 years ago, A. Y. Dubelman pulled out of the small and quiet *shtetl* Rawicz, a *shtetl* that was near Chelm – pulled himself into the larger world.

While still a young man Dubelman aspired to go to a large Jewish center, where Jewish life pulsed. Dubelman was drawn to the large Jewish center, New York, and one day he left his home *shtetl* and went into the world.

Dubelman did not succeed in entering America and he remained stuck on the way, in distant Cuba, where has lived for nearly 30 years. Dubelman made his home in Cuba with the intent of developing the Jewish community there and publishing the Yiddish word.

Dubelman published two books in Cuba, *Dertseylungen fun Kubaner Lebn* [*Stories from Cuban Life*] and *Havaner Lebn* [*Havana Life*], for which he was also an editor. He was a contributor to many Yiddish newspapers in other countries.

Leibele Stol

M. Tenenboim, Israel

Leibele Stol was well known among the Chelemer youth in general and among the progressive youth, in particular.

The progressive youth were extremely active in Chelm, equipped with extraordinary daring at filling the assignments from the Communist Party.

Although the Communist Party in Poland was dissolved because many of its members were branded as traitors, the progressive young people in Chelm did not cease their Communist activities nor abandon the connection to Moscow. With great stubbornness, they continued their illegal activities and fought the reactionary [actions] without interruption.

One of these young, stubborn people was Leibele Stol. He worked with a tailor on Lubliner Street. He carried within a fervid belief that a brighter morning would come from the east and all those persecuted would become free and happy.

The atmosphere in Poland was strongly anti-Semitic and reactionary; the ideal for the young Christians was to attack Jews and to see broken Jewish heads. It felt as if the casks of gunpowder would be thrown open and the cursed hand of venom and hatred would on any day throw the world into a burning torch.

[Page 366]

The city garden in Chelm was the meeting place for the young of various shades of opinion. There various ideas were debated, about thinkers and their schools of thought. The Zionists youth, the *Hashomer Hatzair* [Socialist Zionist movement] and the progressive youth would come together.

Leibele Stol often appeared in the garden with his group. He was the one who set the tone in all discussions and he argued for his political opinions with great zeal and enthusiasm. Leibele Stol would hectograph [reproduce by means of a gelatin duplicator] leaflets. I remember how he distributed them on the 1st of May and threw them into workshops where the workers produced agricultural implements. He and his group would knock out the window panes and throw proclamations inside calling for the workers to join the struggle against the despised capitalism.

When the war broke out, he and all of his comrades escaped. However, the Hitlerist pestilence headed them off. He returned to his birthplace, broken and sad and hid for a time. He was forced to leave his hiding place because of hunger and pain and was caught by the Gestapo.

Honor his memory!

Mendl Stam

The first murderous German edict – the Chelm-Hrubieszow-Sokol death march – showed that the delusion held by some of the Jews about the Germans, that they were not so brutal, was false. The face of their wildness was stripped naked and clear. The reverberation of the shooting in the Hrubieszow forest, the spilled blood on the Chelm-Hrubieszow-Sokol highway shocked the Chelemer Jews and the Jews in the neighboring towns and cities.

A group of young people did not take part in this death march. They hid in a cave. The nights were dark and they would go out of the cave at night and infiltrate the shops, taking food.

The Polish shopkeepers noticed that the Jewish businesses that were transferred to their authority as soon as the German entered were being opened at night. They organized a group of Poles under the leadership of the well known enemy of the Jews, Akola Bulak, the baker and they trailed the Jews to the cave when they would come out at night. The Poles took a long rope and one of them let himself down into the deep cave with the rope. However, their "scout" did not return. The young Jews quartered him into pieces with sticks and iron crowbars.

[Page 367]

The Germans and Poles conducted a police raid of this cave and the entire group fell into the murderous-fascistic hands.

At the head of this group was Mendl Stam. He was rebellious and possessed a great entrepreneurial spirit. He was not helpless within the walls of the prison; he attacked the Gestapo and escaped with a revolver.

The Germans nailed up notices promising a great reward for those who caught Mendl Stam. A search was made for him. The Gestapo led him away to prison. The Germans took revenge on him. They administered a violent death on him – he was tortured to death.

Let his memory be blessed!

Dr. Yisroel Oks

Dr. Yisroel Oks was a bright figure, a dear Jew with a sweet Jewish heart that dissolved the fog and then separated out the lines of illuminated light. Thus did Dr. Yisroel Oks shine and radiate with his Jewish perception that brought light into the flickering darkness. Jewish paupers knew that Dr. Yisroel Oks and his old mother and his dear *Yidishe tokchter*,[1] his wife, would not forget the poor and would always help him and on Fridays prepare a *Shabbos* package for him.

This bright personality, Dr. Y. Oks, who perished in the Chelm-Hrubieszow-Sokol death march, worked with my father in the interest free loan fund and I saw his interest in every needy person coming to him for a loan.

With a bent head and broken heart, we must remember his service to the community. His curled head of hair, from which a considerable amount of silver hair shone out, gave him the appearance of a typical Jew, of which he was not ashamed. His smart, dark eyes always smiled good-naturedly.

Dr. Oks was famous in Chelm as a medical doctor and as a city businessman who could also study a page of *gemara*.

Honor his memory!

Translator's footnote:

1. A Jewish daughter – one who fulfills her role as a Jewish woman.

[Page 368]

Yisroel Yitzhak Nankin

Y. Ceber, Australia

Translated by Gloria Berkenstat Freund

Y. Ceber

Yisroel Yitzhak Nankin, the son of Fishl, the tailor, was one of the most active workers in the artisans' union. He absorbed the feeling of justice, of fairness and love of the Jewish masses and was active for years in activities on behalf of the Chelm artisans.

There was a threat of economic danger to the Jewish artisans when the Polish government issued reactionary guild laws in the 1930's.

At that time, the central Jewish Artisans' Organization in Poland began a widespread campaign among the Jewish craftsmen to inform them about the anti-Semitic guild laws. Yisroel Yitzhak Nankin threw himself with heart and soul into this informational activity.

At every opportunity he defended the right of Jewish artisans and the common people.

His was the chairman of the Jewish Tailors' Organization and of the Spoldzielczy Bank [Cooperative Bank founded by *Agudas Yisroel*]. He was also one of the founders of the "*Linat-ha-Tzedek*" [hostel for the poor] and was also active in the "*TOZ*" organization [Society for the Protection of Health].

The "*Linak-ha-Tzedek*" gave him a special memento as an award on his 30th birthday and he received a golden memento from the Chelm Artisans' Union.

In 1936, at the age of 41, he breathed out his soul. His untimely death was a great loss for the Jewish craftsmen and the mass of the people in Chelm.

[Page 369]

The Uncle from Chelm

Sh. Tenenboim, New York

Translated by Gloria Berkenstat Freund

My father had several brothers: one in Zwolen, a second one in Siedlice, a third in Warsaw, a fourth – in Chelm. We, small children, did not know our family. My father had an inclination to move every half year from one small village to another. An old ruin stood somewhere; he rebuilt it, fixing it up with his own hands and brought light and sun into the old ruin. After this, when we had lived [there] for a half year, my father would again rebuild a deserted palace of a count and we would move there. Once my father traded horses; he only bought sick horses. He would come home from the fair with such a sick, wounded horse that it was a pity to look at it. In the course of weeks he would heal it, washing it at the village pond, clean it, cover the wounds with fresh skin. The horse shone in its good home. We all became accustomed to horses; first, my father sold it for a pittance and then bought some sort of bloodied, gloomy horse at the fair and again healed it for weeks.

Once it happened that my father bought a sick horse from the Oblase landowner. The horse lay in the stall writhing in pain.

My father firmly decided to have the horse. He paid and as soon as the horse had been led outside with great difficulty, it fell over and died on the landowner's field. My father was engaged in lawsuits with the landowner for many years. But the landowner still demanded money from my father for bringing a dead horse on his land…

At one time my father was occupied with watchmaking. He would buy old, dead watches, clear them out so that they would go as fast as if they had been given life and he sold them. Our house was always a hospital of dead watches with dirty dials like the faces of corpses. That is the kind of watchmaker my father was.

Perhaps a great doctor who wanted to heal the world was lost in him.

Wandering from village to village, we did not know our family. And this was mostly regretted during the lonesome hours. Now, when they have all disappeared as if into a dark abyss, I am sorry that I did not know them. I would have wanted to describe them. From time to time the familiar face of an uncle, an aunt would suddenly appear and my mother would cry at their leaving and my father would "rejoice" and go back to his dying horses, to his dead watches, to his neglected ruins…

I would want to write an entire book about my father's fantastic character, about his extraordinary talent as a writer, painter, speaker. The walls of the houses, the watches, my father would paint them all in gold and silver paint. He would record events and stories of the dark war times on the edges of the sacred book pages. There was a colorful artist in my father that was lost with him. I inherited my own writing talent from my father. But this is just a spark of the great flame that blazed in his great heart.

[Page 370]

My father's brothers were lonely, sick and poor Jews. They toiled bitterly in their lives. Only the brother in Chelm was a Jew, a rich man. He was named Reb Pesakh. And for as long as I remember, he lived in Chelm. And speaking about him, about his good luck, about his successful children, about his beautiful wife, already well known Chelm stories were told. Wonderful Chelm arose in the spell of the famous, fantastical humor. In the enchantment of pointed jokes, in the grotesque of all the wonderful, soaring, glorious Jews who all took part in the Chelemer uproar of destiny, in the gaudy carnival of lucky and unlucky. From every Chelemer Jew dripped ideas, shrewdness, wisdom and wit; the Chelemer Jews were all covered with the light of the moon, which they captured; wanted to lock the heavenly rose in the barrel as other folk and authors chased after the bluebird of Meterlink, after the blue flower of Novalis [romantic German poet Georg Philipp Friedrich Freiherr von Hardenberg]; in the manner of the pie in the sky that a lover says to a lover in the aromatic lilac night. The Chelemer fools entered my heart with their dreamy-blue eyes, large heads full of wisdom, red, fiery beards, lit by the moon. I loved them, these glorious, great, holy fools from the great, golden Jewish folklore.

My Uncle Pesakh appeared in our home only once in my life. He fell as if from heaven. Expecting to see a happy, Chelemer uncle, it was a sad, Polish Jew who sat at the table. He looked so much like my father that I had the thought that my Uncle Pesakh would, God forbid, not know whether he was really the uncle or really my father.

Perhaps in my heart I wished that my uncle from Chelm would forget who he was and that he would remain with us and think that he is our father and that my father would leave as the uncle from Chelm… Quiet, after so many years, sat the uncle from Chelm. And my father also was quiet. Both brothers had not seen each other for many, many years. They had become grey during that time.

[Page 371]

My mother placed food on the wooden table [covered] with the cut oil cloth, on which there were blotches of ink. (Here we had first learned to write with large letters…) My Uncle Pesakh's pale, gentle hands with a bloodless parchment skin, scraped on the table. He savored food. Instead of my mother's food, he took a package of macaroons from a satchel and with his thin teeth bit a small macaroon and drank from a glass of milk…

– What do you eat for breakfast? – my mother asked, eager to know what is eaten in a rich Jewish house.

– A small macaroon… A little preserves… – answered my uncle.

– And for midday? – My mother further asked.

– A piece of chicken… A little soup… And we snack on macaroons…

– And what is eaten for dinner?

– Very little. We drink a glass of milk with a macaroon…

[Page 372]

We children listened to this great "conversation"… Now we were very surprised by our uncle's wealth. That in a Jewish home one could indulge in eating macaroons at all three meals; this was beyond our fantasy. Only a Czar could indulge in eating macaroons at each meal… If this was so, then the uncle from Chelm was indeed a very rich man…

The separation was sad… At the crooked road near the damp "Olszine" (woods), the two old, sad Jews… With grey beards and quiet faces, and behind them went my mother with we children. It was at dusk. A cuckoo sang its last coo-coo. A golden nightingale trilled a golden love song in the woods…The sun was large, like an enormous eye of God, Who already saw the future crimes across the Polish earth…

– – – Sorrowfully, we went home, as from a funeral… That evening we did not speak at home. We were somehow silently frightened. As if we felt that a great misfortune was coming – that our Uncle Pesakh from Chelm and his entire family would be annihilated with Polish Jewry.

Only in later weeks and months did we talk about our rich uncle who ate macaroons at all three meals…

[Page 371]

Yisroel Moonlit Nights

by B. Alkwut-Blum

Translated by Gloria Berkenstat Freund

Here I spent the night
And I went out to welcome the red beards,
Tin-plated smocks, women in muddy boots,
Homeless young people with ringing fists,
A friend eating a piece of chalk.

I saw, saw the full moon on the mountain –
A whetstone for the nightly knives above them.
Is this the moon that we had once captured
In a barrel of water?

I saw my father over a light
With a bare wick and pure fire.
The whiteness of the walls
Lay on my mother's bed like a skeleton.
The ceilings dripped rusty tears
Over the sleeping children.

Home. Mountain. City of world fools.
True story. A horned cow chewed
The straw from my bed.
An old Jewish *pakn-trager* [1] is your name.

[Page 372]

And as we three brothers are a cadre
Parted all over the world –
How we have carried your need for legends.

A true story. But, from where. Oh,
From where is a Jew?
You are smart, may your light shine, you are smart.
We crowned ourselves
With the laughter of a goat.

Only a word bloomed here,
A plant that still grows in me.
In every person there is a stranger
My fellow townsman who dies.

White night. The face of the night
Passes like a widow's and remains
In the entire emptiness of heaven, alone –

A feather, a quiet scribal quill
Over our street.

Negl-vaser.[2] Morning sighs. *Shemas.*
Here, eating a fruit means being rich
And stepping on a piece of bread
Is a great sin.

Translator's footnotes:

1. Itinerant bookseller
2. Part of the ritual upon awakening in the morning includes *Negl-vaser* – nail water – the washing of one's hands and the recitation of a portion of the *Shema* [the central prayer of Judaism.]

[Page 377]

Memoirs and Notes

Chelm
(Before the Flood)

by Hilel Szargel (Tel Aviv)

Translated by Gloria Berkenstat Freund

My eyes lead me back; it wants to see
Jewish life, sad and joyful,
Where the road is longed for and invites
The poorly clad heart.

Suddenly appears in my city, in Chelm,
With its hilly church *Sobor* [cathedral]
With everything that my mood soaks up
Of the dark year passing like the wind.

Pictures, aromas, dreams
Near the fences of Manczinski's orchard
Enter childish rooms
Of torment and green mercy.

Such a sweet hum buzzes.
A child sees beauty in the world.
God's wonder is present everywhere –
A sun–spot lights up among the trees.

* * *

An aroma intoxicates me,
My mood blooms in remembrance –
Of a cool river on the flowering slope,
A sunflower glows in the sky.

The dew on the green, wet meadow,
The puffed up young yellow flowers,
The river flows with childish noise;
We come from a barefoot world.

We sit on the grey–green stones.
Our feet caressed, purified in the water,
The sun is about to pass,
The blue luster grows duller and dim.

Suddenly, a stone is thrown at us –
The cold monotony broken.
The cry swims in the water,
The blue world becomes harder for us.

Such a sort of suspicion is carried off
From the tree immersed in the river;

[Page 378]

The sky frightened and pale,
Falls together with the night for us.

* * *

Weeks, holidays pass
On the highway of Polish stones.
The street is higher and cleaner,
The beauty of lilac is in the air.

My mother carries around the burden
And walks in a flowery *matinée* [dress]
The home is painted in gold,
Like in a beautiful, wealthy wedding.

But a sadness, a heavy one is spread out
Unknown behind the shoulders of life,
Thus does my mother sew it,
In the "east" in a grey fabric.

My father – he works until late,
But on *Shabbos* [the Sabbath]; a very different face,
His eyes – like a spell that sees
A higher and eternal light.

"*Sholem Aleichem* [welcome or hello] – angels!" –
He turns to the children with a blessing
And after everyone sings,
Hanging off bent walls.

* * *

And the holidays come again,
Swimming freely from the memory,
And the shadows cannot steal
The reflection of the childish years.

A forest is beautiful and it is green,
A forest enveloped in summer,
The road drawn straight
To the noise of the steam mill.

The mill sings and it has magic,
And such a sweet aroma of bran,
Gentiles refreshed in white,
Are busy there and they bustle.

[Page 379]

And songbirds and swallows dazzle,
The *kheder* [religious primary school] is difficult and tired,
With King David whom the rabbi anoints,
King David, is also a Jew.

Shavous[1] speeds here with a cake,
A cake and holiday singing,
The summer, like a golden carpet,
Haunts in a drawn out walk.

Tisha–b'Av[2] – children in sadness,
With carved wooden swords,
Dark melodies of regret;
Lamentations, evening places.

Crying, Yom Kippur–like funerals
Shatter in the street like a flood
And then the new year is torn
With autumn–like leaves.

[Page 380]

Life is bitter and hard,
But the winter gives familiar strength,
The childish spirit near the ovens,
The past wonderfully confided.

The *Baal–Shem*[3] came from Hispania
On a cloud, on Friday night,
Himself understanding the wonder
And again causing sadness.

Therefore, the synagogue
And the low, iron gate lie low there,
Hidden, they again are closed,
[So that] the fear will rock our hearts.

When – the Gentiles – would – come – with – axes
The synagogue would close…
Thus we possessed worlds
Molded in our own forms.

L. Malach's visit to Chelm

A corner of the Chelm state garden
The photograph was taken during the stay in Chelm by the [now] deceased poet, L. Malach, who appears in the center of the group

Translator's footnotes:

1. *Shavous* – spring holiday commemorating the Jews receiving the Torah at Mt. Sinai.
2. *Tisha–b'Av* – ninth of Av, commemorating the destruction of the 1st and 2nd Temples in Jerusalem.
3. *Baal–Shem* – Master of the Name, kabbalistic rabbi who performed healings, miracles, exorcisms and gave blessings.

[Pages 381-382]

Those I Remember

By Pinye Lerer

Translated by Miriam Leberstein

In memory of: My brother, Moyshe Lerer, who died in Kivioli Concentration Camp, Estonia, end of 1944; my sister Alte Sore Lerer; my cousin Tshipe Kohn (born Lerer), her son Leybl Kohn and her daughter Blume Kohn, martyred in Chelm, Hrubiewszow, Vlodove.

After the horrifically tragic deaths of millions of brothers and sisters, and the destruction of all the places we lived, including our hometown Chelm, our minds and hearts are flooded with thoughts and images of what occurred and our ears still hear the last cries of our flesh and blood rising to the heavens. Did it really happen? Did the foul world do such things to us?

How will we get over the extinguished lives that dwell within us? How will we get over the mountain of murdered doves that look at us with open eyes?

From among the stars scattered across the deep dark heavens let us select a few, call them by their names, so as to know how to proceed in the light they cast. Let us tell about them and know what we have lost.

My strongest impressions from my childhood and boyhood in our town are connected with Jews immersed Judaism – the Sabbaths and holidays, Torah study, the *besmedresh* [house of study and worship]. I feel that there I saw people freed from all the bad spirits, even the most oppressive, that afflicted them; there they had on weekdays a taste of the sacred, of the Sabbath. Something like a flaming hoop held them securely together, letting go of them only for the purpose of making a living, and then gathering them together again. No formal learning could have brought them the kind of full, free joy, like a law of nature, that they experienced from, for example, a Passover seder, a Yom Kipper prayer, or immersion in the Torah. Such spiritual exaltation is the highest perfection, a work of the art of life, and our Chelm was not after all, a perfect place. Nor was it an exception; we need only mention Brisk, Lublin, Vilna or Zamosc to understand what they tell us. But now we can turn to our own wonderful Jews, the great Jews with whom we lived, without any danger of being laughed at.

When I think of Chelm with its market place, the ring of shops near the Polish church, I keep thinking about that example of an "ordinary" Jew, Shmuel Hilfnbeyn, a cigarette seller stationed near the small market. "When I think of him my bowels rumble and I feel pity for him." [In quotations in the original]. The way he sidled quickly around , with his head and neck outstretched, swallowing in terror as one does while fasting; his sad smile, his deep, soft voice, like a caged bird from another sphere who cannot find a place to settle. I knew him from the *besmedresh*, from prayers during the High Holy days, when his voice never stopped from *slikhes* [penitential prayers] to *neile* [closing prayer on Yom Kippur]. My child's heart would melt from the sweetness. With what refinement his pale hand would pull up his prayer shawl over his head during an especially fervent prayer, as he shouted and pleaded in God's house:

"I call to mind, O God, and I moan, when I see every city built on its mound, but the city of God [Jerusalem] degraded to Sheol beneath it."

One could clearly see how here, "hidden by the shadow of God's hand under the wings of the *shekhina*" [quotation marks in the original] he was overcome by pure devotion.

Among those whose names were uttered with great respect, and who added luster to the town was my father, Reb Yoske Lerer, Yoske Reb Tudrusl's, as he was called, a descendant of renowned generations of rabbis in our area. He was a grain merchant, a man of refinement, sensibility and clear thinking. He had a reputation for honesty among Jews and non–Jews alike. When there was an error or doubt regarding an accounting, people relied more on his notebook than on the accounts kept by the bookkeepers. They would consult him on matters between friends, rely on him to resolve disputes and would simply come to him to hear a good word, a word of comfort, a word of Torah. He had many religious books in his home –Talmud and *midrashim*; Rambam's *Duties of the Heart*; *Turim* by Jacob Asher, printed in Sfad in the year 300; Isaac Luria's *siddur*, with *shmoys* [second book of Bible] and *tseyrufim* [Kabbalah]; Rabbi Emdin's *siddur*; the philosophical work, *The Binding of Isaac*; and more such books.

But what he relied on most to warm his difficult yet radiant, deeply Jewish life were his books on various areas for which he had an exceptional love and attraction: philosophy, astrology, mathematics, grammar and the works of medieval poets: *The Measure of Heavens*; *Deeds of Tuvie*; *He Who Enlightens*; *Tower of Strength*, Luzzati's *Poems*; even a Hebrew grammar by the Vilna Gaon; and Malbum's Poems.

If I'm not mistaken his book cabinet emitted the scent of generations–old spices and gave the clear impression that one was protected by a great fortress spread over many eras, generations and lands. He loved astronomy, and had gotten as far as Slonimski's book and could calculate when an eclipse would occur. Sometimes on hot summer days he and his brother in law, Reb Binyomin Shur (Gorlovski) from Lemberg, a *dayan* [religious judge] and intellectual, would go down into the cellar and there diligently study astronomy. He understood medicine and could read prescriptions.

Rebe Reb Pinkhesl Lerer, e"h, who was well known and loved in Hasidic circles in Chelm

[Pages 383-384]

His sons usually studied with the best *melamdim* [teachers of young children] and he himself taught them *midrash*, books of ethical and Biblical interpretation, Hebrew and grammar; they knew the works of Rabbi Ben Zakkai by heart. But his girls also received a good education. They studied the bible, as well as German, with special teachers. And when the *melamed* came at the beginning of the term to take the boys to *heder* [religious school for young children] the father invited him to examine his 12–13 year old daughter.

—Well, Altele, what is the meaning of *ha'ez* [Heb.,the goat]?

—Gather up, came the [wrong] answer.

One evening around Khanike, my father brought home and joyously showed us an unbound book in two halves that he had bought from the book peddler. It was *Sefer Elim* by Joseph Solomon Delmedigo [1591–1655] about higher mathematics, a rare antique. Our household rejoiced over the purchase. (Later, I learned that he had paid four rubles for it.) Another time, he came home more exultant than usual and showed us a treasure that he had found in an old book–storage attic at our relatives the Kupers. The little boys jumped out of bed and read by the light of the kerosene lamp that hung from the door molding. It was *Sefer HaTishbi*, a very rare book, a dictionary of 712 unusual Hebrew Talmudic terms by the renowned Italian grammarian and the author of the first Yiddish romance, Elihu Levita, from 1541. On the spot we read the artful definitions and marveled at the rhymes in the Yiddish and Hebrew text, for example, one couplet rhyming a Hebrew phrase ending in "the letter *giml*" with a Yiddish phrase ending in "himl" [heaven].

His esthetic sense was also keen and deep, a natural amalgam of intelligence and emotion. Some of that could be detected in his physiognomy, in the sharp lines and creases around his nose, mouth and eyes. His stiffly combed beard had an air of leonine earnestness, like a lion that weeps. This was the impression given by the sad longing expressed in his eyes, a slight movement of his nostrils, a tear hovering in his eye. When he recited the well known monolog by Luzzati or the prophetic verses from the *shemona esri* prayer, he could never get through without his voice quavering from suppressed tears.

When the pretty women in the family would come to our houses, Renye Kuper, for example, or Tshipele Kohn, the beauty from Zamosc, you could detect a change in his expression and in the color of his face when he offered them a chair. I remember how he once skillfully etched a face, the head of Venus, on an expensive pocket knife, a gift from Karlsbad, with an inscription in Hebrew.

For a time on winter Sabbath eves there would come to our table a raggedy, barefoot, feeble–minded man. We children were at first repelled by him. After father had delivered a talk on an ethical matter, the man would remain seated by the side of the table and eat the Sabbath stew. Once, he started to sing the Sabbath songs aloud, and came to the verse: "That they may be privileged to see children and grandchildren learn Torah and *mitzvos* for their own sake." Father gestured to the children asking if they had noticed the words "for their own sake" and his eyes filled with tears.

For forty years, in the heat of summer and the cold winter dawns he trod the road of Hrubieszower Street to support his large family. His life was embittered by evil competitors, Christians who defiled the house with smoke, whiskey and cursing. A refined man with a delicate body, he nevertheless lived to be very old, thanks to his healthy life and his piety.

On his gravestone his oldest son Moyshe Lerer wrote the words of his most beloved poet:

Here lies
A prince, humble spirit, thought
And deed, of few words,
R. Yosef Aryeh who is called Reb Yoske

I remember another hard working Jew, Shimele Treger, how he stood with his shambling, massive body at the end of the sidewalk near the shops, a rope around his neck, dusted with flour as he waited to be summoned to carry something. Usually on the Sabbath he sat with his prayer shawl over his wide hat at the western wall near the hand basin, where people went in and out and washed their hands. Next to him on the bench sat the water carrier, who cheated his customers by bringing them pails that weren't full; Itshele Aynbinder [bookbinder], who had the habit of mixing up pages, sticking them together and sewing them in such a way that the prayer books kept closing, making up for it by adding long curls of lovely pink paper to the cover and back; Yehusiel Shtrikndreyer [rope winder], who secretly brought his spinning rod into the vestibule of the shul so that it could be used to make noise when Haman's name was mentioned during the reading of the Megilla.

The empty space where the big synagogue stood. One can see a part of the besmedresh that remained

[Pages 385-386]

Once a year the *gabe* asked Shimele what name he wanted to be called by when he was called to read the Torah, and Shimele was thus summoned: Reb Shimen Bar Eliezer Klunimus. People helped him a bit in to say the blessing and the cantor quickly started reciting in a subdued tone as if guilty for doing things irregularly.

Before *kaboles shabes* [prayer welcoming the Sabbath] Pinye Traytls would stand, freshly bathed, hair washed, in his torn Hasidic satin caftan, facing the golden flames of the candles at the Eastern wall, looking at the artistically rendered deer and the inscription: "A man worries about the loss of money and doesn't worry about wasting his days; his money doesn't help, his days do not come back;" then sweetly chanting Yedid Nefesh [Beloved Soul Mate]. It was difficult to believe that this was the same Pinye who worked in the butcher shop all week. Now the *shekhine* [spirit of God] shone upon him and the spirit of the Sabbath entered him. He was a poor man with many children, but very hospitable. He invited home boys from the yeshiva who ate there on certain days of the week and Jewish soldiers from the regiment stationed in town, sometimes 10 or 15 of them. I remember a very snowy winter Sabbath, when an extraordinary stranger appeared in the *besmedresh*. He was a Yemeni emissary from Jerusalem, wearing a fez and curled side locks. People looked at him as at a wonder, didn't understand his

Hebrew, pointed to his fringed garment, asked about his version of the prayer *sh'ma yisroel*. Uncomfortable with such a guest, they packed him off to Pinye Treytls.

When it was time for Lekha Dodi [song welcoming Sabbath] you could see Shimele coming from the bath, with his little broom under his arm, with leaves sticking to it. His large boots were freshly smeared with black pitch, which he obtained every Friday from a box set out on the sidewalk in front of a shop in the business district. That's where Shimele stationed himself most of the week. Jews looked up from their prayers to see the coarse young man who was going home so late. And Shimele, to spite them, walked slowly until he reached the Rubiszower *rogatke* and the alley where he lived in a basement among the organ grinders with their parrots and others birds, and other such people.

Tshipele Kohn

A summer day. The child is on his way to the *heder* of Reb Vove, who teaches translation, somewhere on the top floor of a courtyard building in the "Nayer Tsal." On the way is a man holding a binocular box in which you can see various scenes, from Gehenna [Hell] to Gan Eden [Paradise]. The child looks and sees Gan Eden; in a large orchard stroll tall men with canes and ladies with hats and open umbrellas. The scene is similar to that of the orchard of the pedagogical school on the other side of the stone fence that you can see through the *heder* window. The child has not seen the pictures of Hell. Further on, a magician standing on a square of fabric spread out on the roadway turns somersaults, sticks daggers down his throat and bends a child over his arm like a basket. Near the gate to the *heder* stands Pesakh Sakharmarozhnik with his long white beard, wearing a white apron, selling delicious ice cream in glasses with bone spoons.

In the *heder*, the *rebe* stands in the middle of the room, ready to leave. Seeing that once again, the boys had forgotten to bring tuition money, he began groaning and shouted, "God in Heaven, what do you want from me. Have mercy." And he went out looking to borrow money to get something to eat. The Yadishliver *rebe's* wife was careful to make sure that the milk for her 3 year–old Khayele should not run out. But suddenly, the milk spilled and the whole *heder* rushed to rescue Khayele's milk, as if it were blood. "Swollen with hunger," the boys said with pity, of the chubby Khayele. The *rebe's* wife helped support the family by baking beans for the students.

[Pages 387-388]

Once the child saw the *rebe* writing a request to God for money and other things and a bit seriously, a bit in jest, let it fly away with the win

Hasidic bookkeepers at their desk. One man is writing a promissory note.

I remember an elderly Jew, a carpenter with "golden hands." He was observant, a bit bookish. He worked in the same room where he lived with his family. It was crowded and didn't really have room for a bed. So he would take the first part of a piece of furniture that he was making, a cupboard, for example, and used it as a place on which to put the bedding. This created a concern that bedbugs might be left in the finished piece.

The older sons helped the father with the work and were afraid of his anger and anxiety. The younger son, 10 years old, would spend most of the winter lying on planks set over the oven, wrapped up, not washing because of cold and hunger. He would be called over to help his father pull the saw. He was a master at this and people foresaw that he would grow up to be a skilled craftsman. His mother would serve some potatoes in a tin dish and the young boy would eat it standing up in the workshop, coughing (he was asthmatic), and return eagerly to his work. Once, the father awoke from his customary afternoon nap in an angry mood, talking to himself, to the board, working furiously and shooting dirty looks at the workers, and frightening them. Suddenly, in his fury he threw his big wooden hammer and injured the boy's foot. A commotion broke out; cold water and bandages were brought. The old man quickly changed and with great love and compassion assumed his fatherly role. The storm passed. Evening came; it was quiet in the workshop. The workers left. The boy crept up to his place on the chest in his dark corner, seized his injured foot in both hands and began shaking it back and forth while singing with great feeling: "Mother, my dear, my heart, my love; be quiet a little while; extinguish the hellish fire that burns in me, and give me [for a wife] whomever I want." I am sure that he was referring to the next door neighbor's darkly attractive daughter, whom he loved very much.

Who can forget the brothers Yankl and Moyshe Roznblat, the photographers? They were confirmed bachelors who strode around Lubliner Street from their house to their photography studio in their fluttering capes, soft black hats with broad brims and long, artistic hair. Their profession brought them into artistic circles and they took part in the first amateur theater groups, music circles, artists' groups and philanthropic undertakings along with Itshe and Rivke Luksenburg, Fishl Ilivitsky and others. They never travelled because they suffered with lung disease. No one knew about their lung problems. My brother Moyshe once wrote me that once, when he came home to Chelm from a holiday in Vilna the brothers enthusiastically told him about the sunny letter I had written from Eretz Yisroel, quoting entire passages like songs which one knows by heart. This expressed their yearning for the sun, for Eretz Yisroel. These quiet doves were murdered on the death march somewhere on the Rubiszower Road.

Hashomer Hadati [Religious Guard] in Chelm, 1935

Two yeshive boys after eating "days" take a walk

[Page 389]

Why Y.L. Peretz Did Not Deliver his Lecture in Chelm, *Shavous*, 1912

(and other episodes and events of a long forgotten time)

by Shmuel Winer

Translated by Gloria Berkenstat Freund

A great cultural holiday was celebrated in all corners of the world, wherever a Jewish settlement is located. It was the 100th anniversary (1851-1951) of the birth in the Polish-Jewish city of Zamosc, of the father of modern Jewish literature. For all of those, whose cradles stood in Poland, this name has a special significance. Yitzhak Leibush Peretz, the great writer, humorist, passionate fighter for social and national justice, for a new free man, personified the very finest and best in historical Polish Jewry. Peretz represented the most mature fruit of the Jewish cultural collection in Poland over the course of generations and generations before its tragic death. The name of Yitzhak Leibush Peretz will shine the clearest on the collective headstone of the annihilated Polish Jewry.

Shmuel Winer

Therefore, now at this opportunity, it is the most appropriate moment to reveal an unknown episode in Peretz's life of forty years ago, in 1912, three years before his premature death. An episode to which both Chelm and I are connected. An episode that could have led him into deep trouble during the difficult times of Czarist despotism.

After the revolutionary spurt in 1905-1906, there came years of strong reaction, which suffocated and choked. The struggle against Czarism was strongly weakened; its pulse could barely be felt. However around 1910 a revival began again. The revolutionary parties began to rise *tekhayis hameisim* [be resurrected from the dead]. There was also movement among the Jewish illegal workers parties.

It was winter 1911-1912. A cluster remained of the former large *S.S.* [Zionist Socialists] organization in Warsaw. The helm of the workers movement that the intelligentsia had left in the difficult years of the reaction was taken over by the workers themselves. A generation of intelligent workers grew up during the years of the revolution. They sacrificed, were often arrested and it happened that they suffered years in the difficult conditions in the CZarist jails and in exile in the most distant, coldest corners of Siberia.

[Page 390]

The sadder the surrounding reality, the stronger they huddled together, the warmer, more sincere was their friendship.

One of the heaviest cares then among those who were free, was: how do we obtain sufficient means to be able to take care of the most minimal needs of the comrades in jail and in exile. I, too, an active member of the *S.S*, did not stop thinking about this matter. I then hatched a daring plan in my head that, if realized, could bring in a significant sum for us. After I thought about all of the details I confided the plan to the two experienced communal workers in the organization, my closest comrades and friends, the two young intelligent workers, Mordekhai Birman and Avrahamel Kosman. In short the plan consisted of this: I would go to Peretz and invite him to Chelm for one or two readings. And if he agreed, the income that would remain from Peretz's appearance would be a great help in relieving the needs of the arrestees and exiled comrades. After long deliberation, weighing and measuring the arguments for and against the bold plan, we saw no other way out and I was wished luck in my mission. Naturally, it was agreed that the entire thing would remain a deep secret between a few people. No further peep.

A few days before Passover (1912) on a gloomy, rainy day, I found myself at the famous house in Warsaw, Ceglana 1. I went up to the first floor; I looked at the brass sign on Peretz's door with the Hebrew lettering indicating when he received guests. I saw that I had come at the correct time. I stood at his door and wanted to ring. However, I became paralyzed with fear and lost my courage. True, since I had been in Warsaw (autumn 1907), I had almost not missed one of his appearances, unless I had been arrested. I also was one of the exalted young men who would every *Shabbos* [Sabbath] in summertime sit on a bench on Igalkowa Aleje in Saxon Gardens and wait for when Peretz would stroll by with one or more of the young writers – Peretz Hirshben, Menacham and others. With his characteristic Peretz smile, he would greet us all on each side and we were in seventh heaven. However, here was something else, here I needed to meet the great master by myself face to face – and one needed to know how to speak to Peretz.

Standing and thinking at Peretz's door also had a limit; finally I took courage; what would be would be; and I strongly rang with great excitement – and fright at the same time.

[Page 391]

It did not take the blink of an eye and, to my great astonishment, Peretz stood at the open door. He himself had opened the door for me. This again confused me. I did not expect Peretz would open the door himself. He invited me to come inside and excused himself that he could not take me into his office. *Erev Pesakh* [on the eve of Passover] they were cleaning and they were washing the room; he had nowhere to go. There being no other choice, we had to remain in the antechamber. He was wearing his brown velvet jacket, looked gloomy like the weather outside. I, too, became depressed and I thought: I came at the wrong time! I would have run away if I could. Peretz did not let me think for long and asked in a very friendly way what was my desire.

Meanwhile, my equilibrium returned and in a few words I told him that I had come to invite him to Chelm for either one or two evenings. I hoped that he would not refuse. We were sort of neighbors. How far was Zamosc from Chelm? And both cities – in Lublin *Gubernja* [province] and Chelm was not strange to him and here was the proof: His *Chelemer Melamed* [*Chelm Teacher*], his *Shabbos Goy* [*Sabbath Gentile*], his *Iber a Shmek Tabak* [*A Pinch of Snuff*].

Speaking to him in this way, I noticed how his face became clear, his eyes lightened with that particular Peretz look. I began to see that he was simply waiting for me, for my invitation. True, Peretz was not then yearning for an appearance. He had then reached his high point. It was after his triumphant trip through the great Jewish centers. The three Peretz-days several weeks earlier in the Jerusalem of Lithuania, in Vilna (in February) had been transformed into a great people's holiday and into a powerful demonstration for Yiddish literature, such as Vilna had never seen.

When I was finished, he smiled that, in fact, he would be interested in making a quick trip to Chelm and he was happy at the opportunity. Why did he seize this; he did not tell me and understand that I did not ask him. Who knows? Perhaps it was because it was Chelm – the most famous and well-known Jewish city in the world?*[Page 392]*

After a minute or two of thinking it over, Peretz told me that he had the date for his appearance in Chelm. He was free of his duties in the community on *Shavous* [spring holiday celebrating the "Giving of the Torah"]; therefore, he could be in Chelm for *Shavous*.

With the date decided, I told Peretz that I was going home to Chelm for Passover and I would immediately start the preparations there for his appearance. Meanwhile, I asked him to prepare a Russian synopsis of his reading in order to receive permission for the lecture; the regime had to be provided with a synopsis with the exact contents of the lecture in Russian. I promised him I would be back in Warsaw right after Passover and would conclude all of the other matters in reference to his appearance. Peretz did not say one word about money.

I said goodbye to Peretz and left his residence. I breathed more freely. I felt fortunate and inspired by the warm reception I had received from Peretz and that my mission so far had been crowned with success. Yes, now we would be able to help the comrades in need and, yes through me, my Chelm would have the privilege of welcoming Peretz – to see and hear the great master.

S.S. committee in 1906

Top row, standing from right to left: Shmuel Winer, Bishka Mandlbaum, Fayga Wilder and Yair Mandlbaum
Second row, sitting from right to left: Josl Cymerman, Chana Wilder, Leibush Malier
In the very front of the first row – Yankl Birnbaum.
Of the entire group, two are alive today – Shmuel Winer and his wife, Chana Wilder.
They have been in New York since December 1912

I immediately gave a report of my visit with Peretz to my closest comrades, Mordekhai and Avrahamel. It is superfluous to say that they were happy about my first success with Peretz. However, the work first began.

I parted with my comrades; on *erev Pesakh* [on the eve of Passover] I went home to my parents and I entered Chelm at night just before the Seder.

In the morning, on the first day of Passover, I began to take my bearings, to arrange a plan about how to start the work. I met with a few old comrades and told them that we would need to immediately begin to prepare for Peretz's appearance in Chelm. They naturally were very surprised by the news. I said that we would need to prepare such an impressive welcome for Peretz that he would remember it, to show him what Chelm could do and, also, so that Chelm would never forget it. Now imagine the stir that this would create in the city as soon as the great news became public. However, until then, we had to be quiet (two of those comrades are now in America: B. Binsztok in New York and Kh. Zemelman in Los Angeles).

First came the thought about getting the appropriate hall. We had to have the largest hall in the city. This would have to be no other than the *Syreny* Cinema on Lubliner Street. It was resolved that this was the only hall that would be able to best serve our purpose … A day or two later I met with the owner of *Syreny*. He agreed to yield the hall to us for *Motzei Shabbos* [the conclusion of the Sabbath] *Sukkous* for this elevated opportunity and we began to prepare a solemn appeal to the city in honor of this extraordinary event.

[Page 393]

Meanwhile, I wrote a letter to Warsaw in order to inform my comrades how I was progressing with the preparations, several lines, naturally in a disguised manner, so that no one else would guess. Peretz's name was not mentioned. I wrote the few words to the address of Moshe Sztywelman, also from Chelm, who shared my room with me in Warsaw. I signed the letter with the initial Sh.

* * *

The years of *strum un drang* [storm and stress] of the Russian revolution (1905-1906) awoke the wide masses among us in Chelm to a new life as in all of the other cities and *shtetlekh* [towns]. We had struggled with all of our strength since the Middle Ages in which Chelm, as most cities and *shtetlekh* in Poland was still deeply seated. The short struggle for freedom brought out a new type of young worker. This new restless generation no longer wanted to and could not return to their earlier indifferent and boring lives. With their first steps, the Jewish workers parties awoke an interest in culture among the workers, a thirst to know, planted the habit of reading in them. Taught them to look at a book with respect. This, which the Enlightenment did for the middle-class children, was done for working masses by the Jewish workers parties beginning in the present century (20th century). A true cultural revolution occurred among them.

The reality in that pitch dark time was sorrowful. Poverty and need. The prospect of a better tomorrow was muddled. The reaction raged. True, the waves of bloody pogroms in the Jewish cities and *shtetlekh* were declining – pogroms in which bloody Czarism wanted to bury the revolutionary movement in Jewish blood. However, the cold pogrom did not end for a minute. Oppressive edicts that embittered our lives even more dropped on our heads every day without end. It became more difficult for the Jewish people to breathe. The hatred of the oppressed was without limit. However, we did not give up and we hoped for better times, which must finally come.

Meanwhile, we devoted ourselves with fervor to the Yiddish book, to self-education. We diligently read the modern Yiddish literature that blossomed then so beautifully. It brought the holiday spirit to the grey realities and beautified life a little. The reverence for the creations of the Yiddish word, particularly for Peretz, who was already a legend, was implicit. The fervid wish among everyone was to see Peretz themselves.

We could barely conceal what Peretz' appearance would have meant then for Chelm!

However, how does the folk saying go: "Man thinks [plans] and God laughs." And the blow that soon had to fall did not wait for long.

During *Khol Kamoed Pesakh* [the intervening days of Passover], I received a telegram from Warsaw with, I thought, an entirely innocent content: "My mother has become ill; I await a letter with more details." It meant in the disguised language of that time: an arrest had taken place and I should not move from my place until I received a letter. And finally, the dream was gone of Peretz in Chelm. And the troubles began to spread. A Chelm girl, Bayla Wilder, a distinguished activist with the *S.S.*, had sent the telegram from Warsaw.

[Page 394]

There could no longer be any talk about preparing an appearance by Peretz. Now I had to wait for a letter; the letter did not keep us waiting for long. Several days later, I received the much awaited letter and it turned out that it was a great deal worse than I could imagine.

To make it short, this is precisely what happened. There was a meeting *Khol Kamoed Pesakh* of the leading workers at the Warsaw *S.S.* in order to put together a 1st of May proclamation. Naturally, everything was done secretly – highly conspiratorially, as it was then called. Yet the Okhrana (the Czarist political secret police was named the Okhrana) invaded the meeting and arrested everyone. The mystery of how the Okhrana knew about and invaded the meeting – was revealed in 1917. (After the revolution, when the archive of the Okhrana was opened and the names of all of the provocateurs, bought souls were released, among them was the name of the provocateur, Dovid Landa, an active *S.S.* worker, who had betrayed that meeting.) The earlier mentioned Moshe Sztywelman, to whom I had sent the note about the preparations for Peretz's appearance in Chelm, had the accidental misfortune to "go astray"; I say "go astray" because he was not supposed to be there. He was not called to that meeting. They did not want to send him away; he was one of them. So he was arrested there with everyone else. And here the misfortune started.

Moshe Sztywelman, as mentioned earlier, was a Chelemer. He came from the deepest poverty; he was orphaned early. At first, he was in Warsaw for a total of about a year or maybe a little more. He worked at his trade – carpentry – quite passably and lived well. We divided a room at Marjagska 8. He was an uncomplicated, honest comrade and a devoted friend, quiet and withdrawn. He was satisfied and felt elevated by the warm, friendly environment in which he now lived and he appreciated it. He now first began to savor life. It was a bit of redress for his bitter childhood and years of his youth. Yet, at times he fell into a paralyzing melancholy from which he tried to free himself, but with little success. He was approximately the same age as I.

In short, my above-mentioned comrades, Mordekhai Birman and Avrahaml Kosman, were among the arrested. A day or two after the arrest, Bayla Wilder already had an appointment with Mordekhai Birman at Pawiak [Warsaw prison] at his request. He was a handsomer type of young worker, full of energy, with a clear head on his shoulders and a strong and warm heart. He could scarcely wait for her. There was great trouble. At the investigation at the Okhrana, Moshe Sztywelman could not bear the great pressure and revealed who the Sh. was that had signed my letter that had been found with him. Mordekhai told her that I should be informed immediately and forthwith that the Okhrana knew that I was in Chelm and what I was now doing there. Several days later, when Bayla Wilder was again at Pawiak for an appointment with Mordekhai Birman, Moshe Sztywelman had a visitor, his brother, just at the same time. She almost did not recognize Moshe Sztywelman at her first look at him through the bars that divided the arrestees from the visitors. He was no longer the same as he was several days earlier before his arrest. [He was] disheveled with a wild, confused look in his eyes. He noticed her and the idea came to him slowly to cleanse himself. He called her over. He had to talk to her. With a sad, guilty smile and choppy phrases, full of regret, he quickly began to explain: When they found my letter with him at the Okhrana, they forced him to say who Sh. was who had signed the letter and where I was now. The Okhrana now knew everything. I should be warned in time; I should know what I had to do.

[Page 395]

Little by little we learned more details about this sad case.

During the arrest, on that fatal night, Moshe Sztywelman immediately fell into a panic. Yet he did not have to be there. How, with his own free will had he crawled into fire?

Immediately after his arrest, at the investigation by the Okhrana, he was completely stupefied by charcoal fumes. They hammered at him that he should reveal who was the Sh. was who had signed the letter that had been found on him and where he was now. They turned their "tested" means on him. They tried with anger and with good, with false, cunning spiteful remarks. He could no longer bear the inquisition and capitulated. As if in a trance, he told who Sh. was and where he was, what he was doing there.

Woe to he who did not possess the spiritual and moral strength to be able to look the enemy right in the eyes. However, most were like the earlier mentioned Mordekhai Birman and Avrahaml Kosman. They grew up when they fell into the paws of the enemy. In jail, they worked to catch up with the education that they had not had the opportunity to pursue when they were free. They showed such courage and human self-worth both during the trial and after the trial that they evoked respect even from the enemy. (Now in America, I carry out a correspondence with them. My letters are smuggled to them in Pawiak and their letters are smuggled out and sent to me in New York.

[Page 396]

Their letters to me in which they describe very interestingly the then difficult life of the political arrestees in the Czarist jails, were published by Dr. Chaim Zhitlowski in his monthly journal, *Dos Naye Lebn* [*The New Life*] in the issue of March 1914 with an introduction and explanations by Moshe Katz, the respected publicist and literary critic.

Alas, our fellow townsman, Moshe Sztywelman, was not kneaded from that same dough. Immediately at his first face-to-face meeting with the enemy, he lost his physical strength and he gave in.

After the "interrogation" by the Okhrana, he was led, side by side with the other arrestees, up into the Pawiak and they were placed in one room. There in the jail room, he sobered up from the charcoal fumes; his mind began to clear; he saw for the first time with complete clarity what he had done! To so betray his dearest comrades and friends! But there was no longer a way back – it already was too late! He wrestled with himself and desperately looked for a refuge somewhere – and he did not find it. He could not endure it any longer and broke under the heavy burden, which was unbearable for him. Thus, not seeing any other way out, in order to save himself from the hellish suffering, in order to escape from the unbearable reality, he was seized little by little by darkness, until it reached so far that he became wild and in the middle of the night he even attacked his closest comrades, Mordekhai and Avrahaml, with whom he was in the same cell and he began to choke them. Once, and then again. Despite the fact that they covered themselves and blocked everything. They were afraid that removing him from their cell would be worse. The watched him as if he were a helpless child and helped him in any way they could. They sympathized with him in his catastrophe and suffered with him in his great misfortune.

Moshe Sztywelman

The end was tragic. Little by little, little by little, his reason completely left him. He was taken from Pawiak to an institution. He was brought to his trial, a scant two years later (December 1913), but there no longer was someone to judge. While my closest comrades, Mordekhai and Avrahaml and others, were sentenced to eternal exile in Siberia and others in the group to various prison terms, Moshe Sztywelman was sent to a state institution in Warsaw for the deranged.

He did not regain his sanity before his quick, premature death at the young age of twenty-plus years. Six weeks after the trial in the middle of the summer of 1914, on the eve of the First World War, he breathed out his last breath. He had yet to begin to live and clung fast to life. And under normal humane circumstances he would have been able to live out his given years. Let us here mention our unfortunate townsman, Moshe Sztywelman, upon whom fell the dark fate to be one of the thousands of innocent victims of Czarist despotism.

* * *

We return to Chelm.

As already said earlier, all the preparations for Peretz's appearance ceased and all traces disappeared, as if there had been nothing. Naturally, I did not return to Warsaw. And I began to prepare for the inevitable visit by the Warsaw Okhrana.

[Page 397]

I was certain that I would not get off so easily now. I was branded by them. I was in their hands twice during the last two years. In the middle of March, 1910, 10 to 12 of us Chelm young men and girls in Warsaw came together on a *Shabbos* night to spend a joyous evening in honor of Purim. Agents of the Okhrana and the police already were concealed in the room from before and when someone opened the door and stuck in his head, he immediately fell into their ready hands – no none came out of there alone. The entire thing was a mystery to us. First we were dropped into real trouble at the "hearing" (investigation) at the Okhrana; then we were scattered for more than four month in the worst jails. It was crowded and packed in the jails, so we suffered for most of the time, in the wet, cold holes in one of the forts – in the Aleksejewski fort – in the Warsaw fortress. Not having any evidence with which to bring us to trial, we were sent out of Poland for six months. We were taken away to Kowle with "pageantry" in a procession of convicts. (Chana Wilder also was among those prisoners – she was later my wife. Still alive from that group also are: Hillel Szmaragd, in Paris; Ester Wilder in Paris and, I think, Rayzl Luksenberg in Canada).

When we returned to Warsaw six months later, the mystery of our ambush on was solved. A certain young man from Berdichev wanted to have an "easy income" – all kinds of reptiles swarm in a swamp – he became a denouncer for the Okhrana, a bought soul. He gave into their hands the Jewish young people – right and left. He did not know us – I did not know him; by chance, he was a frequent visitor in that house where we were supposed to come together and he learned that we would come together there on *Shabbos* night and that was enough for him. Not knowing any of us, he threw us all together in one pot and "designated" us as anarchists. Why anarchists? They [the Okhrana] paid the highest price for anarchists. He was paid per head.

The truth was that more than half of us were not connected with any illegal revolutionary movement. This was a person of that type, from which was recruited years later, in the days of Hitler, may his name and memory be blotted out, the greatest human-dregs, the shame of the Jewish people – the accursed *kapo* [a concentration camp prisoner recruited as a supervisor of forced labor]. (A few dozen years ago, I heard that this debased denouncer lives very calmly in New York.)

I was taken the second time in 1911. It was on a *Shabbos* day, in the middle of May when the Okhrana attacked the general meeting of the Jewish Literary Society in Warsaw. The Okhrana "sifted out" around 30 people from among the several hundred assembled and gave me the honor to be counted as one of them. And again the well known investigation and again jail. However, the extent to which the Czarist regime had considerably decayed can be demonstrated by this characteristic fact. Among the arrestees was an engineer Heler, a Bundist, the chairman of that meeting. He came from a rich family in Riga. His father came to Warsaw and bribed none other than Rachmaninov himself, the great inquisitor of the Okhrana, with a considerably large fortune. He freed several other arrestees along with engineer Heler so as not evoke any suspicion toward him. It fell upon me to be one of the lucky ones. This time I had languished for several months.

[Page 398]

The main thing, is it not remarkable that I was not now very eager to meet them again? However, they did not let me wait long.

It was a day or two after Passover. A mild spring day. My father had just left me alone in the middle of the day to give attention to his iron business (in Leibele Kupersztok's courtyard entrance on Lubliner Street). I noticed how the gendarme with the beard – he was call "the beard" because of the long respectable beard he wore – was prowling, smelling and sniffing around the shop. He even stuck his beard in the shop – this because he apparently was making sure that this was really me. This gendarme with the middle class beard and with his leisurely gait always walked among Jews. He knew everyone – large and small – knew where everyone lived and everyone knew him. His religious worship was to sniff out if it was necessary to bring one in. Meanwhile, before anything [happened], my little sister, Bluma, who was with me in the shop, disappeared from sight. She ran home to warn our parents. As young as she was, not yet a full six years old, she knew what this meant. We lived in Avraham Gecele's house at Seminarska Street across from the Belzer *shtibl* [one-room synagogue]. At the same time my mother learned that "the beard" had been to the house owner today ostensibly to record the names of all of the residents in the house and exactly where everyone lived.

At night it already was very dark; I went home through Lubliner Street. I recognized several Warsaw Okhranakes [members of Okhrana] strolling so pleasantly. In short, all signs showed that it would happen today, at night. There could no longer be any doubt.

Coming home I found my family very worried. I even tried to calm my parents, but naturally it was useless. After eating in a heavy mood I left our home, leaving everyone in distressed expectation on the strange night watch that was before them. I strode away with quick steps to my hiding place.

A long, sleepless night; barely lived to see morning come. It did not take long and my father sneaked into my hiding place. He told me that he had looked very carefully the entire way to see if they were following him. One look at his very pale tortured face immediately gave witness to the inquisition that he had endured that night. Without further delays he started to relate:

[Page 399]

That night we did not close our eyes. With quivering hearts, we awaited the 'uninvited guests.' The time draws out as if from resin. And it was night – when their custom was to drag the [people] out of their beds in the middle of the night – it already was one in the morning. They knocked on the door and it began. The key inside fell out of the lock from the banging on the door. With dread my father searched for the key. They began to rage on the other side of the door with oaths and vehement curses and threats that they would immediately break the door. My father finally found the key and unlocked the door. An entire gang burst in with an uproar with the gendarme with the beard as their guide. They also had a large bloodhound with them. After they asked my father if he was Hersh Leib Winer, the father of Shmuel Winer and also my mother if she was Sheva Winer, they went to "work." Under the leadership of the "beard" they immediately went to the beds – the first was my brother Pinkhas' bed. With his first look, the "beard" saw his "disaster" and with an almost crying voice he groaned to the caught one "*Etonya tot*" (It is not him). They also went to the beds of my sisters, Gisha and Bluma, looked for me under their beds. (My brother Pinkhas and both sisters, Gisha and Bluma, are in New York today.) They also asked about my brother, Benyamin, who was then in Yekatrinoslav [Dnipropetrovsk]. Then they turned to my father – he should immediately say where I was hiding. He told them that I was in Warsaw. What do you mean, Warsaw? – They tapped with their feet – you such and such.

Had we not seem him today with our own eyes? They again started to curse and to threaten him; he must immediately tell them where I was hiding. Despite their threats, my father stood fast: I was always home for Passover and, as always, immediately after Passover, I returned to Warsaw. They all had a fit of rage – they had the net ready, everything had gone as if oiled and here the fish had slid out from under their hands, he was gone.

They did not spare my mother. She also was terrorized.

They now went to "work" with fury. They looked, rummaged in all of the corners of the house. They looked for me, the "sages," under my mother's bed. A few went into the courtyard, they forced open the rooms and they searched for me there, too. A police guard even stood around the house – no one came in and no one went out. The "work" in the house continued. They looked for *trayf* [non-kosher, in other words, illegal] literature, proclamations. They scattered; they struck everything that was in the house. They looked through my father's religious books; they looked through the pages of the High Holy Day prayer books, the Five Books of Moses, until they came to my mother's woman's prayer book and there they finally discovered the right "subversive literature." They pulled out a prayer – one page that lay in my mother's prayer book, printed on both sides. With a look full of triumph, they began to wave the prayer right in my father's face: "What is this? You should answer immediately." Sensing that a misfortune was moving on him, he began to move backwards and answered them shaking that this was a *molitve* [Russian – prayer], (a *Tkhine* [Yiddish book of prayers for women]) belonging to my mother.

[Page 400]

Well, he did not need anything more. They started to roar with blood-curdling curses: "You rogue, such nerve – to deceive us before our eyes! Are we blind? Do we not see that it is a *Zydowska* [Jewish – a pejorative word] proclamation!" And the scoundrels threw themselves on him and they began to beat him with a hail of fists. (My father was a weak man and he began to suffer with heart problems after this brutality and the terror and pain. Little by little, he constantly lay sick until the last day of his life, 15 Tevet [3 January] 1923.

Ten of my notebooks from the Hebrew journal *Reshafim* (*Sparks*) were in our house. Several of the notebooks had colored covers of thick paper. The notebooks were in a small parchment pocket. They began to choose several notebooks with great joy – now they had the right goods. Why only these few? Because they had red covers! It is enough to say that the editor of *Reshafim* was none other than Dovid Friszman and the journal was published in Warsaw with the permission, naturally, of the Czarist censor.

But this still was not everything. When they finally were finished with the search, they swarmed to cut to pieces everything that fell into their hands – then they used their last trump card. They attacked my brother, Pinkhas, told him to get dressed and go with them. True, they did not really mean him – but as I was not here, they took him as a hostage. It should be understood that with this they had in mind to break the stubbornness of my parents. They were not completely stupid. After everything, they had no doubt that my parents knew of my hiding place. However, my parents also resisted the psychological attack on their nerves. Shooting their last bullet, they finally ended the inquisition and left, actually taking my brother with them. They did not forget to take my mother's *Tkhine*, the *Reshafim* notebooks and more with them.

One can imagine the situation in which my parents and sisters found themselves. (After a day or two, realizing that their strategy was a failure, the Okhrana had no other choice than to free my brother.)

In short, for the present, I came out the victor in the first uneven contest between me and the Czarist gendarmes, police and agents dressed in civilian clothes. However, now what? This question stood before me in its true intensity. With the particular stubbornness with which they had chased after me, I realized that I was playing with fire. It is certain that my letter, which they had found with Moshe Sztywelman about Peretz' appearance in Chelm was to blame and they sharpened their teeth for Peretz himself. True, Peretz' name was not directly mentioned in my letter – however, they now knew who and what, after the disclosures by Moshe Sztywelman. Only with this, I think, can the more than usual perseverance with which they chased after me, the only one directly implicated in the matter, be explained. My arrested comrades in Warsaw, too – with whom I stayed in contact, in secret, naturally – warned me that my name also figured in the case that was being prepared against the Warsaw *S.S.* [Zionist Socialist] organization.

[Page 401]

They kept urging me to leave the country, quickly, to not give the Okhrana the opportunity to catch me. Their devotion was truly touching, how they took my fate to their hearts – more than their own difficult situation.

However, it was not as easy to do as to say it. In addition, the thought of emigrating then pressed on my spirit as it meant saying goodbye to those closest and dearest for eternity – never seeing them again. But, since the corrupt Czarist, despotic regime was considerably decayed, we could calculate that in five years this giant on clay feet would lay on the garbage heap of history.

In short, time does not stand still. Through the window of my hiding place I often saw the gendarme with the beard prowling on the opposite sidewalk. He was lying in wait for me at the entrance to Chana Wilder's house. He divided his time between my home and her home. It already was almost after the summer and it appeared that the gendarme with the beard was beginning to get tired. I began to earnestly prepare to leave. However, sneaking across the border was too risky. Often [people] were caught and sent home under escort. At the advice of Goldfeld, a Chelemer ship-ticket agent, we would travel on the Russian ship-line from Libave[1] [Liepeja, Latvia] for 25 rubles. No matter what legal peril, the governor's office issued a passport for traveling abroad. This Russian ship line helped with this, so they also could profit from the great storm of Jewish emigration that made the German and English ship companies rich.

The beginning of November. A dark *sof khoydesh* [end of the Hebrew calendar month], a very cloudy sky – the wind outside cried cold tears – and I quietly sneaked into the house of Chana Wilder. Here, a quiet wedding would take place, without *klezmer* [musicians]. We would be led to the *khupah* [wedding canopy]. In addition to our parents, there were only a few guests from the closest family at the secret wedding. The entire scene, near the thickly covered windows, muffled lights, worried faces and quiet whispering – looked more like a Marrano *Kol Nidre* scene, gathered in a deep cellar at the time of the Spanish Inquisition[2] – than like a wedding. Incidentally, this was a double "celebration" – both, so to say, a wedding and a farewell for our departure for America. Naturally, there was no lack of tears at the "celebration" – everyone separately thinking – would we see each other again?

A day or two later we were both, my wife and I, on the way to Libave – the harbor of our hopes. We arrived there after around 30 hours without any pitfalls on the way. The paper in my pocket that I had taken out a few days earlier at the [provincial office] in Lublin – the small piece of paper, which qualified us to receive a passport in Libave, warmed me. It turned out that there, in Libave, I was not an only son. [There were] other passengers, such I, also Jewish runaway soldiers.

[Page 402]

A day before embarking on the ship. The passengers assembled in a giant room, *chinovnikes* [Russian functionaries] sat behind small windows and gave out passports. It was the turn of my row, I presented my paper and 25 rubles and – there was a calamity: The *chinovnik* found a blemish in my paper and – and nothing helped – I did not receive our passports and we could not sail with our ship.

This blow, however heavy it was lowered on us, did not leave us despondent. Now that we had come so far, we must not panic. The next morning I already was sitting on the train which carried me speedily back to Lublin. Chana, my wife, remained waiting in Libave. Having traveled about three quarters of the way, everything had gone smoothly. It was evening; the train stopped at the Malkin station, not far from Bialystok and – a rush, turmoil, gendarmes, militiamen, a commotion. Just then, no other than Czar Nikolai the last, himself, had a whim to be there with his general retinue and government officials. He was, just then, present at large scale military maneuvers in that area. Multitudes of gendarmes entered into the turmoil in the wagons and they carried out searches and they led out everyone – no matter whom. And again, a lucky accident – there is a lot to tell – and I exited unscathed. After the train had been held for many hours, it finally moved. I finally arrived in Lublin peacefully the next morning. I received the correct paper from there – for a ruble naturally – and I traveled to Chelm. I again said farewell to my home, again tears. I immediately went back to Libave peacefully.

Now there were no more difficulties. We received the well-guarded passport and a few days later we were on the ship. The irony of the story was this, that our ship, which withdrew farther from the shores of the "Land of Blood," as Jews then referred to Czarist Russia, and began to cut the waves of the sea on its way to America, - this ship that now saved a few people from the Czarist jail and persecutions, - that the ship itself carried the name "Czar."

Our trip took 13 days. There were no great storms. On the 14th day, on the 8th of December 1912, the "Czar" landed in New York Harbor. As fast as we left the Russian ship and set foot on the hard New York ground, we finally, for the first time in a long time, breathed freely.

* * *

I returned to Chelm nine years later and naturally, in addition to the great experience of seeing my parents and family again, there also was the happy satisfaction over the bad end that had ensnared all of the Czarist satraps, hangmen and executioners who so embittered our lives in Russian during the revolution. A justly earned end – *keyn yovdu* [may they all come to the same end – said upon learning of the misfortune of an enemy]!

[Page 403]

The last drops of joy seeped out quickly upon seeing the practical result for us of the newly resurrected from the dead Poland. When one compares the earlier Czarist pogrom regime with the present bitter anti-Semitic Polish regime, one can only say: if not yet worse. They even go as far on the road as Hitler with their concentration camp in Kartuz Bereza [detention camp for opponents of the Polish regime], where the best sons of Poland are tortured with such savagery that a number are tortured to death. They have the qualities for pogroms against the Jews. Jewish blood again runs like water: in Pinsk, Vilna, Przytyk, Brisk and others. Jews are thrown out of moving trains, Jewish beards are torn out by the skin and there are other persecutions and harassments. Anti-Semitism and boycotts are the official policy of the Polish feudal regime. They tear the last bit of bread from the mouth. The tax policy completely impoverishes us. We are very visible to them – too many Jews in Poland – *Zydzi do Paestyny* [Jews to Palestine] – is the official state slogan. And this after over 800 years of living on Polish soil, deeply woven into the history, into the economic, social, cultural and political fabric of the nation.

Here is a characteristic incident from that time. In the middle of the day, my father came running home, very agitated, pale and simply falling to pieces. We had to put him to bed immediately. What happened? He was friendly with a Pole with whom he would carry on trade. They would go to each other's homes. That day my father was supposed to be with the Pole, but before he crossed the threshold, the Pole grabbed him with great rage, took a hunting rifle down from the wall and aimed at him, raising a cry that he [my father] should leave his house immediately or he would immediately shoot him on the spot. My father barely escaped with his life. A few hours later, the Pole came running to us and, with tears in his eyes, begged my father to forgive him. He told him that just when my father came in to him, a representative from Warsaw, who had been specially sent to strengthen the boycott movement against the Jews in Chelm, was sitting there. He said he had been denounced because he trades with Jews. In order to save his life, he had to take the extreme step – play the tragic-comedy.

I arrived in Chelm at daybreak, as I said, *erev Sukkus* [on the eve of the Feast of Tabernacles], 1921. By night I already had given out to around 50 Chelemer families the few thousand dollars that their relatives and families in America had given to me for their sake. "Relief" in New York, in which I was active, had sent a good sum with me for the institutions in Chelm – for *Linas-haTzedek* [society providing a place for the needy to sleep], *moyshav-skayneym* [old age home], *Talmud Torah* [religious elementary school for poor boys], Peretz Library and others.

This time, coming back to New York, I say goodbye to my father forever. After my father's death (15 Tevet [3 January], 1923), we, my brother and sisters, brought our mother to New York. She lived out her last years with us (she died on 20 Cheshvan [14 November], 1939).

* * *

[Page 404]

Forty years have passed since that strange spring, 1912. Could it occur to us that my forced emigration carried such terrible far reaching consequences – and not only for me? The very richest (or wildest) fantasy could not have suspected it!

It was in that period of *sturm und drang* [turmoil], at the beginning of this century (the 20th). The young in Chelm – as in other cities and *shtetlekh* – tore away from the narrow homes into the larger world – for us it really meant, to Warsaw. There was for these young people then an unwritten law, an inviolable law that whatever happened, all must return dressed up to the home nest on Passover for the Seder [ritual meal describing the Exodus from Egypt], loaded with the newest literary publications. It had to be that for certain reasons, Bayla Wilder (my wife's sister) did not come home on that Passover and, therefore, as mentioned earlier, could immediately inform me about that fateful arrest in Warsaw (Bayla Wilder and her husband, B. Binsztok, are today in New York). Understandably, if not for this lucky chance, I, today, probably would not be writing these lines. How only thanks to this chance, not only were my bones saved, as well as the body and souls of my wife, Chana, daughter, Ruth, and son, Milton (Mendl), from Hitler's crematoria and gas chamber, and another few dozen Jewish souls and their future generations avoided the tragic fate of our unfortunate six million sisters and brothers in the Hitlerist death factories.

Hersh Leib and Sheva Winer – parents of Shimeon Winer[3]

* * *

To this day, after so many years, when the melancholy coincidence of my inviting Peretz to Chelm 40 years ago reaches my imagination – I become puzzled by the great mystery as to why the Okhrana would have undertook such an expensive mouthful. After everything, Peretz was "stamped" by them for a long time. It is certain that they kept an eye on him from 1899, when he was imprisoned for three months in the Warsaw Citadel, after he was arrested at an illegal workers' gathering.

[Page 405]

It is now difficult to say conclusively if Peretz knew that his appearance in Chelm would also by used to create aid for the political arrestees – a heavy crime in the eyes of the Czarist regime. While I arranged with Peretz to come to Chelm, I did not say it to him directly and he also did not ask any questions. However, while that conversation was so ephemeral, talk did occur of the attack almost a year earlier, which the Czarist regime made on the Jewish Literary Society, of which Peretz was the president, and made a short end to its rich existence… This first mass society for spreading Jewish culture was very popular and beloved by the great mass of the young in Warsaw. Incidentally, it is the greatest surprise that no earnest attempt has been made to research this highly stimulating chapter in the life of modern Jewish culture, over 40 years ago. The society was the prototype and precursor for all later movements and societies that had the same purposes. (The Literary Society was born in the autumn of 1909 and was ended during the earlier mentioned attack in May 1911.) In short, during that attack on the general meeting of the Jewish Literary Society, in the Harmony Room, at Nowigiarski 12, on a *Shabbos* day, in the middle of May, 1911, the Okhrana arrested about 30 people from among the several hundred assembled.

[Page 406]

The arrestees were all members of the general workers parties, all those for whom the Okhrana already had a record of an earlier arrest. It is also a fact that I was one of that group of arrestees, which I recalled during my talk with Peretz. He knew precisely to whom he was talking. Can it be possible that Peretz did not at all suspect something? However, on the other side, naturally, no one can vouch that he did have some sort of premonition.

Consequently, the mystery as to why the Okhrana left Peretz alone – now when they had such a good pretext to bother him – can in the light of the circumstance of that time, I think, be cleared up only with this, that in 1912, Peretz was, even for them, no longer the Peretz of 1899. Not only had Peretz now reached the highpoint in his creation of the great classics of Yiddish literature – but, in addition, he was then perhaps the most prominent and the most impressive figure among the Jewish people in all parts of the world. And even the blindly brutal Czarist regime had to consider this and to take account of it and no longer dared to touch Peretz. He was now too big a bite for them to swallow. Now, they simply did not succeed in picking a quarrel with the world. (And I, my humble self, must have all the more reason to feel lucky that Peretz at that time escaped from the great calamity.)

New York, 1952

Translator's footnotes:

1. Someone has crossed out "Libave" in the New York Public Library copy of the book and handwritten the name "Libau" next to it.
2. Spanish Jews who had nominally converted to Christianity saying the prayer recited on the eve of Yom Kippur – the Day of Atonement.
3. Someone has crossed out "Shimeon" in the New York Public Library copy of the book and handwritten the name "Shmuel" under it.

[Page 405]

Spring in the Old Country

by Hilel Szagel, Tel Aviv

Translated by Gloria Berkenstat Freund

A red rose blooms,
Planted [by nature],
Where my house stood
For many generations.

A [blade of] grass sprouts
On the broken threshold,
Where the house was,
It is clearly in shadows.

A tree grows;
Spring invites
And it smells of sobs,
Of the final thought.

And it smells of sobs
And here rots a hole,
A brick, a stone,
Reminding one of a house.

[Page 406]

A stone and a bloom,
Painted gold

And it is still quiet
As if someone were dying.

A cat runs past,
A wild and black one,
Dread and awe,
Comes from my heart.

A mouse comes
From a hole somewhere,
A sign of a catastrophe
That befell my house.

Clay is scattered
From the remembrance of a wall,
Where my house stood
In the Polish land.

[Page 407]

Kalayev, the Great Russian Revolutionary – A Chelemer…

by Y. Milner

Translated by Gloria Berkenstat Freund

I myself knew his old mother in Chelm. And I was a close friend of one brother, who was a pharmacist at the Second Polish Pharmacy opposite the *kościół* [church].

I remember him as if through a fog, his tall figure, his blond head of hair, his beautiful, deep-blue eyes. He was a student in a *gymnazie* [secondary school], in the upper class and, later, we learned that he was a student at Moscow University and an important member of the Socialist-Revolutionary Party, which would be called S.R.

The Grand-Duke Sergei Aleksandrovich, the uncle and brother-in-law of Nikolai II and (his wife was a sister of the Tsarina, Nikolai's wife), then reigned in Moscow. He [the Grand-Duke] had a great influence in the tsarist court and his governor-general of Moscow was equal to being his "viceroy." Sergei Alesandrovich was the symbol of the Russian reaction and an enemy of the Jews, to whom there was no equal in the land of [Tsarist advisor, Konstantin Petrovich] Pobedonostsev and [Minister of Justice, Ivan Grigorevich] Shcheglovitov. When Sergei arrived in Moscow, he declared that the holy city needed to become "*Yidn frei*" [free of Jews]. And here began decrees and persecutions, until in the well-known year of 1892 came the "expulsion of the Jews," when they drove all of the Jews out of the capital city. And our literature was famous for the songs of the Hebrew poet, Menakhem Mendel Dolitzki, who wrote the real poems of lamentation about the misfortune.

However, the Chelm *gymnazie* [secondary school] student, [Ivan] Kalejev, took revenge for all of the Jewish calamities. The *S.R.* [Socialist Revolutionary] Party threw on him the responsibility to make an end to Sergei Aleksandrovich. And a few days before Passover, in 1904, Kalejev threw a bomb at Sergei as he was traveling in a carriage from the Kremlin. The Grand Duke, the horse, the wheel and the coachmen all exploded and were mixed together into a kasha [buckwheat dish]…[1] Kalayev was arrested. He acted like a hero at his trial (Sergei's wife came to him in jail and said that she would intervene for him so that he would be given his life if he confessed and he refused the offer of mercy). He was hanged. And for a long time his mother would stroll through the Chelm streets dressed in black. A year later, in 1905, the First Russian Revolution broke out… A new era had begun.

Chelm Becomes a *Gubernia*

[Page 408]

To make Chelm a *gubernia* [province] was a dream of the Russian reaction. It was a strong blow for the Poles and they mobilized world opinion against it. In 1910, the project of a Chelm *gubernia* even appeared in French socialist newspapers and the act was called "the Third Partition of Poland…" In 1912 it was pushed through and proclaimed by the *Duma*, which had a majority of reactionary elements, and the main inspiration for the new law was the Metropolitan Jevlogi, who was a deputy of the specially created "*Pravoslavner* [Russian Orthodox] *Curia*."

Chelm became (and artistically created) a *Pravoslavner* center, with the *Sobar* [cathedral] and with the seminary for priests. Am *otpusk* [vacation] would take place there every year (on the 8th of September), where the peasants would come on foot from all corners of the nearby *gubernias* to worship in the cathedral. They wanted to create a "Czestochowa" to spite the Poles…[2] The area itself was called "Cholmskaia-Rus" and it originated in the year 1240 with a Galicianer Duchy (with Duke Daniel). Around 1569 the Catholic influence was strengthened here. After the First Polish "Rebellion" (1831) the Russian regime began to bring back the "Uniates" [members of the Ukrainian Catholic Church] to the *Pravoslavner* [Russian Orthodox] church and Russian assimilation was strengthened. And thus the idea idea of a Chelm *gubernia* so that the area would be completely isolated from Poland.

Jevlogi had triumphed. And the first governor of Chelm was [Alexander] Volzhin, the Siedlce governor, an enemy of the Jews, who organized the Siedlce pogrom, well-known in our history. They made great plans for million of golden rubles. They needed to build a new Chelm and they began to lay the foundation of a new, large administrative house; new streets began to appear… The new administration completely ignored the Jewish population; in the best case they called on us when they needed money for new city expenses. Jevlogi was an anti-Semite himself, as only a bishop can be, and, in addition, a *Pravoslavner* in Russian times can be… He had a weakness for an old couple, poor Jewish people, who had received a *koncesia* [concession] for the apples in the garden, a Berdichev Jew who lived in Chelm, Avraham Riszberg, who was a frequent visitor of the bishop. He considered them the most beautiful and best Jews, the remaining were…revolutionaries. He told a delegation of the Chelm "local elite," who came to him to ask for mercy, that a pogrom not take place on the day of *otpusk* [military furlough] (which fell on the first day of Rosh Hashanah). That day all of Chelm trembled in fear of a slaughter.

[Page 409]

However, there was no "peace" between Jevlogi and Volzhin: Jevlogi considered himself a bit of a Chelm "king" and Volzhin still wanted to be governor. It came to this, that Jevlogi threw out the "armchair" that Volzhin brought to the *sobor* [ecclesiastical council]… It became a scandal. The "Holy Synod" of Father Burg intervened: Volzhin left, and Jevlogi, too. And the latter became Bishop of Zitomir. When the war broke out in 1914, Jevlogi undertook a mission to create *Pravoslavia* in the Lemberg area (along with General Ivanov, which even included Przemsyl) and Volzhin became the *Ober-Procurator* [head of the Most Holy Synod], which was the highest *Pravoslavna* administrative official. However, after the October Revolution, he left for Rome (where he died) and Jevlogi for Paris (where he died in 1949). In Paris, Jevlogi surrounded himself with all of *Pravoslavia* in Europe, outside the borders of the Soviet Union. He played the role of a liberal, of a friend of the Jews and very much wanted to forget the past in Chelm. It is true that at the time of the [Nazi] occupation he did everything to permit the *Pravoslavna* priests to issue false papers to the Russian Jews with which they could save themselves. He even went a step further; he approached the Moscow Metropolitan. I knew many Parisian-Russian Jews who were in contact with him. They told me that he always remember his Chelm years with a moan and often spoke about his… Jewish friends in Chelm!...

Tsar Nikolai the Second in Chelm

What happens, happens to everyone… Thus it was destined that Chelm would have in its barracks the 65th Russian Infantry (*piechota*) Regiment, which had the red *kolishkas* (as we would call the stripes on the sides of their circular *furaczkes* – hats). Nikolai the Second personally served in the first company of the regiment because he was still a *tsarevitch*, a crown prince, and his father, Alexander the Third sat on the throne. He learned military wisdom in the regiment and his rabbi [teacher] was a staff sergeant with a large, wide moustache and his chest was covered with medals. So to say: "His chest"… When the regiment would march through the Chelm streets with the First Company in the lead, right after the colonel who rode on a horse walked the sergeant covered with medals from head to foot. It simply was awe-inspiring. However, on the sidewalk stood our Chelm Jews, looking at everything with a contemptuous smile and in the end they were correct because it was nothing of significance.

[Page 410]

Suddenly all of Chelm learned that the Moscow Regiment would celebrate an anniversary: its existence for 200 years. The Warhaftig family, still remembered by old Chelm, were the "caterers" (*podraczik*) for the regiment. The colonel, himself, told Yisroel Warhaftig that such an event would become a holiday, so he [Yisroel Warhaftig] should prepare good meat and every soldier would receive an entire rye bread and a large piece of meat with kasha [buckwheat] on that day. The news spread quickly; it was talked about in every house and in every corner. The prominent men in the city were summoned to the city hall; the chief of the police (Raczdestwinski, who had a "price list" of three rubles for his pocket [for the bribe he required]…) gave a speech. It was decided that Tomaszow Rabbi would welcome Tsar Nikolai with a Torah scroll (along with the Russian Orthodox bishop and Catholic priest).

I was then 11 years old. Dressed as a *gymnazie* [secondary school] student, I received a special card, thanks to which I was permitted to enter the cathedral, where Nikolai was to make his first visit. We were informed by a special courier on a horse when the train arrived at the train station and the bells of the cathedral began to ring. A shiver went through the bones of everyone standing in two rows at the edges of a long and wide red carpet that covered the floor of the cathedral. The gates opened and Tsar Nikolai entered. Later we boasted the we had stood near him, able to touch him with a finger… He walked in front. I remember that I immediately recognized Baron [Woldemar] Freederickzs, who was his Imperial Household Minister, General [Aleksey] Kuropatkin, General Minister, the Lublin governor and… near its conclusion, the staff sergeant of the first company with all of his medals and a smile.

A fragment of Chelm

It was said later that when the tsar left the train station and the "delegation" with the bread and salt approached him, he stopped and smiled in front of Reb Meir Najhaus, the Chelm rabbi, whom we would call "Tomaszower" [someone from Tomaszow]. Old Jewish women would than say, "What a wonder? He [the rabbi] is still handsome as gold!…" True, in his satin *kapote* [coat worn by pious men], with his large *shtreiml* [fur hat worn by married men in many Hasidic sects], with his long, white beard, with his still youthful, black, clever eyes, and with the Torah in his hands, he had such a stately appearance that no one could cold-bloodedly pass by, not even the Russian Tsar.

Tsar Nikolai II and his retinue spent two days in Chelm; businesses were closed for two days, a holiday for the Jews and non-Jews. Then we saw Nikolai 10 times a day. He simply became boring… And we were happy to be rid of him so that Chelm life could again flow with its usual rhythm.

[Page 411]

The Four "Nikolayevsky" Soldiers in Our Chelm Past

– What is a "Nikolayevsky Soldier?"
More than 100 years ago Nikolai the First, the Russian Tsar, the great despot, had a weakness of wanting to make "people" out of the Russian Jews! His peasants were slaves (they were freed after his death, in 1861), the entire land and all of its people languished under his yoke; he also was entangled in various wars and was the "policeman" of Europe and yet he had only one concern: how to make "his" Jews into people…

And so that they would become worthwhile he believed that first of all they needed to be turned into soldiers. And they would grab small Jewish children in our cities and *shtetlekh* [towns] and they would be turned into soldiers. Jewish mothers did not sleep through the night, entire families lived in fear; they hid their babies in any way they could… But nothing helped. There were frequent victims. And the children were given to peasants in the distant provinces of Great Central Russia. They became shepherds and they were beaten mercilessly so they would become *Pravoslavna* [members of the Eastern Orthodox Church]. The majority maintained their Jewishness. However, others, the weak children, would give in and convert. This continued until the end of their military service and this took 25 years of the Jewish child's life when he was in service of the tsar, may his glory be exalted (said ironically)! However, we must tell the truth: that he [the soldier] endured the temptation. According to Russian law, he received equal rights as a citizen. He had the right to live in all Russia and "Nikolayevsky soldiers" were found in Moscow and Tambov, in Irkutsk, everywhere, everywhere, one from a city, two from a family.[3] They were all very pious, illiterate (and how [were they all very pious]…? I do not, God forbid, say it in order to rebuke them. On the contrary, I have the greatest respect for them!) and Russian Jewry of the past created hundreds of excellent jokes about them.

…there were four of them with us in Chelm. They stand before my eyes as if alive. Two converts and two Jews, Nikolai (I only remember his name but not his family name) and Kashe (the family [name] reminds me of the family name of the French communist leader, but I do not remember his name). Like all Nikolayevsky soldiers, I do not remember where they came from and who their parents were. They probably went astray to Chelm by accident. Nikolai was a house painter and when he exerted himself a great deal, a kind of *Borukh Atah* [Praised are You] or *Shema Yisroel* [Hear O Israel] crawled out of his brain… It is characteristic of the Chelm Jews that they would be drawn to Kashe with a feeling of sympathy. It was not the type of hate as to a convert. They were considered as "Marranos…" However, Kashe was an official… a government functionary. At that time he was the "only letter carrier" in the city of Chelm; all the Jews knew him and he knew everyone. When he would bring someone a *Hatzefira* [*The Siren*] or a *HaMelitz* [*The Advocate*] (at that time, in general, there were two subscribers for the first newspaper and one for the second one), he would show that he knew Yiddish letters and would search, for example, for a *hey* ["h"] or a *lamed* ["l"]. And the women stood around him and marveled [at him].

[Page 412]

The two remaining were pious Jews. The first, Reb Mordekhai, with a white beard, a poor Jew; he would go to the houses [to ask for donations], but with pride. He could give a "Russian blessing" to the most prominent men, as if he were still in the barracks. One could not bother him. If he became angry, he could hit someone over the head with his cane. And yet, he was called Reb Mordekhai; he had something in him above the ordinary and not all of the Nikolayevskys had the respect so that the area would give them the honorific of Reb… The second one was a hero of the Sevastopol War (of 1855). They were a sort of "aristocracy," even in Russia proper. In general, they were only about ten survivors living in the entire [Russian] empire. The Tsar himself gave them modest privileges; all doors and gates were open for them and they received in perpetuity great areas of ground. So, our *Pravoslavna* was the owner of an entire stream where there was a *kopike bod* [a bathhouse for which one paid one *kopike*] and he parceled out his land where a *shtetl* [town] was almost built in the city and the quarter was called "Palestine." In later years, a bit of Jewish life came from Jewish Chelm.

My First Correspondence from Chelm

Neye Tsal [an area of Chelm] was "our Chelm ghetto." The irony of Jewish fate was thus that in my childhood years at the *Neye Tsal* (it was officially called Pocztowa Street), a priest lived in house number 1 [the first house] with a fruitful garden and the last house with two Greek columns was the post office. However, the Chelm Jews lived in the kilometer between the priest and the post office in the most terrible sanitary conditions and [each family] in one small room, according to Avrom Reyzen's song, *A Gezind Zalbe Okht* [*A Family of Eight*].

In January 1898 a misfortune took place there. A Jewish woman made a fire to warm herself a little during the great frost and the clothing of her young son caught fire and he was burned instantly. Everyone from *Neye Tsal* came running as a result of the terrible shouting of the unfortunate mother. A few hours later all of Chelm was at the cemetery. The city was agitated… and this made on me – and I was not yet 12 years old – such a strong impression that I took a pen in my hand and wrote a correspondence (my first "literary" activity…) and sent it to *HaMelitz* [Hebrew newspaper]; and imagine, it was published immediately!... In total perhaps 10 lines, as I remember. The four letters that I saw published in the correspondents column, with the orthography of that time: *Khelm* (they added: Lublin district) [Chelm is spelled with four letters in Hebrew –*kaf, ayin, lamed, final mem*] was so beautiful and so lovely that I could not tear myself away from them. The typesetter made an error with my name. I had written "Y. Milner," but he printed it as "V. Milner" (with a *vov* [not a *yud*]). However, the terrible accident of the child of the *Neye Tsal* could not even for me, a child, be considered as an "event" and not as a celebration at seeing my name published and it was not the "typesetter" alone who caused a stir, but a sensation was created because *HaMelitz* had published a correspondence from Chelm.

[Page 413]

– And do you remember the steps from Lubliner Street that would lead to the *Neye Tsal*?

There, Jews were hidden under the steps, under the Nazi-Germans, and a Christian baker would bring them food. Once an "ear" heard that there were voices under the steps. The Germans came and shot 17 hidden Jews and the baker was hung.

Daybreak in the Old Chelm Synagogue

Such a fact needs to be registered in the *Pinkes* [book of records] of our city, in our *yizkor* [memorial] book. It was August 1919, Poland arose from the dead and such a historic event had to take place in an atmosphere of great ideals that were crystallized by the French revolution and with which Poland helped restore its freedom. However, the Polish anti-Semites had completely different opinions. [Jozef] Haller's soldiers, the *Poznanczikes* [from Poznan] and the remaining Polish reactionaries from all regions, decided to eradicate the Jews in the country. Waves of pogroms began. Jews were afraid to travel on trains and, in general, to appear in the street. The world shuddered. The "allied" governments decided to intervene. [Prime Minister Ignacy] Paderewski began to make excuses. England sent a special emissary, the brother of Lord [Herbert Louis] Samuel, to carry out an investigation on the spot. And [Woodrow] Wilson, the American president, decided to do the same [and] sent a special envoy, his close advisor, [Henry] Morgenthau [Sr.], to Poland, (Wilson's advisor Morgenthau was the father of [Franklin Delano] Roosevelt's Secretary of the Treasury, [Henry] Morgenthau [Jr.]; the father was a well-known diplomat and the American Ambassador to Constantinople).

[Page 414]

On the 9th of August 1919 Morgenthau arrived in Chelm and my brother Shimeon Milner and his family arrived from Moscow on the same day. Morgenthau went to the "community" and there he met my father who welcomed him. The news spread lightning fast through Chelm. All of the Jews in the city gathered at the old synagogue. Morgenthau, my father, my brother and Reb Anshel Biderman arrived. The Poles sat in their residences out of anger… They understood that this was not a Haller Purim play [this was not something frivolous], but something serious. My father asked my brother, that is, his son, to go up to the desk from which the Torah is read and to give a welcoming address (all of the Jewish newspapers in Warsaw immediately described it). My brother gave one of those speeches, which can only be created in a human language at such a sublime moment. The Jews cried and Morgenthau [cried] with them and among them. In general, he was astounded to see such people in such a city impoverished by the war and to hear such words from their mouths, which could cause a shiver in every soul.

Morgenthau accepted my father's invitation and came to our house from the synagogue. Our Pokrowska Street was flooded with Jews. Morgenthau expressed his great satisfaction that there were such communities among us Jews. From that moment on he became a friend of my brother and they later were closely connected in New York and the friendship carried from the Chelm synagogue to Morgenthau's son.

Chelemer in the Land of Israel

On my last visit to Israel I was very interested in our Chelemer in the country. All of our memories are connected to our struggle for *Eretz-Yisroel* during the [Theodor] Herzl era and also after his death. Jews yearned to leave Chelm to go and build the land.

In 1909 when I visited *Eretz-Yisroel* I met one Chelm Jew there, Mordekhai Lederer, about whom I have written here. However, in 1949 I could not see all of the Chelemer because there were approximately 300 families spread across the entire country. They were in Tel Aviv, in Jerusalem, in Haifa, in the Negev and in colonies and *kibbutzim* [communal settlements]. There is a *kibbutz* in the Negev, *Yad Eliyahu*, all of whose *hakhshore* [training to prepare for emigration to *Eretz-Yisroel*] occurred in Chelm. As they learned about my arrival at the *kibbutz*, they simply did not know where to seat me and how to welcome me.

I met old comrades such as Simkha Beker, to whom Solel Boneh [one of the oldest construction and engineering companies in Israel] is indebted, because the majority of its buildings were built thanks to his work; Yehosha Orenstein has a publishing house, Yavne, on Allenby Street in Tel Aviv and [Chaim Nahman] Bialik himself had steered him on this way. In the town of Kfra Haim I met Shimkha Turkeltaub's son, a Jewish farmer, better said: a Jewish peasant!... I could not tear myself away from him (I still remember when he was born) because I rejoiced at meeting such an idealist. With such people the country could be revived.

[Page 415]

Our Chelm is very well represented in this country [Israel]. And we even have diplomats there. The representative from Cuba in Israel is Rafael Zilber And he himself is the grandson of our *shoykhet* [ritual slaughterer], Reb Moshe Mendl!...

But Israel also has – imagine – its Chelm. This is the Ekron colony. The Baron Rothschild built Ekron in 1884 for the former Jewish colonists from Ruzhany (Grodno *Gubernia* [province]). An entire 16,000 *dunam* [land measure in Palestine – a *dunam* equals about 10,764 square feet or 1,000 square meters]. And folklore was created in Israel about Ekron, which was inspired by the Chelm stories. They actually are called the Chelemer from Israel... They even have shutters in their attics. And when someone from Ekron is asked from where he is, he answers you:

You are smart yourself! –

Hersh Sziszler

Chance would have it that I would write these lines in 1950 when it would be 25 years since Hersh Sziszler, our Chelemer Hersh Sziler, had begun to print his creations (because he had begun to write when he was still almost a child). He himself, who loved to make fun of the area and of himself, writes: "At age 15 I already wrote well; on all of the walls and on the backs of my friends..." This was characteristic of Hersh Sziszler: the material boiled in him. He would write day and night. Not in vain, we Chelemer, can emphasize that he truly inundated the world [with his writings] – today he is a coworker at dozens of Yiddish newspapers and journals, almost all of the Yiddish press of the terrestrial globe.

The future literary historian of the Yiddish word will, using the works of Hersh Sziszler, be able to put together an anthology of the Yiddish press.

However…I am sure that when Hersh Sziszler becomes tired paging through all of the newspapers and journals for which he has written – he will stand with a sweet smile for the edition of the *Chelemer Shtime* [*Chelemer Voice*] in which in honor of *Sukkous* [Feast of Tabernacles] 1925 (that is 25 years ago) his first featured article appeared. "There is the smell of *skhakh* [green branches covering a *sukkah* – temporary structure in which one has meals during *Sukkous*] in Chelm… and thus he remains, like several of our group, with great longing, call it if you will, "nostalgia" for our Chelm, for our environment, for our *shtetl*. One must come from Chelm to feel that in its humorous stories one hears the laughter of the Jews of our alleys and "that laughter should be laughed," as Hersh Sziszler said himself in his last book: *Shmeykhl un Gelekhter* [*Smiles and Laughter*]…

Hersh Sziszler also wrote using all kinds of pseudonyms. He had Eysre's names [Eysre was the father-in-law of Moses, who had seven names]. A man cannot write under the same name in one issue of a newspaper, so he had to think up other names. And he wrote about himself: "My pseudonyms are: Sender Hersz, Sender *Khoyzek* [mockery], *Nisht Ikh* [Not I], *Der Griner* [*The Green One* – an immigrant], *A Higer* [A local one], *A Yid* [A Jew], Hershl, *Hey Shin* [Yiddish initials, H. Sh. in transliteration], *Shtam a Yid* [Just a Jew], Ahronzon (his father, who perished with his entire family in the ghetto, was named Ahron Sziszler), Tsvi, Ben-Ahron [son of Ahron], *Knapeser* [eater of very little] and "*Khapt im der vatnermakher*" ["The devil take him"]…

[Page 416]

And here finally, I want to reproach the dear Hersh Sziszler: (why did he never sign his name as A Chelemer [someone from Chelm]? Really not "You are a sage," but simply, A Chelemer!.. One must read between the lines of H. Sziszler's humorous stories in order to comprehend that this is a Chelemer.

Luboml (Libevne)

A *shtetl* [town] that, according to the statutes of the "Four Lands," belonged to the "land" of Belz-Chelm. That is what the administration of the Jewish *kehilus* [organized Jewish communities] wanted in that epoch. Reb Yoe

l Sirkish, the *Bach* [abbreviation of *Bayit Chadash – New House* – Sirkish's book of commentaries], who was the rabbi in Luboml (as well in Brisk and Krakow), in his famous *Bayit Chadash* (in 1600) wrote a great deal about the situation of the Jews in Luboml (which is considered one of the oldest Jewish communities in Poland). The synagogue in Luboml was known all over the world for its magnificent glory. In 1729 there was a large fire in Luboml and the synagogue, the Catholic Church and the *Pravolavna* [Eastern Orthodox] Church remained whole. There is a list of "survivors of the fire" (Ben-Tzion Kac, Aleksander Harkavy and Meir Balaban have written a great deal about the Jews in Luboml), according to which we can learn the professions of the Luboml Jews 250 years ago: tailor, barbers, jewelers, glaziers, in addition to shopkeepers. There were 1,200 Jews in Luboml who would pay taxes in 1765; in 1947 [mostly likely it should be 1847] – 2,000; in 1897, up to 4,470 residents. There were 3,297 tax paying Jews in Luboml. Their number before the last war had doubled.

I was in Luboml in 1913 at the invitation of our Chelemer, Feywl Frid (who was a teacher there). It was the 20th of Tamuz and I spoke to the Jews in a full and packed synagogue – in the old, historical synagogue. The following day, I was elected as a delegate from Luboml to the 11th Zionist Congress. Thus, there are threads present that bind me to the old *kehile* [community] of the "Land of Chelm!"…

[Page 417]

Our Jewish history also has its caprices. Before the First World War, a Luboml Jew, Tarlo, settled in Portugal. He was an important Port wine merchant, well connected in Portuguese government circles and he made a proposal: Portugal should atone for the Inquisition, not more and not less! And as Portugal possessed a colony, Angola, in Africa, it should open its gates and let in Jews, but not just immigration, but a Jewish territory would be created there. He wrote in the Jewish press that in Angola there are diamonds and coffee and other products. In short – this is a "land of milk and honey." The entire Jewish press, in every nation and in every language, wrote about this and the name of the Luboml Jew, Tarlo, became known in all of the Jewish communities in the world.

The synagogue in Luboml, which was built in the 16th century

From Dubno – Across Dubienka – To Chelm

Reb Shlomo Dubno was one of our greatest philologists and one of the pioneers of the Enlightenment. He was born in Dubno in 1738 and died in Amsterdam in 1813. And yet he had a connection to our Chelm. He lived for several years in Chelm, where he had settled in order to study Torah with Reb Shlomo of Chelm, the author of *Merkivet ha-Mishneh* [*Second Chariot*]. The latter also was known as a famous pedagogue and Reb Shlomo Dubno published the book, *Sha'are Ne'imah* [*Gates of Melody*], which was a great scientific work about our Hebrew punctuation, about accents. Reb Shlomo wrote many remarks (*heores* – comments or remarks), several improvements, as well as a "substitute introduction" of a large poem in honor of his beloved teacher because of whom he had left Dubno and remained in Chelm for a long time.

* * *

As is known, the *shtetele* [small town] of Dubienka (in Hrubieszow *poviat* [county]) is not far from Chelm. A *kehile* [organized Jewish community] of 3,000 Jews. And it seems that the world famous *magid* [preacher], the *Dubner Magid* was called that by the Jews only by mistake[a]). Because who in the world knew Dubienka?... Dubno had a reputation. And the *magid*, in truth, was named Reb Yakov from Dubienka (despite the fact that he lived in Dubno for a long time). Because he married in the small Dubienka and lived with his father-in-law *oyf kest* [support given by a father to his daughter's husband so that he could study Torah]. He was born in a *shtetele* near Vilna and he died at the age of 65 in Zamość (He spent a few years in Wlodowa.). Zamość, with its intelligentsia and with its contact with Lemberg, and, in general, the Galicianer Enlightenment, had the greatest influence on him. In Zamość he changed his name to Reb Yakov Kranc and we knew his grandchildren and great grandchildren, who belonged to the Zamość Polish-Jewish assimilated of the *Izraelita kheder* [religious primary school].

[Page 418]

One of his grandsons was Mieczyslaw Kranc, the director of the Lodzer Bank in Chelm (in around 1900), to whom all of Chelm would point at that time; he lived with a non-Jewish wife and did not even appear in the "German synagogue" on Yom-Kippur.

Reb Yakov Kranc was in contact with Moses Mendelssohn himself; he was called the "Jewish Aesop." His allegories and fables were known in all of the Jewish Diaspora. Yitzhak Ber Lewinzon himself wrote about him in his books, which were well-known and popular.

Ruda-Opalin

A small village, one station from Chelm on the railroad to Brisk. During the summer, it had a rare landscape covered in green, with flowers and tree-lined paths all around. There were two Opalins: the gentile village where no Jews were seen and the *huta* [glassworks], the beautiful glass factory with its workers and administration. The latter was Jewish. The owner was a Jew from Odessa who brought with him directors, bookkeepers, correspondents, traveling salesmen, all Russian Jews. During the early years of the Zionist Congresses there was a very active Zionist organization there, which was under the authority of Chelm. It would sell Zionist memberships and shares in the "Colonial Bank"... A share cost one pound, that is, 10 rubles, which was then a large sum of money and not everyone could buy one. And yet 50 shares were bought there!... I, myself, more than once dropped in on a visit in around 1903 or 1904 and appeared at meetings or was present for *glezlekh tey* [glasses of tea – at gatherings] to "rouse" the audience. I have to add that among the Russian Jews at the *huta*, the traditions of Russian Jewry were strong; all members knew what was being discussed [Zionist ideas] and there was no lack of internal enthusiasm…

Yosef Barac, himself from Radomyśl, a member of the Jewish intelligentsia, a great idealist, a rare Jew, was one of the most active members there. And a very special and courageous memory remains with me. In Barac's house in Ruda Opalin, I met his cousin, Ginzburg. Although a fine name, a famous Jewish name, he was an extraordinary person. The entire world knew him as "Port Arthur Ginzburg." That is what he was called everywhere. Like Barac, he was born in Radomyśl, but left for China. When the Russo-Japanese War broke out he earned millions as "supplier" for the army. Later, he settled in Petersburg. One only had to be from Radomyśl for him to help a person in need; that is how much love he had for the *shtetl*. And later, Jews were enraged when he gave money to build *Pravolavna* churches. (He also built a synagogue in Radomyśl.) He was an original type who could only be created during our exile… He died in Paris where he had settled after the "October Revolution." And in Paris he continued to support the Russians and gave money to Eulogius for his ecclesiastical tasks. At the same time, he put on *tefilin* [phylacteries] every morning and worshipped wrapped in a silk *talis* [prayer shawl] made of pure Chinese silk…

[Page 419]

Krasnystaw

The decrees of 1584 (from Stefan Batory himself), 1664 and 1774 are well known in history, in which the government made sure that Jews would not, God forbid, settle in the center of the town, but in the outskirts. Was this why Krasnystaw truly was a beautiful *shtetele* and the "gentiles" simply did not want to see the face of a Jew there?... And this awoke in Jews the tendency to settle around Krasnystaw, in the small *shtetelekh* and even villages, so that the percentage of Jewish residents in the surrounding places was much larger than the non-Jewish ones. In general, we can record that before the Holocaust there were around 5,000 Jews in Krasnystaw.

Krasnystaw is considered one of the historic Polish towns. History states that once during the time of His Highness Kazimierz the Great there was a noble Polish fortress and a legend went among the residents that Kazimierz himself had a villa here, where he would at times come with Esterka, his Jewish lover.

The Grobla [poor Jewish area of Krasnystaw], which was separated from the city by the Wieprz River, was the neighborhood in which lived the poorest toiling artisans, Jews as well as Christians. At the beginning of the 19th century when it was forbidden for Jews to live in the city, Grobla was the ghetto.

Religious life was concentrated in two houses of prayer. One [was] in the city and the second was in the Grobla. In addition, [there were] two Hasidic *shteiblekh* [one-room houses of prayer] – the Trisker and the Gerer. There were merchants and small business owners union, an artisans union, *gemiles-khesed kase* [interest-free loan fund], a *folks-bank* [people's bank] and a *khevra-kadishe* [burial society].

The class differences and communal temperament were shown during the elections to the city council, the *kehile* [organized Jewish community] and in choosing the city rabbi. The poorer class – the toilers and artisans – almost always had the upper-hand.

Thus lived the Jewish *kehile* in the *shtetl* Krasnystaw for over 200 years, with scholars, Hasidim, followers of the Enlightenment and idealists, nationalist [Zionist] and social. Some hoped for and waited for *Mosheikh* [the redeemer]; some dreamed about a Jewish state in *Eretz-Yisroel* and some fought for a better tomorrow.

Until the brown [shirt] monsters came in the form of the German Nazi murderers and almost the entire Jewish community of the *shtetl* Krasnytaw was annihilated like all other Jewish *shtetlekh* in Poland.

[Page 420]

Wlodawa

Although the *shtetl* was in Siedlce *gubernia* [province], it was very close to Chelm, at the mid-point between Chelm and Brisk, and Jews from both *shtetlekh* felt "at home" in each of the locations. A story was even told (and they swore by their beards and *peyes* [side curls] that it was a fact) that could enter our folklore. As is known, a train appeared in the area for the first time and this was the Chelm-Brisk train. As the first train left, all of Chelm was at the train station to see the wonder. The "chief" of the train announced:

– In honor of such an important day, everyone can travel to Wlodawa for free!...

One can imagine how they pushed themselves into the train wagons. However, the "chief" had only said to Wlodawa. They had to buy tickets to travel back and no one had any coins in their pockets. The most respected Chelm businessmen had to go to the Wlodawa houses to ask for donations in order to buy tickets to return home…

There already were Jews in Wlodawa in 1589. It was a *shtetl* where [Bogdan] Khmelnytsky had annihilated all of the Jews (in 5408 [1648]) and even the Jews who had come to Wlodawa from the surrounding *shtetlekh* to save themselves. Before the last war there were around 12,000 Jews, with Jewish institutions, with a fine Jewish life. As is known, this all became an utter ruin. (I will add that before the First World War, the Russian Jews, many from Odessa, chose Wlodawa *poviat* [county] and settled there at large and very rich "estates" (*giter*). Thus, at that time, a Jewish landowner, Gurewicz, lived there and his son was a professor at the Sorbonne. Today they are all in New York.

Sawin

The *shtetele* Sawin belonged to our Chelemer *poviat*. Jews had had the right to live there from ancient times. The *shtetl* was small and I know that it possessed a thousand Jews before the last war (in 1897, 458 Jews lived there). [They were] very poor, with a bitter income and they dreamed of Chelm… and America. These were the greatest dreams of a Sawin Jew. The former came to New York and remember the latter in their old home…

Trawnik

Who among us can think, traveling through the station with the red bricks from Trawnik that there once was one of the most terrifying limekilns of Polish Jewry?... In general, there were very few Jews there. However, during the death of Polish Jewry, Jews from all over the world were concentrated there: French Jews perished in Trawnik!... It is one of our largest cemeteries, a thing that could only have been thought of by a wild imagination and a criminal mind…

Original Footnote:

a. a.There also was a popular *magid*, the *Kelemer Magid* and by mistake he was very often called the *Chelemer Magid*, but he had no connection to our city. He came from Kelm, a *shtetl* in the Kovno area.

Original Footnotes:

1. In his book, *History of the Jews in Poland and Russia*, Simom M. Dubnow writes that the assassination took place in February 1905.
2. Czestochowa is the location of *Jasna Gora* – a monastery that is the home of the Black Madonna – a Catholic site of pilgrimages, a shrine to the Virgin Mary.
3. The phrase, "one from a city, two from a family" comes from Jeremiah 3:14: "Return, O wayward sons – the word of Hashem – for I shall be your master. I shall take you, (even) one from a city and two from a family, and I shall bring you to Zion."

[Pages 421-422]

Hrubiewszower Street
(As I Remember It)

by Shloyme Wasserman, New York

Translated by Miriam Leberstein

There was a town in Poland with many Jews; the town remains, but without Jews. Chelm had prestigious streets, like Lubliner Street, which extended through the middle of the town. It was lined on both sides of its cobbled road with beautiful stone buildings, businesses selling all kinds of merchandise and various institutions that were part of the social and cultural life of the Jews.

Very different to Lubliner Street was the street called the "Naye Tsal," known for its ramshackle houses, dark basement dwellings, cramped workshops, heders [religious schools for young children] and all kinds of small houses of worship where tradesman and other workers prayed.

There were side streets and alleys, each with its own character, that often bore the name of one of their residents, for example, Leyzer Pak's Street. Although the street had had a Russian and then a Polish name, for many Jews it was Pak Street.

And then there were back streets with narrow alleys that at certain times had a bad reputation because some of their residents were thieves, beggars, cripples, organ grinders and simply rowdy fellows.

Shloyme Wasserman

This was all in the past, when Jews in Chelm, worked, did business, built, created, studied, fought with the perpetrators of pogroms, raised new generations and hoped for better times. Today, after the evil storm of the Nazi murderers, all hope has been extinguished, along with the lives, and the streets of Chelm have no Jews.

But long before this tragedy, Chelm was a legendary place for most Jews and had entered the folklore and literature of other languages, as, for example, in English, in The City of Wise Men and *The Treasury of Jewish Folklore*, by Nathan Ausabel, published in New York in 1948. He devotes more than 20 pages to Chelm stories, with a forward in which he explains the reason for the term, Chelm Fools. He points out that Chelm is not the only town in the world with such a reputation. Before Chelm, there was a town of fools in England called Gotham, and in Germany a town called Schildburger, with innumerable stories about its residents. In 1597 these stories were translated into Yiddish and since there were already Yiddish stories about fools in general, it became clear that the Jews also needed an address for a town where these stories could take place.

So they chose Chelm. Why, in fact, Chelm? Well, if they had chosen Lublin, wouldn't people ask the same question? And, as the Yiddish proverb goes, you don't ask questions about a story.

Chelm occupies a very eminent place in Yiddish literature. Jewish writers of various periods have strived to produce an improved version of the folktales about the fools of Chelm. It is important to note some of the writers who have eternalized the town in Jewish literature. These include Aaron Zeitlin who wrote *The Wise Men of Chelm*," which was staged in New York by Maurice Schwartz's Yiddish Art Theater; *The Wise Men of Chelm*, Collected Stories, compiled by Ben Mordecai; *The Wise Men of Chelm, or Jews from the Wisest Town in the World*, by I. Trunk, published in Buenos Aires; and most important, our great classic writer I.L. Peretz, who artistically interweaves the legendary material about Chelm in his three stories, "The *Shabes* Goy," "Because of a Sniff of Tobacco," and The "Chelemer Melamed [teacher in heder]."

There are also quite a number of high quality poems, stories, jokes and anecdotes about Chelm in the text books of the Yiddish children's *shules* [afternoon and weekend schools teaching Yiddish]. Thus, Chelm, more than all the other towns in Poland, has remained in the folk spirit and has constantly been revivified in the creative folk imagination.

But Chelm is entirely different for its townspeople who at various times left their home and wound up overseas, and also, more recently, for the Jews who survived the death marches, the Chelm ghetto and the death camps. For all of these Chelm is their home town, where they were born and where they were rocked in their cradles, took their first steps and absorbed the melody of their mothers' singing "God of Abraham;" where they would get their ears pulled by the teacher in their stuffy heders; and where their fathers sternly taught them how to show respect. It was the place where they devoted the springs of their lives to working in shops and workshops and dreamed of love. Everything is etched in their memories — the bitter and the sweet, the bad and the good — and they don't want to forget any of it.

[Pages 423-424]

Although I am writing for this yizkor book, which must serve as a part of the inscription upon the memorial, which we, the living all over the world, must erect for the lives that were extinguished, a memorial for everything that was Jewish and now no longer exists, my heart does not want to recognize that. My heart is still interwoven with that once vibrant people before they were wiped out by the German murderers and their henchmen. My heart still sees the faces of those near and dear, family, friends and acquaintances. They are all with me, everywhere; they are with me in the packed underground trains of the noisy world city New York, and on quiet streets, at stormy mass meetings and homey family dinners, they are with me when I work and when I dream, they come, like witnesses to the 6 million who were killed and they demand: Do not forget, do not forgive.

I will not forget, not forgive. I will try with the help of my memory and with the information I have gathered, to recreate just a part of my hometown, Hrubieszower Street, where I grew up and which I left in 1922.

From the time I left, it seemed to me that everything remained as it was – the people, the houses, the trees, the goats feeding in the ditches along the road. Still, it might be that my descriptions might not be entirely correct, or that I left someone out. If so, please excuse me; it wasn't intentional. Also excuse me for the nicknames that I use for some people from my street, because I don't remember their family names and also because no one will know them without their nicknames.

The Street

Hrubieszower Street extended from the forest, the "Borg," to the *rogatke*, the crossroads of Lubliner Street, Potshtover Street, Hrubieszower Street and Voyslavitser Road. On one side of Voyslavitser Road stood Nokhem Shos's stone building. Across the road in a small alley in a poor little house lived an old shoemaker who was renowned for his mastery in placing a patch upon a patch.

At the top of the street stood the house of Yehudis Kupershtok. In the summer you could see her two daughters sitting on a bench on the porch, both with velvety black hair, black eyes and smooth, clear faces. Although they were quiet and modest, it was almost impossible to walk past the house and not notice them. (I don't know what happened to the two daughters, a son and their mother during the Nazi era.)

Aron Tukhshnayder (I think his father was called Fayvele Shnaps) lived in the Kupershtok house in a basement. Aron didn't spend much time at home; he would wander around, come home, then disappear again. His wife Hinde, a small, emaciated, worried woman, tended to the children. Their poverty was great, their little room small, but everything was clean, tidy and sparkling as if the sun always shined in. (She and her husband were killed by the Germans; accordingly to the latest information, one daughter survived and lives in Lodz, Poland.)

Off the courtyard of the Kupershtok house lived Eydlshteyn the clockmaker. He followed modern ways and provided his children with a secular education; his eldest son Yoske learned the printing trade. (He now lives in Canada with his sister and mother). The youngest son Khaim took over his father's trade. (He lives now in New York). I can still see the clock maker Eydlshteyn in his 3/4 length jacket, wearing a Jewish–Polish hat, with a well–groomed little beard, walking along the soft shoulder of the road once a week on his way to wind up the clock of the Voyener hospital, near the forest.

And while I'm thinking about that part of the street, I can't fail to mention "Crazy Volodye." I think he was the son of a priest. He didn't display any special characteristics of insanity except that he wore the belt of his trousers high up near his rib cage, had a weird look in his small red eyes and waved his arms horizontally as he walked along. This was so particular to him that when people wanted to describe someone who walked oddly, it was enough to say, "Just like Volodye." He was known far and wide throughout Hrubieszower Street.

A little further down was the house owned by Moyshe Pinieles. A tall, blond, quiet man, Moyshe Pinieles always seemed very busy. (His two daugherts, the younger of whom was Miriam, live in New York; I don't know what happened to the other children). In Moyshe Pinieles building lived tradesmen and laborers. I remember the red–headed shoemaker who lived in a basement apartment. He had many children, but I remember best the oldest son, Asher of whom the other boys his age were afraid.

In another cellar dwelling lived Shimele Vasertreger. Shimele was short and thin like a boy who hasn't finished growing. But the sparse blond beard that adorned his sorrowful face revealed the secret known by everyone on the street: that he had to labor hard to support his wife and children, each smaller than the other and all beautiful. Where did Shimele get the strength to carry water to people's houses? It was a riddle the answer to which could be found in his own boasting, which he enjoyed like a hungry man enjoys a good meal. His eyes would light up with a childish naivete. Did any of his many children survive the Nazis?

[Pages 425-426]

A few houses from Moyshe Pinieles' right next to the road, stood the pump. The water from the pump had the habit of drying up in summer and freezing in winter or simply becoming stubborn and refusing to provide water. On both sides of the well was a smithy, a lively and cheerful place. The bellows kept inflating and deflating. The blacksmiths banged on the glowing iron on the anvils. Others pulled iron hoops onto the wheels of Polish wagons, hammered nails into horseshoes. In those days, the smithies were the heavy industry of Hrubieszower Street.

Sore Beyle's grocery store stood opposite the pump. Sore Beyle was a small, hardworking anxious woman. Her husband, Aron Holovetsh, was a brother of Mendl Holovetsh, whose wife, Freyde Ide's also had a grocery on the same street. (During World War I, Freyde Ide's and several of her children died of cholera.)

Another grocery on the street belonged to Khinke Kalmans. They had four children and lived like everyone on Hrubieszower Street. The two older daughters were drawn to education. Of that whole hard–working family only one daughter survived. According to what I have heard she was in hiding with Christians in Chelm the entire time of the war. She now lives in Uruguay.

From what I've related to this point, one could think that Hrubieszower Street consisted mostly of groceries and residential buildings along the road. But that was not the case. On either side of the road, the street spread out deep and broad, branching off into narrow alleys and muddy paths, which led to courtyards and small houses, with basements and attics. These places housed tradesmen, beggars, criminals and people of unknown means of support. Often they had Christian neighbors — Poles, Germans and Ukrainians – and in most cases got along with them.

The street had its own distinctive appearance at different seasons. In winter it was covered by deep snow. A frosty wind blew in from the surrounding fields into chimneys and through the windows, which often had rags instead of panes. The side streets were covered with snow and to reach the pump to get water was like climbing a mountain of ice. In summer the street revived. The surrounding fields blossomed with rye, wheat, oats, barley and white buckwheat flowers. The gardens blossomed in the Christian courtyards – like those of Shindetski, Wilhelm, Shutkovski and the old retired "General." The old chestnut trees around the brick "Old Hospital' were laden with juicy, healthy color. The willows at the ditches on both sides of the road turned green, cast pleasant shadows on sunny days and in the evening quiet, on the web of moonlight, and dropped their blossoms on the green grass for couples in love.

The street also had different aspects at different times of day.

Early Morning on Hrubieszower Street

Morning usually began with the clip clop of horses' hooves and the screeching wheels of loaded wagons which the residents of the street were driving to the railroad station. The wagon drivers, hearty Jews dressed in padded vests girded with red belts and sporting hats with tall crowns, arrived at dawn. After them came peasants on foot and with horse–drawn wagons from neighboring villages – Strakhaslav, Strupin, Kamin, Udolits, Voyslovits and others. Often the peasants were accompanied by a Jew who lived in the village.

The residents of the street got up to do their daily work, to earn their living, some by working, some by doing business. They lived in houses owned by the "*katsapke*" [Russian woman;perjorative], which extended along the breadth of the road; in Shloyme Ivri's stone building; in Rokl Kasriel's building with its courtyard; in the buildings owned by the German Yavorski and the Pole Shindetski.

Coming to meet the peasants on the road were the buyers, Jewish men and women not just from Hrubieszower Street but from other Chelm streets as well. Of the grain merchants I remember best the Langs, Jews with long beards and long caftans who had their own grain warehouses, whom the local peasants knew well. There was also Zelig Erlikh, who lived on Hrubieszower Street near the road. He was a short man, always busy with buying and selling. His wife, Fride, a dignified looking woman, was busy with running their household and raising their only child Leyzer. (After World War I they all left for America and live now in Augusta, Georgia.)

All of the buyers hurry down to the forest, the Borg; each wants to be the first to meet up with the peasants. They besiege the peasant wagons, knock on them, ask what they have to sell. There, at the forest, they meet the Jewish residents whose houses were situated between the forest and the Voyener Hospital. There was an elderly couple, Reb Itshele Izhbitser and his wife, who lived on the money sent by their son in far–off Argentina. Another was Reb Leyzer Varman, a tall man with a long beard who seemed to be immersed in thought over important matters; his wife and youngest daughter Tsirl had a grocery. The father and his son did business along the road. Their eldest daughter Etl was known for her beauty. She left for America before World War I.

[Pages 427-428]

The third resident was Der Grober [fat] Borekh (Bornshteyn, also known as Borekh der Gotekes.) He acted like a rich man. His eldest son studied to become a doctor; for his other sons he engaged private teachers. The teachers also helped out with household chores. Often you would see a teacher with one of the boys in a two–wheeled wagon, pulled by a donkey in harness, carrying a big water barrel, going to the pump. Borekh had an only daughter, a beauty; her parents watched over her as if she were a dream come true. I don't know what happened to any of them during Word War II. One of the teachers, Wolfson, left for America after World War I. One of Borekh's son lives now in Johannesburg, South Africa.

They all made their living on the road; they bought everything – poultry, potatoes, onions, radishes, millet, buckwheat, cows, calves. If the price was too high, they wouldn't pay it. They let the peasant drive off a little way – "Well, you're not the only one at the market!" – but would still watch to make sure no one else was buying. And when the buyers started fighting with each other, they would come to an agreement and wind up partners in the deal.

Another person who tried to buy on the road was "Cool Yaye," a short, thin Jewish woman who spoke very poor Polish. Her husband had gone to America before World War I and she was no longer receiving letters and money from him. So until the war was over, in order to stay alive, she bought and sold and also raised a few goats, which her youngest son Shloymele pastured on the nearby fields. After the [First World] war, she and her three children – Sholem, Miryem and Shloymele – went to America and settled in Chicago.

From time to time Avrom Nakhaners, called "the Nakhanakha", a nickname derived from mispronouncing the name of the shtetl Ukhan, dabbled in business on the road. He was very thin, had a beautiful white beard and a refined manner. He lived in General Jaworski's building. He had two daughters, Rokhl and Perl. Perl was renowned for her beauty and they said that rich boys were crowding her doorstep. But she was in love with a Bessarabian boy who was a soldier in the barracks on Hrubieszower Street. Quite often you could hear a Jewish soldier singing from the barracks window; one such song remains in my memory:

"At home, I wore shoes, comfortable old shoes[1]
Now I have to spend the Sabbath with Fonye *Ganev*
Fonye, Fonye *Ganev*, Fonye is a *ganev*, 1,2,3

The people on the street knew that Perl met up often with the Jewish soldier in Freyde Ide's store, where they spoke of love. And Perl succeeded. She married the soldier and went away with him to Bessarabia leaving behind romantic legends on Hrubieszower Street. Today she lives with her husband and children in Philadelphia in America.

One of the regular buyers on Hrubieszower Street was "Shtume" (silent/dumb) Rivtshe. She was a bold and hardworking woman who contributed a lot to the support of her family. Her husband, "Shvartser" [dark] Aron, was engaged in religious study, a quiet man who led the prayers with great feeling. I can still see his dark, sharp–featured face poking out of his prayer shawl. When he read from the Torah, the melody expressed consolation and pleading and engendered faith in the congregation that held its *minyen* [prayer group]in Hrubieszower Street.

Aron and Rivtshe raised their chidren to be traditionally observant, but the children were also well versed in Yiddish literature. They also raised an orphan, Shayele, the son of their daughter, treating him like their own child, even though their home was very crowded. Khaim, the oldest son, watched closely over the child, as well as his younger sisters and brothers. Shayele was a gifted and dear child and Khaim taught him his trade of making boot tops. Then came the Nazis and their henchmen who destroyed almost the entire family.

Here are the names of those they killed: Avrom, the eldest son, who lived somewhere near the *rogatke*, I think, not far from Khaim Tintnmakher; according to reports, Avrom's son, who studied in Paris, survived. The daughter, Pesl and her husband, Dovid Mordkhe Hendl and their 6 sons were all killed. The youngest son, Butshe, lived in a village near Chelm; I don't kno what happencd to his wife and children.) The youngest daughter, Khane, married to Dovid Gross, Yankl Bashlegers son, died there. Of the large family only Khaim Sobol, the boot top maker, survived. (His wife, Miryem, two daughters and son were killed.) (I was told by my esteemed townsman Berl Kelberman, who now lives in New York with his wife and son, that he, along with Khaim Sobol, Mani Tsitron, a boot top maker; and Shloymele Levetover, a tailor, were among the last thirteen Jews in Chelm. They were imprisoned by the Nazis as the best tradesmen and were forced to make clothing, shoes and accessories for the murderers and their sweethearts. Because the Nazi's had to flee from the Red Army, these last Jews remained alive. Khaim Sobol lives in Israel.

Among the buyers were those who engaged in trade only from time to time, when things were bad, or before a holiday when it was easier to make a profit. Among these were Der Grober Srulke and his wife (their son Yisroel is in Israel) and Shloyme "Terk's" wife. (Their family name was Kesler; I think their two daughters survived the Nazis.)

There were problems with the fat policeman who was called the "Spudnitse" [skirt] because he was so fat around the waist that it looked like he was wearing a skirt with many pleats. When he appeared there was a commotion among the buyers, especially the poor ones. They ran away with their goods, to escape the policeman's punishment and the confiscation of their goods.

[Pages 429-430]

Some of the frightened buyers hid in the home of Reb Volvele Shnayder. The house had a kitchen, bedroom and workshop. Reb Volvele usually sat at the table where he prepared his work. He would be wearing his yarmulke atop his head with his *payes* [sidelocks] hanging down from the yarmulke, and they would become entwined in his well–groomed, reddish beard. Around his neck hung long pieces of paper or thread which served as measuring devices, with the measures marked by the shape of a cut in the paper or knots in the thread – his own inventions. On the table was an *arshin* or a wooden *ayl* [units of measurement] to measure fabrics or linen, and chalk to mark the various parts of a garment.

At Reb Volvele's there were a lot of children –"yours, mine and ours." He had five children from his first wife; his wife had three from her first husband, and together they had five. The three sons were half heder students and half tailors, working in the shop together with Christian boys from villages who were learning the craft. Reb Volvele didn't make a lot of money but he had a lot of faith and so he was mostly in a good mood; whatever happened, his response was "This is also good. It could, God forbid, be worse."

Reb Volvele liked to talk about the world, the times and events; about the Sambatyon River and the Red Jews; about Joseph and his brothers. As he talked, he looked over his spectacles, which he bought from Sholem Hirsh Khaskes along with the accessories he needed for his tailoring. His spectacles barely stayed on his nose; his youthful brown eyes looked at the pictures that hung on his whitewashed walls as he spoke to his sons and the Christian apprentices who already understood Yiddish, about the Vilna Gaon or about the twelve tribes which were portrayed symbolically as signs of the Zodiac. He told wondrous stories about Jewish bravery and wisdom. On Friday he would give one of his sons a few cents to go to Yoysef Itshe Hindes the bookseller to buy story books to read on the Sabbath.

The buyers who hid out at Reb Velveles felt safe with their goods. If the Spudnitse should pursue them and find them at Reb Volvele's, Reb Volvele would say, "This string of garlic (or this chicken, or these 60 eggs) were brought to me by the peasants as payment for my work. Look, here's the fabric for the jacket I'm making, which I have to finish before the peasant goes home."

Among Reb Volvele's children – "mine, yours, and ours" – none felt they were stepchildren, but rather true sisters and brothers. Almost all of them were killed along with their families:

All of the children of the eldest daughter, Zelde, who died long before the Holocaust and who lived in Hrubieszower Street ; her family name was Waksman.
The second daughter, Eydl Shtam, lived sometimes in the building owned by Rokhe Noakh Shtikendreyer and sometimes in the *katsapke* [Russian woman's] houses, was killed along with her children Henie and Henie's family.
Son Shloyme Shtam and his wife and children.
Son Elye and family.
Son Efraim.
Only one daughter and her child survivied. Her name was Tsharne Vayntraub and she lives in Ramallah, Israel.
The third daughter, Hinde Tukhshnayder who lived near the *rogatke*, was killed with her family, except for one daughter who survived and lives in Poland.
Volvel's third daughter [sic] Esther Gorn, married to Itsik Gorn, called Itsik Pokrivker, was killed along with the rest of her family. They lived in the house owned by the German Jaworski. Esther's children were Alter, Feygele, Nekhele and Velvele. Their son Lozer, who lived at Shindetski's and who died in World War I, had two daughters who died in the Holocaust, Sore and her family and Freyde. Lozer's son Khaim Varzoger survived with his wife and child and lives now in Lower Silesia, Poland.
A son [of Volvele], A. Hersh, and his wife, who lived in a village, were killed by the Nazis.
Three sons surivived; one lives in Poland and two in the Soviet Union.
Another son of Volvele's, Sholem "Beker" who lived near the steps in the Naye Tsal, survived with his entire family and lives in Israel.
Of Volvele's sons who emigrated at various times, two live in Argentina, Menashe Wasserman and Shniur Wasserman. Volvele's eldest child, Yosel Wasserman, or as they used to call him Yosele Shakher, lives in Philadelphia; Shloyme Wasserman lives in New York.

Hrubieszower Street During the Day

During the day, when the buyers were already seeking out customers for their goods among the well off Jews, and the peasants were going from store to store to spend the money they had made on things for their village households, Hrubieszower Street quieted down. In the quiet you could hear the grinding of the wheels of the ropemakers, one of them at the circle that stood in an open field, spins the flax which is handed to him by another from large pockets in his apron. The flax is turned into rope and the rope is made into reins for the peasants' harnesses.

There was one ropemaker, an old man with a white beard, whose name I don't remember, but I remember his person, the way he pulled the flax while walking backwards further and further from the wheel. At the wheel there often stood his grandson, Avraham "Plioder" (I don't know why he had that nickname or what it means). Avraham was a sturdily built fellow with a strong desire to attain a better position in life. He grew up to become a fine tailor and reached a high level of self education. After he got married he lived in Dubenko. I don't know what happened to him.

[Pages 431-432]

On the other side of the street lived another ropemaker, Kasriel Rokhl Noyekhs. He was a quiet unassuming man. He and his wife wanted their daughters to marry men who continued their religious studies, but the daughters were attracted to a modern, secular life. However, the parents' wishes were mostly fulfilled. The older daughter, Beyle Tsirl, married Velvel Fridling, the second daughter, Margalit, married Volvish Liberman, and the youngest, Sheyndl Rivke, married Leybl Weber, who was not only a religious scholar but a tradesman who had his sights set beyond Chelm. At the first opportunity he set off for the wider world and finally got to America and later brought over his wife and son Khaiml. They live in New York.

(Of Kasriel's family the following were killed: His wife, Rokhlele, his daughter Beyle Tsirl and her husband. A son who was a partisan and spent the entire war hiding in the woods, returned after liberation to his house to see if anyone was left alive and was shot by Polish Fascists. One son, Abba, survived and lives in America. The second daughter Margalit was killed with her children. Her husband, Volvish Liberman, survived and lives in Israel.)

Kasriel owned his own home and had many tenants. One was Khaye Tile Burshtok, whose husband Moyshe worked in the mill on the same street. She and her husband were murdered by the Nazis. The only one of her family who survived was her daughter Perele, who had gone to Brazil before the war.

Itsik Katarinazh [organ grinder] also lived in the same building. A tall, erect man with a neat, small beard, he lived piously. He would buy an *aliyah* [call to read theTorah] and would sing along with the cantor and he liked to participate in religious discussions with members of his *minyen*. But he wasn't well–regarded by other Jews on the street, and this was mostly because of other wandering organ grinders who would stay with him. This made his sons much appreciated by the younger people on the street. The sons were Leyzer, Bertshe and Elye Tsener. (Tsener was a nickname because he had a broad flat brown face that looked like a *tsener*, a copper ten–cent piece.) They wandered around with organs on their backs, with parrots and white mice that picked out lucky fortunes for everyone. And when they came home, the street became jolly, and you could expect a fight to break out.

In a side building lived Crazy Suzhe with his sister. He was a thief, and went around barefoot.

Chelemer Madmen

A madman known as Saltshe

Suzhe, as he was called, a strong, fine looking man, but sadly, not quite right

Avremele "Gelus: Had a weakness for trying to make marriage matches

[Pages 433-434]

He went hungry in winter. He had pearly white teeth. Very often he would express a very clear thought, making you think that it was an evil lie to call him crazy and that he had returned to sanity and you could have a discussion with him. Then suddenly something would go wrong in his brain, his eyes would take on a strange look and he would break out in a loud, crazy laugh.

On summer days, when Hrubieszower Street had a dreamy feeling, you would often see the young widow Khaye Tove, like a shadow. The mother of two daughters, Henie and Khane Sore, her dark thin face could barely be seen from under her headscarf. She went about the fields to collect rags and bones to sell to the ragman for a few cents to buy bread. Things went a bit better for her after the harvest, when she gathered leftover stalks of grain. Her old mother, Yekhoved, also a widow (Elye Dripak's wife from Dubenke) always helped her with her work. I don't know the fate of her daughters.

In front of the fence of Jaworski's building stood Mendl Glas's grown up daughters. They looked at the quiet street as if to ask, "What do we do now?" No one answered them, no one cared that they came from a prominent family that had lost their fortune and had to move down to Hrubieszower Street and live among tradesmen and organ grinders. The street didn't like people who looked down on them, especially when those people fought among themselves in a very coarse way and the shouting could be heard in the street.

A bit further down, one could find Alte Yoysef Erlikhs, the weepy, fearful daughter of parents who were very protective and didn't let her do any work. So she stood there all along, all dressed up, with a book under her arm, observing the people going back and forth. Her father, Yoysef Erlikh and his wife Rokhele, lived with their daughter in an alley near Yashek "The Kilivatsh." Yoysef looked like someone who had come down in the world. His bedraggled coat still bore signs of former wealth, giving him somewhat of an appearance of a Germanized Jew. He was a sign painter, but seemed to consider himself an artist. Long hair peeked out from under his Jewish cap. He said that he knew several languages, even English, and liked to talk to the young people about worldly topics. His wife, always anxious, hovered over her cherished daughter.

With time, Hrubieszower Street became more developed and acquired a mill. The mill had previously been one of two barracks. Zalman Lemberger rebuilt the vacant barracks and rented it out to tenants – Sheyndl Herts, Mates, Kleyner, Berish Handlsman and Avraham Shroyt. Of these I best remember Avraham Shroyt, when he arrived with a wagon full of children from the village Radzheyov and settled near the Russian woman's house. The neighbors looked at the newcomer and counted the children as they got out the wagon wearing wooden shoes; there were five daughters and one son. Avraham died of cholera during World War I; his widow Leye Shroyt, or as they called her, Leye Bishke's, moved with her children into town. Her son Yankl Shroyt remained an employee at the mill. Yankl lives today in Santo Domingo. His wife and three children – Feygele, Avrom and Sorele — were killed by the Germans. The widow Leye and her daughter Sore and Sore's husband Yankl Trager and four children, and her daughter Khane and her husband Shmuel Winik and two children were all killed. Three of Leye's daughters live in the Americas, Miriam Felhandler and Esther Varzoger in Montevideo, Uruguay and Rifke Wasserman in New York.

The second barracks later belonged to Shloyme Ivri whose children grew up to be folk–intellectuals and active participants in Jewish communal life. All were killed by the Nazis and their helpers. His eldest son, who served as a doctor with the Soviet army, was killed by Polish Fascists. Yosl Goldhar, one of the survivors who visited Chelm after liberation and who lives in America told me that Itshe Luri's son, a lieutenant in the Polish army, fought heroically against the Polish Fascists and died in Chelm. A son of Shloyme Ivri who has lived in New York since before the war told me that out of the entire Ivri family there survived one grandchild, the daughter of a daughter, who lives in Warsaw.

Shabes [Sabbath] on Hrubieszower Street

On *shabes* mornings in spring or summer the townspeople came for fresh "*povietshe*" [Pol., air]. They walked along the side of the road. The gardens of the Christians would be in bloom, the wheat fields gave off sweet scents, the street was still asleep. Not far were the woods, with all kinds of trees, a bit further a copse where berries grow, and even further, a place where you could buy fresh milk and butter, and where there were swings. All of these were rare in town.

When you returned, the older people would be coming home from praying. After prayers and the *shabes* meal, the street was quiet. Shops were closed, the windows curtained, a goat tied to a tree lazily nibbled at the grass. Gradually, young people began to come outside, some with a book, some with a newspaper, and they gathered around Shaye Glezer's porch.

[Pages 435-436]

Shaye Glezer's house stood opposite the former barracks. It wasn't very large, but it was a center for young people. First of all, Shaye Glezer sold pumpkin seeds and soda water (you paid for them during the week). Second, his oldest son Dovid loaned out good books for six cents for two weeks. Dovid was a house painter. He was short and had a dark skinned face. From one side, he appeared gloomy, as if he was terribly offended about someone or something and was on the edge of anger. But on the other side of his face a smile played that was calming and reassuring, as if to say, "Come on, I'm only joking." His manner of speech was also unique. He didn't begin in the usual manner, "first," then "second," but immediately proceeded to "third, what is there to say?" At prayers on *shabes*, he would chant one of the blessings to the melody of "The Internationale." He had read a lot and the young people who were attracted to culture made use of his books.

All week his father, Shaye Glezer, carried on his back a box of glass, as well as mastic and a "diamond" ready to cut glass for new panes, and bore the burden of making a living as well as worrying about providing dowries for his daughters. But on *shabes* and holidays he became a new person and a moving cantor. I remember the soft, pleading melody of his chanting of the penitential prayers at dawn. That melody evokes his appearance – his serious face encircled in a gray beard and eyes that pleaded on behalf of those who didn't care to recite the prayers.

Although Shaye and his wife Tsirl kept an observant home, you could hear coming from that home the sounds of young people, of modern life, which was knocking at the doors of Chelm like a joyful announcement: "We are coming to enrich and beautify and improve the life of Chelm's inhabitants." Some of these sounds were rehearsals by the amateur actors who were preparing to put on theater productions in Chelm. The actors came from town to Hrubieszower Street during the day on

Saturday, and arrived dressed in holiday attire. The young people [of Hrubieszower Street] looked at the boys and girls walking together and envied them. "That's the life!" Of the visitors, two stood out: A tall, handsome boy, Ruven Molyer (Ruven Shekhterzon) who lives now in New York) and Yankl Melekh Hirsh, a youth with a broad, straight back, black hair and black eyes, about whom they said on the street that his father takes his shoes away to keep him from rehearsing on *shabes*, but the son finds a way and comes anyhow. (Today Yankel Melekh Hirsh – Yankl Breytman – is a well known cantor in New York.)

Another of the group wass Fayvl Dreksler, short, vivacious, with fine artistic features. Later, he lived with his parents and siblings on Hrubieszower Street. After World War I, part of the family went to various countries. Yankl (Hersh Tsheslers) went to Palestine, Ita to Argentina, another brother whom I'm told is a fine actor played with Maurice Schwartz and is now in Argentina. I don't know what happened to the other children. Fayvl Dreksler performed his entire life until he was killed by the Nazis.

The group rehearsed at the home of Moyshe Pitshke's daughter, who lived in Shaye Glezer's building. There they studied how to perform, sometimes *The Binding of Isaac*, sometimes Song of Songs or another popular play, and through the windows you could hear monologs, prologues, and songs, as, for example:

> I haven't forgotten my childhood
> I used to hear the sound
> Of my mother sitting by my cradle
> And singing me a song.

> Or

> —Children, do you know the *brokhes*[blessings]
> —Yes, we know them well.
> —Can you answer all my questions?
> —Yes, why wouldn't we?
> —What *brokhe* do you say over new clothing?
> —*Malbush arumim* ["He who clothes the naked"]
> —And if a wife is constantly spewing curses?
> —*Matir asurim* ["He who frees the captive"]

Shaye Glezer's youngest son Mendele had a good voice, artistic talent, a good sense of humor and a keen wit. When he would come home from Warsaw for Passover, he would be elegantly dressed, with a broad brimmed hat, high quality suit, and a watch of dubious accuracy. He would recount the wonders of big–city Warsaw, the theater performances that he had seen. He called the actors by their names and described their appearance; this excited the imagination of his listeners, especially when he sang out: "*Yidele dayn kroyn is dos pintele Yid…*"[Dear Jew, your crown is the tiny spark of Jewishness inside every Jew.] Or "Figure it out; be smart and figure it out. Such things are easy to understand." [Both songs from Boris Tomashefsky's play *Dos Pintele Yid*. At those times you would be ready to go to Warsaw, even without your parents' knowledge.

But after World War I, when Mendele was stuck in Chelm, where organizations of various kinds were being established, he organized a drama group on Hrubieszower Street and established a relationship with the Poalei Tzion party. The Party had its workers' headquarters in Kuper's house on Lubliner Street. The group was determined to prove to the town that it shouldn't look down on the drama group from Hrubieszower Street, which didn't have a great reputation. With a few exceptions, the group's members had little understanding of theater. That's why they believed that "if you want to you can," that they would be able to use the stage to bring truly literary works to the Jewish audience. So they selected the play *Near and Far* by Peretz Hirshbeyn. Mendele, with his love of theater and artistic taste worked hard with the novice actors to achieve the right tone, a refined gesture, or a stage presence. They got the experienced actor Fayvl Dreksler to help, and finally in 1919 notices appeared on the kiosks of Chelm that the new drama group would be presenting a performance at the Town Hall. To the surprise of the performers, the members of the longstanding drama group in town attended and with true collegial friendliness assisted the new group by sharing with them their collective experience.

Of the actors I remember best Tovele Hertz, a dynamic, gifted performer. Here is a picture of the members

*[Pages 437-438]*the drama circle and the participants in the first and last production.[2]

Mendele soon went to America to join his brother Sholem. (Of Shaye Glezer's children, Dovid, Peshe, Rivke, and Gitl and their families, and Freyde, were killed by the Nazis. I think one of the daughters, I think Rivke, had a son who survived who must be in Israel.)

During the years of the Austro–German occupation [during World War I] people struggled with hunger, epidemics and homelessness. Refugees from war zones gathered on the community–owned plot on Hrubieszower Street where a hospital was supposed to have been built but never was, and they died there of hunger and illness. Later, during Polish independence, the Jews had to fight the Hallerites [followers of General Haller, anti–Semitic leader], and all kinds of pogrom–waging bands, and life for the Jews became more difficult with every day. By that time it had been a long time since there had been frequent fights between Jewish boys on Hurubieszower Street. Mostly the fighting was between everyone else and the sons of Volvele Shnayder, who were village boys and not so well bred as the boys born in town. Later, the status of both groups was equalized and a cultural bond was established. Volvele Shnayder's was the meeting place where the rehearsed, discusses and often danced. Among the participants was a person I haven't yet mentioned, Osher Leml Vaynshteyn, Feyge Vaynshenkerin's son. (He lives now in America; his mother and one daughter, Eydl survived; Eydl lives, I think in Israel. The oldest daughter, Sore, was killed with her family.)

In those days of storms and upheaval in Poland our Christian neighbor, "Sadolke" appeared on our street. He was a short, pockmarked, dissolute man poisoned by debauchery and anti–Semitism. He caused many problems for the Jews of Chelm and the surrounding area. I mention him because it may be that he was the forerunner of the Nazis, who ended what he began.

At that point, young Jews began to look for the reasons behind every event. They looked for ways to defend against and to protect themselves from what was happening and those who could escape in time ran from their birthplace, Poland. In 1922 I escaped but the street on which I was raised and its inhabitants became part of me. May what I have written become part of the history of the Jews in Chelm, who were so tragically murdered. May our pain, anger and hate be recorded, may it go from generation to generation as an oath of vengeance. May this yizkor book eternalize the memory of the holy martyrs of our town. May my pages serve as a reminder for the survivors of Hrubieszower Street that we will not forgive or forget those who murdered our own, near and far.

Translator's footnotes:

1. "Fonye" is a diminutive of Ivan and was a derogatory term used by Jews to refer to the Tsar or to Russian rule in general. "Fonye *Ganev* [thief]" enhances the insult.
2. Photo not provided in this article.

Volunteer firefighters of Chelm, who had a large number of members from the Jewish intelligentsia in the years 1916–1918

[Pages 439-440]

The *Shtibl*[1] of the Belzer Hasidim

by Moyshe Grinberg, Tel Aviv

Translated by Miriam Leberstein

When people write about Chelm, they write about the town with a great history, the town that was rich with institutions, organizations from the far right to the far left, the town that produced prominent personalities from various areas, such as art, politics, science, etc. But this book would be incomplete if it didn't describe, if only briefly, religious Chelm: the town of Hasidim and religious scholars, of many religious institutions, beginning with the great Talmud Torah and yeshiva that served as the first place of learning for a large part of the youth of Chelm and its environs, and the many Hasidic *shtiblekh* where every Hasidic *rebe* had his own followers and every Hasidic group had its own particular customs and practices. I will try to write what I can remember about one of these – the *shtibl* of the Belzer Hasidim.

* * *

The Belzer *shtibl* stood on Shedletske street, far from the *shtiblekh* of the other Hasidic groups, like the Kazmirer, Trisher, and Radziner, which were located near the *besmedresh* and Shul Street. There it seemed as if it had the task of protecting all of the Jewish residents of the neighborhood. The tall Belzer *shtibl* building with long, wide windows stood out from among the various buildings, tall and low, small and large, where Jews lived. From it you could hear, from early morning to late at night, pleasant voices in prayer, or a *nigun* [melody] from the *khevre shas* [Talmud study group] which studied *gemora* or *mishna* every day, or you would hear a *zemerl* [tune], a dance at a celebratory feast or the commemoration of a rebe's *yortsayt*. [anniversary of death].

Inside, the building was divided. Almost half was devoted to the women's section, which on *shabes* [Sabbath] and holidays overflowed with women, each of whom had her own permanent seat. In the large men's section, on the eastern wall stood the famous Torah ark, which was renowned for its artistic ornamentation. On the western side the walls were adorned with tall cabinets holding thousands of religious books, old and new, which for many years had remained in the hands of various scholars. Scattered through the pages of the old *gemoras* were silver white hairs left behind by one or another scholar as he studied, his eyes sparkling as he recounted a story from generations ago.

In winter, two large ovens warmed those who came daily, those for whom the *shtibl* was a second home. Along the walls were long tables and benches which, with great patience and pleasure, served loyally, daily as well as *shabes*, the many Hasidim at prayer or study, or eating the third *shabes* meal or making *shabes kiddush*.

the elite of the town, the rich Jews, the *shabesdike yidn*, i.e. the Jews who appeared only on Saturday. This is where we saw Reb Berish Kuper, a fine, upstanding Jew and a man of privilege; Reb Mateseyu Kleyner, who was a great scholar as well as a man of wealth and a great philanthropist; Reb Shloyme Roytman, a man of power and influence, who was close to the *rebe*, and who was a *bal tekie* [blower of shofar] during the High Holy Days; Reb Shloyme Yitshok Rozenberg, a man of noble character, who enjoyed best a good debate on a Talmudic question; Reb Berish Landau, a man of religious learning and business who was highly respected and esteemed by others. There was also Reb Yeshue Melamed, an unusually interesting type, whose wealth consisted in his contentment with his lot. A very honorable person and very modest, he always saw the good in people and was a peacemaker. He considered it a sacred obligation to distribute "tobacco" that he had made himself with great skill and taste. He led the morning prayers during the High Holy days and when he sang "hamelekh" everyone trembled in fear. But he never looked joyful. He was unable to father children. And there was Reb Mendele Shmuele Harsh's, who as boys we called the "wicked holy man" because he was always getting angry at us.

On the south side were seated (in accordance with the rule of our sages, "Whoever wishes to be wise will dream,") men who weren't as wealthy, but were more learned, who would come to the *shtibl* every day and even several times a day. Here we had great scholars, the very pure, the well known group of Reb Yankev Mordkhe, a great scholar and pure soul who always led the *musaf* prayer on Rosh Hashone and Yom Kippur; Reb Yudele Stav, an expert in music and an intelligent man; Reb Shmuel Hakatan, who in contrast to his name ["small"] was a great Hasid and scholar; Reb Moyshe Horodler who had adorned the *shtibl* with his wonderful drawings; Reb Yitshak Yeshaye, a person who was completely uninvolved with worldly matters, of whom it was said that he couldn't distinguish one coin from another; Reb Simkhe Amerikaner (he got the name because his father had lived in America; he himself was a *melamed* and far from rich). One of his habits was to refrain from speaking until prayers were over and he never called his wife –my mother – by name, not wanting to mention the name of a woman aloud, but instead, when he had to tell her something he would say, "tell me," or "say" and my dear mother, a true saint, took it as a sign of affection.

[Pages 441-442]

The Hasidic group described above was known for its solidarity. A happy occasion for one was a happy occasion for all and if, God forbid, something bad happened, everyone sympathized, everyone helped. Together they celebrated, for example, a *maleve malke* [end of *shabes* ceremony] and their devotion to each other was great. Their faith in God was constant; they never had any grievances to the Almighty, even though they lived in great poverty they accepted his will and when their bodily or spiritual pain became intolerable, their best advice was to go see the *rebe* in Belz, give the *rebe* a *kvitl* [written request] pour out the pain in your heart. Year in, year out, they would visit the *rebe* three or four times a year, and each time would return home completely changed, satisfied and joyful, having received the rebe's blessing.

* * *

Although all the Hasidic groups officially lived together peacefully, there was a certain separation that went as far as arrogance between the Belzer and the other groups in Chelm. The Belzers took no position on political matters. When there were elections to the *sjem* [Polish legislature] they received directives from "above," i.e. from Belz, and as is known these followed the rule, "Follow the law of the land…" One had to vote for the Christians and in fact there were actually Polish deputies seated in the *sjem* who were elected by the Belzer Hasidim. At a time when the other Hasidic groups had taken a different position, and had gotten closer to Jewish political organizations, only the Belzer considered every political organization as "*treyf*." Even the Agudah [ultra Orthodox group] was alien to them. Mizrahi [Zionist Orthodox] was heretical and if one of the Hasidic boys got "infected" [with Zionism] he lost his seat in the *shtibl*. Zionism was like *chometz* at Passover, not to be seen.

* * *

No matter how difficult their daily lives were, their spiritual life was wholly satisfying. The holy Sabbath was compensation for their suffering during the six week days. On that day they found the most interesting and meaningful aspects of life. On Friday nights and Saturday mornings or on a holiday the Belzer Hasidim and their *shtibl* took on a completely different appearance – joy and happiness shone on everyone's faces and a great shining light poured from the windows and illuminated all of Shedletske Street.

Friday afternoon, after going to the *mikve* [ritual bath] in order to greet the Sabbath in cleanliness, they dressed in *shabes* clothing–beautiful silk caftans and velvet hats. (The custom of wearing the *shtrayml* [large fur hat] like the Belzer Hasidim in Galicia and the Gerer and other Hasidim was not adopted by the Belzer in Chelm). In the *shtibl* they recited Lecha Dodi and their ardor was so great that it seemed like everything was singing along – the walls, the books, everything rejoiced to great the guest, the holy *shabes*.

Saturday morning before prayers the tables were filled with various study groups. At one such group they studied the *daf yomi*; at another table with older people, they studied *perek mishanyes*; at a third one could hear a pleasant melody, someone singing the *sedre* of the week, two bibles and one translation."

On the south side near the door was Reb Chaim Yosl whose specialty was reciting psalms. He was an honest simple Jew for whom anything more than psalms was foreign, and he was in seventh heaven when he stood at the pulpit and could recite psalms with the congregation. And so, not thinking about day to day worries they studied and later prayed with great joy and enthusiasm, feeling the true taste of life and the spiritual pleasure of the great gift of the holy Sabbath.

But they couldn't always avoid weekday worry on the Sabbath. The *shtibl* had various expenses and almost always had a deficit. Not able to employ the normal means of requiring a monthly contribution from the Hasidim, the *gabes* [administrators] created a unique method to collect money from the congregation, and in fact on the Sabbath. When the prayers ended, the gabes closed the exit doors and blocked them with tables, and everyone was required to leave behind his prayer shawl. It didn't help to complain; everyone, rich and poor had to comply. In this manner, they collected dozens of prayer shawls, and the Hasidim, requiring the shawls for prayer the next day, were obliged to redeem them after the end of Sabbath or early the next morning. It was more difficult to do this with those Hasidim who had another, "weekday," prayer shawl.

Reb Pinye Meyer Geltshes (Pinkhes Tenenboym) a Belzer Hasid

[Pages 443-444]

The height of joy and emotion was reached at the third Sabbath meal on Saturday evening. The sun had long set. Darkness reigned in the *shtibl* but that didn't interfere with the meal. All the Hasidim sat around the tables, each taking a small piece of challah. Reb Shmuel Hakatan had a custom of distributing pieces of fish. Everyone, in the dark, took his portion in hand and imagined he was partaking of Leviathan [legendary giant fish that will be eaten after the coming of the Messiah]. Slowly we sang all the Sabbath melodies. Each singer knew which melody belonged to him and as soon as one melody ended, another began, until "Dror Yikve" [He grants release] which belonged to my father, Reb Simkhe Amerikaner.

We grew more enthusiastic by the minute, rejoicing in the Sabbath Queen, and we, the holy sheep, joyously accompanied the singers and the songs carried far. Later, very late, well after stars had appeared in the sky and the last singers had ended with Shir Hamayles [Song of Ascents], a ray of light suddenly illuminated the *shtibl* and those around the tables were forcibly wrested away from the exalted world of the Sabbath.

Sabbath was over; its departure was a great sorrow even though it would soon come again. Right after Havdalah [ceremony ending Sabbath] the scholars' group began to prepare for *melave malke*. This was much more intimate; each person contributed a few cents, enough to provide bread and herring, and if there was any money left, one of the women would cook up a dish of groats. And a group of Jews, having shed the trappings of the world, enthusiastically sang songs about the Sabath and told stories about Hasidic *rebes*, and engaged in serious discussions interpreting current or past events. Well after midnight, the singing of Ish Hasid [devoted man] accompanied the departure of the Sabbath Queen.

* * *

Today this corner of Chelm is filled with sorrow. No longer do you hear the melodies of the chanting of *gemora* or psalms. There are no longer any Jews in the street, or in the entire town. They have been shot, burned, buried alive. No one even had a Jewish burial. That tall building, the Belzer *shtibl*, is dark, empty, ruined, the thousands of books it held burnt, not a trace of them remains.

Jews, pure souls, who strived the entire year to do right between man and man and even more between man and God, Jews who were careful a whole year not to fall into bad habits, who sinned perhaps once in the year and yet on Yom Kippur beat their breasts and said, "*ashamu, bagadnu, gazalnu* [we have sinned, betrayed, robbed.]" It was a lie, a big lie, when they wept during the prayer, "we have sinned among nations." They – they are more sinful than other people? More sinful than those sinners and beasts, the murderers of six million Jews, old and young, woman and children, who are the true sinners?

And how sad that it was precisely on the holiday Shavuot, the day of the giving of the Torah, that the martyrs of our town were led by the Nazis, with the help of the Poles, to their murder in the woods, and never returned.

Translator's footnote:

1. small Hasidic house of worship

Chelm

(author unknown)

Translated by Miriam Leberstein

My town!
Everyone who remembers you
has to smile
because of the folktales about the Jewish life
that was once lived in you.
But when I remember you,
my town, I remember only suffering
and endless pain.
How could it be otherwise?
Your rabbi, renowned for his wisdom,
driven barefoot on a winter day,
the blood dripping from his face
onto the glistening snow,
his splendid gray beard
spread out by the sharp wind;
the rejoicing of the Christians
as they looked on.
Your old rabbi, ordered to dance,
remained in one spot,
began to recite "Pour out your wrath"
word by word.
Then the old man began to feel
that death would be his fate
and with "Shema Yisroel" he honored God.
But a line of bullets
cut off his prayer and his life.
The holy man was left lying
On the snow covered street.
The snow fell thickly
from the gloomy sky
and covered him
like a white shroud.
Chelm mourned its aged rabbi
And the congregation felt
that the final hour had come.
A short time passed
and all was destroyed.
Where Jewish life once had bloomed
Only earth and ashes remained.

[Pages 445-446]

A Page of Memories
(pictures, lives and personalities, 1897–1917)

By B.Binshtok

Translated by Miriam Leberstein

The town lies buried in a deep, dry, dazzling white snow. Although a crackling frost has persisted for several weeks, life and activity continue as normal. Paths and roads of trodden snow connect the city streets and alleys just as if someone had laid them out in advance.

Workers, poor people, wagon drivers, and porters keep warm in cheap quilted jackets, altered military overcoats, patched jackets, worn lambskin coats belted with rope, fur and padded hats, shawls around their necks and hoods covering their ears, and on their feet *voylikes* or boots wrapped in rags instead of galoshes. Poor women and girls are dressed in quilted skirts, cowls, a shawl on top of a bonnet or *shaytl* [wig], a big shawl over their shoulders, and tall laced shoes or men's boots.

Young people as well as rich shopkeepers and merchants and their families wear nice modern clothing, elegant fur coats with matching hats, high laced up shoes with full– or half–length "Petersburg" galoshes.

* * *

The night of the third candle of Khanike was a big holiday in the alcove where Reb Shimen Yankev and Marmerivtshe lived. Their only son Shloymele, a thin and sallow but lively little boy was turning three and preparing to go to *heder* [religious school for young children]. He is a fearful child and cries a lot. Once, when he was very sick, they got the rabbi to agree and "sold" him [symbolically] to Brayndele "the cat" [to fool the Angel of Death]; may it never happen again. Brayndele was called "the cat" because she would open other people's food cupboards in the middle of the night to get something to eat for her little fatherless children. She lived in the basement of Froyim Kore's house near the old bath house on Seminarski Street. Marmerivtshe used to keep her cupboards unlocked on purpose every Friday night, leaving a piece of fish, some challah, or some rolls for Brayndele.

Today, the night of the third candle, Marmerivtshe is radiant and happy. She is getting her little boy ready to go to *heder*. She hugs and kisses him, straightening his *talis kotn* [fringed undergarment], tidies his 8–cornered hat and curls his thin little *payes* [side locks] with her moistened finger.

Shloymele knew a bit about *heder*. He knew that today he would turn three and would start going there to learn Torah. Many weeks ago his father began to prepare him for this sacred beginning. Every evening after prayers, Shimen returned home from his hard job on the ramp of the train station, and right after supper he would take the boy on his lap, open a large prayer book and point with a pocket pointer, while singing a poignant tune: "This is how a little boy learns Torah. Say it again, my dear child, *alef* and *bet* and *giml*." Shloymele liked the sweet singing and sang out loudly, "*alef, bet, diml* [sic]."

Shimen Yankev also lived in the basement of Froyim Kore's building. They called him "Kore" because he was rich, the landlord of a building. He was a miser and heartless and inhumane; he would hit people. Shimen Yankev was ten years younger and the second husband of Marmerivtshe. She had run away from her first husband of ten years, Pinkhes Shelishtshekh, and her nasty mother–in–law. Although there were only 3 people in the family, there was a lot of work to get done. They had their own house, horses, a cow, chickens, a large establishment. That would have been tolerable if not for the mother in law, an old, sick and angry woman. She would torment Marmerivtshe constantly, cursed her viciously, calling her a dismal, barren woman and caused her great heartache. Marmerivtshe had had no children with Pinkhes.

When Shloymele started to walk, Marmerivtshe would take him by the hand and stroll over to Moyshele Palievshi's store, where Pinkhes used to load his wagon.

It was already 1 P.M. Reb Shmuel Ber, one of seven subtenants who lived in alcoves on the other side of Shimen Yankev's "Spanish wall," came home to eat lunch. He wondered why Shloymele had not yet gone to *heder*. "It's so late already," he announced. Little Shloymele felt very guilty and ashamed by Reb Shimen Ber's remark and asked his mother, "When will I go to *heder* and learn Torah for real, Mother? At that moment the door opened and Moyshe Shloymele Hirzhe's – the *belfer* [teacher's assistant] – entered. He was wearing a nice padded overcoat with an astrakhan collar and an astrakhan hat pulled over his ears, and high boots with full, deep galoshes. In his hand he held a basket full of little pots from which you could smell fresh cooked lunches for the children in *heder*. It wasn't long before Shloymele was dressed and wrapped in a shawl. The *belfer* took him and carried him under his arm the quite short distance to Shloymele Hirzh, the teacher of beginners in *heder*.

[Pages 447-448]

Shloymele Hirzh's *heder* was in his own house, a sunken ruin that had been that way for many years. The main entrance was from a little alley behind the slaughterhouse. Behind the house was an area where the children played in summer. A garbage bin stood next to the fence with a gate that led to Seminarska Street. Along the west side of the house was the brick wall of the seminary where the future Orthodox priests of Russia studied and prepared to be God's emissaries and spiritual leaders for the people of Russia.

When they came in, the *belfer* unwrapped Shloymele's shawl and presented him to the *rebe* [teacher]: "Shloymele Shimen Yankev Marmerivitshe's!" Shloymele Hirzh was a broad boned man of average height, with a broad, full face with a short, thin gray beard. He was wearing boots with high, wide bootlegs, where his cotton trousers were hiding themselves along with his leggings; a dirty white undershirt over his big woolen *tales kotn*; and a yarmulke on his head.

Shloymele Hirzh bent down, patted Shloymele on the head and was about to say something to him when the door opened wide and a cold wind rushed in, along with a woman carrying a chicken. This was a neighbor, a tenant of Pinyele Yosele Beker, who lived on the other side of a wall of the heder.

"Excuse me, Reb Shayale, may you live to see the Messiah, tell me if this chicken has an egg, it keeps flying around my room." Shloymel Hirzh took the chicken, which was squawking loudly, blew into it somewhere, stuck in his finger, scrunched up his eyes and stretched out his mouth. "Yes, she has an egg," he announced the good news. "You should have great *nakhes* from your children," the woman shouted joyfully, taking back the chicken, and she left the room.

Shloymele and all the children in the *heder* had looked on eagerly and greatly enjoyed the scene with the chicken.

Shloymele Hirzh's *heder* consisted of one large room with two windows which almost lay on the ground. A large table stood in front of the windows with chairs on both sides and a long high bench facing the windows. On the table lay pieces of bread, challah, bagels or *pletzls*, dry or smeared with butter, prune preserves or schmaltz, which the children had left over. The *belfer* would stave off his hunger with these pieces; the remainder was fed to the hens, geese and ducks which the *rebe's* wife raised to sell.

The three year old children sat on several very low, long benches and played with their own fingers, their caftans or their *tales kotns*. Other children sat on the floor and napped. On the other side of the room stood two high beds where one or two hens would often be sitting. When a hen would break out in song —"kop–kop–kop" – Shloymele Hirzh, very pleased, would hide the egg, take the hen off the bed and put it in the storage space under the chimney opposite the beds. A large barrel of water stood by the chimney, near the narrow door where there was also a bucket and a broom.

Shloymele Hirzh, as soon as he was done with the woman with the chicken, picked up Shloymele and sat him on the high bench, near the table, in a row with several other children, ready to start studying. The *rebe* kept each child at the prayer book for two to four minutes. When it was Shloymele's turn, the *rebe* tenderly took his chin and guided it so that his eyes would focus directly on the alef–beys. The *rebe* then sang in his hoarse voice, "A little boy says *alef*. And what is this? A *beys*! And this? A *giml*." Shloymele sang out in his thin little voice: "*Alef! Beys! Giml!*" The *rebe* again sang, pleased that his pupil was able to learn, "That's how a boy studies Torah," and ended, very prosaically, "when your children are as old as me, they should know as much as you, Shloymele."

Shloymele's father did not rely solely on the *rebe*. Every night after supper he studied *alef–beys* with the child. Thus the child made exceptional progress, so that by the week of Passover his mother took him out of Shloymele Hirzh's *heder* and signed him up with Reb Shaye Kozak."[Cossack], the *traf* [second stage of learning to read] *melamed* [teacher]. At Reb Shaye's every child had to hit the mark; if not Shaye Kozak would poke his fingers at their bottoms. Shaye Kozak's *heder* was on the same street, several steps from Shloymele Hirzh, behind the ritual slaughterers. It was also in the rebe's own house, a half-sunken ruin, with two low windows looking onto the street.

Shaye Kozak had to put up with a lot of trouble from his building; that is, not from the building itself, but from the area across the street, opposite the house, which didn't belong to him. Every Monday and Thursday [idiom., very often] the police would come and drag him off to jail for nothing.

There were two different schools of thought in Chelm about why he was called Kozak. Some people said it was because he was tall, had an elongated, sorrowful face, a long sparse grey beard, long limbs, and a hernia; and he coughed, snorted and wheezed – like a Cossack. Others held that it was because of his wife, who was a shrew, a scoundrel, a Cossack. Shaye Kozak was terrified of his wife. Whenever something bad happened, he would call on her, relying on her to take care of it. To support this theory, they told the following story in Chelm:

[Pages 449-450]

One lovely summer Sabbath morning, when they were reciting the blessing for Rosh Khoydesh [new moon] Elul, Shaye Kozak was coming home from prayers, walking sedately, with his hands gracefully clasped behind him, when he encountered his son and rebuked him: "Goy! Why are you running? What's your hurry? You got to shul late, you goy. Your mother, the witch, is praying at the third *minyen* [prayer group] and around 1 P.M. she'll bring home someone's cold, sour Sabbath stew, may her bones ache. Why are you rushing?"

Berating his son and cursing his wife, Shaye Kozak arrived home and what he saw caused the poor fellow to almost faint. This is what had happened. While he had been in shul, several Christians had arrived, bringing blocks of wood and boards, and after digging a ditch near his door they began constructing a "Gate of Triumph," because Tsar Nikolai was supposed to come to Chelm for the big holiday that occurred at this time of year when thousands of peasants from near and far Russia would gather in Chelm in order to drink the holy water from the well on the hill.

When Shaye Kozak, who already had enough worries, saw this he became very angry and began to shout in Russian: "This is my Sabbath! This is my place!" And to his son he said in Yiddish: "Stay here and I'll go get your mother."

When he was barely five years old, Shloymele began to study *chumesh* [first five books of the Bible]. The entire membership of the society *hakhnose kale* [aid for indigent brides], with whom Shimen Yankev prayed, was invited to celebrate the event. People crammed into Shimen Yankev's alcove. Shloymele looked like a tiny little Jewish man, dressed in a cut-down caftan with a belt, a silk 8-cornered hat and a velvet yarmulke. His face was pale, adorned by two long, curled *payes*.

After cake and whiskey and good hot noodles, the *melamed*, Reb Itshe Sheyfeles, stood up and called for silence. You could hear a pin drop as they began.

Itshe Sheyfeles asked, "What are you studying, little boy?" Shloymele didn't answer, but displayed the middle finger of his right hand.

Itshe Sheyfeles asked, "Ha! You're studying a finger?"

Shloymele: "No!"

"So what are you studying?"

"I'm studying the third book of Va'aykre."

"What does Va'aykre mean?"

"And he called."

"Who called?"

"And God called to Moyshe Rabeynu."

Shloymele didn't study long with Itshe Sheyfeles, because it was hard for Shimen Yankev to pay tuition. At five, Shloymele entered the middle class of the Talmud Torah, where poor children paid a small amount of tuition or even none. The Talmud Torah in Chelm had three classes: beginners up to *chumash*; *ivre* [reading] up to beginning *gemora* [Talmud]; and *gemora* up to tanakh [entire Jewish bible].

Reb Shmuel Hersh, a nervous, sickly, nasty man, was the teacher for the first class. He spoke Yiddish with an accent of the Volin region. He held the children in fear, calling each one "Mama's little baby."

Shmuel Hersh's classroom was one large room with six windows. It had a long narrow table with two long benches for the children. At one end sat Shmuel Hersh, and at the other the *belfer*. There were 50–60 children who studied in the *heder*. The children sat on long low benches or on the floor. In the summer the children played in an area in front of the building. The *heder* also had several high modern school desks – usually unoccupied — where Leybl Lerer gave lessons and taught the poor children to read and write Yiddish and Russian. These desks were there because they were required by Russian law governing schools. The Talmud Torah was a legalized state institution and everything had to be done according to law. It would happen that when the head of the city education committee came to inspect the conditions there, the children would run out, warning others, because the number of children exceeded the lawful limit. Only 8 or 10 children would remain in the classroom, and they sat at the modern desks. Reb Shmuel Hersh and the *gabe* [administrator] of the Talmud Torah, Reb Nisn, or one of the other teachers would go every Thursday to the town offices to collect the weekly subsidy for the Talmud Torah.

Shloymele started with the second class, with Reb Borekh the *chumash melamed* and when he turned 8 he went on to study with Reb Moyshe Libivner, the *gemora melamed*, the highest level teacher. Moyshe Libivner was a Trisker Hasid and a tidy man, well versed in his subject. He had three daughters and one son, Yitskhok, who sold lottery tickets. He talked people into buying tickets for the lottery of the Gerer *Rebe* in Warsaw.

[Pages 451-452]

Shimen Yankev, the hard working laborer, had great faith in the lottery and every year he would lose some money playing. If, with God's help, Shimen Yankev won a stake in the game he was in seventh heaven. In such a case – which occurred only once or twice in his life, he treated himself by buying a drink of brandy and a whole wheat roll from Moyshe Pondrik, who kept his wares inside his coat and sold them at the entrance to the synagogue. He was a very poor man, but cheerful. He would make faces and screw up his pug nose. At weddings he would disguise himself as a rabbi, joke around and sing a song from "The Seven Wives." The crowd would sing along, laughing until they cried. This is the first stanza of the song:

> My first wife Trane
> was quite a noble lady.
> She cooked and baked
> made stew and chopped fish.
> She was a nasty gossip
> and she would tell lies.
> And before she'd finished
> cooking a spoonful of food
> she'd eat up more than half of it.
> A glutton, woe to her.

And the audience would sing along: "A glutton, woe to her."

Chelm had other such merry–makers, like Motl Tuvies. He used to conduct the first shabes blessings on Friday night. When there was a wedding on Friday night (often in the synagogue courtyard, without musicians) he would sing to the bride and groom and lead the in–laws in a "mitzvah dance" like this.

> Who am I singing about?
> Reb Chaim Kirer has come to grace the wedding
> Sing a *freylekhs* [kind of dance] for the groom's side

And the audience would sing: "tay ray ti di di di"

or

Here comes Aunt Beyle Yone
Aunt Beyle Yone, shush, now, shush
Everyone falls for her
Let's sing a *freylekhs* for the bride's side.

Shloymele started to earn money while he was still studying with Moyshe Libivner at the Talmud Torah. On Purim, he went around performing with the Purim players and delivered *shalekhmones* [gifts of food]. Before Passover he measured flour for matzo baking, and worked his way up to the point where at the age of 11 he was a skilled kneader and quite a good oven tender. Before Passover poor people in Chelm worked making matzo. Women and girls got blisters and calluses rolling out the dough and couldn't move during Passover. The kneaders, rollers and oven tenders slept through the first seder. They were glad that they could make money and didn't have to ask for aid from the community, something that the poor of Chelm really hated to do.

Late on Friday, Marmerivtshe told Shloymele to go the "vinegar maker" and buy four groshens worth of wine in honor of the Sabbath; she told him not to forget to first rinse the bottle at the pump. The vinegar maker, a man with swollen cheeks, would walk around the large, tall barrels which the water carriers filled with fresh water from the market place pump. His wife, a short stout woman drew wine from the barrels. On a Friday late afternoon, the store was crowded, mostly with children, who, like Shayale, had been given a 10 groshen coin and instructed to ask for 4 groshens worth of wine and to get 6 groshens change. In the rush, Shayele asked for 6 groshens worth of wine and wound up with the original 10 groshen coin as well. As soon as the Sabbath was over, Marmeritvtshe returned the 10 groshen coin to the vinegar maker, even though she always complained that the wine was watery and didn't taste good.

* * *

Marmerivtshe had given birth to 13 children but only three had lived. Child mortality was very high in Chelm despite the fact that the town had so many institutions of higher learning that produced highly educated people – doctors, priests, technicians. This demonstrated how isolated and backward Jewish life was in the town.

Shimen Yankev sought additional sources of income so as to be able to pay tuition for Shloymele, who ws a good student. He worked for the landlord Tankhen Kashemakher, in whose "house" lived 8 families in alcoves separated from each other by Spanish walls, except for Khatskele Shuster who had his cobbler's workshop in the front room near the door, as well as place for "a wife and a bed" near the shared chimney. Shimen Yankev was responsible for supplying the lodgers with water and with wood to heat the oven for baking and to cook the Sabbath stew, and had to see to it that the "*piekalik*" [receptacle for hot coals above the stove] kept the Sabbath chickory coffee warm.

[Pages 453-454]

The *piekalik* once almost caused Shloymele's death. This is the story. Shloymele had crept onto his Spanish wall and was able to reach the ceiling, which was crumbling with age so that pieces of plaster hung down like a fringe. Shloymele noticed a sparkling, round piece of plaster hanging down from the ceiling and took it down, cleaned it off, and revealed a 40 groshen silver coin. It seems that someone in the attic had lost the coin and stepping on it had pushed it into the surface of the ceiling. Shloymele told no one about this windfall. It happened on a winter "short Friday." Shloymele spent two groshen to buy candies from Yankl Penzik and four groshens to buy pumpkin seeds, which he stuffed into two pockets of his padded coat. He kept the remaining 34 groshens in his vest pocket, in 2, 6 and 10 groshen coins.

He prayed with his father in the little shul and didn't tell about the money. After the Friday night meal, Marmerivtshe would throw anything that came to hand over the *piekalik* to insulate it so that the chickory would stay warm. She took Shloymele's padded coat and threw it on top, and the pumpkin seeds spilled out onto the floor; it looked like a whole sack of seeds had spilled.

Marmerivtshe became suspicious and began questioning Shloymele: "Where did you get so many pumpkin seeds?" "I bought them at the market." "Where did you get the money?" she asked, putting her arm around him. At that moment she heard the clanking of the coins in his vest. She took the child into their alcove, took off his vest, and shook it out onto the table. The copper coins made such a loud noise that everyone in the house was startled. Marmerivtshe cried, "Money on the Sabbath!" She delivered several strong slaps, asking "where did you get so much money?"

All the lodgers gathered around the *piekelik* and looked at the pumpkin seeds in amazement. Each one suspected that Shloymele had stolen from him. Shimen Yankev, who had looked on in a daze, felt ashamed. He pulled the leather belt from his trousers and began beating the child, yelling, "Tell me, where did you get the money?" Shloymele wept, poor boy, and with arms outstretched sought his mother's protection. The neighbors joined in shouting, "Where did you get the money?" Shloymele finally said, "I found it." "Where did you find it?" the entire group yelled. "I found it in the ceiling," Shloymele said, crying bitterly. But here Shloymele made a grave error. Shimen Yankev was completely stunned by this answer. And he continued to beat him with the belt, shouting, "In the ceiling! You non–Jew! Money on the Sabbath! And a liar to boot!"

Marmerivtshe could no longer tolerate the situation and took the child under her wing. Shloymele sobbed and became feverish. His mother sat by his bed all night in the dark. He got so sick that he almost died.

Shimen Yankev and Marmerivtshe were like thousands of other parents. They were very devoted to and loved their children. But if a child violated one of the essential laws, such as the sanctity of the Sabbath, or committed theft, etc. then the foundation was shaken and there was no place for sentiment. In addition to parents, the *melameds* beat them furiously. It is certain that the teacher's state of health and mood were significant factors in punishing the children, which happened with and without the parents' knowledge.

There was another story involving Shloymele. At the time he was studying with the great private *gemora* teacher Reb Shloyme Woslewitsker (from a shtetl near Chelm). He was a Trisker Hasid in his forties, thin and straight as a ruler, with a short yellowish beard. He walked lightly, quietly, barley touching the ground and leaning a bit to the side. The Chelm police chief in those days, who wore a corset and very fitted clothing, also walked leaning bit to the side. Shloyme Woslewitsker smoked cigarettes that he rolled himself. He had long hands and long bony fingers. His *heder* was in the same alley as that of Shloymele Herzh, next door to a family that made paper purses, using a paste to which they added sand, which made the purses heavy.

The *heder* consisted of one small narrow room with two windows. On one side of the table stood a bed–bench and on the other sides long benches where 10–12 students and the *rebe* sat crowded together. Two beds stood opposite the chimney, and a small barrel of water and a broom and a pail stood by the door. The *rebe* didn't have a wife, but he had a grown daughter and a grown–up only son, Shayale. The *rebe's* middle daughter, Sore, was as pretty as a picture and sold soda water on Lubliner Street. Sadly she left Chelm for Lublin because of shame over an unhappy love affair, and she did there at a young age.

[Pages 455-456]

The first cinema came to Chelm and set up in one of the shops in the *ringplatz* in winter, around Khanike. People were talking about the great wonders you saw there. All the boys from Shloyme Woslewitsker's *heder* agreed that on Khanike, when they didn't have to attend *heder* at night, they would all go to the cinema with the Khanike gelt that they

would receive. They bought tickets and each held onto his own ticket. Shloyme would look at his when no one could see. His had the number 40 printed on a blue cardboard square. The number was rubbed off a bit and Shloyme filled it in with a pencil so that it became a very distinct number 40. When Shloymele arrived at the cinema the man at the door thought the ticket was false. He tweaked Shloymele's ears and threw him out with such force that he fell on the snowy sidewalk.

A lodger of Shimen Yankev saw how Shloymele was thrown out into the snow and told Marmerivtshe. When Shloymele returned home, saddened by this mishap, he got hit by his mother for "wanting to go to the circus." But that was just the beginning. The next day in *heder*, Shloyme Woslewitsker whipped the boys one after the other. It was a regular bloody pogrom. You wouldn't have recognized the peaceful, soft–treading *rebe*. Like a wild animal he attacked his students and hit them wherever he could. Yosel Froyim Kores got away and with a stone broke several window panes of the *heder*. Several boys did not come back to the *heder* after that morning. Who knows? Maybe the blows that they used to deliver in those days was the "charm" that caused Chelm to raise so many prominent intellectuals and socially conscious people.

* * *

Summertime, when the splendid colors of the sun made Shloymele restless and upset, his father took him after the Sabbath nap to shul to recite psalms. Shloymele found himself in a very difficult situation. On one side, he saw before him the old yellowed cloth covered Book of Psalms, the cantor at the pulpit drawling out the verses with a sad melody and the echoing recital by the congregation. On the other side, the symphony of the sun through the high stained glass windows called to him.

Shloymele could not resist the strong pull; he snuck out from under his father's arm and ran out of the synagogue, even though he was certain he would be smacked for that.

The winters in Chelm would start early, right after Sukkot. Snow, blizzards, great cold lasted until just before Passover. The summers were very lovely, mild and pleasant. The early morning, evening and nights were splendid, beautiful and enchanting.

Every day of the week, like every holiday, had its own special charm and beauty.

A celebration of the enlargement and renovation of the Chelm synagogue.
In the center is a row of rabbis, dozers [community officials] social activists, the synagogue committee and others.)

Girl students from the Beis Yakov school

Chelm and its Environs

by Benyamin Orensztajn

Translated by Gloria Berkenstat Freund

Benyamin Orensztajn

When I write the word Chelm, the word falls apart into separate letters. Each letter represents for me an historical aspect of Jewish life, struggle and death.

The city of Chelm is the only one in the world that created the largest treasure of Jewish folklore, legends, stories and jokes. Entire generations spiritually fed themselves from the creations that brought bright and joyous beams to Jewish life.

I became acquainted with Chelm from a very different aspect – from an ethical-moralistic basis. This was in September 1939. The night before *Erev Rosh Hashanah* [the eve of Rosh Hashanah], I wandered from Wlodawe to Chelm. My bicycle did not last through the long march and I led it like a fainting sick person and went on foot. A mass of people flowed. A Hasidic young man walked ahead of me, who was constantly bothered by a Polish anti-Semitic student. The anti-Semitic student kept cursing the Jews: "The Jews provoked the war, the Jews were lumber merchants, they cut the trees and disturbed Poland's beautiful landscape, Jews were communists (*zyda-komuna* [Jew commune]), Jews have no ethics and no morals" – and the entire anti-Semitic lexicon screamed out of him. I moved closer to the student and I quieted him with a few words. I said to him: "Jews are fighting on the front for Poland's freedom and where are you? You are a Polish patriot? You are a traitor! A Hitlerist agent!" The anti-Semitic student lingered as if showered with a pail of cold water. The Hasidic young man helped me lead the bicycle and asked that we stay together. He actually beamed with satisfaction at the few words that I had said to the anti-Semitic student.

When we arrived in Chelm, a Jew stood at a large kettle and distributed coffee with which he refreshed those wandering. I looked around and saw the anti-Semitic student waiting in line for coffee. I asked him: - Well! Who has ethics and morals? The anti-Semitic student "went to the ends of the earth" in shame.

Despite the fact that the coffee was not of the best kind and was also not sugared enough, the coffee had an effect on the dry throats of the tired, exhausted wanderers like the best refreshing kind, like the best wine.

[Page 458]

Shmuel, the Hasidic young man who had wandered with me, told me that he wanted to go to pray in a group. All of the houses of prayer were full of tired travelers. Therefore, he entered a private house where Jews prayed in a *minyon* [10 men needed for prayer]. Meanwhile, I went to fix my broken bicycle and promised Shmuel that I would come to the house to meet him.

I went to Shmuel when my bicycle was finished. He had one and a half rolls and pushed them into my hand, I should take them. I asked him – where had he received the rolls? He answered me that the owner of the house where they had prayed had gone to the baker and bought rolls for everyone. He had a total of 45 pieces. He divided the rolls, three each, among the 15 worshiping wanderers. My host had left nothing for his family members, saying that the residents could manage to cook food, but the wandering Jews did not have any possibility to buy food. I was very moved by the noble, ethical deed of my host and also by Shmuel who wanted to divide the food with me. I did not take the one and a half rolls, arguing with the verse: "It is the host's duty to care for his guests."

Shmuel decided to remain in Chelm for Rosh Hashanah and I continued my wandering with the repaired bicycle.

I traveled, moved fast with tired feet, over the roads and paths. I entered a village. A peasant greeted me and before I had a chance to speak, he said to me:

"*Shikata Abrama? V'tim budinku.*" (Are you looking for Abraham? In the building?)
Several minutes later I was with a farmer named Avraham. To my surprise I saw a Jew with an imposing appearance and a long black beard with the countenance of a learned man.
– *Sholem aleykhem*[1] Reb Avraham, I greeted him.

– *Aleykhem sholem a Yid*, came the answer.

We began to converse. My throat and lips were dry. My face covered in sweat, my body suffering from the difficult road and, in addition, dead hungry.

–May I have a glass of water? my mouth unintentionally said.
[Page 459]
– With me you will not drink any water. We have here, *Boruch HaShem* [Blessed is God], enough milk, replied Reb Avraham.
Several minutes later, I was sitting at a table lavishly set with plenty of good things and I ate; actually swallowing delights with my eyes.

Reb Avraham introduced me to his family: his wife, sons, daughters, sons-in-law, daughters-in-law and small grandchildren. A family, *keyn eyn hore* [may there be no evil eye], like an entire tribe. Everyone healthy, firmly built, thriving, developed and they multiplied like the fruit in the fields. We carried on a conversation and we created an idyllic friendship between us.

I immediately learned that there were small Jewish village communities all around that also had a rabbi and that a Jewish landowner lived not far from here. The rabbi and all of the Jews would go to him to celebrate the holiday. Reb Avraham was his *khazan* [cantor]. He made the last preparations, looked through the *makzorum* [Rosh Hashanah and Yom Kippur prayer books] and told his choir, which consisted of his sons and sons-in-law, that they should not sing in a flat tone.

At night everyone had to go to the landowner. I was immediately taken to have the opportunity to speak with him.

I entered the estate, a true landowner's courtyard, a large building (a castle) adorned all over with carefully planted flowerbeds blooming in various colors, rows of trees and tidy paths which led to the entrance to the castle. I saw an entire row of household buildings and stalls filled with cattle, poultry and wheat.

The landowner learned about me and wanted to speak with me immediately. I was led into a washroom. I washed myself, dusted off my clothing and shoes. I was led from there into a room where a table was set for me. I could not eat. I was irked by the fact that I had eaten so arbitrarily at Reb Avraham's. However, when I thought that a half day earlier I had simply fasted because I could not buy things and that I had exclusively found nourishment from a few carrots that I had pulled out of a field, I felt justified.

The landowner's wife appeared before me. She made the impression on me of a princess. She looked half the age that she actually was. There were golden beads hanging at her throat from which shone diamonds. Her fingers were adorned with rings from which blue-white diamonds sparkled. Her ears shone with costly earrings. She began speaking to me. My glances and attention were turned to the landowner's wife, to the Jewish princess. Her oval face, naïve eyes and snow-white teeth presented a prototype of a godly appearance. She asked me not to tell the landowner any bad news so that he would not worry. She asked why should he be disturbed on *yom-tov* [holiday]? She took offense that I had a human earnestness on my face. Was the truth, God forbid, as bad as I present it?

[Page 460]

Yes! I answered. Perhaps it is worse then I present it. How can I show a smile on my lips or contentedness on my face after the atrocious pictures I have seen in the course of my days of wandering?

In the calm atmosphere of life, in the lap of nature, where an idyllic harmony reigned between heaven and earth, my pictorial episodes had the effect of shocking the landowner's wife.

I told her that in Kaluszyn I saw how Shimeon Haranczik's son was simply ripped into small pieces by an attacking German airplane; I saw the air assault on the 33-kilometer area that demarcated Kaluszyn to Siedlce and the detonations had deafening affects. The houses in Kaluszyn shook and quaked like children's cradles. It was thought that the entire area had been severed from the earthly globe.

I told her how I had been in the city of Siedlce. No living person was seen. An entire row of houses was still burning and those who had set the fire were devouring everything possible. The smells of the burning houses and human bodies choked our throats and eyes.

It was the same in the *shtetele* of Zwolen. Noteworthy things took place there. All Jewish houses were exclusively destroyed there. The Aryan houses and the church remained standing on a firm rock, triumphant and victorious, as if they had defeated the Jewish houses and Jewish life.

Several kilometers before Wlodawa I saw a garden in which the all the heads of cabbage were shot through. The German pilots thought that people had hidden in the garden and these were human heads. In the morning, I met Professor Moshe Szor on the Wlodawa-Hrubieszow highway. He sat in a peasant wagon wrapped in hay, shivering from the cold.

He took me to his library room. The landowner with his patriarchal appearance, dressed in velvet and silk, as well as the library, were a pleasant surprise for me.

This was the second time in my life that I had met a Jewish landowner. The first time was in 1937 in Polesia. That meeting was during normal times. The few days I spent then were in harmony with nature and daily life, in a carefree atmosphere, with entertainment, humor, wine and song.

This time it was with a solemn mood. Firstly, because of the general situation and, secondly, because of the Rosh Hashanah holiday.

[Page 461]

The landowner was influenced by radio communications that he had heard about the ruthless bombardment by the Germans of "open cities" in Poland and about the great losses of human life and material estates.

The landowner asked me: "Where is the Polish Air Force? Why is it silent? Why does it not react?"

The landowner expressed his satisfaction that I was his guest for Rosh Hashanah and asked me to remain at his estate for a longer time. He took me by the hand and led me into the synagogue.

All of the Jews from the surrounding village settlements were present in the synagogue with the rabbi at the head. The praying began with the landowner going to the lectern and reciting the first three verses. After him, the rabbi recited three verses, then the *khazan* [cantor] took over the praying.

Reb Avraham prayed the *Maariv* [evening prayer] and *Musaf* [additional prayers added to morning service] services accompanied by a choir that consisted of his sons and sons-in-law. His lyrical tenor voice evoked wonder in me. The Hebrew reading – amazement. The words of the prayers from his mouth acquired a picturesque content. He moved the men as well as the women to tears. Who knows, perhaps his ecstatic praying was the result of a boring, secret thought that this was the last Rosh Hashanah for which he was the messenger of the community? After the *Maariv* prayers, all, according to their prominence, sat at the long tablecloth-covered tables and celebrated the holiday food and banquet that lasted until late into the night. After, the landowner, the Rabbi, Reb Avraham and a large number of Jews sat down to study.

I became acquainted with the landowner's courtyard and with the abundant family. The landowner's wife also asked me not to leave after the holiday, but said I should remain at the estate.

On the second day of Rosh Hashanah, when Reb Avraham prayed *Musaf* and showed his cantorial talent, two Jews came running from Chelm. One knocked on the Torah stand and called out:

"Jews, save yourselves! The Germans are in Hrubieszow; they are shooting from all sides in Chelm. The Polish military and the administration have run away. We are in danger. The Germans could arrive at any hour."

Praying was interrupted and there was great confusion. The women began to cry and shudder; the rabbi called out in a sorrowful voice:

"Our Father, our King, tear up the evil decree of our verdict."

* * *

In the evening I again took my bicycle and wandered farther. I arrived in a small *shtetele* [small town] at the conclusion of Rosh Hashanah. I was tired and sweaty from the difficult road. The road was like a small sandy desert. Not only could I not ride on my bicycle, but I had to drag a paralyzed patient in the deep sand.

[Page 462]

When I arrive in the *shtetle* and saw the first small wooden houses, I met a Jew who stood near a house and wore an armband with the inscription: *L.A.P.* (*Liga Obrony Przeciwlotnicze* – League for Air Defense).

– *Sholem Alecheim a Yid* [literally, hello a Jew – a traditional greeting by one Jew to another] – we reciprocally greeted each other. The Jew led me into his house. First, I washed myself a little. Washing in the house was not an easy procedure because they still did not know about water management. The entire family immediately became busy. My host brought water from the well. My host's wife prepared a bowl for washing and the daughter brought a towel and soap.

Meanwhile, the table was prepared as if for a holiday and I was delighted with the food. We spoke about the general situation until late at night, which created a sad mood. The family came from Chelm. Therefore, they constantly asked about Chelm relatives and acquaintances. By chance, they asked me about the Chamski brothers, who I knew well. They were photographers in Warsaw.

In the middle of the night I went to sleep in the bed prepared for me.

I woke up in the morning, when the sun shone on the eastern side of the sky and the rays burst into the small house, filling the small room with light. I did not rejoice then in the splendid nature because in those days a disharmony took place between nature and Jew. With the sun shining brighter, the suffering in Jewish life became darker. I lay awake and thought about the situation of the last days, about my wandering – where I spent the night, not the day and where I spent the day, not the night. My thinking was interrupted by a light knock on the door. My host notified me that the rabbi wanted to speak with me. I began to dress more quickly. I took me shoes in my hand and I did not recognize them. My shoes had been dusty from the sand and now they shone like new. The same with my pants; they were cleaned and pressed as if just taken from the tailor. One thing was very conspicuous to me. My entire clothing had disappeared from my sacks. There were no shirts, no handkerchiefs, no pocket cloths; my tie was missing, my socks were gone. What could I do? Meanwhile, I entered the vestibule to wash. There was a hand towel hanging, a piece of soap lay for washing and I washed myself.

The kitchen door was open and to my great wonder and surprise I saw that the wife of the host was standing at the table with an iron and was pressing my underwear, my socks and ties. I remained without words and did not know what to say and how to thank her. She had washed my clothing the entire night, polished my shoes and suit and continued to iron.

I put on the washed and ironed shirt, socks and tie and went to the rabbi with my host.

[Page 463]

The rabbi was an older Jew with a stately appearance, a long white beard; his high forehead with deep wrinkles were those that adorn the countenance of a sage.

The rabbi questioned me, posed various questions, among others a pointed question, namely: What are the signs that Jews need to leave a city? I immediately answered the question that the moment when the police and the archives will be evacuated, the city will be threatened by the general enemy and the Jewish life will be threatened, too, by the resident anti-Semitic population that was searching for such a moment as an opportunity to stage a pogrom and loot the Jewish population.

The rabbi immediately sent the *shames* [synagogue official] to learn what was happening in the *shtetl*. The *shames* returned quickly with the news that the police and all of the officials and the documents were evacuated on trucks during the night.

The mood was sorrowful. The *khazan* stepped to the lectern to pray. After praying, with grest effort I turned away all of the invitations from the city's middle class worshippers. I knew that if I did not go to my host for breakfast, the entire family would be upset, particularly the wife of my host, who had washed and pressed my clothing all through the night.

After breakfast, the wife of my host, no, this is not the right designation, the Jewish mother, the Jewish folk-mother, asked me to remain until the afternoon and, indeed, she busied herself preparing lunch.

I accepted the invitation and remained for lunch. I had a thought that my host should go with me, that is, leave with me. However, he could not decide. Therefore, he went to confer with the rabbi. The rabbi was very worried about the situation and felt under a heavy burden of the Jewish people, for which he could not find an immediate solution. The rabbi said: "It is a state of emergency and at such a time I cannot give any advice; everyone has to do as they understand, but I will not leave this place. I will remain; I will not leave my community."

My host returned broken from the rabbi. He felt the seriousness of the situation. Until this minute, he had not believed in the coming horrible storm and yet he decided, like the rabbi, no to leave.

In the afternoon I took leave of the noble family. I wanted to pay them back with something for their sincere and friendly welcome. However, I had nothing that would attract their consideration.

In the morning, after a night of wandering, I saw an orchard. The fruit trees proudly exalted in their ripe fruit and teased my appetite.

[Page 464]

I entered the orchard and a short Jew with a black beard and brown countenance, burned by the rays of the sun, willingly sold me five kilos of apples for 50 *gorshn*. (A kilo is two and a quarter pounds and 50 *groshn* is approximately five cents). When I left the orchard and had just started to sit on my bicycle, the Jew hurried out and began to call me. I went back to the orchard. The Jew asked me to sit and turned to me with the following words: "Young man! I ask you to do me a favor, if you will, so that my conscience will be clear if you would take back the 50 *groshn*. What right do I have to take money from a wandering Jew for a few kilos of apples? Who knows, perhaps I myself will need to escape and abandon the orchard?

The Jew gave me an entire lecture about the *mitzvah* [commandment] of welcoming guests (*Hakhones Urkhim*), and in taking money from me he had violated the *mitzvah*.

I tried to calm the Jews, saying that I had not, God forbid, come to ask him to give me something and if I had picked out the apples that I wanted, it was my duty to pay for them. In addition, 50 *groshn* was dirt-cheap.

The Jew spoke with me for a long time and I was tired from an entire night of wandering and my eyes were pasted together from sleep. The Jews made me a bed in the orchard among the trees. I deliciously slept in the shadow of the burning rays of the sun and was covered by the widespread growing branches from which the fruit hung down.

When I woke up it was already dusk. The orchard keeper waited for me with lunch and we ate together. I parted with him in a friendly manner and left to continue my wandering. When I neared my bicycle I noticed that it was loaded a little too much. I immediately noticed what had happened. The Jews had sewn a sack from a handkerchief, filled it with fruit, bread, sausages and cigarettes and bound this to my bicycle. The provisions from the orchard-keeper were very useful to me in the farther days of my wandering.

I would, mostly, wander at night, because the roads were filled with mortal danger during the day. The Nazi air-destroyers would drop bombs on the wanderers. Shmuel Haranczik's son was torn to pieces by a Nazi bomb in the area of Minsk-Mazowieck and Kaluszyn.

As I write these lines, more than 30 years have passed. More than 30 years have passed since I became acquainted with Chelemer Jews, of whom each was a world of justice, fairness and integrity, hospitality, humanity and helpfulness.

A shudder fevers through my brain and body when I need to assert that this important Jewish cultural center, the holy *kehile* [organized Jewish community] of Chelm, as well as the surrounding communities exist no more. The dear and beloved Jews have disappeared and have been eternally annihilated, like ripe stalks in a field. The crown and pride of Jewry has exhaled its breath of life in pure holiness, in spiritual and physical sanctity.

Translator's footnote:

1. The traditional greeting among Jews, it means "peace be upon you." The traditional response means, "upon you be peace." *Aleykhem sholem a Yid* – "upon you, a Jew, be peace" – is a way of one Jew acknowledging another one.

[Pages 465-466]

Apolin

by Khaim Furman

Translated by Miriam Leberstein

The Feud between the Trisker and the Stepiner Hasidim

The feud between the Trisker and Stepiner Hasidim began 1908, when it became necessary to select a *staroste* [elder, official] whose job it was to maintain birth records and see to other governmental matters. There were two candidates for the post, Hertsl Kirzhner from the Trisker side and a representative of the Stepiner side. The two sides engaged in a bitter struggle. Each side made efforts to attract more people. I remember how my grandfather, Hershl Furman, who was the second candidate on the Trisker side, invited our neighbor Menashe to a special dinner and paid him 3 rubles to cast his vote for the Trisker.

The feud lasted many years. I can remember several instances that occasioned conflict. The *shoykhet* [ritual slaughterer] Shmerl Tenenboym, who was a Trisker, and Berish the *shoykhet* who was a Stepiner, did not get on at all. Shmerl would declare an animal that Berish had slaughtered unkosher, and vice versa. Each had supporters who would engage in ugly physical fights. These fights would often take place in the *besmedresh*, where both Hasidim and *misnagdim* [opponents of Hasidism] prayed. The women of both sides joined in the fights.

Eventually the two sides made peace. When I studied with Shmerl the *shoykhet* I was present when Berish visited and the two would in a friendly and relaxed manner consider a blemish in an animal to determine if that made it unkosher.

Jewish Tradesmen

My grandfather Hershl Furman was the first tradesman in the town of Apolin. He was born in Ludmir and when he was quite young he had to run away to escape the military kidnappers in the time of the cantonists [conscription of Jewish boys under Tsar Nicholas I]. For some time he wandered from one place to another and during this period he learned carpentry. He had a good reputation among the peasants and estate owners. He hired workers for his workshop and also taught the trade.

By 1914 there were already a couple of dozen Jewish tradesmen and workers in Apolin. The first tailors and shoemakers came to Apolin from other towns. They were mainly Trisker Hasidim, but a few were Stepiner.

Hertsl the Staroste

Hertsl Kirzhner was the *staroste* of Apolin and held a respected position in the town. First of all, he held a government post, and second, he owned two houses and a large orchard, along with a herd of sheep for wool and a dairy business. He had these sources of income until World War I, but after the war everything changed. He was left with only the two houses and the orchard.

I always enjoyed talking with him and hearing his stories about the revolutionary days of 1905. Although he was an ardent Trisker Hasid, he liked to read books in Yiddish and was a devoted follower of the *Haskalah* [Jewish enlightenment] movement. He liked to be active in the community and for a time was a member of the American Jewish committee of Apolin.

Shloyme Kayser

Shloyme Gikhman had the nickname Shloyme Kayser [emperor]. He was born to poor parents; his father was a shingle maker. He got the nickname Kayser because as a boy in heder he acted in a domineering manner toward the other boys.

For a short time he studied carpentry. While he was in the Tsar's army in Kharkov he learned Russian. After the military he was a sales agent for Singer sewing machines.

In 1914 he went into the army and was taken prisoner by the Germans. He quickly learned German and became a supervisor in the prison camp, which also held English and French prisoners, and he learned those languages as well. He returned home from internment during the Russian Revolution. He was taken with the Communist idea and became active in the movement. He evacuated with the Bolsheviks during the Russian Polish War and settled in Gomel where he did well in the medical school and became a doctor. He remained in the Soviet Union and according to reports, became a prominent Communist Party activist.

Borekh Shames

I don't remember his family name. Shames [synagogue beadle] was his nickname because when he was young he was an assistant to Berl the *shames*. His father was poor, a dealer in agricultural products he bought from the village peasants. He was orphaned very young. In 1915 he went to Minsk and became interested in getting an education. He learned Russian and read a lot. He was also taken with the Communist idea and fled to Russia after Poland became independent. There he achieved the rank of general in the Soviet army.

[Pages 467-468]

Yiddish Theater

The first theater performances took place as soon as the Germans left town [after World War I]. Avrom Shuster form Mezeritsh came to town and inspired the formation of a drama group. He was the director. At that time, parents didn't allow their daughters to act in theater, so men had to play the female parts.

They put on "The Binding Of Isaac," "Hertsele the Meyukheses" [woman from a prominent family], and "Khesie the Orphan." They had great success. Young people came from nearby villages to see Yiddish theater.

Over the course of time a good drama group developed. Meyer Chaim Goldberg was a talented director and performer. From time to time, they asked the Chelm drama group to stage various plays.

The religious fanatical element in town impeded the development of Yiddish theater. One time the drama group was preparing to put on "Bar Kochba" but the religious Jews didn't allow it. This greatly discouraged the theater people.

The Library

In 1921, thanks to the initiative of Meyer Chaim Goldberg and others a Yiddish library was established. The religious element under the leadership of the *dayan* [religious judge] fought the library. Among the young people there was a difference of opinion. Still, the library existed openly until the *staroste* shut it down.

Afterwards, we kept the books in our homes and distributed them to readers illegally. Later, Menukhe Milshteyn took over leadership. During the political arrests in 1930 the library was completely liquidated.

The Jewish Workers Movement

Our town also had a small workers' movement. The first strike took place during the intermediate days of Sukkot in 1921. A worker's activist from Chelm's Left Poalei Zion came to town. He summoned the workers to Oystsher Street, where our young people would stroll, and presented a report about exploitation and Socialism, calling them to strike against their bosses.

News of this event spread quickly. The strike took place and all of the workers' demands were met. From then on, the workers were under the influence of the Left Poalei Zion from Chelm, which would supply Apolin with party publications and brochures.

During 1924 Zalmen Rubenshteyn from Libevne and Henekh Kupershtok from Agrusin came to Apolin and conducted Communist propaganda among young workers. Zalmen Rubenshteyn came from a bourgeois home. He knew Ukrainian and was a good speaker. He had already served four years in a Polish prison and then crossed the border into Russia, where he took a course in illegal political activity. The Soviets then sent him to work on the political front in Poland. After they visited Apolin, contact was established with the Communist Party in Chelm and in 1926 Apolin had a many–branched Jewish Progressive Organization which dominated the other parties.

The Polish defense vigorously tracked us and made arrests. As members of the above mentioned progressive workers party, I and others were forced to flee overseas.

Some of our comrades were arrested and freed shortly after. During World War II some of them were in the Red Army and partisans who heroically fought the German Fascist executioners. The grandchildren of my grandfather Hershl Furman were among the. Two of them, sons of Yoyne Furman, were awarded the Lenin Order from the Soviet government.

Finally, I want to mention the progressive worker activists Shloymke Bok, Ide Nekhe's youngest son, and Henekh Kupershtok. Every Chelmer knew the dark cellar where Ide Nekhe raised her four sons, who played such an active role in the workers' progressive movement. Hundreds of workers in Chelm will remember this Jewish mother, similar to [Maxim] Gorky's mother, and her children, especially Shloymke, who attained such a high level and who so tragically lost his life.

When Henekh Kupershtok was arrested we couldn't imagine that he would stand so firm. We had feared he would give up other comrades, but we were amazed when we learned that he stood up in court like a courageous fighter. When the Polish regime condemned him to death after his second arrest, the workers in North America organized a large protest in which my father took part. The death penalty was reduced to life imprisonment. He was freed in the first days of World War II and was killed by a German bomb while trying to escape to Russia.

[Pages 469-470]

Chelm in the Years 1924 to 1931

by Chaim Worzoger, Montevideo, Uruguay

Translated by Miriam Leberstein

At the end of 1923 and the beginning of 1924, our town Chelm experienced a big change. Parties and movements began to come back to life. Among these, the youth movement Poalei Zion [Workers of Zion] quickly emerged.

The Jewish workers' parties in Chelm, including Poalei Zion, had a history going back well before the dates noted. I have a photograph of Ber Borochov [1881–1917, founder of Zionist Social–Democratic Workers Party] that is inscribed, "Poalei Zion, January 20, 1918 – Chelm." On the back is a stamp, "Jewish Social–Democratic Workers Party, Chelm," and in the middle of the stamp, "Poalei Zion." Thus, the Poalei Zion was alive in 1918 and certainly spreading its influence to a large circle of Jewish workers. Quite possibly the Poalei Zion existed even earlier, but unfortunately I don't have any information about earlier dates.

I am interested in proving that the Borochov youth movement, which produced hundreds of socially conscious young people, among them a large number of intellectuals who were and still are active today in Jewish national life, did not spring up by itself, from its own skin, but had its origins in the Poalei Zion movement, which first prepared the way.

The precursors were the families Winik, Fisher, Frukht and Beker of Reformatski Street. My first steps took me to the premises on Lubelski Street where there was already an active cultural and social life. This meeting place was a destination for many like me. It was already considered a true people's university by many young people. It hosted lectures and programs on culture, science and literary topics, literary discussions, political actions, meetings and conferences of a general social and labor organizing nature. The audiences included not only local residents, but visitors from the Jewish literary center, Warsaw. Whenever "Warsaw" was mentioned, it referred to the intellectual Warsaw with its hundreds of writers, poets, political leaders, artists and simply intellectuals.

The first lecture I ever attended in my youth, when I still wore the round Hasidic hat, was by Melech Ravitch. I remember it as in a dream. I see before me a handsome, imposing figure, his face framed with a small Christ–like beard, a leather belt cinched at the hips. He stood erect on the stage and his white face stood out in the poorly–lit hall. His speech, if I am not mistaken, was "From Ettinger to Peretz Markish," a giant leap in the history of Yiddish literature. I understood something of the lecture. I had already been for some time a member of the I.L.Peretz Library on Piarski Street, where the well–read, gray–haired Khishele was the librarian. I don't remember any more about that evening. The figure of Ravitch stayed with and intrigued me for a long time. I had not yet had the pleasure of personally meeting this poet–speaker of my first literary conference in Chelm. I am certain that it was among my first literary events and served as a sort of introduction to future wider cultural and educational work.

Our local people were already quite active. Ruven Frukht was an active participant in literary discussions. From a well–off family, he was a handsome, sturdy boy with thick copper–colored hair. He was a good speaker and knowledgeable about literature. He would often quote German poetry while gazing at a portrait of Heinrich Heine, as if calling on him as a witness in support of his opinions.

Shniur Wasserman was a head taller than all of his comrades. Clad winter and summer in a white collar, with dreamy poetic eyes, he was never without a book under his arm. He was a reader and an assiduous student. His talks were very interesting, infused with poetic melancholy. Today Shmuel Wasserman is a well known Yiddish children's writer. His poems appear in the readers of almost all the Yiddish *shules* [part time after–school programs] and they are recited or sung with feeling by thousands of Jewish children. But in those days, I saw his poetic quality only in its external expression.

Fayvl Frid was a person with a volcanic character. He was also a walking encyclopedia. He had a stormy past, dating to the revolution of 1905. When I knew him, he was still in full flame. He was a gifted speaker, interesting in both form and content. His talks and lectures were always interesting, interwoven with quotations from the Sages and from Yiddish literature. His outstanding characteristic was his folksy language which had all the charm of our mother tongue. He spoke plainly and expressively and without mixing in all the different foreign words which Jewish intellectuals so often used. In addition, he was both thorough and able to make the hardest material easy to understand. Fayvl Frid spoke about everything – politics, literature, art and much more – and all with ease. His varied experiences brought him to the highest levels of the town's Jewish intelligentsia, in contrast to his contemporaries who held themselves apart.

[Page 471-472]

Fayvl Frid was also my Yiddish teacher. He told me that he and Zalman Reyzen, when the latter was serving in the 7th regiment in Chelm, worked together on a Yiddish grammar. The project took a long time to complete. But when Reyzen published it in book form he omitted Fayvl Frid's name. I don't know how much of this story is true and how much imagined. In the course of preparing this memoir I remembered it. I also remember his wonderful stories about the time of his banishment to Siberia. He didn't tire of recounting them and each time added another detail. I remember how his fiery eyes sparkled when he would illustrate his stories with pictures of groups of Jewish political exiles. One of the pictures showed Gershon Pludermakher, a renowned Jewish intellectual in Vilna. I had the good fortune to be a student when Gershon Pludermakher taught Yiddish literature in the Jewish Teachers' Seminary in Vilna. May these recollections serve as an expression of gratitude for my wonderful Yiddish teacher.

Moyshe Lerer was another member of Chelm's Jewish intelligentsia. He was a friend of Fayvl Frid. He was the literary *shames* [caretaker]. He also received Jewish writers when they came to Chelm. He took them around town and showed them the people, the antiquities and unique sights. He also was the de facto connection to the greater Jewish intellectual world. His profession was the same as his name [teacher]. He worked for poverty wages in the Yiddish public school on Shedletski Street. He devoted his time to collecting objects he thought had historical or scientific value. He would climb into the attics of the Old Shul, the besmedresh, and old houses and search and rummage. Chelm had only one such passionate collector of sayings jokes, old expressions, song, stories.

Lerer was steeped in his heritage of generations of rabbis and Talmudic scholars. In the 1930's he went to Warsaw and was hired by the bibliographic department of YIVO [Yiddish Scientific Institute]. In 1941 when the Soviets invaded Poland, Lerer, who as far as I know was far from a Communist, became the head of YIVO in Vilna. He shared the fate of thousands of Jews of his birth town.

Dovidl Goldraykh was among those who were involved in Yiddish literature and followed its development. He was from a rich family and received a traditional Jewish education – *heder*, *yeshive*, *gemora* – and surreptitiously read, hidden under the religious texts, the classic Yiddish writers including Peretz, Frishman, Sholem Aleichem and Mendele. He entered the Poalei Zion movement and served it with devotion and enthusiasm, with Hasidic ardor. He gave lessons to young people. He led a lecture group and was considered one of the best speakers. Some of the members today occupy the most prominent cultural positions in various parts of the Jewish world. Dovidl would also participate in mass meetings. His favorite subject was the life and work of Peretz. According to my information, he now lives in Israel.

Wide horizons and tremendous opportunities for work and influence opened up for the Poalei Zion. Everything was ready for political action. The Jewish Communists were also preparing. There ensued a struggle between the two groups for hegemony over the young people.

Leading the fight was Yankl Beker who had taken a central role in political work and cultural activity. He had all the requirements; he was a good organizer, a fiery speaker, young and unafraid of any eventuality. He began in the tailors' union, which was under Communist influence. There they [Poalei Zion supporters] formed a youth section, which became the basis for building a workers' movement.

Then began the offensive. They held a series of meetings, secret meetings, conferences with members of the union, etc., all of which took place in late afternoon and evening. The very first point from which things spread out was a group of young people, almost all girls. All attention was focused on this new spinoff.

Today after the passage of a quarter century, one might think it wasn't very important, the victory of a group of 15 or 20 children. But for those times it was a very significant matter. It was a struggle for an idea, an ideology and to understand the importance of that struggle it is necessary to remember that the Jewish Communists were generally assimilationist and cosmopolitan. They denied a lot of things that today they consider important and necessary. Then, however, every kind of Jewish activity, even in the field of unionism was seen as "nationalistic" and "reactionary." They fought against every form of Jewish cultural activity, such as schools and evening classes. I remember a proclamation the Jewish Communists made against the sole Jewish elementary school and evening courses on Shedletski Street, where young workers were taught to read and write Yiddish, and learned about Jewish history and Palestine. The Reds maintained that such work weakened revolutionary ardor and diverted attention from the social revolution that was waiting at the gates of the town. Of course, the idea of territorial concentration of Jews in Eretz Yisroel was completely taboo.

[Page 473-474]

As I write this today the quandary has been resolved by the tragic Jewish reality on one hand and by the new heroism of our generation on the other. Those who opposed the national perspective and national ideas shared the same fate of all Jews under the Nazis. The enemy wasn't choosy and sent everyone to the crematoria of Majdenek and Sobibor. But our generation was also the generation of great visions. It saw beyond the confines of its time and made preparations; it worked, built, created, and at the cost of Jewish tears and blood achieved their own Jewish land, the land of Israel.

But to be true to the portrait I am describing it must be said that at the time it was a struggle to educate that generation for great national feats, a struggle also for basic ideological principals.

The victory of the few young people within the Communist tailors union later grew into a movement which put the Poalei Zion of Chelm in the ranks of the most important cities of the movement in Poland. The victory served as a signal to establish independent Jewish trade unions.

Within a short time, there were established unions of retail workers, bakers, millers, porters, boot–top makers, printers and our own tailors' union led by Feyge Boym. In the Communist unions the nationalist followers organized and established Borochov factions.

At that political movement, the Borochov youth set off on the road to a mass organization. That was also the time of my entry into the youth organization.

The youth committee was put together by a group of young intellectuals, infected with dynamism and a great desire to control the hundreds of young workers and students. The prime example of these was Khaim Bibl, called Bibl for short. There was no peace for him in his home. His father was busy as a *melamed* and studied day and night. So he chose to adopt the group's premises as his home, staying there day and night. He was always the first to arrive and the last to leave. Bibl was very daring and brave, one of those people who cannot tolerate wrongs and who react immediately. His reactions in the heat of the moment could be very fiery. He didn't make any good friends this way but everyone, even his "enemies," greatly respected his courage and his honesty.

Shmuel Shargel, another member of the youth group, served as its "permanent" secretary. He was as bold as Bibl, and a bit mercurial. A very dynamic person, he was involved with and took responsibility for the whole town. In his briefcase he had office documents from Dazman's brandy distillery, as well as the supplies for half a political party — copies of "Free Youth" to distribute, circulars, letters from the central committee, accounts of all the youth sections – a book to read, a flower for his Khanele. He juggled everything in his head. He was everywhere in all the government offices and hung around a long time until he obtained a position in the town hall. In that position he was also very energetic and won advancement for his productivity. In addition to all this he had provide for his whole family.

The young people relied on discussions to process what they read. They also conducted the famous "box evenings" where all kinds of questions were placed in box and then selected for discussion. Usually the discussions were held in the library. Our cultural history has not yet given due appreciation to the role played by the Yiddish–Hebrew libraries in the shtetl between the world wars. They were not just places to exchange books, as with other ethnic groups, but educational institutions designed to serve the masses.

The young people also read the publications of their own party. Poalei Zion had a very popular and well–edited political–literary publication, "Fraye Yugnt" [Free Youth]. The editors and staff included such people as Yankev Kener, the father of the youth movement in Poland; Dr. Emmanuel Ringlblum; Dr. Rafoyl Mahler; Zrubel; Buksboym, Shakhne Zagan; Yoysef Royzn; Peterzayl; and the best of the young poets.

All the workers' holidays were celebrate with zeal and youthful enthusiasm, turning them into political action against the reactionary and anti–Semitic forces in the country.

The youth organization also extended its influence into nearby towns – Reyvits, Rudi–Apolin, Krasnitsov, Grabaviets, and others. Youth organizations were established in almost all the towns, the only points of light for Jewish youth in those far flung corners of Poland. All thee organizations later became important sources of support for the multi faceted political work in all parts of the Chelm region.

[Page 475-476]

The work done by the young people in all the elections — to town councils, the kehila [organized Jewish community] and the *sjem* [Polish legislature] – was very important. The towns and villages around Chelm had a large Ukrainian population, which had suffered greatly from the renowned Polish program of "pacification." The struggle of the Ukrainian population in eastern Galicia for their rights as a national minority drew them closer to the struggle of the Jews against the Polish regime. Actually, the General Zionists had had an alliance with the Ukrainians in eastern Galicia. After the death [in 1926] of [Symon] Petlura [Ukrainian political leader]the alliance fell apart. The Ukrainian population was psychologically and politically ready to take up a common struggle for political and cultural rights for the national minorities living in Polish territory.

They began to carry out an enlightenment campaign in the towns and the whole region. Dozens of emissaries, mostly young people, spread out into small towns and villages and groups, urging people to vote for the united slate of the left Poalei Zion and Sel–Rob [Ukrainian Peasants and Workers Socialist Alliance].

Youth group of Poalei Zion, Khaim Worzoger in the center

Their campaign was full of dramatic moments. They encountered many unusual events that stirred them up. They came into their fullest selves, knowing that they were participating in a struggle for the most basic human and Jewish rights.

The coalition slate won tens of thousands of votes. This was a statement to the political reactionaries, a message that Jews can also have allies in the struggle for rights. It is true that they did not succeed in electing any deputies to the *sjem*. Itsik Lev, the Poalei Zion candidate, lost by very few votes. If they had had 40 more votes in the Krasnistov electoral district *Haftsirah* [Zionist newspaper] in Warsaw would have announced a victory.

Even without winning a deputy, the party grew to the heights of its power in Jewish Chelm, leading to its big victories in the *kehile* and town council elections. In the *kehile* the Poalei zion council members played a important role and helped to conduct Jewish communal life in such a way that the poor and working class was not subject to mistreatment or injustice. They truly fought for the common people.

Shmuel Barg was a singular figure in the *kehile*. A simple water carrier, he rose to the position of *sheliekh– tsibur* – a representative of the community. He richly deserved the post by virtue of both his integrity and his deep belief in the ways and truths of Poalei Zion. He was directly connected to the workers. If he had to attend a meeting of the town council in the middle of the day, he would set down his water cans at the pump, and still in his work clothes, rush to the meeting. The same thing happened when he had to help someone, do a favor or intervene on someone's behalf. With his strong instincts Shmuel Barg did not permit Jews to be mistreated and considered that his greatest mission in life.

Itsik Kornzeyer was the first Jewish employee of the municipal government; (others came after him). He was a devoted activist in the party. In contrast to Akslrod, who was a fine raconteur, optimistic even at the most tragic moments, and had a lot of folk wisdom, Kornzeyer always appeared tragic and wore an expression of shaky pessimism. He was reserved, reluctant to speak, although when he did speak, he did so clearly and logically. What he had to say was measured and weighed, as was his writing. If he managed to write something it was learned and interesting. He was an intelligent fellow, possessing a solid Jewish and secular knowledge. He was a bookkeeper, and was in charge of bookkeeping for the party and all of its branches and institutions. There were many accounts and sufficient headaches. But he did everything with his characteristic calm. With his reserve and patience he endured his personal troubles so as not to affect his work for the community.

Thanks to the Poalei Zion faction the town council turned into a body where the demands and requests of the Jewish population were expressed and their interests were well defended.

When detailed, comprehensive monographs will be written about Jewish towns in Poland and the part played by Jews in town administration Chelm and its Poalei Zion will occupy an important place.

[Page 477]

Chelm As I Remember It

by Faivel Zygielbojm

Translated by Gloria Berkenstat Freund

How do I begin? That such a large cemetery lies between Chelm now and how I remember it. Chelm, a city in Lublin County, like many other cities in Poland and yet different. [It is] literally world famous. Who has not heard of the "Chelemer Sages" who added the true Chelm charm to our folklore? Around what other city have hovered such wonderful Jewish folk stories, which are deeply rooted in the folk epic and will be told forever. Poets, musicians and artists such as Ben Likhtensztajn, Y. Trunk, Kipnis, Henekh Kon and so on have described the stories, illustrated and authored music (to Jakub Glatsztajn's *Josl Luksh fun Chelm* [*Josel Luksh from Chelm* – a poem]), published books that will always tell of Chelm the city of wonder, of the "fools" who saw how the markets take place in Lublin. Packed stage coaches from the "entire world" are drawn to Lublin, passing Chelm and here in Chelm Jews go about without income. And none of those passing by stop even to pay a penny's ransom. The "fools" decided to draw the attention of the "by-passers" and they succeeded. Well, well! A Jew on a wagon says to another passenger, why are four Jews carrying the old man on a reader's desk over the snow? Very curious, let us stop the wagon and ask them. It is our *shamas* [rabbi's assistant]. So, why are you carrying him? You do not see that a fresh snow has fallen? In order that he will be able to awaken the Jews for the divine service we carry him on the reader's desk so that he will not dirty the snow.

Faivel Zygielbojm

Ha, ha, ha, gasps everyone on the wagons, around the wagons. Ha, ha, ha, do you hear the "Chelemer Sages?" And why do the women carry their shutters into the synagogue? Because the *shamas* is old and sick and he cannot go around knocking on the shutters on the houses, so he can sit in the synagogue and knock on the shutters. Ha, ha, ha! Coachmen and merchants from the four corners of the world in Lublin after the market gasp, "Do you hear the 'Sages?'" Merchants sit in the inn with a cup and talk about the wonder of the Chelemer "fools" and they decide to return to stay longer and see what the Chelemer are capable of in order to have something to tell their children's children.

The Chelemer waited for the return trip of the *yaridnikes* [those going to the fair].

[Page 478]

As soon as they saw the merchants, they began to carry heavy logs from the mountain down to the highway. The merchants stopped to look and wondered, Eh, Chelemer! They are dragging logs down from the mountain? We throw them down and are finished. Really? The Chelemer say innocently, but with a purpose, say – the Jew is correct and they begin to carry the logs up the mountain and throw them down. The merchants laugh until their sides hurt and the Chelemer stand on the mountain and think: there will be income…

Thus the Chelemer with their foolishness began to draw more people. Each time they thought of a brand new foolishness – [people] began to run to Chelm to see the "fools." The inns became full of strangers; cobblers toiled until midnight because there was no lack of mud. The Chelemer again saw such pleasure. So many people were stretched out across the market around the synagogue with stands of goods and little by little Chelm became the market center.

Two Chelmer carried on a conversation near a cluster of strangers: What kind of shoes do you think the Kaiser wears? Golden. Well, if it is muddy, do they then get soiled? He puts on galoshes. Then can the golden shoes be seen? He makes holes in the galoshes. Does the mud get in? He stuffs them with straw…

Thus the wonderful Chelm stories were spread. And Chelm was built up. A large, Jewish city, full of sages. Chelemer "fools" or Chelemer "deceivers…" who fooled others and embellished the great panorama that was Jewish life in Poland with a particular local color and shared with it the fate of annihilation.

Chelm, from the Hrubieszow forest to Palichonke, which led through Sobor, Lubliner Street to the garden and further, where couples in love would stroll arm-in-arm and forget the world around them; this territorial Chelm remained. But the Jewish magical city is not here any more. The beautiful Chelm institutions, the *Linas Hatzedek* [organization to care for the sick], People's Bank, Old Age Home, Talmud Torahs [free religious primary schools for poor boys], Yiddish *Folks-Shuln* [secular primary schools], *Tarbut* [network of secular Hebrew language schools] schools, Jewish *gymnazie* [secular secondary school], the Peretz and Gros libraries, chess club, worker unions, literary circles, drama circles, parties, the rich men with the beautiful shops on the wide *Rynek* [market] and the poor people with the small shops and stalls on the market. The Hasidim-*shtiblekh* [one-room prayer-houses] are no more; the rabbis with their genuine homey humility and the artisans, porters, butchers and their toiling are no longer the Chelemer Jewish embellishments. The old woman's synagogue with its painted window panes, the small butchers' synagogue for the "common folk," the house of prayer and study where the young men would sit and study, and the nearby shopkeepers would pop in, revel in the voice of studying, do a *mitzvah* [commandment, a kindness] to buy and offer a frozen apple to a young man, a little *kvas* [yeast based drink], a flat roll.

[Page 479]

There is nobody to be afraid of the wide open doors of the men's synagogue that frightened the children during the night because the corpses came to pray, read the Torah and they barely call you and you even hear them in deepest sleep but they no longer awaken…

The anteroom above, with torn religious book pages, where the *Golem* [creature created by magic to defend the Jews], cursed by the old Chelemer Rabbi, lies transformed into a mountain of torn religious book pages, is no more. There are no more *kheder* [religious primary school] boys with *peyes* [side curls] who would spring in a circle on a bit of ground not far from the house of the dark *soyfer* [scribe] and actually heard a church [bell] ringing deep underground because it was said that a church once stood on that spot and the bell would ring in spite when a Jewish funeral passed by. But when Leibele Linczner died and the church bells rang during his funeral, Rabbi Leibele sat up on the *mite* [board on which a corpse is carried], muttered with his lips and the church sank…

The Chelemer peculiarity is no more, its simple, "common" Jews, such as Abele the water-carrier, a Sabbath-observer and a Bundist, who prayed with the melody of the *Marseillaise*; Chaim Hoptasz and his son, who helped his father in Fartaszne's carpentry workshop and in the evening played the violin, tapping with his foot to the cadences at evening parties and beamed with joy to see the "common folk" dance; Wewtshe, "the shoemaker" with a beard that covered half of his body, a toiler who knew the Psalms by heart; Chaim Lang who stole from the pockets of Polish officers and brought [what he stole] to the Bundist party; the crazy Berele who would sell fruit during the winter and rebel against the abhorrence of Rabbi Gershon [of polygamy, divorcing a woman without her consent and the opening of correspondence by a person to whom it was not addressed], recite the Torah in Russian and curse Nikolai in Yiddish, and still more of a collection of crazy men, Shuzsha, Wowo and others, who completed the picture of Chelm with their crazy characteristics. The common doctor Motye, who wrote a prescription for every sick poor person: a pot of *lukhshn mit hinershe yoik* [noodles with chicken soup]. There is no gallery of the types of women, the *palewtchebe* [a strong woman who excels in business], the rich widow with the strength of a man; Sprintse the butcher, ran a large business, always provided for the poor for *Shabbos* and the holidays; the tall Frayda-Nekha, Menashe'khe and Rokekhe – triplets, who on *erev* [eve of] Yom Kippur did everything possible in the synagogue courtyard; Malkale Winik, a small, weak quiet woman would rely on the cries of the triplets, standing near them and contributing her quiet tears; the Blumensztrochs, an aristocratic half-assimilated family, whose daughter, Zlota, played the piano and was a mother of urbane elegance; the Dubkowskis, whose house was a true spiritual center; the Luksnburgs, a family of musicians and engineers; the Rojznblats, an intelligent family with bohemian, artistic inclinations; the comrades Nusan Baum and Gershon Basz, two quiet students, studied together and became "worldly" together, studied, read a great deal, their parents became impoverished at the same time. Nusan became a proletarian in Warsaw and perished with his family in the ghetto there; Gershon studied in the Warsaw Art Academy, a rare, delicate painter, he died before the war; the Lerer family and their respected Moshe who was betrothed to the Yiddish language, a Yiddish researcher and philologist, was one of the most devoted workers in YIVO [*Yidisher Visnshaftlekher Institut* - Institute for Jewish Research] and perished there; Joska Goldhocher, a rare musician, a popular joker and magnificent teller of stories, the darling of the city; Bentshe Lang's family, of whom only Moshe the Zionist activist in America and Perl in Israel survived.

[Page 480]

Faivel Winik

Who can enumerate all of the figures and groups who each separately gave something to Chelm and created the entire picture? The butchers, for example, the oaks who protected the Chelm Jews from anti-Semitic attacks. I remember when the *Hallerczikes* [anti-Semitic followers of Polish General Jozef Haller] entered the city and began to go on a spree, cutting beards along with pieces of the face, murdering, robbing. The local anti-Semites ground their teeth and waited for a true pogrom to flare up in order to be able profit from it. Suddenly the heroic butcher youths appeared in the alley with knives and axes, maimed a few *Hallerczikes* and drove them from the city. This happened on a winter Friday. All of the shops were closed. Some were looted; women could not buy food for *Shabbos*. *Erev Shabbos* [the eve of the Sabbath] was disrupted; but not *Shabbos*. In the evening, the butchers called the Jews to the synagogue and welcomed the *Shabbos* Queen. The butchers guarded the doors.

Chelm possessed rare dramatic strengths. There were often Yiddish performances and they stood at an artistic height. They should be remembered in this yizkor book. They were: Ailiwicki, Meir Torn (Fentak), Faivel Dreksler, Yisroel Zygielbojm, Shura Helper, the dark Chaim, Tseshe Helper, Tseshe Bojarski, Tanya Sznajder, Sheva Binsztak, Fanya Goldsztajn, Bornsztajn, Yisroel Lewinsztajn, Moshe Zygielbojm, Pinya Zygielbojm, Moshele Karlik, Itshe Luksenburg, Avraham Bernfeld, Hertz Chaim Lang, Avraham Jakov Krotman, Bluma Argun, Dwoyra Wajc, Serke Tudrus, Cymerman, Avraham Zajde, Berl Goldman and Sholemke Goldboim the prompter. There were certainly still more names that my memory cannot reach. We performed *Cyrano* in the city hall room, in the chess club and *Polonia* Theater. Professional theater troupes often came to Chelm, among them Ester Ruchl Kaminska and her troupe. A theater performance in Chelm was a holiday for everyone. Pious young people would transgress in the company of frivolous people and go into a Yiddish theater.

[Page 481]

The gathering point for the young intellectuals was at the Orguns'. The literary circle of the Jewish *gymnazie* [secondary school] also had its club there. Every *Shabbos* they would meet, reading their own writings, or reports about Yiddish and Polish classics.

The owner, Faivel Orgun, would listen with pride to how the young people were excited with new ideas and presenting the new Peretz, Mendele, Wispianski and Mickewicz. My dearest young friend Faivel Winik and I were the only "civilian" members of the *gymnazie* circle.

The work of the circle truly brought the Polanized [assimilated] Jewish young closer to Yiddish and Jewish creativity.

Chelm also had *halutzim* [pioneers preparing for emigration to *Eretz-Yisroel*] such as Wowke Gotlib and others and a strong idealistic leftist youth who drew many students into their circle and carried on widespread activity among the Christian population as well, rented premises under various names, were often betrayed and fell into the devilish hands of the secret agent Wykusz: a sadist who was famous for his torture. The name Wykusz was [like] a scarecrow. Yet the movement grew and grabbed a large portion of the Jewish youth. The great role that the Bund played for many years and how it was involved with almost every branch of life in Chelm is, of course, described separately.

* * *

Among many Chelm memories I remember this version of the *Golem* legend in Chelm:

Nathan Ausubel asks in his book, *A Treasury of Jewish Folklore*, which was published in New York, in 1948, if Mrs. Mary Shelley, the author of *Frankenstein*, knew about the legend of the Chelemer *Golem*?

I will record the Chelm version about the *Golem* in the Chelm yizkor book as I heard and *saw* it in my *kheder* years.

There was an attic room over the women's section of the old synagogue full of discarded religious books. The "room" frightened all of the *kheder* boys. We were afraid even to look into the "room." Because of the scarcity of *kheder* rooms in the *Talmud Torah* building, I was destined to study in the women's section for a semester. We held the *tsitsis* [fringes on the *talis* and four-corned undergarment worn by pious men] in our hand when we went by the few steps that led to the "room" and said:

[Page 482]

Golem, golem, do not awake
Disgarded religious books are your end.

Our Rebbe, Hershl "*Pipke*" (because he had a wart in the middle of his forehead, we called him Hershl *Pipke*[1]) warned us not to approach the room. It happened one morning the rebbe became ill and his daughter came to us to say that we should repeat the theme of discussion until lunch, that is, until 12 and afterward go home. My friend, Moshe Tarbiner (a village boy, a little older than me), said to me in the synagogue courtyard: "Up, let us see the *Golem*." I could not resist the temptation of committing the sin and started following him with the *tsitis* in my hands and with shaking steps. My friend was the first to open the door of the room. We both murmured the prayer:

Golem, golem, do not awake
Disgarded religious books are your end.

I saw a full room, a mountain of discarded religious books.

Everyone knew that the pile of discarded books was the *Golem's* body.

It was said: –

Many years ago the gentiles created a practice; every Tuesday during the fair, they got drunk and beat and maimed the Jews, driving them from the small shops. The old rabbi could not bear this. The rabbi fasted and a made a giant man out of snow, blew the breath of life into him so that he would defend the Jews. The next Tuesday the drunken gentiles began to rampage as earlier, beating, killing the Jews. Suddenly the *Golem* appeared with an axe in his hand. Ten gentiles threw themselves on him, stabbed him with knives, but no blood ran, just as if stabbing snow. However, the *Golem*split their heads and they ran bloodied to every hole. A fire broke out in the *shtetl*; the *Golem* dragged barrels of water and put out the fire. No one knew who he was, from where he came, to where he disappeared and what his name was.

It became quiet at the fairs. The gentiles did not bother any Jews. The opposite, they acquired respect for the Jews and were afraid to speak loudly. Chelm was quiet for a long time: no fires and no beatings. Jews said quietly among themselves that it was the prophet Elijah who had saved them.

Once the same *Golem* appeared in the market with an axe in its hand and began trampling to the right and left, Jews and gentiles. There was turmoil in the *shtetl*. A few days later – the same thing again. People hid in their houses. The *Golem* tore off shutters, broke windowpanes. The old rabbi possessed great sorrow and grief. He fasted again, afflicted his body. He cursed the *Golem*, that his body shall become a pile of dirt and he become a mountain of discarded religious books.

The *Golem* spread out on the ground in the women's section of the synagogue and he turned into a mountain of discarded religious books.

* * *

This is some of what I remember from Chelm, the city where I spent my very young years and it is good that the "Chelm Sages" are being immortalized in the columns of the memorial book.

Translator's footnote:

1. A *pipke* is a tobacco pipe in Lithuanian Yiddish. A variation of the spelling is *pupik* meaning belly button, the more likely meaning of the word in the above lines.

[Pages 483-484]

Some Memories

by B. Alkvit

Translated by Miriam Leberstein

B. Alkvit is my pen–name; my birth name is Eliezer Blum. I was born in the valley of Jewish poverty – on the "Naye Tsal," that is Pocztawas Street, in the great center of Jewish life and culture, Chelm, on December 7, 1896. (The date is uncertain. That year it was the last day of Khanike. In the Khanike lamp made from hollowed–out potatoes, the oil had already been exhausted, and the wicks extinguished.)

I was the eldest son of Sholem and Henie–Beyle, who had I don't know how many children. That is, there were three of us. But in those days there went among us a tall, dark, taciturn man, who carried hung over his shoulder a longish chest covered with black cloth. We saw him only when a child had died, when he appeared like a shadow of the unseen. He would rush into a house and rush out into the street with the child inside the chest. No one ran after him. Funerals were not held for small children.

How many times did this man come to our house? Often enough. Once our mother packed up a few things, gathered the children and put a lock on the door. But she didn't want the Angel of Death to think that we had just gone off for just a short visit to our aunt, who lived at the far end of town on the way to the forest, and would return the next day. So she gave my father a piece of chalk and told him to write.

My father took the chalk and with a flourish, began formally with *b"h* [*barukh hashem* –blessed is God] and the date in Hebrew. He continued : "Be informed that we don't live here anymore. Therefore you need not exert yourself to come here anymore."

We did not live in fancy surroundings. But who can forget the spaciousness of a house in Chelm? And it wasn't just the house – there was the street as well. And we had a window that looked out on a courtyard that ran uphill, where our father kept his paints, ladders and tools. For Father, who was called Sholem Pineles, was a painter, a painter in summer and a glazier in winter.

That Chelm was an old, a very old Jewish town I didn't learn until later, when I was already far from home. Still later, a friend gave me a picture of Chelm, an etching taken from a book named "Ghettoes of Poland." This friend, a colleague, knowing that I came from Chelm, gave it to me as a gift. But the picture truly stunned me. Chelm looked so old, so antique, as if unchanged from the Middle Ages, and so sunken in despair. That was not the Chelm I knew. I had never seen that kind of poverty. Our poverty had a bit of grass. In our poverty there was color and laughter, and the hill and the courtyard outside our window. And the hill, which was bare on top, was a hill for children. It was a young town – a town of mothers and fathers and aunts and uncles and good food to eat on the Sabbath.

I thought that the artist who made the etching was a depressive. He had not been to the market place and seen the people of Chelm in the crowd of peasants and soldiers at the stalls with ribbons and beads; and the market women sitting over their fire pots selling bagels and hot beans. He hadn't heard of our artisans, our boot–top makers and hat makers, who made hats for the army officers – all of whom worked together and shouted together, along with the cobblers and tailors, "Down with the Tsar."

He had never entered the Hasidic *shtiblekh* [one room prayer houses]. Or the factory, the foundry where Jews did not in fact work — they weren't allowed to — but which provided us with its whistle. When the factory whistle went off we knew it was noon, they were having lunch now.

Still, the etching was a picture of the neighborhood where we lived. What had happened? Had the town changed so? Had I changed? Without having contact with the life of the town, could I even be certain that I had been born in Chelm – I mean in Chelm itself — or maybe just in one of the tales about Chelm.

In any case, the famous tales they tell about Chelm are after all, also Chelm. But given that there are no children in the Chelm stories – probably because children aren't taken to meetings, and where are meetings so talked about as in the stories about Chelm — we return to Chelm itself.

The education I received was the kind that is called "traditional," except in one respect – the *melamdim* [teachers of young children in religious schools] had no memorable influence on me, either good or bad. I can't complain that someone in Chelm ate my bread and jam, or that the teacher's wife sent me on an errand to buy a groshen's worth of sour cream or potshmetane with tsharvetshane cheese. Potshmetene is probably sour–milk, but the cheese? I've eaten all kinds of cheese, Swiss and French, Dutch, Italian and cheese of unknown origin, but the tsharvetshane cheese of Chelm that one could buy for a groshen is for me a riddle to this day.[1]

What I retained from my studies during my years in *kheder* is what my father taught me. In general, my impressions of those years, I mean my impressions in retrospect, are mostly of moments with my father. For example, every Sabbath in summer he would study a chapter from the Bible or Talmud, just when I ought to have been playing outside with my friends; he couldn't find a more suitable time. Those times, when my mother came out of the house and called to me, that my father needed me, I began to understand why people wanted to overthrow the tsar.

Once on the second day of Shevuot, he woke from a short nap to go to synagogue.

[Pages 485-486]

It was well before the evening prayers. I ran after him. He asked if I wanted to go with him to say Psalms; today, he said, was King David's *yortsayt* [anniversary of person's death]. King David's *yortsayt*? That made a strong impression on me. The *yorstayt* established a connection between King David and dying – this had the effect of actually bringing him back to life, resurrecting him. In another minute and I'd have hear him playing on his harp.

But it was cold in *shul* and there were so few people. I was the only boy in that big cold *shul* with its heavy chandeliers hanging on chains over the men reciting psalms. The voice of each worshipper had another voice, an echo that repeated after him, "*anshey ha'ish*" ["Blessed is the man," Psalm 1]; that recited and reverberated over the chandeliers among the chains, "Why do the heathens rage," [Psalm 2] and "For the conductor of music, a psalm of David," [Psalm 4].

I trembled with cold. My father led me by the hand. Outside, we were embraced by a delicious warmth. He took me on a bit of a walk, up to Lubliner Street and then further up to Rubieshower Road, to the Chelmer forest, where people regularly gathered wood and mushrooms and in the summer days of Shevuot picked lilac and berries, and where they would sing revolutionary songs. And to me it seemed that walking that road we were also commemorating King David's *yortsayt*.

We were three brothers and when the fourth child, a girl, was born, my mother died. And that ended our life as a family. The girl, my sister Henie– Beyle, named after my mother, died in childhood of hunger during the war [World War I]. Father was already gone; he died shortly after my mother. I, already grown, a 12–year old, was sent to live with an aunt in Lublin. From there I went to Warsaw, where I also had relatives, then on to Vienna. There I plunged into loneliness as into deep water, over my head. But there in Vienna I became acquainted with a young revolutionary, Eliash Gutorinski (Bragniski in his home town near Kiev) and this was my first friendship with an adult.

In 1914 I arrived in America and until 1920 when I got to know Yankev Glatstein, there was no friendship that influenced me as much as the one with Eliash. In New York I went to night school, worked in a shop, then studied in preparatory school. In 1920 I began to publish in the journal "Inzikh," [Introspective] published by a group of poets —Yankev Glatshtein, A. Leyeles, N.G.Minkov – who along with other arrivals had formed the Inzikhist movement of Yiddish poetry. I was drawn to the group, and later became co–editor, became a teacher in the Sholem Aleichem Folks Institute and contributed poetry, stories and literary criticism to Der Feder [The Feather], Fraye Arbeiter Shtime [Free Voice of Labor], Undzer Bukh [Our Book], Kinder Zhurnal [Children's Journal, Kern [Kernel], Kultur, Hamer, Oyfkum [Rebirth, Emergence],Yidish, Di Prese [Press], Yidishe Kempfer [Jewish Fighters], Tsufkunft [Future], Der Tog [The Day].

And so life proceeds. Bu among all these facts and accomplishments, my memories of Chelm remain fresh to this day.

Translator's footnote:

1. The errand referred to seems to be an occurrence in one of the fictional stories of Chelm.

[Pages 485-486]

Woislowicz

by Yisroel Kelner

Translated by Miriam Leberstein

Twenty kilometers from Chelm lies the town of Woislowicz, which had 300 Jewish families. The Jews lived a life of poverty, but they were very religious. There was a *besmedresh* [house of study also used for worship], a synagogue, and a number of Hasidic shtibls [small house of worship], each for a different Hasidic group – Gerer, Trisker, Radziner, Belzer, Wlodovker and Kotsker.

Yisroel Kelner, industrialist and social activist in Capetown

Woislowicz had a rabbi who earned his living by selling yeast. He also made money from ritual slaughter, even though the town had three *shokhtim* [ritual slaughterers] who were well learned in religious matters and fine leaders of prayer.

The Jewish occupations were the same as in all the shtetls in Poland. There were shopkeepers, merchants and artisans. There were a lot of orchard keepers who rented orchards and sold fruit in the area.

Life was quiet and idyllic after World War I. During the war the Jews had evacuated to Berdichev. In 1918, life changed radically. New winds began to blow. The young people became Zionists and various organizations and parties were formed, which maintained contact with groups in Chelm.

Woislowicz had friendly, good hearted Jews who helped each other in time of need. Notably, Sholem Kelner and his wife Taybe were very hospitable. They took into their home beggars and couriers, giving them food and a place to sleep. There were many such good hearted people in my town

[Pages 487-488]

Reminiscences

by Tsadek Ayzen, Melbourne

Translated by Miriam Leberstein

The Khevre–Kedushe [Burial Society] and the Founding of the Talmud Torah [free elementary school for poor children]

The *khevre–kedushe* in Chelm was run by artisans and laborers. It was their practice, when a rich person died, to require the payment of a large sum of money for his burial. If that payment wasn't made, the corpse could lie unburied for three or four days.

When Gutele Khones, a well–known wealthy woman died in 1910 the town was in an uproar. The *khevre–kedushe* wouldn't agree to bury her until the amount of money they demanded was paid. My father, Leyzer Yankele i, who was the *gabe* [administrator] of the *khevre–kedushe*'s synagogue and Melekh Hirsh, who was the *gabe* of the *khevre–kedushe*, both agreed with the rabbinical court that it was forbidden to shame a corpse.

Tsadek Ribayzn (Ts. Ayzn)

The situation was tense. The majority of the *khevre–kedushe* didn't want to give in, so the family of the deceased had no choice and turned over the amount demanded. The *khevre–kedushe* rejoiced in its victory and conducted the burial.

With the money they received the *khevre–kedushe* built the new Talmud Torah where 150 poor children studied and each child was provided with clothing. Because of the rich woman's death, a few poor children were set on their feet and there remained a fine memorial to the woman – the Talmud Torah.

Der Langer Shmuel [Tall Shmuel]

We once had a relative who worked for us, Langer Shmuel (Shmuel Ribayzn). He was a ruffian, had served in the tsar's army as a dragoon, and always hung out with his kind. No matter how much people rebuked him for his improper behavior, it made no difference. He would answer: "I was born a Jew and I'll die a Jew. And if a non–Jew insults a Jew, he won't come out of it in one piece." And so it turned out.

A peasant once came into our store to buy tools. He bargained with my mother over the price and insulted her "Jewish mug." This shocked Langer Shmuel and he beat up the peasant. Whether other peasants and a policeman attacked Shmuel, he gave them the same treatment and ran away. The police looked for him for a long time. My father helped him out with a few rubles, but Langer Shmuel continued to maintain that "a Jew should not allow himself to be insulted."

Averting a Pogrom

In 1918 the Poles seized power from the German–Austrian occupiers of Poland. It was winter on a Sabbath day. I was in the Workers' House of the Bund in Chelm, where I saw Dr. Fensterblau speaking with a group of workers who were very agitated. It was a serious matter.

Poles in the town were preparing to carry out a pogrom, to attack the Jews. They said that the bloody act would take place on Sunday morning, after church services, with the help of peasants in the vicinity who would come to town especially for that purpose.

Dr.Fensterblau and others with him were very anxious and upset. There wasn't much time to act, to organize self–defense; it had to be done in a hurry. The young people who were there in the Bund headquarters were designated to be messengers to call together representatives from various Jewish organizations, as well as certain private individuals, doctors and people who could administer first aid.

To the quickly arranged conference came representatives of all political groups with the exception of the Right Zionists and the Orthodox. The proceedings were held in strict secrecy. All night they prepared to provide every Jewish street with a defense post and a first–aid station. They needed several safe places to hold weapons and the Kuzmir shtibl was designated to be one such place. But the men of substance in the town refused and wanted to inform the police about the entire matter. So people went to the little synagogue of the butchers, which was next to the big synagogue. There they hid guns and grenades among the torah scrolls.

[Pages 489-490]

The aroused Poles got word that the Jews were preparing to defend themselves, that they had weapons and an organized self–defense. The Poles their desire to attack and the planned pogrom was averted.

Getting Rid of a Jewish Informer

At the outbreak of World War I in 1914, the Russian military headquarters was in the building owned by Herr Berish Kuper at 27 Lubliner Street. A Jewish soldier from Kiev was stationed there, working as an informer. His assignment was to denounce Jews.

Once, the informer encountered on the street not far from the Russian headquarters, a Jewish artisan (Fishl Shnayder's brother, who sewed cheap clothes) and asked him where the headquarters were. The Jew didn't understand anything, didn't know he was in danger, especially since the question was asked by a Jewish soldier. So he pointed out the headquarters and was immediately arrested, taken from his family and imprisoned.

The Jewish artisans in Chelm decided to teach the informer a lesson. Risking their lives, they locked him up until the Germans occupied Chelm. Then they turned him over to the new powers.

Jews of My Town

by Rivka Szrojt

Translated by Miriam Leberstein

In 1905, in my hometown Chelm, people were expecting something and that something frightened them. And then suddenly, there was joy: a constitution had been granted. Kith and kin, young and old went into the streets, singing and joyful. But suddenly, quite soon, people began to run in great panic, not knowing where to hide from the soldiers and police who were attacking them murderously.

When things quieted down, people in Chelm began singing a folk song that went like this:

> Tsar Nikolai gave us a constitution
> then quickly took it away.
> He wanted to stop the revolution
> with his filthy politics.

In Hrubieshower Street there was a voyener [state?] hospital with its own water authority and clocks which a Jewish clockmaker wound once a week. Further up the street there was the "old" hospital for civilians, and after that a home for Christian orphans. On the other side of the street were the barracks where the "Moscow Regiment" was stationed. Quite often we'd hear a Jewish recruit singing of his loneliness from a window opening onto the street.

> At home I wore shoes, comfortable old shoes
> Now I have to spend the Sabbath with Fonye Ganev[1]
> Oy, Fonye Ganev
> Fonye is a Ganev, 1,2,3.

The residents of Hrubieshower Street, who were poor artisans— cobblers, tailors, rope makers, glaziers, peddlers, organ grinders and thieves, listened to the song with compassion and wanted to take the recruit home as a guest for the Sabbath.

There was also a water pump in that street which dried up in the heat of summer and froze in the winter cold. And when it was working it was the object of conflict between the Jews and the Poles, over who had arrived first.

Hrubieshower street ended at Rogatke, where two other streets started. One, Lubliner Street, on a hill, the other, the "Nayer Tsal," in a valley. That began with a technical school and an ironware factory and soon petered out into small crooked houses with deep, moist *sitarines* [?] with small windows that looked out onto the ground, through which one could see and hear people walking by.

Here, in the poor Jewish part of town there were sewing workshops, carpenters, lathe operators, small synagogues and Hasidic *shtiblekh*, with constant fights between the Trisker and the Kuzmir sects. The Trisker *rebe* laid a curse on the Kuzmir *rebe*, that he should not have any children and the Kuzmir *rebe* laid a curse on the Trisker *rebe*, that he should have no beard. Although they later both regretted the curse, by then it was too late.

But the Kuzmir *rebe* stuck up for the people. On Simchat Torah he led the procession that carried around the Torah in the big synagogue. Although he had a limp, he didn't get tired of the singing and dancing. Afterward, they sang his newly crafted *nigunim* [Hasidic melodies.] They would continue to sing them in the workshops and also at weddings.

[Pages 491-492]

In the "Naye Tsal" lived Chaim Gergele, the petition writer. He was short and walked fast, lost in thought, seeing nobody. His caftan open, his head stretched out like a rooster, bent over the ground, looking for scraps of discarded pages from holy books, picking them up and putting them in his pocket, just as his father the rag picker would put scraps of fabric in his sack.

Between seeking and finding he would pluck at his beard. His cheeks were streaked with blue, like the quills of a plucked goose feather. But he wrote good petitions.

He wrote with an old pen on the back of the papers. He didn't need to ask many questions of his clients; the less he heard, the better, because he knew, as if from the air, everyone's complaints and legal issues, as well as their origins, their family and address. The peasants would pay him in homegrown food products. And in the middle of writing he could get up and go inside and check to see if the hens had laid an egg.

Opposite the "Naye Tsol" was Lubliner Street with the cathedral that stood atop a high hill, the loveliest hill in town, with trees and flowers surrounding the cathedral, although no Jews were allowed there.

***

Lubliner Street continued on with beautiful stone buildings with gates and courtyards with nice shops, hair salons, and barbershops with many mirrors on their walls.

One such barber was called Moyshe Pitshke the Royfer [non–credentialed medical personnel] Most of his clients were peasants and the poorest of Jews. Once a young fellow found his way in, wanting a haircut. He emerged with one side of his head shorn like a convict, the other half with his hair barely trimmed.

Moyshe's medical treatments were similar. When he was called to attend to a patient he would take their pulse and begin asking questions:

—If you cover yourself with bedclothes do you feel hot?
—Yes.
—If you take off the covers, are you cold?
—Yes
—If you look down from a mountaintop do you feel dizzy?
—Yes.
—Well, that settles it. We have to do cupping or apply leeches and you'll feel better.

Despite this, people loved him like one of their family. He came when he was needed and he didn't quibble about payment. They didn't like going to big doctors, like Lutshkoski or Genrekh, a Jew who had converted and who gave himself airs. Genrekh believed in the immortality of the Jewish people, citing as proof that Jews can eat *cholent* [Sabbath stew], which remains in the gut from Sabbath to Wednesday, and still survive; therefore, they must be immortal.

Chelm also had a large synagogue and a *besmedresh*. They said that in the attic of the synagogue a golem lay among the discarded religious books. Since no one could come near him, it wasn't possible to renovate the synagogue. The cantor was a fine, quiet man well–versed in music. One of his former choir members is today the well–known New York cantor Yankev Brayfman.

Opposite the *shul* was a small market place, with butcher shops and stalls selling fish, baked goods, pumpkin seeds and hot chick peas and beans. In an alley lived Yoysef Itshe Hindes the bookseller. In addition of sacred books he also had story books like Tsentre, Ventre, Eli Royber with Six Fingers, the Pretty Bird and the wonderful stories of G. Achim.

In time the readers of the story books grew up to become subscribers to Dubkovski's private library which had books from both Yiddish and other literatures. Dubkovski also had a newspaper kiosk in the very heart of Lubliner Street. Not far was the *magistrat* [town hall], a church, and the Saxon Gardens where young people strolled in the evenings, fearful of being attacked by Christians.

So Chelm lived, with its *gymnazie* [academic high school], teachers' seminary, yeshives, Talmud Torah, weekly fairs, and with its police, including the policeman they called "*Spudnitse*" [skirt] because he had such a fat belly, he looked like he was wearing a skirt. People were as used to them as they were to Meshugene [crazy] Berele who went crazy in the summer heat and set off into the street with his long blonde beard and black caftan, complaining to God and the world in three languages – Polish, Yiddish and Hebrew.

And Crazy Suzhe was of course also a citizen of Chelm. He was a giant of a man, lived in hunger, went barefoot in winter. In the middle of the night he would stop and roar, say something and then burst out laughing. Sometimes he would speak in such a way that it seemed he had come to his senses, but then something would get tangled in his head and forced him to become crazy again.

When Chelm was about to become a *gubernie* [province] the First World War broke out. A year later, Germany and Austria occupied Chelm. After that, there appeared political parties, bourgeois and proletarian. Shmuel Ziegelboym took his first political steps there. There came workers' housing, libraries, drama clubs, our own weekly newspaper. Hunger raged. Cholera and influenza took entire families. The *linea hatsedek* [aid to the sick poor] organized young Jews who risked their own lives to care for the sick in poor homes, feeding their parched mouths.

When Poland was liberated, Jews took a prominent role. But soon they were obliged to organize against Polish pogromtshiks. The youth of Chelm even assaulted a group of Halle–ites. [followers of General Halle, prominent anti–Semite.]

Translator's footnote:

1. "Fonye" is a diminutive of Ivan and was a derogatory term used by Jews to refer to the tsar or Russian rule in general. "Fonye Ganev [Thief]" enhances the insult.

[Pages 493-494]

Light and Shadow

by Reyzl Tseber, Australia

Translated by Miriam Leberstein

Who can forget grand Lubliner Street, which ran from the Ravitser Forest, through the suburb of Pulitshanke to Hrubieshower forest. Lubliner Street and surrounding streets teemed with Jew and Jewish life. That is where the exchange was situated, and the famous "ring" of 70 Jewish owned shops which extended to the small market place next to the Jewish butcher shops. From there ran streets that were exclusively Jewish.

In Spring 1927, there were rumors that the Radomer Train station would be transferred to Chelm. In order to achieve this, the *starostve* [local government] donated the land adjacent to the *starostve* and to the Hrubieshower Forest as a site for the necessary administrative buildings and for connecting the streets of the railroad administration with the train station. The people of Chelm hoped that the transfer of the station to Chelm would bring thousands of new residents, businesses and employment that would improve the town's economic situation, and that of the Jews.

In the summer of 1927, construction businesses, engineers and architects arrived and work soon began on a large scale. Thanks to the construction many Jewish workers and businesses did well. Economic conditions improved. The Jewish merchant bank, a division of the Joint Distribution Committee, experienced strong growth in membership. At the same time a small business bank was founded.

Jewish organizations in Chelm were very active. Jewish cultural life developed greatly. Two Yiddish newpapers — Chelemer Shtime [Voice] and Chelemer Vokhnblat [Weekly] appeared regularly. Three Jewish libraries enriched our supply of books and the best Jewish theater troupes and lecturers visited Chelm.

Jewish youth studied in the Jewish and state–run high schools, like the Tarbut *gymnazie*, business school, Jewish–Polish *gymnazie*, teachers' seminary and others. People traveled to study in the universities of Warsaw, Lemberg, etc.

In the course of the several years that the administration building was constructed the town expanded into the new neighborhood.

Reyzl Tseber, nee Rikhtshrayber

The Town Council of Radom opposed the transfer of the administration to Chelm and got the Polish Sium [legislature] to intervene. As a result the Kontrol Koleyova [?] was transferred from Bidgashtsh and moved into the new building. The officials were real Nazis. They settled into the lovely, comfortable building. Along with them came Christian merchants who settled into the heart of the Jewish town center and caused enormous harm to the Jewish merchants.

The material conditions for the Jews got worse and worse. The tax burden became intolerable. The new tax official who was appointed to Chelm levied huge taxes on the Jews. Many Jewish businesses had to close, especially shopkeepers and tradesmen. This also badly affected the Jewish bank. In 1935 the merchant bank failed, the crisis in town worsened and many young people left for Warsaw and other places to seek work.

1939 was the most difficult year under the Polish Fascist regime. A few years before the terrible war there were burdensome government edicts aimed at Jews and the Jews in Chelm felt it the strongest. At the time there was the "urbanitske linie," a so–called beautification project. The Chelm Town council also undertook beautification efforts, and their first undertaking was to get rid of all the poor Jewish houses. The renowned "ring" of businesses, consisting of 70 Jewish shops which was the source of livelihood for hundreds of Jews fell victim to the "urbanitzatsie".

The order to demolish the ring evoked an oppressive feeling among the Jewish population. They tried to have the edict retracted; delegates visited the town authorities, appealed to the council, to the president and others. But they were unsuccessful.

While efforts to persuade the authorities were still underway, the town council ordered the fire department to tear off the roofs of the Jewish shops and to destroy the ring. As moral compensation the council voted to give every Jewish merchant a symbolic zloty. This was a painful insult and a great humiliation.

[Pages 495-496]

A Day in Chelm
(A chapter from memoirs of the First World War)

by Eliezer Shindler[1]

Translated by Miriam Leberstein

On Tisha b'Av, 5675 (1915), during the first year of World War I, I was wounded and fell into the hands of Fonye [the Russians].

Tsar Nicholas's armies were at that time experiencing defeat after defeat and they took out their anger on the prisoners of war. The sick and wounded among us were in a terrible situation. Our new caretakers didn't even think of providing medical treatment, cleaning infected wounds, or changing dirty bandages.

They encouraged us with Russian curses and beat us with Cossack whips. A group of us wounded prisoners dragged ourselves under Cossack guard over the sandy Polish paths like living corpses, until we got to Chelm. There we were driven into the garden of a church, with guards posted at the gates with whips and guns.

Spotting a well, I dragged myself over to get some water to clean my pus–filled wound and wash my dirty bandages. Suddenly, a priest appeared in his clerical garb, a pock–marked swine with a fat red neck and a belly like a German beer barrel. He began shouting at me angrily for dirtying the trough that stood near the well; because I had washed my wound and bandages there, his cows would not want to drink from the trough.

I looked at this servant of God and said: "When I saw you, I thought that you were a student of Jesus of Nazareth, come to bring help and consolation to the sick, wounded and homeless. But from what you just said, I see that you belong to those about whom our prophet Jesus said – "They kiss the calves, but they slaughter the people.' Instead of cleaning our wounds you think about your calves."

The fat Polish priest had not expected such a response and quickly left. Sitting near the pump in great suffering, afflicted by pain and hunger, without any idea of where to turn for help, I saw at one of the iron gates a Jew dressed in traditional Polish Jewish clothing. He was speaking to the Cossack guard, asking him for something, and put a gift in his hand. I thought to myself, the Jew is looking to do business; probably wants to buy or sell something to the priest, and is asking the Cossack to let him into the courtyard.

As soon as the Jew got inside, he ran over to me with his pack. He greeted me with a "sholem aleichem," and stretched out a brotherly hand. "I saw you among the prisoners, and recognized you as a Jew, so I'm bringing you a bit of food, a fresh shirt and a little cash. Your journey is just beginning. Who knows how many miles you will have to go until you get to a camp. Take my modest gift and forgive me for not being able to give more. We Polish Jews are in great poverty and trouble. On one side, we face the enmity of the Russians, on the other, the Poles. The town is filled with refugees, there is famine, the poverty is terrible but we mustn't forget you prisoners. All Jews are responsible for each other."

I forgot about my hunger and pain and marveled at the Jew who had come to help a brother. He had put his life at risk by approaching a prisoner, since the Russians thought every Jew was a spy and thousands of innocent Jews had been accused of espionage and shot.

The priest, the Goerings and the Goebbels, the killers of men, loved dogs and worshipped calves, loved animals and slaughtered six million Jews, men, women and children, including the Jews of Chelm.

We whisper, remember these pure and holy souls.

From right: Dr. Dovid Valberger, Mordkhe Ivre and Shmuel Guterman, in Polish uniform in 1920

Editor's note in the original:

1. Eliezer Shindler, well–known Yiddish poet and writer was in the Austrian army in World War I and was a prisoner of war captured by the Russians, who took him to Chelm.

[Pages 497-500]

Mayn Shvester Perl

by Yankev Tsvi Shargel, Petach–Tikvah

Translated by Miriam Leberstein

In a village between Chelm and Lublin
(the ground that the Germans profaned)
amid forests and fields of green
there lives Perl, my sister.

Her visage is dark and charming,
but her hair too early turned gray,
alone as a stone in the village
she yearns for a far–off place

She's a simple and quiet woman,
mother to eight little ones.
Her heart is filled with prayer.
She gives help and counsel to all.

On frosty nights by the oven
she sits and spins her tales.

Perl can cure anything
with the power of her love and faith.

She can repel the evil eye,
apply leeches, *bankes*[1], compresses,
but her children have little to eat
though her home abounds in goodness.

Though her village neighbors are wealthy
her house is small and low
and in the night she lies weeping
and she is skin and bone.

Her little girls are growing up;
the youngest now wears a braid.
Their mother's skin is wrinkled,
her cheeks like shriveled apples.

She's well acquainted with bad luck;
she knows what fate holds in store.
Perl sends her girls to work as maids.
With head bowed, she still has hope.

Perl knows the forest and the dirt road
and her neighbors, the arrogant Germans.[2]
She hears their fearsome singing at night
and their horses' cries when they're beaten.

***

Her husband Ruven is a redhead,
with thickly grown eyebrows and beard.
Though the village pains him, like an illness,
he still loves it and holds it dear.

With long and heavy steps
Ruven hurries on his way,
a coarse, unmannered village Jew
content with all that surrounds him.

He doesn't ask any questions,
not "why" or "how" or "what for?"
The village admires his good nature
as it does the fields, grain and straw.

He travels to fairs with the Christians.
In his pack lie faith and belief.
He comes to life when he meets fellow Jews
who sweep through the fair like doves.

He came to the village with Perl
with love for her and the land.
Their fate is enmeshed with the village,
with a life from which Jews are banned:

with trees laden with pears and apples,
with cows and calves in their stalls,

with the land and all of its perils,
with fields and clean water in wells,

with grass at the windows and thresholds
with the wind and the chill of the field,
ready to do what others tell him,
to open the door to all.

But rarely does anyone visit;
the Germans don't like to mix.
It's only when one of them sickens
that they come to seek help from my sister.

" Ruven, dear," they say, "darling,
the wagon awaits at your door."
And they tell their son Mundzye [dim. of Mundlayn]
he mustn't hit Perl's children anymore.

But Mundlayn likes to hit people
and he gnashes his teeth in rage,
and one terrible dawn in September
he shoots and hits his mark.

The highway runs past the house
and leads to roads that stretch far away.
Perl closes the shutters
she knows that a storm's on the way.

* * *

Like horses all in a lather
in a frenzy of looting and lust
the brazen German colonists
churn the road to dust.

From towns and villages all over
they come to load their wagons with loot.
Pious Christian women make the sign of the cross
as Jewish blood flows.

Rings, still attached to fingers,
earrings, along with ears,
the bells on their horses still ringing,
the gates of the colonists crash.

Pillows bloodied in slaughter
still wet with children's tears.
With beastly eyes ablaze
the murder–train draws near.

The older children run away
to their savior, the Red Army
At my sister's house, no one slept.
Woe to the mother and father.

Terror entered their cottage,
stole the smiles from the children.

The father crawls away to hide.
The mother takes leave of her senses.

Why did she lock all the doors?
Why did she shut us up in the room?
Who will take us to the field?
Why is father trembling with fever?

The robbers brandish their swords,
the air is filled with lamentation.
But Perl, with wondrous enchantment,
waits for God's deliverance.

It will come, that great moment.
How can the world go so mad?
My sister believes in miracles,
believes she can escape fate.

And her neighbor, the murderer Mundlayn,
rages with poison and gun.
The wind carries the cries of my sister, the midwife
who delivered the village's children.

In a village between Chelm and Lublin
(the ground that the Germans profaned)
amid forests and fields of green
there lives Perl, my sister.

II

In the village Bekeshe the snow is falling.
My Perl stands watch on the porch.
She stifles her screams.
The highway leads from here to Maidenek.

The little ones are hungry and weak;
how can they make the journey there?
She stands and watches them as they sleep
on the road between Chelm and Lublin.

The vines are dry and thin;
they can't hide the light from the porch.
My sister tells her grievances to God,
gathers her troubles in a pack.

The tree in the orchard
stretches out a limb, like a hand.
The rope on the crank to the well
calls her to the other side.

The empty, gutted barn
is like a toothless mouth
that whispers to her Sabbath shawl
as her eyes fill with tears.

"We lived so many years with our neighbors,"
my Perl complains to God.

"This village, with all its charms,
has mocked and degraded your daughter."

We had just dug up the turf
and scattered straw around the walls,
though the village laughed and mocked us
and shook their fists.

We gathered aprons–full of sorrel.
The nights are so long.
The children got fish from the pond.
Outside it was stormy and dark

We went to say *slikhes*[3] at midnight
to serve you with honor and awe.
Now they've killed the Jews who lived here.
Who will now dance with the Torah?

They snatched Ruven from his bed
and threw the dying man on a wagon.
Who will now come to the *minyen*?
Who will now pray to you.

It states clearly in the holy books
That it's not the dead who will praise you, my lord.
What use to you the countless graves,
the biers of horror and sorrow?

Her orchard whispers in terror
in a foreign, hostile tongue,
and the frogs are strangely splashing
near the well on this autumn night.

The stars go out over the village.
The porch is flooded with mourning.
My sister wipes away her tears
with her black Sabbath scarf.

In the village the night is ending.
My sister and the children on the porch.
Bekeshe has finished its slaughter.
The highway leads there, to Maidenek

The village awakens to snow.
The Germans laugh on the porch.
My sister and her children are on their way
to join the Jews in Maidenek.

Translator's Footnotes:

    1. *Bankes* are vessels used in cupping, a traditional remedy.
    2. The Germans referred to here are colonists of Austrian–German origin who settled in Chelm and surrounding villages, dating from the time Chelm was under Austrian rule (1795–1807). During the German occupation in World War II many aided the German forces. This poem describes the experience of living as a Jew in a village among German colonist neighbors before and during the occupation.
    3. Slikhes — prayers for forgiveness recited in the period leading up to and during the High Holy Days.

[Page 505]

Destruction of Chelm

The Slaughter of the Jews in Chelm

by Lazar Kahan, America

Translated by Gloria Berkenstat Freund

This was written as soon as the news of the death march reached America.

A slaughter of Jews took place in Chelm on the first day of the month of December [1939]. The Hitlerists shot hundreds of Chelm Jews! At the beginning, nebulous rumors circulated about the gruesome death; it was difficult to find out the truth about this violence. Of course, we were unable to learn any facts. Chelm, of course, lies far from here. The city was also severed from the Soviet realm, so that Jewish refugees seldom emerged through there. And if a Jew from that area did sometimes escape from that *gehenem* [hell], he remained in a small *shtetl* in Wolyn or in Galicia and the world did not know what happened there.

In the beginning of January 1940, we first received conclusive information about the ruthless slaughter of the Chelm Jews. Several young *halutzim* [agricultural pioneers, whose goal was to settle in *Eretz-Yisroel*] from Chelm arrived who had actually left there before the slaughter of the Jews had been carried out there. However, they received the news from there from several Chelm Jews who were saved from the slaughter. In addition to this, a woman also came, who had been in Chelm until the middle of December and herself had been present for all of the horrible events in Chelm.

On the basis of this information and particularly on the basis of what was said by an eye witness to everything that occurred in Chelm, I now have the opportunity to tell the world all of the frightening details of the slaughter of the Jews in Chelm.

The slaughter of the Jews was carried out on the first day of the month of December, as said. However, the Germans had occupied Chelm at the beginning of October. In the course of two months, the Nazi youth in Chelm did not have idle hands. Earlier, they did "something" to the local Jews before their savage death.

Let us first acquaint ourselves with the persecution that the Hitlerists imposed on the Jews in the first two months. We will not stop at any "trivialities" – on grabbing Jews for work, on arresting Jews and torturing them, which, for example, happened to Dr. Zajfen, a popular Jewish community worker in Chelm. He was arrested because he was said to have declared that a Hitlerist newspaper was a rag… He was tortured terribly in jail and it is said that he no longer is alive…

These were all "trifles." And here we will jot down several events that were characteristic of the Hitleristic administrators in Chelm. Similar persecutions also took place in other cities in the German area of occupation. However, Chelm was a bit of an exception in the forms and manner of torture.

[Page 506]

The first fear was tossed down onto the Chelm Jews by an announcement that was posted on the Chelm streets on the 7th of October. A fat line, "We warn the Jews," published in German and Polish, drew attention. These words were published with bright white letters both in German and in Polish. With smaller letters it was announced that whereas the Jews were spreading rumors that the Russian army would ostensibly return to Chelm, the German commanding officer disclosed that all of the rumors were false and the Jews were warned not to spread such lies…

A thick, dark cloud in the sky was cast over the Chelm Jews. They felt that now would begin a series of decrees and persecution against them and so it was. A few days later the Germans began to grab Jews for work, both men and women. A series of wanton plundering began. The Germans also were occupied with "Europeanizing" the Jews, that is, with cutting and pulling beards.

An eye witness in Chelm told me the following particulars of how this Hitlerist "work" appeared in Chelm: By chance, I was then at a dentist at the market. Suddenly we heard a tumult. We ran to the window and we saw such a picture of arbitrariness and moral as well as physical torture. A horde of Polish boys and girls as well as older Poles stood at the market and German soldiers and officers arranged a "spectacle" for themselves and for the Poles.

Jews were caught at first to clean and to polish the German autos that stood at the market. Poles also helped to catch the Jews or pointed: "*Jude*"… Then the Germans, again with the help of the Poles, grabbed Jews, mostly with beards, and forced them to push motorcycles and autos… If a Jew did not carry out this work in the way the German wanted, he would leap from the motorcycle, beat the Jew and step on him with his feet… They plucked out the beards of many Jews… The Nazi brutes even tore out a beard along with the flesh of one Jew…

Here, by chance, the rabbi of Chelm passed. He was a young man, tall, good looking, had graduated as a Doctor of Philosophy from a Viennese university and received rabbinical ordination from his now deceased father-in-law, the previous Chelm rabbi. The Hitlerists had a weakness for tormenting good looking Jews and for torturing rabbis. The Germans found both things in the Chelm rabbi… a rabbi and a good looking one… It was no surprise that they so vilely tortured him.

First of all, the barbarians shaved off the rabbi's beard. The mob of Poles, who stood around, were delighted with pleasure… Then the rabbi was asked to push an auto; when he did not carry out this "work" well – they beat him… Later, the Hitleristic inquisitors forced the rabbi to clean out the horse manure from the market…

[Page 507]

And he had to do this dirty work with his hands and clean it out so that there would be no sign [of dirt] left over… To great laughter from the mob, the sadists forced the rabbi to pack the horse manure in his hat and to immediately put on his cap…

This shameful spectacle, which was carried out at the market opposite the City Hall, made a shocking impression on the Jews in Chelm. The representatives of the *kehile* [organized Jewish community] ran to the German commanding officer to intervene, but it was of no help. Meanwhile, the "performance" continued.

When the Germans released the rabbi after the shameful torturing they caught Jews with beards, they cut and tore out beards and even set fire to the beards of several Jews. Then they dragged Jews with burning beards to the fence and poured water on them without end… The Jews were drenched and, as it was cold, they caught colds from this "shower" and became sick…

It is easy to picture how the Chelm Jews felt after such a "spectacle" at the market… A few weeks passed calmly – an uncommon event. Then, atrocities again occurred.

This was in the beginning of November. A flying brigade from the Hitlerist assault troops with the insignia of the black *totenkopf* [death head] entered Chelm. In one day this punishment expedition carried out a pogrom against the Chelm Jews and administered severe torture.

The flying brigade was divided into groups; each group had a list of a score of rich Jewish men and rich businessmen whom the Storm Troopers had to "visit." They announced their "visits" through soldiers. They set aside a separate hour for each rich Jew. And ordered all of the residents of a house to be in the home at the appointed hour – if not it would be bitter…

The task of the Storm Trooper flying brigade was: rob the money, gold, silver and the objects of value from all of the Jews in one day. And this happened after the *kehile* had already paid contributions twice: once 140,000 *zl.* and the second time – 180,000 *zlotes*…

However, the Nazi Youth had information from their local *Volks-Deutschen* [ethnic Germans living in Poland] and from Polish "informers" that more money was still with the Jews in Chelm – the *S.S.* had to rob it. They went from house to house and robbed money and other expensive objects from the Jews.

As soon as they entered a Jewish house they tore off the rings from the fingers and took the watches and other things of value. Then they began to make audits. Everyone had to get completely undressed – even the women and small children.

When Jewish women did not want to undress naked, the *S.S.* bandits cynically said:

[Page 508]

– "We do not need your body… You have nothing to be ashamed of… we are only looking for money and jewelry…"

If they found large sums of money, more or less appropriate to the information they had about each, they took it and left. If they received less than the Jew should have possessed according to their information – they began to torture and beat all of the residents of the house.

Their tactics were then thus: For example, they took the man in one room, the woman in a second room and the children in separate rooms. In another way, in each room they beat, tortured, threatened with shooting. Jews were thus beaten and wounded during these executions so that they lay sick in bed for many days after…

The murderers tortured one weak Jew extraordinarily ruthlessly. His wife could not bear her husband's moans and screams. She jumped to the balcony in order to throw herself from it and commit suicide. The brutes caught her by the clothing, pulled her back into the room and began to cruelly beat her and trample her with their feet, why did she want to take her own life…

In the morning, the Storm Troopers left and after the pogrom, it was again quiet for a few weeks.

Then the following ruthless slaughter of the Jews took place:

On the 30th of November, the German command gave orders to the *kehile* managing committee that on the 1st of December in the morning, all of the Jews 15 to 60 must appear at the market. No one knew what this would signify. The *kehile* managing committee immediately informed all of the Jews about this order. This order evoked an understandable unease and panic among the Jews. The rich and the more secure Jews immediately decided to escape. A few hundred Jews left for the surrounding *shtetlekh* and villages in order to hear from afar what the Germans had done with the Jews at the market. Hundreds of Jews hid with Christian acquaintances, or hid in closed up cellars, in stalls and did not appear at the market on the 1st of December.

However an enormous group did appear. The number that was found at the market was estimated at 18,000. This was at 9 o'clock in the morning. The hundreds of Jews at the market had to stand in rows. The Jews at the market did not know what awaited them. The Hitlerists had spread rumors that the Jews would be exchanged for Germans in the Soviet realm and that those assembled would be sent to the Soviet Union. Many Jews were satisfied with this, that they would be finished with all of the Hitlerist edicts. Not all of the Jews at the market were desperate.

When the Jews were already assembled and standing in rows, a German officer arrived and gave a speech – a speech full of defamations and curses on Jews.

[Page 509]

Then an entire horde of Gestapo agents arrived on bicycles. They checked all of the assembled Jews and took all the money that people had with them from everyone, as well as their passports and documents. During the pause, several Jewish doctors who also had appeared at the market turned to the officers [and said] that they had to go to the hospital to the sick and asked to be let out. They were freed. The officers also let out a score of Jewish craftsmen who showed notes that they worked for the Germans…

However, the great mass of Jews remained at the market where they were held until 12:30 in the afternoon. When the Germans had bullied the Jews enough, searched and robbed them, they ordered the gathered Jews to sing Jewish melodies… But not one Jew opened his mouth to sing… The Gestapo agents were angry and began to beat the Jews so that they would sing… The Jews sang…

They sang "cheerful" melodies, mainly *Rebeka*, which the Gestapo agents had demanded… But this was not a cheerful song. This singing was soaked through with blood and tears.

At around 12:30 in the afternoon the gathered Jews were told to stand in rows of four people and to begin marching out of the city. The Jews were taken through the main streets to the road that went to Hrubieszow, 50 kilometers from Chelm. They were not led quickly in the city. As soon as they reached the highway, the Gestapo agents on the bicycles began to ride quickly and forced the mass of Jews to run after the Germans on the bicycles.

The Jews were accompanied by 60 armed Gestapo agents. If a Jew lagged a bit behind the group, he received blows. A few hundred Jewish women ran behind the group. They wanted to know what would happen to their husbands and children. The Gestapo agents forced the women who staggered from behind back to the city. However, many women hid on the side roads and followed for a score of kilometers after the Jews being dragged away. These women, who returned to the city in the evening, brought appalling news about the "march" of the mass of Jews…

They said that they heard shooting several times, that they themselves saw a few score corpses in graves even in the middle of the road…

There was a tumult in the city. What could be done besides crying and shouting? On *Shabbos* many women went away in small wagons to look for their husbands among the corpses. But they learned from the peasants that the Germans had immediately buried those shot – 50 men to a grave… The women only saw blood stains on the road… Jewish wounded were found in several villages. They had been taken away to surrounding *shtetlekh* and many of them were saved.

[Page 510]

Sunday in the morning, a peasant brought a letter from the 16-year-old, Mietek Welczer to his grandfather stating that he was still alive and was with the peasant. The peasant was immediately asked to bring the grandson, changed into the clothes of a gentile boy, back to Chelm. The peasant was well paid and on Monday he brought the young boy. Mietek, the young boy, was the first one who described the facts about the murderous slaughter of the Jews for the Chelm women and old men. The following is what he described:

"My father, Hersh Welczer, a rich Jewish manufacturing merchant, and I found ourselves in the middle of the large marching group. As soon as we arrived beyond the city, the Gestapo agents began to chase the Jews. Not everyone had the stamina to go through the march. If a Jew just stopped and remained behind the group, he was shot without hesitation.

"When we found ourselves 10-12 kilometers from Chelm, the Gestapo agents stopped the group, chose 20 of the youngest and best looking Jews in the group and the group was again chased. The 20 chosen Jews were taken away by several agents into a woods. We then heard several shots… Then nothing… We were not permitted to turn around. We were threatened with shooting… Later, we only saw that the Gestapo agents returned without the 20 Jews… We understood what had happened to them…

"In around half an hour, the Germans again stopped the march, again chose the 20 best looking Jews and also led them to a woods. This time we only heard screaming and not shooting…

"When we went 30 kilometers and found ourselves not far from Bialopole, my father became so tired out that he whispered to me: he would remain behind the group and I would go further… I understood what this meant and said to my father that I would die with him… We were then located at the end of the group.

"Suddenly things became bad for my father. He remained behind. I also stopped and led my tired father to the side. A Gestapo officer came galloping and began to beat my father. Everything became clear to me – I delivered a push to the officer and he fell down… However, the officer immediately stood up and gave me a terrible push, so that I fell into a grave… He shot several time at my father. I lost consciousness.

"However, I heard two bullets fly by my head… As in a dream, I saw that the grave was being lit with reflectors… I recovered in a few minutes. I saw that the group was far away. Apparently, the Germans thought I was dead. Several corpses lay around me. I began to search for my father and found him severely wounded. I wanted to save him.

[Page 511]

"By chance, an auto went by in which sat several Poles. I asked them for a little benzene to wash around my father's wounds. However, they did not give any benzene. I saw cottages in the distance; I ran to ask for a little water. But the peasants were afraid to give me a little water… Finally, one peasant gave me water and he himself went to help me save my father. The peasant and I carried my dying father to a Jewish villager. They tried to save my father, but the agony of death did not last long; he died… I remained with the peasant and, later, sent a note with him to the Jews…"

This is the terrible account of a 16-year old young boy who was saved from Nazi bullets by a miracle. And what happened to the crowd of Jews? The others who were saved said: More than half were shot by the Germans and murdered on the road. Many were wounded and escaped to the surrounding villages. A sum total of 300 living Chelemer Jews arrived in Hrubieszow… There they were held in a stall for 24 hours without food and without anything to drink. Then the Germans in Hrubieszow also organized a bloody game at the market, took the 300 Chelemer Jews and a few hundred Jews from Hrubieszow and dragged them together to the Bug. At the bank of the river, the Germans stopped the dragged Jews and forced them to go over to the Soviets. However, the Red Army did not permit the Jews to cross. Scores of Jews threw themselves in the Bug. The swimmers somehow went over to the Soviet side and were not stopped by anyone. The Jews who could not swim were drowned in the Bug… A few hundred Jews, who remained on the bank, were then taken away by the Germans to somewhere in a concentration camp…

[Page 512]

In addition to the already mentioned Hersh Welczer (his widow and his orphans later escaped from Chelm to Wolyn), the following popular Chelm Jews were shot during the slaughter: Dr. Oks, the photographer, Rozenblat, the three Lewensztajn brothers – rich iron merchants, Gamulke, a former lieutenant in the Polish military and Itshe Sznicer, owner of the perfumery, Sklad… Their dead bodies were then handed over by the peasants who knew them to their orphaned families. The other Jews who were shot were, as has been already said, buried in mass graves of 50 men in a grave…

Lipe Goldman, may he rest in peace, .
Perished in Chelm from the Hitler tragedy

Reb Matye Finker, of blessed memory
(brother of Chene Zigelboim), whom the
Hitler murderers annihilated

Chene and Chana, the daughters of the shoykhet
[ritual slaughterer], Reb Pinye Szajdwaser, may the
memory of a righteous person be blessed, who were
annihilated by the Hitler murderers

Tzipe Gewant with her children all perished in the gas ovens of Sobibor

Betzalel Goldman, of blessed memory

[page 513]

The Death March – Chelm-Hrubieshow-Sokal

by Ben-Tzion Bruker, Israel

Translated by Gloria Berkenstat Freund

My hands tremble writing and my heart hurts from all that has been told of the destruction of Chelm. Nightmares, specters and pictures of the annihilation of my blood and flesh appear, of people who are close with whom I was brought up and lived… Every language is too poor and pale to describe the death of the martyrs and will be too mild to express the brutal stories of the murders. The survivors, Shlomo Atlas and Ahron Josef Wajnsztok, suffered through the Chelm-Hrubieshow-Sokal death march.

I heard how their voices trembled as they spoke… They could not forget each horrible day of slaughter that took place only a few years ago…We Chelemer Jews also must not forget…

I write the savage facts told with bloody words. All of our brothers and sisters, who are spread across the world, need to tell their children and their children's children these recorded stories, so that they will be engraved in their memories for eternity. The Chelm-Hrubieshow-Sokal death march, which was a depraved chapter of martyrdom, was the vicious start of the destruction of Chelm.

Ben-Tzion Bruker

* * *

Shlomo Atlas and Ahron Josef Wajnsztok told me the following horrible details of the death march:

"The autumn of 1939 was uncommonly beautiful and did not permit the entrance of winter. It was usually dreary and cloudy but, in 1939, it was sunny and bright. Everyone wanted the weather to be the way it was in their hearts because the heart of each Chelemer Jew was then in pain. Death lay in wait from everywhere. Screaming was heard from the tormented Jews and clouds were wanted; that the world should storm… But no! Despite the fact that it was the 1st of December, 1939 – no autumn rain jarred the window panes of the Chelemer Jewish houses. But the "hostages" knocked on the doors and said to be at "Okrąglak" at 8 o'clock in the morning…

[Page 514]

The "Okrąglak" (Rinek [marketplace]) is a round place where the center of Chelemer commerce was located. There were always merchants, customers, brokers, assessors and ordinary Jews who told of "news" and heard "news." In 1939, just before the World War, the Polish government – from Koc and Pristarowa[1] - worried little that Hitler was sticking out his paw towards Poland, but worried a great deal that a bunch of Chelemer Jews could have their poor livelihood and under the subterfuge of beautifying Chelm, tried to destroy economically the Jewish merchants; one of their methods was: liquidate the "Okrąglak." All of the Jewish protests and pleas did not help. The *Owshem*[2] Premier, Skladkowski, with one stroke of the pen ordered that the shopkeepers on the "Okrąglak" be thrown out and in their place a park would be created. However, the Polish government was not successful in placing a park in this place. Therefore, the Hitler devils had an empty spot for the Chelemer Jews.

No one wished to go to the "gathering." They went to neighbors and sought advice: why would they be calling the men – from 15 to 60 years old? One said that it probably was because of the yellow patches, a second interpreted it as a new contribution [money demanded from the Jews]. They consoled themselves with smelling salts, but for several, their hearts beat fiercely. They had premonitions of the maliciousness. Some stubbornly decided not to go, considered where to hide, run to the other side. But a number went to " Okrąglak" out of "curiosity."

At 8:30 in the morning, several score of Jews were assembled at the " Okrąglak." The arriving Jews consoled themselves: Well, lost, we will see what will be; what happens to all of the Jews will also happen to us. And thus the Jews gathered and the number gathering grew minute by minute.

At eleven o'clock in the morning a group of about 2,000 Jews was already assembled and immediately realized that they were in a dark vise. A thick cordon of armed *S.S.* men surrounded them on all sides and the tragic spectacle began.

A band of *S.S.* men were let out on a rampage against the Jews. With sadistic pleasure they "enjoyed themselves" with the Jews with beards. The doctors were immediately murderously beaten: Walberger and Oks. The red crosses on their arms were spat upon. The screaming and crying from those beaten reached to the very heavens and they were joined by the crying and laments of the wives and children who watched from the balconies and windows. Each thrust from the wives and children who tried to snatch their unfortunate fathers, husbands and brothers was pushed back by the blue-eyed beasts. There was crying and shouting: men, women and children.

[Page 515]

But no one heard their shouts. The *S.S.* men and the Poles watching with hate responded to the shouts of the Jews with cynical laughter. This was not only a *gehenim* [hell] because this word is too poor to explain, too modest to record the dramatic scenes which took place then.

The violence and the beating stopped the moment when an *oberleutnant* [senior lieutenant, a commissioned officer], whose strange face was deeply engraved in our memories, appeared. The *oberleutnant* ordered: "Everything you have with you should be freely given up! If not when we – on the road – find somebody with something, we will shoot 20 Jews as punishment."

Entire sacks of Jewish possessions were gathered by the *S.S.* beasts. It was decreed that everyone stand in rows of six people, take off their hats and sing. Meanwhile, the *S.S.* men surrounded everyone. The bangs of their rubber clubs, their wild animal screams resounded and at 12 o'clock, the 1st of December, 1939, the great, great grandchildren of the "mourners of Zion" with bare heads were forced to sing *"Deutschland, Deustchland über alles"* ["Germany above all"]. They left the city Chelm where they were born and lived so many years. All of those who had just set foot on the "Okraglak" were taken out of the city. With them went many Jews whom the cannibals caught in the streets and found in their homes. The procession was accompanied by wives and children who were brutally repelled.

The *S.S.* bandits, who rode horses and went on bicycles, constantly chased the Jews. We were not allowed to go slowly. They followed in autos with ammunition. They were also accompanied by heavy machine guns. We saw that those who stopped were lined up to be the first victims. And right outside the city, the first victim fell. This was Menasha the headstone engraver's son (Mandelbaum). He, alas, was lame and could not keep up, so his fate was immediately sealed.

But those not lame and other invalids stopped. It was impossible for everyone to endure the pursuit by the *S.S.* animals. Therefore, many "stopped" and in fact the bullets from the pistols were heard. With each shot a Jewish victim fell and remained lying on the road. The road was covered with the dead… Birds of prey went to help – the Polish and Ukrainian peasants – and began to rummage in the still bloodied pockets, removing the last remaining things from them and then they took off the clothing and carried home *dos groyse gevins* [the jackpot]. The peasants came from every village and watched the bloody show with pleasure. But from one village, the peasants came with bread and wanted to give it to the barely living Jews, but the brown beasts repelled them.

[Page 516]

Josef Wajnsztok related: " A peasant woman wanted to give me a piece of bread, but she could not give it to me and she did not want to throw it in the mud. But I told her to throw it in the mud. When I received the muddy piece of bread, I shared it with Lipe Herc's son. The muddy piece of bread was like bread and butter or marmalade for we hungry ones then."

"When the death procession was 13 kilometers from Chelm – at the Poplawicz Forest – the *oberleutnant* ordered that they stop, declaring that the Jews had tried to escape and as a punishment he would shoot 25 Jews. Said and done. The *totenkopf*[3] heroes chose 25 Jews, among them the Rozenblat brothers (owners of the photo-business, Sztuka), Zajdenfeld the tailor and my sister's son. The Jews were driven five meters deep into the forest and immediately shooting was heard. Twenty-five martyrs fell then with *Shema Yisroel*[4] on their lips…"

"The six *S.S.* men returned from this 'work' calmly, with a casual smile, and the 'death march moved again. We actually ran because knowing that stopping in the line meant death,' everyone tried to run, to push themselves ahead. One ran after the other; the road was narrow and everyone could not go on it. Therefore, many ran in the ditches and every Jew who fell in a ditch was shot. And thus the ditches became full of corpses…

An episode occurred: The tailor, Berl Guterman, bound his white beard with a piece of cloth.

Living witnesses of the death march
From the right: Ahron Josef Wajnsztok and Shlomo Atlas, who survived and are now in Israel

[Page 517]

The old Jew could not go farther, so he sat and cried… An animal, who was born from a human stomach, ordered him to stand up. The old Jew asked for permission to rest a little, but a bullet was the answer to his request and a red stripe of blood flowed over the white beard.

"The elder of the purse making guild, the *parnes* [elected member of the organized Jewish community] Herszberg, also fell. His wide coat spread out and the bullet only made a hole in the coat. But Herszberg fell unconscious from fear. The *S.S.* member thought that he had shot him. Herszberg remained lying there, then he escaped to the Russian border and crossed it in peace.

"We ran with our last strength… We threw off our coats and jackets. Our feet became covered with *pokhires* (blisters); we took off our shoes… The wounds opened and blood colored the black muddy road. Large puddles of blood gave witness that an unfortunate one of the 'death march' had passed. I, Wajnsztok, had trudged with him, but an *S.S.* man shot him. For helping the doctor, I received an iron glove over my head from an *S.S.* man…[5]

"The *S.S.* men were 'humanitarians' – they were unable to look at the dead bodies. They ordered two Jews to bury the dead. The Jews dug graves with their last strength and when their graves were completed, two shots were heard and the gravediggers fell into the graves…

"Our strength ran out: no eating or drinking for the entire day. Toward evening a peasant wagon appeared with bread; the *S.S.* men purposely threw the bread in the air so that it would fall on the heads of the unfortunate. The bread actually bounced off their heads and fell into the mud. The people grabbed the bread and divided the last morsel. We took water with our hats from the mud and that is how we drank. Two Jews tried to go to a well, but they were immediately shot.

"Night fell. The *S.S.* men lit the way with search lights so that no one would dare to escape. A Jew dared to run into the woods, but a German caught him and stuck a dagger through the Jew's spinal cord. Everyone ran unconsciously; we did not know where we were going and how we were going and from where we got the strength… 'I, Shlomo Atlas, with my own strength led Helfer, the perfume merchant, and another Jew.

"The wild screaming of the Hitlerists quieted down a little. The crack of the rubber clubs was also quieter. Only the rush of the autumn wind, the heavy breathing of the tortured Jews was heard…

[Page 518]
"From the distance small fires appeared – these were the lamps in Hrubieshow. We neared Hrubieshow. It was exactly four o'clock at night.

"A storehouse, where the Jewish merchant kept his flax, stood a kilometer before Hrubieshow. This storehouse was the 'night hotel' for the Jews surviving the 'death march.' But entering the 'hotel' was not so easy. The *S.S.* men again had to count how many living victims they still had and they counted with whips. Each Jew entered the 'hotel' bloodied. From the counting it was shown that only 800 remained of the approximately 2,000 Chelm Jews who had left Chelm on the same day at 12 o'clock. All of the old and weak were dead somewhere in the ditches and the living in the 'hotel' envied them.

"The few Jews just squeezed together in the storehouse and in the attic. They did not sleep; they lay unconscious. They could not breathe and they also could not move. They wanted the night to last forever. But the world remains the world: the night disappeared and in came the dawn which threw streaks of light through the small crevices and holes in the warehouse. The points of light threw fear in the squeezed together, helpless Jews. Everyone, being sure that the end of their life would come today, said *Vide* [confession of sins on Yom Kippur]. But they could not think for long; the wild screaming of the *S.S.* men – "*Heraus, heraus*! [out, out] ..." interrupted the thoughts of the Jews and they met the morning with an anguished feeling. However, they had to go again.

"There was a small river on the way. Going over the bridge, many Jews threw themselves into the water. The *S.S.* men shot after them and the water became red with blood. From the distance, we saw many people. These were the Hrubieshow Jews who were people in the same situation as us. And the sadistic whims against the Chelm and Hrubieshow Jews began to be repeated. Jews with beards were chosen for dancing and the impartial lens of a film camera noted it all. One Jew was forced to lower his pants. Yairn, the treasurer of the old age home, was placed to clean the boots of an officer and when he had polished the boots, the officer constantly beat him with a whip. There was no help; the heavens did not hear the shout of Israel and the earth did not shake. Everything remained as it was.

"But it again became worse. The shooting did not cease. Large numbers of victims fell. But all of this did not satiate the blood thirsty sadists.

"The *S.S.* men dug a pit and threw in the living iron merchants – the Lewensztajn brothers, the perfume merchant Sznicer, Helfer and another Hrubieshow Jew.

[Page 519]
"The continuation of the march was unbearable. There was a downpour from above and underneath, there was terrible mud up to the knees. Shoes, boots remained in the mud. Whoever remained stuck in the mud was shot. One tried to help another. I, Josef Wajnsztok, helped lead Jakov Wlodower (a hairdresser) and Arkel Tenenbaum."

We looked around a little at the straight road. Our rows were very sparse and many were weary from our pains. A few had the idea of staging a revolt. It should be understood that the idea of a revolt was not connected with saving one's own life, but we only thought of an honorable death – "Let me die with the Philistines." And in the midst of running, an idea was carried among all of the Jews: "Maybe something should be started, if we dare?" But a quiet, sorrowful look was the answer to the question, that is: "And what will become of our wives and children? – They will shoot all of them!" In the last moments, the worry for their wives and children still lived among the unfortunate, and therefore, the idea of a revolt was tainted.

Hitler assassins shoot at Chelemer Jews during the Chelm-Hrubieshow-Sokal death march

Another day of sorrow, of pain and death passed. The rows of the Chelemer and Hrubieshow Jews became even sparser. Night came again.

After everything, the road was very muddy. The *S.S.* men thought of a place – for the Jews to "go to sleep" and, of course, in the mud. The *oberleutnant* ordered everyone to lie down in the mud with their faces down. The entire area was fenced in with barbed wire. Whoever wanted to raise their head was immediately shot. And the *S.S.* men stood around and warmed themselves at a bonfire. The searchlights lit the muddy area. A downpour came down from above and everyone murmured in the quietness: - "Look down from heaven and see!" See, God, how the sons of Israel, who said, "*Ata Bichartanu*" [You have chosen us], sleep here!

In the morning, right with the coming of dawn, the order came to wake up. Every Jew was transformed into a muddy mass, from which a pair of eyes looked out in deadly fear. One recognized the other only through his voice.

[Page 520]

We again went over the muddy, dirt roads accompanied by the shooting, bangs of the rubber sticks and wild voices. The rain poured down without interruption and this greatly sharpened the joy of the blond barbarians who enjoyed seeing how the rain cascaded over the Jews. The "provisioning" took place in the same way – by throwing bread on the heads and water was given at night when we entered a village.

With precise German accuracy, a plan had already been worked out about how to cause even more humiliation and to cause internal torture. There was a club in the village with a stage. The *S.S.* members chose the club for a night's lodging and the entrance had to be through the stage. It should be understood that entering had to be by counting and beating with whips. The Jews, not knowing that there was a stage, entered the club quickly and continued to run so that everyone fell off the stage and one fell on the other. They remained lying thus the entire night. It was impossible to move; even to take care of natural needs, one had to empty himself on another. The air was foul, but the Jews were already indifferent to everything. They lay half dead and asked God that the end come even quicker.

However, the end did not come. In the morning, we went to the window to swallow a little of the rain water which freshened the smell a little. We were not permitted to stick out our heads too far; we were threatened with a bullet.

The Nazis chased everyone out onto the street where there was still a downpour. Everyone was arranged on a square, face to face in two rows. The *oberleutnant* then announced: "Now the time has come and we will no longer chase you – now we will shoot everyone." A bitter feeling enveloped everyone. Many thought – Would it not have been easier to fall on the road. Several received the announcement with indifference. Children ran to fathers, brothers to sisters; they wanted to be together at the last minute. But the *S.S.* men did not allow this. A machine gun was erected, ready to shoot. Meanwhile the lieutenant summoned Tenenbaum, the Chelemer photographer, and asked him to take off his coat and lie down on the ground. Tenenbaum lay down with his face up, but the lieutenant ordered him to lie with his face down. He took out his revolver and said: "Now I am shooting you!" Tenenbaum awaited his death. A shot was immediately heard. However, the shot was in the air. But Tenenbaum's black hair turned grey-white. He became an old man.

[Page 521]

The *S.S.* men again began to count. Only 406 Jews remained. Six more Jews were shot so that the figure could be rounded off. The remaining – it was declared – must go to their "holy land" – to Russia. In addition, they sadistically consoled that they would have the occasion to cross a river that would not be deeper than their chests. One row needed to go through Belz and the other through Sokal. We went in the row that went to Sokal.

The farther road again led through mud up to the knees. There was no strength to go farther. In the last 10 minutes, another 50 Jews were shot. The remaining Jews saw a *shtetl* in front of their eyes and this was actually the German zone of Sokal.

Very few Jews remained. They were all ordered to sit on the ground. The Poles, who were permitted to enjoy themselves at the expense of the bloodied souls, looked at the Jews as at an amazing site. The Nazi amateur photographers left no stone unturned… Finally an order came to open the bridge and the Jews were let through to the Soviet side. The *S.S.* members told them that if they came back they would be shot.

The Soviet border guards were surprised by the half-naked, muddied and barefoot Jews… The border guards were frightened and blocked the bridge, not letting anyone go farther. The Jews immediately tried to throw themselves into the water, but the soldiers threw grenades there. The Soviet Sokal garrison was mobilized, taking control of all of the outlets from the bridge.

The news about the Jews on the bridge spread lightning fast among the Sokal Jews. The entire *shtetl* of Jews came to the bridge. One great joint cry was heard. The Jews of Sokal cried together with us. The terrible picture of the unfortunate Jews demanding their due: "Shout, Israel!" and the Sokal Jews left for the Soviet city commandant asking that the remaining Jews be saved. The request was rejected. Meanwhile the Sokal Jews – young and old – men and women – gathered near the bridge and threw bread, sugar, fruit and so on, over to the bridge Jews. The Jews on the bridge bared their muddied hearts to the Red Army, shouting: "It is better if you shoot us than return us to the Germans!"

A committee of the Soviet boarder guards turned to the Germans asking the reason that the Jews were being deported. They received an answer that the Jews had mounted a rebellion: they attacked the Germans and demanded that they be taken to the Russians. So the cynical answer did not solve the problem and the Jews had to go back. The Jews lay down on the bridge declaring that they would not go back. Because of this, the Soviet commandant decided that two members of the Red Army must take each Jew by the hands and feet … and thus they were carried over to the German side.
[Page 522]

It was already pitch dark when the small remnant of Jews found themselves face to face with the Germans. Several *S.S.* members assured the Jews that in the morning they would be able to go home. Now they told the Jews to go to the train station. The *S.S.* was waiting for the Jews at the train station, accompanied by violent blows. The Jews immediately dispersed and arrived in the nearest village where the village magistrate permitted them to sleep in the school building.

The *S.S.* assassins could not rest… They set out for the synagogue and chased out all of the Jews to the river. A number immediately went into the water. Those who could swim swam across and others drowned. Others ran along the shore of the river.

"I, Shlomo Atlas, swam to a broken bridge. But with luck, a board from the bridge lay on the other shore. I went onto the posts of the bridge and going deep into the water I reached the other shore. Then the rest came over to the other shore in such a manner.

Wandering on the other shore, we met Jewish members of the Red Army who took us to the office of the border guards and instead of giving us a bed for the night, they arrested us. Despite all efforts by the Sokal Jews, we sat in jail for a month and in the end, the commandant instructed that we be sent back to the German border. While being led by a Soviet patrol for a distance of 40 kilometers to the other border point a message arrived that there was an order from the Sokal commandant that we should be taken back to the part of Sokal in the Soviet realm.

The Sokal Jews welcomed all of the survivors from the Chelm-Hrubieshow-Sokal death march like their own brothers. They gave us clothes, shoes and fed us for a long time. The first *Shabbos*, the saved Jews went to the synagogue and *gebentsht goyml* [said the prayer for escaping from danger]. Alas, five Jews who had been lucky in coming to Sokal died from their wounds in the Sokal hospital.

* * *

At the conclusion, the above mentioned narrators – Atlas and Wajnsztok – ended with the following thank you to the Sokal Jews: "We hold it as our duty – at this opportunity – to express our sincere thanks in the name of the surviving Chelm Jews wherever they are found, all over the world. We stand firm that the Sokal Jews at that time showed full humanity and national solidarity and mercy.

[Page 523]

The Death March

by Y. Herc, Canada

Translated by Gloria Berkenstat Freund

Thursday night, the 30th of November, 1939, there was a great panic among the Jewish population in Chelm. The Jewish *kehile* [organized religious community] let it be known that all of the Jews – men from 16 to 65 – should gather in the morning, Friday, the 1st of December, 1939, at 8 o'clock in the square where the stores of the small market stood (the *Okrąglak* [*Rynek* or marketplace]) and any men found after that time outside the gathering spot would immediately be shot.

A strong fear fell on everyone. One ran to the other for advice on what to do: go or not go? Why were they calling only the men?

Anshl Biderman, president of the Jewish *kehile*, personally went from house to house to inform the Jews calmingly that the formal notice from the Germans was only a formality and after everyone listened to the decrees, the Germans would free everyone.

As in every Jewish home in the city, it was also gloomy in our house. No one went to sleep. My mother, sensing the worst, cried without stop through the entire night. All of the men in the house – my father, two brothers and I – did not speak among ourselves. We communicated the fear, pain and worry and anxiety about the fate of the women left behind in the home without any support – a mother and two sisters – with each other only through looks.

We decided that I would go alone to the *Okrąglak*. The women would remain in the house or go away for a few hours to Christian neighbors and the men would hide for the day.

The morning of the 1st of December, 1939, was cloudy. I said goodbye to all of those dear to me and to my unforgettable parents – Lipe *ben* [son of] Yehoshaya, may he rest in peace, and Chana *bas* [daughter of] Nakhum, may she rest in peace, as well as my dear sisters, Chaya, may she rest in peace (she was 18 years old), and Feyge Leah, may she rest in peace (she was nine years old), whom I saw no more, as well as my two brothers Shalom and Fishl – and went with a heavy spirit to the *Okrąglak*. There was a large group of Jews already assembled: small and large, young and old – fathers and grandfathers with their grandsons. The number of Jews grew larger with every minute. And when the *Okrąglak* became full of Jews, heavily armed *S.S.* men marched out from every street and alley to the collection point and surrounded all of the gathered Jews.

[Page 524]

We immediately had the most frightening premonition, understanding that we were called here not to hear any German orders and arrangements. But we could no longer go back. They immediately stood us in long rows and the Polish police went among the Jews, ordering us to give them everything that we had in our pockets, that if anything were found in someone's pocket, he would immediately be shot. Then an *S.S.* officer gave a talk, declaring that they were taking "the worthless, lousy and dirty *Juden* [Jews]" to work. This same officer ordered us to dance and sing songs. I remember how Motele the cabinetmaker (I do not remember his surname) was harshly beaten by an *S.S.* man during the dancing and he was a strong man, but he could not even go one mile with the death march before he was shot.

Before we moved on the road of death, the *S.S.* men selected the *kehile* member, Dr. D. Wlaberger, a small number of craftsmen, such as shoemakers, tailors and others and they remained in Chelm.

After the selection the death march began. The shootings started right after the city hospital and the following first victims fell: the above mentioned Motele Stolier, Mandelbaum (the gravestone engraver who was lame), Palewski and so on. The *S.S.* ran wildly among the rows of Jews like blood thirsty animals beating with whips and chasing us so that we would run quickly – and anyone who just stopped was immediately shot.

German trucks with armed machine guns drove before and after us. We ran like a flock of sheep clustered together and frightened, ruled by just one feeling: "Run, run – perhaps we will escape from the Hitleristic dogs." Today, while the international tribunals free the German criminals sentenced to death, it will probably sound laughable and anachronistic, but then each one wanted to survive for only one purpose, in order to see the German defeat and have revenge on them. We exerted our last strength to run ahead and ahead… Shlomo Frajman, who worked for my father, was in the ranks near me.

We were counted in the Poplawiczer Forest, 16 kilometers from Chelm, and the first 20 people were shot by the *S.S.* a few dozen steps from my row. I heard the cries and pleas of the unfortunate people asking to be allowed to live. After every shot, their cries became weaker, quieter, until it became entirely deathly still. One *S.S.* officer boasted that he had shot "20 swine." Among these 20 martyrs who were shot in the Poplawiczer Forest were: Ben-Tzion Salon, Feywl Rozenblat and his brother Yakov Rozenblat, Dovid Kornfeld, the photographer with the long hair, Aba Feldmois.

[Page 525]

The shootings lasted in this way until Hrubieszow. The number of victims grew larger and the pits along the road from Chelm to Hrubieszow were seeded with the bodies of Jews who could not run, who had been shot. These Jews were particularly those who had sat over a page of *gemara* [Talmud]; not being able to run, they were among the first victims to fall. It is as if engraved in my memory how Moshe Rozenbaum's brother – lame – ran with great effort, perspiring in only a shirt and with a great panicky fear in his eyes until he fell, crying out: "Jews, save me! They are about to shoot me; Jews save me!" A shot was soon heard and a young Jewish life was annihilated by the beasts in human skin.

Not far from me, Yakov Tenenbaum stood with his father Pesakh, who began to lose his strength near Biala-Pole (25 kilometers from Chelm). Two Jews took him under the arms and dragged him with them. Yakov, his son, could also barely walk. He entered my row and I took him under the arm and "pulled" him with me. In order to encourage him, I also gave him a piece of *challah* that I kept in my pocket. But he divided the morsel of *challah* with his father who was being led by the two Jews and they all fell. But it did not last long and they were both shot. It was at a difficult spot to pass over and the son helped the father go over and the Germans noticed this and they killed them.

Children sacrificed their lives to save their parents and the following facts say this very clearly: Grunwald the hatmaker marched with his two sons: one 22 years old and the second – a 15-16 year old. The two sons pulled their father with all of their strength, but the moment arrived when he could not go farther and he pleaded with the children: "Children, leave me, I cannot in any case go another step; I am already old, save yourselves." The children, crying, pleaded with him to strengthen himself because it was not far to Hrubieszow and they would rest there. Regrettably, the *S.S.* man observed this and immediately shot the old Grunwald and also the older son who did not want to be separated from his father. The younger son went among the crowd, running with a heart-rending lament for the deaths of his father and brother.

[Page 526]

Ephraim Meler (an owner of the import business on Lubelska Street, near the hill) ran with his 15-year old son. At night, when we ran through a thick part of the woods and there were trees along the way, the Germans – out of fear that we would try to escape – increased the speed of our run with more continuous shootings. He, Ephraim Meler, did not have any more strength to run and a tall *S.S.* man – in a steel helmet with a badge of a skull and hung with medals and awards – took him out of the row, shot him in a ditch near the highway. The *S.S.* man had first shouted out to the son: "Jew, get your father" and also shot him.

Hersh Welczer, Yehoshua Barnholc's son-in-law, ran with his 16-17-year old son, Mietek. They marched together until sundown. At night the Germans began to shoot into the crowd and Hersh Welczer met a bullet. His son, seeing that his father had fallen, ran into the forest and waited until everyone had gone past. After, he looked for his father who was still alive and he dragged him deeper into the woods. He tried to save him but, after a few hours, his father breathed out his soul in his son's arms. His father informed him before his death that he now needed to be the father for the entire family and he should take care of his mother and his younger brother.

Moshe Cwiling, who was called *Dwadcat Kopeyeknik*[6], when he felt he was losing his strength and the end was approaching, took out a stack of 100 *zloti* banknotes from his fur and while walking continuously tore the money into pieces, calculating that the Germans would not later benefit from this. Those who walked with him said that in those moments, he had lost his mind.

* * *

At night we arrived in Hrubieszow. We were led into the oakum storehouse of Warman, the Hrubieszow Jew, where we spent the night. We made an account of how many Jews were murdered during the course of the day. It appeared that hundreds of Jews were shot on the way. It is difficult for me to calculate all of the names of those shot along the road. I only remember the following murdered: Berele's son, Fishl's two sons (Lewensztajn), Yakov Yehoshua, the owner of the hotel – Achtman, who worked with the notary public; Moshe Wilder; Beyle Trayst's son, Yakov; Yitzhak Szlechter (came from France); the alderman Szajn; the bookkeeper Fryd.

I was side by side together with Shlomo Frajman in the storehouse. We were all hungry and very thirsty and tired. No one could fall asleep because we did not know what would happen during the coming day and the atrocious scenes and experiences during the course of the day floated before our eyes.

The night passed with great and difficult cold sweats and the morning came. This was early *Shabbos*, the 2nd of December, 1942. We were again arranged in rows and taken to a place in Hrubieszow where Hrubieszow Jews stood arranged in exactly the same number as in Chelm.

[Page 527]

Then we were taken together and we were chased and shootings again took place. The weaker, older Hasidic Jews in their traditional costumes lagged behind and they were shot.

We were taken from Hrubieszow by the Storm Troopers (*S.A.* [*Sturmabteilung*]), who leaving Hrubieszow, had dug a pit and thrown in six living Jews who could no longer walk: Josef Lewensztajn, Gomulke (Lewensztajn's brother-in-law), Sznicer from the apothecary storehouse on Lubelske Street, Avraham Helfer (apothecary storehouse) and two more Jews whose names I do not remember.

Leibel Szajdwaser, son of the shoykhet, Pinkhas Szajdwaser, who was murdered by the Nazis

Pinkhas Szajdwaser, Chelmshoykhet, perished at the hands of the Hitler murderers

The director of the Chelm *Tarbut* school, Bloch, wrested himself from a young, blond German's hands, who wanted to shoot him because he wanted to take care of his physical needs. To this day, the picture floats before my eyes of how the young *S.S.*-man pulled Bloch to the pit and shouted: "Jew into the pit!" And Bloch asked: "I have one wife and one child; give me her life." And the murderer still dragged him to the pit. Abruptly, he broke from the Hitleristic assassin's hands and ran into the ranks. The German chased him and losing him from his sight he substituted another shot Jew for him.

The road from Hrubieszow was a bloody one. It rained and snowed and we walked with our last strength, until we came to the *shtetl*, Uhrin (I think that is what it was called). We were given "food" in such a manner: a goods truck arrived with bread and the Germans threw it in the air, photographing how the Jews caught pieces and morsels of bread. They derived pleasure from this spectacle. Then we were again chased. I almost lost my strength.

Night came again. We were driven to a place for the night in a school in a small settlement. It was very crowded and we had to stand on our feet until dawn. And standing this way we took care of our physical needs. The stench from the human excrement was very heavy and we dared not open a window.

[Page 528]

The Germans bolted the doors and windows of the school premises. I was very thirsty because I had swallowed pieces of mud instead of water and in order to quench my thirst I licked the moisture from the window panes. It was a nightmarish night and we could barely wait for morning to come.

We were again placed in rows and chased. Going through villages, the Ukrainian residents wrung their hands over our fate and threw bread.

* * *

Sunday, the 3rd of December, was the third day of our death march. We walked across marshes, mud above the knee and often up to the stomach. I wanted to throw away my coat, but Shlomo Frajman took it from me and wore it for a few hours until it became easier for me.

Hundreds of victims fell on the third day. The *S.A*-members [storm-troopers] shot almost without interruption. One young *S.A.*-man distinguished himself with his savagery. I heard how he begged for bullets from one of his comrades because he had none.

I remember well the following savage picture: Feywl Rozenknop – a butcher, a tall, solid person, went into deep mud and sank even deeper. He shouted and pleaded that we offer him a hand, but no one wanted to go to him because they feared for their own lives. He was shot and the large body of Feywl Rozenknop remained stuck in the mud a little bent over and red streams of blood trickled from him without stop.

Seeing all the horrible things, I also became indifferent to death. On the first two days I ran as if crazy and made a superhuman effort in order to remain alive, but then my will to live dulled. Looking at those shot, I imagined that clothing or dead objects had fallen, not people.

I remember when we stopped to rest for an hour, not, God forbid, because of us, but because of the exhaustion of the Germans. Leibl Lewensztajn (Fishl Berele's son), who was half a corpse, came to me then, with a broken hand, holding it in a kerchief tied across his chest and without a coat (he had thrown away his skunk fur coat because it was heavy) and he said to me: "No one can help me any longer. You see that my three brothers were shot in two days, now my turn is coming because I can no longer go along. I will be shot after another kilometer. At least I have been lucky that my son, Motek, is on the other side of the Bug [River] and his life is secure. Yes, it was worthwhile to return from Italy." (I studied medicine in Italy with his son and we returned home a few months before the war). I tried to calm and console him, but during the second rest stop, he was already in the World of Truth [dead].

[Page 529]

I want to relate these facts: Among the *S.A.*-murderers was one with the name Buchholtz who could not watch the bloody actions against the Jews and did not laugh at and did not shoot any Jews. In the evening of the third day of the death march, he came to a group of Jews and quietly said: "Have patience, it is not far to the Russian border. We are taking you to the Russians." His talk encouraged us a little, although we did not have any confidence in any German. As has been told, in the morning, the same German shot Jews on the last day of our march.

Once the Germans got lost in the marshes and night came. The weather was frosty. It snowed a little and the ground was frozen. We lay to rest on the muddy earth. We huddled next to each other seeking a little warmth because the majority of us had thrown off our coats and even our jackets when walking. Many of us also did not have shoes, which lay stuck in the marshes. We were happy that we had pulled our feet out of the marshes. We were very thirsty and, consequently, we sucked the dampness from the mud. The desperation was very great. Several pious Jews, because of bitterness, spoke about God and of his anointed, that God was not just, and concluded that there was great doubt if He was anywhere here.

After the night here we again went. This was Monday, the 4th of December. We were again chased and again we were shot. We came to a village, Zulabicz (I think) at 12 noon where we were counted and seeing that according to their plan of annihilation there were too many Jews, they removed Jews from the rows to shoot.

There, near a whisky brewery, the 400 Jews were divided into two parts, seating us with one group opposite the other. The owner of the brewery began to befriend the Germans, calling out that the "*Zydes*" had still not been killed enough and that they are guilty for everything. The German officer stood two machine-guns opposite us, aimed at each group of Jews. He gave a speech, concluding that this was now our end – we would soon be shot and, on the spot, he ordered, "Shoot." Both machine guns sprayed fire and bullets flew over our heads, several centimeters higher. Each of us bunched together and twisted our bodies in order to make ourselves smaller, even with the earth. This probably amused the Germans who had great pleasure from the fire-spectacle and took photographs of our various poses.

Finally the officer ordered a stop to the firing and gave us a short speech that we would soon be taken to the Russian border and one group of Jews would march in the direction of Belzec and the second group would go to Sokol. But he underlined that during the coming night everyone would need to cross the border because whoever was found in the morning would immediately be shot, adding: "And this is not a joke – you have had one example."

[Page 530]

The Jews began to thank the officer and several shouted, "*Heil Hitler*," for which they received a considerable portion of whips because "The dirty Jews should not mention the name of the *Fuehrer*."

* * *

My group went to Sokol. In a few hours we were there. The city was divided into two parts by the Bug River; the suburbs and the train station were in German hands and the Russians had the actual city. We were on the German side until darkness. No shootings took place; they had absorbed enough of our blood. The above mentioned small blond murderer decreed that Juar, the treasurer of the Chelemer old age home, lick his boots with his tongue and he beat him during it.

When it became dark, we were again counted. Then we were taken to the bridge and told to run to the Russians, while they shot over our heads. We ran with cries and shouts and with upraised hands, as a sign that we were not armed. The Soviet border guard stopped us and demanded clarifications. When they saw our desperate situation and heard the entire tragic path, they calmed us, saying that they would immediately ask their commander who had to decide if we would be permitted to enter the Soviet side.

Soon the Jews of Sokol knew of our situation and their loud crying could be heard from a kilometer's distance. The Soviet soldiers gave us food, drinks and the bloodied, frozen Jews, bandages. I remember how a young Soviet soldier seeing a barefoot young Jew without a coat (I think this was the youngest son of the hatmaker, Berish Grunwald), with bloodied feet who looked like one piece of gelled blood, gave him his great coat, made him a bandage saying, "*Zapatim im*' (we will pay them).

The procedure for letting us in lasted a long time. Several managed to mix themselves in among the soldiers and entered the city of Sokol illegally. Bloch, the director of the Tarbot School [a secular Hebrew language school] also did this. Each time different village chiefs came with questions. In the end one Soviet office came and gave a speech to us: "We have sent a telegram to Lemberg about your matter and also communicated with Kiev. The answer was – Do not allow them in, motivated [by the fact] that first we do not know if there are spies among you and secondly we cannot do this because Hitler could send us all of the Jews who are under his government."

[Page 531]

The officer asked us to go away on our own in order to avoid undesirable measures.

Hearing the talk, we lay down on the bridge, calling out that we would not move from the spot and it would be better if they shot us because in any case death awaited us from the Germans. But this declaration of ours did not alter the decision of the Soviet guard. The Soviet soldiers carried us one by one back to the other side of the bridge, which was not guarded by the Germans.

Groups formed immediately. Several decided to go back to Chelm and other groups looked for a way to swim across the Bug River and go over to the Soviet side.

Shlomo Frajman and I searched for an opportunity to ferry ourselves across to the other side of the Bug, but reaching the other side involved great difficulties. The peasants did not want to ferry us across at night because the Soviet guard was larger then and there was the threat of death. One peasant advised that we go a half kilometer on the shore of the river with the tide until we found an old bridge that had been blown up. There, he said, the water was at a depth up to our neck and we would be able to go across.

Thus we did. We grabbed the beams of the bridge and we swam from one scaffold to another. We tried to stand up, but we did not feel the ground. So with great weariness and danger to our lives, we swam. The water was torrential and cold. It was then the night of the 4th into the 5th of December. We just barely reached the shore.

[Page 532]

Wood piles smoked from the Russian guards in the distance. We heard their voices. We lay for, perhaps, half an hour in the great silence. Waiting until the guard withdrew a little farther, we then crept into the alleys of Sokol.

We knocked at the first Jewish door with a *mezuzah* [small box placed on door frames of Jewish homes containing the *Shema Yisroel* – Hear O, Israel – the central prayer of Jewish worship]. We were let in right away. The residents of the house took off our wet clothing and gave us food and gave us their own beds.

The owner of the house was the owner of a brickyard. He kept us in bed for three days until we regained our strength and until the Soviet regime in the *shtetl* stopped looking for illegal residents.

A committee was created in Sokol to help the homeless Jews. I also received several *zlotes* from the committee for a train ticket to Luboml (Libivne) from which, through a messenger, I told those at home that I remained alive.

Many of those who took part in the death march became sick with infections and with pneumonia, as well as having frozen feet. Several of us were sent to Siberia by the Russians because they had crossed the border illegally.

* * *

The above mentioned horrors and the ruthless deaths took place in the year 1939 when there were not yet any gas chambers.

The rynek in 1900-1905, where the Polish regime later erected a Monument of the Unknown Soldier

Translator's footnotes:

1. Colonel Adam Koc was associated with *OZN* [Camp of National Unity], an organization many considered Fascist, and Mrs. Pristarowa was instrumental in restricting kosher slaughtering.
2. *Owshem* – Our Own, a government policy of a general boycott of Jewish products and workers.
3. "Death head" or skull, the insignia used by a division of the *S.S.*
4. "Hear, O Israel" – the central prayer of Jewish worship.
5. It is unclear as to the identity of the doctor whom Wajnsztok mentions.
6. 20 Kopeyeknik – a kopeyk or kopeck is a Russian coin.

[Page 533]

Lipa the Butcher from Chelm

by Schneur Wasserman

Translated by Pamela Russ

This event, that is described here, took place at the beginning of the Nazi occupation of Chelm

I.

He came from generations of butchers
Lipa the butcher, in the city of Chelm
He inherited the meat market in the marketplace
From his bearded ancestors – the Jewish God.

His surroundings: the meat market, the slaughterhouse, the marketplace
Early Shabbath morning – in the *Beis Medrash* [Study Hall];
A *minkha* [afternoon prayer] and *maariv* [evening prayer], sometimes a *kaddish* [prayer for the dead].
Not religious, but a Jew, as a Jew should be.

Today's world is not strange to Lipa,
The ins and outs of today's world,
The youth, may you live and be well!
Smart – already a little too smart, and they understand …

"Classes" and "parties": "Reds" and "Bund" [socialists]
"*Petzekes*" [*Poalei Tziyon* Party, Jewish Socialist Labour Party], Zionists, and who knows what else!
And each person wants only with his own horse
To bring the Messiah to this generation.

Also, Lipa is an expert at listening to a speech,
On the eve of the elections to the city council , to the *Sejm* [Polish parliament].
He would have thrown the pelts off the lords,
But he loved to get things done in Chelm, his home.

Lipa's own home town is Chelm,
The muddy market place, the cows and the horses,
The Christian drunk-shaven chins,
The Jewish busy, dishevelled beard …

The clogs [wooden shoes], the colorful peasants' scarves,
Tuesdays and market days, in a holiday time.
The Greek Orthodox church was on Lipa's own hill,
In the front, on Lubelski – the old Polish church.
The Christian "cemetery" and – ten times to differentiate –
The Jewish cemetery, against the night, may we not think of it.
The old *Beis Medrash* [Study Hall], religious-Jewish-humped
Goats that dance across the roof.

II

How Lipa loves his home town,
And loves more his own home and his child

His Rokhel'e – the only eye in his head
And – may nothing untoward happen to his child:

A child, a contemporary child "attends classes"
Speaks Polish, even the Kaiser can understand!
A smooth tongue, sharp as a knife,
Also – may no evil eye befall her – "stately" and beautiful.

[Page 534]

Deep in her studies, busy, embedded,
Just as all those in today's times.
A girl – Lipa smiles into his beard
And smart, a little too smart and respected …

III

Just as the Nazi's non-kosher foot
Stepped on the homey earth of Poland
Lipa took into his own hands
The fate that was set out for him.

Lipa sharpened his butcher's knife
To protect his home, his child, and his people,
(These butchers have strong hands
They broke the bones of more than one hooligan…)

IV

There were teary, grey autumn days
That lazily rolled around the streets of Chelm.
The sun covered its face with clouds
Its head covered with grey ashes.

On a day such as this, one autumn day,
With tear-filled eyes, and clothed in mist,
In a deathly terror, Lipa saw on his doorstep
A senior Nazi accompanied by a soldier.

"You're a Jew, correct?" "Yes, Sir, I am a Jew."
Lipa replies and quickly glances to the side,
To Rokhel'e behind him – a flick of the hand
Which means: "Daughter, leave here, as fast as you can!"

"Stop!" shouts the senior Nazi – with such a grin,
From which one's blood freezes in the body:
"The hand of the victor reaches everywhere.
The wine and the wife belong to the winner!"

"What is your name, girl? What do they call you?
"Rokhel! Oh! Your name is a great one!...
"The mother, ha ha, of the Jewish nation…
"Yes, fine!" Winks to the guard: "Get her out quickly!"

"A greater mission is prepared for you,
"Than your elder grandmother; think about it clearly.
'You can be a mother to a Nazi man!
"A Nazi with tar black hair eyes and hair…"

"Racist behaviors? Yes, it is a sin.
"But you are great, Rokhel, you are great, honorable!
"Double ration of bread and of meat
"You will get, and even more: an Aryan passport…"

"Better in a good way… Too bad, you are young…
"You can live …" And he takes her freshly {roughly] in his hands…
But not with modesty, a white body of a girl.
A knife, a sharp one, flashed in front of his eyes…

[Page 535]

Lipa's kosher butcher knife
Sprayed itself with non-kosher Nazi blood.
Rokhel, her father's butcher hands,
Kissed her with tears of joy and happiness …

That same night was just waking up
To echoes of guns and choked voices.
Dawn awoke with unrest
With curiosity and fear and misted glances.

[Page 536]

With joy, the streets of Chelm
Looked over the fences
At tens of Nazi dead bodies in the market place,
Contemptible, Nazi blood on the bridge.
* * *

The goat's smile became red
From Lipa's open wound.
The streets bowed in awe
In front of the heroic martyrs, they uncovered their heads.

[Page 535]

Whose Am I, Who Is Left for Me?

For each soft bed – a sister, a dishonored one.
Deathly hungry, a brother – for each spoon of food.
Where can I lie – on my soft warm bed, lie?
How can I come to the table, sit at the fully prepared table?

The small, lonely chairs are waiting quietly around the able,
The bread is becoming stale and the knife is rusting.

[Page 536]

At my table – forever embarrassed –
My sister will not sit, nor my brother, nor my friend.

My heart will no longer have to celebrate with the worries,
With the sweet worries of helping when a beloved one
With the last crumb of bread, with the comfort of tomorrow…
To whom? To whom do I belong now? Who of mine are left?

[Page 535]

Today it is spring on Earth,
Whoever has blessings should recite them –
Once I also had
Blessings for the world and for its people.

Today it is spring on Earth
And my heart is rising with thorns
My lips – snake venom –
Can curse only in rage.

That means. I have only curses
I will throw them like rocks
Into the face of the world,
Into its shameless face.

All the smart, beautiful words
I will throw into the trash
And my proud human head
Will bow before a wolf in the shadow…

The almost four thousand years
Of the words "do not kill"
Did not make the person nicer
Did not make the hearts better.

[Page 536]

From the fiery words
That were engraved and written out
On the tablets of the world
Remains only ash for us…

So, my daily bread I will
Only knead and mix with the ash

And it will become bitter in my mouth
For me and for everyone, this same food.

And it will chase away the pleasure
From the smoke covered tables,
As the person has long ago
Chased his mind from his heart.

And the satisfied rhythm of rest –
Has been wounded with my thorny words.
Sleep from the eye will be shunned
As the day's light shuns the blind person.

* * *

Today it is spring on Earth
And my heart is rising with thorns
My lips – snake venom –
Can curse only in rage.

[Page 537]

Chelm at the Time of the Hitler Occupation

by Yitzhak Groskop

Translated by Gloria Berkenstat Freund

The author of this article, who through a miracle escaped death, lived in Chelm during the German occupation. He describes his own experiences and observations as well as episodes and facts from other Chelemer that were told to him.

On Friday, at dawn, on the 1st of September, 1939, German airplanes appeared over Polish cities that warned of the coming ruthless war. Chelm was bombed on the 2nd of September. Many people died. The population ran outside the city to seek protection from the bombs.

A week later, on the 8th of September, Chelm was heavily bombed by hostile airplanes, mainly the "Kalejawa" and the neighboring streets. 250 people were killed then – Jews and Christians. Mr. Soloweitchik and other Jews perished then in the bombing. Their bodies were not found.

On Monday, the 7th of October, at nine o'clock in the morning, a division of the German motorized army appeared in the city. The Germans first visited the *beis-hamedrash* [synagogue or house of prayer] and whoever was found there was beaten and all of the religious books were thrown into the street. Hitler soldiers stood outside and dishonored the books. Then groups of soldiers went to the Kuzmir *shtibl* [one room prayer house] No. 2 that was found in Yehoshua Binsztok's courtyard. The wild Hitlerists broke open the door and dishonored all of the Torahs.

At the same time, the Germans began to grab Jews for work. Every morning the members of the *S.S.* would go across the city in pursuit of Jews. They forced those caught to clean toilets, gutters and to do other dirty work with bare hands.

The Jewish population in Chelm immediately had a premonition about the Hitleristic regime and all of its horrors. Jewish houses and businesses were plundered by the Germans. A great deal of goods and articles were immediately sent to their families in Germany. The Gestapo immediately took hostages, demanding that Jews give one payment after the other. In addition to this they themselves went through Jewish houses to rob the belongings.

[Page 538]

They saw every opportunity to extort money from the Jews. It happened that someone stole a horse from a German; the Rabbi Gamaliel Hochman was immediately arrested, making him responsible for the theft. Yakov Sztol paid the Germans a ransom and the rabbi was freed.

In addition to the persecutions, the Hitler regime took care to defile the Jews in public. A Chelmer newspaper was published in which they mentioned the Jews with the most insulting words, such as: dirty one, mangy, lousy and unclean. This newspaper was spread in many copies and it was also distributed in the city and its surroundings. The Germans' purpose was clear: to incite the Christian population against the Jews.

Gestapo forcing Jews to pray outside

On the 30th of September, 1939, the sorrowful, well known German general, Franko [Governor General Hans Frank] came down to Chelm. The doors of the Jewish houses were bolted. The Polish police went through the Jewish houses and warned the Jews not to go out in the street because it was strongly forbidden by the Germans. The same General Franko arranged to "reduce" the Jewish population in the city because there were too many Jews in Chelm.

On Thursday, the 31st of November, 1939, *S.S.* men came to the Jewish *zoklandinkes* (hostages) at night and ordered that on the 1st of December all Jewish men from 15 to 60 gather at the *Rynek* (market place) where the German commandant would give a speech to them in which he would declare how the Jews needed to behave under the German occupation regime. There was then a warning that each Jew should come in his nicest clothes.

[Page 539]

The Jewish population was alarmed by this news. The *zoklandinkes* ran through the city at night, telling the Chelemer Jews that they should go to the market and if they did not fulfill the decree, the *S.S.* men would themselves search for the men in the Jewish houses and whomever they found would be shot.

A panic arose among the Jews. They did not know what to do. They asked each other. Despair was great. Many Jews ran to the surrounding villages, others – to the Soviet border. I, myself, ran to the Soviet border, but at the border, the watchmen forced me to return.

Approximately 2,000 Jews assembled in the city center at the *Rynek*. When the Nazi bandits saw that the square was already filled with Jews, they surrounded the *Rynek* with armed *S.S.* men and vicious dogs. The Jews understood that a great danger lay in wait. The *S.S.* men first called the youngest Jews to them and they were heavily beaten. Then they decreed that all of the Jews should give them everything they had with them: money, jewelry and documents. One Jew did not move quickly enough to give up his things; therefore, he was heavily beaten until he lost consciousness. The victim was Motl Bakalczyk of Lubliner Street.

The Jewish wives and children of the detained men stood from afar in great fear and when they started to cry, the *S.S.* men shot in the air and decreed that the Jews should stand in lines and march away on the road to Hrubieszow, ordering them to sing Jewish songs. The women also wanted to march with them, but they were not permitted to do so.

Outside the city, the *S.S.* men shot at every Jew if he did not march fast enough. The Jews threw off their hats, clothing, shoes so that it would be easier to walk. The *S.S.* men on motorcycles chased the Jews faster and more quickly. And each Jew who stopped on the road was immediately shot.

Several kilometers from the city, the *S.S.* men removed 25 Jews from the first rows and ordered them to go into the forest. Shooting was immediately heard: the 25 Jews were killed. Among the murdered were: Salan, Dr. L. Aks, Shmuel Kac (from Szeliszcz) and others. The German city commander was present at the action and later declared that the dog-like Jews wanted to escape, and therefore had to be shot. The same commander warned that whoever escaped would be shot… The entire road was seeded with Jews who had been shot. The peasants from the villages buried the murdered Jews in the forest.

[Page 540]

Chona Nisenbaum, the son of Reb Yakov Nisenbaum, may the memory of a righteous man be blessed, who fell as a victim of a Nazi bullet during the Chelm-Hrubieszow-Sokol death march

Reb Yakov Nisenbaum and wife

Thus were the Chelemer Jews chased by the Nazi sadists. Fathers fell arm-in-arm with their sons. When the three Lewensztajn brothers stopped on the death march, they were placed on a wagon and taken to a nearby place where there were pits and they were shot there.

Upon arrival in Hrubieszow, barely 600 souls of the 2,000 Jews remained. On the second day – this was *Shabbos* – the *S.S.* men in Hrubieszow prepared the same *aktsia* [an action, usually a deportation] as for the Chelm Jews. They were gathered together and chased toward Sokol with the Chelm Jews – to the Russian border. The earlier procedure was repeated again on the way: They shot into the Jews from Hrubieszow and from Chelm. Of the Chelemer only 400 remained. In Sokol, there was the Russian border. However, the Russians did not want to let the Jews enter and the *S.S.* drove the Jews into the river. They stood thus for a considerable time. It was then a cold winter day – a number of the Jews secretly swam across to the Russian side. Others perished in the river and a still smaller remnant of these unlucky Jews returned to Chelm weak and exhausted. Many of them then died from the cold and atrocious conditions.

In the morning – after the death march – the Nazi executioners issued an order that all Jewish women whose husbands had left on the march for Hrubieszow-Sokol should report to the Germans because they needed to be sent to their husbands. A new panic arose in the city. They did not know what to do. The women and the children cried in desperation. Knowing what had happened to their husbands, they had great fear of reporting to the Germans.

* * *

In 1940 the Hitler regime began to arrange *Juden-Ratn* [Jewish councils]. Jews then were not supposed to buy from Christian businesses. The Jewish badges with the *Mogen-Dovid* [shield of David – the Jewish star] were introduced. Young and old had to wear the "yellow patch." There had to be a *Mogen-Dovid* sign on each Jewish house or shop. Jews became entirely forsaken and had to take off their hats and bow for each German.

It happened that if a Jew forgot to wear the "yellow patch" on his clothing, he was taken to the Gestapo from which he did not return. Jews were not permitted to wear any shoes with leather soles, only wooden in order that they could be heard, that *here goes a Jew*.

[Page 541]

A true hell for the Jews began in 1941, after the outbreak of the war between Germany and the Soviet Union. Jews then became completely cast off. The Hilter regime immediately created a ghetto which ran from Uscilugska Street through Pocztowa, Szedlecka, Katowska, half of Lwowska to Podgurna – near Lederman's mill. On the other side of Lederman's mill – the Pakrowka – was located the camp for Russian prisoners of war. All Christian residents from the above-mentioned ghetto streets were moved to other quarters of the city and they were given Jewish houses – outside the ghetto – to live in.

All of the Jews from Chelm and the surrounding *shtetlekh* were driven into the Chelm ghetto. Others were deported to Chelm from outside the country, such as Czechoslovakia, Hungary and other countries. The *Judenrat* had to send the Jews to work every day – according to the decree of the German regime.

Ukrainian *sitchevekes* [recruits] were then in Chelm for *marshirungen* (military exercises). They were being prepared militarily in order for them to be able to fight against Russia. These Ukrainian groups extorted still more money from the Jews, threatening them with excesses and pogroms. The Germans ignored it when the Ukrainians robbed and terrorized the Jews in the city.

A certain person unexpectedly appeared in Chelm passing as an administrator of Jewish possessions. At the beginning it was not known if he was a Jew. Later it was learned that the "administrator" was a Jew. He was called "the Jewish overseer" – Reb Pinkhasl. He had a dislikable appearance, was of short stature and with a shaved head – a true German. He always held a whip in his hand like every Gestapo-man. To the Jews he said that he was defending their interests; he was their "overseer," but, in fact, he worked with the Gestapo.

[Page 542]

Once, the "Jewish overseer" entered the ghetto and told those Jews there that he was authorized – by the German regime – to create a Jewish self defense group – Jewish police, so that the Jews could defend themselves. A Jewish police [force] of 150 people was created, over which there was a commandant. The jail was on Pocztow Street and there were arrests for every trifle. If a Jew escaped from the jail he was then shot by the Gestapo. The "Jewish Guardian," Pinkhasl, caused the Jews in the ghetto a great deal of trouble.

Jewish police with Polish labor foreman at the entrance to a labor camp in Chelm

Erev Shavous [eve of the holiday commemorating the Jews receiving the Torah at Mt. Sinai], 1942, this Reb Pinkhasl came to the Chelemer *Judenrat* with a demand for the surrender of 3,000 Jews who were not capable of useful work. The representatives of the *Judenrat* were then, among others, Meir Frenkel (son-in-law of Dovid Liberman), and Anshel Biderman. They called an urgent meeting of all the members of the *Judenrat* and of the Chelmer businessmen. The meeting took place in the butchers' synagogue and lasted an entire night. It was a bitter and dark night. They did not know what to do. There was great despair. They wrangled for a long time, but in the end they decided to surrender the demanded Jews to the Gestapo.

On the 22nd of May, 1942, on the first day of *Shavous*, the most sinister attack was carried out. Terrible screams and loud noises were heard in the morning hours, when old and sick Jews were taken out of their beds. These Jews were sent to the women's *beis-hamedrash* and the Belzer *shtibl* [one room house of prayer]. The Jewish police stood guard over them. At nine o'clock in the morning the members of the Gestapo came to the courtyard of the *beis-hamedrash*. The person, Pinkhasl, reported with flattery that the decree had been carried out and the Gestapo men cynically laughed at that.

Uniformed Gestapo men, Ukrainian bandits, *Volks-Deutsch* [ethnic Germans] and other angels of destruction immediately appeared on the Chelm streets and grabbed Jews, young and old. Jewish blood ran through the streets. Those Jews who were caught were led to the train; they were loaded into dirty box cars like cattle. The Jews were held in the riveted closed box cars for two days – without food and water. They had to stand due to the crowding. Then they were taken to the gas chambers of Sobibor. Many Jews breathed out their souls – were suffocated in the box cars.

The *S.S.* men constantly carried out hunts for the Jews. They were sent to work in the gas chambers for the Russian prisoners of war who were in the jurisdiction of the *S.S.* regiment. The Jews were forced to pull those murdered out of the gas chambers and remove their clothing. Several days later, these Jews were murdered to blur the traces of the horrible murders. Thus did it happen. Every few day there were several hundred Jews missing from the Chelemer ghetto.

[Page 543]

* * *

In June, 1942, the second *aktsia* began in Chelm. On a *Shabbos* day a Gestapo delegation from Sobibor appeared in the city which demanded several thousand Jews for work. For appearances sake, the Chelemer Gestapo argued with the Gestapo from Sobibor, saying they themselves needed the Jews to work in the city. Understand, they came to terms… A decree was issued that everyone had to assemble on Szedlecka Street, near the Belzer *shtibl* within half an hour.

Although there was great turmoil among the Jews – the significance of the *aktsia* was understood – there was no alternate choice: they assembled on the square. Those who did not report were shot. The Gestapo went through the houses and shot those not reporting, even those with work cards. Around 600 Jews were chosen on the gathering place for Sobibor.

After the second *aktsia*, life in the Chelemer ghetto became more savage with each day. The remaining Jews understood that their death was unavoidable. The streets in the ghetto became desolate and empty. The Gestapo automobiles like wild destroyers caught Jews for Sobibor from which no one returned.

* * *

The Germans called the third *aktsia, auszidlung* [deportation]. General Frank, the hangman, specially came to Chelm and decreed that 3,000 Jews be "deported" to Wlodawa. The 3,000 Jews were forced to go to the location of the railroad management, forced to go to Wlodawa – on foot.

The destroyed Jewish street, the Nei Tsal, on which the ghetto was located

[Page 544]

The Gestapo wanted again to assemble the Jews on a false pretext for the last *aktsia*. The Jews knew what such an aktsia signified and they dug caves and bunkers. The Gestapo searched for all of the Jewish bunkers, taking the Jews out of them. The Germans shot into or threw grenades into those bunkers that were very deep, in which the "enclosed" Jews were annihilated.

After the "Poczt Steps" – on Pocztowa Street – at Zalmele's bakery – 40 plus Jews were hidden in a bunker. The entrance was through the bakery. The Germans learned of this and entered the bunker from which the hidden Jews were led out. The Germans crucified Zalmele the baker with nails, dipped him in tar and burned him.

The last *aktsia* in Chelm was called by the *Judenrat*. It began on the 6th of November, 1942, and lasted 24 hours. For an entire day the *S.S.* members – together with Ukrainian and other dark elements – searched for Jews and ransacked every Jewish house, dragging out all of the Jews from the bunkers. All of the Jews were forced to go to Lubliner Street, to the courtyard of the Catholic Church; the Jews from the surrounding *shtetlekh* and villages were driven here, too.

The day was rainy, bleak. The street cried, too, at the Jewish catastrophe. The screams and wails reached to the very heavens. Jewish children were flung from high windows to the thick church walls by the Gestapo.

Chelemer Jews, after digging a hole and completely undressing, were shot by columns as forced by the Hitler murderers. This took place in the Rejvicer woods. The Jews in the photograph, from left to right: the first, name unknown, second, A. Binsztok, Mendele Kowal, Bel Helga, the child his grandson is nearby and Feywl Hiz, a worker in the slaughter house in Chelm. The civilians are Polish police and Gestapo

When the *S.S.* members had assembled everyone, they ordered the Jewish policemen to be taken away to Saxon Garden on Lubliner Street where they were shot. (Pinkhasl, the "Jewish overseer," disappeared.

[Page 545]

It was said that he allowed himself to become a groom for Danutsie's daughter and he escaped with his wife.)

All half-dead Jews were led to the train. A camp of Jewish workers was located near the cemetery. The German camp commander chose several hundred healthy Jews from the mass "deported" Jews, leaving them in the labor camp. The remaining

Jews were loaded into sealed boxcars, just as cattle and sheep and they were held there without food and drink. There were all taken to the gas ovens of Sobibor. A large number of the deported Jews died in the boxcars.

After the last *aktsia*, those Jews caught were not deported elsewhere, but they were shot on the spot. The murdered Jews lay on the Chelemer streets and the Germans' dogs tore pieces from them. Several days later, the firemen came to bury them.

[Page 546]

Only the Jews in the above-mentioned labor camp remained. The work consisted of pulling down Jewish houses. The Christian population would buy the wood or bricks from the German commandant. For their hard labor the Jews were given a dry piece of bread. They were counted several times. Hungry and barefoot, they worked from dawn until late in the evening. If a Jew became ill he was immediately shot. No medical help was given to any Jew, so therefore, they would keep silent about their illnesses. With a temperature of 40 degrees [104 Fahrenheit], with their last strength, they barely dragged themselves to work, one Jew holding up another.

Thus they worked for four months. Half of the remaining Chelemer Jews died, and the remaining Jews were taken to the death camp, Sobibor.

[Page 545]

About the Last Two Actions In Chelm

by J. Grinszpan

Translated by Gloria Berkenstat Freund

On the 5th of November, 1942, still in the dark before daybreak, some of the *ordnunsdinest* [auxiliary Jewish police in the ghetto] started to go through the ghetto in Chelm calling out: "Everyone needs to go to the assembly grounds! Jews, everyone go to the assembly grounds for the selection!"

A beautiful day dawned; a pure sun meandered still higher. The day was radiant, but not for the Chelemer Jews. The day was a dark one for all of us. What took place in the two days – the 5th and 6th of November – no one had imagined before. Even Dante's fantasy could not imagine such savagery.

The hundreds of *S.S.*-men, the *S.A.* [storm troopers] gendarmerie with their murderous Ukrainian and Lithuanian assistants stood against the powerless and unsupported Jews. Their orders were heard that every paper and thing of value, foreign currency, gold and silver should be turned in.

At this moment, mothers pressed their children to their hearts. Children cried bitterly; hands were raised to heaven that God above should have pity on the innocent children.

However, the fascist murderers did their murderous trade. First they took 200 children out of the lines. The spasms of crying from the children, mothers and fathers had no effect on the hearts of the Nazi devils. The children were taken to a nearby house through which they [the Germans] shot and which they set on fire along with the children. A volcano of fire tore toward heaven.

[Page 546]

Fathers and mothers screamed: "Oh, our children are burning! Oh, look, look there in the fire! Oh, God in heaven."

The 3,000 assembled Jews on the square were placed in wagons and taken to Treblinka, Sobibor.

On the second day, the 6th of November, 1942, the same ruthless spectacle was played again and 2,000 Jews were taken to Sobibor.

* * *

On the 6th of November 1942, the total deportation took place. The order from the *S.S.* was that 100 Jews should dig mass graves at the cemetery… When this work was finished, the *S.S.* men told them to sit on the ground with their faces to the graves. The Jews, knowing what awaited them, did not carry out the order and began to escape. The murderers opened fire from a machine gun; all of the Jews except for two fell dead like chopped down trees. The Jews who survived were: Shlomo Margolis and Yankl Goldberg who perished in the partisan struggle several days before the liberation of Chelm.

On the above mentioned day, the Germans led 3,000 Jews to Sobibor. Chelm remained almost *juden-rein* [free of Jews].

Several Chelm Jews avoided this deportation, thanks to the fact that they were hidden on the Aryan side and in the forests. Those who escaped to the forest fought in the partisan camp with great heroism.

[Page 547]

Eyewitness Testimony of Iser Zilber

by Iser Zilber

Translated by Gloria Berkenstat Freund

The cry of my Chelemer Jews echoed in the distance. The air was full of sorrow and rage. Women and children and the surrounded ghetto Jews cried. The day was beautiful and the sky was blue. I was on the roof of the Czarniecka *Gymnazie* [secondary school], where I worked. I observed my brothers being led to slaughter, and the echoes of rapidly running German military shoes were carried to me.

I could no longer work. My head hurt. My feet shook. I was afraid that I could fall off the roof, but the day passed. I left for home carrying a box of tools, in the evening, under the watch of Nazi guards.

I entered the house. It already was dark. Those in the house were crying. We cried about today's death march, about the destruction of the city and about my fate. My wife advised me to escape immediately to save my life.

The Szmern brothers, Avraham Las and I left our homes in the grey fog of the autumn morning. We avoided the central streets and, going through the back alleys, we arrived outside the city. We went through side roads and paths, through marshes and small damp woods. We went to the Bug [River] – [separating us from] the "other side," where the German angels of death did not rule.

We arrived in Dorohusk, where we met many Jews who wanted to go over to the "other side." It already was night. We were dead tired. A good Dorohusk peasant offered us hospitality. His entire house was filled with Jews. We also found a place there and we fell asleep in great fear and weariness.

The morning chased us out again. We came to the Bug in a half hour. We met many Jews there who were carrying on negotiations with the Ukrainians to arrange for them to take the Jews to the "other side." We also negotiated with two Ukrainians and came to an agreement about the price, but they were sorry because they wanted dollars and, given that we did not have dollars, we had to return embittered to the peasant in the cottage.

We lay on the floor and we did not sleep. The idea about what to do now tormented us. I did not think for long and I said that I was returning to Chelm because it did not make sense to save myself and let my wife and children perish. No! What happens to my wife and children will also happen to me! We all decided to return to Chelm.

The road was full of danger and we tried to go with side roads to avoid the Germans, but nevertheless we came upon two *S.S.* men. They approached us with triumphant expressions. I fell over in fear. My box of tools opened on the ground. They stepped on my body.

[Page 548]

A Jewish woman from Chelm, who was going with us, woke me from my faint and led me into a Jewish house. But there was also gloom. The *S.S.* member had paid a visit and warned the Jews not to take in any Jewish strangers because they would be shot for doing this. However, a Jew remains a Jew. He took us into a stable. I lay down on the straw and cried bitterly. The *S.S.* members led away the remaining Jews and they were forced to do the heaviest work in the Dorohusk sawmill. Despite our despondency, in the morning we decided to return to Chelm.

I lay in bed for three weeks after returning home. I could not move. The "trip" to [go to] the other side and back had its effect. My feet were swollen and I had pneumonia.

Meanwhile, the *Judenrat* [Jewish council created by and beholden to the Germans] needed tinsmiths. They sent for me to come to work. I could not move, had pains. However, they did not believe me. Dr. Walberger was sent to me and he also established that I was incapable of working.

I barely stood up after lying in bed for three weeks. My workplace then was in the "Gestapo." The chief of the Gestapo – *Pan* [Master] Walter – liked my work and he ordered me to remain there to work.

The *S.S.* once took me to work in the hospital for the insane. The Gestapo chief, Pan Walter, argued with the *S.S.* and demanded that they bring me back to the Gestapo. However, the *S.S.* did not want to and the Gestapo was sent Yosef Goldberg, who did his work badly in my place. Therefore, the Gestapo chief threw him from the second story. He barely returned home, bloodied and broken. After this, the Gestapo sent a vehicle to the hospital for the insane for me and succeeded in removing me from the *S.S.* I again went to work at the Gestapo.

Day after day passed quickly in great hardship. Gloom hung in the Jewish houses. We did not sleep at night, fearing the arrival of the day. Every day brought new edicts on Jewish heads. Although it was spring, it had the face of the gloomiest autumn.

[Page 549]

After spring came the summer of 1940, which brought the ghetto edict to Chelm. The Chelemer ghetto began in the quarters and streets of Krzywa–Kopernika, a part of Seminarska through Szkolna, *Przychodnia* [Clinic] Usciługska, *Neye Tsal* to the *Neye Welt* and Lwowska Streets. There the surviving Chelemer Jews were forced into that part of the city. To them were brought the Czech Jews, their companions in misfortunes, who even earlier than all of the Chelemer went to the sacrificial alter of Sobibor.

We were not supposed to leave the ghetto without permission. Everyone had to wear a white armband with a *Mogen–Dovid* [Shield of David – the Jewish star]. A Jewish milk seller and his wife had left the ghetto at one in the morning to receive milk. They met two members of the *S.S.* on the way and they were shot on the spot.

The Jews in the ghetto drew some of their income from the little bit of possessions that remained from before the war. Poles entered the ghetto and bought everything for pennies. A large number of Jews were hungry and died, among them, I remember, was Manis Beker, the *gabbai* [synagogue sexton] from the synagogue in Chelm.

The Poles did not always enter the ghetto to buy something from the Jews because the Germans also did not spare the Poles when they were in the ghetto. Poles also were shot by the Germans, among them the former city president, the lawyer, Tomaszewski.

The annihilation of the Jews of Chelm began. The first victims were the children. One morning, *S.S.* members and Jewish policemen appeared in all of the Jewish homes. All of the children were removed and taken to the synagogue. From there they were taken to the Chelm train station from which they were taken away to the gas ovens of Sobibor.

My eight–year old son Dovidl also was caught by the *S.S.* We were informed of this by my daughter, who came running to me at work and brought me the "good" news. I immediately went to the chief of the Gestapo, *Pan* Walter, and asked him to free my child. The dog "consoled" me that the same would happen to me. I told him that if my child were killed I would not work. He told me to go to the sadly well–known Raschendorf, who led the children's *aktsia* [action, usually a deportation]. Arriving at the train, I reported to Raschendorf that the chief, *Pan* Walter asked that my child be given back. He laughed at me cynically and asked two *S.S.* youths to chase me away. The *S.S.* hooligans did not let him ask for long and "served" me with the handle of a vending machine. I fell in a faint. One bit of luck was that my daughter had gone with me and she revived me and led me home.

My wife ran in front of my house with joy that Dovidl was home. It turned out that my child had escaped while being led to the train and hid in the attic of Yehiel Fiszer's house on Szkolna Street.

[Page 550]

The Jewish police, dressed in black round hats with *Mogen Dovids* and carrying rubber sticks at their sides, paraded in the gloomy streets of the ghetto.

The synagogues and houses of prayer were closed. Only the small *hakhnoses–kale* [organization providing help to poor Jewish girls whose families could not provide a dowry] synagogue was open (near the slippery steps), but the *S.S.* bandits stormed in often and carried out a pogrom on the worshippers. The fate of the Jewish women was particularly difficult. They had to work at heavy labor in the water system. They dug canals, dried swamps and they did not receive anything to eat.

The second *aktsia* in Chelm arrived unexpectedly. Now it was the turn for the surviving older Jews from Chelm and of the Czech Jews. The *S.S.* murderers and their Jewish assistants, with their elaborate lists, went to all of the older Chelm Jews as well as the Czechs and drove them out of their homes and took them to the Belzer *shtibl* [one room house of prayer]. They were held there for the entire day and at nightfall they were taken to Sobibor.

The last *aktsia* took place on the 6th of November 1942. This *aktsia* had the purpose of making Chelm *Judenrein* [free of Jews]. The 6th of November was a Friday. All of the Jews in Chelm knew of it by Tuesday and the city was in turmoil. Everyone ran wherever they could. They mainly ran to the neighboring villages. The women who worked in the *kasherne* (military barracks) went there with their children to hide. However, the hands of Hitler reached them.

Chelm was surrounded by all of the bloodhounds on the morning of Friday, the 6th of November 1942: members of *the S.S.*, the usual Germans and Ukrainians. All of the Jews were chased from the ghetto in the direction of the church square. Many Poles had gathered there and watched the spectacle with pleasure at the great Jewish pain and great misfortune.

An *S.S.* man came in the afternoon and ordered all artisans and intellectual workers to go with him. A larger number were led to the train station. We were all shoved into a small room and we stood in terrible conditions and waited for the night to end.

[Page 551]

In the morning we were divided into two groups. The intellectual workers were sent to the heaviest labor and the artisans to various work. At the *bahnhof* [train station], or as we called it, *toythof* [death station], Abish Szpan, Shmuel Oksman, Bertsha Faygbaum (a carpenter) and a Czech Jew and I were sent to the directorship of the Gestapo.

Almost all of the Jews were deported to Sobibor. A few Jews still worked at the *bahnhof*, but 20 often were taken out and they were shot in the Hrubieszow forest (near the military hospital). I again worked in the directorship of the Gestapo. I was sure that I was the only one [left] in my family. My wife and children must surely be in Sobibor. If so, of what use is it for me to live?

A Pole came to me at work once and told me that my oldest daughter, Chaya, was alive. The Pole gave me a short letter from her and in it I read: "I am naked and barefoot. *Tatele* [Daddy]!" I decided to do everything possible to help my daughter.

Chelemer Jews being led to an aktsia accompanied by the Jewish police

At night I specially made a key to the *S.S.* storehouse of stolen goods. And the next night I entered there and took out a packet of women's clothing. I understood that these things came from the Czech Jews. I buried the things and, wanting to see the Gestapo chief to receive permission from him to go the barracks where my daughter was, I did a bit of work and damaged the water pipes. Immediately afterwards, the chief called me to repair the water system and then I succeeded in receiving permission to go to the barracks on Sunday.

I actually did go to my daughter with the things on Sunday. She was in terrible condition. Both of us cried like small children. My daughter consoled and calmed me. I learned that several more Jewish girls and women worked in the barrack. Saying goodbye to my child was not easy, but I had to leave. I visited my daughter several times in this way. Later I learned that the Jewish girls and the Jewish women were taken to Sobibor and among them was my dear and unforgettable daughter.

The number of Jews at the *bahnhof* became smaller and fewer. I still remember those who were the last victims, such as: Ahron Fus, Goldman's son, Yona, Welwe Cymryn, Shaul Walter, Rafal Dech and Abish Szpan. Each of us waited in the ranks for when we would be taken to the "mountain" to be shot.

[Page 552]

They did not wait for us on the "mountain." One day, vehicles waited for us in front of the *bahnhof*. There was a heavy guard from the *S.S.* on the vehicles. As always, we thought that this meant our last hour. The vehicles took us further on the street of the train to the jail.

The gate of the jail opened and we immediately found ourselves in the jail courtyard. We were taken to a dark cellar and we were thrown into it with great brutality. We could not see; we felt that we were falling on human bodies. We were horrified when we learned that this was the death cell of the Chelm jail There were 23 Jews here and they were waiting for their fateful hour. We all cried bitterly.

There was a knock on our door in the morning. We were afraid. However, a little piece of bread and cigarettes fell in and we had the first greeting from a group of Jews who still were here and could move around more freely. They threw bread and cigarettes to us. The always courageous, Shlomo Bubys, was among them.

Every time we were called, we thought that death had come and I also thought this. On a certain day there was a knock on our door and Tantshe Nisbaum and I were called. We were called by the jail chief who sent us with a guard to the *bahnhof* to make "stretchers."

We were taken to work for several days and in the evening we were brought back. On the way I once met Mrs. Libhober going under the guard of the *S.S.* members. Her son was in the death cell. As I learned, Mrs. Libhober, who was a good seamstress, told the Gestapo that if they shot her son she would under no circumstances work – and her son did remain alive.

At work I once met the regrettably famous Raschendorf. He carefully considered our work and said to us that the Jews in the death cell would remain alive. Returning "home," I told this to my suffering brothers. However, no one believed it. Certainly, there was no one to believe because in the morning we were all led out and [we were told] to undress down to our underwear. We understood that these were our last minutes. However, we again were led to the death cell. Our only food was that which we received from Shlomo Bubys.

Several days passed and a group of Jews was separated from [us in] our jail and did not return. We remained few in number and indifferent to everything. Yet, we no longer wanted to remain in such a condition. We called to the director of the jail and and said that he should either shoot us or take us out to the working Jews. He agreed to the latter condition and we left for work.

[Page 553]

Fifteen Jews worked with us in the jail workshops. These were: Shlomo Brustman, Moshe Neiman, Kelberman and his wife, Hersh Boksenbaum, Shlomo Bubys, Gitl Libhober and her son, Ben–Tzion Micfliker, Tantshe Nisbaum, Yehiel Szczipak, Manis Cymryn, Golda Laks, Chaim Sobol, Binsztok and me. Life was more or less bearable. We often went into the city under guard and bought various things for the workshops. We did not recognize Chelm. There were no Jews; there were Poles in all of the Jewish businesses. We returned broken from the city. The electrician, Binsztok, had informed us that the Germans were suffering constant defeats. We were afraid that the defeats would [land on] our heads.

The front came all the more closer to Chelm and with it also the danger for us. Meanwhile we were called to the Gestapo to work for the chief. We arrived there at night. It was very merry there; whisky and wine flowed like water. The noisy and impudent laughter was tempting and exciting. Half–naked women lay around drunk. The chief came to me and ordered Tantshe Nisbaum and I to make crates in which to pack things. We began to work and we understood that the Germans would not be with us for long, but what would happen to us – would they let us live?

We finished the work late at night. We were given a bottle of wine to drink and were taken to a Russian prisoner, Misha (Misha actually was a Jew), to spend the night. There also were set aside all kinds of good things on the table with Misha. He treated us to everything and told us that the Germans were leaving and we needed to escape.

We again made the crates in the morning. An *S.S.* man ordered us to pack the crates in the vehicles. Bramiler, the vice chief of the Gestapo came to see if everything already was in the vehicle. He got into the vehicle and called over to the guard. I heard the way he ordered: "*Kalt machen die Juden!*" [Bump off the Jews!] I was terrified. My only wish was to perish with everyone in the jail and not here at the directorship. However, we immediately were ordered into the vehicle with the people and Misha. We were taken to the jail. On the way, Misha jumped out of the vehicle. The Germans chased after him and did not catch him. I enjoyably breathed the fresh air and thought: how long would I breathe such air?

Arriving in jail, I told my suffering brothers what I heard from the vice chief, Bramiler. Everyone lowered his head listening to me. Immediately after this, we again were chased into the death cell.

[Page 554]

We were not in the death cell for much longer. The Russians came closer to the Bug and the ground burned under the German feet. They prepared to leave. They again needed more workers. Therefore, they again called us out and ordered us to help them pack. To our good fortune, the Soviet troops began to bomb Chelm and, particularly, the train station and close to our jail. The members of the *S.S.* departed like mice for the air–raid shelters. We were left without a guard.

I told everyone the situation, told everyone to save themselves. I said to go to the cellar of the water system and hide. We did go there and hid.

There were constant bombardments for three days and three nights. The entire fence [around] the jail was destroyed; dust, soot and scraps covered everyone. We were all close together. I did not understand what power maintained us then. Finally the bombardments ceased. We no longer had any strength. We decided to explore what the situation looked like and, again, the daring Shlomo Bubys told us that a guard stood near the broken fence, a member of the Red Army.

He went over to the Red Army man and told him that there were 15 Jews in the jail. The Red Army man told him that we should leave the cellar and told us we were free. A movie camera was taken out and filmed us.

I immediately went to the city with Shlomo Brustman. The first greeting I had was from a Pole who welcomed us with mockery and shouted: "The Jews again are here. They have not yet all been shot!" We went further on our way to the Red Cross where we washed a little and received coffee.

The city hall took us in and gave us the house at Post Street number 39 to live in and a little bit of [food]. We immediately created a kitchen and the women Kelberman and Libhober cooked.

We created a committee and Shlomo Brustman was the chairman. Our house became a place of refuge for all Jews. Jews from the Aryan side with Aryan papers, partisans and Jews from Russia arrived. I was indifferent to everything. Just as I earlier had the desire to live, now I wanted to die. However, the constant letters that arrived from Russia searching for relatives also brought a greeting from my son who was looking for me. New blood poured into my veins. An impulse to live again awoke in me. I began to work again and awaited my son, the only survivor of my large family.

[Page 555]

Witness Testimony of Gitl Libhober

Translated by Gloria Berkenstat Freund

No. 38/12 15-XII-1946

Minutes of the *Voivodisher* [provincial] Jewish History
Commission in Lublin Archive of J.H.C. Minutes no. 2112.

This relates: - Gitl Libhober, born 11/18, 1897. Possesses middle [school] education. Trade – a dressmaker. Before the war – lived in Chelm at Lwowske Street, no. 4, and she now also lives in Chelm at Pasztowe 39.

Recorded by Irene Szajewicz.

There were 18,000 Jews in the city in 1939 when the Germans entered Chelm. I had a husband and a 15-year old daughter and a son of 17. The Germans immediately began to bully the Jews, grabbed them for work. Mainly they employed the Jews for cleaning the toilets with their bare hands, and after the work they ordered the Jews to beat one another. S.S. members Ralfink, a tall blond, 30-year old man, and Dr. Selch, also of the same age, particularly tortured the Jews. A month after the arrival of the Germans, a *Judenrat* [Jewish council] was created according to their [German] procedures with the merchant, Frankel, at the head. Members of the *Judenrat* were: Biderman, Dreszer, Tenenboim, Frajberger.

One day the *Judenrat* ordered all of the Jewish men from 15 to 60 to assemble at Luczkowski Square where he [Frankel] would speak to them. The Jews gathered. The *Wermacht* [German armed forces] surrounded them and, pointing their guns at them, ordered that they surrender their money and expensive things. First they took everything from the assembled Jews and then they began to beat them murderously. The worst scoundrel and murderer was the above mentioned Ralfink who directed this *aktsia* [Nazi military operation usually associated with rounding up and deporting Jews]. The women and children also came from distant streets wanting to hear what the leader of the *Judenrat* would say. In a moment, Ralfink went over to a Jew named Motl Bakalczyk and asked him to dance. When the women and children seeing it all began to cry, the Germans began to shoot in the air and the assembled men were driven in the direction of Hrubiesow. I was also present for all of this because I did not let my husband and son go out of our house and, therefore, I wanted to know what would happen here. If there would be any bad consequences. The desperate women went to the *Judenrat* and begged to be told what had happened to their husbands.

Then the women left on the Hrubieszower Road and saw that the road was sown with dead bodies. There were traces of blood and pieces of clothing everywhere. One thousand Jews were killed then on the road to Hrubieszow.

[Page 556]

One of those who successfully escaped told me that the Germans had ordered the Jews to dig holes and then told them to lie in them and other Jews were forced to bury them alive. Eight hundred Jews reached Hrubieszow; from there they forced them to Keldz on the Bug River and told them to go to the other side of the river. Three hundred Jews were successful in reaching the shore of the other side of the river and approximately 100 Jews returned to Chelm in very bad condition. The Germans wanted to arrange such a spectacle with the women, but the *Judenrat* did not want to summon the women and the Germans gave up on this. Many Jews attempted to escape to the Russian side. The Jews were treated horribly (by the Germans). We received food cards; everyone was forced to work. When it was possible, they ransomed themselves with money. This lasted until 1941. The *Judenrat* had to fulfill all of the German demands, which was not so easy and, therefore, the *Judenrat* had to extort everything from the Jews in order to placate the Germans, but the murder of Jews had not yet started.[1]

At the beginning of 1940 we were forced to put white patches with the *Mogen Dovid* [Star or Shield of David] on our right shoulder… Still in 1940, I reported as a foreman and became a dressmaker for the *S.D.* (*Sicherheits dienst* [security service]).

Once, a member of the *S.S.*, Schteinert, a terrible murderer, and his wife approached me and ordered a dress from me. He demanded that the dress be finished the next morning at 11 o'clock. I answered him that it would be finished at 3 o'clock in the afternoon. After long words, they agreed. The dress was sewn by the morning and I, myself, carried it away. Schteinert met me and asked at what time was I supposed to bring the dress. I answered that I clarified this last night that it could be finished at 3 o'clock and it was now just 2:30. Without saying one word, Schteinert began to hit me, so that I fainted. Then he told the Jews who worked for him that I should be carried to the cellar. When I came to, Schteinert's wife was standing near me and asked how I was doing and said that she was delighted with the sewn dress. Agitated, I said: And why did your husband beat me so if this was true? She began to scream that nothing had happened to me and he had beaten me very little and now I should sew three more dresses. When I categorically refused, she threatened that if I did not sew the dresses, she would immediately bring the dogs, which would bite me, and she said that her husband had especially not killed me because my work pleased her and as long as she had me sew dresses I would live. Knowing that I had no other option, I agreed to take on the additional work. My husband was the pharmacist for *TOZ* [Society for the Protection of Health]; my son also worked in the pharmacy. My daughter sewed with me.

[Page 557]

In May 1941, a transport of Jews arrived in Chelm from Slovakia. They had a great deal of baggage with them. The things were laid out in the synagogue and then the Germans removed it all. Each Jewish family took several people from the transport. They were at the mercy of the *Judenrat* because the Germans had stolen everything from them. Jews were not supposed to be taken care of by Aryan doctors or to make use of the pharmacy. Jews organized medical help in their own area. There were also Jewish businesses because the Aryan stores were not supposed to be entered. A Jewish militia was organized.

One day a member of the Gestapo came to me and demanded that I sew a dress for his wife during the course of three days. I did not have the time because I had the work for the *shishkes* [big shots] from the Gestapo and I could not be even a minute late with their work. The *Judenrat* gave him another dressmaker. Three days later I was called to the Gestapo by a Jewish militia man. There I found the member of the Gestapo with his wife in a new dress and also the dressmaker who had sewn it. Schlezinger, the member of the *S.S.*, asked me if the dress had been sewn well. Although the dress had been sewn with many defects, I do not want to say this and I gave an evasive answer. Then Schlezinger gave his whip to the dressmaker, ordering her to give me 15 blows.

In Autumn 1941, the Jews had to transfer to a separate quarter. These were the streets: Szkolne, Unjejacka, Pocztowa, Siedlecka and Katowska. Only the Jews who worked in the city could go outside the limit of these streets. Jewish militia men and armed Poles stood guard over the quarter. I lived on the corner of Kopernika and Szkolne Streets. There were two entrances, one for we Jews and a separate one for our "clients" from the Aryan side. Other tradesmen lived in the same place.

The plight of the Jews became more difficult with each day. Spring 1942, the Jews were deported to Wlodawa from the small *shtetlekh* around Chelm: Dubienka, Wojsławice, Siedliszcze, Sawin and from others. All passed through Chelm. I saw how the Germans bullied them. I saw their terrible need and misfortune. In Chelm, it was said that only the working Jews could remain there.

The first *aktsia* was in May, 1942. The Jewish militia and the *granatowa* [*granatowa policja* – Blue Police, popular name of the police organized by the General Government] went with the *S.S.* members through the houses and took the old, mainly the Slovak Jews. Toymer of the *S.D.* led the *aktsia*. The Jews were deported on the train to Wlodawa, but some of them were off-loaded in Sobibor where there was a death camp, but we did not know that then. Letters arrived from Wlodawa to which the deported were sent and we were sure that they would meet the same fate as those from the small *shtetlekh*. That is, that they would be rounded up and deported, that the majority would be annihilated. Staying alive was more difficult for those who did not have any work to do.

[Page 558]

Two months later in July, after the first *aktsia*, I remember that it was a Friday, the second *aktsia* broke out. The Germans and the *granatowa* police exclusively carried it out. The Jews were gathered from their workplaces (from the city hall, from the water facility and from others); they were bound together in groups of 5-6 people and were driven in the direction of Wlodawa. Several escaped in route and the remaining were taken to Sobibor. No one reached Wlodawa. We then first learned that they had perished and we knew that things were bad.

On the 14th of August a Jewish militia member came to me and said that all Jews must go into the ghetto and I, also, could not live in the same house in which I had lived until then. I ran to the *S.D.*, to my "client," and I asked what had happened. Then I was told that I should hide everyone of mine because those who did not work for the Germans would be deported to Wlodawa. I hid my husband and son with a Ukrainian acquaintance in a bunker. I remained in my apartment with my daughter and with the women workers. The Jewish militia violently removed us from the house and took us to the square on Siedlecka Street. There were many Jews there. My daughter escaped from the square and ran to the *S.D.* She explained that I had been taken and that all of the clients' goods remained in the house. Meanwhile, terrible things happened on the square. A Jew, who had held a piece of bread in his hand, was brought. The bread was torn from him and the Jew said that "the world is no longer for him." Then, when the German asked him what his last request was, he answered that he wanted to eat the piece of bread. The Germans gave him the bread and when he placed the bread in his mouth, they shot him. One of the Germans standing on a balcony showed a Jewish child to those gathered beneath and asked if the child pleased them. Then he smashed the small head of the child, banging it into the wall and, tearing the head in half, he threw it on the square. It is difficult to write about the terrible, horrible events that took place then on the square. Several tradesmen, it seems the more praise-worthy, were taken from the square. The *S.D.*, who had been informed by my daughter, came to take me from the square. All the Jews who had been brought together, about 3,000, were deported from the square to Sobibor, where there was a death camp. I remained living in my apartment. The Jews who were left after the *aktsia* remained in the Jewish quarter, went to work and some time passed that seemed quieter to us.

[Page 559]

The first day of November 1942, repression began again. It became clear that something would again happen.

Two day later, before the *aktsia* broke out, I brought work for the *S.D.*, finding *S.D.* Horn completely drunk. He then told me that only the Jews who were needed tradesmen would remain in Chelm and the rest would be deported. I asked the date; he answered that he did not know exactly.

On the 6th of November, Taymer[2] and the *S.S.* member, Roshendorf, (the worst hangmen over the Chelm Jews) came to the apartments of tradesmen who needed to remain and marked their doors with chalk as signs that they were to remain with the workers and their families. At the same time, they ordered that the doors be bolted and that no one be allowed in. I did what I was ordered to do.

[Page 560]

In half an hour the *S.S.* came and took me and everyone, except my husband who had hidden the last moment. My protests and all of my talk about the chalk mark on my door did not help me. I was brought to the square that was on Kopernika Street. On the way the daughter of *S.S.* Horn saw me. I called to her; she should tell her father that I had been taken. A member of the *S.S.*, hearing my talk, called out to her: "Do not say anything to your father. All the Jews must die," and at this, Horn's daughter answered: "All of the Jews can die, but not Mrs. Libhober. She must sew my new dresses." And she immediately ran away. There were several thousand Jews at the square near the Russian church. The Germans beat them with whips, tortured and bloodied them. The walls of the church were red with blood. Horn came with several *S.D.* and said to me that I should go with all of mine to the other side where a group of the chosen tradesmen stood. The Jews at the square were ordered to line up in rows of three and they were taken away to Piarske Street. Six thousand Jews were taken then. Many bodies of murdered children and several adults were laid out on the square. The population of Chelm stood on the other side of the church calling out: Good for them; long live Hitler! Wagons immediately came and the bodies were taken. They were thrown in the wagons like sand. The *S.S.* surrounded our groups of tradesmen and told us to go. On the way we met the other Jews. They were taken in wagons and we to the camp on Kalajover Street. They were taken in the wagons in front of our eyes.

Signed: Libhober Gitl. VIII.25.1950, in Warsaw

Translator's Footnotes:

1. There is a contradiction in the statement that the "murder of Jews had not yet started" as is evident in the previous paragraphs.
2. This name is spelled as both Toymer and Taymer.

[Page 559]

Not a City, but a True Cemetery[1]

by Ester Bas-Meltser

Translated by Gloria Berkenstat Freund

…so I am in my birthplace Chelm. This is, alas, a true cemetery. Every stone – a headstone, each house – a witness to the murdered martyrs.

If we could understand the language of the wind that shakes the leaves on the trees in the emptied streets, we would certainly learn about many tragic scenes that were played out when the hangmen drove our parents, sisters and brothers to death.

Everything chokes with the heavy, oppressive picture of the nightmarish day. Our Polish neighbors greet us with an open hate in their eyes. We see, literally, a resentful astonishment when they look at us; from where did we come and how did we survive?

"Yet, a small number of you were saved," a Polish acquaintance said to me with a tone of suspicion.

[Page 560]

Day in, day out, I roam around the emptied Jewish streets. Only the strange, unfamiliar eyes of Polish children, who surely are wearing the clothing of those who perished, now look out of the windows from which the faces of Jewish children with dark, sad eyes would look out. I stand on Kopernika; the sun starts to go down. The redness reminds me of the flames of the destroyed Jewish houses.

It looks to me as if the blood of the tortured runs from its rays… I instinctively close my eyes and I think that I hear their voices. It begins to get dark; the moon appears in the sky. Its bleached brightness also frightens me, remembering the bleached out dear faces, the frozen eyes of my husband, Kuba, who fell asleep forever along with the Chelemer Jewish community.

Original Footnote:

1. An excerpt from the book, *In the Fog of Death* by Ester Bas-Meltser, which was published in 1950 in Montreal, Canada, published by a group of newly-arrived Chelemer.

[Page 561]

Eye Witness Account

by Yoel Ponsczak

Translated by Pamela Russ

An excerpt of a diary – from the archives of the Historical Committee in Warsaw

Number 104/VII

At the end of July 1942, a luxury car with five murderers entered the building of the *Judenrat*. They approached the chairman and demanded that by 2 pm all the Jews should be assembled in one place, and each person could take 15 kilograms with him. All left to the Ukraine. I quickly left the *Judenrat*, went home and delivered the "good" news. There was tremendous panic. People began to hide. I and my wife and child went into hiding as well. Our hiding place was one of the best ones in Chelm. It was a room in a German school, by a certain Professor Zeiger. It cost plenty, but it was worthwhile because we were safe there. I, having had a good work card with a green ribbon, could go freely in the streets. Within about one hour, you could not see even one Jew in the streets. At 12 noon, our streets were enclosed. They already did not allow me to leave these streets and I could not come back to my family. The *Judenrat* signaled to me that I should go somewhere else. But I had nowhere to go. I went into a shoemaker's home, he was one of the "aristocrats." He worked for the murderers, and we sat there in great fear.

Through the window, we saw how the murderers were chasing all the Jews to one place. At 4 pm, there were already about 2,000 Jews assembled in that place. Frequent shooting could be heard. The city labor officer, along with Inspector Heldhas, were strongly involved in this *Aktzia*, and a large number of people were released. Three hundred people were taken to Sobibor, mainly the elderly, and 70 men were shot in the city.

These tragic summer days dragged slowly under the heavy load of work. Fall arrived, then cold. Many people were barefoot, naked, and hungry, and that's how we had to work in the muddy swamps. We were resigned to our fate. We felt that the ground was burning under us.

October 26, 1942, there was great pandemonium. All the workers of the factories were detained, and that was the clearest indication that the *Aktzia* would take place at night. You could not leave the area because of the late hour (Jews could only go out until 7 pm), so my family and I could not hide in our regular place in the above-mentioned school. We waited for the murderers all night, but the night was calm. As soon as it became light, we went to the school. The professor greeted us quite nicely, even though we disturbed his sleep. Within half an hour, there were already about 15 Jewish families in the school. The professor made a small business out of this, and with each *Aktzia* he raised his price.

[Page 562]

The morning passed calmly. Not one Jew was seen in the streets. On the odd moment, you would see a Jew running in a state of nervousness.

I went to the chairman to find out was going on. He was very agitated and did not hear what I was saying to him. But I did not let up and his reply was a tragic one: "It's bad." It was already 11 o'clock. I went home to be able to take something for the family. At that very moment, the SS men were guarding those few streets and I could not continue onwards. This time, one of my neighbors created a good hiding place, so I went to hide there and he gladly took me in. It was now 12 o'clock and the murderers searched through all the streets. You could hear the incessant shooting. I was very nervous that I was not with my family.

It was evening, no shooting was heard, patrol cars were heard going through the streets. The region was small and there were more than 20 people there, and it was very wet. Finally, it was day. The murderers stormed through the Jewish streets. The entire time, you heard shots and explosions of grenades. The *Aktzia* lasted all day. In the evening, there was pounding at the door. We thought it was the patrols, but apparently it was Mr. Mandel from the *Judenrat*. He gave us gruesome news about the two days of the *Aktzia*. Eight hundred people died as sacrifices in that place and 3,000 people were evacuated on foot to Wlodowa. The entire time, I was thinking about my family hiding in the school. My daughter came in the evening, and with tears in her eyes she told me that her mother and Dovid'el were taken away. I heard this news as if a hammer had pounded on my head, but I calmed down and decided to save my wife and son at any cost. After leaving a payment, I settled my daughter in the home of a Christian, and I left for the *Judenrat*. All the members were in the *Judenrat*. I told them about my tragedy and asked for help, but sadly, they could not help me. They told me that my wife had been evacuated with the entire group of Jews and taken to Wlodowa, and she was together with the child.

The *Aktzia* was over, but I did not see anyone in the streets, other than the murderers who were wandering around. I decided to go to Wlodowa in order that, maybe, I would be able to save my wife and child. Six kilometers outside of Chelm, in the village of Horodyszcze, the peasants told me that some Jewish women were there who ran away during the night when the peasants were asleep. They told me that among these women was a tall brunette holding the hand of a young child. I was certain that this was my wife and my son Dovid'el. Like a wild man, I ran from house to house. The village was big. Finally, I found two Jewish women and a child, of which one was actually my wife and child Dovid'el.

[Page 563]

The following morning, my daughter Pelye, whom I had left at the home of a Christian, kissed and hugged and cried with her mother and her darling Dovid'el.

Sadly, this joy did not last long. The murderers did not rest. They were already discussing the next *Aktzia*. I went to my Professor Zeiger, discussed the price with him, which as usual he raised again, this time more than others, and then we agreed. The week passed in terror. There was a panic, but things calmed down.

November 5, during the day, I was informed that there would be an *Aktzia* that night. In the evening, I and my family, along with sisters and brothers-in-law and their children, and there were also two Czechoslovakian Jews with us as well, and a certain Shmuel Schwartz and his wife, and we all went to the school. As was done previously, we were given a room, and there were Jews also in the other rooms. It seemed that Zeiger's school was popular in town. All the Jews were my good friends. All night, we went from one room to another, visiting as guest. As day broke, the murderers began to become wild. In the streets and on the smaller roads there was a real slaughter. The shots of the machine guns and the throwing of grenades did not stop. This did not stop all day. Only in the evening did it quiet down. In the late night hours, Zeiger visited us, but he became wild. We could not even speak to him. He kept screaming about how bad it was, and then he left.

[Page 564]

His cold visit was suspicious for us, but what choice did we have. We held a short discussion with all those present and we decided to leave the school and to hide in the attic. We were now over 100 people. It was daylight. There were also a few Orthodox Jews among us. It was Shabbath. We blessed the new month of Kislev, and in town, it was once again the same as the day before. The shooting and the bombs from the grenades did not stop. Everyone was tense. The children cried, but thankfully, they could not hear this on the street.

At 10 am, the Germans found us in the attic. They took down 55 men. As sheep to the slaughter they took us to a designated place in the center of town. There they beat us mercilessly and then separated the men from the women. Then they chased us in the direction of the train station. We thought that they were taking us to the wagons to go to Sobibor. As we were going, I was holding the hand of my brother-in-law Avrohom Yakov, and we decided to escape. We ran towards a yard, and a friend ran after us. No one shot after us, I think because they did not notice us. Fate wanted that I should not struggle for 22 months, wandering without rest.

[Page 563]

Eye Witness Accounts

by Manis Zitrin

Recorded by: E. Winik

Translated by Pamela Russ

On the eighth day of the war, the Germans bombed Chelm ferociously. There were many wounded on that day. From the first day on, when the Russian army entered Chelm, a military comprised primarily of Jews, was created immediately. The Poles did not join. In the villages, the militia were the Ukrainians. After eight days, the Russians left the town voluntarily. There was chaos. The Jews were terrified to go into the streets. The Polish good-for-nothings began their looting and even broke down doors of the shops. The local military of the magistrate themselves were looting as well, set fires, and even killed a few Jews.

The Poles began to spread a rumor that they were killing Polish officers and Polish police in the cellars of the prisons. The rumor was spread everywhere.

A great number of civilian Germans came from the villages, and they immediately became militia men. As the German military authorities took over the city, they they designated Mr. Kamentz, an owner of a mill and a steel foundry, as mayor.

[Page 564]

Very quickly, the Germans snatched up Jews for work, collected all kinds of taxes, and they sold the materials from the Jewish stores for pennies to civilian Germans who ran away from the villages.

In about six weeks, the Gestapo already arrived. The first *Judenrat*, which was established by the Polish magistrate, was headed by Mr. Meyer Frankel, the son-in-law of Mr. Lederman and a brother-in-law of Itche Meyer Lederman. In essence, the *Judenrat* was good for the Jews, because they organized Jewish life somewhat. The Germans beat the Jewish *Judenrat* members for any small thing.

Later, some *Ratnikes* [name for those in the *Judenrat*] began to use their situation more for themselves – for their own families and for their material needs, at the cost of others.

In November 1939, the Gestapo demanded its first taxes from the *Judenrat,* in the sum of 100,000 zlotys. The *Judenrat* members went to each house and collected the huge sum, and we paid the tax. A few weeks later, the Gestapo demanded that a few things be put together, primarily winter clothes and electrical items. Once again, we collected as much as possible and delivered everything to the German thugs.

[Page 565]

At the end of November 1939, the Gestapo offensively once again demanded another tax, now 1/4 of a million zlotys, which the Jews could in no way produce.

Then came the demand that the Jews, primarily the men, must present themselves … "to work" early in the morning, on Friday, December 1, 1939, on the *Rynek* place [market square]. The *Judenrat* went into all the Jewish streets and told the men to present themselves for work, they themselves not even knowing to what type of work. About 2,000 Jews, the aristocrats of the city, gathered at the market square at the designated time. Not one of the Jews had any idea what was prepared for them.

At a set time, the Gestapo commandant arrived, and asked who was a skilled worker. He selected a group of ten men from the crowd. In the blink of an eye, the entire worried mass was surrounded by German Stormtroopers on motorcycles, and all 2,000 Jews were chased into the Hrubieszow forest. For three days, the tragic brothers were chased, beaten, and murdered, and all those others were shot. The road was quickly sown with the dead.

Interesting, that for a short time the Russian border was open, but no one wanted to escape. The Germans spread rumors, false ones, that they were leaving Chelm ... This created great confusion in everyone's minds...

On the German holiday, November 9, 1939, the new German mayor, Mr. Haga, who was brought specially from somewhere else to Chelm, delivered a speech, where he publicly announced that he would make the city *Judenrein* [cleansed of Jews].

After the "march," the city was as if dead. The *Judenrat*, whom the Germans considered as hostages, began to "be a little bloated' about themselves, and it began to be a privilege, a merit, to belong to the *Judenrat*. Anshel Biderman, Bash, and others did not reveal what they knew about the German acts. Frankel was the head of the *Judenrat* that began to protect their relatives and their own people.

In Chelm, there was no enclosed ghetto, but it was divided into two areas: In the first area there was Poctowa [post-office] street, Sziedlice, Katowska Street, until Motye Levin's house. The second area: Szkolna, around the synagogue, Kwisza, part of Seminarska Street, and Kopernika Street.

The *Judenrat* organized a merchandise warehouse for the needs of the Gestapo. They would buy the materials in Warsaw. As escorts for the Gestapo, two Jews from the *Judenrat* went to Warsaw to make these purchases. The Jews – in the Jewish area – brought materials with the help of the Christians, sold the materials, and even made some money. Some even brought materials from Russia (before the Russo-German War). There was a lot of smuggling, and the Germans closed their eyes to this. Paper money increased for everyone. There were some Jews who earned a lot of money and lived very comfortably.

[Page 566]

The *Judenrat* created its own post system, offices, and so on. The director held himself to be "great," a complete "manager," a "Kaiser," and the Jews had to remove their hats for him.

The Germans set up Pinkhas Szwartzblat from Libewna as the Jewish commandant. Previously, he was an agent for the Poles.

* * *

The issue of worker's outposts was a real problem. When the Germans had to clean out a house, or sweep out the garbage of a house, the Gestapo immediately called the *Judenrat*, that they must provide so many and so many workers, presenting the numbers as they demanded, for example: once - ten men; another time 40 men and women, another time even 100 people for work. The *Judenrat* had to assemble the required numbers of unskilled laborers and skilled workers for the Gestapo. The poor people labored hard and bitterly.

When the Russo-German war broke out, the situation for the Jews worsened daily. In March 1942, there was already a terrible slaughter of Jews in Lublin. Many Czechoslovakian Jews were brought to Chelm and they shared the same fate as the Jews of Chelm.

On Passover 1942, the chairman of the *Judenrat* gave a speech to the Jews in the yard of the Old Age Home, saying that whoever would not work would certainly die. Every morning the Jewish police chased the Jews to work.

The Germans created a new street that stretched from the Seminary Street to the train station. With their blood and sweat, the Jews paved this new street, where a new prison was also built for prisoners and for Jews.

The Germans twice set fire to the large, old synagogue, that was already 700 years old. The German vandals forced the Jews to remove the stones from the synagogue and clean the place up, make the ground smooth, so that no one would be able to tell that once a synagogue had stood in that place.

The staff officers of the Gestapo needed people, skilled laborers who would work for them, make suits for them, coats, shoes, boots, and so on. And not for the officers only, but also for their loved ones and mistresses. Therefore, they chose people from every vocation, arrested them in the new prison not far from the train station, organized special factories in the prison, and the craftsmen had to work continuously – understandably, unpaid, but only for enough food to sustain their lives – and do everything that the Gestapo ordered.

[Page 567]

These are the names of the 15 people, craftsmen which the Germans selected for slave labor and who, miraculously, survived in the Chelm prison:

Shloime Brustman – a tailor (today in Israel); Berl Kelberman – a tailor (today in America; Rokhel Kelberman, Berl Kelberman's wife (today in America); Tankhum Nisenboim – a carpenter (today in Brazil); Khaim Sobel – a spats [gaiter] stitcher (today in Israel); Isser Zilber – a tinsmith (today in America); Shloime Bubes – a shoemaker (today in Israel); Hersh Buxenboim – a shoemaker (today in Israel); Bentshe Mitzfliker – a tailor (today in Canada); Gitel Liebhober – a seamstress (today in Poland); Golde Laks – a seamstress; Manis Zitrin – a stitcher (today in Israel); Samuel Liebhober (in Poland); Moishe Najman – a tailor ((in Israel); Yekhiel Szczupak – a cap maker, died after the liberation.

Other than these 15 martyrs, there was also a sixteenth person, Yakel Binsztok, a radio technician. He fled right before the liberation from prison and died during the Polish resistance in Warsaw.

[Page 568]

Thanks to Yakel Binsztok, who fixed the officers' radio apparatuses, he had an opportunity – as he regulated the apparatuses – to often hear news which he gave over to his friends about what was happening on the war front. Also, the doctor of the Gestapo comforted them so that they would not lose strength and hope.

On July 20, 1944, the Germans ceded from Chelm. The Gestapo had received an order from Lublin to burn the prison with all the prisoners inside. But the commandant did not carry out the order, and miraculously, the fifteen Jews survived.

The last three days were the worst, because the Germans were no longer in the city. But the men heard shooting, so they hid in the cellar of the prison and lay there without food or water, without light, and without air to breathe. When they finally decided to crawl out of the cellar, because their lives were no longer manageable, they just happened to crawl out onto the feet of a Russian soldier, a guard, who, miraculously, did not shoot them, but he summoned the higher Russian officers who – after an investigation – gave them food and photographed and filmed them.

[Page 567]

Eye Witness Accounts of Shloime Brustman

Recorded by: E. Winik

Translated by Pamela Russ

After the liberation of the German tyranny, the few Jews of Chelm decided to remain together. They found a Jewish home and settled in. The house was on Pocztowa Street, number 39. Very quickly, the house was turned into a center for the Jews coming in from the entire area. Of those Jews who were hiding by the Aryans, there were several Jewish daughters: two daughters Baden (they once had a laundromat); a girl Butshe – a daughter of Goldstajn; Avrohom Berland's daughter, Lederman's daughter, and some other women.

At the first meeting, there were already eighteen Jews, Chelmer, and at that time the mayor Mr. Gut, photographed all of them.

The first Jew who returned from Russia was Mr. Bibel. Today he is in Israel.

Life continued under all these conditions and loneliness. They used the women's section of the Beis Medrash [Study Hall] as a place for these newcomers to sleep.

The new Polish government instituted some new actions against those who were active Polish collaborators with the Germans. I, in the name of the Jews, also instituted some actions against those Poles who had taken the property of the Jews in the community. They had taken the seniors' home, the *Talmud Torah* [school], the cemetery, the baths, and so on.

The Polish village elder recognized a group of Jews as the new Jewish municipality. This Jewish committee was made up of:

[Page 568]

Sh. Brustman, Manis Zitrin, Ponczak, Alegant, Yisroel Kuper, Gedaliah Bakalczuk, lawyer Hersh Derfer, Yosef Rolnik. They organized significant aid work; opened the *Batei Medrashim* [Study Halls], provided the Jewish soldiers with food, especially for the Jewish holidays, and so on. Later, they already received a subsidy of 10,000 zlotys a month from the Jewish Central Committee in Lodz.

In 1945, when the situation became unsettled in the land, some Poles began to attack the Jews in the streets. They even began shooting at some of the Jews in the town. It was then that the thought came to flee from Poland. I left to Germany at that time, where I remained for some time, and then got to Israel with the illegal *Aliyah*.

* * * *

Twice, the Germans set fire to the synagogue. The first time, the firemen put out the fire, and the second time, when the woman ran out – from Borukh Tzale's yard – and she began to scream and to cry about the fire, and she ran to save a Torah scroll, the German murderers threw her, a living human being, into the flames of the synagogue.

Later, the Jews had to remove the stones from the synagogue, smooth out the place, as if nothing had been there before. In the synagogue, the Jews found the bones of the woman Laks, who had been burned in the fire.

[Page 569]

Between Life and Death
(A Chapter of Pain and Demise)

by H. Akhtman, Canada

Recorded by: E. Winik

Translated by Pamela Russ

The soldiers surrounded the Jews and herded them over to the churchyard. People were coming from all directions. They were herding the rich and the poor, old and young, small and big. You heard bombing. In those places where the Gestapo could not find any Jews, they threw grenades and killed those who were hiding.

It was already nine in the morning. My brother, Moishe, came with a group of people. We asked him for news. He told us that he left the city with another family, but the Ukrainians caught them in the fields. They were forced to undress and then they were searched for money. But when the Ukrainians did not find any, they quickly chased my brother and his group into town and brought them to us in the church.

In this place, there already were Dr. Welberger and his entire family, all the officials of the administration, all the workers of the official German work sites. Everyone was brought here, without differentiation. No longer did they look at the work permits, they were now worthless. If you were Jewish, then the fate was the same – to come to the churchyard, where hundreds of soldiers were standing and filming us.

I looked and waited: Maybe they would bring my parents. But we wished more that they would be killed on the spot. At least they would not have had to see the horrific tragedies that were befalling everyone.

It was already eleven o'clock. They were bringing people without end. Next to me stood my cousin with a smashed up head. He tried to turn away, but a soldier immediately fixed that thought. He did not feel the blood that was running from his head. "It's nothing," he said. But when they brought the *Judenrat* at noon, everyone understood that now it was serious, we would all be evacuated. But the soldiers set aside Chairman Frenkel, and near him – the technician Tenenboim, and their families. A new thought arose. Maybe they would not evacuate all the Jews and maybe we would actually be the lucky ones. They also brought Anshel Biderman and they set him near us.

He began to scream and beg Frenkel to save him. But Frenkel did not even look at him. He now had no more energy. The soldiers calmed Biderman by showing him their gun.

Rivers of people were coming and coming, but the Germans remained calm. It was lunchtime. They left behind a small number of soldiers with us and then they left.

My brother Moishe had a small package of food with him, and a bottle of milk. We took nothing with us. He took out small pieces of *challah* and shared them with us and told us that we should save the bread for a darker time. He believed that even worse times would come.

I was happy with one thing, that I did not see my parents I wasn't sure that they were alive, but at least they were not watching this terrible tragedy.

[Page 570]

Two pm. All the Gestapo men and their chiefs were present. My heart was beating. Who will have the fate to live and who will have to die? Some faces were pale, tired – some, strained some – indifferent.

The chief and his officers went around and looked at the crowd. Our lives were in their hands, and really only the strongest, healthiest, youngest were selected to remain alive. There was already a small group in the middle of this place, and they now had some hope of remaining alive. The chief saw my husband and called out his name, and he pulled me along. But my hope was very small. The chief looked over all the people, the lucky ones, saw me, and ordered that both of us should go back and be sentenced to death.

We went back. There was tremendous chaos, screams, cries. Nothing helped. One Gestapo man approached the young Levenhertz and ordered him to go to the selected group, but he said that he would only do so if his wife and child came with him. Understandably, the Gestapo man did not take well to this, and Levenhertz remained with his family among the so-called dead. This was the only incident where a man did not want to save himself without his wife. All the men left their wives, children, mothers, fathers, anything so that they would save their lives.

Dr. Wolberger also wanted to rescue himself, so when someone took him out earlier, another person, with one beating, pushed him back into the "dead" rows. In the end he was successful. He and his son were included in the living.

Time passed, and the group of people sent to their death grew, becoming larger. They were still bringing people out from hiding places. I begged my husband to save himself, it would be terrible for both of us to die. But he did not change his mind. We calmed down, were watching the goings on, and at the same time waiting for our death. I didn't know where my brothers were, I was only watching people fighting for their lives. In a minute, a familiar officer passed by my husband and winked at him. I pushed him out of the rows, and I heard only his voice: "Hela, save yourself!" I tried to do that right away, I looked at the officers thinking how could I fool them, how could I sneak into the group of the living. I tried to take just a few steps, but the evil eye already saw my efforts and was now watching me. It was getting dark. The soldiers began to form us into four people per row. I looked around and searched for my relatives. Yes, I found Moishe, my brother, and I asked about my two younger brothers, Yankel and Borukh, and he told me that they were lucky to be among the living.

[Page 571]

It did not take long, and 6,000 Jews, set in rows of four, marched out of the churchyard and went down with the *piarske* ["clerics"] Szenkowycz and Kolejewa to the ramp. The lines were surrounded by soldiers. The rifles were loaded, ready to shoot, positioned downwards, pointing at us. I went near my brother. I couldn't let go of the thought of fleeing. The words "Hela, save yourself!" did not stop ringing in my ears. I heard them and I had to do something. In front of my eyes, I saw the houses that we passed, and I could see nothing but the angry eyes of the Gestapo men and the points of the rifles. But I did not lose hope.

It became dark. A soldier passed nearby. With my eyes, I tried to plead for mercy, but he moved the edge of the rifle closer to me. And that's how we approached the ramp.

The train was not yet there. The Germans organized us so that we sat down on the ground and waited. Once again, people were trying their wiles. They took out their papers from German places and showed them to the officers, who pretended to read them and then ripped them up. They [the Jews] said that they had been working all the time, they mentioned the names of important German officers, but it made no difference. Children were crying, mothers were crying along with them.

Suddenly, I saw a young, beautiful girl. Her name was Gross. She was speaking to a soldier, and the soldier took her and left with her. We believed that he took her back into the city. She left behind her mother, a cripple, and she was gone.

I walked through the rows [of people]. Morgenstern's wife and two children were sitting quietly. Not far from there was Wolbergerowa and her daughter, and Pesha, who had worked all the time for Dr. Wolberger. Wolberger's wife told me that she was trying to run away. Then Dubkowski's daughter approached me and asked why I was here and why I had not saved myself. I told her that I had my Polish ID card but I wanted to see what would happen to my family, and that is why I was waiting until the last minute. But then after that I would save myself. And in that actual minute an officer passed by, and I asked him where I should go for nature's needs [to relieve myself]. He took me aside, I sat down, and he was holding a loaded gun. In a flash, I grabbed him and said these words:

"You are a human being, you have a heart. I want to live. I am still young. Let me live!"
"Run," he said to me. "But I have to shoot." At that moment, another officer approached and he asked what I wanted. The first officer said that I wanted to die. He slapped me on my feet, I crouched and crawled back to the group. Now I am resigned, I knew that I had to die. I looked for my brother Moishe, and they were calling for everyone to stand up and get into line.

[Page 572]

The train arrived. As before, together we approached the living grave.

At the door of the train, there were soldiers standing on either side with clubs in hand, and whoever approached the door's entrance was beaten by them. When I had already stepped across the entrance, I heard a cry: "Oy!" and my brother was clutching his head. The club had found his head.

The trains were for animals, filthy. In each car, more than 200 people were packed in. There was nowhere to sit. Everyone had to stand. I leaned gently onto my brother.

Soon someone found a match, and then there was some light. I cannot forget the scene of a young girl, maybe 15 years old. She took out a piece of bread, began to eat, and then said: "This is not yet the last time. I have stood before death three times, and I am still alive." I stared at her and was amazed at her courage to live. My brother also took out some milk and bread and shared them with me. I told him to give some to others as well, and he replied that we had to remember the dark hour [that would be coming]. My brother had a true Jewish heart, never able to decline anything for anyone, so I wondered at his words.

I said to him: "Moishe, it is easier for you to die than for me. You do not have This World, so you will have the Next World," because he really believed in the Next World. But he answered that he did not know. He broke away from this belief. I asked him what he believes in now, is it better that he jump through the small window and meet his death? But he said that he believed in Sobibor there could be a camp, and maybe he would be selected to go to this camp. With this, I stop talking to him.

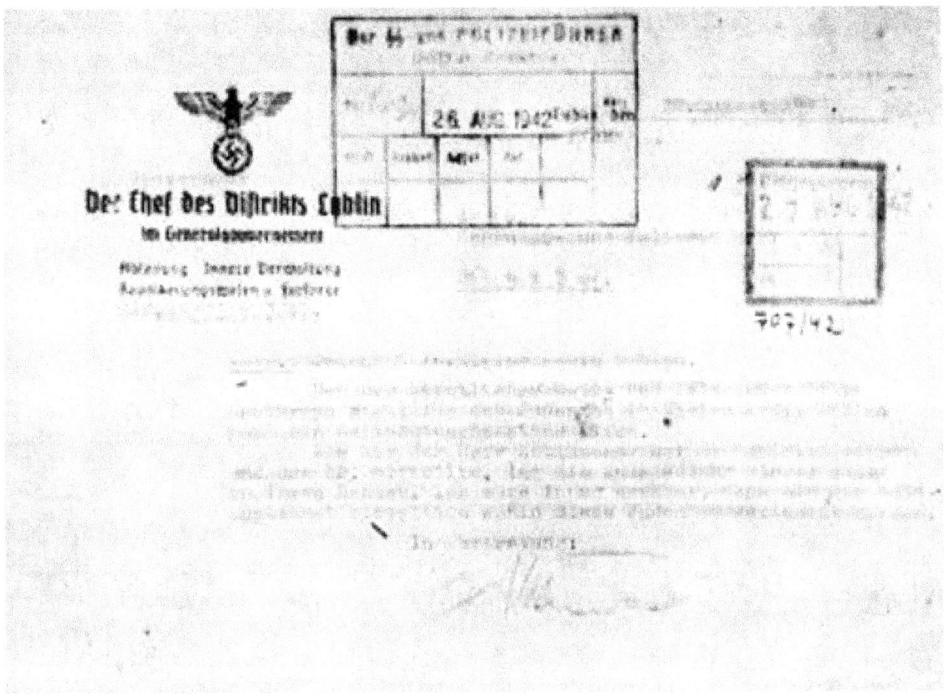

A document from the Hitler tyranny

There were people standing around us, children were crying. It was dark. We were locked in from outside and the train began to move. We heard voices, and we felt people pushing closer to the window. I asked:

[Page 573]

"What is going on?" They told me that two people jumped out of the window. I now also wanted to try, but the person next to me said I should not go because the officer already noticed and he was holding his gun ready to shoot at anyone who was looking out [of the window].

The train was running at full steam, the clanging of the wheels slowly put everyone to sleep. We were being taken to certain death. I felt nothing, I am indifferent, let's do it as quickly as possible. Once again I heard whispering and there was pushing. I learned that once again someone jumped out. I asked my brother if he also wanted to try, but he declined. I did not answer him, I did not say goodbye, and I stepped right through heads, feet, and bodies, and I was right near the window. The train was running very quickly. I asked myself: How should I jump? I heard a voice saying that I should jump in the same direction as the train was running. I asked for help to push me out and strange hands pushed me to the window. My feet were already hanging out, I am only holding on with my hands on the window, and am hanging on. I was not thinking, only going by instinct. I felt nothing, and only heard voices. I knew nothing, and with one push against the wall of the train, I jumped down.

I don't know how long I lay in a faint. I opened my eyes and began to remember where I was. I saw a figure approaching from a distance. I asked her soon, is it true that we were going to Sobibor? And she replied, yes. They approached the gate of Sobibor, and when the train stopped, she was able to jump off the car [of the train]. She left her mother behind in the train, and her mother threw out a winter scarf after her, so that the girl would not be cold.

I looked around. My bag lay open and my house keys had fallen out. I gathered everything together and, unknowingly, I felt a lot of wetness. I look – a puddle of blood. I move a little, and feel my chin. I put my hand there, and I had a hole under my chin. It seemed that when I jumped out [of the train] I fell face down on a rail and cracked open my chin. I removed my scarf from my throat and tied up my chin so that it did not hang down. Until this very day, I have a scar under my chin that remains from that time.

I do not remember the name of the girl. We both decided to get off the rails and stay there for the night. We both sat down near a bush and we covered ourselves with her mother's scarf. I was shaking, either from the cold or from the loss of blood. I could not stay in one place. We waited that way until dawn and then went wherever our eyes took us. Neither one of us knew the area. Suddenly, we saw a farmer's hut. My friend was very afraid that they would recognize her as a Jew. She did not speak Polish too well. I told her not to speak too much, that I would take care of that. When we entered the house of the non-Jews, they became frightened of us. I quickly made up a story for them, that the Germans wanted to take me to Germany for work, but I jumped off the wagon and got hurt. They gave me water to wash myself. I washed out the scarf and then put it back on. My coat was completely bloodied, but I could do nothing about it. I looked into the mirror and saw that my face was totally cut up and swollen. The Christians gave us warm soup and pieces of homemade bread. My friend ate well, but I could not swallow even one spoon.

[Page 574]

I wanted to pay these peasants and took out 20 zlotys but they put the money right back into my pocket. They showed us the way to Chelm, so we left the house and went on our way.

We were going and going, and it was already getting lighter. We arrived at a small village near Chelm, I don't remember the name. We wanted to have something to drink or to find a place to stay overnight. But my face, it seems, told the truth. Everyone sent us to the village magistrate for permission to stay in the village and to get something to eat. But after many tries, we resigned ourselves to the situation and went into the forest where we found a deep ditch. We collected many fallen leaves from the ground and lay down to sleep. I was very cold. It was a beautiful day with sunshine, but I could not warm myself. We stayed like that for many hours. Then, in the afternoon, we left to go to Chelm. But just as we started on our way, the farmers, who were just on their way home from the weekend annual market day, warned us that we should not go to Chelm, because terrible things were happening there. They were still hunting for Jews, and when they found the Jews, they were shot on the spot. But it seems that my bloodied coat and wounded face revealed who I was.

But this did not stop us. We had no other way to go. We arrived in Chelm in the evening. When we arrived in Oblonski, a Christian approached us and shouted that the Gestapo was not far from the metalworker's place. We went to medic Prukhnyok's place, with whom we had lived for many years, but his sisters did not want to let me in, even though I asked for medical help.

We continued on Oblonski to Kopernika Street, and were soon near Szenkewicza Street, when a watchman stopped me and learned that I was Jewish. Meanwhile, my friend moved away from me and left without me. But, with all my courage, I reply [to the watchman] that he had no proof that I was Jewish, and on the contrary, I could prove to him that I was Polish. I took out my Polish passport and showed him. He let me go and I ran after my friend. From far I see that he was taking her away. At that moment, I was separated from her and never heard from her again. I went back to Kopernika Street, and thought that Liebhober's wife was taken out of the group because she used to sew for the wives of the Gestapo men. I would certainly find her at home, and she lived in Akhtman's hotel. She and both of her children actually did survive, and I saw her in Chelm in 1945. But before I could get there I was stopped by an officer. He looked me over, from head to toe, but he did not arrest me. I calmly went into Liebhober's house, where there was no one to be found. The beds were still made, and everything was still in order… The clock on the wall was still ticking. It was six o'clock in the evening. I removed my bloodied coat, and threw myself onto the bed in my dress and shoes.

[Page 575]

Not long after I was lying there, about half hour later, I heard footsteps on the stairs, heavy steps, and of many people. The door of the second room was opened, and two officers with one young non-Jewish woman came in. From their conversation I understood that this non-Jewish woman was looking for clothing that she had left behind to have sewn. I heard how they opened drawers and were looking into the closets. I did not move, and at the same time, I covered myself with a pillow. They came into my room, turned on the light, looked around, and did not see me, even though my feet were actually poking out of the bed. I saw them: two tall military men and a non-Jewish girl. After a few minutes they left the room and locked all the doors. I didn't think about it and soon fell asleep.

When I woke up it was still dark. The clock was no longer ticking. I was not lying there for long when it began to dawn. I was afraid to put on the light and when I was already beginning to be able to recognize objects I got off the bed and looked around the house. I did not find my coat in the same place. Seems like the Germans thought about it and then returned it. I tried the doors, but they were all locked. I did not see any way out. I was in a living grave… I went from one room to the next with the same result. I did not know what to do. I tried again, but all the doors were steeled shut, not able to be opened. Suddenly, I saw another door, it was only chained. I opened it and entered a small room with one broken window and I saw that there was a balcony right at the window. The balcony had steps and they led into the courtyard. I did not think any further, I grabbed a man's black coat and put it on me, leaving my bloodied coat in the house, and crawled through the window. A piece of the pane that I touched, fell off. For a moment, my heart stopped. But I didn't hesitate and climbed through. I was now in the yard and ran through the gate. The watchman just happened to be sweeping the street. I edged my way up to the wall like a shadow and very soon, I was on Kopernika Street. I was finally free!

[Page 576]

I ran as fast as I could. My own steps frightened me. I was already on Pocztowa Street. I didn't look around. My feet were moving by themselves and my eyes were looking out on their own. I already passed my own house. I had a quick look and no more, and went through the fields to Zolvanez where my *shikse* [Christian female] that I knew lived, and on the last day she had gotten me a passport. A Jewish girl wearing a scarf ran ahead of me and told me that it would be better for me to go back because the peasants in the village would inform on me. I did not answer her, but continued on my way. I did not know the exact route. Only once did I go with this *shikse* for a walk and she showed me the way. But at this moment, I felt that I was going by instinct. I could have found the right way even with my eyes covered.

I came to the house in about an hour. I snuck in through the door of the courtyard. No one was in the house except for the *shiksa*'s mother. I asked her where was Zhenni, it was Sunday morning. She had to be home at this early hour. I said that I wanted her to sew something for me. The mother sent her small son to find Zhenni and in a few minutes she came in. She cried when she saw me. She immediately put me to bed in a second room where no one would come in. She gave me water to wash my wounds again, and then she gave me warm milk. After two days of starvation, the warm milk was very delicious. I told her about my tragedy and said that I did not know if my parents were still alive. I had 900 zlotys and gave her 200 for her father and I told her to hide the other 700. I told her about all the things that were hidden in my house, and then asked her to try and get them out.

At night, she put me in the attic with some hay. She organized a place for me to sleep in the hay, and she made a small wall of the hay so that if someone came up they would not see my place under the hay. I stayed in hiding there in the attic until the 17th of November. That means, from Sunday, November 8, until Tuesday the 17th. Zhenni came to me twice in the day, in the morning and at night, and brought me food and told me about any news. She was afraid to come during the day in case neighbors would see her. On Monday night, Zhenni came as usual, and brought me food. She told me that my parents were alive. She had been in my house and had spoken to my parents through the walls and gave me their regards. They were very hungry. I begged her to give them some bread and milk. She agreed. In the morning, when it was still very dark, Zhenni woke me up and gave me her mother's clothing, and like two peasants, we went to town. She told me that she would not even approach my house because just for crossing the border into the ghetto she would be shot. I had a small basket of food with me. The German guard was standing 10 meters from my house. I went in, knocked on the locked door and called out "Mama!" I do not have to write how I felt at that moment. There are no words to describe this. I was not afraid. A quiet voice answered, it was my mother-in-law. "It is Khaya, our Khaya…" And then my father's voice: "Give us water!" I left the basket behind and went, in the dark, to try to get a cup of water, but everything was dried out. I went to a neighbor of mine, and I almost fell into the open cellars from which they had dragged out the people who had been hiding there. I did not find any water. I had to go into the yard to the well and collect a bucket of water that I had to carry over. I called "Mama" again and I heard my father say to my mother: "Say something so that she will hear you." The first words from my mother were to ask if the children were alive. I told her that all her children were free in the Gestapo, and that Moishe, who was already burned alive, was hiding, and that I too was well hidden. We would still have to wait until Sunday the 15th when they would open the ghetto and then we would go back home and all be together again. I left them with that hope and went with Zhenni back into the attic.

[Page 577]

And now my mind began to work about how to help my parents. What could I do, how could I save them? Not even one single idea came into my head. I did not sleep, I could not eat. At that moment, even though I was not a believer, that God should shorten their pain with their death. Yes, I asked for my parents' death so that their suffering would stop.

My Zhenni began to complain that she was getting scared. She was not able to get any more bread and no more milk either. I pleaded with her, and she agreed to go one more time, Friday at dawn. I disguised myself again, and brought them [my family] some bread, milk, and borscht [beet juice]. They did not ask any questions, said goodbye quietly, and again I left to my place.

I knew nothing about my husband and two brothers who had not come with me. I had no contact with them. I began to plead with my *shikse* that she should come with me into town, but once again she was frightened. After much pleasing, her brother promised to come to town with me on Sunday to try to find out where my brothers and husband were.

Sunday morning, I once again disguised myself, and at 10 o'clock, I and the *sheygitz* [non-Jewish male] went to town to find my dear ones. I came to Lwowska. It was quiet because not many people were in the streets. I went passed my house and just glanced to the right where my parents still lived. I had just come to Pocztowa Street, that once was a lively street filled with children, parents, with great activity and liveliness, now all died out. Not even one soul, not even one step was heard. Broken windows, destroyed benches, tables, seats, dishes in the streets. Thousands of pages from books, thousands of papers flew in the streets. It was terrifying just to look at the street. Everything was dead.

[Page 578]

Not long ago the streets were noisy with thousands of voices, with the center of the ghetto. But today – no sign of life, only the white papers. If the winds could speak, they would tell of the tragedy of Jewish life. With a downcast head, silently, I walked through the Jewish grave of the former life.

We went back in the direction where I hoped to find Jewish life and when I came to the public new school near the train center, there were Jews there, standing with shovels and axes, working. It made a strong impression. These were faces that were already not alive. The faces were still moving, but death was already etched on their faces. With my eyes, I looked for acquaintances. I heard a whisper: "There is your sister." I looked around, and I still did not see a face that I knew. In a minute, two faces separated themselves from the ditch and looked up at me. I recognized them. They were my two younger brothers, Yankel and Borukh who saved themselves and did not go to Sobibor. A soldier stood at a distance. We turned off the road slightly, and we began to talk. The first thing they said was that our parents were dead. I assured them that our parents were still alive, but that our oldest brother Moishe was dead. We were not able to speak for long, but they told me that my husband was working back at the Gestapo and when he could, he would bring them a piece of bread. My husband was better off then they were. My heart ached looking at my youngest brother, without a coat, frozen solid, brown and blue. But I could not help them. After a few minutes, they left me and went back to work. I never saw them again. In about three days, I learned that they were both shot.

I continued on to the Gestapo, but I did not see my husband. The *sheygitz* was getting restless and he wanted to go home. He was afraid to go back with me so he sent me through the woods and went home the regular way.

In the *shikse*'s home, it seemed that the parents had discussed me and decided not to allow me to stay any longer. When I came home, they told me that they were frightened to keep me any longer. I had no choice and I promised them that I would leave that week.

Monday night, once again Zhenni, the *shikse,* came up to me again, and brought me the real news. Her brother was in town on Monday morning, and saw how they had taken out a group of Jews from our house. She told me about certain details, and I was certain they were my parents and my mother-in-law. What I felt then, I cannot describe, but still, I begged her to come with me once more to my parents and see what had happened there.

On Tuesday morning, I changed my clothing, took a small basket of food and went on my way.

It was still dark when I arrived there. As usual, the *shikse* with me remained on the other side. With an empty head and without any thought I entered the house and I will express, in my own words, what I saw.

[Page 579]

The door to the hiding place was open. I did not call out "Mother! Father!" any longer. I entered the kitchen. The windows were covered with sacks (seems that my parents believed that they would come out [of hiding] on the 15th of November) but when they came out [of hiding] they were afraid of the light, that they should be seen, so they covered the windows. There was freshly brought in wood in the kitchen, on the table were freshly grated white beets, which they usually fed to animals. Seems that they were hungry, but they would not have the opportunity to eat.

When I left the house, I saw a rubber boot that my father had lost when they led him to his death. I did not cry, I did not speak. A rock was in me when I came back with the basket to the cemetery where the *shikse* was waiting. To her question of how were things, I responded with nothing. I left the small package in the cemetery and went to look for my husband. Now I no longer had to remain in the city. Nothing was keeping me there.

Jews doing slave labor under the Nazi government

[Page 580]

Calmly, we went into the city. It was still very early, but when we passed the train depot the Jewish slaves were already working. I looked around, searched, and did not find my brothers. They likely worked in a different place. My husband was not there either. We went to the Gestapo, into the lion's den. The Gestapo men knew me very well because I had worked there all year, but I was not afraid. We came to the Gestapo gate at 8:30 in the morning and we hoped that if one of the workers would come out then we would ask him to bring out my husband. We waited like that until 12 o'clock, but no one came out. The *shikse* did not know my husband. I had only a small picture of him. She took the picture and approached the windows of the Gestapo and looked in. Suddenly, she saw a face in the window and she winked at him. He came down. When he heard her out and came down from the Gestapo, she approached him and showed him the picture. She asked him if he knew the person in the picture. That person was my husband, and she told him that I was waiting for him at the gate. They came out together. I saw my husband, but he no longer looked familiar to me. His head was shaven, he was blackened, with scars on his face. I could not believe that in such a short time he could change that much. We did not speak a lot. He had only one request, that I stay with him for just one day. He would sneak me into the cellar and we would be there together. But I declined, I do not know why. Maybe I felt that life was no longer a life, but on the way to Kielce I was sorry that I did not stay with him. I told him about the death of our parents, we squeezed each other's hands tightly, and parted without any hope of ever seeing each other again. I went home to the *shikse*'s house, took along the 700 zlotys with me, and nothing else. At seven in the evening, I left Chelm.

I went to Kielce because my husband had two sisters in Stasow, near Kielce.

* * *

This was one episode of Chelm during the time of the *Aktzias* [roundups]. How I came to Kielce and how I saved my husband is a different chapter of the unnatural episodes and events.

[Page 581]

In the Chelm Work Camp

by Yoshe Akhtman, Canada

Recorded by: E. Winik

Translated by Pamela Russ

When they separated me from my wife, I remained with another 200 or 300 Jews. As was usual for the Germans, they screamed at us and beat us and set us in rows, and then ordered us to go, without looking around, just to go. The large group went on Pijarska Street, and we, the smaller group, went a little onto Lyubelska Street until Perockjega Street and the train station – past the Jewish cemetery.

It was a labor camp, where they crowded us all in, one on top of the other.

When we organized ourselves a little, and became calmer, night had fallen. We had no light, there was no window. Everyone sat with his own thoughts. Quiet, no one was speaking.

Suddenly, we heard footsteps. Thousands of feet, and a familiar German yell: "You lice! Lice! Get up, you cursed dogs!"

We heard sticks beating heads and people screaming: "Oy!" We began to move. One person wanted to get out, then another, but they did not allow anyone to go out. We were all men, and suddenly a cry is heard, as if everyone had planned this. One cry from all 300 men, but a quiet, choking cry, because everyone was afraid to cry loudly. The Germans hated the cries. In these cries, you could hear complaints to oneself: "Why did I not go with my father or with my mother, with my wife, with the children? We know that they will keep us only as long as they need us, and then the same thing will happen to all of us. So why do we have to suffer? Isn't death for all of us better?" The thudding [of feet] became quieter.

In about two hours, when everything calmed down, they began to set us out in three different rooms.

The room I was in once held hay. It was obvious that there was once hay since there were many tiny stones left behind, and we had to lie down on these. We lay one on top of the other. With us here was a Jew and his son from Germany. The small rocks were digging into the Jews. He cried, it was not comfortable for him. There was also a porter from Chelm, I do not remember his name, but he was a strong young man. He was stabbed in the side with a switchblade by a German. It hurt the man terribly. He was not able to lie down. He cried out of pain, but no one could help him.

Suddenly the door opened and the camp elder entered with a question: Whoever was not feeling well or was sick and wanted to go into another room should go with him. Understandably, the German man and his son and the wounded porter left with him. We never saw these people again. They were shot that same night.

[Page 582]

On the second day, that was Shabbath, all of us were let out into the yard, each one of us received a piece of dry black bread and some bitter coffee. It is noteworthy: We were not guarded by any Germany military but by the Jewish militia. A Jewish police was standing at the gate, and at the fence, the same. This was our entire guard setup because the Germans were sure we would not try to run away because we really had nowhere to go. If a Jew was found in the city then he was shot immediately; if a group was found then they were taken to prison until they became a larger group, when they were taken to the field on the way to the lake, and there was a large dugout ditch. And when a group was brought there, they were spread out with their faces looking down into the ditch, and from behind them the shooting began so that they fell with their faces downwards on the ground. Earth was then shoveled over them from the top.

There were no more Jews from the city coming into our camp. There was nowhere left [in the city] to hide because if you were seen by a Pole he would immediately hand you over to the Germans. There was no food, so that the Jews gave themselves up on their own.

As we went out we were counted and the same when we returned. Once, this happened: On the second day of being in the camp, right in the morning, a shout was heard that everyone should line up. The camp elder (the camp elder was a civilian German from Germany) approached, and called out the name of one of the Jewish militia and then he asked that one of the death cells be opened. There, people who tried to sneak into camp or committed other crimes were kept. From these cells, the people were taken out and shot.

The camp elder demanded that a woman be brought out, and this was the wife of the Jewish militia. He called out loudly, that the Jewish militia had committed a crime by sneaking his wife into the camp, and now both he and his wife would be shot in our presence so that it would be an intimidation for others, so that they would remember this.

[Page 583]

After he shot these two young people, he left and told us that they had to remain lying there in the middle of the place all day and then he told everyone to disband. I passed one of the death chambers and I hear my name being called: "Yoshe! Yoshe! I beg you, give me a piece of bread! I haven't had a piece of bread in my mouth already for three days. I am together with my brothers-in-law." We summoned a few more people and we made a human wall. The one in the back kept an eye out so that we should not be seen. I looked around carefully and gave the woman my entire loaf of bread. I and my brothers-in-law were placed into one group of workers. We left to work and when we returned the woman was no longer there.

We worked on the road that led to the direction of the large *shul* [synagogue]. It was very cold. My two brothers-in-law, two young boys, one 15, the other 17 years old, were also working. When they left the house it was still warm so they did not dress themselves warmly. My heart could have exploded as I watched them. The cold shriveled them. Once, something good happened to them: Once, we were there working, and we saw how a group of Jews was being led by young Hitlerists. When they saw us they began to laugh and taunt us. The group of Jews was comprised of 15 people. I remember how one mother was holding her child's hand and was carrying her other child in her arms. Not far from us, all the Jews in the neighborhood had been shot, and these thugs, with smiles, were staring right into our faces, preparing for other victims. They removed the coats from these dead and put them on the living dead.

As we were working on the road, we saw every day how they took wagonloads of dead Jews to the Jewish cemeteries where a large ditch was dug out, and all the bodies were thrown in.

This work was headed by a Gestapo man. That means, that the workers were Jews but his job was to watch whether we Jews would search in the pockets of the dead Jews. That means that all the dead were searched to see whether they were taking money or gold with them.

After working for a week in the camp, they took me back to my old job, where I worked before the camp, in the Gestapo. My job was to polish boots, heat the ovens, and keep the cupboards clean. We were four Jews who did this. Each one had to serve eight men. Some also had to take care of the wives and children. The Gestapo tried to replace me with a Pole, but he did not work like the Jews and everything was very filthy, so they had to ask for me to come back. I now had to do alone what was earlier done by four Jews.

The Jews working in the camp. On the sides, you can see the Kapos [a prisoner assigned by the SS to become supervisor and functionary] guarding them.

[Page 584]

When I entered the house, I found other Jews there. These were skilled workers. I will try to mention them by name: Chelm carpenters by name: Yosel Milkhman, Aharon Hos and his son, Tantshe Nisenboim and a cabinetmaker from Kalysz. Of those, the only one who survived was Tantshe Nisenboim. One tinsmith – his name is also Blekhermakher [which means 'tinsmith"], he also survived; two painters: Lipa Goldman, and Stolnik. I don't remember his second name; one upholsterer – Yosele Eisen, a brother-in-law of Lipa Goldman.

At this time, I want to describe how Lipa Goldman's brother, Mottel, died. He was a stitcher of gaiters, as I was. He was a major figure in the handworker's union. Everyone remembers him. This is how he died: The entire time, until the final *Aktzia,* he was working for the German gendarmerie. They detained him during the last *Aktzia*, not allowing him to go home. Two weeks before the *Aktzia*, the Germans told him that they would shoot him, but that he could save himself with money. He said that he had no money with him but he had some money hidden at home. The Germans were not lazy, and they went home with him. When he took out the money and gave it over to the Germans, they beat him and shot him on the spot. In the Gestapo, I found a very nasty person who was like that from before the war, and during the time of the war, he also did terrible things. He was one of the worst informers – this was Abish Kershenboim. They used to call him "the yellow Abish." He had his own shop in the "*Rynek*" [square]. The Gestapo kept him because they still wanted to found out everything they could about the Jews through him. After two weeks, we noticed that two Gestapo men left with him and came back without him. This was the end of an ugly creation, Abishel Kershenboim. His brother Fishel, deaf, died in the first group along with all the other Jews.

Now my work was four times greater than before, and much more, because after the frost it became warm and it rained. Every day, I saw through the window how they were taking groups of Jews to be shot. The Gestapo men would come back with their boots smeared with blood mixed with mud. Sometimes I had to scratch off the blood with my fingernails, and sometimes I had to clean off the blood from the uniforms. Some had blood on the sleeves, past the elbows. I had to scratch with my nails because the Germans loved cleanliness. I had 28 pairs of boots and I had to polish them from seven to seven thirty and to heat up the offices because the Germans also liked when it was warm. I had to get up before dawn so that I could do all this.

We all slept in the carpenters' warehouse. Once a week we went to wash in the prison that belonged to the Gestapo.

[Page 585]

Once, as we entered the prison yard, we saw two familiar Jews, beaten up. Seemed that they had just been brought here. One was the "fat band" but he was no longer fat. Everything was hanging from him. The other was the son of Warsaw's cake baker. He was called Bakh. Both were terrified, blackened, half-dead people. We never saw them again. Near the bath where we washed ourselves there was a cell for captured Jews.

Once, when we arrived, we saw this picture: We had to wait for a while. As we were standing there, we heard moaning. We looked through the peep hole, we saw men, women, children, and girls all completely naked, without shirts. Among them we recognized the older daughter of the woman Horowyc who had a perfume store on Lyubelska Street. Later we found out why they were keeping the people there. Because during the time that they were in the room, their belongings were searched for hidden money or gold. When everything was ready, they were chased out and everyone had to quickly dress in their clothes. All this time, they were hit over the heads with clubs, so that there was no time for anyone to find his own clothes. A tall person grabbed short clothing, and a short person grabbed long clothing. Everyone looked ridiculous. Then they were taken across the city, into the field, and shot. All along the way, they were chased and beaten, just as a pig beater would torture the pigs. With an earlier group, I saw how they were taking men, women, children, and among them I saw the old man Moishe Tukhman. He, tall and thin, she, short and heavy. He was leading her by her arm. He went straight ahead. But the Germans could not tolerate that a Jew would be walking straight. They began beating his head with clubs, but he did not bend. The Germans became upset and began to beat the wife. The elderly Moishe Tukhman bent over to his wife to protect her, but he did not bend for the German beatings. I never saw them again because they left on the train to Sobibor.

[Page 586]

To us in the Gestapo, a barber by the name of Yankel Karp would come twice a week. I did not see him any longer at the last *Aktzia*. Our boss asked for him. He said if he were not hiding then he would take him back to work. Once we heard a scream and a laugh. They were taking out a group of Jews and among them was Yankel Karp. The laughter was because they had caught him. We waited for our boss to take him out, but he was standing there, laughing and cursing: "Cursed Jew!" because he had been able to hide himself so well and they had not been able to shoot him sooner. That was the prize for working for more than two years. Yankel Karp the barber was shot in the field on the route to the lake.

* * *

Finally, I was able to flee, and my wife and I were able to save ourselves with Aryan papers.

[Page 585]

Revenge! Revenge!

Translated by Pamela Russ

Nights of pain, days of anger
For months and for years,
Do not give my tired body any rest.
Nights filled with nightmares
Of the *heimishe* [homey] places
Wind themselves into me
And with them, those closest to me.
Here, I see my mother,
She decided
Not to go on the Death March
And if she dies, let it be so,
In her own home…

There she lies, shot, on the stone,
Which for years, the first step onto it
Was from the house into the street.

And next to her, my father
Who had just come from work
Filled with pain and tears.
And after that he was

[Page 586]

in the death factory Sobibor
Where they made Aryan soap
From human fat and limbs,
The call for revenge, not for one minute
Comes out of the mouth.
And when those sentenced to death
Decided to stand up and resist
Even though everyone knew
That it would only bring death.
With only hands and force
He died a heroic death,
As is appropriate for Jews.
That's what a survivor
Told me.
My father's last words
He gave over to me
As his soul left.

(Unknown composer's name)

[Page 587]

In Those Days
(unusual events of the death years in Chelm)

Translated by Pamela Russ

Zalman (Zalmele the baker), when he heard that they had shot two Jews whose sin was that they found some potatoes on them, became very frightened that they might find some sacks of flour on him, which he had hidden in his bakery, under the set of stairs.

When they herded together the Jews of Chelm into the narrowest streets of the poorest quarter, such as the New Goal, New World, and into the neighboring, dark small streets, it was decided that Zalman's bakery would bake bread for the ghetto Jews.

The bakery was in a cellar where there were two ovens – an old one and a new one. The old one had been with Zalman for many years, and even though he did not bake in it, he did not throw it out because it served as a hiding place for Zalman to hide the flour when the tax officer would come. No one knew that behind the old oven there was a cellar under the set of stairs…

There, Zalmele hid several sacks of flour during the German occupation.

When the shooting and deaths repeated themselves often in the ghetto, a terrified panic gripped the Jewish population. Then Zalmele the baker thought that he could hide some Jews in his cellar. He related his plan to one of his relatives.

Several weeks went by and the Gestapo came to Zalmele in one rush and circled the ghetto. Zalmele's relative Frayde and her daughter were taken through the broken oven into the cellar under the stairs. They found another two women there and another man.

Several months passed, and only a few Jews remained in the ghetto. The majority of the Jewish population was evacuated to Sobibor and were shot there on the plains of the New World. There only remained the capable workers.

There were eight people hiding in Zalmele's cellar. He himself would crawl in there when it became rowdy in the ghetto, trying to comfort the Jews who were there, saying that they should never lose hope, and that with God's help they would outlive Haman.

* * *

For many years, Zalmele had a worker named Vasil. It was a winter night, when Zalmele noticed a ragged and unconscious person on the steps of the bakery. He took him into the house, sat him near the oven and gave him some food. This was the non-Jew, Vasil.

Since that night, Vasil remained with Zalmele. He used to carry the water, heat the oven. He spoke only short, mumbling words, appearing to be somewhat mentally unbalanced.

[Page 588]

At the beginning of the German occupation, Vasil sustained himself through Zalmele. But later, when the order was given that a Jew could not employ any non-Jewish workers, Zalmele told Vasil that he had to leave. When Vasil heard the words of his boss, he managed to acquire the right words and asked Zalmele for mercy, and that he should keep him, and that he was ready to go to the Germans to ask for permission to remain there.

Vasil actually did go to the Gestapo, to the chief Schwamberger, who was the cruelest of the cruel. He thought about it and said to Vasil that he would give him better work. After giving him a pat on the back, the Gestapo chief asked him if he was able to shoot, and if not, then they would teach him how to shoot.

That same day, Schwamberger took Vasil into prison for his first lesson. Eight Jews who were captured in a bunker were sitting there. He gave Vasil the loaded gun, and ordered: "Shoot these cursed Jews!"

Out of fear, Vasil shot them, and just as he saw that these Jews had fallen to their death, pouring with blood, the gun fell out of his hand. Schwamberger ordered him to take the gun back into his hand, and if not, then he would immediately be shot himself.

Vasil picked up the gun, and remained working for the Gestapo. He was always seen half drunk, accompanying the Gestapo chief.

In the ghetto, the name Vasil became the strongest term for ghostliness, and Zalmele became frightened for himself, knowing that Vasil knew about the old oven and about the steps that led to the cellar.

His fear was not for nothing. Once, the Gestapo chief told Vasil that he should accompany him to Zalmele's bakery in order to do a search there.

Coming into the bakery accompanied by Vasil, immediately Schwamberger kicked Zalmele with his boot, and then threw him down onto the ground. He then ordered Vasil to shoot his former bread provider. He, the Gestapo chief, went over to the old oven and noticed the path to the cellar. Soon, choking screams were heard and the terrified Jews appeared.

Vasil was holding his gun aimed at Zalmele, but you could see that he did not want to shoot him.

They removed the Jews from Zalmele's bakery. The Gestapo chief told Vasil that a bullet was an easy death for Zalmele, and he called in a soldier from the street to take the cursed Jews to prison, and Zalmele as well.

[Page 589]

The following day, the Jews were shot in the prison yard, and for Zalmele, an especially awful death was contrived because he dared to hide Jews.

Opposite the stairs there was a pole, and the Gestapo chief had ordered that a public crucifixion of Zalmele take place… The Jews of the ghetto were assembled, and non-Jews came as well, and stood on the steps as if watching a circus performance.

They brought Zalmele from prison and took him right to this execution place. His small body had become even smaller, and his gray beard had become snowy white. He stood at the stairs and mumbled a prayer.

The Gestapo chief soon arrived accompanied by Vasil, and in a few short words, Schwamberger said that this Jew was going to be crucified because he dared to hide Jews, and whoever hid Jews would be put to death this same way. Then he turned to Vasil saying that he should avenge himself with his Jewish bread provider.

After these words, Vasil uncertainly approached Zalmele, and led him to the steps of the pole, where he tied him up to the pole, and then poured a bucket of tar onto the pole and ignited it. The flames enveloped Zalmele's body and suffocated him.

[Page 590]

Soon, an order was given that was posted on the walls of homes and all public places that no one dare take down the crucified Zalmele.

The following morning, there was no trace of Zalmale's body on the pole. They accused the Jews of having done this. An order was given for the Jews to bring forward the person who had defied the order of the Gestapo. And if not, they would all be killed. The ghetto was surrounded. Everyone thought that Schwamberger himself had done this in order to get rid of the rest of the Jews as quickly as possible.

But it did not take long and it became clear. A peasant came to the Gestapo and told them that in the Jewish cemetery, a uniformed non-Jew was hanging on one of the trees. Immediately, a Gestapo unit rode out to the cemetery, and they saw Vasil hanging on a tree, and under his feet there was a fresh dugout mound.

They dug out the mound and found evidence of Zalmele's body.

Vasil had brought the burned remains of Zalmele's skeleton to a Jewish cemetery, and then, on his own, hanged himself.

Y.G.

[Page 589]

Habeit Mishamayim U'Reeh
["Look upon us from heaven and see"]

Translated by Pamela Russ

(The Jews sang this in the Chelm ghetto; the writer is unknown)

Oy, Habeit Mishamayim U'Reeh
Look down upon us from Heaven and see,

Ki Hayinu L'Ag VaKeles
L'Ag VaKeles BaGoyim
We are so ridiculed by them
Nechsavnu KeTzon LeTevach ["We are considered as sheep to slaughter"]
Oh, Creator, how can You watch such a thing?

We are never tranquil,
But always going to the slaughter.

Chorus:

Therefore we always ask:
Help us, Protector of Israel,
And accept our tears.
We shout out *Shema Yisroel* ["Hear O Israel"]
Please accept us, Protector of this one nation.
Show all the nations that You are our God,
We have no one except for You
Whose name is One God.

Strangers say: There is no purpose, no hope.
The nations say that for us there is
No hope at all.
They can chase us
They can torture us
We have no one

[Page 590]

To complain to.
But still we know
That You are there in Heaven.
The verse about You is
"You do not rest nor do You sleep."
You have to protect
Your children.
Therefore, we know
That You are in Heaven,
With wonders, with miracles.

Khose H' aleinu ["Have mercy on us"]
Ve'al titneinu beyado ["Do not hand us over into their hands"]
Have mercy on us, do not hand us over
Into their hands:
Lama yomru hagayim ["Why do the nations say"]:
Ayei elokeihem ["Where is your God?"]
That is always their cry.
Oh, little Jew, little Jew, what can you do here.
Take your pack and go to Tzion.
We would have fled
But the road is not open.
Why do You let them do this to us?

Chorus

[Page 591]

Sobibor
Eyewitness Testimony of Moshe Hochman

Translated by Gloria Berkenstat Freund

Minutes: Melakh Bakaczik-Pelin
Linz Bindermichl, Austria, 18th September 1947

Up to 1939, the Jewish population of my home city, Zolkiewka, numbered 500 to 600 souls. When the war broke out, approximately 10 to 15 families escaped to Russia.

On the first day of the German occupation twenty Jews were shot by the Germans due to their denunciation by Poles that they were communists. Grenades were thrown into Jewish homes in order to frighten the Jewish population and, therefore, many of the Zolkiew Jews dispersed: some to Lublin, some to Chelm and some to other places. Later, when it became a little quieter, many of the Jews who ran away returned to Zolkiewke [the town name is spelled in three different ways].

It again became turbulent in 1942. I remember how I came home frightened on a Friday night. I learned from the *Judenrat* [Jewish council created by the Germans] that Krasnystaw Jews informed the *Judenrat* that the gentiles in Zolkiewke had seen a great deal of Jewish clothing in Belczec. With tears in my eyes, I told this to my wife and said to her: " Ester, light a candle; it is bad, we have to part." We kissed each other with a heavy sobbing.

The entire *Shabbos* [Sabbath] day passed with trembling and fear. At night on *Shabbos* the Gestapo entered the [home] of the most respected Jew in the *shtetl*, Avigdor, and he scaped in a hurry. A gendarme chased after him and shot him. He remained lying in a pool of blood on the road that led to the church.

A few days later, in May 1942, there was a great turmoil. It was four o'clock in the morning. The Gestapo drove the Jews from their houses and Jews were grabbed in the street. They brought everyone to one place. Poles with rifles also helped catch the Jews, searched and rummaged in every corner. There was a great downpour at that time, a storm with thunder and lightening.

One of the boys asked a German where they were being taken and he was shot immediately. A woman of 50, who also asked something of a Gestapo member, was shot, too.

I had prepared a bunker earlier that was located outside the city where huts had been erected in which to live when a fire took place in the *shtetl*. On the eve of the war, my wife and children and I escaped to the bunker in the middle of the turmoil. My daughter later left for the *shtetl* to see what was happening. She told us that all of the Jews were standing at the market square, surrounded by *S.S.* and Gestapo men and by armed Poles. We did not know what to do. I went out to ask a Pole who lived near the huts. He said to me:

[Page 592]

"*Moszek zie niema rady was Wysiediajon.*" ("Moshek, it is bad; I have no advice; you will be deported.")

We left the bunker and went to the marketplace. I said to my wife: "What happens to all of the Jews will also happen to us."

We were driven from the marketplace in storms and rain. We dragged ourselves the entire night with sacks on our backs and at around one o'clock in the afternoon we arrived in Krasnystaw. The storm and the rain did not stop. We all wanted to die on the spot; preferably let them shoot us.

From Zolkiewke to Krasnystaw is 28 kilometers. We left many dead on the road. We already knew that they were driving us to Sobibor, which is 90 kilometers from Zolkiewke.

In Krasnystaw we met Jews from other *shtetlekh*, such as Trabin, Wysoka and Krasnystaw Jews.

We all stood outside for an entire day until the next morning and the rain continued to pour down. Then we were taken to the railroad. Transports already stood there. Germans stood with two pails, loudly ordering us to give up our gold, silver and everything we had before we were allowed into the wagons. Meanwhile, we were photographed.

Six thousand Jews were driven into the transport. The doors of the freight wagon were sealed. There was not a bit of air and many people, mainly children, lost consciousness and died.

We arrived at Sobibor on Thursday at six at night. Sobibor is one kilometer from Wlodawa. This was a small train station of only a few old buildings not far from the Las Kresowy forest. There was a sawmill and not far away a deep, thick forest extended for many miles.

The Gestapo set their dogs on us as soon as we left the train wagons. Each member of the Gestapo was one meter and 80 centimeters [five feet nine inches] tall. They set the dogs on us and they tore pieces of flesh from our bodies.

The camp was right at the station. It was located on a smaller plot. It was enclosed by wire. The women were ordered to go to the right, the men to the left. Men and women and women and children were separated brutally. There was a great uproar and cry to the very heavens. The strong outcry of "S*hema Yisroel* [Hear O Israel – the central prayer of Judaism]" could truly have split the highest heaven. They also took my wife and children from me by force.

After this "work," we were placed in rows and the Gestapo declared: <u>Whoever wants to work should step out</u>. We did not know which was better and what we needed to do. Eighty men stepped out and I, too, was included. We were taken to another camp.

[Page 593]

There was a pit in the second camp where clothing belonging to the Jews who had been shot was burned along with body parts. Under the guard of armed Ukrainians we lay one after the other and we each expected that death would come at any moment. We said goodbye to one another. We lay down on the ground, stretching one head to another and in such a state we lay an entire night and an entire day. We preferred death rather than living like this.

Twenty-four hours later we were taken away to the previous camp that was near the railroad. Of the 6,000 transported I did not meet anyone there. I did not track down my wife and children, my brother, Hershl, and Zawl Hochman. I only found my son, Yisroel, my nephew, Hershl's son Yeshayale and my cousin Matys, Zawl's son. They told us that everyone already had been gassed.

We worked for a time at sorting the clothing of the dead and then we were given various work.

We saw how they were bringing transported Jews. 5,000 to 6,000 Jews were brought in a transport. Jews from Poland, Czechoslovakia, Holland and from Ukraine were brought to Sobibor. During the winter, transports arrived with frozen children and adults. They would be severely beaten when they left the train.

The frozen ones in the wagons were taken in carts across the *shines* (rails) to be buried. Later, there were special machines with teeth (*lorkes*) that threw out the dead bodies from the wagons and scattered them in the fields.

I remember how once a transport arrived of several thousand Jews in striped suits with *yarmulkes* [skullcaps] on their heads and with bottles at their side. They were all numbered and stamped with Majdanek Camp. We did not know why they had been brought here because if it was to kill them, they could have been gassed at Majdanek. They looked like corpses. Extinguished eyes protruded. They asked us to give them a piece of bread and water. When the Germans gave them a piece of bread, 20-30 people threw themselves on it. They asked us what kind of camp this was. We were afraid to tell them. I recognized several of them; they were from my *shtetl* of Zolkiewka and from the neighboring *shtetlekh*.

They waited in the yard for a long time. The Gestapo and Ukrainians came at night and they began to heavily beat them. In the morning, at dawn, we counted 3,000 dead. At 8 o'clock in the morning, they were taken to the gas ovens where they were burned.

I was in the hell of Sobibor for 18 months. There were two barracks in the camp at the very beginning of my arrival. Later the death camp was enlarged, There were 20 barracks erected. The gas chambers were in a separate place. They had a sloping floor and when a door was opened the people slid down. Five hundred men were let in at one time. A member of the Gestapo watched to see if the victims were dead through a small window on the roof. Then they were removed, buried or burned. They were buried during the first half-year. After the German defeat at Stalingrad, they brought a machine and it drew the dead from the earth to be burned.

[Page 594]

All of Sobibor was a field of dead people and dogs dragged hands and feet before my eyes.

When they would bring the transports to Sobibor they would sort [the people] into three camps. The first camp was for tailors and shoemakers, carpenters, plumbers, bakers. The second camp was for workers to sort the clothing and items from the dead. Therefore, they had to work naked. The third camp was for those taken to be gassed.

* * *

I worked in the second camp and then I worked as a tailor in the first camp.

When things grew worse on the front and the Red Army was approaching Kiev, a smaller transport arrived in Sobibor. We saw and sensed that our end was near. In great secrecy, we, approximately 100 men, organized to take revenge on our murderers and, perhaps, some of us would succeed in saving our lives.

It was impossible to escape from the camp. There were three walls around the camp with barbed wire. On two high guard booths also stood armed Ukrainians. Two hundred Germans stood on guard around the camp who were organized in three shifts. In the background of the forest stood a division of armed Ukrainians with an *S.S.* man.

[Page 595]

The Germans had mines in certain places. It was even difficult for a bird to fly out, even more so for a person.

Therefore, we were ready for everything and the thought of rising up in a rebellion was very developed. We did not know how to do it because we did not yet have any weapons.

A young man from Warsaw worked at sorting the clothing. He hid tin cans of benzene among the clothing and he wanted to ignite the barracks full of clothing and himself at the designated moment of the beginning of the rebellion. He was still young, but he said with determination: "It would be better to die *kiddush haShem* [in the sanctity of God's name – as a martyr] than to perish at the Germans' hands, but perhaps as a result you will be saved." We called off the project because we learned that our hypothesis was incorrect that setting fire to the barracks would create chaos among the Germans and Ukrainians and perhaps we would be able to escape during the uproar. We calculated that first they would murder us and then run to put out the fire in the barracks.

Several days passed in hesitation and reflection about how we should begin the uprising against the cruel murderers. We finally came to a decision that we, the professional men, should [be the ones to] begin.

Shimeon Yakov – Marmeriwtshe Binsztok, Shlomola Binsztok with his wife and children, perished in the gas chambers of Sobibor. Bayla Joba Szmoragd-Binsztok died in Paris in 1936.
May their souls by bound in the bond of life.

There were 20 Gestapo men in the camp itself who administered the camp internally with the Ukrainian guards. We thought if we succeeded in suddenly attacking and murdering them it would create panic among the Ukrainians and then we could break the wire fences and disappear into the woods. Since recently each *S.S.* man had been assigning work to the artisans because of the defeat on the Russian front, it we discussed among us whether we should call each of the *S.S.* men at the same time to be measured or to see the completed work, or to see if something needed to be repaired.

There were separate workshops. There were several workers in each workshop. We would find a solution with one *S.S.*-man…

I led my tailor's table with nine workers. We were entrusted to make the start.

This took place at *Sukkous* time [at the time of the Feast of the Tabernacles], 1943.

We were sewing a civilian suit for the *untersturmfuhrer* [second lieutenant] Neumann. I let him know that he should come to be measured for the suit because it already was finished. He came immediately, riding on a horse, tying it to a fence.

When the sadist entered my workshop, I shouted: *Achtung* [attention]! All of the workers in the workshop stood up. He took off his belt with the revolver, laid it down on the table opposite him and stood erect.

The workshop had three rooms and a kitchen. One room was for sleeping, one room for the hatmaker, where a Jew from Turobin sewed hats for the murderers.

A mirror stood in the room where I did the measuring and in order that he not see what was happening behind him I earlier had moved the mirror a little.

[Page 596]

A Russian Jew, who fell into captivity and had been deported to Sobibor was given [the task] of killing Neumann. This Jew was hiding with the hatmaker with a sharp, small hatchet in his jacket. The *S.S.*-man noticed him when he entered my room and immediately asked: "What is this man doing here?" I answered: "He is here to smooth down the hatmaker's table." When

I buttoned the jacket, the Russian attacked Neumann from behind and split his head with the hatchet. He fell immediately and we stabbed him with a sharp knife in order that he not make any noise and we dragged him, dead, into the hatmaker's room, covering him under the bed with rags.

We needed to liquidate the *S.S.*-man in the kitchen in the same way. However, he did not have time to come.

Other *S.S.*-men were also "liquidated" at the same time. The *obersturmfuhrer* [first lieutenant] Gretschus had slaughtered the above-mentioned Warsaw youth. The *S.S.* man Beckman had a Warsaw servant. Three concentration camp inmates entered and they stabbed him and his servant with a dagger.

Eighteen *S.S.*-men and Beckman's servant were killed by our fighting group. Two members of the *S.S.* remained in the camp.

A group of 30 Jews worked in the forest under the watch of a member of the Gestapo. They came straight to the roll call that took place once a day. Since we already had weapons from the murdered *S.S.*-men, we immediately shot the member of the *S.S.*

A commotion began at the guard posts when the Ukrainians heard a shot. However, they did not know what had happened. We began to cry out in Polish: "*Czerwona Armia w Warszawie*" ["The Red Army is in Warsaw."]. The Ukrainians were confused and attacked us. We entered a second camp where the weapons arsenal was located and [gathered more weapons]. Meanwhile, a *Volks-Deutsch* [ethnic German], a Pole from Lublin, began shooting at us with a revolver. We shot him. However, shooting at us by the Ukrainians at the guard posts and by the Germans who stood around the camp began immediately. However, the Ukrainians each had only five bullets. They were not given many bullets because they were not trusted by the Germans. They immediately fell silent. The initiative was in our hands. The two *S.S.*-members hid in the cellar, afraid that we would make an agreement with the Ukrainians.

We began to run to the wire. Several 100 wormed their way out of the death camp, but about 30 Jews fell dead at the wire because there was a great deal of shooting by the Germans. We ran into the forest and divided into groups. I escaped with eight men. I lost my son, Yisroel, from my hands. I learned after the war that my only son perished with my nephew Yeshayale, Hershl's son.

[Page 597]

The fate of the escapees to the forest was difficult. It was worse that we had separated into small groups. The Poles attacked the Jews in the forests. Approximately 40 Jews who had escaped from the Sobibor camp lived to see the full revenge against the Germans. In my group were: Leib Feldhendler, the son of Rabbi Yosele, and Jews from Izbica and Krasnystaw. However, they suddenly disappeared from among us and I never saw them again.

* * *

I remained in the forest only with the above-mentioned Russian Jew. He was named Moshe. He began to ask me to go with him because he was in a strange country and did not know the Polish language.

We wandered together through the forest and steppes. I looked around at night, as we were not far from the train line near the Wieprz River. I could swim across the river, but he could not. We wandered around for two days without food. We tried to find long poles and tie them together with the laces from our shoes so that we could use them to cross the river. But the sun began to rise … We left for the side where there was a bridge. He said: "With God's help, we will cross the bridge safely. He had left his hat on the Sobibor wire, so he made a hat for himself with his striped scarf that was seen from afar.

We went to the bridge. There was a hill near the bridge, and when we went up on it we saw two German civilians speaking to each other. We ran by them and safely crossed the bridge. This was at *Minkhah* [after noon prayer] time. We changed direction on the right side of the Wieprz River, went across the cemetery and highway and out on into the fields where we found beets. We snatched some to eat and we took several beets with us.

We ran constantly in great haste until we went out onto the highway from Zolkiewka. We knocked at a peasant's [door] and asked for a piece of bread. However, he did not give us any. A second peasant opened a small window and gave us bread and milk. The Russian Jew paid him for it with a gold chain from a watch.

Night fell again. There was a beautiful full moon. We rested in a woods near the "Biala" court. However, we heard shooting from a machine gun. I wanted to go in another direction. The Russian Jew advised me that we should go straight with the road. I obeyed him.

Immediately on the road opposite the court, six members of the *S.S.* sprang out with a shout: Halt, hands high, hands high! We raised our hands and stopped.

[Page 598]

They surrounded us and led us into the court – From where were we coming? They asked and we answered that we were Poles and were going to Krasnystaw. The searched us to see if we had any revolvers and they found a few beets and pieces of bread. They found a thimble on me and they laughed.

They understood that we were Jews. They calmly asked us if we wanted alcohol. The Russian Jew jumped in with Russian words, saying that we were traveling from Krasnystaw and going to Gorzkow to work. When they asked: "Why are you traveling at night," we answered: "We want to arrive at work before dawn." "Good," they answered and they deliberated among themselves whether to shoot us in the forest or to send us to the head man in the court for him to decide.

Finally, the entrance to the court was 100 steps away. Four *S.S.* men remained on the highway and two members of the *S.S.* led us to the court. I went several steps in front.

There was a barrier to the court in front and a military hut. On the right were bushes, a garden and a few stalls. Approaching the barrier, I sprang into the bushes. The guard shouted, "Oh-oh!" and began to shoot with his rifle. The two *S.S.* men also began to shoot at me. However, I ran with great haste. I fell into the swampy marsh where I could sink in.

I barely crawled out from the swamp and went onto the highway. I ran approximately four kilometers until the day was beginning. Outside of the village of Wisniow that was near Gorzkow, I entered a deep valley and I lay under a bush for an entire day. People passed by and did not notice me. At night I approached the village of Poperczyn, where I had a peasant acquaintance. Coming to his house, I saw his son who shouted: "*Jezu kochany, powiedz mi Moszek skond ty sie wzionl?*" "Dear Jesus, tell me, Moszek, from where have you come?"

I told him that I had escaped from the Sobibor death camp, but he should advise me what I could do now and I asked him to let me stay in the barn a day or two. He told me: "Crawl in the haystack and I will bring you food." I gave him a string of pearls, brought from the camp.

I was with him for two days. Then he advised me to go the Lublin woods because there were Jewish partisans there and the woods were thick.

Not far away on the road, four kilometers from the above-mentioned village, was a peasant acquaintance of mine, Ganslowski. I went into his attic quietly and snuggled into the straw. It was a hundred steps from the German gendarmerie. At night I went down and woke him. "From where have you come," they all asked. They covered the windows and asked me to speak quietly. I asked them if I could stay with them for two weeks. Ganslowski explained that the house was not far from the highway and the gendarmerie was nearby. I drank a glass of tea, said goodbye and left. He asked me to tell him where I was going. I did not tell him the true direction because I had hidden my things [at his house] before the deportation.

[Page 599]

From Ganslowski I left for the village of Gany. I went to a peasant. His dogs attacked me. I knocked on the window and called "*Panie Stechirzu, otworz!*" ("Mr. Stechirz, open!"). He did not know who it was and he came out with his wife and children, undressed. He recognized who I was. They gave me food. He put me to sleep in the house, but I immediately went into the stable attic to sleep better.

In the morning, the peasant consulted with his entire household about what they should do with me. The son-in-law felt they should chase me away, but the old peasant said that Moszek is not a dog and if he has come to me, he is destined to survive. It was decided that they would keep me. They kept me for seven months. I did a little tailoring. During this time various searches took place. However, I was not found.

A month before the liberation, a German requisition division arrived in the village, surrounded the village, searched and rummaged. I was in the attic and I covered myself with chaff. The female peasant came in and searched for me with great difficulty, saying that I should quickly escape because if not they would all be lost. However, I did not come out from under the chaff and I only came out after the departure of the German requisition division.

[Page 600]

The front came closer to the village. It was harvest time; I hid in the fields among the grain. Shooting started, I lay for a time among the rye until the Soviets arrived. Amidst the rye, I heard the Russian language and the peasant's wife came running, telling me the news that I was free.

* * *

I left for my *shtetl* Zolkiewka. I did not meet any Jews. Everyone looked at me with sorrowful eyes. I found a Polish tailor and went to work for him. With him I earned a pair of pants and a jacket. However, I was not in the *shtetl* for long. A young gentile entrusted me with a secret that the peasants were contemplating killing me and the priest reproached the peasant in the village of Gany for hiding me.

I reached Lublin. Because of the events in Poland, I left Lublin and went to Austria.

When I traveled to Lublin, I stopped in the court where the *S.S.* men had kept us at night. There, a young gentile told me how the Russian Jew had been heavily tortured until he was shot. This Russian Jew, Moshe, actually was the one who began the revolt in the Sobibor death camp.

[Pages 599-600]

A Bottle of Ashes

by Avrohom Lew, Israel

Translated by Pamela Russ

Nineteen fifty four is already counted
The wounds are not yet healed
And may it never happen
That the wounds should ever open
And they bleed and they become infected,
G-d, how can I go on living?

Near these large graves
I stand, small and poor.
Near these holy martyr children
I stand, blinded by the torment
Broken, stooped,
I see them as if fresh before my eyes.

A teacher from "there"
Brought along from kindergarten
In a bottle, a little bit of ash.
It is standing here in my table
Like a sad, black flag
As a bloody reminder;

Of those vast years
That could not be clearer,
And death lurks again

Across mountains of the killers.
The world is sharpening its knives already polished
Ready for a new massacre.

Nineteen fifty-four is already counted,
Counted and almost over,
The wounds are not yet healed
And the graves are not yet covered.
Because who can cover
Our holy millions?

Now, to a new massacre –
The world is preparing for a new style,
And we are in the middle.
Whether you want it or not,
We go on the same sleigh - - -

The bottle of ash is honored
On my desk, as a weight.
If that bottle could speak
What would it say to the world?
Just as Hillel, it would call out:
"In the end, they who drown you will themselves be drowned."

I am taking the bottle into the palm of my hand
I inhale the torment
That is left of the millions
That darkened our shine.

Nineteen fifty four is already counted
The wounds are not yet healed.
Years, bloody and difficult,
Can this wound ever be healed?

[Page 601]

A Conference on Social Self Help

Translated by Pamela Russ

From the archives of the Jewish Historical Institute of the Central Jewish Committee in Poland Folder 50 (Chelm)

Protocol
(translated from Polish)

From the negotiations at the conference of delegates of the Chelmer region and of the Regional Provisions Committee of the Jewish Social Self Help, that took place in Chelm on the 25th and 26th of January, 1942, on Kopernik Street 8.

The conference began its meetings on January 25, 1942, at 13 o'clock and 30 minutes.

Those present:

Dr. Tish Eliyahu; member of the presidium of the Jewish Social Self Help in Krakow.

Frenkel Meyer; chairman of the Provisions Committee of the Jewish Social Self Help in the Chelm District. He was also chairman of the conference.

Druker Mauritzi; secretary of the committee of the Jewish Social Self Help, and secretary of the conference.

Shein Yosef; member of the Committee of the Jewish Social Self Help, Chelm.

Oks Khaya Roza; member of the Committee of the Jewish Social Self Help, Chelm.

Katz Nosson; member of the Committee of the Jewish Social Self Help, Chelm.

Dr. Gorin Shimon; member of the Committee of the Jewish Social Self Help, Chelm. Was not able to attend because he was ill, and Dr. Yelen Avrohom, director of Unit VII, attended in his place.

Other delegates of the Committee of the Jewish Social Self Help in the District of Chelm:

Las Khaim Yisroel and Esther Gelbord	Chelm
Kohen Avrohom ………………	Wlodawa
Kraft Bezalel and Zinger Efraim …….	Rejowiec
Lerer Shalom and Kruk Leibe…….	Siedliszcze
Kruger Yitzkhok, Berger Faivel, Sajkewycz Bunim …….	Wojszlowyc
Perelstajn Moshe……….	Swarzhevo
Fuks Alter ……………..	Sawin
Tziberman Yitzkhok, Kozhukh Shaindel	Uhrusk
Goron Akiva ………	Sielec

[Page 602]

Stajnwurtzel Akiva ………..	Zmudz
Magistrate Beler Khava, Gerstajn Avrohom	Cycow
Roter Pinkhas, Migdal Yitzkhok ….	Dubienko
Rozenboim Khaim ….	Pawlow

Other delegates from the Jewish Councils:

Biderman Anshel, Freiberger Aryeh, Reiz Mordekhai, Tenenboim Yeshayahu, Zilberman Yeshayahu…..	Chelm
Blatt Volf ….	Rejowiec

Zeidfoden Shimon …..   Pawlow

Kesterman Aharon ….   Krzywiczki

Delegate from Provisions Unit and representative of the fixed estates in the Jewish district:

Szwarcblat Pinkhas ……   Chelm

Guest, doctor representatives from Unit VII of the Sanitation and Hygiene Supervisors:

Dr. Oberlander Noson, Dr. Wolberger Dovid   Chelm

Dr. Springer Avrohom …..   Wlodowa

Dr. Firt Yoilish ……   Rejowiec

Dr. Bieler Maximilian …….   Cycow

Business of the Day:

1. Opening.
2. Reading the Protocol of the previous meeting on February 16, 1941.
3. Issue of fighting the epidemics, also to improve sanitary conditions.
4. Financial and activity reports from all units of the Jewish Society Self Help for the year 1941.
5. Issue of child care.
6. Provisions for the newcomers and for the workers.
7. Issues of food supplies.
8. Receiving financial aid.
9. Free advice.

…

[Page 603]
Re the first point of the business of the day:
The chairman of the Chelm committee as well of the conference greets the delegate from the presidium of the Jewish Social Self Help, in the persona of Dr. Eliyahu Tish, and he also greets all the other guests, the delegates from the departments of the Jewish Social Self Help, from the Jewish Councils, and also the representative doctors. He announces that Dr. Alter, as the counselor of the Jewish Social Self Help, head of the District of Lublin, and Dr. Ziegfried, as the representative of the provincial legal guardianship committee of the Jewish Social Self Help in Lublin, reported on their absence – the first because of important official efforts, and the second because of a difficult sickness – and they wish the conference success. He honors the memory of Dr. Mauritzi Kleinhoiz, member of the Chelm committee of the Jewish Society of Self Help and representative of the Department of Sanitation and Hygiene supervision, who died on September 18, 1941, and delivers the following: "A great meritorious person has left us, a person with an unblemished character, who devoted his entire life for the benefit of individuals and for the society. One of his wishes before his death was that there should be no speeches about him, and that we part from him quietly and without fanfare." And in agreement with this, the chairman requested that the memory of the deceased be honored with a three-minute silence.
Those gathered, while standing, heard the speech, and a silence began, which lasted for three minutes.

The chairman then explained that the goal of the conference of February 16, 1941, was to create units of the Jewish Social Self Help in the entire region, and this now was a report-conference for the period of the previous year.

The chairman gives to Dr. Tish the podium.

Dr. Tish Eliyahu greets all the participants of the presidium of the Jewish Social Self Help, and in his own name, he says: "I have come to you not as a wealthy uncle, but as a friend to a friend, as a comrade to a comrade, as a brother to a brother, in order to discuss and decide the means of working together. The presidium understands the conditions, needs, and requirements of the Jewish people in the general governing area, gives whatever possible, rushes forward with help wherever and for whatever is needed. In a few weeks' time, the presidium will announce through a circular, a report of their activities of the entire year. The presidium cannot be alone in its work. The activities have to be built on collaborative work with all its units in the General Government region. That means, with the committees of the Jewish Social Self Help and delegates, and the negotiations of this conference should take place and will take place on this platform."

The secretary of the meeting announces that the *Kreishauptmann Abteilung Innere Verwaltung Bevoelkerungswesen und Fursorge* [German: "Department Chief of Internal Administration of the Population and Welfare"] was duly informed through the committee about the conference, and a letter was sent on January 24 to publicize at the conference:

"General Government region – Lublin. The department chief in Chelm, office of internal administration. Chelm …
[Page 604]
… January 24, 1942. To the chairman of the *Judenrat* [Jewish Council] H. Frenkel in Chelm, at the conference of the delegates of the Jewish Social Self Help, that will take place on the 25th and 26th of the same month in Chelm, you should announce: The *Judenraten* and delegates of the Chelmer region have to accurately fill out all the instructions of the chairman of the *Judenrat,* as well as the chairman of the Jewish Social Self Help, H. Frenkel. Every counteraction will be severely punished by us.

The Official *Kreishauptmann*: Dr. Bohrman.

Re Point 2 of the Item of the Day:
They reviewed the protocol of the conference of February 16, 1941.

Re Point 3 of the Item of the Day:
The financial and activity report of all the Chelmer regional delegates for the year 1941 – presented by Mr. Yosef Shein.
The Chelmer region includes about 21 municipalities, that include:

Delegates from the Jewish Social Self Help	16
General number of Jews	29,942
Number of Jews needing help	13,449
Number of kitchens	16
Number of people who used the kitchens	6014
Number of meals distributed during one year	73,537
Main products used	92,912 kilograms
Help for homes used in about 7 months in town of Chelmno	385
Families	1925 zlotys

During the period of the reports, the committee held about 23 meetings, other than well-attended meetings of various departments and committees. Members of the committees conducted 18 inspections of the activities of the delegates of the Jewish Social Self Help in these places. They composed 1,646 letters.

In November of last year, they organized a department for non-profit loans, whose goal it was to distribute constructive aid to financially lacking people, and gave them an opportunity to rescue themselves from their needs using their own strength. Thanks to the volunteerism of the people, they collected 3,000 zlotys. To date, about 20 or so people of Chelm were able to make use of loans of about 100 zlotys. When greater funds will be available, the activities of the department will also be more spread across the region.

A unit of help for relatives out of town was also organized, which serves the city and region. From its very beginning, this department showed lively activity. With our collaboration, 122 people made use of this.

[Page 605]

We are always in touch with the German Red Cross with the collaboration of the local *Kreishauptmann*.

In October, a special *esrog* [for Sukos] project was undertaken. Thanks to those sent here by the presidium of Krakow, there were 30 *esrogim*. Around 3,000 zlotys were collected from this.

There were 528 articles of clothing distributed to 432 people, and 462 ½ meters of material to 263 people. In total, 695 people made use of this.

Other than 100 and some tens of pairs of shoes that we received as a charitable gift, the committee bought and distributed 300 pairs of shoes to the needy. Efforts are being made to acquire a purchasing permit for 1,000 pairs of shoes.

Activity Report in the City and Region For the Year 1941

Place	General No. of Jews	No. of Needy	No. of Kitchens	No. that Used Kitchens	No. of Meals Distributed
Chelm	12,500	6,928	3	2,164	383,998
Wlodawa	5,586	1,710	1	1,200	144,000
Rejowiec	2,379	717	1	350	66,611
Sziedliscze	2,026	1,000	1	350	49,497
Wojslowic	1,377	813	1	340	2,600
Savin	840	200	1	100	31,068
Sosnowic	831	250	1	100	24,000
Dubenko	648	200	1	100	5,000
Cycow	511	158	1	50	1,994
Swierz-Roda	476	240	2	60	16,107
Wereszczin	394	160	1	100	5,000
Urusk	377	270	1	50	3,000
Rakolupi	398	250	1	50	2,500
Turka-Zhmudz	307	130	-	-	-
Krzyworzeba	295	100	-	-	-
Olchowiec	239	43	-	-	-
Pawlow	238	86	-	-	-

Zmudz	182	119	-	-	-
Stav	132	-	-	-	-
Krzywicki	56	25	-	-	-
Wiroki	150	50	-	-	-
TOTALS:	**29,942**	**13,449**	**16**	**5,014**	**735,375**

Received, among others, from the presidium in Krakow – 36,000 kilo potatoes; 100 liters cod liver oil, 100 shirts, 100 covers, 100 containers of condensed milk, 100 kilo beans, 75 sack cloths, also herring, marmalade, soap, soap powder, pork meat, and so on.

In this year's report, these were given out: 1 man's coat, 3 women's coats, 1 child's coat, 27 sweaters, 100 pairs men's shoes, 3 children's shoes, 3 rubber boots, 2 winter boots, 2 scarves, 15 winter hats, 16 pairs of gloves, 10 knitted suits for women, 10 knitted suits for girls, … 53 knitted suits for children, 12 men's suits, 12 boys' suits, 2 blouses, 1 jacket, 16 women's jackets, 9 girls' jackets, 6 furnishings for babies, 42 children's jackets, 42 pairs of women's stockings, 6 children's stockings, 1 men's stockings, 101 blankets, 5 sheets, 2 vests, 49 men's shirts, 11 boys' shirts, 462 ½ meters of material.

Of the 101 blankets, 65 were distributed in the Chelm region, and 31 in the hospital in Chelm.

[Page 606]

Other than that, there was also distributed in Chelm and the Chelm region 100 liters of cod liver oil, 36,000 kilogram potatoes, 150 kilo pork meat, 100 shirts especially for the newcomers, marmalade, herring, and a series of life's products.

Activity Report of the *Apotropsim* [Guardian] Committee
Of the Jewish Social Self Help

The City of Chelm, for the Year 1941

Doctors:

Ambulatory – 8370 persons; patient home visits - 2271 persons.
Hygienists:
Ambulatory – 2910 persons; patient home visits – 197 persons; service aide – 581 persons.
Doctors' Treatment:
12,518 adults; 2439 children; 3155 free examinations; 8216 dispensed medication, of these 2488 free; gave 5754 persons preventative injections; sanitary units visited 25,943 homes; shaved 1226 persons for free; 18,037 persons visited the baths.
Nutrition:
Children and the sick – 7174; of these, 691 babies; of these, for free 1588. Gave out sugar – 2116 kilo and 52 decagram; 3223 kilo rolls; kasha – 72 kilo and 60 decagram; biscuits – 150 kilo and 10 decagram; in the kitchens, a total of 383,998 lunches were given of which 213,251 were free.
[Pages 607-608]

Financial Report
Income

Place	Local Taxes and Donations	Subsidies from the Jewish Social Self Help, and Others	Subsidies from the Jewish Councils	Payments from the Supporters	Sundry Incomes	Totals
Chelm	30,739.38	26,050-	40, 199.32	66,288.99	4,699.11	167,976.80
Wlodawa	1,165.50	22,200-	28,329.18	15,708.65	9,981.88	77,385.21
Rejowiec	1,739.80	9,794.10	5,638.30	1,721.90	4,628.30	23,522.40
Sziedliscze	2,474.50	10,050-	11,328.18	5,461.58	3,659-	32,973.26
Wojslowic	4,933.60	7,200-	-	3,792.47	6,067.39	21,993.46
Sosnowic	123.05	8,200-	830-	254.55	168.50	9,576.10
Swierz-Roda	-	-	-	-	5,629.92	5,629.92
Savin	6,123.65	7,150-	70-	159.30	-	13,502.95
Urusk	2,373-	4,300-	-	1,102-	497-	8,272-
Rakolupi	1,132.80	1,900-	60-	35.30	513-	3,641.10
Turka	-	500-	-	-	535-	1,035-
Zmudz	204-	350-	-	-	320-	874-
Cycow	-	-	-	398.80	1,785.51	2,184.31
Dubenko	2,740.50	2,300-	-	-	9,202.50	14,243-
Weresczyn	1,457.20	1,900-	2,059.60	-	-	5,416.80
TOTAL:	**55,206.98**	**101,894.10**	**88,514.58**	**94,923.54**	**47,687.11**	**388,226.31**

Expenses

Place	Maintenance	Dispensed Products	Financial Support	Help for Homes	Sanitary Aid	Administrative Expenses	Sundry Expenses
Chelm	98,172.52	16,450.43	93.37	2,291.50	16,950.94	16,542.82	9,257.50
Wlodawa	35,676.19	-	12,355.90	158-	6,089.40	20,732.90	3,450.06
Rejowiec	9,084.40	2,892.45	897.90	418.90	6,251.33	795.45	2,917.32
Sziedliscze	10,738.94	8,129.15	3,535.20	258.-	7,140.94	336.-	2,828.70

Wojslowic	13,821.08	1,706.90	610.70	70.40	2,697.05	1,038.06	91.30
Sosnowic	4,308.88	-	2,993.55	13.50	1,171.32	769.67	646.-
Swierz-Roda	-	-	1,370.50	150.-	250.-	-	3,625.63
Savin	10,148.86	-	1,648.49	-	1,395.80	791.10	-
Uhrusk	1,410.0	3,583.-	2,661.-	125.-	596.-	397.-	416.-
Rakolupi	243.65	831.53	1,925.-	-	100.-	164.50	-
Turka	-	535.-	500.-	-	-	-	-
Zmudz	-	-	400.-	55.-	-	30.-	445.-
Cycow	1,205.85	-	577.-	-	-	127.70	-
Dubenko	3,894.60	-	-	-	-	-	11,127.50
Wereszczyn							5,498.97
TOTAL:	188,704.97	34,128.46	29,568.61	3,540.30	42,642.78	31,725.20	40,303.98

Subsidies from the chief of the district of Lublin, by the *Kreishauptmann* for the year 1941: Chelm – 2850 zlotys; Wlodawa – 950; Rejowiec - 650; Wojslowic – 400; Savin – 300; Sosnowic – 200; Uhrusk – 200; Turka-Zmudz – 200; Swierz-Roda – 100; Cycow – 100; Wereszczyn – 100; Rakolupi – 100; Dubenko – 100; Krzyworzebo – 100; total – 7,000 zlotys.

With regards to the report, these were the comments:

Mr. Cohen Avrohom (Wlodowa): The numbers that were presented in the report are not actual, because the needs and expenses increase daily as a result of the growth in poverty of the state population in Wlodowa, where the number of those being supported has already reached 3,000. The delegation also does not have any great pretenses against the presidium of the Jewish Social Self Help, despite that the presidium is feeding the delegation with circulars, and it is not reacting precisely nor in a proper manner to that which is presented by the delegation's unquestionable needs and requests.

Mr. Kraft Bezalel (Rejowiec): I cannot agree with the critic from the Wlodowa delegation. We are doing everything that is possible, regardless that the conditions are very difficult. We have complaints to the Chelmer committee only because they favor particularly the city Chelm, and they have done nothing for Rejowiec.

[Page 609]

For example, for the need of fire wood. The situation in Rejowiec is worsening and the poverty is increasing. And now the needy who require support are those who have not needed help in the past.

Mr. Lehrer Sholom (Sziedliscze): In Sziedliscze today there are 2,100, of which 800 – these are the newcomers – find themselves in exceptional need. The whole town is very poor. Every day, we distribute three meters of bread among the poor, and this is done at the expense of others, as it is removed in parts from their expected regular [provisions]. 375 people use the public kitchen, and several hundred other poor people also request help from the kitchen, but without any result. We know that the Chelm committee is using their energies to the limit and is doing everything that is possible, but it is not in any position to do more here. I appeal to the presidium for more permanent and substantial aid.

Mr. Krieger Yitzkhok (Wojslowic): First I greet the delegate of the presidium and I thank Mr. Frenkel, the chairman of the committee, for organizing this conference. We are working exclusively with our own strength. We do not receive any subsidy from the *Judenrat* [Jewish Council]. We are not arguing about the views of the Wlodowa delegate, this is not the time to criticize. We want to find a way to work together, particulary with means for addressing the sanitation and hygiene needs. We contribute to the lunches of the public kitchens about a liter of soup daily - a few decagrams, and Fridays – 20 decagrams of bread for everyone. We ask that all these products be compensated for, and especially potatoes, according to the contingency prices, because if not, then the public kitchen will cease to exist. At the same time, both sugar and wood are very much needed. Thanks to the fact that the "distribution center" gives us provisions, the kitchen still exists, and more so, for this same reason, the Jewish Social Self Help also has an income from these consignments.

Mr. Berger Faivel (Wojslowiec) joins in the tasks of Mr. Yitzchok Krieger, and also asks for medical help, asks for provisions of flour and primarily potatoes for the public kitchen. The city pharmacy has very high prices for ordinary medications. The prices are 10-15 times higher than the same medications that are in the stores of Chelm.

Mr. Perlstein Moshe (Swierz) in Swierz-Roda expresses tremendous need. Only ten families are barely taken care of, and these are the workers. The others are hungry and naked. The local economic conditions make it almost impossible to survive. The population is relying for assistance from the outside. Because of the shortage of potatoes, flour, wood, we cannot conduct a public kitchen – one in Swierz and the other in Roda. We ask for help with food products, clothing, and wood.

Mr. Fuks Alter (Savin): We are asking for help with food products, clothing, wood, and also ask that there be a Jewish doctor set up in Savin.

[Page 610]

Mr. Steinwurzel Volf (Zmudz): We ask for help with food products, clothing, wood.

Magister Bieler Eva (Cycow): The delegate of Cycow began her activities on April 1, 1941. And within nine months she got only 600 zlotys from all types of sources and we had to support ourselves. We run a public kitchen, first and foremost for children, because we could not sustain adults with what we earned. If we will not receive provisions of flour, potatoes, wood, and so on, the kitchen will be forced to shut down.

Mr. Roter Pinkhas (Dubenko): Asks for help with food products, clothing, heat, and sugar, soap, and a financial subsidy. In the region of Hansk, to which the delegate in Dubeczno also belongs, there lives a total of 661 Jews, of which 14 people possess special certificates.

Chairman Frenkel Meyer (Chelm): In summary of all the speeches, I see that there is no exceptional overload thrown against the presidium, nor against the committee. The speeches had only suggestions. About the wood, the distribution of it has no practical value because the price of one cubic meter is anywhere from 10 to 20 zlotys, but the transport will cost 80 zlotys. About subsidies, every *Judenrat* will be obliged to pay the delegate from the Jewish Social Self Help every month and in the next few days a circular will be sent to all the *Judenraten* in the region, whose task will be to organize a budget for the last six months, and also to indicate if the individual *Judenrat* has paid the subsidy to the local delegate and how much. A copy of the letter from the *Kreishauptmann* of January 24, 1942, will be attached to the circular.

The delegate from the presidium, Dr. Eliyahu Tish: The presidium knows exactly the statistics and the needs of the individual delegates of the Jewish Social Self Help, as well as the means and levels of activities of the individual regional committees, among which the Chelmer committee has acquired a name as one of the best functioning; a committee that works with fire, energy, and intelligence. The presidium knows that the Chelmer committee did not use one thing for themselves at the expense of any delegate. But it is unquestionably necessary that the *Judenraten* collaborate to recognize the sacrificing work of the Jewish Social Self Help, which frees the *Judenrat* in a large way from the social provisions activities. The public kitchens themselves are a living example of the wonderful and useful activities of the Jewish Social Self Help. I appeal to you for mutual understanding, help, collaboration, because you are both institutions of the Jewish kibbutz and you have to supplement each other.

[Page 611]

Re Point 4 of the Item of the Day:

Instead of Dr. Goren who became sick, Dr. Yelen Avrohom represented him in the fight against epidemics and the establishment of sanitary conditions.

> 1. The fight against epidemic is a fight for cleanliness, for improved sanitary-hygienic conditions, and the fight against typhus is, other than that, a fight with lice which is the sole transmitter of this disease.

2. In the case where the doctor discovers a contagious disease, the sick person must be removed from the home immediately and taken to hospital or to the isolation house. Of these points, if there is not Jewish doctor then you must go to a non-Jew – a doctor – or to the closest Jewish doctor.

3. Those close by must be isolated in a designated location within 24 hours. In this situation, if there is a bath or a tub, you have to wash those who are nearby, and have them change their clothing for clean ones. If there is no bath or tub, then those who were near the sick person should be washed. If there is lice in their hair, it has to be cut and burned. In the home of the sick person, you have to do a sulphur-gas disinfection. If there are several rooms, then all the things have to be gathered up in one room where there has to be a gas disinfection, and the other rooms should have a general disinfection.

4. You are not allowed to transport a sick person from one town to another – under the personal supervision of the delegate of the Jewish Social Self Help or the *Judenrat*.

5. In order to put in sanitary conditions, the regional committee of the Jewish Social Self Help is creating a "Cleaning Week" under the banner of "Let's get rid of the lice!" To this goal, there will be special placards and instructions. The Jewish distribution center will send a significant amount of soap powder to distribute to the population.

6. In each community, the delegate from the Jewish Social Self Help, during the "Cleaning Week" will provide the sanitary needs to the appropriate situation.

    a. In the homes, you must wash the floors, doors, windows, beds, and other household items.
    b. The bed linen and personal clothing must be boiled.
    c. The straw and the hay stacks have to be changed for new ones.
    d. If there is a bath, a ritual bath, or a tub, you have to use them as such, meaning if possible, the entire population should bathe there during Cleaning Week.
    e. The yards, steps, balconies, etc., have to be cleaned to a proper condition.

7. The task of organizing and completing the above-mentioned belongs to the delegate from the Jewish Social Self Help.

[Page 612]

The local population that does not follow these instructions will be strictly punished.

Dr. Shpringer Avrohom (doctor from Wlodowa): The contagious diseases, especially typhus, was brought into Wlodowa and the surrounding areas, from the work camps in Savin, Krikhof, Sajczyce, and so on. The shortage of soap, soap powder, bicarbonate soda, alcohol, and so on, make the fight against sickness harder and sometimes tragic, and the delegate asks that we instruct him on means and ways against this fight that will bring results, especially with the eradication of these lice. In Wlodowa proper there is no epidemic because, for example, now there are nine sick with typhus, but the fight and the means are absolutely necessary to prevent the sickness from spreading. The delegate asks the presidium and the committee to try to acquire the above-mentioned materials for personal bathing and laundry washing.

Dr. Furt Yoelish (doctor of Rejowiec): There is an infirmary in Rejowiec. The medications are very expensive if you buy them in a pharmacy. Therefore we ask that you distribute the contingent medications to the poor in the Jewish population.

Dr. Bieler Maximillian (doctor of Cycow): There is no typhus among the Jews of Cycow. There were only a few cases of abdominal typhus. In the region there are a total of 500 cases of typhus and abdominal typhus, but among the Jewish population, to date, there is not one incident. We are doing everything to eradicate the disease, but we ask that you distribute soap and bicarbonate soda.

Dr. Eliyahu Tish (Krakow): To answer Dr. Springer, I will say that two other doctors at the conference have already described the means and ways to conduct a fight that will bring results. This is already part of the area of the professional doctor's work. Other than that, he recommends that we connect with the epidemiology specialist Dr. Wolberg, employed in the Czestchowa Judenrat, who, with good results, put into place methods and means, among which were also communiques and open appeals. The speaker asks that all local doctors from the region should request from the presidium their orders for medications, which, as much as possible, will be fulfilled.

The chairman Frenkel Meyer (Chelm): With the consent of the government organizations this committee of the Jewish Social Self Help will organize in the entire Chelm region a "Cleaning Week" with the goal of eradicating the lice. This event will take place everywhere as well and will be under the management of the government organizations, of the delegates of the Jewish Social Self Help, and of the *Judenrat*. They will air out, wash, and scrub people and items. Soon, we will send soap and soap powder to each person for washing and for all the needs. And the price will be one *zloty* and 12 *groshen* for a piece of soap and soap powder. Other than that, we have to organize …

[Page 613]

… publicity through communiques, notices, and also announcements, at every opportunity. The committee will compose the text of the publicity material that will, in appropriate numbers, be distributed among the delegates of the Jewish Social Self Help, or to the *Judenrat* in the places where there is no department of the Jewish Social Self Help. Because of the late hour, the speaker concludes the meeting at 18:30 o'clock until the following morning at 9.

The ongoing business of the conference of the delegates of the Jewish Social Self Help, January 26, 1942, 9 am.

Attendees: As yesterday, with the exception of the out-of-town doctors, members of the delegation of Cycow and out-of-town *Judenrats*.

Addressing the 5th point of the order of the day, the chairwoman Oks Chaya Roza speaks:

One of the most important tasks of the Jewish Social Self Help must be the children's care. The term "child" contains all our hopes, our future, our existence. If this war business and radically altered social and economic conditions, which the adult population understands and feels and the younger generation will not break under and will withstand, then we will exist. When, before the war, needs among the Jewish masses spread more and more, the internal and external consequences were first evident in the child, because for him the sanitary and hygienic conditions left it stamp in the first line. This already then attracted the attention of the society "TAZ" – this society is for protecting the health of the Jewish population – and it acknowledged the primary task being for child care. TAZ began its activities for care of school age children, and organized child centers and half-centers, care centers for mothers and babies. During these two years that the Jewish Social Self Help was conducting its work, the care of these babies, among others, came as providing milk, sugar, and booties. Care for school children – as provisions (bread and soup). For the summer, a half-center was organized for 110 children of school age. They were given meals twice a day, and were under special supervision from the morning until 4 pm, and the result was that they gained weight to about two kilograms. The physical conditions were very good, because the children were clean, happy, and had smiling, glowing faces. This happened also because they were removed from the atmosphere of the home's pressures and stresses, from the damp and small cellars and attics, where the sun never shines, and they were taken into the fresh air.

[Page 614]

We therefore appeal to you that we want to expand the care for the child, and in order to carry this out we need, among other things, to organize women's committees. We have to strive to support the mothers, organize care centers for babies and children, and protect them with a permanent sanitary and hygienic facility. We have to organize centers and homes where other than provisory and medical help the children should be provided with supervision under the direction of educators, and the children should find themselves in a warm and clean atmosphere. Organizing summer kindergartens where children can spend their free time in the fresh air under responsible supervision, will not create great challenges. In every city, town, or settlement, there will be one house – one large room – clean and sunny, where the poorest children of those being supported will be brought. There, under guidance of a designated person, the children will have their care, and great attention will be paid to the hygiene of each child, they will be bathed, hair will be cut, and so on.

This outlined program of providing care for the poor child and mother is not just in the realm of dreams, because with good will this can be accomplished in real life, even in the smallest town.

Mr. Kraft Bezalel (Rejowiec): In full agreement with the activities of Mrs. Oks, but in Rejowiec these provisions and possibilities of organizing child care do not exist. There is no location to be had, and there is a shortage of wood. Eventually, we could set up the children with other families, and organize a special child center in a more conducive time.

Mr. Lehrer Sholom (Sziedliscze): I am in agreement with the presentation of Mrs. Oks, that the child has to have priority over the adults. In Sziedliscze there is an absolute shortage of homes, and the possibility to be involved with the children becomes worse because of the shortage of potatoes, firewood, and means for bathing and scouring. The residents of Sziedliscze, with few exceptions, are exceptionally poor. There are many who have come here. He asks to demonstrate the possibilities and means of acquiring child provision.

Mr. Cohen Avrohom (Wlodowa): In Wlodowa there are 700 children aged 8 to 12. The delegation, under its own initiative, takes care of the children, and it does so not with the account of the Jewish Social Self Help, but with the funds of its own members. Generally, the children are immediately taken under care, food is not sent to the home. But the shortage of shoes and clothing for the winter completely depletes the provisions on the spot.

Mr. Berger Faivel (Wojslowiec): In Wojslowiec there are no homes, there is a shortage of basic provisions, and in clothing and shoes, money. We ask that these be provided for us, and especially important is sugar.

Mr. Fuks Alter (Savin): Presents the same as Mr. Berger Faivel, but also asks that a doctor be sent to Savin, as well as medications.

[Page 615]

Mrs. Kozhukh Sheindel (Uhrusk): She speaks and presents, as Mr. Berger Faivel, and says that there are 30 children in Uhrusk, between the ages of six and eight, and in the entire district, there are 100 children. The working conditions of the delegates are very difficult, particularly because the support of the *Judenrat* is not there. In spite of that, the delegation will now step forward and organize the child provisions, and we ask the committee to help us from time to time in the form of suggestions, instructions, and publicity.

Mrs. Oks Chaya Roza (Chelm): The lacking within a house cannot be removed by forcefully overtaking a house. With the dearth of clothing and shoes, one can figure things out by having a collection event, and the women's committee will then mend and adjust; sugar, which is designated for the older ones, and then passed down to the children, because sugar is good for the children's bodies; sugar and coffee and a roll, in worst case scenario, would be enough for a meal.

The chairman Frenkel Meyer (Chelm): He confirms that Mrs. Oks completely accurately presented the issues of child provisions. From these speeches, you can see that houses and firewood are lacking. For these details, the committee will turn to Mr. Treuhaender, that the houses which are used for the tasks of the Jewish Social Self Help should be rent free, the same for child care, and also if houses are lacking, they will give permission some from the Jewish Social Self Help. The committee will also turn to the *Fostinspecteur* to designate for the delegates a specified amount of provisory wood for the kitchens and similar goals. The committee will also try to distribute amounts of sugar, especially for the children.

Re Point 6 of the Item of the Day

This report was given by Mr. Shein Yosef (Chelm) and in agreement, the chairman Mr. Frenkel Meyer, set up that special material and moral supplies must be distributed to all locations that are part of the activities of the Jewish Social Self Help for those who had moved [fled, been evacuated, etc.,] and for the unemployed. What to give those who moved – make them comfortable in every detail in line with the local population that has always lived here. The same principle understandably applies to the workers, and this is relevant not only to those who are working on local projects, but also in the working camps, and to those who as a majority or exclusively come from Warsaw. Among other things, we are providing them with sanitary care and sometimes with food and clothing.

Re Point 7, Reported by Chairman Frenkel:

From the presenters' reports and from the delegates' speeches, it is clear that all branches of the projects and activities of the Jewish Social Self Help are rooted in food, and this problem is the most prevalent. In …

[Page 616]

... every region, and we must run tight housekeeping, because our funds are limited, and other than that, it is possible that the situation with food provisions will worsen. For the entire period from the war until the present, the region did not receive any provisions for those who need support, or the Jewish Social Self Help was not considered. Other than that, individual locations did not receive anything for their people. As you can see, for example, from the previous year's report, the delegate from Roda-Swierz received 2.10 kilo of cornmeal per person per week. There was no talk at all about wheat flour and other articles.

After great and numerous efforts by the dependable authorities of the materials distribution office in Chelm, it seems that they did not distribute 2.10 kilo weekly, but 550 grams of flour per person. Regardless of that, there are special amounts of cornmeal for kitchens, those who need support, and for hospitals.

Other than the normal provisions that are distributed to the population for those who are supported, for the kitchens, and for the hospitals, it entered my mind to provide for all the locations in Chelm, with the exception of Wlodowa, who had already received 5,000 kilogram of wheat flour. For this the delegates have to go to the distribution office.

At the same time, I wish to report that after strong and numerous efforts, I was able to get 2,500 kilo of sugar, exclusively for those places in the region and for those who are being supported (with the exception of Wlodowa) where, for the entire period of the war no sugar was given out to anyone. (Applause.)

I also received a special amount of noodles and gruel for the hospitals.

Questions come from the hall, can you get salt. The chairman: Yes, you can get it in smaller amounts and the people's representatives can come forward and ask for this, and they will get it according to provision prices. Yesterday, I already shared that I decided also to give a designated amount of soap and powder soap that will be enough to wash one set of clothing per person, and it will cost one zlot and 12 groshen. The delegates or the *Judenraten* have to pay for this into the fund of the committee or directly to the distribution office. About the sugar, I ask the delegates to first give it to the children, the sick, and those being supported. About potatoes, unfortunately, because of the frost, there can be no discussion of the possibility to provide. That is, I have permission to provide the city of Chelm with 2,000 meters of potatoes, but we cannot fill this because of the frost. But I want to say that of these 2,000 meter, even though this is designated to the city of Chelm, we will give 200 meter to Sosnowiecz.

At that point, the chairman turns to the representative from Wlodowa, Mr. Cohen, and says that following the example of Chelm, Wlodowa should also distribute what they can to the surrounding delegates, because from Mr. Cohen's statements, it is clear that Wlodowa is not suffering from lack of food provisions and is managing quite well. It is not known at all, if ...

[Page 617]

... our catastrophic situation will occur tomorrow in Dubeczne, Sosnowiec, and so on.

Then the chairman turned to the representatives of the delegations, if they accept the direction of the work of the committee. Voices: Yes! Yes! Now the task of distributing amounts of wheat flour for matzo is waiting for us. In general, I well understand that financial assistance will not address your needs if you do not get the food provisions according to the allocation prices. If even Krakow and America would allocate subsidies to you, this would not appease your food needs. As an example, I will say the following: I have heard that some of the delegates have reported that they are not able to pay 20 zlotys for a kilo of sugar. If you will multiply 2500 kilo by 25, you will get a sum of 65,000 zlotys at a time when this has to cost the distribution office 4,000 zlotys. This is like a subsidy of 58,000 zlotys for January. I am doing this and figuring this out because of my love for people, and I will keep calculating this in the future in the same way. I ask that this be a collaborative task among the *Judenraten* and the Jewish Social Self Help.

Re Point 8 of the Order of the Day

The reporter Mr. Katz Noson (Chelm): From the delegates' speeches, I get the impression that among the *Judenratens* in a relatively large number of places and their delegates, there is some antagonism, which is important to mention because, on a large scale, this can hurt the work of the representatives of the institutions, as well as the interests of the population. On the contrary, a collaboration, a positive one, a friendly one, will be useful to both sides. As an example, I will take the city of Chelm, where the *Judenrat* is making every effort to help the Jewish Social Self Help. Among other things, the council gives out a regular monthly subsidy of a few thousand zlotys. The delegates, from their side, have always to try to find sources of funding appropriate to the local conditions. And the council gives regular subsidies to these sources, monthly payments, voluntary taxations, projects, events for the Jewish holidays, and so on. All this has to be instituted and evolved.

Mr. Cohen Avrohom (Wlodowa): As the representative of the chairman of the *Judenrat* in Wlodowa, I promise you that the *Judenrat* will collaborate with the delegate from the Jewish Social Self Help. He asks for a copy of the letter from the *Kreishauptmann*, from January 24, No. 111 710-42, which was addressed to Mr. Frenkel.

Mr. Lehrer Sholom (Sziedliscze) and Migdal Yitzkhok (Dubenko) confirm that the *Judenrat* in their locations are doing everything they can to support the delegates, but their efforts are from time to time fruitless, because the means are not available, since the Jewish population there has become completely poverty stricken. If there would be no help …

[Page 618]

… from outside sources, then the situation would be even worse and it would be difficult to emerge from it.

Mr. Kraft Bezalel (Rejowiec): Asks that potatoes and fire wood be donated to Rejowiec. He reports that soon, a course in agriculture training will be organized, which is very important for Rejowiec.

Chairman Frenkel: We have to accept as an absolute claim that: A) all the profits that the *Judenraten* received for their provisions distribution will be paid to the delegates of the Jewish Social Self Help. B) The *Judenraten* must distribute regular monthly subsidies, and the amounts of the subsidies are to be determined based on the budgets of the last six months. C) You cannot provide to those who are being supported with individual help in the form of money, but can only give dry products or another form of help, such as rent, firewood, etc. In exceptional conditions you can digress from this last order (probably for two points).

Dr. Eliyuha Tish (Krakow): The goal of the conference was to find a way to collaborate on resolving the situation, put into place means and ways that could help support the projects of the Jewish Social Self Help. I would now like to discuss the relationship of the *Judenrat* to the Jewish Social Self Help. We do not see any basic reason that should interfere with the collaboration of these only remaining two Jewish institutions. The *Judenraten* are obligated to and must recognize the important sacrificing work of the Jewish Social Self Help, which, on a large scale, frees the councils of social provisionary work. Living examples of the beautiful and useful work of the Jewish Social Self Help are the public kitchens, treatment centers, and hospitals, food centers, and child care center, the "Drop of Milk," and several other institutions that bear a benevolent and constructive character. I invite understanding, assistance, collaboration, because you are both institutions of the Jewish People and you have to complement each other's jobs. With the goal to prevent the Jews from completely going under, the term "self-help" was thrown onto the Jewish street [street jargon], and this term has become the goal of our institution, to bring aid to the poorest masses, among those whose needs are the greatest – and the aid – the most unquestionable. With this term, we come to the Jewish masses and we want to help them.

But it is impossible to find one remedy for all the problems which the delegates presented here. Everyone has to find ways that will relieve these local conditions and situations. We are doing everything humanly possible, but the means are small and frail.

In such a situation, the main goal of our activities should be – child care, because the child is the foundation and the future of our People. Through applying these mentioned strengths the child care situation can be managed in the right ways, even with the most modest means and conditions.

[Page 619]

The work of the Jewish Social Self Help is also a battle for the Jews. I appeal to everyone that this work be carried out, so that after the war it should be an honor to be able to say about oneself that he participated in this work.

Re Point 9 of the Business of the Day

(Open Suggestions)

The following suggestions are presented:

1. Suggestion by Mr. Lias Khaim (Chelm delegate) about setting up a single, simplified accounting for all the delegates of the Jewish Social Self Help according to the examples provided. He maintains the suggestion be applied in the following ways: Whereas every month I have to become acquainted with reports of the individual delegates, I can show many errors in their notes of profits and expenses, that makes it impossible for them to prepare the correct reports. Because members of the delegation are not familiar with the general principles of accounting, therefore, some delegates are not presenting reports. The system that I am presenting does not require any specific vocational skills, and also not any expensive books. It is enough to have two books: a fund book and an accounting book, demarcated in a specific fashion.

Setting up the following system of accounting and monthly reports that would bring all the totals of the required individual rubrics, would give the regional provisions committee an opportunity to set up monthly reports for the entire region. After testing this system for a few months in the area of the Chelmer region, we would be able to pass the project by the presidium of the Jewish Social Self Help, as the accounting of the delegates in the entire General Government area.

2. Suggestion by Mr. Kraft Bezalel (Rejowiec) about interventions of the government organizations, that the locales that are active with the Jewish Social Self Help should be freed from rent.
3. Suggestions by the member of the delegation: Yitzkhok Ciberman (Uhrusk), Sholom Lehrer, and Leib Kruk (Sziedliscze), Alter Fuks (Savin), about raising the salary of Mauritzi Druker, the secretary of the regional committee of the Jewish Social Self Help by five hundred zlotys a month.

It was decided to give over all the suggestions to the Chelmer regional provisions committee of the Jewish Social Self Help.

Whereas the business of the day was completed, the chairman thanked everyone for their collaborative work and for participating in the discussions, and with a call to further intensify the work in the field of social conditions, he confirmed [and closed] the businesses of the conference on January 26, 1942, 13 o'clock, 30 minutes.

[Page 620]

An Administrative Meeting

From the regional provisions committee of the Jewish Social Self Help, this took place in Chelm on February 11th, 1942, 11 am.

Present were the members of the committee of the Jewish Social Self Help: Frenkel Meyer-chairman; Shein Yosef, Oks Khaya Roza, Katz Noson, and Dr. Yelen Avrohom – representatives for the sick Dr. Shimon Goren.

At the meeting, they addressed the above-mentioned opened suggestions that were brought in to the meeting and the following decisions were made:

Re the first suggestion:

It was decided to accept the project of the monthly fund reports and accounting according to the included samples, to print and send them to the individual delegations in the Chelmer region with the request to provide the reports and books on April 1, 1942.

Re the second point:

The chairman Mr. Frenkel informs: A memorandum about this issue was given to Mr. Treuhaender in Chelm in the name of all the delegates to free from rent all the locations that are used by the Jewish Social Self Help, and also about providing new locales.

Re the third point:

With the consent of all those present, it was decided that from the fund (account) of the regional committee of the Jewish Social Self Help, as of February 1, 1942, every month, the secretary of the Jewish Social Self Help, Mauritzi Druker should be paid 300 zlotys for his work for the region, and this is independent of the earlier agreed monthly salary of 600 zlotys for his work for the city. Other than that, to pay secretary Druker 300 zlotys as a one time payment for his work in the year 1941.

Chairman of the Committee of the Jewish Social Self Help – Meyer Frenkel

Secretary of the Committee of the Jewish Social Self Help – Mauritzi Druker

Jewish Social Self Help
Jewish Chelmer Regional Provision Committee
Of the Jewish Social Self Help

This is a copy of the original
A. Blum
Warsaw, August 1, 1950

Stamp:
Jewish Historical Institute
Of the Central Committee
Of the Jews in Poland

S 20a.

Page 621]

During the Days of the Destruction
(several memoirs)

by Khaim Sobol

Translated by Pamela Russ

I am not a writer but I will try – as much as my memory will serve me – to describe all that I saw and experienced from the first day that Hitler-Amalek [enemy of Israel] stepped foot into our town with his bloody boots, until the liberation, when the Red Army chased out the Hitler murderers. During all of that time, I was in Chelm.

September 1, 1939. The dark war breaks out, and every Jew feels the terrifying times. The events link themselves to a powerful rhythm. Already in the first days, Chelm was viciously bombed, about 200 people were killed by these bombs – Jews and non-Jews alike. People were leaving the city, running into the villages where the situation is also not safe.

Two weeks after the German occupation of Chelm, rumors circulated that the Soviets were coming to town to replace the Germans. The Jewish population hears this miracle with joy. The Red Army marches into the city, but according to the agreement with the Hitlerist authorities, they leave the city and go back to the other side of the Bug River.

Once again, the city is in Hitler's hands. Fear and chaos reigns. The Red Army – before they left Chelm – warned and told the Jews to go with them. With the greatest regret, only a small number of people took seriously the warnings of the Red Army. Only the Jewish youth, the left-wing, left the city. But the majority of the people and groups of the Jewish population remained in Chelm, thinking that nothing bad would happen to them and that the Germans would not do anything reproachable to the Jews.

But the worst happened. As soon as the Hitlerist occupiers once again retook the city, they created a horrifying terror among the Jewish people: murders, taxation, robberies, happened day and night. In particular, the SS units went from house to house, searching and killing, stealing the best possessions. A *Judenrat* was formed, and they took Jewish hostages.

The members of the *Judenrat* were reassured that thanks to the fact that they would collaborate with German authorities, nothing bad would happen to them and they would live in peace. But they were fooled by the refined thugs. The Germans captured Jews for work, left them broke, and in the end, killed them off.

Robberies took place on a grand scale. All the Jewish residents of Lublin Street were chased out of their homes and they were placed in the Jewish streets – Post Street and others – where later that was the Chelmer ghetto.

On December 1, 1939, the Gestapo in Chelm ordered the *Judenrat* to assemble all the Jewish men …

[Page 622]

… ages 16-60, in the market place, where the "circle" of Jewish business once lived, to hear a Gestapo chief's speech. The Chelmer Jews were thinking that maybe this really could be just a speech and not executions, and so about 1,800 Jewish men came to the above-mentioned place.

When they came to the "circle," a strong guard of the Gestapo surrounded the Jews. The order was passed that everyone should give all their belongings [which they had on them] over to the Germans. Then they were ordered to get into lines and march to Hrubieszowa Street.

The marching Jews soon realized their death sentence. They cried and pleaded with the Germans that they be freed.

The 1,800 Chelmer Jews were herded to Hrubieszow and from there to Sokol – to the Soviet border, saying that if the Jews love Russia then they must go there. On this death march, many Jews were shot. For the smallest infraction – not being able to march quickly, Jews were shot. Only a small number of Jews crossed the Bug River – to the Soviet side – and a portion of the Jews returned to Chelm.

From that bloody death march until the *Aktzias* [roundups] in 1942, Chelmer Jews went through very dark days and nights, hunger and deathly fear, seeing death at every moment and at each step. There were deportations to the death camps in Sobibor. The chaos was so great that there were incidents when Jews told the Gestapo that they wanted to be shot rather than be tortured.

In 1942, when the final *Aktzia* took place, the SS selected the 50 of the most skilled workers – from all vocations. I was chosen from the gaiter makers [spats or shoe makers]. Under heavy armed guard, we worked for the SS officers. By that time, the city was already emptied of Jews.

So, they took to "liquidating" our work team as well. Of the 50 Jewish workers, we remained no more than 15. They took us over from the Block to the prison.

For 16 months, as we saw death before our eyes, we worked in the prison. There was not one single Jew left in Chelm. We also preferred death at that point and waited for it as if waiting for a miracle that would free us from the clutches of the German murderers.

On May 17, 1944, Soviet airplanes bombed Chelm, also the train station and the prison where we worked. The prison guards and some of the prisoners were killed at that time. The prison building was destroyed. During this bombing, we – the same 15 – fled. One of us was shot by a guard.

On the second day, May 18, we, 14 Jews and 70 non-Jews, were led away to be shot. Until this day, I cannot understand why they shot the 70 Aryans and we, the 14 Jews, were sent back to work in the prison.

[Page 623]

We worked until July 21, 1944. Then, when the Red Army did its great offensive and crossed the Bug River, Chelm was the first Polish city that was taken over by the Soviets, and we were liberated.

This happened so quickly, that the prison administration and the Gestapo, in great chaos and fear, fled during the night. At dawn, we noticed that we were without guard. But the Germans were in the city. There was still fighting and a lot of intense shooting.

[Page 624]

After that, we were afraid to leave the prison, so we tried to find a hiding place in a bunker of the prison. We stayed there for three days – without food or drink. We did not know that the Red Army had been in the city already for two days.

As we left the prison, one of our Jewish workers – Yekhiel Szczupak, a hat maker, died immediately. We learned of the great tragedy of the mass destruction only after we were liberated. Some of us felt a terrible solitude and the gruesome tragedy of the Jewish nation.

[Page 623]

Chelm

by Shlomo Wahrzorger

Translated by Pamela Russ

Wherever I lay my head – my tragedy hunts me down.
O, my hometown, with hilly streets, with ups and downs –
As
"Its" curse, as a thunder, rolled across the city.
The paved road that leads to the forest lies there isolated.
Brokers, wheat merchants in rusty coats –
Quicksilver in the wind –
With "*Ma tovu*" ["how good it is…" part of morning prayers] on the lips, at the same time as the blue,
The few peasants went out – to rummage
… in the hay …

Now they are crying blindly
The stone highways, for Stival'e's wagon driver, at the side
Of the wagons, with creaking and groaning.
The market is faint – thirsty.

For bales and barrels, which --- added color
Every Tuesday at the fair.

They are crying as well:
The crooked back streets, the quiet houses, as teeth left in a mouth,
Empty of old age.

O, my fellow toilers – honest butchers,
Jewish from the Eastern Wall – and silver adornment [of the *talis*]…
All, all, there at the bottom of the field …
The sky is crying over your open grave –
Wherever I put my head, your tragedy hunts me down.

There is no trace of the *Beis Medrash* [Study House] that was in the middle of the city.
The courtyard, the small street with narrow sidewalks, that had calm

Routes
From grandfathers, son --- with grandchildren – taken away.
No sign remains
Of the second shul, the "simple" one, that is opposite here,
Where, every year, the cantorial *Kol Nidrei* [recited on Yom Kippur]

[Page 624]

Would make the Christians all around tremble,
And to distinguish – the large church
That shoots its shining bare head arrogantly to the sky
With bells ringing loudly …

As the "steel circle" filled with Jewish shops
With hands chapped from the wind – brown, blue – swollen,
Faces – rusted as tin and steel,
That wander around the shelves of the shops.

Where are you, smithies of the "new goal"?
Clumsy porters of the "New World" –
The Shabbath eve – the flames of the burning candles
Tables covered in white, the candelabrum is set.

The Shabbath, heartfelt tones of Shabbath songs,
The mother's "G-d of Abraham" [prayer said by women as the Shabbath ends], her pale face – wrapped
In sadness.
At the first glimpse of the first star in the home – the dark
Navy.

There are no blessings for the new week.
Wherever I put my head – the tragedy hunts me down.

* * *

When they nailed Zalman the baker to the post
And poured pitch on him and then burned him alive,
Jesus looked through the church windows and watched
And cried out of embarrassment, as his name is put to shame…

* * *

A robed person came to him to purify himself
And "his" priest forgave him, and his priest blessed him …

* * *

And the church bells from the tall mountain saw this
And rang on the Sundays, and the holidays, as if nothing
Had happened….

[Pages 625- 626]

The Last Action

By Malka Milchtajch- Lorber Z"L

Translated by Blima Rajzla Lorber

The Last Action

I

In the Ghetto of Chelm nobody remained.
The inhabitants were taken during dawn,
under an intense rain, like animals, to an unknown place.
They were nude and barefooted.
The lines were huge,
they crawled slowly and also slowly they prayed while walking.
The day went away and also did the night.
A new day was breaking.
Their feet and their bones seemed to be broken.
They could not walk anymore.
Even so, they did not surrender.
They went on, they did not surrender.
What will happen, nobody knows.
There were old men, children,
parents carrying packages of sadness and bitterness,
together with the yellow strips around their arms.
Everything very painful.
They walked without rest, without bread nor water.
The streets were dark and it was cold and humid.
The sky cried rivers of tears.
In a low voice, crying, the Jews asked themselves: "What will happen to us?"
"It does not help crying," they said.
They were pushed with weapons, but their strength was at the end.
Nevertheless, they were forced to walk.
"Our enemies are riding at our side."
"Where will they take us?" They asked with their eyes, crying.
Mothers held their children, hugging them strongly.
They remained silent, but their hearts protested:
"How did we let them take us like animals to die?
We cannot suffer anymore! Whatever will happen needs to happen."
When somebody was late, he was shot.
The second, the third… the hundredth and in their lips words of fear and anger burned.
Nobody saw anything in the darkness.
They only heard shots.
Old men and young men just like trees fell down.
If someone was left behind, a tremor went through his body.
From the ones that were behind, few remained.
A mother shouted: "Please, what was our sin? Pity! You stepped on my little child."
They were no more silent and they heard a cry:
"Do not kill my child! Only kill me. It is better to kill me."
The weapons went on shooting.
The soldiers beat people with their weapons.
There was no more salvation.
The S.S. soldiers ran and with rage they screamed:
"Here, your unfortunate ones, you are blamed for your own misfortune."
Again, a child cried and was still being dragged.

"Father, I am not able to go on anymore! I stay here in the forest."
The father begs: "Be strong, a little more. Do not stop, walk my son!"
And he was already looking his only son, a child, being eaten by dogs.
One more day went away with a lot of suffering.
What will tomorrow bring?
Will the Germans will still be alive?
"If parents and children do not die tomorrow,
still these unfortunate Jews will be free," the soldiers screamed.
The hearts beat afraid.
Oh God, soon life will end.
With range and dark the night fell again.
It rained, rained and rained.
A sharp wind blew: the end will be very sad.
And it turned dawn.
In the forest, a plain.
No, it was not imagination, the last hour beat.
We cannot waste time and we should say the last prayer.
The hole was big and fresh.
It will shelter people's sadness.
A soldier's voice was heard: "Get to the edge of the hole."
Suddenly, an aged hand raised and turning the face to the bandits,
with the his fist closed the old man spoke:
"Innocent blood spilled will never remain silent.
Put an end to this fight, you will not win.
My curse will get to you like a strident blitz."
With all his strength the old rabbi screamed:
"Look at me, I will jump first in the hole.
Do not be afraid, because when one cannot live, death is also beloved."
Shots began to be heard and a voice recited "Schmá Israel…."
Everything was quiet.
No screams were heard anymore.
The earth covered all of them, hiding deep inside the last pain.

To where?

II

If I still will be able to return.
Destiny I will take me back to my country.
Who will listen to my first cry ?
The one who comes in front of me will give me a warm hand ?
Who will wait for my return from so far ?
Whom will I hug, crying, embraced at his neck, whom ?
The streets were destroyed by the enemies' hands.
Shots were like hail.
The streets I knew so well.
They will be ashamed!
The houses destroyed , in ruins. Broken homes.
The tough stone roads painted with blood and human insides.
In front of me there are graves and shrouds
that will call me for a saint revenge –"They will pay!"
Sometimes, I will not find not even shrouds.
Other times there will not be signs of human bones.
My return is horrible.
The feeling is what will I find.
I will find the tombstones in ruins,
written with the martyrs' blood,
who in Eternity will remind what the murderers did.
All decapitated. No one remained!.

I will neither find my mother nor my father,
nor sisters or brothers, nor friends or relatives.
My town is a desert.
It seems a cemetery, after a gale has destroyed everything.
I will be depressed and pain and suffering will wake up my sadness.
It can be that in Majdaneck crematorium
I will need to seek for a rest of ashes,
in plantations as fertilizer, in Treblinka.
Or to seek in a third death camp or can it be in the tenth.
No powder remained from these of my people who had fallen.
I will not see any writing, tombstone or sign.
To whom will I ask when sadness comes?
So weak and nobody to console me.
I swallow my rage.
They who took everything of good from the martyrs
With a hateful look and with all my anger I can now spit.
As a flame which illuminates the way of the wanderer,
Strong it will bind. Poor wanderer!
For my youth's sad and bitter years,
I will again have to leave my destroyed old home.
From the one who dreamed to return soon.

The Young–Old Man Ballad

III

He was together with thousands of people,
waiting to be taken to the gas chambers.
He felt his mother's hand pressed his warmly.
"See, soon they will take you for the sad action."
He did not see nor listened to anything.
He was feeling his mother's tremor.
"Oh God, we didn't deserve such a death!"
The look was pale and embittered.
"Show us a miracle, we do not deserve such a punishment.".
Mindless, her lips murmured:
"Worse than death is the mother's suffering."
The voice was suffocated.
He opened his shirt.
Only destiny wanted to play a game on him.
"Oh, bad luck! Do not separate us both now!
Oh, foolish boy! You still have a lot to suffer.
Mother, may we not be separated before death."
Glances of envy accompanied him.
"Why was he luckier than the others?"
But his fate did not bring him happiness.
Inside of him, tears burned as fire.
He was nineteen years old,
with the impulse of youth.
The head, a brown forest.
And the eyes aimed at dreams in the sky.
He knew how strong he was,
he hoped to be a great man.
The only child, he was his mother's pride
and she believed the world would hear from him.
A vigorous body,
firm hands as tree branches.
The chest inspired with energy.

He could not see anybody to be harmed,
he could not silence.
Now, he was feeling as thousands of them.
Fear was on his face.
It is more difficult than death, more difficult!
He felt so depressed with the executioners.
They ordered him and two other boys to go to the place of the slaughter
in order to select and to organize clothes
so that they could be transported in the wagons.
The three friends made a pact.
When the wagons were full,
they, at night, would enter quietly and there, amid the clothes, they would hide.
The train left fast as a ray and in a wagon, hidden, three hearts beat together.
The eyes shone in the darkness, burning.
The way for the station was getting shorter.
A deep sound, cutting as a handsaw, could be heard.
The wind blew the night breeze,
The faster they fled from death's claws.
With thousands screams, the quiet night calls.
He was the first one to jump.
Just as the roar of a shot at night.
The two other ones also fell,
for the prison guards were taking care wagons' roofs.
The train swallowed the night's noise.
It was already dawn.
He walked silently.
He was cleaning up his mouth when he came to and he felt like reborn.
He was alive and the earth his feet stepped on was free.
He approached the two boys and saw them wounded.
"You, friends, can not stay here, because the day is breaking.
Look, I am well and healthy and I will take you both with me."
It is as soon as he said that he felt he would not be embarrassed,
and the swollen eyes started opening up, a pain groan kept silent.
"Oh!", both of them said at once.
They looked at him but they did not recognize the old man
They jumped all of a sudden and looked at him.
"You are well and healthy, you said! Oh, Schmá Israel!
In one hour you got old."
Without believing in that, he pulls some hair off his head.
"Oh, Great God, my brown hair is white as snow."
At the age of 19, in blooming of youth, the youngster became an old man.

[Pages 629-630]

Jewish Heroism

By Khananie Binsztok

Translated by Miriam Leberstein

Several Chelemer Jews died in battle against the Nazi murderers. Yashe Kratke died in a battle with the Germans near Warsaw on the second day of Rosh Hashonah in 1944, while we were crossing the Vistula late at night. We were surrounded by the German army and very few of us survived.

There were two young brothers, Bolek and Yurke Ivre, whose mother, Tanye, was a well-known dentist in Chelm and whose father, Y. Ivre, died during the death march from Chelm to Hrubieszow. Both brothers, well-trained officers, fought the entire time of the war. They were wounded many times, but still survived the war.

After the war ended, they were sent back to Poland. The elder brother was appointed the leader of a group assigned to fight the remnants of roving bands of thugs and was killed in the course of fighting. After this tragic event, the younger brother could find no rest and thirsted for revenge. At his own request he was transferred to the same city where his brother had died. There he fought for an entire year against the treacherous bands and on the very anniversary of his brother's death, on the day of the elections to the first Polish *sejm* [legislature], he was killed by an enemy bullet. We were deeply shaken when the sad news reached us at the Jewish Committee in Lublin.

A young boy from Chelm, M.N. Liber from Hrubieszower Street, was at the battlefront all through the war. He distinguished himself and participated in the most difficult and dangerous battles. He was killed while swimming across the Oder River.

Another young boy, Leyzer Roznblum, fought the entire time of the war in the Russian and Polish armies. In battle near Berlin, Roznblum was on assignment in the forest when his group was surrounded by Germans and he died a hero.

* * *

Many Jews from Chelm died in battles and struggles with the Nazi serpent. It is difficult to tally up each name.

Finally, I want to mention a young man, Mordkhe Brayer, a painter by trade. He and I served in the same division in the fiercest battles deep in Germany. In the city of Kohlberg he was assigned to a division of mine-throwers. Mordkhe Brayer did not leave the battlefield until he had fired all the mines. After two weeks of heavy fighting, one of his officers stated that Brayer had made a major contribution to conquering Kohlberg. He was awarded the highest medals and honors for his heroic fighting.

[Pages 631-632]

A Gruesome Summation

By Y. Fainsztok

Translated by Miriam Leberstein

In September, 1939, Chelm had 18,000 Jews, approximately 60% of the total population. The town had two Yiddish newspapers, a Jewish *gymnazie*, a Tarbut school. There was an entire street of *besmedreshim* [houses of study and prayer] and *shtiblekh* [one room houses of prayer] for various Hasidic sects, such as the Kuzminer, Trisker, Lubliner, Radziner, *et.al.*

On October 9, 1939, the Germans invaded. Persecution started on the first days. Jews soon lost all protections. Local sinister elements took advantage of the situation. In addition, every evening the Gestapo drove around and searched the homes of the more prosperous Jews. Many Jews were beaten. Women were ordered to strip naked and do gymnastic exercises. Then the Germans would pick out the best of the household possessions and drive away. This lasted for weeks; people got used to it.

The cold winter sadly dragged on. In the town hall, engineers were planning how to enclose the Jews in a ghetto. But the Judenrat, led by Frenkel, managed to bribe the head of the Gestapo, Hager, and the plan wasn't carried out immediately.

Jews moved around the town more freely, breathed more freely. There were no more beatings or forced labor. Somehow they managed to make a living.

Suddenly, like a hammer blow, in August 1940, the Judenrat announced that people should be careful, that something was about to happen. People arranged various hiding places and did not sleep at home.

One night, 4,000 S.S. men spread out among the Jewish population, going house to house, and arrested 483 men, while the others remained in hiding. The Judenrat vigorously intervened for two days, exploiting every form of influence and they managed to free 411 men; 72 were deported to a camp in Belzec.

The Judenrat organized a relief committee to help those who had been sent to the camp. Each week a couple of men travelled legally to Belzec, bringing food for the Jews, as well as valuable tiems as gifts for the soldiers guarding the camp. On Yom Kippur, 71 people returned home from Belzec. One had died.

The summer ended. Transports of wounded and frozen German soldiers began to arrive from the Eastern front. The brutes began to grow anxious and we felt it immediately. The Gestapo warned the Judenrat that Jews should participate more in work, rather than politics or strategizing. Soon, they resumed beating people in the street, seizing people for forced labor, and threatening to establish a ghetto.

In December, 1941, in the course of two days, the Jews in the more beautiful streets were evicted and forced into small, muddy, dirty by-streets. Jews were forbidden to use the main streets. Conditions worsened again. A rumor spread, that the ghetto would be established on January 1, 1942. The Judenrat and Frenkel again made huge efforts, distributing money and valuable gifts, and they did not establish an actual ghetto. But they did force the Jews to crowd into a few small streets. Three to four families shared a room with a kitchen.

Suddenly, we got the news that Lublin was being "cleaned out." That was the greatest blow. We knew that our turn would be next. The Judenrat came up with an idea and offered up 6000 workers for the water system. In April, 1942, 5,000 to 6,000 workers, men and women, stood in water up to their waists and dried the swamps and flooded meadows near Chelm. They toiled long and hard, but that did not help.

In August, 1942, quite early on the Sabbath, a luxury car drove up t the building housing the Judenrat and five unfamiliar Gestapo officers [not from Chelm] got out. They told the chairman that at 2:00 P.M., all the Jews must assemble at the square with 15 kilos of baggage, because they were being sent to "Pinsk." Frenkel immediately intervened with the local German authorities and was somewhat successful .The local authorities declared that all the Jews still in Chelm were essential workers. The other Germans, however, didn't want to go away empty handed. They went into the streets, seized about 300 people, shot 50 on the spot and took the rest with them.

On October 23, 1942, a large group of S.S. men and Gestapo surrounded the Jewish quarter. The *aktsie* [raid,operation] lasted two days; 2800 people were taken to Sobibor and 800 were shot in town. Within a short time, on November 6, the last *aktsie* was carried out. Chelm was declared Judnrein [free of Jews]. For several days, the town was a real battle post. A lot of Jews were actually in good hiding places, but the Gestapo had search dogs and found them and shot them or sent them to Sobibor.

Of the more than 18,000 Jews [before the war], by November 1943 about 700 Jews – mostly tradesmen — were left, hidden away in *platsvukes* [German workshops]. But every few days these were reduced and then only 70 were left.

In May, 1943, they liquidated the *platsvukes*, but the Gestapo prison selected 15 tradesmen – tailors, cobblers, furriers, boot-makers – who were miraculously saved. For the convenience of the Gestapo they were left until the end.

On July 21, 1944, the Red Army occupied our town and freed the 15 Jews in the prison and about 50 Jews who were in partisan groups and in the forest.

Thus, of the 18,000 Jews, there emerged from the forests and camps about 100 people. A number of Jews, mostly young people, had escaped to the Soviet Union. That is the final summation.

9. Januar 1942

Unser Zeichen:
Ref. II R./We. C 2

Der Gouverneur

An die

Kreishauptmannschaft
und Bevölkerungswesen u. Fürsorge

C h o l m.

Betrifft: 2.000 Juden aus M i e l e c.

Ich bestätige, das am 6. Jan. 1942 mit Ihnen geführte Telefongespräch in obiger Angelegenheit und übernehmen Sie für Ihren Kreis 1.000 Juden, davon 400 Juden mit Zielstation Wlodawa und 600 Juden mit Zielstation Parczew. Ich bitte Sie, unbedingt dafür zu sorgen, das auf bei den Zielstationen die Juden empfangen und richtig dort hingeleitet werden, wo es von Ihnen bestimmt wird; nicht, dass es so passiert wie in anderen Fällen, dass die Juden ohne Aufsicht an der Zielstation ankommen und sich nun über das Land verstreuen.

Im Auftrage.

(—) podpis nieczytelny.

Facsimile

[Pages 633-634]

The Avenger, Esther Terner

By A.Y. Kornblit, New York

Translated by Miriam Leberstein

Esther Terner is her name; I remember her from before the war. She was a pious Jewish girl, raised in the spirit of Beis Yakov [Orthodox religious schools for girls] by pious Jewish parents, refined and protective; an only daughter, who had been, as they say, tied to her mother's apron strings. Yet this refined girl possessed the courage and pride to understand that since God had preserved her life and protected her in the German death camps, so that she emerged alive from the Sobibor uprising, she was obliged to take revenge for the torture and murder of our people.

Even before liberation she kept in mind the written notes she had found in the clothing of the Jews who were gassed: "Remember, you who remain alive, to take revenge for our innocent Jewish blood." After liberation, her conscience tormented her, she could not rest. By coincidence, while in Germany, she recognized one of the chief murderers in the Sobibor death camp and turned him over to the justice authorities, who sentenced him to death.

As we see in this photo, Esther Terner, whose last name is now Rov [?], identified many other Nazis in the German courts.

I recently encountered Esther with her husband and newborn child in New York, where they are rebuilding a life for themselves in the free land America. She feels she has repaid a significant part of her debt by obtaining revenge against one of the murderers of the Jews of Chelm, most of whom were killed in the gas chambers of Sobibor. But she considers her debt to be even greater. "I will never forget the German murderers. Jewish blood will not have been spilled in vain. If revenge is not accomplished in our generation, we will transmit the same feelings to our children and grandchildren: to remember what Amalek [anti–Semites] did to us! Never forget!

[Pages 635-636]

Jewish Avengers

Translated by Miriam Leberstein

On a rainy evening, a Pole drove a wagon full of hay into a partisan camp in the forest.

We hurried to empty the hay out of the mysterious wagon. Before us we saw flecks of frozen blood. There were black, bloodied sacks, which held the bodies of five Jewish partisans who had been killed in battle. Their names were: Moniak Shafran (born in Otvotsk); Yekhiel Bronshteyn (born in Polenits, on the Otvotsk railroad line); Ber Gingold (born in Chelm); Avrom Tikatsinski (from Garvoln); Arye Blumenshteyn (from Warsaw). They had been on their way to carry out a partisan mission when they were attacked by the Polish Fascist organization, NSZ (National Armed Forces), and were killed after a four–hour battle.

Moniak Shafran came to the forest right after the deportation of the Jews from Otvotsk in August 1942. Yekhiel Bronshteyn escaped from the Warsaw Ghetto in on January 18, 1943. Ber Gingold came to the "Regut" forest right after the liquidation of the Jews of Chelm. Blumenshteyn and Tikatsinski came to the Regut forest after the Warsaw Ghetto uprising on April 29, 1943.

Within a few days of arriving at the partisan post in the forest they distinguished themselves with their daring attacks upon S.S. guards in the ghetto, and leading the Jews out from the ghetto into the forest.

On August 17, 1943, there was an oppressive feeling among our squad. We had heard rumors about the Kalushin ghetto. The Jews there had been deported in 1942, and in 1943 the Germans announced that they were creating a new ghetto there. This was a ruse to lure Jews who remained to come to Kalushin and to kill them. Many Jews were deceived and came to Kalushin, relying on the fact that the announcement had been signed by the German governor, Hans Fischer.

We partisans knew what the Germans intended and put out propaganda telling Jews not to go to the ghetto, that the Germans would kill all the remaining Jews – we estimated that there were 20,000 Jews left in various places. But our efforts had little effect.

"This is the murderer who helped to kill over a million Jews in the gas chambers of Sobibor." Esther Terner point to Erich Bauer (third from right) in a Berlin court

By August 17, we had received word that regiments of S.S. troops and Polish police grenadiers were pouring in from the area around Kalushin. The Jews in the ghetto were in a panic.

Fearing an uprising in Kalushin like the one in Warsaw, Generals Tropp and Brand sent large military regiments into Kalushin. Although the S.S. commander had announced that nothing bad would happen to the Jews and that the Germans were there to prevent a pogrom by the Poles and Ukrainians, his words did not calm the Jews

We sent out the five partisans named above, who were supposed to penetrate the ghetto and persuade the Jews to run away and not to rely on false promises by the Germans. They travelled by bicycle. On the way, four kilometers from Kalushi, they encountered the NSZ, who attacked them with heavy fire. A shooting battle broke out and two of the five soon fell dead. The remaining three ran deeper into the forest and the NSZ, who were numerous, pursued them. Having no more bullets, the partisans set fire to the forest in order to chase away their Fascist pursuers. But that didn't help and all three were killed.

When the five comrades failed to return from their mission in the afternoon of August 17, fifteen of us set out to look for them. The forest was still burning and Polish fire fighters were driving in to extinguish it. On the road we saw entire divisions of S.S. riding trucks and tanks in the direction of Kalushin, and German Messerschmidt airplanes were circling over the forest, looking for our tents, that is the homes of the "Jewish bandits." After that came other airplanes called "Henke" and Messerschmidt 109.

The planes began to bomb the forest. The Germans intention was to frighten the Jewish partisans as well as the Jews in the ghetto, who would know that the forest was not a refuge for them.

Once again, five partisans went to look for the five who were missing. One of them, Shloyme Lederman from Zamosc, was killed by a bullet fire by a Polish policeman. The remaining four came back with the news that S.S. divisions were still travelling in the direction of Kalushin.

We emerged from the haystacks where we had been hiding and set off for Kalushin. Our plan was to break into the ghetto shooting, to make a way for Jews to escape. At 10 P.M. we began shooting at the German guards at the ghetto guard posts. We were deafened by the German shooting. Not until 1 A.M. were we able to chase the Germans from one of the guard posts. Out of the ghetto came Jews, young and old; children of 5–6 years old ran as quickly as the adults. I remember how a small child dragged his mother along, saying, "Come, let's run faster." Until the Germans were able to recover control of the guard post, 200 Jews escaped.

[Pages 637-638]

We began slowly to retreat from Kalushin. We were pursued by the polish police and German field gendarmes. After an hour–long struggle we managed to evade our pursuers. Five of us were killed: Moniak Bialekman from Kielce; Zise Kats from Chelm (his partisan pseudonym was Zigmund Kot); Motl Pasternik from Zamosc; and Melekh Rozenberg from Chelm.

As soon as we returned to our partisan camp in the forest we learned that five murdered partisans lay in a nearby village. Partisans hurried to the village where saw five sacks in which their bodies lay; these were brought to the forest in a Polish wagon.

When we opened the sacks, we saw a frightful sight. Moniak Shafran's body was so riddled with bullets it looked like a kitchen grater. Yekhiel Bernshteyn lay peacefully as in a heavy sleep, as if he would soon wake up, an ironic smile on his young face. Arye Blumshteyn's body was partly burned. Ber Gingold was holding a gun in his hand, as if unready to give up the fight with the Fascists. Avrom Tikatsinki's right hand and both ears had been cut off as if with an ax and his genitals were gone. His teeth were tightly clenched, indicating that he had been tortured alive, and had clenched them to prevent himself from revealing the secrets about the partisans which the torturers were trying to extract.

We buried them all in one grave. On the grave we placed a wooden memorial carved with their names and the Inscription: "For your and our freedom," and we whispered "Revenge, revenge, revenge."

Somewhere in a military cemetery in Germany, among the crosses, is this stone on the grave of the Chelemer Jew, Meyer Meler, who fell in battle with the Nazi murderers

On the Tenth Yortsayt of the Slaughter in Chelm

By Yekhiel Yoykenen, America

Translated by Miriam Leberstein

They were driven to slaughter,
the upright and the lame
and among them all
was my pious mother

Khane Maytes –
everyone remembered her.
Who in Chelm
did not know her?

The murderers beat them,
and laughed and mocked them,
and ordered her to say:
There is no God!

The best of mankind
will avenge them.
And God in heaven
will have his revenge.

That they will be punished
that is certain.
But we must wait
until the time comes.

[Pages 639-640]

The Miracle of the Last Jews in Chelm

By Ben Tsion Mitzfliker, Montreal

Translated by Miriam Leberstein

June 18, 1944 was a lovely summer day. The sun reached even our narrow prison courtyard and warmed with its rays. Suddenly we heard: "Get up!" We recognized the voice of the head prison, the sadist and murderer Oberschafuerer Kenig, may his name be wiped out. "Today let's drink to brotherhood," he said in German. This request was unexpected. We were not accustomed to such words from such a monster.

At the time, I was walking around the courtyard, looking at the high gray walls and thinking how I could escape from this hell. Suddenly I was summoned. The head was in the shoemaking workshop, holding a bottle of whiskey. "Well, Mitzfliker," he said when I was still on the threshold, "Don't you want to have a drink to brotherhood with your chief?"

"Why not?" I answered. "But, excuse me, I don't drink alcohol." I believed that in those horrific times, our torturers should drink and we should stay sober. I took the opportunity to ask the chief to permit me to say something. "Bitte schoen," he replied. My comrades exchanged glances. I saw they were not pleased with my request. I gathered my courage and began to speak.

"Herr Chief: As you know, we are the last Jews in Chelm and our fate lies in your hands. If you want, we could remain alive. We are the last of the last."

I don't know if he understood this to mean that I was giving him the opportunity to rehabilitate himself. But he answered: "Yes, you are not the last. I know many more Jews from Chelm. One thing is clear. If I remain alive, you will remain alive; but when I die, you too will die." Walking drunkenly, he left the workshop and we remained alone.

Some of my comrades were very upset that I had spoken so openly to the chief. Others were pleased. Until now, we had discussed and thought out all of our conduct. But my conduct was spontaneous and mine alone; that was what had displeased some of them.

The chief's response gave us a lot to think about. Obviously, his answer did not reassure us. The words "If I die, you too die" gave us a bit of encouragement; they meant that he thought his life was not so secure, that he too could die.

The Gestapo in the meantime was preparing for evacuation. Our hearts rejoiced but at the same time we were sad. We rejoiced because we, the last Jews of Chelm, had lived to see the rays of the rising sun that would free the remaining Jews in the forest and hiding places.

In the distance could be heard the dull roar of cannons regularly going off every minute. Then night fell.

The night was full of nightmares for us. We were locked in a single cell, not in barracks as previously. They took anything we had that was valuable. We knew what this meant. We expected to be shot any minute. The sound of cannon fire grew even louder.

When they summoned two of us to help pack the Gestapo's things, we thought that our final hour had come, that they were calling us to kill us one at a time. Our feelings in those moments are easy to imagine, even though we had prepared ourselves. When our two comrades returned from their work, it was already broad daylight. We were assigned to pack up the workshop, preparing to evacuate, to Radom as the Gestapo tried to convince us.

The sound of cannons was for us like a beautiful rhapsody, just as if nature wanted to present a magnificent concert with our long time torturers. The compositions of Beethoven and Bach paled in comparison to the music that we heard that day. We wanted to look into the eyes of the Germans, to see their nastiness mixed with fear.

After that feverish day night fell, the last night for the murderers and torturers of our dear Chelemer Jews. While in the West, the sky over the Lubliner forest was already dark, in the East, toward Brezna and Sobibor, it was infused with a phosphorescent glow. Over the semi–dark skies of eastern Chelm flew the steel birds of the Soviets and they began to bomb the evacuation points of the Germans. It is impossible to describe the chaos, especially the nervousness of the Gestapo whom we observed out of the corners of our eyes. They were simply out of their minds. Our nerves were strained. What would happen?

[Pages 641-642]

Would they forget about us in the midst of this great chaos? The question tormented us.

During one of the air strikes in the evening, we went down into the cellar, to the heating room for the prison where we were allowed to go during air raids. After an hour, we left the cellar and went upstairs and we didn't see any Gestapo. We thought they were hiding somewhere. It turned out they had run away like mice, but we didn't know that.

Only in the morning did we realize that we were alone, without our masters. But we had other guests – German soldiers from the battlefront, tired and broken down; they could barely walk. We didn't reveal ourselves to them and went right back to the cellar, which they couldn't have known about.

Some of the comrades didn't want to hide in the cellar, thinking that they would search for us there. Others thought that we should use the opportunity to hide in the lion's jaws. The latter position prevailed.

The cellar had a catacomb, 4 meters square, 1.2 meters high; to occupy it we had to stay in a seated position. At the entrance to the catacomb someone had placed a cupboard and an old sofa which served to conceal the entrance. We all got inside the hiding place, all squeezed in together. The last to enter, who were near the entrance, moved the sofa closer, so we were safe from any searchers. Now began the suspenseful waiting: life or death?

We hadn't brought any food with us; no one had even thought of that. After a few hours, we heard loud explosions. We quickly understood that before they left, the Germans were demolishing important objects and buildings. Our prison had to be among these and we believed it would be destroyed, so that we would find our grave here, just as if we had been directly killed by the Germans.

Heavy artillery battles interrupted us. We could tell which shooting came from the Soviets and which from the Germans. The thunderous noise from the east dominated with its high baritone. The German response grew less and less. Then the shooting stopped. We didn't know if it was day or night.

A while passed and we heard a fight with rifles and machine guns and the noise of heavy tanks. We knew they were tanks, but which tanks? We couldn't determine if they were the Germans. We had lost contact with the outside world.

We figured that the town was already in Soviet hands. We decided to do whatever we could to establish contact with the world and decided to send one of us out as a messenger – like a dove sent to see if the flood had ended. The person we selected was the shortest of us, a former singer in the choir of the Chelemer cantor. He quietly slipped out and returned with the news that he had seen people in military uniforms but he could not determine if they were Soviets or another military force. He hadn't seen a red star on their hats, but he was sure they weren't German. We waited again for a long time.

Again we sent our messenger. He quickly returned with the news that at last we were free. The prison courtyard was packed with Russian soldiers. With superhuman effort we began one by one to extract ourselves from the catacomb. I looked back at our oasis, our hospitable catacomb, and said goodbye with a glance.

The bright light dazzled us. The Russian soldiers could not believe that we were Jews. A Russian officer, a Jew, told us to go into town and pick out a house where we could live for the time being.

I still remember that day. It was July 22, 1944, a lovely, warm day. The sun shone brightly, or maybe that was just what we thought. But where would we go? Where was our home, where were our families and friend, where were our people, where were our good Chelemer Jews? The town was empty. A town without Jews, and we, the last of the Mohicans, the last Chelemer Jews, now felt the entirety of the tragedy, the heartbreak.

I will end with a list of those with whom I survived: Shloyme Brustman (tailor); Manis Tsitron (bootmaker); Gitl Libhober seamstress), and her son and daughter; Berish Kelberman and his wife; Isser Zilber (tinsmith); Khaim Sobol (bootmaker); Hersh Boksnboym (shoemaker); Shloyme Bubis (shoemaker); Shtshupak; Khaim Kirzhner; Nisnboym; Tantshe (carpenter); Moyshe Nayman (tailor); Ben Tsion Mitsfliker.

[Pages 643-644]

The Suffering, Death and Heroism of Chelemer Landslayt

By Abish Goldman, Porto Alegre, Brazil

Translated by Miriam Leberstein

As one who fought the Nazi brutes on the battlefront, I want to note some of the heroic acts of our *landslayt* who fought in the liberation armies of Poland and the Soviet Union, as well as in the Partisan divisions in the forests.

In 1939, Chelm was for several weeks under Soviet rule. It is difficult to describe the terrible impact of the news that the German barbarians were taking over the town. The Soviet authorities announced that the Red Army was retreating to the Bug River and gave us two weeks to cross the border into the Soviet Union. The very next day many people, mostly young, left Chelm, fearing revenge from the Polish anti–Semites and even more from the Germans.

Some Chelemer Jews settled in nearby towns like Luboml, Kovel, Ludmir, Lutsk, et.al. At the time, I was with my friend Dovid Shlakhtman in Ludmir.

Abish Goldman, as a soldier, received many medals for his heroic acts against the Germans

Later that year we heard horrific news about our town. Chelm had already suffered numerous deaths under Nazi occupation. We learned of the mass murder that occurred when the Germans drove thousands of Jews to the market place, telling them that they would be taken across the Bug to the Soviet side. Instead, they murdered the majority of them on the way.

The several hundred who crossed the Soviet border were detained there. The Soviets did not trust them and sent them to work camps in Russia. Chelemer Jews who had already settled in the Ukraine were in a difficult situation because of the large influx of emigrants. Many of them voluntarily registered to work in Soviet Russia.

I managed to get work in a government printing shop in the city of Lida, near Baronovitsh. Later, in 1940, because of the distrust of Polish citizens, they began to arrest refugees from Poland. I was arrested in May and sent to the Lida prison and from there to a work camp in Russia. With me in the same camp in Opalukhe was my landsman Mendel Tsimerman. He was lucky to have a special assignment there and he had it better than I did.

In 1941, when the Germans attacked the Soviet Union, all the Polish citizens were granted amnesty. After being freed from the work camp I travelled to the Caucasus, where I found many Chelemer landslayt working in various places. But because of the German offensive in the Caucasus we were evacuated deeper into the Soviet Union. Passing through Samarkand, Tashkent and other places I encountered Chelemer landslayt everywhere; all felt a deep yearning for our home town.

I settled in the city of Prunze in Kirgistan. There I heard about the horrific extermination of Polish Jewry. We were shattered by the bitter news about the death camps –Auschwitz, Treblinka, Majdanek, Sobibor, *et. al.* A terrible thirst for revenge, a burning urge to obtain payback for the murders of our parents, sisters and brothers, impelled us to join the armies fighting for liberation.

In 1943, the First Polish Division, "Kosciusko", was formed in the Soviet Union. I entered the Polish army and was immediately set to the First Tank Brigade. There I met two more Chelemer landslayt, Yosek Kratke and Beniek Tshesner. We often chatted about our home and were glad to be able to attack the Germans in our tanks.

I met with Beniek Tshesner often. He told me he has left his wife and child with a Polish family in Lutsk and that when we liberated Lutsk he would seek them out Tshesner was already an officer and worked as a clerk at the army command. Yosek Kratke was also a high ranking officer and was transferred to another regiment. I was soon transferred to tank training and later office school, where I was the first deputy of the leader of the first tank battery.

[Pages 645-646]

The Jewish soldiers serving in the Polish and Russian armies were united in their drive for revenge. The Jews in the First Polish Division felt we were well treated there.

In 1944 we entered actively into battle. Many Chelemer landslayt served voluntarily in the army. After heavy fighting our division reached Kiverts (near Lutsk). There I again met up with my landsman Beniek Tshernin who with tear filled eyes showed me the wedding ring of his wife whom he had left in Lutsk, and told me, "This is what remains of my wife and child." The wife and child and the wife's sister were brutally murdered and buried in a mass grave outside Lutsk. The Poles told him that the earth over the grave continued to heave, moved by the still living victims buried there. I shuddered at the thought that I had left behind my parents, sisters and brothers five years ago. What had happened to them?

Then, we prepared to march into Warsaw in a quick offensive. We were already in Luboml, close to Chelm. The Germans attacked us with heavy artillery but nothing could stop us; we marched into Chelm. We entered Koliever Street late at night. The town was ablaze with fire. The train station had been bombed and was burning. Adolf Dorman's factory was burning. We drove through the Jewish cemetery but it was unrecognizable ; it was just an overgrown field.

We drove along Oblanske Street. From there, I cut through Narutovitsher Street to Potshtover Street, where my family lived. My tank comrades waited for me as I knocked on the door, my heart leaping with anxiety and hopeful anticipation. The door opened, but instead of beloved faces, I saw strangers, Christians who were now living in our house. They described the death of Chelemer Jews, taken by the thousands from the Chelm ghetto to a place outside town near the slaughter houses, where they were shot and lay buried in a mass grave. Chelm was "Judenrein."

Dejected, head bowed with deep pain in my heart, I left my home, swearing to avenge the blood of my family, my landslayt, and the Jewish people.

We marched into Lublin and to Majdanek, the death factory where millions of Jews were killed. We liberated the famous Lublin prison, Zamek, where we found many Jews and Poles who had just been shot. We marched quickly to Warsaw. During heavy fighting in the Praga neighborhood two landslayt fell: Shaye Krotke and Binyomen Naymark.

In 1945 during the big offensive against the home of the Nazi barbarians, I encountered many landslayt in various divisions fighting on the front in Berlin. Many of them were awarded medals and decorations for heroism.

I participated in many battles. I was wounded twice and received many medals and decorations including the highest Polish medal, the Cross for Heroism.

We Chelemers who fought on the front, like Jewish fighters in general, thirsted for revenge. We didn't forget for one moment our tragically murdered sisters and brothers. In the battles we took thousands of German prisoners of war. On one German officer I found photos of dead Jews taken in Tarnow, Poland in 1940. He had kept these photos as a memento of his "heroic acts." I told this murderer that I was a "Jude" and that now he would pay for these killings. Two bullets rendered this criminal harmless. I kept the photos. On their backs were inscriptions written by the murderer himself.

Chelemer Jews took an active role in the Polish and Russian army in Berlin. We were happy to see how the thousands of soldiers in the "undefeatable German army", barefoot, hungry and defeated, were sent to prisoner of war camps in Siberia. They paid for their crimes but we had arrived too late to save more Jews from death.

As soon as the war was over, I got a pass to go to Chelm. I still had the illusion that I would find someone from my family. The Jewish Committee was already at work and I found just a small number of landslayt who had survived. Our town, without Jews, looked like a big cemetery. Where the old synagogue had stood was an empty lot. The *besmedresh* was boarded up. The cemetery was destroyed, everything wiped out.

I met a landsman, Mone Tsitron, who told me how my brother Motl was shot in his home and my brother Lipe was the last victim. My whole family, together with thousands of others, was taken on the death march. But I found the crippled beggar who used to sit cross legged at the market square, crossing himself and asking for alms, at the same place, as if nothing had happened.

[Pages 647-648]

At the Jewish Committee I also met landslayt who had just returned from the Soviet Union. All of them were in need of assistance. Jewish partisans worked for the Committee: Gedalye Bakatshuk; Shaye Herts and his wife; Mrs. Levenshteyn and many others. They strived to serve the needs of the arrivals and to alleviate their condition.

Among others I met Serl Shishker and her children and her sister Sorele. They asked me to accompany them to their previous home on Oblonska Street and help them dig up gold items that they had hidden before running away. As a soldier, I obtained permission from the police But our labors were in vain. We dug up the entire cellar and found nothing. The Poles had beat us to it.

The Polish anti–Semites still pursued the small group of survivors. Armed bands were still raging and killing Jews. The fear was indescribable. It became impossible to stay there. I visited our house and Chelm for the last time.

As in a sweet dream I recalled my childhood, my dear parents, sisters and brother who were so tragically killed here. I recalled the life of Chelm, the political parties, the young people, the sports organizations, where for many years I attended sports competitions. It was all a dream! Only smoke and ashes were left.

I left my town forever with a deep wound in my heart that will last forever. Later, I got married and with my wife emigrated to Brazil to join my only surviving brother, who helped me establish my own printing shop.

The Goldman family at the Passover seder in 1927. Of the entire family, only Abish and Avrom Goldman survived. They live In Brazil.

The Great Catastrophe

By Shimshen Brayer

Translated by Miriam Leberstein

When the terrible war broke out and the Nazi brutes attacked Poland in 1939, I was already in my second year of service in the Polish army. I was 23 and participated in the battle with Hitler's armies. The polish army was quickly defeated. A chaotic mood reigned. Our fight with the Nazis last until the Soviet army began occupying Ukrainian territory in Poland.

At that time I returned to Chelm, which was now occupied by the Soviets. After three days in Chelm, I was obliged to leave. The Russian army left Chelm after the [Molotov–Ribbentrop] pact with Hitler. The Bug River became the Soviet border. Many Jews left with the Soviet army; I joined them and because of that I am alive today.

At the outbreak of the war with Germany in 1941 I was in Kiev and would receive letters from my mother. The letters were sad, soaked in blood and tears. My little sister would write that she no longer had the strength and courage to live under the Germans. She was hungry and tormented, worked hard at breaking stones. She was 15 years old. Before the war she had finished 7th grade, worked and helped my mother, and now she was enduring so much suffering. She didn't mention our other sister.

In 1946, when I returned from Russia to Chelm, I didn't recognize the town. There were no Jews. Poles worked in the formerly Jewish businesses and lived in the Jewish houses. Many Jewish businesses were boarded up, the streets were empty, the market place deserted. Shul Street was full of ruins, the *besmedresh* boarded up. Jewish Chelm had disappeared. Every corner wept.

I found out that the Nazis had killed my mother and sisters, my uncles, aunts and cousins, along with all of Chelemer Jewry.

I served in the Soviet army for more than a year, seeking revenge. I did take revenge, but that was not enough, after I saw the great catastrophe, the great Holocaust.

[Pages 649-652]

Chelm During the Ghetto Uprising

By B. Alkwit

Translated by Gloria Berkenstat Freund

With all that the yizkor books, chronicles and scrolls tell of their cities and *shtetlekh* [towns], they describe Jewish Poland in depth, describe, so to say, the hinterland of the great Jewish uprising: how was it possible, from where did it get its strength that those suffering and bowed rose up, that they became fighters, became heroes - they, the heroes of eternal tolerance, the carriers of Job's patience - heroes and martyrs in the struggle against the enemy in a time when the entire world hit them in the face.

One of the cities was Chelm - the first ghetto uprising was in Chelm.

Chelm, yes, Chelm of the Chelm stories. Who had not heard of Chelm? It was a small city, a poor one and, it was said, a foolish city, as in the stories - of fools, and they also say, sages. But there is no sage whose wisdom is as famous in the world as the nonsense of Chelm - unless, indeed, the wisdom of King Solomon.

B. Alkwit

The glory of Chelm is like the glory of a wonderful story. There are people who even think that Chelm is itself a story, a fable. But it is here, there was such a city - and for the Chelemer it was a city not just of jests. But the uncertain truth, which gave the city its name, can sometimes be the cause of a mistake that Chelm is also Chelmno, or the opposite - that it probably is motivated by the publisher of a Yiddish book - it is quite a distance from here to Posen [Poznan] on the other side of Warsaw. Chelm is also east of Lublin, not far from the Bug River; Zamosc, where Y. L. Peretz was born, is to the south.

Chelm was a very old Jewish city, on a mountain - just as in the stories, but Jews lived in the valley in great Jewish poverty. There was one street there with stairs. It was the oldest Jewish street, but it was called *Neye* [new] *Tsal* and the stairs led down to the market, to commerce, and to *Minkhah-Maariv* [afternoon and evening prayer] in the large synagogue, in the ancient House of Study. In the 1930s, the population of the city numbered 30,000 souls, approximately half Jewish.

The beginning of the history of the Jews in Chelm is in the wall of the synagogue. Here in the wall is hidden the grave of the groom and bride who perished under the *khupah* [wedding canopy] in the synagogue courtyard during the slaughter by Chmielicki's Cossacks. The Cossacks slaughtered 400 Jews. With the strength of a new Jewish generation, Chelm restored itself. The famous Chelemer *Yeshiva* [religious secondary school] grew. Reb Elihu *bel-Shem* [miracle worker] arose. And in our time, a Shmuel Zigelboim (Arthur). Zigelboim was the manager of the worker home, which the Bund founded in Chelm.

[Page 650]

How the treasure of folklore was created here is hard to say. Researchers have found that by the 16th century stories were told in poor Chelm about other foolish cities - Gotham in England, Schildberg in the former Germany - settled by Jews. But the Chelm stories are different, different in their morals, their general fantasy - there communal assemblages.

A meeting is called about all of this. The rabbi is here; the *parnes-khoydesh* [monthly city official] is here; but Chelm, Jewish Chelm is the oldest democracy in Europe. Even if someone would come in with an idea, as for example, let us capture the moon in a barrel of water, he is heard and the *parnes-khoydesh* calls a meeting.

The bloody scroll of the events after the meeting is now assembled. The first news, the yellowed clippings that lie before me like sacred old documents, was written by Yitzhak Fajgenbaum, a well known worker for *Poalei-Zion* in Poland, at his return to America at the beginning of January 1941.

He described:

"This that happened in Chelm has no equal in the entire martyrdom of the Jews of Poland under the Nazi regime because in Chelm there was something that could not be expected, namely, an armed resistance of Jews against the Nazis; there the Jews fought like lions…

"This was in November, when the Nazis hung out announcements across the entire city that all Jews in Chelm must leave the city during the course of three days and go in the direction of Lublin. Chelm is not far from Lublin, but a spirit of rage and opposition enveloped the Jews and voices were heard that they would not go. The Chelemer Rabbi turned to the Nazi commander asking to be permitted to call several businessmen to organize the departure from the city.

"There were three opinions among the Jews who assembled with the rabbi. One - obey and surrender to their bitter fate. A second opinion was that it is better to die here before dragging themselves on the roads and being tortured by the Nazis in an unfamiliar place. And the third opinion was - fight against the Nazis. Yes, there were those who said that they would not let themselves be chased like dogs. Before they would leave the world, they would give the smell of gunpowder to the Nazis. They would fight and take as many Nazi bandits with them to the other world as they could."

[Page 651]

Yitzhak Fajgenbaum says that the representatives at the "third meeting" were "two prominent Chelemer Jews, one a doctor and the other a lawyer." No one tried to argue with them, against them. "There were no arguments." The situation was just discussed a little; the bestiality committed by the Nazis in the city, the looting, the violence and rapes, were described.

Now, however, the Nazis began to go through the houses, to violently drag the Jews to Lublin; they had to "respond with a blow"… and the murderers were answered with fire.

The uprising was carried out with guns. The guns and a few bullets were brought home from the army when the Polish army crumbled, by young people, former soldiers and reserves.

The power that the Germans then had in Chelm was not enough when the Chelemer opened fire. The Nazis called out reinforcements to defeat the uprising. And here is a report from the *Silesian Zeitung* [*Newspaper*], dated the 12th of January 1940.

"In Chelm," the Nazi newspaper relates with sadistic pleasure, "our fighters had both a difficult and an easy assignment. The easy assignment was when they entered the Jewish houses in order to send the Jews to Lublin, It was discovered they had committed suicide. The Jews did not wait for us to be done with them, but eliminated themselves. Others presented a fight against the government and shot at our soldiers with Polish guns. These were reservists who were dropped from the Polish army and did not surrender their weapons. The local regime immediately set the houses on fire, smashed and annihilated the attackers."

Thus the great regime of the Third Reich, in its conquering march across Europe, also led to the uprising of the Chelemer Ghetto and the Chelemer Jews. The *Silesian Zeitung* writes, "The Jews 'received a lecture about how to conduct themselves against the German army.'"

Those who remained alive were forced on the road to Lublin.

But the plan for a "reservation" for Jews in Lublin collapsed and some of the Chelemer returned to Chelm. In time, Jews from the surrounding *shtetlekh* began to arrive - and later - also from other countries.

At first it was not known what this meant. Some time passed and nothing was heard - there was enough to be heard, so they did not ask about Chelm. But frightening rumors began to arrive and then confirmed reports that the world, as well as the non-Jewish bloodied world, actually became struck with fear about them.

[Page 652]

The Germans transformed Chelm into a death-center for Jews not only from Poland. Jews were brought here from the Russian Ukraine, from White Russia, from Holland, Belgium and Czechoslovakia and Greece. It was a slaughterhouse and here they experimented on the Jews with scientific death. They tested gases; Jewish old men, women and children were gassed in order to see how they worked, if they could be used in gas attacks and before finally - annihilating, exterminating the Jews from Poland, from Europe.

This was seen while seeking and researching chemical methods of war, which Hitler's chemists worked on for gas attacks on the Allied armies or also on the population.

Anthony Eden, England's Foreign Minister, read to Parliament the reports about what was happening in Chelm in the form of a declaration and the American Secretary of State included the declaration among the State Department documents, which he presented to the public.

This was at the beginning of 1943. Later when Hitler's collaborators were tried in Nuremberg as war criminals and criminals against humanity it was learned what they had done in Chelm.

Then an issue of the German journal *Di Handlung* [*The Action*] arrived in America with a memoir by the German, Paul Herzog, who served in the German army in Chelm. His memoir is called: *Chelm - a Mountain of Skulls*. And this "mountain" was received in America as the first confession of regret by a German.

In his confession he describes the systematic routine savagery of the Germans on crushed and trampled people, when they fell at work. He describes the camp of prisoners, how beaten and wild non-Jews were incited to take revenge on the Jews for the debasement they endured, for the blows they received from the Nazis; how the imprisoned were held in earthen stalls in the camps and literally were transformed into cannibals.

Part of this memoir by Paul Herzog needs to be included in the scroll of Chelm, the nearly legendary city, on a mountain that once swarmed with stories about fools, stories of jests. But the German devils made a mountain of skulls out of the mountain of stories and a valley of death out of the valley.

This was in 1943. At the end of May, in that year of destruction, a famous Chelmer Jew - Shmuel Zigelboim, the Jewish representative to the Polish government in exile in London - united the hearts of the world with his suicide in protest against the indifference to the annihilation of the Jews in Poland.

[Pages 653-656]

Chelm Right After the Liberation

By Moishe Gantz

Translated by Gloria Berkenstat Freund

It was in the month of July 1944. I was then in the ranks of the Red Army in a forest in the Kowaler area. One night the strong movement of people was heard. This was a Polish military division that occupied a place in the same forest area. Only the dirt road divided them from our members of the Red Army.

The leader of the Polish soldiers reported then that Chelm was freed of the Hitler hangmen.

After several shots of salute, the Polish and Russian soldiers came together, sang, danced, played harmonicas together.

When I heard that there were no more German murderers located in Chelm, I began to think of various ideas. I had a great desire to go to Chelm to see who remained alive. But the idea was disrupted - I was in the military, at a position and the military duties were colossal.

On the same night, a member of the Red Army came to us with seven German captives. I observed the Germans by a weak kerosene lamp. I asked them from where they came. One, a *yeke* [derogatory term for a German, often a German Jew] from Leipzig, told me that he had been taken prisoner in Chelm. I immediately asked him how long he had been in Chelm and through which streets he had gone. From him I learned that Jewish Chelm was *juden-rein* [free of Jews].

At daybreak we loaded the vehicles with ammunition and food and started on our way. We drove past Ljubomil; I remembered the *shtetl*. In 1939, when I left Chelm I had been there for several weeks. I looked and wondered: where are the Jews? The *shtetl* was enveloped in deathly quiet. The windows of the houses were sealed with boards. The *shtetl* was emptied with no bit of life.

At the crossroad stands a member of the Red Army, directing heavy military traffic. We travel farther, in the direction of Chelm. We stop in Jagodzin. I go to a peasant, take from him - for we soldiers - a few potatoes and sour milk. Our group eats, smokes an inferior kind of tobacco. I want to know if we were going to Chelm, but we are not supposed to ask because only headquarters knows the routes. This is a great military secret.

My every limb trembled. My thoughts were taken by my home city. I then went to our chief, a first lieutenant, and in fear asked him if we are going to Chelm. I asked him cautiously in order that he not have any suspicion. I told him that I was a Jew from the city of Chelm, born there and had lived there until 1939.

[Page 654]

The chief pleasantly answered me that we were going to Chelm, adding that he would help me look for my family.

We crossed the temporary bridge over the Bug River. Our vehicle went fast. I looked around; at first everything looked unfamiliar. But I immediately recognized several roads and woods, Chelm's neighboring villages.

The former *Sobor* [cathedral], the tips of the Catholic Church were visible in the distance. My heart began to beat quickly. We entered Chelm through the train street. Our vehicle stopped on the corner of Sienkiewicza and Szkolna. I exited the automobile, looked around me; my first look fell on Szkolna Street. I looked into the large courtyard of Mr. Borukh Wajnrib (Tsales) - a deathly silence. Where were the many Jewish families of the courtyard? Where were the *shoykhetim* [ritual slaughterers], the butchers, the fur pelt traders and artisans? I sought, searched, perhaps I would notice someone, but there was no sign of life.

I looked at the other side, in the direction of the *Talmud-Torah* [primary religious school for poor boys]; I was looking with a great thirst for a Jewish face, straining my eyes, I searched for the Jewish children who made noise here day and night, strained my ears, perhaps I would hear a childish voice, a Jewish voice from the open windows of the Jewish homes. But it is dead silent. Everything is dead, no trace of a soul.

[Page 655]

I went farther along Szkolna Street, closer to the center of the city. I went by the spot where the large old synagogue had been located for centuries. It was a ravaged square with clods of earth and stones. I stood with a grieving heart.

I went to the corner of Szkolna-Lubelska Streets; it was quiet here, too, no living soul. From the *Rynek* [market place] I noticed that our house was no longer here and the entire Przechodnia Street, the opposite from Berish Kuper's building, stood in ruins.

I move closer to the location of our house. I see a little pile of stones and scraps. I go to my chief and lead him to the house where my family and I had lived until 1939.

I go across the "skating ground steps." I look for the Jewish women, the women merchants, the young *kheder* [primary religious school] boys, the Jewish water carriers, the artisans, the tailors, the shoemakers, the cabinetmakers, the bakers - where are they all?

I went to Josef Goldhaber's apartment. I entered; a Polish family lived there. I asked them, what happened to the Chelmer Jews? The Polish woman answered that she had been living here only a year and she did not know anything...

Empty square and the ruin where the Kuzmir shtibl [one-room prayer house]
of the Kuzmirer Rebbe, may the memory of a righteous man be blessed, was located

[Page 656]

I entered the house of the *Shvartser Bekerin* [the dark woman baker]; Christians lived there, too. I stood as if my feet had been knocked out from under me and saddened. [It felt as if] there was drilling in my brain: Where can one learn anything? Where can one find a Jew?

A Pole suddenly arrived from somewhere; I asked him if any of the many thousands of Jews who had lived here were still alive. The Pole indicated that a few Jews lived at Pszczowa Street, number 39. I went there immediately. In the courtyard I met Izer Blachermacher, who stood in fear. I told him that I was a Chelemer Jew; I mentioned my family. A few more Jews immediately appeared, skeletons, among them: Monis Cytrin, Yehiel Szczupak. At first they did not recognize me, but they immediately fell on me, hugged, kissed and cried heavily with hot, boiling tears.

I asked if they knew about my family. Crying deeply, they told me that no one survived; their close family members also perished; the Hitler murderers brutally annihilated all of the Jews, young and old.

Then I understood and clearly saw the dark end of more than 18,000 Jews.

[Pages 655-656]

That Which I Lost Will Never Return

[the author is unknown]

Translated by Miriam Leberstein

Ten years have already passed,
but still the wound bleeds.
I hear as if it were now
my mother's cry to me
through stifled tears:
"Farewell!"

It was the second day of Sukkot
when I brought home the news
that the Russians were leaving the town
and the Germans were arriving.
My father sat in gloom at the window
and looked at the sun shining outside
as if he wanted to ask it:
Would you let a beloved son
go wandering in foreign parts?
The sun kept smiling as if to answer him:
I shine everywhere,
so why should you grieve?
My father always said
A child will do as he wishes.
He said to me, uncertainly:
You've been my son for 18 years,
Do what you think best.
These are hard times in goles [diaspora]
Things worsen by the day.
A father cannot even give advice
to his own son.
So if you choose to leave
I will not stand in your way.
May you go in peace
and in better times,

may you quickly come home.
I strode through half the world
and never wearied,
through hunger, want and toil.
I never forgot my dear home,
held it always in my heart.
And when the happy time came that I returned,
my heart felt nothing but pain,
weighted as if by a stone,
oppressed by the catastrophe.
But I could not shed a tear.
My sorrow drove me away
like a beaten dog.
I found no place to rest.
My sorrow found no voice.
I kept searching, though I well knew
that which I lost
will never return.

[Pages 657-658]

When Chelm Fell

By Yankev Tsvi Szargel, Petah Tikva

Translated by Miriam Leberstein

It was the end of September, 1939. A copper–red sun shone without warmth (like a stepmother, as the mothers of Chelm used to say), looking down over the town with sorrowful rays.

At the former *ring–plats* [Jewish business district] in the middle of town stood a group of terrified Jews, like calves led to slaughter, surrounded by The German criminal bands of the SA and SS. The Jews were singing *zmires*, songs, as ordered by the Nazi wolves. A cloud spread out, the red of the sun disappeared, a light snow began to fall and crept into the upturned collars and the holes of their shoes. A biting wet cold assaulted them. Tears ran from their eyes and melting snow from their beards. The uniformed soldiers, dressed in their metal helmets and ammunition belts as if on military parade, armed with bayonets and machine guns, surrounded the former market place and cast an aura of terror and despair.

Across from the square, from various streets – Lubliner, Lvover, Kopernik and Shul streets – unhappy mother and girls wrapped in blankets and bedcovers stuck out their heads in painful suspense. Orders were shouted, motorcycles and trucks sounded their whistles and roared, adding their noise to the screams and shrieks that came from every direction. There were beatings and chasing and shooting. People fell dead – dead mothers, fathers, sons, brothers. The death procession spread out. At Hrubieszower Street there was shooting. No more Jews in Chelm; no more Chelm.

No more Chelm?

No more?

What is Chelm?

For a long time now, Chelm has not been the legendary town of wise men and fools, who challenge the religious leaders with jokes and stories. Chelm is a beautiful, hilly town, surrounded by thick forests and a vibrant Jewish life, the living Jewish expression of the struggle for existence – young people, political parties, schools, classes, lectures, libraries, theater. Chelm is the Hasidic groups – Belzer, Kuzminer, Trisker, Tomashover, Kotsher, Husiatiner and Radziner, as well as the Left Poalei Zion, which sends the largest percent of town council members to the anti–Semitic town council.

Chelm is arriviste assimilationists, competing with the Tarbut schools and kindergartens. It is a combative and creative Yiddishist movement which is already erecting a building for its elementary school and runs evening classes, a children's home, and a chorus. Chelm is the kibbutz, Hechalutz, Zionism and a daring, risky Communist movement. Chelm has a Shtern, a Hapoel, a Macabee and other sports clubs. It has a large Talmed Toyre and an even bigger yeshiva, a large, modern Barachov Library with thousands of Yiddish and Polish books for the young people and workers; a large Peretz library which lends out Yiddish, Hebrew and Polish books. It has a bourgeoisie and a deprived, ignored and illiterate underclass.

Chelm expels an upstanding Jew from a Hasidic *shtibl* because his son has stopped wearing the flat, round cloth cap , *the* Jewish hat, while the sons of other men from the same *shtibl* – Beker, Goldraykh, Kuper and Szargel – organize both Jewish and Polish workers!

Chelm sends the first Poalei Zionist deputy to the Polish *sjem* [legislature] – Dr. Yitzhak Sziper.

Chelm produces artists, actors, journalist, poets and political activists. Let me note just some of these whom I remember: A.Goldberg, editor of "Haynt;" Moyshe Lerer, Secretary and staff–member at the Vilna YIVO; Shniur Wasserman, poet in Argentina; Yisroel Levenshteyn, poet, translator, co–editor of the Warsaw "Shriftn;" the famous singer Dora Dubkowski; the renowned actors from the Warsaw Yung Teater – Fayvele and Pinyele Ziglboym; their brother Arthur, renowned labor leader and central figure in the Bund, member of the Polish National Congress in London, who will be forever remembered for committing suicide in protest against a world that did nothing to stop the murder of the last Jews in the Warsaw Ghetto; the famous Hendler family, the father a painter in Paris, the daughters violinists, the concerts of Ida Hendler hugely successful in European capitals and in Tel Aviv; the famous painter Sheymi Monshteyn, whose international prominence was a source of pride for the Polish government; the brothers Shimen and Yoysef Milner, Yiddish and Hebrew writers and cultural activitists. There are many more but my memory is dimmed by pain and sorrow and I am unable to give them the tribute they deserve.

The heroic boys who languished for years in Polish prisons for their dedication; the network of trade unions who defended the interests of the Jewish as well as Polish workers; the fighters for civil rights for Jews in the town council and *gmines* [small towns]; the disseminators of the idea of *shivat tsion* [return to Zion] and more and more young activists who contributed to Jewish culture in various fields – that is Chelm.

Chelm published two Jewish weeklies at the same time – one by the Left Poalei Zion called "Folksblat", the other the bourgeois Zionist "Chelemer Shtime" which was published up to the time of the Holocaust.

Chelm had for many years a highly professional drama group led by Fayvele Dresler, who brought theater performances to nearby towns.

[Pages 659-660]

Chelm had a handworkers' union and a *gmiles khesed* fund [free loan society] and a *lines hatsedek* [housing for the indigent sick] and *biker khoylim* [aid to the sick] and *hakhnose kale* [aid to indigent brides] and more, and more, and more.

And the town was proud of its *shul*, hundreds of years old, that had been fashioned from a church, and its Jewish cemetery, where the renowned miracle worker Reb Eliyohu Bal–Shem had lain buried under a heap of stones for hundreds of years. And if it should happen that bad times should befall the house of Jacob [i.e. Jews] in the holy city of Chelm, people will run to the holy man's grave, cry and pray, light candles at his head and the evil decree will, with the help of God, be annulled.

Then what had been the ring–plats became the *former* ring–plats. Everything there was wiped out. What does that mean – the "*former* ring–plats?"

It is the shame of Fascist Poland, that is, the dark, bloody politics of Jozef Beck [Polish Minister of Foreign Affairs] that opened the gate and paved the way into independent Poland for the Schwabian barbarians [Germans] who trampled and crushed centuries of human effort, hundreds of thousands of lives, and in the first ranks were the confused, lost and defenseless Jews.

I myself never saw the "*former* ring plats" (It is possible that it already has a new name,) but this is what my friend Shmuel Szargel wrote to me in July, 1939:

"You have probably heard about the sadly renowned "*urbanizatsie*," the effort to reconstruct and modernize Jewish commercial areas and make them more like "big town" centers. As with every misfortune, you don't want to believe it, think it will never happen. But then the holiday Shevuot arrived along with a huge rainstorm, odd for Shevuot – in spring to have such a wild rainstorm. And our government found it necessary to carry out its *"urbanizatsie"* in three of the poorest Jewish houses in the poorest Jewish neighborhood, the "Naye Tsal." A band of peasants came in and with noise and fury threw out the meager belongings of 24 Jewish families out into the pouring rain. We, the Poalei Zion comrades, quickly "intervened." We opened up the classrooms of the Talmud Torah and packed in the unfortunate families with their possessions.

"Now, the religious people are angry at us for having disrupted the children's religious education."

"But in the end, in the oldest Jewish street in the heart of the crowded Jewish section stood peasants with iron bars and hammers and spades and shovels who tore down Jewish houses on a rainy Shevuot."

"But that is not all. Do you remember the *rinek* (the ring–plats)? Do you remember the historic building, built in the style of the town halls at the end of the Middle Ages? – a big building, long and rounded like an egg, with a roof like a hat with a visor – and around it 80 Jewish shops with round niches and tin–clad doors. On weekdays the merchants tug at your coat – 'Mister, cheap shoes, pants, shirts, buttons, yeast, poultry, soda water.' On Saturday and holidays when the stores are closed the *rinek* looks like a giant with a huge belly circled by an iron sash over its hips."

"Do you remember this source of livelihood for Jewish Chelm? Now not a trace of it is left. The *"urbanizatsie"* by Polish anti–Semitic military officers demolished the building as well as the 80 shops and left an empty space in the middle of town."

"A smoky dust hangs over the entire town, as if after a terrible fire. A whole town full of Jews walks around in mourning and are too embarrassed to look at each other."

"What will so many families do now? Who can they turn to? Who will help them?"

"In the meantime, we provided lodging for the 24 families until the community can do something. But what can we do for the 80 families whose source of income was destroyed by *urbanizatsie*?"

"June, July, August, September, October, November – on November 30, 1939 the Nazi authorities in Chelm issued an order that tomorrow all men between 15 and 60 must assemble on the former ring–plats, that is located on the main street of the town."

"The old Krasnower rabbi told us to light black candles: 'It is the end, Jews, the end'."

And we know what the end was. Woe to us.

Dora Dubkova, renowned singer; murdered

[Pages 661-662]

Eyewitness Account

By Bela Szargel[a]

Translated by Miriam Leberstein

The war broke out when I was 5 years old, living in Chelm, Poland. On a Friday afternoon 8 days after it began the Germans mounted their first air attack. Terrified, we left the house through the windows and hid in the fields until the bombing ended. Then we left Chelm and went to stay in a village for a few weeks, before returning to Chelm. When it became clear that the Germans were nearing Chelm, we crossed the Bug River into the Soviet Union, where we settled. My parents found work and sent me a Jewish kindergarten.

We lived in the town Lutsk for 7 months until one summer Saturday at dawn, they rounded up all the Jewish Polish citizens and sent us to Siberia. Along with others we were stuffed into a truck, taken to the train station and loaded into train cars. We didn't know where we going a

nd felt very despondent. It was in the heat of summer and there were many people in the train cars. It was hot and airless; you couldn't catch your breath. There wasn't any water to drink. They said they were taking us to the "*vayse bern,*" [lit."white bears"; a punning synonym for Siberia]

I still remember one horrifying image. At one of the stations, someone jumped out of the train to get hot water. At the same time they started to rush people back into the train, and he fell, scalding his entire body. He screamed in pain and threw himself down on his belly, like a snake. They left him in a hospital and our group kept going.

After traveling for three weeks we arrived in Siberia. It was evening when we were unloaded from the train. We sat down among our baggage. When night fell it became very cold. In the dark, Soviet trucks loaded with wood drove up and distributed the wood. We lit fires and warmed ourselves and told stories. Our first night in Siberia my parents wrapped me and my little sister in bedcovers, but we couldn't sleep. I lay and listened to the despairing words of the people sitting near us. The next day they brought us to the bank of a river called T*shul*im. There we and our baggage were taken to a very large barracks where we lay down, and extremely tired, quickly fell asleep.

We were awakened by the whistle of a steamboat that was approaching the shore. It was raining hard. I saw the NKVD, who were waking people up and ordering them to carry out their baggage. In the morning another boat came and we shipped out. We traveled for two entire days and finally arrived at our destination, a village that extended for two kilometers along the river T*shul*im, called Berie Gayeve. There we were assigned places in a large barracks, very dirty and in disrepair. When we lay down to sleep, bedbugs rained down from the ceiling. We couldn't stay there and spent the night outside. But even during the day we couldn't rest; the mosquitoes sucked our blood mercilessly.

Gradually we got used to all of it. We did heavy labor, despite freezing temperatures which reached –60 degrees [Celsius], as well as heavily weeded terrain. We lived this way for 16 months until we were freed and left the taiga.

Finally we arrived in a warmer climate in Central Asia, in Kirgizstan, in the city Osh. We arrived in winter and there was frost on the ground. We were taken to a kolkhoz [collective farm] and were given a clay house and settled in. My father worked, and I and my sister went to a Polish school.

The first winter was very difficult. Many people died of hunger and cold. In this way we survived the difficult time of the war, living to see the defeat of the cursed Nazis.

We then returned to Poland. As soon as we crossed the border, we knew that a horror had occurred there. We didn't stop in our hometown, but went directly to Silesia, and from there to Berlin, from which we will go to Eretz Yisroel.

Original note:

a. Born Jun 4, 1934 in Chelm, Poland, now living in Israel. This piece was written in the Jewish Displaced Persons Camp in Berlin–Schlachtensee run by UNRAA (United Nations Relief and Rehabilitation Administration) during the time she was a student in the Hebrew language school there.

[Pages 663-664]

Chelm

By I.I. Sigal, died May 1954 in Canada

Translated by Miriam Leberstein

I

Even Chelm, the Chelm of childhood,
even dreamy Chelm, my friends,
was crippled and destroyed,
stone by stone, by the Germans.

How will its genteel refugees,
those who managed to survive,
find a place, a corner,
in the cold, prosaic world?

How will they get used to
their vapid languages, their talk,
to the way they sorrow, like aged children,
to their joy that is splendid but coarse.

How will their peaceful wisdom
get along with our cunning and fraud?
They will be destroyed, brothers,
lonely, diminished, and adrift.

So let us call a meeting
and let us consider the matter
and see to it that our town Chelm
is provided with walls and a roof. Let the other places
wait a bit — you hear!
And let's restore our brothers of Chelm
to their rightful place on earth. And let us lift up our small
wooden *shul*
from the ashes.

And let us restore our rabbi
to his holy seat. It won't take us long to do this.
It takes only a bit of cash.

And Chelm will again become Chelm
and put forth a new generation. And from afar we will hear
again
of the piety of the rabbi of Chelm,
and news of all kinds of good things:
the wisdom of the *dayan* [religious judge], the wonder of the
merchants,
smiling and praising God
for preserving the existence
of this holy Jewish town.

II
The rabbi of Chelm teaches *mides* [section of Mishnah]
but he writes no holy books
and when he starts to explain religious law
every Jew becomes pious.

Every Jew becomes quiet
and lowers his head.
Isn't that enough? After all,
we already have gray hair.

Some of in their 30's and 40's,
the rest even older.
Praised be God for another *shabes*,
for another day, another week,

for another morning prayer,
for the prayers at evening and night.
Your song makes each small day exalted
and every good hour a gift.

Why do we deserve your gifts?
Perhaps because we don't ask much.
A Chelemer Jew doesn't seek riches;
a Chelemer Jew just goes to the fair

because all the other Jews go there
and he wants to meet up with his kind,

> to hear the voice of another Jew,
> to look another Jew in the eyes.
>
> and to assure himself that there are
> other Jews everywhere
> who observe all of God's laws
> and are honest, good and pious.
>
> And that's enough for him.
> And he returns to his home,
> to his thatched roof and to the stall
> where his goat awaits him.
>
> And on the roof a white rooster
> stretches out his neck and crows,
> a crow that signals cooler weather
> and even perhaps some snow.
>
> He quickly goes into the house
> and washes his hands
> and slowly chants: "And he is merciful,"
> an evening prayer after the fair.

[Page 665]

Witness Testimony

Translated by Gloria Berkenstat Freund

Name and family name: Ruth Englender
Residence until the war: Chelm
Education: Student in the 6th class of the Hebrew Public School in Berlin, Schlachtersee.

I was born in Chelm, Lublin *Voivodie* [province] in 1933. The city was not large, but it was interesting to me.

We lived in Chelm until the outbreak of the war. The war with the savage Germans began in 1939. Chelm was the first city in Poland that was bombed by the Germans. I was then six years old. Although I cannot remember everything or impart it all in writing, I will try to communicate several memories and facts that I can never forget.

When the first bombs fell on the city, everyone – in the confusion – ran to wherever they could. We ran to an orchard and crawled on the ground in order to save ourselves from the bombs. I was running then and became separated from my mother, not knowing where she was. I lay completely still, with a neighbor. I only whispered this question to him: "I beg you, tell me if we will stay alive?..." I repeated these words several times in deadly fear.

The terrible bombardments lasted for several hours. When things became quiet, I saw the destruction of Chelm and the blood of shattered people.

We escaped to a village to a Polish acquaintance on the second day in order to calm our nerves a little and to free ourselves of the fear of death that floated over us. It was calmer in the village than in the city. We hid in the village for a month. Then we returned to the city where great anxiety and fear reigned. It was continuously said that the Germans would enter in a week.

However, the Red army entered and urged everyone to go to Russia where it was calm, quiet and there was no war.

My mother decided without wavering to go away to Russia. She folded a pack of things and we left Chelm with other people in overflowing trucks and arrived in the western Ukraine.

In about a month an uproar about passports began. Every refugee had to apply for a passport that only provided the right to live in a village. Therefore the large majority of escapees from Poland did not want to obtain passports because it was said that they would be sent to Siberia with these passports.

Finally, one day the Soviet regime brought together all of the Jews without passports and they were sent to Siberia by transports with up to 50 people in a train wagon. It was very suffocating and difficult to breathe. There was no water to drink in the wagon.

[Page 666]

We traveled under guard – in such conditions – for more than a month until we arrived in Siberia. It was winter. We lived in barracks that were crowded and dirty. Several built barracks and others worked in the forest to earn a piece of bread.

It was very bad for us there in Siberia. People walked around swollen from hunger. Through a miracle, we were only in Siberia for a few months.

We left Siberia for the Urals. Life there was a little easier. My mother was employed in construction work and I went to study in a school.

The German-Russian War broke out in 1941 and all of the Jews were freed from the barracks and the camps. After living in the Urals for a year, we were permitted to live anywhere in all of the Russian cities where anyone wanted to live. We then traveled to Asia.

In Asia we settled in a *kolkhoz* [collective farm]. My mother spun cotton and I helped. However, it was difficult to live from this work and my mother was forced to sell several of the things she had brought with her from Poland in order to buy a little barley flour.

We lived in Asia for four years. In one regard it was good for us there because I had the opportunity to study in a Polish school. However, we waited impatiently for the end of the war in order to return to Poland.

When the war ended in 1945, the happy news arrived that we had waited for during our long wandering – that we could be repatriated to Poland. We left for Poland immediately, but we also found that our home had been destroyed and saw the destruction with our own eyes. We learned the facts of the terrible slaughter of the Jews. Therefore, we immediately decided to leave Poland as soon as possible.

Now we are in Berlin and I am studying in the Hebrew school with which I am very satisfied. We now wait for the day when we will leave here, from the land of the assassins and murderers.

[Pages 667-668]

Poems

By Sholem Shtern, Canada

Translated by Miriam Leberstein

Arise, Dear Jews, to Serve the Creator[1]

Elul, the time of *slikhes* [penitential prayers]
The Jews of the town are sleeping in the valley of death
Morning unfolds, as always, cool and red.
The bloodied grasses wilt in the garden.
The *shames* is hanging from a wire fence.
Hungry, screeching crows peck at his skin
Who will wake the dead?

Who will summon them to serve God?
The Almighty may yet, God forbid,
Grow angry and punish the congregation.
Jews, why are you still sleeping?

The *shames* is dead.
I will wake you
before the first red tinges of morning
flame out.
Dear Jews, don't you hear me,
Knocking on your shutters:
"Arise, arise, dear Jews, to serve the creator.

No one awakens.
The bright lamps burn in the *shtiblekh*,
In the *besmedresh*, in the old *shul*.
God waits on his throne of mercy
for the prayers which do not ascend.
The wood merchant Moyshe Shmuel, stares face–up,
his tongue a loosened screw.
I bang on the closed shutters:
once, twice.
A terrifying echo resounds
in the frightening void.
In the market place Jews
lie like slaughtered sheep.
I stumble on Moyshe Shmuel's broken body.
My tears moisten his cold brow.

Where can we run? From whom can we plead for mercy?
One, two, fearsome blows on deaf shutters.
God, I will not move from this place.
Stiffen the hammer in my hands.
The blood freezes in my body.
I want to lie down near Moyshe Shmuel
I want to rest in the valley of death
together with this holy folk.

Tears

In the land of Poland
in Jewish cities and towns
the *shekhine* [divine presence] dwelt.
The river blossomed, as clear as a mirror.
Green were the open roads, the plains,
and the quiet, grassy hill.
The hometowns, cozy and wistful,
snuggled up to the forests.
In spring, the lilac branches
caressed like warm fingers.
A true joy shone on the meadow,
on the shepherd's tent.
Light and love, courage and faith

poured out from pure Jewish hearts,
from students and apprentices.

Now, the sun, ringed by smoke, is like a glowing brick.
Jews lie slaughtered on their thresholds.
Horrifying images – a bloodied cradle,
rusted bolts, paintings ripped from the eastern wall.
And the *shekhine* flutters with broken wings
and sobs over the holy martyrs
and my tears flow over the great destruction.

Footnote:

1. In the shtetls of Eastern Europe, the *shul* knocker (Yiddish: *shulklaper* or *shulrufer*), often the synagogue's *shames* [beadle], would wake up his fellow congregants in time for morning prayers and in the middle of the night for *slikhes*, the penitent prayers recited throughout the month leading up to the Days of Awe. He would rap on the shutters with a hammer and call out some version of this poem's title: Arise, Dear Jews, to serve the Creator. The Yiddish word used for Jews in this case is "yidelekh," a diminutive denoting affection.

[Page 670]

The End of a Jewish City

Translated by Gloria Berkenstat Freund

Histadrut [General Organization of Workers] Zionist-Socialists in Chelm

Sitting in the center from right to left: Sh. Szafran, Retich, M. Sztajn, Y. Zilbersztajn, Chaim Feldhendler, M. Lang, Berl Liberman, (unknown woman), B. Feldhendler

The heart has become empty and hollow.
The joyful nights – a sad morning.
A deep tear brings pain somewhere –
A dark cloud sways over the head.

Memories run, run back through the years,
To the *shtetl* [town], to the alleys, struggle with memories!
There was spring, there was youth – and it is not there –
A former Jewish city is lost…

Deep in tears, the wound infected,
What happened to everyone, to our own?
What did the enemy, the monster want? –
Our fists clench in grief, in rage.

Where are our comrades, young, dear friends,
With whom we wove dreams,

[Page 671]

Studied with Reb Avraham Yitzhak the *melamed* in the *kheder*.[1]
Learned to be pious, to not commit any sins.

And pale Jews, driven in multitudes,
Driven to the gallows, to dug out pits:
Small children, babies, shot on the sidewalks –
And in flames: synagogues, Jewish houses and rooms.

It was the devil who shot and murdered them:
Fathers and mothers, sisters and brothers.
Our hearts have become empty and hollow –
A Jewish city left only with graves.

H. Sziszler

Chelm Jews in a camp in Austria in 1948 during a memorial service for the Chelm martyrs

Chelm Jews in Berlin-Marendorf in 1948 during a memorial service honoring Chelm Jewish martyrs

A group of Chelm Jews with their wives and children, who are in Toronto, Canada, during a memorial service for the Chelm Jewish martyrs

Translator's footnote:

1. A *melamed* is a religious teacher; a *kheder* is a religious primary school.

[Page 677]

Chelemer Landsmanschaften

The Chelemer *Landsmanschaft* in South Africa

by H. Y. Monti

Translated by Gloria Berkenstat Freund

H. Y. Monti

Our *landsmanschaftn* [organization of people from the same city or town] consists of a small Chelemer colony because few Jews emigrated from faraway Poland to South Africa. The first emigrants from Chelm to South Africa were Dovid Alter, may he rest in peace, and Hersh Dreksler, who left *Eretz-Yisroel* and wandered away to Africa. This was a bold objective on their part. At first these emigrants could not acclimate themselves and quickly went back. However, a few years later they returned to South Africa and began to adapt to their new home.

It was difficult for the Jewish emigrants to adapt as citizens of South Africa, to anchor themselves and establish roots in the country because the language was strange for them. The emigrants from Poland and from Chelm had to apply themselves until they established their economic positions. It was a long evolutionary process.

The Jewish immigrants in South Africa, as in other countries, created unions for communal work that were principally bound to their old home. The nostalgia and the everyday interest and connection to their home beyond the sea stimulated the creation of an entire series of *landsmanschaftn* in South Africa, including the Chelemer *landsmanschaft*.

Because the number of emigrant Jews from Poland to South Africa was small, the "Club of Polish Jews in South Africa" was created, which still exists. It unified all Jewish emigrants from Poland. Those whose initiative founded the club were: Y. Gerszt, N. Winik, Y. Poliak, W. Flaksman, the Getc brothers, Szuster, Kejwan, Jarszin, Shlomoh Metz, Later, the Chelemer Aid Union was organized when several more Jews emigrated from Chelm. Their aid work consisted of sending help for the Chelemer needy and to institutions.

The social-economic condition of the Chelemer Jews at home was then difficult because of the growth of anti-Semitism and *Owshem* [Our Own, government policy of a general boycott of Jewish products and workers] politics. We in Chelm received the first aid with great gratitude and the Jewish press in Chelm warmly, full of appreciation, published activity reports from our South African Aid Union, such as the following:

"In August, 1936, a Chelemer Aid Union was founded.

[Page 678]

"The purpose of this union was to help relieve the needs of the Chelemer Jews who had become impoverished in the old country.

"The founding meeting took place in the residence of Hersh Handelsman. A large number of Chelemer *landsleit* [people from the same city, town or village] were present at the meeting. A managing committee was immediately chosen of the following people: Motl Alter, H. Sziszler, N. Winik, Hersh Handelsman, Shmuel Berger, Chava Biale and Ruchl Alter.

"The elected managing committee appealed to the assembled group to immediately impose a tax on themselves for the union. Almost everyone present agreed to the tax. A significant sum was raised then and there."

In a second correspondence from H. Sziszler in the *Chelemer Shtime*, dated July, 1937, is the report on six months of activity of the Chelemer Aid Union:
"The Chelemer Aid Union in Johannesburg works with the greatest intensity and self sacrifice. There are conferences each week and new ways to collect a few pounds are sought. It is truly admirable that in the short time the small group has existed, it has been shown to carry out undertakings that were accomplished with success.

"The entire so-called Chelemer colony that is quartered in Johannesburg consists of barely two *minyonim*[1] of Chelemer countrymen and, perhaps, scarcely a *minyon* of them work with devotion and sacrifice to gather aid.

"The work of the Chelemer Aid Union in Johannesburg is becoming admired and valued highly by older, longtime societies there, which are very backward in this regard. It is not an exaggeration to say that many communal workers were inspired and expressed recognition of the Chelemer Aid Union in South Africa.

"The Chelemer Aid Union arranged an impressive family evening this past *Shabbos* evening. The program consisted of 1) an activity report, 2) a literary-musical part and 3) a dance. The evening was arranged in the house of Friend [a term often used among *landsmanschaftn* members] Jakov Alter, at beautiful serving tables.

[Pages 679 - 680]

It is interesting that all Chelemer countrymen along with the Yiddish press in Johannesburg were invited as well as many acquaintances and friends who came with help for the *landsmanschaftn*. The evening was a successful one."

In a later correspondence by Ben-Ahron (H. Sziszler) published in the *Chelemer Shtime* of October 1938, we learn the following facts about the first yearly gathering of the Chelemer Aid Union:

"Sunday, the 23rd of October, the first yearly meeting of the Chelemer Aid Union took place in the home of Hersh Sziszler in Johannesburg. The meeting was called for the purpose of providing an activity report, to elect a new managing committee and to strengthen the work of collecting support for the poor in Chelm.

"Nakhum Winik was elected as chairman of the managing committee and H. Y. Monti as secretary.

"Shmuel Berger gave the activity report showing the work carried out by the Union. The treasury report for the entire time of the existence of the Aid Union was given by Hersh Sziszler, showing that the small group of Chelemer *landsleit* in Johannesburg had succeeded in collecting the sum of more than 200 pounds in a short time from which the needy in Chelm benefited with over 120 pounds for Passover and the rest was sent to Chelemer institutions and individuals.

"A new managing committee was elected of the following: M. Alter, Y. Alter, N. Winik, Leizer Sziszler, H. Sziszler, H. Handelsman, Y. Zigelboim, Shmuel Berger, Mrs. Biale and H.Y. Monti.

"M. Alter was again elected as chairman, Y. Zigelboim as treasurer and H. Y. Monti (Monczarsz) as secretary.

"A women's committee was elected of Rayzl Sziszler, Rikl Alter and Ruchl Alter."

As we see, the Chelemer Aid Union, which later became the Chelemer *Landsmanschaft*, was only a young institution compared to the long-term societies whose members emigrated to South Africa many years before the Chelemer pioneers set foot on African soil. Thus we can assert that the superb work, which was judged with words of praise by our home city, was carried out by the small group of Chelemers until the Second World War.

The Union would arrange two activities a year until the war: a winter collection to provide wood and clothing for the needy and a collection for Passover.

The Chelemer Colony in South Africa

First row: sitting from the left: Leah Sziszler, Leizer Sziszler, Motl Alter, Hersh Handelsman, H. Y. Monti, Yakov Alter, Josef Palman, Moshe Rajkhbind, of blessed memory, and Mrs. Rajkhbind
Second row from the left: Yisroel Zigelboim, Sheva Winik, Rayzl Sziszler, Mrs. Monti, Rikl Alter, Feywl Rajkhbind, Ruchl Alter, Rywka Palman (Alter), Brukha Handelsman and Rayzl Monti
Third row, from the left: Bune Rajkhbind, Berish Biderman, of blessed memory, Gershon Monti, Akiva Winik, Nakhum Winik, Bayla and L. Waksman and Chaya Fajerman

[Page 681]

Erev-Pesakh [on the eve of Passover] 1939, almost the entire Chelemer colony energetically took part in the carrying out of a great aid campaign that began with a general meeting in H. Sziszler's house.

This was the last Passover action for the needy in Chelm. Thanks to the energetic activity of F. Zigelboim, Haim Luksnburg, Meir Celniker, a famous artist from London who starred in South Africa, an impressive people's concert was organized, which brought in a significant sum to help the poor Jews in Chelm. A banquet took place in M. Alter's house after the concert. The press and communal and cultural workers were invited to the banquet.

The war broke out and there was no contact with the old home and no new immigrants came to South Africa.

Jewish immigrants from Poland only passed through South Africa during the war. Also in 1945, Polish Jews came who had escaped to Russia from Hitler's sword and joined Anders Army, which arose on Russian territory in accordance with General Sikorski's[2] Polish-Soviet pact. They were with Polish soldiers (there were 4,000 all together) in 1945. They turned up on the shores of South Africa, traveling farther, to Iran (Persia). These Polish and Jewish soldiers were housed in the military barracks in Pietermaritzburg (Natal).

As soon as we learned of this, representatives from the "Polish Club" were delegated to meet with the Jewish soldiers from Poland. Representatives of the Chelemer Aid Union were also in the delegation.

The first encounter with these Jewish soldiers from Poland, who numbered about 84 men, was very moving. Although we already knew about the calamity to our people, a small hope was smoldering in our hearts that perhaps there was a larger number of survivors and perhaps we would receive some news about the survivors, their names and families.

With broken and aching hearts, the delegation was informed precisely about the atrocities and the sadistic slaughter of the Jews in Poland and in Europe.

The delegation carried out a registration of all of the Jewish soldiers and from where they came and where their relatives were located, their names and their families. This list was published in the local Yiddish press and in the foreign Yiddish newspapers. Akiva Winik, the Chelemer *landsman*, occupied himself with searching for the relatives of the soldiers.

The Chelemer Aid Union along with the Club of Polish Jews organized aid for the Jewish refugee children who were brought from Russia with the homeless Polish children. The children settled in Oudshorn, Cape Province. Among these children was a Jewish girl from Chelm who was brought to Johannesburg by the Club for Polish Jews and who later was sent to Israel, where her parents who had escaped from Chelm to Russia before the Germans arrived in Chelm were located. They emigrated from Russia to Israel. The Chelemer Aid Union helped a family from Poland that survived emigrate to Australia.

[Page 682]

* * *

To our deep pain and grief, there was no longer any opportunity for our Aid Union to send aid to Chelm where the city had become *Juden-rein* [cleansed of Jews], but it was bound to the several hundred Chelemer Jews who, by a miracle, survived and were spread in various camps in Germany, Austria, Italy and for those who reached *Eretz-Yisroel* with assistance from *Hapoel* ["the worker"], we organized an aid campaign, sending them food products, money and clothing.

Under the leadership of Mrs. Ryfka Alter-Palman, a committee was created concerned with sending packages of food and clothing to the surviving *landsleit* in the camps and in Israel. We also provided packages to the Chelemer Jews in Russia through American firms. Later, the committee itself bought food products, which were much cheaper, and a greater number of packages were sent.

The Aid Union would receive hundreds of letter from the surviving *landsleit* who thanked the Union for the help provided and for the display of interest in their cruel fate. They described the horrors of the Nazi slaughters and their survival.

Then the idea developed to memorialize the Jewish community of Chelm in a *yizkor bukh* [memorial book] that would recall the old home with its institutions, parties, groups and organizations, the Chelemer Jewish people, the meritorious community workers and cultural workers and also the destruction of Chelm.

An initiative-commission was created that published a call to all of the *landsleit* in the world to send in material and descriptions for the Chelemer *Yizkor Bukh*.

In December 1950, a brochure was published – a schematic draft for the book. A second appeal was also published to the Chelemer Jews throughout the world:

Distinguished and Dear Chelemer *Landsleit*!

The Union of the Chelemer *landsleit* in Johannesburg, South Africa, has taken the initiative to publish a yizkor book consecrated to our annihilated Jewish city Chelm and its surroundings, where thousands of our own brothers, sisters, relatives, etc. were so brutally annihilated by the Nazi hangmen.

[Page 683]

Our city, Chelm, had a rich and very interesting past. A full-blooded life pulsed there with a network of institutions and diverse organizations and movements.

Very notable and interesting cultural, communal and religious personalities lived and created in Chelm. There was a well-established Jewish national way of life with great experiences and themes. According to the assertions of historians, Jews lived in Chelm from the 13th century.

The many generations of the Jewish population's existence in Chelm and its surroundings, the savage death of about 18,000 Jews in Chelm itself and the thousands of Jews tortured to death in nearby cities and towns demand from us their redress, a *matzeyvah* [headstone] and a monument.

Over the past year since our correspondence, *landsleit* from destroyed Jewish cities and towns have erected monuments by publishing *pinkasim*[3] and yizkor books in memory of their unforgettable cities. The idea that the memory of their cities could be entirely forgotten over the course of time tormented them. Therefore, with great skill, love and responsibility, they erected *matzeyvus* [headstones] in the form of books and monuments.

This preoccupation and concern stimulated us to publish the Chelemer Yizkor Book.

As is explained in the enclosed prospective, we have created the format for the materials that will be published in the yizkor book.

However, we are determined that the story be more deeply and voluminously illuminated and, therefore, it is a clear necessity that the Chelemer *landsleit* must accumulate still more materials that have a connection to all the themes described in the brochure and also that they themselves write, because every detail and even the smallest item will enrich your and our memorial book.

It is unquestionably a colossal, gigantic work that demands sufficient effort and intensive activity. We must not stop for any difficulties because the yizkor book is the most important work remaining for us for the holy memory of our fathers, mothers, brothers, sisters, relatives and friends, who perished so unmercifully in our unforgettable city, Chelm. We will see to it that more historical documents and testimony from the tragedy of the Holocaust in the Nazi era, photographs and biographies of our landsleit, both dead and from the Chelemer Jews around the world and in Israel, may their lives be prolonged, will be published.

Our desire is that the Jewish cities and *shtetlekh* around Chelm also have a respected place in the book; the economic, cultural and communal life of all of the Jewish communities that existed for generations should also be illuminated. These *shtetlekh* were also closely bound to Chelm geographically, such as, Staw Lubelski, Krasnystaw, Apalyn, Szelszcz, Wlodawa, Hrubieszow, Dejwic, etc. Their history is restored in the Chelemer yizkor book.

[Page 684]

However, we must stress that the yizkor book also requires financing. It will cost more than 2,000 pounds.

The number of Chelemer *landsleit* in South Africa is very small (that is, a few dozen families). Without your direct financial support it will be very difficult for us because the book will be published shortly.

We turn to you as the committee of Chelemer *landsmanschaftn* [organizations of people from the same city, town or village] and individual *landsleit* and ask that you designate special commissions whose task will be to collect documents, articles, memories, pictures and photographs, literary creations, folksongs and ethnographic material (about Chelm) and sums of money for the Chelemer yizkor book.

It is just a few years since the tragic death of our Jewish kinsmen in Europe and it is still not too late to revive our memories of many of the facts and matters that bind us to our old home. With the passage of time it will not be possible to accomplish our holy mission.

The famous Jewish historian, Prof. Shimon Dubnow, called out to the surrounding Jews as he was led to the Nazi scaffold, "Remember and set it down in writing for the future generations!"

Let us all put our testimony in writing, and remember and record the great scroll of suffering of our dear home city, Chelm!

Chelemer Aid Committee in Johannesburg: Y. Alter, M. Alter, B. Biderman, B. Bojdek, H. Handelsman, N. Winik, E, Winik, Y. Zigelboim, Ch. Y. Monti, Y. Palman, H. Sziszler, L. Sziszler.

P.S. We ask you to obtain subscribers for the Chelemer Yizkor Book. The price of the book: two pounds or five dollars. Please, compile biographies of *landsleit*, necrologies with photographs that will go into the book, including "who is who" – one side costs 20 pounds; a half side – 10 pounds; a quarter – 6 pounds; an eighth of a side – 3 pounds.

Johannesburg, December, 1950

After publishing the call, hundreds of *landsleit* in various countries, such as France, Australia, America and Israel spoke up with much appreciation for this book idea. In France, thanks to the special interest of our distinguished countryman, Josef Milner, a committee was created consisting of the following Chelemer countrymen: Josef Milner, Y. Torn, Dr. Arlan, M. Szpejzman, Y. Murowiec, Y. Staw, Mrs. Parobek and A. Globen. This committee proceeded to collect money and subscribers to the yizkor book, even from *landsleit* who live in Holland, Belgium and elsewhere and published the following call:

[Page 685]

To All Chelemer *Landsleit* and People from the Vicinity of Chelm in France, Belgium, Holland, England and in Europe

The great tragedy that befell our people also destroyed Chelm, our old historical city, and its neighbors. Tugged and spread over the entire world, they created a Chelemer Society in almost all of the nations where Jewish communities are located. And one of these societies from distant Johannesburg (in South Africa) took upon itself, with the assistance of all of the Chelemer societies around the world, the fulfilling initiative of publishing a yizkor book that will immortalize our birthplace.

It is already more than a year since the founding in Johannesburg of the committee, which took upon itself the holy duty to carry out this work.

They were successful in gathering and creating extraordinary material and the book and its contents will adorn not only every home of our *landsleit*, but will also enrich every Jewish library and increase knowledge and will provide vast material for future historians.

We turn with our appeal to all Chelemers in France, in Belgium, in Holland and in England. We need to help our *landsleit* in distant South Africa carry out their undertaking, which will be an honor for our former city of birth and will be a monument that will remain for generations. We turn to all *landsleit* from the surrounding area (Zamoczsz, Tomaszow, Lubomyl, Hrubieszow and so on) because all of these communities will have a respected place. Such a book will need to cost over 2,000,000 francs (this is the amount that the Lubliners devoted to their "yizkor book," which is in print). A minimum of 500,000 francs must be reached and that falls on us. There will be more than 250 illustrations and pictures in the book that will remember our old home; several hundred articles about the former Chelm, which alas was once a Jewish city that was annihilated in the Holocaust.

The Chelemer Society in Paris organized a special committee to awaken our *landsleit* that we do everything so that the yizkor book is published quickly.

The committee-members were

Y. Torn
Y. Staw

Szpejzman Madam Parabek[4]
Y. Murowiec
A. Globen

    a. Each Chelemer must subscribe to a minimum of two copies (each copy costs 2,000 francs) one for himself, for his children, for his home, and a second to give to someone close to him in order in that way to immortalize the city where our cradles stood.

    b. Create a fund for the yizkor book.

    c. Each *landsman* can contribute necrologies with photographs of their parents and relatives who perished. Each *landsman* is asked to contribute for the book and his name will be published in the book with the sum [that was contributed].

    d. Everyone who has memories of our city should record them and send them to the address given below.

We call on you, dear *landsleit*, to go to work at once.

And we hope that no *landsman* will remain indifferent to this sacred work that will be an eternal monument for all of our martyrs and will contribute generously for this purpose.

In all instances you can write and send your orders or checks to this address.

A. GLOBEN, 16, Bld. Des Filles du Calvaire, PARIS. Tel. Rog. 22-11.

Committee for the "yizkor book" of the Chelemer Society in Paris.

Similar book committees were organized in Australia, Canada, Israel, and so on, that sent in material, photographs, writings and testimonies about the Holocaust and also money.

The interest in the yizkor book was observed by all landsleit in the Jewish world. A special "Chelemer Yizkor Book Committee" was created in America that published the following call:

Chelemer Yizkor Book Committee in New York
Chelemer Memorial Book Committee [in English]

Endorsed by:

Chelemer Branch 585 *Arbeter Ring* [Workman's Circle], First Brotherly Aid Union.

Dear *Landsleit* of Chelm and its vicinity:

The Chelemer Yizkor Book is about to go to the publisher. This book will be a monument, a collective *matzeyvah* [headstone] for Chelm, our birthplace, for the 18,000 annihilated lives of our parents, sisters, brothers, relatives and friends who fell at the bloody hands of the murderer, Hitler, may his name be erased. In addition, the yizkor book will also reflect the distant and recent past of Chelm, where our cradles stood.

Important and interesting historic material, memories, monographs, histories were collected and many pictures of our ancient Jewish city and also material about the bloody, sorrowful chapter of the annihilation of the Jews in Chelm and its vicinity.

[Page 687]

Now we are giving you the last opportunity to acquire this yizkor book because the number of books printed will be those subscribed for in advance or ordered. You must hurry and send in your five dollars or more to our treasurer, A. Rozenboim.

You can order more than one book – it will be a gift valued by everyone, even those not from Chelm; Chelm was from ancient times a symbol of incisive humor and hearty cheer for Jews all over the world.

Considerable sums of money are still lacking for our yizkor book to emerge as impressive as it deserves. There have been much larger expenses than could have been foreseen. Actually, the book will cost almost eight dollars. For this reason, a larger sum of money has already been contributed by organizations and individuals in all corners of the world, including New York with around 600 dollars. It is an interesting fact that the smaller Chelemer community in Paris provided almost twice as much as New York in the number of subscriptions and contributions.

The yizkor book is mainly dedicated to immortalize the name of our martyrs. With a minimum of 10 dollars and more, each *landsleit* can erect a *matzeyvah* for those closest to them.

[Page 688]

The city of Chelm is *Juden-rein* [empty of Jews], the cemetery was destroyed. The ashes of our Chelemer Jews and those from the surrounding area, who were burned in Sobibor (between Chelm and Wlodawa) or other crematoria, were carried by the winds to all seven seas. The memory of these martyrs lives only in our hearts. Let us record and publish the sacred names of those close and dear to us in the yizkor book, which will be found in all of the libraries in the entire world, in all of the houses of our Chelemer *landsleit* in every nation in which they are located.

Let us immortalize their names and in this way not permit their memory to be erased from the world, as the murderer, Hitler, may his name be erased, wanted. The names of *landsleit* who died in America or elsewhere need to be immortalized in the book. Hurry up and let us know before it is too late. You should know that without the small Chelemer community in Johannesburg, in distant South Africa, the Chelemer Yizkor Book would never be published. They, in South Africa, voluntarily took this colossally difficult task upon themselves and we, at least, should help them to finish this sacred work.

Make out a check or money order in the name of CHELEMER MEMORIAL BOOK COMMITTEE
and in the enclosed envelope, conveniently send what you can, giving the number of books that you are ordering, as well as the names that you want to have immortalized on the collective *matzeyvah*.

[Page 689]

With respect,

Chelemer Yizkor Book Committee
in New York

B. Binsztok, Cantor Y Brejtman, K. Boldman, Y. Hercman, Sz. Waserman, Sz. Winer, Sura Wodzilowski, Y. Yorfest, J. Mitelman, A. Rosenbaum, M. Sztejn.

A. ROSENBAUM, Treasurer
3971 Governeur Avenue
Bronx 63, N.Y.
Phone: Kingsbridge 6-3478

Members of the Book and Editorial Committee

Sitting from the right: Hersh Sziszler, Hersh Handelsman (chairman), Y. Palman (treasurer)
Standing: Akiva Winik, H.Y. Monti (secretary), Yisroel Zigelboim and Nakhum Winik

Yisroel Zigelboim's visit to the countries of South America was also used as an opportunity. He interested the Chelemer Jews there in the book and also the publisher of *Dos Poylishe Yidntum* [*The Polish Jewry*], because we thought about sending all of the material to Argentina so that the above-mentioned publisher would publish the book. However, for technical reasons, this idea could not be realized.

In 1951, Akiva Winik took a great deal of time collecting material for the yizkor book on a visit to Israel. A special meeting was called about the book by the Chelemer *landsleit* in Israel.

The Chelemer Aid Union or the Chelemer *landsmanschaft* in South Africa established a book and editorial committee with the following composition: Josef Milner, Hersh Sziszler, H. Y. Monti, Akiva Winik, Nakhum Winik, Hersh Handelsman, Y. Palman, Yisroel Zigelboim.

The pedagogue and editor, Malekh Bakalczuk Felyn, was invited to edit and put together the yizkor book.

Of course, the undertaking to publish the Yizkor book was daring on the part of the small group of Chelemer in South Africa and it required many achievements and much effort. We ourselves did not foresee the difficulties that were involved in publishing such a book and therefore, it could not be published on the announced date. We also did not receive any material from the *shtetlekh*, although we turned to individuals and the press many times.

An interesting notice in the name of "The Chelemer International" - in connection with the Chelemer Yizkor Book – appeared in the Parisian newspaper, *Arbeter-Wort* [*Worker's Word*] by A. Briksman:

"…the Jewish tragedy truly has no borders… A Yizkor book for Chelm is proceeding to publication in Johannesburg. A group of *landsleit* in Johannesburg could not create such a yizkor book alone. This was more than they were capable of and Chelemers from New York and Chicago, from Israel, from France, from Canada, from Argentina, from Mexico, from Cuba, from Australia grouped themselves around the yizkor book.

[Page 690]

A true 'ingathering of the exiles" of Jews from a Jewish *shtetl* in Poland, who were widely scattered throughout the entire world. The groups created among the *landsmanschaftn* a great and intensive correspondence. It was learned where this one, that one or another Chelemer lived. Contact was made. Solidarity was created. Such a fact should not be forgotten and, even more, should not be neglected. It can create the terrain for a federation of Jewish *landsmanschaftn* on a worldwide scale. An organization can be created that should include many countries. A '*va'ad*' [council] of many '*aratzot* [lands]'[15] that would have an influence both in the cultural and in the material sense. In short, a 'Chelemer International.'"

A small number of Chelemer Jews are in South Africa now, in total a few *minyonim*. The harsh immigration laws of the South African government and the outbreak of the Second World War prevented the bringing of relatives and friends from Chelm. Only a few individuals succeeded in entering the country after the last war. However, despite the small size of the Chelemer colony in South Africa, it is active in all spheres of communal and cultural life.

The majority of the Chelemer immigrants were good artisans and workers at home. Each *landsman* had to work hard to make a living during the first so called "*griner*" [literally, green – the years before cultural assimilation] years. Then many of us "worked ourselves up." Several attained a stable economic position. However, their unpretentiousness and traditions did not disappear even in the best economic conditions. The Yiddish language also was preserved in the homes of the Chelemer Jews. Several of us occupy a very respected place in the various communal institutions. Chelemer Jews in South Africa respond with aid and with actions for all campaigns and undertakings.

Malekh Bakalczuk-Felyn

[Page 691]

In the course of all the years of existence of the Chelemer Aid Union or of the Chelemer *landsmanschaftn*, the following people, who have already died, were also active in the work:

Dovid Alter, of blessed memory

Dovid Alter, of blessed memory

He was one of the first Chelemer pioneers in South Africa and thanks to him the Chelemer colony in distant South Africa arose. He came to South Africa in the 1920s with colossal entrepreneurial vigor. In his years as a *griner*, he created a furniture factory. Later, he moved on to construction in which he progressed. He always showed an interest in his home city, Chelm, and its townspeople and he took part in the work of the Chelemer *landsmanschaft*. He died prematurely at age 48.

Honor his memory!

Fanya Zigelboim, of blessed memory

Fanya Zigelboim, of blessed memory

She was torn away during the best years of her life. She was everyone's beloved and devoted worker for the Chelemer *landsmanschaft*.

She was one of the most active and devoted women of the Chelemer *landsmanschaft* and showed a great interest in the poverty of the Chelemer Jews, devoting much effort and time to each aid activity carried out by the Chelemer *landsmanschaft*.

[Page 692]

Fanya Zigelboim also was very active in our Jewish societies and institutions in South Africa.

Honor her memory!

Berish Biderman, of blessed memory

Leibush Biderman, may he rest in peace, father of the deceased Berish Biderman

He was active in collecting the first sum of money that was sent to our old home. When the Chelemer Aid Union was created, he was one of the most active founders and activists.

Berish Biderman was much beloved in our Chelemer colony and greatly valued both because of his good virtues and because he preserved his Chelemer way of life here in South Africa. He was a fully religious Jew and preserved the Jewish traditions and religious conduct of Chelm. His bearing and *Yidishkeit* [sense of one's Jewishness] reminded each Chelemer *landsman* of the patriarchal, handsome, innocent figures and types in Chelm.

May his memory be blessed!

* * *

To this day, the Chelemer *landsmanschaftn* is in contact with the Chelemer *landsleit* and sends them help, but the yizkor book was the crown of all of our achievements. However, without the help of the *landsmanschaftn* in the Diaspora and in Israel we would not have been able to fulfill this idea.

Our messages and letters had a warm reception with all Chelemers everywhere and this encouraged us in our work, which was very difficult, considering the small number of Chelemer families in South Africa.

Translator's footnotes:

1. Barely 20 people, a *minyon* consisting of a minimum of 10 men. *Minyonim* is the plural form.
2. Wladislaw Sikorski was the Prime Minister of the Polish Government in Exile and died in a mysterious plane crash in 1943.
3. A *pinkas* (singular of *pinkasim*) was originally a register of names and events in Jewish communities. After the Holocaust, many *pinkasim* were published, providing the history of various destroyed cities and towns.
4. Earlier spelled Parobek
5. a reference to the *Va'ad Arba' Aratzot* – the Council of the Four Lands that was the central authority governing the Jewish communities in Poland from 1580 to 1764.

[Page 694]

Chelm in America

by Ben Binsztok, New York

Translated by Gloria Berkenstat Freund

The emigration of Chelemer Jews to America must be divided into two emigration periods:

1. The first emigration that lasted until 1905;

2. The second emigration that extended from 1905 until the Second World War.

The first emigration brought Jews who were "risk takers" to America, that is, Chelemer Jews who took a chance and "left for America;" Jews who "had to escape" from Chelm, where "the earth burned under their feet" – Jews who ran seeking "luck in America." There were Jews who escaped after the "oath[1]" because they did not want to go "to serve Russia."

The second emigration began in 1905-1906 after the failure of the first revolutionary outbreak in Czarist Russia. Chelemer Jews – together with the Jews in all of the other cities and *shtetlekh* [towns] in Russia and Poland – left en masse that year because they could no longer or did not want to live under the severe Czarist regime. Among them were found socialists, revolutionaries, who lived under the shadow of Article 102, which meant long years of hard labor; socially conscious workers, the intelligencia and followers of the Enlightenment [*maskilim*] who had felt humiliated and fell under the special exception laws.

When the new independent Poland arose after the First World War, a time of new persecutions of Jews began: cutting Jewish beards with swords, throwing Jews out of trains, excesses, riots and pogroms. It was the time of Grabski's sadly famous "hearse" that looted Jewish possessions through taxes and the Polish economy had proclaimed "*swoj do swojego* [support your own]" and "*Zydzi do Palestini* [Jews to Palestine]" policies.[2] On one side, the economic restrictions, the baiting of the Jews and, on the other side, the longing of the Chelemer *landsleit* [countrymen] in America for their relatives and families was the driving force of the last Chelemer mass emigration to America.

The Chelemer landsleit during the second emigration were younger and more modern. They were the Chelemer with seniority in communal activity, people with responsibility for the community at large who had a healthy influence on the local *landsleit* and existing Chelemer communal institutions in America.

* * *

The needle trades in America that were concentrated in New York absorbed the great majority of Jewish immigrants of that time.

Other Chelemer *landsleit* from the first emigration – with small exceptions – brought with them poor spiritual baggage.

The first 10 years of this century [20th century] in this country – mainly in New York – were years of "cutting teeth" – pioneer years, which placed their stamp on the immigrants. Other Chelemer were "cooked" in the American melting pot, but they came out only partially cooked. America, the land of unlimited possibilities, helped a share of the emigrants become rich, but only materially.

The beautiful American democratic virtues, traditions, the glorious American history, literature, art and science – our Chelemer drank very little (with a few exceptions) from this well. Little pieces and crumbs of so-called local customs and the partly democratic system lulled our Chelemer to sleep and they did their duty. And thus was shaped a kind of uncooked and unbaked, half Chelemer-half American element.

The difficult "green" years through which the majority of emigrants passed brought them closer together and united the Chelemer *landsleit*. The solitude, the loneliness and the "longing for home" brought our *landsleit* together under one roof, where their general problems and communal needs, their daily anxiety and worries would be debated spontaneously.

These common problems led to the founding of the "First Chelemer Brotherly Aid Union" in 1906.

The mission and purpose of the Union has remained almost the same to this day:

1. To support the enrolled "brothers" in case of need (including charity);

2. To help him in case of illness, God forbid;?

3. To help in case of death, when the society will assist with funeral expenses, a grave and one dollar for each enrolled member will be paid to the widow.

All of the benefits listed are the minimum that a Jewish society in America provides for its members.

Only three of the founders of the Chelemer Aid Union are still alive today – may they live to be 120 – in New York.

Sholem Lederer, one of the main founders of the society, was one our most intelligent *landsleit* [people from the same town] in the first emigration. He wrote multi-volumes of interesting short stories and novels. He died at age 92 in 1952.

We Chelemer *landsleit* of that time lived communally in an intimate way in and around the society. Doors and windows were firmly closed to all international and national American problems.

In addition to the above mentioned obligations, the society also made sure "to satisfy" the members <u>spiritually</u>. To attain this purpose the society would organize a picnic for a summer Sunday, where each one brought a package of food. The society provided a keg of beer and our Chelemer "frolicked" the entire day in the "park" along with *landsleit* from other cities and towns.

[Pages 695]

The society would hold a banquet, a kind of *melave malkha*[3] that would usually take place every first and third Sunday of the month after its meeting. The group would come because it was an attraction and everyone would greatly enjoy themselves.

The greatest and most important undertaking that the Chelemer Society would carry out was the yearly ball during the winter. This ball was arranged in a large, beautiful hall with a beautiful orchestra. Our *landsleit* and their wives felt as if they were at their own wedding – in the manner of important in-laws, and they paraded, each wanting to surpass the other. There was rejoicing and simple happiness, when a "*grine*" [green one – newly arrived immigrant] family would appear in the hall. Everyone was ready to "do their thing," clapping the "*grine*" on the back and speaking to him in English.

The organizing committee wore bright, colored ribbons – like generals – and badges with the inscription "committee" pinned to their lapels. They would bustle about in the hall, keeping order and circling with the American and society flags.

These proceedings – one of many that our Chelemer *landsleit* found somewhere and introduced as a part of their communal ritual – did not find favor in the eyes of the young Chelemer immigrants. Through these rituals and strange conduct, our old Chelemer *landsleit* of that time actually wanted to suggest the new manner of life in the free land, America.

The regular twice a month society meetings were carried out under the popular parliamentary rules.

The agenda – a strongly local one – would be very fervidly debated. The question, if this or that brother-*landsleit* was entitled to receive the payment of his health insurance, would be heatedly debated, often until late at night. One brother reported that he had not found the sick one at home; a second said that he met him eating a small dish of "*kliskelekh mit bebelekh* [small dumplings with small beans]." All of our brothers exchanged glances and murmured: "Ah… *kliskelekh!... bebelekh!...*

These debates did not interest the young element that had begun to "run" to America at the beginning of 1905. Among these Chelemer emigrants were found very highly intelligent *landsleit* who clearly understood very well the new world and the new time in which they were living. Understandably, for the new arrivals, the organized society of the First Chelemer Brotherly Aid Union was not enough and the new emigrants organized a youth club that was established as the Progressive Chelemer Branch 585 of the *Arebeter Ring* [Workmen's Circle].

The following statement of principles (published in a journal), written by the writer of these lines, shows the new, widespread communal scope with which the younger element of Chelemer *landsleit* were involved and lived:

16th Year of Communal Work of the Chelemer Branch 585 *A.R.*

Our branch is a link in the great chain of social-political organizations that the post-war period encountered and very much needed.

Worker problems, both national Jewish and international, questions and events that have communal, economic or cultural worth occupy the head of the table at our meetings.

Our meetings are interesting, lively and have a social-political educational worth, thanks to the idealism and intelligence of the active members.

Our national orientation in light of revolutionary developments is clear and of consequence.

We materially support: workers' struggles, children's schools, various "aid" undertakings here in this country and in the old home.

Our branch strongly fights communal apathy, emptiness and monotony, which recently threatened the existence of many similar organizations.

The Chelemer Women's Club, which our branch recently established, bubbles with activity and is able hold its own; the journal and ball would not have been possible without the Chelemer Women's Club.

We heartily greet all of our friends, sympathizers and members. We say thank you for all of the compliments that are published in the journal.

We call: Join as a member of our branch."

This is not the place to record and list the names of all the individual *landsleit* who achieved an eminent place in American and Jewish communal life through their communal activities.

* * *

The Chelemer *landsleit* in America and mainly the Chelemer colony in New York recorded a glorious chapter in the history of communal activity, of self sacrificing aid work for the last 35 years.

Members of the Chelemer *A.R.* branch 585, where the younger, international element of Chelemer *landsleit* have grouped themselves, have influenced and led these communal activities in the course of the turbulent and bloody events of the last 30-35 historical years.

The meetings of the Chelemer *A.R.* branch 585 are carried out in the best parliamentary way. The meetings, which are held twice each month, reflect almost every important American, Jewish and worker problem – both national and international. The debates at these meetings often have a highly academic, instructive character.

[Page 697]

Finding themselves constantly in a whirl of communal activities, the people planned, roused and called upon the Chelemer *landsleit* not to stand apart, but to take an active part in the great historical events of our era.

Understand that such a group of young people did not avoid the plague of dividing into left and right.

The Chelemer *A.R.* branch 585 was the first organization in America to buy an *Eretz-Yisroel* bond, although only a few members were disposed toward Zionism and only one – of those I know – was a *Poalei- Zionist*. This was Itshe Fiszelson, a graduate pharmacist in Baguszewski's pharmacy in Chelm. He came to America in 1913. He was a member of the "Young *S.S.*" (Socialist Territorialists). Here in America he was a *Poalei-Zionist*. A highly intelligent, energetic person, serious and honest, he fought and defended his viewpoint and ideas at the Chelemer *A.R.* branch 585.

In 1929 he organized a group of members who left our *Arbeter Ring* branch with him. They founded branch 280 of the Jewish National Worker's Union (a *Poalei-Zionist* fraternal order]. He was a restless communal man with a sense of fairness and justice and the suffering of the masses in America in the difficult economic crisis of that time pushed him farther to the left. He left the *Poalei-Zionist* order and became a member of the Jewish branch of Left Worker's Order. At that time, he was also in the leadership of the Birobidzhan movement [movement for an autonomous Jewish homeland in the Soviet Union] in America. He died of heart disease in 1948. He was eulogized at his grave by a representative of the Communist Party in America.

* * *

During the first few years of its existence, the Chelemer branch 280 of J.N.A.P.[1] was a lively *Poalei-Zionist* organization. In 1930 the name "Chelemer" was changed to *Akhdes* [unity]. I do not know the exact reason for this, just as I do not know why other Chelemer *landsleit* in New York say that come from Lublin or Lublin *gubernia* [province].

The Chelemer *A. R.* branch 585 also had members who were not from Chelm.

In all situations, *Akhdes* branch 280 was in contact with the Chelemer institutions. In 1934 they published *Der Chelemer* [*The Chelemer* – person from Chelm], a compilation of interesting material about Chelm. Itshe Fiszelson was the editor of the journal. I hope that the name "Chelemer" will again be used because according to what I hear there has been no *Akhdes* – unity – there for a long time.

The Chelemer *landsleit* in New York, Newark and Montreal demonstrated a great deal of devotion and self-sacrifice to the relief problem.

[Page 698]

Chelemer Relief was actually founded in New York during the course of the First World War. Our distinguished *landsman*, Avraham Rozenboim, is one of the key founders of Chelemer Relief and of the Chelemer branch *585 Arbeter Ring*. The mail and correspondence with Europe was interrupted then because of the war. Chelemer *landsleit* in New York were very worried about the fate of the Jews in Chelm. Chelemer Relief was organized then in order to be ready to provide support as soon as the war ended.

The first relief money was brought by our distinguished *landsman*, Shmuel Winer, to Chelm *erev Sukkous* [on the eve of the Feast of Tabernacles] in the morning in 1921. The sum that was sent then was only for institutions in Chelm: *Talmud Torah* [elementary religious school for poor, young boys], *Lines haTzadek* [poor house], the old age home and for the Peretz Library.

Chelemer Relief first took on its proper character and importance in the 1930's. Anti-Semitism in Poland flared up. The bitter economic condition of the Jews in Chelm forced the annihilation of the existing communal institutions, which were so important and necessary in the city.

Serious and responsible Chelemer *landsleit* in New York evaluated the situation in the light of the events at that time and decided that:

"Greater support, more often and for a longer time was arguably needed in order for the Jews in Chelm and the communal institutions there to be able to repulse and survive the difficult economic attacks by the so-called independents and "Free Polish Government."

Chelemer Relief, which until now consisted of individuals, was reorganized under the name "the United Chelemer Relief" and was joined by all existing Chelemer organizations in New York.

Thanks to the experience and intelligence of the new, younger Chelemer immigrants, "United Chelemer Relief" was rebuilt on new foundations.

This "going to the city" to gather contributions with a "red handkerchief," in which the collected money was held on the basis of "me-you" accounts was changed into well organized "money campaigns" for Chelm. I provide my report about the relief activity in 1937-1938 here as a concrete example:

Relief for the Year 1937-1938

The very new, serious and bitter condition of the poor Jews in Chelm mobilized and united all isms, all organizations, all *landsleit* in New York, Newark, Montreal (Canada) in one "United Relief Committee" and the result was a great moral and material success. True, at that time we did not reach all of the *landsleit*, but those we reached generously gave their support, more than once, or four or five times, directly and quietly, at each opportunity and again at other kinds of opportunities. The detailed financial report mirrors the heartfelt connection to our Jews suffering from need in Chelm. Over 218 dollars were raised from several card and house parties that were given by H. Rozenfeld, G. Rajf, A. Bron in New York and by Y. Sztajn, J. Czenser, B. Zamelman and Sh. Blajer in Newark. One designs an "arm chair" to raffle, another - a "bedspread" and a third - delicious kasha knishes.

[Page 699]

There are more interesting features from this year's campaign: Mrs. B. Hertc collected 4,500 dollars for ads in the journal. Ten or 12 devoted members of the committee in New York and Newark collected over 800 dollars by completing visits to the houses of about 200 *landsleit*. Newark would contribute about 30-40 dollars to support earlier campaigns. This year - over 340 dollars. Montreal never had a relief campaign - this year we established a permanent relief society, to which *landsleit* pay 25 cents monthly dues, come to meetings, are interested in Chelm and we have actually received the first 100 dollars from Montreal and a balance remaining of 10 dollars in the bank there - a promise of further support. At the high point the oldest and most sympathetic Chelemer society, the branch 585 *Arbeter Ring*, branch 280 Jewish National Workers Union, together contributed over 150 dollars. It would be very interesting to mention each person's cooperation and devotion. However, this is technically difficult.

May we be spared today! After the first "point of order," our communal meeting adopted parliamentary procedures. Our president, G. Rajf, very quickly and skillfully found his bearings so that he could be proposed as chairman of the "League of Nations." G. Rajf was not only "a ___ [5] and representative of," he was also a responsible, earnest relief work volunteer. In short - we have a very sympathetic chairman. Y. Tukhman, our treasurer justifiably earned our trust and appreciation. B. Hertc, H. Flug, M. Sztajn, Y. Dreksler, A. Karp, Kh. Rozenfeld, W. Dublman - worked like bees. The Newark committee amazed us with their successful work. Montreal, Canada, was truly a great surprise - let us applaud them all.

We ask our *landsleit* in Chelm to accept our help - although not great - not as charity, not with lowered eyes, because we here are the lucky ones and, as such, we must help.

We wish you a better and hopeful future.

We greet the new committee in Chelm and we hope that the manner for dividing the money will satisfy us in America and you in Chelm.

Greetings from Chelemer *landsleit* in New York, Newark, Montreal and Chelm.

Ben Binsztok

[Page 700]

Financial Report for 1937-1938

Income

First Chelemer Aid Union	$150.00
Chelemer branch 585, *Arbeter Ring*	$105.00
Branch 280, Jewish National Workers Union	$100.00
Support from *landsleit*	$804.90

Card and house parties organized by Chelemer Women's Society

At H. Rozenfeld, Brooklyn	$50.00
At G. Rajf, Brooklyn	$53.45
At A. Bron, Brooklyn	$29.00

Organized by Newark Committee

At Y. Stajn, Newark	$30.00
At Sh. Blojer, Newark	$23.00
At Ben Zemelman, Newark	$20.96
At Yakov Czesner, Newark	$12.00
	$218.41

Raffles:

Mrs. B. Hertc	$45.00

All others combined	$73.50
	$118.50

Journal:

Complimenting Chaim Zemelman	$100.00
All others	$109.25
	$209.25

Events arranged by

The Chelemer Women's Society	$105.40
Newark Committtee	$55.10
	$160.50
Total	**$1,866.56**

Expenses

Protest meeting hall	$23.00
Protest meeting hall	$20.00
Printing	$36.21
Postage	$32.10
Montreal Society	$16.00
Newark	$3.36
	$130.67
	$1,735.89

State of Finances

Distributed for those suffering from need in Chelm	$1,200.00
In bank, New York	$382.35
In bank, Los Angeles	$10.00
Debts of 27 *landsleit*	$143.75
	$1736.10

The raffle will take place at another opportunity, because not all of the stubs and money have been received.

All contributions are officially acknowledged in the Journal.

Ben Binsztok.

The new manner of collecting money demanded planning, publicity and appealing, informative-literature.

The work was difficult and painstaking. Personal interests often suffered because of communal activities.

In the beginning, it was a little difficult to collect the funds. Certain *landsleit* and even entire organizations wanted only religious institutions to receive support. Free-thinkers did not want religious institutions to receive "even one *groshn*."

[Page 701]

There were times during the first years of Relief when we had to use strategic methods in approaching some of the *landsleit* as well as organizations.

In the beginning, the leaders of the first Chelemer Society opposed the relief work. However, thanks to the tireless informational work that was methodically carried out by frequent postscripts, letters, lectures at various large and small gatherings, or entertainment evenings specially organized by the "United Chelemer Relief" – thanks to this, hearts softened and the money purses of many skeptics of relief opened.

In the last summary it must be said here that the Chelemer *landsleit* in America recorded a hearty and superb chapter of history in the realm of aid to our unfortunate poor brothers and sisters in Chelm.

The slogans of "*tzadekah*" [charity] and "constructive aid" went hand-in-hand with aid for "political arrestees" in Chelm.

All Chelemer *landsleit* remember the case when the Polish government arrested two Chelemer young workers and sentenced them to death.

A call for help reached us in New York, which requested moral and material help.

We accepted the call and organized the Chelemer *Patronat* – an outspoken political aid organization of that time.

The work was difficult: first, because of the purely political character, and secondly – because of the fact that one of the two arrestees was a Ukrainian (the Jew was named Kupersztak).

Money was provided for the attorney and petitions were sent to the Polish government on behalf of the arrestees. The result was that the young men were saved from the gallows.

The *Patronat* also supported the *Botwinces*[6] in Spain. They were the first partisans who went to fight against the Fascists and Hilterists – the bloodiest enemies of the Jewish people.

Here we must remember Shlomo Elboim (a son of Sura-Elke and Yisroel Elboim - a baker-worker in Chelm), who escaped from Poland to France in a remarkable and dangerous way:

In Warsaw he hid under a wagon of the Warsaw-Paris express train and in this way traveled to Paris where he was removed half dead and taken to a hospital. The French newspapers then wrote very fiery reports about this case.

Shlomo Elboim left France for Spain, joined the Botwin Company. He was wounded several times and finally fell on the battlefield, two days before the Botwin Company was called back from Spain.

* * *

Not all Chelemer *landsleit* felt comfortable in specific Chelemer societies. Many *landsleit* departed on their own, or were driven out by the Chelemer environment or because of one or another incident. Here I will remember only one name from this category of Chelemer *landsleit*:

[Page 702]

The *shwartsn* [black or dark] scribe's son. He lives in a suburb of New York and is a music teacher. In 1912 he graduated from the conservatory in Warsaw. Several of his friends organized his first public concert in the Chelmer Circus Hall, *Sirena*. A. Kipnis took part in the program. The purpose of this concert was simply to place several rubles in the pocket of the dark, charming Chelemer young man, who was as poor as the night. Jewish Chelm did NOT come to the concert. The undertaking was a great failure. The *shwartsn* scribe's son, who is now well known in the musical world is America under the name Josef Wardi, avoids the Chelemer *landsleit* in New York.

Captain Milton (Mendl) Winer, son of Sh. Winer – in 1944. He took part in the Second World War. He traveled around the entire globe more than once during the war years, by ship and airplane, with danger to his life. He visited every continent and went to the ends of the earth. He did not forget that he is a son of the Jewish people and looked for fellow Jews in the faraway nations.

On the 22nd of December 1951, the Chelemer branch 585 *Arbeter Ring* celebrated its 35th anniversary with a magnificent banquet and dance in a beautiful, large hall on Broadway in New York.

The Chelemer *Arbeter Ring* branch knows how to arrange a banquet or any kind of entertainment. However, an experienced eye is needed to produce delicate effects. The tiredness, oldness really hurt the eyes. The invited children, the daughters and sons-in-law, sons and daughters-in-law, who so beautifully and cheerfully enjoyed themselves, underscored and brought out the tiredness more sharply. It was noticed that a considerable number of members moved around as if at a stranger's wedding. Friendly joy and family joy was lacking that was natural at past anniversaries. The members are relatively young. I believe 55 is the average age of a member of branch 585 *A. R.* In a society like the *Arbeter Ring* branch, friendship and truly friendly relations actually need to be the *alef-beis* [a, b, c's], the basis of the daily tasks and activities of the Chelemer *landsleit* organization.

Translator's footnotes:

1. The "oath" refers to being inducted into the Russian army. Poland did not exist at this time due to the numerous partitions of the country by Russia, Prussia and Austria.
2. Wladyslaw Grabski was the Polish Prime Minister during the 1920's and reorganized the Polish economy in a way that was very detrimental to the Jews; the wagons of the tax collector's were nicknamed "Grabski's hearse."
3. "Ushering out of the queen" – the evening meal at the conclusion of *Shabbos*.
4. Jewish National Workers Union.
5. This space appears in the original text.
6. Members of the Naftali Botwin Company of Jewish supporters of the Republican side who fought in Spain during the Spanish Civil War. Naftali Botwin was a Polish-Jewish radical, who was executed in 1924 for the assassination of a member of the Polish secret police.

[Page 703]

The First 25 Years of the Chelemer *Arbeter-Ring* [Workman's Circle] Branch in New York

by Shmuel Winer

Translated by Gloria Berkenstat Freund

(This article was printed in a special journal published by the Chelemer branch of the Arbeter-Ring in New York in March, 1941, on the occasion of its 25th anniversary.)

Born in April 1916 in the middle of the First World War, our branch now in March 1941 celebrates the observance of the conclusion of a quarter century of fruitful communal activity in the very fervor of the Second World War. Twenty-five years in which the face of the world has changed completely.

And yet one only needs to close one's eyes and one thinks it is yesterday. Memories come back to the surface and such clear pictures, episodes, events from long ago swim out, which will return no more.

* * *

Together with hundreds of thousands of immigrants who stormed the "golden land" from the four corners of the world just before the outbreak of the First World War, came a bunch of young people from our home, Chelm. They made their home in New York, the greatest city in the world.

The first steps in the cold strangeness were difficult. The struggle for a piece of earth under the sun, for the ability to exist was accompanied by death. The process of adaptation and fitting in was not easy. The road in the new, strange world was full of stumbling. Uprooted from their old home; not yet rooted in the new home. They had a ceaseless longing for those familiar dear faces, for the familiar sky, for that entire way of life in which they grew and matured that was left on the other side of the ocean.

[Page 704]

Under the circumstances, the more lively of that bunch developed the idea to unite, to join in a *landsmanschaft* [organization of people from the same city or town] mutual aid organization in which they could properly live communally and culturally. In as much as a number of them had brought with them their revolutionary and socialist traditions, it was natural at that time to join the fraternal workers' order – the *Arbeter Ring*.

And thus, the progressive branch 585 *Arbeter Ring* was born 25 years ago.

It did not take long for the branch to be safely past the childhood diseases that each new born organism must go through and it quickly stood on its own feet.

The branch constantly grew in esteem and in the number of members. Little by little, all of the youthful, intelligent strength among the *landsleit* was brought in. The new immigrants, after the First World War, brought fresh youthful strength to the organization. Its communal unity and activity grew side by side. The branch omitted nothing. It reacted to initiatives and took part in all of the movements dedicated to the building of the Jewish street in New York – the largest center of Jews in the world. They were everywhere – at every gathering, conference, of every direction and nuance there was. It was everywhere, full of life and momentum.

The meetings, every second and fourth Friday night of the month, became noisier and more interesting. The crowd sharpened its tongues – even more their brains. They slowly became more proficient debaters, speakers. All communal movements and ideologies received their clear expression here. The world was shaken at it foundations. Years, loaded with dynamite, cooked and effervesced during those stormy 20 years; the branch was transformed into a combat arena. One competed against the other in strength. Each deeply confident in his truth threw himself into the struggle with youthful enthusiasm. The struggle became sharper and more bitter. Many times too bitter.

A group of members of the "First Chelemer Sick Aid Union" in New York

First row, sitting: Y. Nodel, Sh. Kuper, M. Sztajn, Y. Kuszerman, (long time secretary of the Chelemer Society), E. Ejzen, A. Stahl, of blessed memory, H. Lorber, G. Rajf (president of the Chelemer Society), M. Long, B. Szternberg, Sh. Blajer, Klajnman
Second row, standing: L. Blajer, women: Feder, Nodel. Stroj, Kuszerman, Fajertog, Kohn, Lorber, Czesner, Herc, Sztajnberg, Rota, Blajer, Klajnman
Third row, standing: Mrs. and Mr. Kh. Berland, A. Berland, Cymerman, Gutharc, Sh. Mandelboim B. Szumlan, Y. Goldman, Y. Zalc, Y. Kaj

[Page 705]

The air became that much hotter. It became more difficult for the various contradictory ideologies to live peacefully among themselves. Personal bitterness also grew among a sizable mass of the members. And thus, the branch was brought to crisis in the 1930's.

Gabriel Rajf, communal worker, untiring social worker and chairman of Chelemer Relief in New York for the last 30 years

Earlier, a group of members disposed to Zionism severed itself and became instrumental in the founding of a Chelemer branch of the National Workers Union (the *Poalei-Zionist* Fraternal Order). Immediately after, a group of leftist members left the branch and joined the International Workers' Order. This accompanied the bitter Hoover depression that also did not do the branch any favor.

At this critical time, our wives came to help the branch.

The children were no longer small; the mothers had a little time for themselves. One after the other our wives began to appear at meetings of the branch. It did not take long and they began to be at home in the branch. They brought fresh life to the organization.

[Page 706]

Here at the end, at this opportunity, our veteran must be remembered with respect, who with his unrelenting stubbornness played a considerable part in the founding of our branch. This is no one other than our respected Avraham Rozenboim (he was known in Chelm as Avraham the Krasnystawer iron dealer's son). During the space of more than 20 years, he served devotedly as secretary of the branch and carried the burden not only of the entire organization, but also was devoted to each particular member with body and life. He never spared effort, time and energy when somone was in need of help in times of trouble. He was not only beloved because of this by the branch members without exception – from the left to the right – but by the local Chelemer colony in general.

* * *

It is now hard to believe that a quarter century has passed since the branch began its existence.

And time passed. Each in his way left deep roots in the native soil [of America]. Built homes, had children, went through difficult paths with them from birth to adulthood. In a word – all have little by little grown intertwined in the web of life here on the native soil.

Certainly there is now great joy. A celebration for all members who have weathered all storms with the branch and in the branch and reached the 25th birthday of their branch 585 *Arbeter Ring*.

New York, February 1941

Maks Sztajn, active worker and secretary of Chelemer Relief in New York

[Page 705]

A Chelemer Story in an American Way

by B. Alkwit

Translated by Gloria Berkenstat Freund

I come from Chelm. Should I tell you about it? This is not a story from the past. It is lost today, but for the Chelemer *landsleit* [people from the same city or town], who are found everywhere, throughout the world – it is a new Chelemer story.

Chelm, who has not heard of this Jewish city? – Who is not a Chelemer? Chelm was an important Jewish cultural center, not because of its size – but Chelm was great because of its name, because of the center that it was – a center of fools, as is told in the Chelemer stories.

Chelm was one of the first Jewish cities that the Germans destroyed, but how Chelm stood up against the devils, how it fought – Yitzhak Fajgboim, a Jew from Poland, a respected *Poalei-Zion* worker, told at his arrival in New York in January, 1941 how the first ghetto revolt was in Chelm.

[Page 706]

And after the revolt, shortly after, Chelm became a cemetery for many Jews from other cities, from other countries. Corroborative reports about this began to arrive in Washington at the beginning of February, 1943, that masses of Jews from various points in Europe were driven to Chelm from the ghettos and there – massacred.

[Page 707]

America's then Secretary of State, Cordell Hull, issued a report at a press conference and Anthony Eden, England's Foreign Minister shocked the Parliament with a speech about the events in Chelm. But…

This is history. Yet I will tell a story from today, about the Chelemer *landsleit* – perhaps the last Chelemer story.

* * *

One beautiful day two Chelemer *landsleit* meet. One a writer, the other a proof reader; they converse. He says: *Nu* [well], what, nothing? I ask him: What, what? I mean Chelm, he says.

He is worried. His quiet, troubled voice becomes a little more troubled: I mean, he says, among fine Jews, *landsleit*, something is being done to remember, to immortalize the memory of their cities, their *shtetlekh* [towns]. They are doing, they are publishing *yizkor-bikher* [memorial books]. But Chelm, wow – Chelm! It is time, I think, to get to work, to collect material. Yet this cannot be done overnight. And if not now, when? If not us, the family, the *landsleit*, who?

Yes, I agreed with him; it is the utmost time; the materials that we must gather are treasures that, I think, have no equal – the documents, historical and culturally historical; personalities and memories, from Reb Eliyiahu *bal Shem* [miracle worker] to the martyred Shmuel Zigelboim, who in his youth lived and fought in Chelm. Today, the stories of or about Chelemer fools, the entire folklore riches and how this influenced Jewish writers – Chelm in the Jewish literature.

Our classical writers have written about Chelm – Mendele Mocher Sforim, Yankev Glatshteyn, Y.Y. Sigal, Ahron Zeitlin and many others – it hurts me that I cannot mention each of them by name – and painters came to see the city and "to paint it." Even music is here. And when Nathan Ausubel published his large collection, *A Treasury of Jewish Folklore*, Chelm occupied a particularly large part with an introduction about the local humor of the stories and…

What a large Jewish cultural work, to collect material and publish a Chelemer memorial book!

However, time did its work; it passed. Years went by, until one night, this summer, I met my *landsleit* in the subway and, here in the heat, in the crush, in the very "rush hour," I fell on him as if from heaven: He asks if I still live at the same address, in Africa?

In Africa?

Yes, in Johannesburg. There they are publishing a Chelemer memorial book. He will send them my address so that they, my *landsleit* from South Africa, can correspond with me about the great work.

Nu, imagine what a person can tell you in the heat, in the crush. In the very "rush hour" in the subway. I shake my head to him: yes, yes, and I ask him to meet with me somewhere else, where we can talk. But he lives in the Bronx, I in Brooklyn and before what, when, there is a letter from Johannesburg.

[Page 708]

The letter is from H. Sziszler, a writer. He requests material and asks for contacts and financial help, because this will cost a great deal and how many are there, the Chelemer *landsleit* in South Africa?

A few dozen families, in all.

* * *

A few dozen families.

How many Chelemer *landsleit* are in New York? I do not know. But the *Arbeter-Ring* [Workman's Circle] has a Chelemer branch with around 100 members. The National Worker's Union has a branch of 200 Chelemer *landsleit* and there is also a society here, a support union and there are surely *landsleit* in other cities in the United States and in other countries of the American hemisphere.

There are also Chelemer in Israel. I know of two poets in Israel for whom Chelm is their birthplace. And there is one other, a new name, Sh. Wazager, who has published his first book after being in Germany.

But the few dozen families in South Africa are publishing the memorial book.

And they have made contact with *landsleit* in America, in Israel, in Europe, that we should send the materials, the documents, pictures, eye witness accounts and local stories, memoirs, songs and stories to Johannesburg – and the necessary funds – and they in South Africa will publish the book.

And it was sent.

Is this not a Chelemer story?

Perhaps the last story of the fools, the Chelemer Jews, who can tell stories about themselves with laughter, with mockery and farce from our wisdom…

I think we need such a story to close the memorial book, that will be published in Africa, while in New York, you see, we did not do it. Perhaps because the New York *landsleit* have so convinced themselves that they are no longer Chelemer.

And perhaps because it is the great New York, because here we have such large numbers, that…we no longer need to do anything. Thus it is in all of communal Jewish life.

Yes, we send materials and the financial means to the few families in South Africa, who are still good Chelemer, with the pure naiveté, that is called foolishness, with the irony and the mockery of the Chelemer stories.

And we will have the moral, that the number, the size of a group, plays a negligible role when cultural work needs to be done.

Small numbers can do greater work than large groups.

Page 709]

The Chelemer *Landsmanschaft*[1] in Paris

by Dr. B. Orlean

Translated by Gloria Berkenstat Freund

Our *landsman* [person from the same city], honorary president and great friend, Josef Milner, once wrote an historical review about the Jewish communities in France and said that the Pilsudski era, as it was known, brought a great number of immigrants to France – the victims of the Grabskis and the Becks.[2] But in 1928, more than 9,000 Jews arrived in France. And that year one of our Chelemer Jews, a person with a noble soul, Szulman, had the idea to found a Chelemer *Landmanschaft*. (Our dear Szulman was deported during the occupation and perished at Auschwitz.) Clearly, at that time, Szulman turned at once to Josef Milner, who did not refuse (we should remember that, in general, he never refused when it was a question of communal work and, particularly, when it involved Chelm). To this day, I remember the first meeting in the Paris ghetto, in the famous "*Pletzl*" [Little Place – the Jewish area located in the 4th arrondissement]. Josef Milner gave, as was his manner, a fiery speech about the necessity for organizing. He called on the old Chelemer in Paris, who were already residents and even "naturalized French," to become guides because in such a large city, in a strange environment and with a strange language, the Jew, the emigrant, needed to have a place where he could meet a friend from his childhood, meet with people who could even teach him how to conduct himself in a new country, sometimes to obtain a loan "when in need" from his own loan society and believe that he is not alone, even though he is far from his old home. Several active community workers were then grouped around Szulman, such as Torn and many others, who alas also perished and whose names are engraved on the *matzeyvah* [headstone] "To the memory of the Jewish Community of Chelm" at the Paris cemetery. He was the son of "*zeyfenzitser*" [slang expression connoting a person who has an easy job or is well situated], Reb Shimkha. He was among those who earned a very fine material position in Paris, but earlier, in 1914, he had slogged in other positions, on the Marne and outside Paris, as a volunteer fighter against the Germans and returned after the war with medals for his heroism. He was also deported with his entire family and they were never seen again …

[Page 710]

In general, there was a tendency then in France (and also in other immigrant nations) to place oneself in a group and organize life around it. Could it be different then?... But the situation was not as it is today, now that the old home has been completely destroyed and the borders are closed and we remained and we were there where fate has already given up. At that time many immigrants were able to travel further, that is, to America, to Argentina and young people as pioneers to *Eretz-Yisroel*. The development of the *landsmanschaft* was affected by the fact that the immigrant element was not a stable one. Alas, we must add that often the immigrant was unable to accustom himself to the new environment and he took his traveling stick in his hand and returned to…Chelm! And how many such Chelm Jews who were already in Paris, lost their courage, returned home and were sent to in Trawnik, or Majdanek or Auschwitz?…

It was very different in 1944, on the morning of France's liberation: the Jews understood that there was no long any "return." And in addition to this, we suffered so greatly during the years of occupation; *there was not a family that did not have a victim* ("…for there was not a house where there was no corpse…" [Exodus, chapter 12: verse 30]) and moreover we grew closer to the French. We finally had the same enemy and the French were so helpful in our rescue that we understood that we must organize our lives here. And in addition, a new generation emerged, the generation of our children, who were born on French soil. And Jewish life in Paris truly began to sparkle.

You must excuse me when I speak more of Paris because it is said in France that "a Parisian is French, but not all the French are Parisians." Paris is everything. The few widely scattered Jewish families from Chelm in Nancy, in Rouen, in Lyon (in the old historic town of Bezie [Béziers], where Reb Avraham Ibn Ezra [1092-1167 - Hebrew poet and scholar] once lived, there is one Jewish doctor and he is a Chelemer: Hershl Erlikh's son!) and in other cities show that in reference to Chelm one must turn to us, in Paris. And not only from French cities; our Chelm *landsmanschaft* is today the only one in Europe. Chelemers from Belgium, Holland and England come to us for a meeting or for an entertainment, for remembering a father, a mother and even a relative.

[Page 711]

Immediately after the liberation, intensive Jewish communal work began to bubble – we went from defeat to the light. French Jewry became the largest Jewish center in Western Europe, the largest Jewish community, almost 300,000 Jews. All of the organizations carried on intensive and widespread activities. And all of the *landsmanschaftn* responded to this; their work stood at the center of this new construction because all of the Jews here had to start from the beginning. And a new constituent joined. The survivors – *landsleit* [people from the same town or city] from the camps. We carried out great work. We supported those who were homeless, found opportunities for them to work and the ministerial permission to work. We had a cash box and gave loans. Thanks to the important communal position of our Josef Milner, we did everything we could to heal the sick through *OZA* [organization offering medical care], to teach new professions at ORT [organization providing vocational training] and gave them opportunities to go to America, Australia, Canada, Argentina and Israel and to receive through HIAS [Hebrew Immigrant Aid Society], for example, the opportunities for emigration and thanks to the "Joint" [Joint Distribution Committee], the needed support for the voyage and also immigrant relief. Here, we want to present a hearty congratulations to all of the organizations mentioned by us. All of our Chelemer who are in new nations as a result of our work can easily corroborate this.

And now I will dwell on our *cultural* activities. Our *landsmanschaft* had a great reputation in Paris and other *landsmanschaftn* were simply envious of us. Our undertakings were a great success. We had a great ball (along with the Brisk *landsmanschaft*). Three or four times a year we organized evenings that were famous and drew large crowds to them. Here we will remember the names of our skillful friends, devoted Chelemer: Torn, Spajzman, Staw, Mrs. Parboek, Mrs. Szrajer, Ahron Glaben, Murawicz, Mr. and Mrs. Micpilker, Goldsobel, Mr. and Mrs. Feldman, both Szmaragd brothers and many others. All devoted, all with heart, with large Jewish hearts.

The old Jewish cemetery in Chelm does not exist anymore…
The matzeyvah* for all of Chelm, for its well known personalities, for the hundreds of thousands who were annihilated, is located at the Parisian cemetery – a monument erected there by the Chelemer Jews in France.

*[Names appearing on the matzeyvah:
Reb Elihu bal-Shem [miracle worker], Reb Shlomo Chelm, Reb Shlomo Yehuda Lederer, Mordekhai Lederer, Reb Yehuda Arya Milner, Dr. Yitzhak Sziper, Shmuel Zigelboim, Dr. Oks]

The Chelemer Matzeyvah at the Paris Cemetery

Josef Milner speaks before the Chelemer landsleit during the erection of the matzeyvah [headstone], "The entire Israelite community of Chelm," at the Paris cemetery

[Page 712]

Here I will cite several of our cultural undertakings:

1) We were the first and the only society of immigrant Jews who entered…*the Sorbonne in Paris!* The entire press wrote about this, both in France and overseas. Imagine that Chelemer Jews organized a historical evening in the Sorbonne dedicated *to the history of the Jews in Paris*!... Chelemer Jews came in order to learn Parisian Jewish history. A large crowd filled the amphitheater. The honorary chairman was the well known judge, Leon Meis, and the chairman was Mr. Georges Wormser, the president of the Paris Consistoire (a former associate of Clemenseau during the First World War and cabinet chief for one of the well known Jews, French minister, Georges Mandel, who perished at the hands of the occupiers). The following were the lecturers: Josef Milner – about the Jews in France since the Romans and until the Revolution; the famous researcher, the greatly educated "Grand Rabbi," Maris Liber – from the Revolution until the Dreyfus Trial; and the great Jewish-French writer Pier Parof – from Dreyfus until the present. It is really impossible to describe the impression made. For a long time after, Chelm was spoken about everywhere, even in French circles.

2) When Josef Milner returned from his trip to Israel (during the first year of the Jewish state), we organized a lecture, under the chairmanship of the same Mr. Leon Meis and with the Israeli Consul in Paris, Avraham Gilboa, in a large theater ballroom. Our *landsleit* Josef Milner was also a splendid speaker and his lecture about Israel was truly an extraordinary literary work.

3) In 1947 we celebrated the 60th birthday of Josef Milner, who was so beloved by all of us. A group of several thousand Jews who are grateful to Josef Milner for their existence stroll around in Paris and in France. Before, during and after the occupation, Jewish societies wanted to celebrate his birthday, but he refused. However, he could not refuse us, those from Chelm, and there was a celebratory "gathering" that could only bring respect to our city, Chelm.

[Page 713]

4) Literary "tea evenings" with Ephriam Kaganowski and Yitzhak Janosowicz took place that were organized by us.

And in conclusion, permit me to end with our destruction. Also, here, our Chelemer *landsmanschaft* in Paris did not forget its duty. At the Paris cemetery, there stands a beautiful, large *matzeyvah* which remembers the destruction of our city and before which almost every day Jews from every city who come to a funeral or for a *yahrzeit* [yearly anniversary of a death] stop and with reverence quietly view the monument which explains how modern Huns, motorized anti-Semites, annihilated a Jewish community, and this is only a small part of a great sea of blood, in which six million of our brothers perished *al kiddush haShem* [in the sanctification of God's name – as martyrs].

Translator's footnotes:

1. An organization of people from the same city.
2. Wladislaw Grabski was a prime minister of Poland [1920, 1923-1925] and reorganized the country's financial and monetary systems. Jozef Beck was the Polish Foreign Minister [1932-1939] under Polish ruler Jozef Pilsudski.

[Page 714][page 715]

Chelm and Surrounding Areas Society for Mutual Aid in Argentina

Josef Eplboim

Translated by Gloria Berkenstat Freund

Our society was founded in the year 1934. At that time, the economic crisis penetrated all branches of industry and commerce and the new immigrants suffered more than anyone else. This propelled the *landsleit* [people from the same country] union which, through its direct activity, also created the loan office that provided the *landsleit* with specific support so that they could get settled.

Let here be recorded the following founders: Bejrekh, Szajer, Hersz Szajer, Motl Sztiglic and Zelik Bobes, who called together the meeting and clarified for those present the purpose of the future institutions that would carry on communal and cultural activities in addition to economic assistance.

At the meeting, the following were elected to the managing committee with the following composition: Welwl Milsztajn (chairman), Meir Herman (secretary), Hersz Szajer (treasurer), Shimeon Nakhman, Moshe Gobel, Welwl Mandlboim, Leibush Lang and Motl Sztiglic. In accordance with its abilities, the managing committee began its activities, which were very prominent in Argentine *landsmanschaft* [organization of people from the same city or town] life.

[Page 716]

We then recognized the need to join the Federation of *Landsleit*-Unions in which the greatest number of the largest groups were members and this influenced our society to strengthen itself with new members and that our institution should take on the challenge to accomplish new tasks. We took an active part in the campaign for the Land of Israel and for the orphans in France.

The first messages that we received from a few of our *landsleit* in Poland depressed us. But we consoled ourselves with the short list of names of the survivors.

Committee members of the Argentine landsmanschaft

[Page 717]

At first we made contact with our *landsleit* and when we received the full list with 700 names of survivors and the report about the convention in Lower Silesia, we published the material in a publication which was received with great interest and love by our members and *landsleit*. (The work of publishing was carried out by Chaim Eplboim.) At the same time, we began to create the opportunity to help out the *landsleit* who wanted to come to Argentina and when they came here, we helped them settle in, providing then apartments and with the most needed things. The most moving encounters were the holiday gatherings which our society arranged for the newly arrived *landsleit* from Poland. Let us here record their names: Yona Szajer and wife, Yoel Engel and Rywka Nodel, Hersh Feldmus and Andje Goldfeder, Motl Feldman and wife, Shimkha Kuper and Mrs. Sztajner, Chaim Sztajner, Shmuel Bakalosz and wife, Motl Cymerman and Mrs. Dajmowicz. The above-mentioned are from Chelm. The following *landsleit* also came to us from Rejowiec: Shmuel Meir Cederboim, Yankl Cederboim, Itshe Cederboim, Szeja Firszt, Zishe Dumkop, Eli Wilder, Shmuel Szlajer, Itshe Frajnd, Leah Rukhwang. From Sielec came Perl Rutker, Motl Szulklaper, Leib Lerer, Kiwa Zylberman.

We held dear the decision that was made at the meeting in Lower Silesia by our surviving *landsleit* in Poland that during the days of *Shavous* all Chelemer and those from the area, wherever they were, should have a formal expression of mourning and honor our unforgettable parents, sisters, brothers and friends, who were murdered in the most horrible way by the Nazi murderers.

This decision was upheld with sacred honor and trembling. Almost all of our *landsleit* came to the act of mourning – both the unveiling of the memorial tablet for the Chelemer religious community that is found on the monument to the memory of the six million martyrs, which Jewish Buenos Aires erected and to the sad evening that we arranged within the confines of our society. And when the news was learned that the Chelemer in Africa were undertaking the sacred task of publishing a book that would immortalize the memory of our destroyed home city, we gave our entire attention to publicizing the idea among our members and *landsleit*. In connection with this, a series of meetings was held at which we clarified the importance of such a book, so that when Y. Zigelboim came with the same task, he found the work for the memorial book already begun and it can be said that all of our *landsleit*, both from Chelm and from Rejowiec, Szeliszcz, Dubienka, Wojslawice, Niechen and Sawin, took part in the important work for the book that would not only share the remembrance of those from our unforgettable city who perished, but would also be an addition to the act of accusation that the Jewish people will yet bring to worldwide judgment against the Nazi criminals.

[Page 718]

As we have shown earlier, we took part in all Jewish communal activities that had a connection to the land of Israel and to our local life in Argentina. Our part in the cultural-communal work that was carried out by *ICUF* [*Idischer Cultur Farband* – Jewish Cultural Union] here was completely separate. We made an effort that not only our *landsleit* should come to performances that *ICUF* arranged, but we arranged evenings with representatives of the Cultural Union.

We also made efforts so that our members would benefit from better Yiddish theater. For this purpose, we hired the better Jewish professional theaters for performances as well as exhibitions of *AIFT* (Argentine Yiddish Folk Theater) that we all visited together. In this way we tried to sow the cultural-communal continuation of our loved and unforgettable home city that was such a firm ring in the golden chain of creative Jewish life in Poland.

The composition of the current managing committee is as follows: Josef Szperling (chairman), Josef Eplboim (secretary), Moshe Nobel (treasurer), Manish Cederboim (vice chairman), Chaim Eplboim (recording secretary), Beirekh Szer, Shimeon Nakhman, Avraham Lindnboim, Sheya Firszt, Shye Yedvabnik, Tovya Bankirer, Efroim Hakhsztajn, Welwl Mandelboim, Mekhl Butman and Itshe Cederboim.

[Page 719]

Chelemer *Landsmanschaft*[1] in Australia

by Reizl Ceber

Translated by Gloria Berkenstat Freund

Before we write about the Chelemer *landsleit* [people from the same town or city], we must stress that Chelemer *landsleit* are found in large number in Melbourne. It is not known about Chelemer in other cities in Australia. Only individual families are located in Perth and in Sidney. Regrettably, they have no contact with we Chelemer in Melbourne.

In order to clarify who were the first immigrants who came here and when they came, we must return to the year of 1920. During the Third and Fourth *Aliyah*[2] to *Eretz-Yisroel* many artisans and Zionist idealists from Chelm traveled to *Eretz-Yisroel*. But when the crisis broke out in the years 1924-1926, our *landsleit* made use of the opportunity provided by the English government which had given permission for immigration to Australia. One of the first who came to Melbourne was our dear *landsleit*, Mr. Yakov Wajnrib, of blessed memory. He brought over a considerable number of *landsleit*, such as M. Szekhter (Shechterson), Moshe Sznajder (Meir Ber's son), W. Gotlib, Berland, Kajfer, and still others from *Eretz-Yisroel*.

The home of Dr. Wajnrib was the center for the Chelemer. Letters for almost all Chelemer came to his address. His home was our meeting point where one was delighted with the remembrances of the old home. Mr. Wajnrib was a man with a phenomenal memory. He remembered everyone by his name and even his nickname.

Landsleit in Melbourne went through all phases for an immigrant: heavy labor, wandering, a struggle for a better income, and so on. It is worthwhile to remember our *landsman* [country man], Moshe Sznajder, of blessed memory, who settled on the land and was the pioneer of farming in Shepparton, Australia.

In the course of time, our *landsleit* became Australianized. They had a stable income. At the same time, economic conditions in Chelm grew worse. The families in the old home bombarded the *landsleit* with letters about aid or bringing them here.

There awakened an initiative among our *landsleit* and we obtained a few "permits," thanks to the intervention of Mr. Wajnrib, of blessed memory. In 1937-1938, many newly arriving Chelemer immigrants were here, for whom Chelm was still fresh in their hearts and in their memories.

Thanks to the initiative of Mr. Y. Ceber and the assistance of C. Eizen and W. Gotlib the first Chelemer committee was created. Its task was to help the old home materially. The first founding meeting took place in Melbourne, in the meeting hall of *Gezerd* [a radical left-wing organization] in November 1938. The following people were elected: C. Eizen, Yakov Wajnrib, of blessed memory, Moshe Wajnrib, W. Gotlib, H. Markman and Y. Ceber. Almost all of the *landsleit* became members, almost 20 families.

[Page 720]

A fund was created of 80 pounds. At that time this was a considerable sum. But the money could not be sent home. In 1939, several people were still successful in coming to Australia. This happened close to the outbreak of the Second World Slaughter… We followed the news that came via the Red Cross with heavy hearts and sorrowing spirits. We learned from the American newspapers about the terrible death march of the Chelm and Hrubieszow Jews. We also learned that many Chelm Jews successfully escaped to Russia. The work of the committee was halted because of the World War.

Meanwhile, a great campaign continued in Australia for sheepskins for the Russian soldiers, organized by the Australian-Soviet Friendship League. With the initiative of several members of the Chelemer committee, the sum of 80 pounds was sent for this purpose.

When the Second World Slaughter ended in 1945 and we learned of the vast Jewish destruction, the feeling awoke in our hearts to help not only our own who had survived, but all of the Chelemer Jews – refugees in the camps. In their time, the Aid Committees in Australia went actively to work. *Landmanschaftn* from the larger cities such as Bialystok, Czestochowa, Warsaw, Radom, Lwowicz and others were created. On the 25th of August 1945, a general gathering was called of all of the Chelemer and Hrubieszower *landsleit* at the home of Mr. Oder and his wife. Both cities went together on the death march, and also perished together in the ovens of Majdanek and Sobibor. In addition, many Hrubieszower *landsleit* had Chelemer wives.

Managing Committee of the Chelemer-Hrubieszower Aid Committee in Melbourne, Australia

Sitting from left to right: Yitzhak Ceber – secretary, Wawke Gotlib – chairman, Chaim Markman – treasurer, and Josef Papir
Standing from the left: Leibl Ribeizen, Ch. Oder and Khenina Binsztok

[Page 721]

The meeting was very enthusiastic; the Friends [term used for members of *landsmanschaftn*] C. Eizen and Y. Ceber spoke. The gathered drafted the nature of the activities of the established Chelemer *landsmanschaft* – the combined Chelemer and Hrubieszower *landsleit* – with the purpose of helping the *landsleit* from the two cities and surroundings. The aid consisted of sending food packages for the Chelemer refugees, as well as "permits" (entry papers). A fund created through assessments (224 pounds) was established. The following people were elected to the committee: C. Eizen (Chelm), treasurer – Mendl Korn (Hrubieszow), secretary – Ch. Oder (Hrubieszow), Y. Ceber (Chelm), Mrs. Berland (Chelm).

The committee contacted all Chelemer committees throughout the world. However, only a few individual committees responded, from Poland, Africa, Paris. The Chelemer Committee in Wroclaw sent us a list of Chelemer survivors, who were located in Poland, in Lower Silesia. Letters flowed in asking for aid and "permits". The committee tried to accommodate each one. "Permits" were obtained for Chelemer and Hrubieszowers. Active work took place. A women's committee was created. Food and clothing was collected and in the evening we gathered in Mrs. Eizen's home and packed the packages. We sent packages to the Chelemer committees in Chelm, Wroclaw, Stettin [Szczecin]. With the support of the Aid Fund, our *landsleit* packed the crates with clothing for Chelemer in Poland. The crates were sent through the "Joint" [Joint Distribution Committee]. In addition, the created fund required a great deal of money, because Chelemer who already had "permits," but no money for expenses turned to us. With the help of our *landsleit* in Africa, five families came down from Poland. We paid for others ourselves.

In 1930, when the economic situation in Poland went from bad to worse, Jews began to run wherever they could. It was impossible to enter America, but those who had relatives there or rich families splurged and they were brought to Canada where it was easier to enter. From 1930-32 about 10 families from Chelm entered.

In 1948 we had a considerable number of newly arrived. Then a new problem arose. As in all nations that took in immigrants, there was a shortage of apartments and getting residences for those arriving was required a great deal of money. To provide our refugees in Australia with a roof over their heads was one of the greatest problems.

The committee did not have much money at its disposal that would enable it to buy a house for the new arrivals as was done by other *landsmanschaftn*. The tide of immigrants in those years was considerable. From 20 families in 1945, our *landsmanschaft* reached 50 families, just from Chelm. The committee contacted the general Melbourne aid fund and the immigrants, who then arrived, received a temporary residence from the aid fund until they received an apartment. Among the new arrivals was a portion who needed basic material aid. For such situations, the committee provided a loan of from 50 – 100 pounds with repayment at favorable rates. An group of people received such loans and this helped them to obtain a residence, set up furniture or even to establish a business. In addition to the material aspect, it was also the task of the committee to support the Chelemer immigrants spiritually. For this purpose, meetings of our *landsleit* were arranged from time to time. Such gatherings took place in the homes of Mr. and Mrs. Korn, Mr. and Mrs. Markman, Mr. and Mrs. Fajfer, as well as several in the auditorium of the *Kadimah* [Jewish Cultural Center and National Library]. All of the meetings passed with great success.

[Page 722]

On the 11th of November 1950, the committee organized a memorial evening in the *Kadimah* auditorium in which a large number of *landsleit* from Chelm and its vicinity took part. The room was already filled at 8 o'clock. Right at the entrance, one noticed the black covered table with two burning lights and opposite hung an illustration of a *matzevah* [headstone] for the fallen martyrs. This made the proper impression and brought tears to the eyes. The *matzevah* had been done by our *landsman*, Shmuel Ceber. The *khazan* [cantor] recited the *El Maley Rachamim* [memorial prayer – "God full of mercy…"]. Then Mr. Gotlib spoke.

Our newly arrived *landsleit* gave greetings from home after the war. After a very successful conference, Mr. Soler from Hrubieszow spoke; Messers Klajn and Goldman provided a short overview of their return to Chelm after the war. Mr. Likhtman read several excerpts from newspapers about Zamoszcz. Then Friend Klajn presented two successful recitations: "A Mountain of Shoes in Majdanek," "Stand Up, Jeremiah" – by Bunim Warszawski. At the conclusion, Friend Y. Ceber gave a very successful report. The evening ended with the singing of the partisan song, *Zog nit keynmol az du geyst dem letstn veg*[*Never Say That You Are Trodding the Final Path* – written by Mordekhai Gebirtog, who perished in Krakow]. Our *landsleit* went home deeply moved.

* * *

After the message from Africa was received about assisting in the publishing of the *yizkor book*, photos, as well as individual articles by our *landsleit* were sent. The committee arranged a meeting in the *Kadimah* auditorium where Friend Ceber read the appeal as well as the contents of the prospectus. The month of May was chosen for action for the *yizkor book*. The committee members visited each *landsman* and encouraged him to provide a necrology and to order a book. All of the *landsleit*, with a few exceptions paid for books and a certain number of necrologies were created.

Right now, the following people carry on the work: W. Gotlib, Y. Ceber – secretary, Mrs. Berland, Josef Paiper. Ch. Ador, Kh. Binsztok, showing a great responsibility and understanding of the important work of our *landsmanschaft*.

Translator's footnotes:

1. Society of people from the same city or town.
2. The Third *Aliyah* took place from 1919 to 1923 and the Fourth *Aliyah* from 1924 to 1929.] From the years 1924 to 1926 there was a financial crisis in Poland leading to increased emigration. Starting in 1882, there were successive waves of immigration, *aliyah*, to *Eretz-Yisroel*. *[Page 723]*

Chelemer Jews in Montreal, Canada
by Itshe Akhtman

Translated by Gloria Berkenstat Freund

Twenty-eight years ago, when I stepped onto Canadian soil and arrived in Montreal, there were only about four or five Chelemer families here. Understand that there was no communal life. We would only see each other from time to tim

In 1930, when the economic situation in Poland went from bad to worse, Jews began to run wherever they could. It was impossible to enter America, but those who had relatives there or rich families splurged and they were brought to Canada where it was easier to enter. From 1930-32 about 10 families from Chelm entered.

Chelemer landsleit [people from the same city] in Montreal, Canada

[Page 724]

There was no communal activity as yet, first, because the families had to settle and, secondly, because there simply was no need for it.

This is how it was until the great calamity began in 1939 and this brought us closer. But then nothing could be done. Meanwhile, a group of Lubavitcher students, escaping from Poland, arrived through Japan, and among them was one of our townsmen, Kramer, a son of Mekhele Kramer, who saw the start of the downfall of our city, Chelm. With us, he threw himself into the work. We began preparing plans for what to do for our city, Chelm.

[Pages 725-726]

In 1945 each of us began to receive letters, information from our own relatives or from friends and even from distant acquaintances and we then began our active work. We sent hundreds of packages to our *landsleit* in the "camps" [displaced persons camps]. When Canada became almost the first country to let in emigrants from the camps, we worked tirelessly in various ways to bring over everyone who wanted to come.

Today, there are up to 120 families in Montreal alone, with children and grandchildren. All, may they be healthy, settled down well, some with work, some in business for themselves. Several even have their own houses. None of the *landsleit* complain, God forbid, that their fate had brought them to Canada. We meet several times a year and together we spend time in a friendly atmosphere.

Thus Chelemer life goes on in Montreal, Canada. If someone makes a celebration, almost everyone is there. Let us hope that our *landsleit* here will long, long maintain the tradition of friendship and with this at least remember our former city, Chelm.

Managing committee of the Chelemer landsmanschaft [organization of people from the same city or shtetl –town] in Montreal

First row, sitting [from right to left]: - A. Karp, B. Naturman, Sh. Diment, Rabbi Kramer, A. Achtman, Mrs. Fruchter, H. Fruchter, A. Herc, Mrs. Herc and Denkop
Second row, standing: W. Kupersztok, Mrs. Kupersztok, Mrs. Diment, Z. Fryszman, Mrs. Achtman, Mrs. Edlsztajn, Y. Edlsztajn, and Perlmuter

[Page 725-726]

Chelemer Jews in Cuba
by Itshe Akhtman

Translated by Gloria Berkenstat Freund

This picture was taken in 1925, while the Chelemer Jews were "temporarily" settled there with the hope of emigrating to the United States. At that time they were united and founded a "Chelemer Jewish Emigration Union" in Havana, Cuba
A number of Chelemer who no longer live in Cuba appear in the photo, among them: Rafal Zilber [Israel], Yeheil Waserman [New York] and so on.

A wedding celebration among Chelemer Jews in Tel Aviv in 1940

[Pages 727-728]

Chelemer Jews in Brazil

by Markus Jakubowicz

Translated by Gloria Berkenstat Freund

Chelemer landsleit in Porto Alegre, Brazil, during the welcome for a guest from Argentina, our townsman, Shneiur Waserman, well known Yiddish poet

We are indebted for the existence of the Chelemer Jewish colony in Brazil to the first two Jews – Jakub Hoizman, may he rest in peace, and Note Laks, who had the strength and the influence on their *landsleit* – to free themselves from their old established home, in Chelm, and to create their new home on the shores of the Atlantic – in the friendly and democratic Brazil.

The Chelemer group in Puerto Alegre was also the avant guard for many Chelemer Jews who are now spread across infinite areas of Brazil. All of them are well established and all Chelemer can take pride in their membership in various communal and political institutions across the land. Everywhere, the Chelemer are the most cultured with the best attitude toward cultural institutions in every city. The name "Chelemer" is no longer a synonym for jokes and mockery. On the contrary: you just have to say the word "Chelemer" and it is already known that a real community worker with the old habits and the customs of the old home is before you.

With satisfaction, I will add that I am proud that my "home" was the first home for the first Chelemer. For many years my house was the first place to which the Chelemer Jew came right from the boat. My reports for *Moment* and my private actions for the first Chelemer Jews in Brazil greatly aided the emigration of Chelmer Jews to the South American lands – and mainly – to Brazil, and thus a large number, who certainly would have been victims of the Hitlerist "Moloch" and would have been still more material for his Treblinkas, Oświęcims [Auschwitz] and annihilating gas ovens.

* * *

With these lines I want to honor those Chelemer Jews who perished, who tore themselves from their thousand year old home to escape and who wretched chance willed that they fall at their cultural and communal positions, leaving after them only the soaring ash that flies securely over the world and envelopes everyone and leaves after it the most sacred memories of Chelm the city once well known to the world.

[Pages 728]

Chelemer Relief in Mexico

by Markus Jakubowicz

Translated by Gloria Berkenstat Freund

A committee of Chelemer *landsleit* exists in Mexico, whose purpose is to help the small number of surviving Jews from Chelm who were saved from the Hitlerist devils.

Members of the committee are – Eliezer Gus, Josef Groman, Itshe Kroman, Yehoshua Dichter, Haim Goldfeder and Gecl Stal. All committee members are active in this aid work.

Immediately after its creation, the first sum that they collected was 45,000 pesos. The sum of 926 dollars was sent to the New York Relief Committee that carries on much activity.

In addition to this, the committee of Chelemer *landsleit* in Mexico sent food packages and clothing for the surviving Chelemer Jews.

L.R.

Perla Safianleder (nee Rozenknopf) *

Lea Rozenknopf *

*Not in original book. Courtesy of Shlomit Beck

Perla and David Mordechai Safianleder (from the right), from left - unknown. *

Leah Rozenknopf (left) with unknown friends *

*Not in original book. Courtesy of Shlomit Beck

Leah Rozenknopf

[Pages 729]

We Plant Trees in "Forest of the Martyrs"

by Markus Jakubowicz

Translated by Gloria Berkenstat Freund

We traveled out of Tel Aviv from the *Keren Kayemet* [Jewish National Fund] Central headquarters in order to take part in planting a forest in the name of the martyrs, killed by Hitler's assassins. The bus with the Chelemer *landsleit* [people from the same city] traveled with a series of buses in which Jews from other cities were traveling. The remnants from each city traveled in a separate bus.

The bus flew, rushed, quickly and fast. We were on the road that leads to Jerusalem. We already felt fanned by the caressing, hot wind.

Here the bus made a detour and we found ourselves on a side mountain path, only just paved. Our bus moved slowly forward. Police officers stood and made sure that we did not go too fast because the road was narrow.

We came to the location of the Forest of the Martyrs. Here all of the white stones were thrust deep in the wild grass. We went to the tract of the sacred forest. The representative of *Keren Kayemet* spoke movingly, honoring the martyrs for whom the trees were being planted. The *khazan* [cantor] recited Psalms and said *Kaddish* [prayer for the dead]. From every heart tears flowed as if streaming from an avalanche. Several sobbed very loud. They remembered the annihilated. Several controlled their spasmodic crying, but tears rolled from their eyes without end. Everyone was still deep in remembrances connected to the untimely destruction of family members. Each broke a cement pot in which was found the young sapling that symbolized a particular *neshomele* [sweet soul]. The sapling *neshomele* was lowered into a prepared hole and it was covered with tear dampened earth.

We said good-bye to the sapling *neshomelekh* [plural of *neshomele*] as with living family trees and deeply sunk in our dark thoughts we went with lowered heads to the buses that would again take us over the mountains of Jerusalem back to Tel Aviv.

M. T.

[Pages 729-730]

A group of Chelemer active Zionist workers, with Moshe Lang

*Dramatic circle of the Linas-haTzedek [society to care for the sick poor] in 1934.
In the center, Josele Rozenblat.*

A group of students and teachers from the Jewish gymnazie [high school], with the Director Lipman and female teacher Cuker

Motl Alter, founder and diligent social worker from the Chelemer landsmanschaft [organization of people from the same town] in Johannesburg

A banquet dedicated to the ending of the school year 1938/39 of the Hebrew Tarbut School [secular, Hebrew language schools] in Chelm. In the photo: Teachers and social workers of the school, in the center, Mr. Josef Rolnik, now in Israel, an active worker in Agud Yotsei-Chelm [Association of the People from Chelm]

Avraham Rozenboim, the "father" of Chelemer Arbeiter Ring [Workman's Circle] in New York

Jakov Alter, a devoted worker from the Chelemer landsmanschaft in Johannesburg

Chelemer Jews – survivors in Germany – during a gathering

Leizer Sziszler, active communal worker from the Chelemer landsmanschaft in Johannesburg

Sh. Eizen and his wife, accompanied by a nurse, leave the hospital in Munich, Germany, having gone through a serious illness. They are now in Israel.

A gathering of Chelemer landsleit in Izrael

Berl Naturman, an active social worker Chelemer landsmanschaft in Canada

YIZKOR

Translated by Gloria Berkenstat Freund

[Page Gimel]

In Eternal Memory

BINSZTOK –
Moshe, Perl, Yakov, Motl.

BRENER –
Avraham, Sura.

BERGAJZER –
Pinkhus, Pesha.

GLAJZMAN –
Brukha.

GROPEN –
Yehezkeil, Zlata.

DUNIEC –
Yitzhak, Shlomoh, Temar.

DIKER –
Bajla, Moshe.

HERC –
Yakov, Ruchl.

WINER –
Dovid, Aizkik, Malka.

WEBER –
Ruchl, Leah, Yakov, Avigdor.

WARMAN –
Shlomoh (pilot in the American army).

JORPEST –
Eliezer (died in Haifa).

KAC –
Meir Ber, Yakov haKohan, Yuta, Chaya-Sura.

MARDER –
Beril, Chana.

FAJL —
Ruchl'e.

FAJGERMAN —
Moshe.

FAJERTOG —
Akiva, Shimkha, Gitl, Maryam,
Feyga, Ruchl.

FISZELZON —
Ezriel, Chana, Moshe, Leah.

ROZENBLUM —
Haim Zev (scribe) Leah, Manasha,
Yakov, Riwka, Sura.

SZERER —
Zisha, Moshe, Szaja, Cipa.

SZTAJN —
Ruwen, Malka, Gitl, Sura, Basha,
Dovid, Moshe, Gedalya, Heika,
Aizik.

SZTAJNBERG —
Ahron, Chana, Masha, Yachet,
Dovid.

New York, America 1954

May the Memory Be Eternal

Of Lipa *ben* [son of] Yehosha Herc, born in 1891, perished *el Kiddush haShem* [as a martyr] in Chelm, wintertime 1942/43. The Nazi animals tortured him intensely to death; there is no pen with which to describe his pain and suffering. Kerosene was poured into his nostrils with his head held down, his nails were pulled with pincers; he was stabbed with bayonets.

He was prominent among the Chelemer Jewish population, was one of the first philanthropists in the city, helping dozens of people in need in a quiet, modest way. He took an active part in Chelemer communal life; he was chairman of the *beis lekhem* [bread for the needy]; *linas hatzedek* [care of the sick] managing committee member, *moshav zakonim* [home for the aged], *gmiles khesed kase* [interest free loan office]; vice chairman of the council of the Jewish *kehile* in Chelm; managing committee member of the craftsworker union; chairman of the butchers union; managing committee member of the merchants union, merchants bank and for the social insurance of the Chelemer city council in his district;

Chana *bas* [daughter of] Nukhum and wife of Lipa Herc, born in 1891, perished as a martyr in Chelm on November 11th, 1942. She tragically perished with her daughter, Chaya, who was born in 1922. They were undressed and naked and the vandals shot them when they stood embracing. The first victim of our Herc family was 12-year old Feigl-Leah who was violently pulled away from her father's hands and sent to Sobibor with other children where she perished in October, 1942.

We, surviving grieving children will never forget you!

Yehoshua Herc, Montreal (Canada) and family;

Sholom Herc, Montreal (Canada) and family;

Efroim Fishl Herc (Shekhunat Borokhow in Israel) and family.

My most beloved and dearest who perished *el Kiddush haShem* [as a martyr] at the hands of the Hitlerists, *yemakh shomom* [may their names be erased]:

Father, Hersh Szporer; mother, Chana-Ita Szporer; brother, Yisroel Yankl Szporer.

Your holy memory will remain forever.

May these lines serve as a headstone for their holy souls as well as for our dear city, Chelm. May their souls be bound up in the bond of eternal life.

Ruchl Szporer-Braun
Canada.

My most beloved and dearest who perished as martyrs at the hands of the Hitlerists, may their names be erased:

Brother, Welwel Brayer, his wife, Golda and daughters, Leah and Chaya; sisters, Basha-Cwia Cwern and children; Hersh Josha and Hendl; Gitl Goldman and daughter, Hendl; Rywka Cymerman and husband, Leibush and son; sister-in-law, Basha Broyer and daughter, Feyga and Ruchl.

May these lines serve as a headstone for their holy souls as well as for our dear city, Chelm. May their souls be bound up in the bond of eternal life.

Mala Brayer-Sztajnberg

My most beloved and dearest who perished as martyrs at the hands of the Hitlerists, may their names be erased:

Daughter, Tatsha; sons, Leibl, Josef, Nusan.

Your holy memory will remain forever.

May these lines serve as a headstone for their holy souls as well as for our dear city, Chelm. May their souls be bound up in the bond of eternal life.

Parents: Shlomoh and Chana Davidson,
Canada

My most beloved and dearest who perished as martyrs at the hands of the Hitlerists, may their names be erased:

Father, Jakov Fligelman; mother, Cwia Fligelman; brothers, Josef, Shmuel-Shimkha; sisters, Frimet, Feyga.

Your holy memory will remain forever.

May these lines serve as a headstone for their holy souls as well as for our dear city, Chelm. May their souls be bound up in the bond of eternal life.

Miriam Fligelman-Szteinberg
Canada.

My most beloved and dearest who perished as martyrs at the hands of the Hitlerists, may their names be erased:

Father Yakov Szifman; mother Yochoved Szifman (Szafran); brother, Moshe Szifman; sister, Rayzl Szifman.

Your holy memory will remain forever.

May these lines serve as a headstone for their holy souls as well as for our dear city, Chelm. May their souls be bound up in the bond of eternal life.

Szifman family

My most beloved and dearest who perished as martyrs at the hands of the Hitlerists, may their names be erased:

Sisters, Chaya Grinszpan and Sheva Berger and their families, may they rest in peace.

Your holy memory will remain forever.

May these lines serve as a headstone for their holy souls as well as for our dear city, Chelm. May their souls be bound up in the bond of eternal life.

Yitzhak Eltster,
Canada.

My most beloved and dearest who perished as martyrs at the hands of the Hitlerists, may their names be erased:

Mother Slowa Boim; sisters Breyndl and Hadassah.

Your holy memory will remain forever.

May these lines serve as a headstone for their holy souls as well as for our dear city, Chelm. May their souls be bound up in the bond of eternal life.

Baras Sara amd Bare Levin
Montreal, Canada.

[Page Daled]

May the Memory Be Eternal

Of my dear mother, Beyla-Royza Frukhter, my dear sister, Pesha-Dwoyra Flik, the children, Yankele, Heykele, sister, Chaya-Sura, may the Lord avenge their blood.

Your holy memory will remain in my memory as long as I live and, until I am united with you, may these lines serves as a headstone for your holy souls.

Your, Berish

Berish Frukhter,

Montreal, Canada.

My most beloved and dearest who perished as martyrs at the hands of the Hitlerists, may their names be erased:

Mother, Rywka, daughter of Yisroel-Pesakh, sisters, Hentsha and Chana.

Your holy memory will remain forever.

May these lines serve as a headstone for their holy souls as well as for our dear city, Chelm. May their souls be bound up in the bond of eternal life.

Yisroel-Itsche Akhtman
Montreal, Canada

My most beloved and dearest who perished as martyrs at the hands of the Hitlerists, may their names be erased:

Sisters: Ester, Dwoyra, Rywka, Sura and her husband and children

Your holy memory will remain forever.

May these lines serve as a headstone for their holy souls as well as for our dear city, Chelm. May their souls be bound up in the bond of eternal life.

Josef Rojhszer,
Canada

My most beloved and dearest who perished as martyrs at the hands of the Hitlerists, may their names be erased:

Mother, Perl Welczer; brothers, Moshe, Haim, Josef; sisters, Zlata, Golda.

Your holy memory will remain forever.

May these lines serve as a headstone for their holy souls as well as for our dear city, Chelm. May their souls be bound up in the bond of eternal life.

Bat-Sheba Welczer, Canada

In holy memory of my dear mother, Zlata, of blessed memory, brothers Yekheil and Shlomoh, may the Lord avenge their blood, who perished as martyrs.

Zelig Friszman and family
Montreal, Canada

My most beloved and dearest who perished as martyrs at the hands of the Hitlerists, may their names be erased:

Father, Sholom Cymerman; mother, Mindl; sisters, Chava, Ruchl; brother, Haim.

Your holy memory will remain forever.

May these lines serve as a headstone for their holy souls as well as for our dear city, Chelm. May their souls be bound up in the bond of eternal life.

Betzalel Cymerman;
Basha Cymerman-Hirsh
Canada

My most beloved and dearest who perished as martyrs at the hands of the Hitlerists, may their names be erased:

Mother, Chaya-Chena Bas; brother, Gershon and wife, Zipa, and little daughter.

Your holy memory will remain forever.

May these lines serve as a headstone for their holy souls as well as for our dear city, Chelm. May their souls be bound up in the bond of eternal life.

Daughters: Pesa and Ester
Canada

My most beloved and dearest who perished as martyrs at the hands of the Hitlerists, may their names be erased:

Father, Yisroel Braun; mother, Rywka Leah Braun; sister, Chana Braun-Kerszenberg; brothers, Yitzhak, Ruwen, Shimeon.

Your holy memory will remain forever.

May these lines serve as a headstone for their holy souls as well as for our dear city, Chelm. May their souls be bound up in the bond of eternal life.

B. Braun
Canada

We will remember you always, our dearest and most beloved, who perished as martyrs at the hands of the murderous Hitlerists, may their names be erased, and our city, Chelm:

Father: Reb Yisroel Yakov Diment; mother: Basha

Sister: Mindl and her children;
Sister: Sheyndl and her husband and children;
Sister: Ester and her husband and children
Sister: Ruchla
Brother: Yitzhak and his wife and children

May these lines serve as a headstone for their holy souls as well as for our dear city, Chelm. May their souls be bound up in the bond of eternal life.

Shlomoh and Freyda Diment
Canada

My most beloved and dearest who perished as martyrs at the hands of the Hitlerists, may their names be erased:

Father, Yisroel, of blessed memory, son of Shabatai Yehuda, of blessed memory; mother, Sura Leah, may she rest in peace, daughter of Reb Moshe Szov, of blessed memory; brothers, Pinkhus, Leibush; sisters, Ester, Malka, Dina.

Your holy memory will remain forever.

May these lines serve as a headstone for their holy souls as well as for our dear city, Chelm. May their souls be bound up in the bond of eternal life.

Son and brother, Borukh-Nota Perlmuter
Canada

My most beloved and dearest who perished as martyrs at the hands of the Hitlerists, may their names be erased:

Father, Shmuel Ben-Tzion Micfliker, mother, Rywka, daughter of Yisroel, brothers, Mekhl and Ezra Micfliker.

Your holy memory will remain forever.

May these lines serve as a headstone for their holy souls as well as for our dear city, Chelm. May their souls be bound up in the bond of eternal life.

Yehudas Micfliker-Zylberman
Canada

My most beloved and dearest who perished as martyrs at the hands of the Hitlerists, may their names be erased:

Sister, Shasha Sznobel; brother-in-law, Haim Sznobel; sister, Beyla Trajst-Bankierer; my sister's only 14-year old gifted son, Avrahamele Bankierer.

Your holy memory will remain forever.

May these lines serve as a headstone for their holy souls as well as for our dear city, Chelm. May their souls be bound up in the bond of eternal life.

A. Trajzt, Canada

My most beloved and dearest who perished as martyrs at the hands of the Hitlerists, may their names be erased:

Brother, Leizer and his wife and children; sisters, Leah and Rywka and niece, Rywka'le and their husbands and children.

Your holy memory will remain forever.

May these lines serve as a headstone for their holy souls as well as for our dear city, Chelm. May their souls be bound up in the bond of eternal life.

Feyga Rojszer-Goldsztajn
Canada

[Page Hey]

In Holy Memory

Reb Ahron and Ruchl Sziszler, parents of Leizer and Hersh Sziszler, Zlata Landsman, Serl Hekhtman and Sura Eizen. Mother, Ruchl Sziszler died on the eve of the Hitler destruction; Ahron Sziszler perished at the hands of the Hitler murderers. Place and date, unknown

You will not be forgotten by your children: Zlata Landsman (Johannesburg); Serl Hekhtman (Australia); Sura Eizen (Israel); Leizer and Hersh Sziszler (South Africa).

May the bright memory of my dear father, Reb Ahron son of Beniamin haLevi, may the memory of a righteous person be blessed, who perished at the the murderous hands of Hitler, somewhere in Poland, the location unknown, be sanctified; of my dear sister, Chana-Doba, and her husband, Hersh Frajnd and their two little sons, of our sister, Liba, my little brother, Yitzhak'l, whom the German murderers killed at his *Bar Mitzvah*; of my dear brother-in-law, Reb Yakov Nisenboim and the entire family, of my dear sisters-in-law, Sura, Ruchl, Malka, Yehudis née Tenenboim, daughter of Reb Meir Gelcze, may the memory of a righteous person be blessed, and their husbands and children; of all my relatives, uncles, aunts, cousins, comrades, friends and acquaintances. My tears fall over their unknown graves or ashes, with boiling blood and it will never be still.

Chana Doba Sziszler-Frajnd, perished through Hitler's murderers with her husband, Hersh Frajnd and two children

Chana-Doba Sziszler-Frajnd – We grieve and mourn the dark fate of our dear sister, Chana-Doba and her dear husband, Hersh Frajnd and their two dear little sons, who the Hitler murderers annihilated before their time.

We do not know where and how they perished; we only know that they were bestially torn from us and they were pure saints along with the entire Chelemer Jewish community and the six million Jewish martyrs.

Zlata, Leizer and Hersh Sziszler, Johannesburg.

*Josele Frajnd and Itshele Sziszler,
who were killed by the Hitler murderers*

Mariam Sziszler, may she rest in peace

*Josele Frajnd and Itshele Sziszler, who were killed by the
Hitler murderers*

She was torn away in the blossoming age, about 28 years old – the good and gentle soul, the graceful, beautiful and sincere Mariam Sziszler, the daughter of Reb Pinkhus Tenenboum (Pinye Meir Gelcze's), well known Belzer Hasid in Chelm.

When Mariam Sziszler came to South Africa in 1934 to her husband, Hersh, she was young, beautiful and healthy. However, she immediately began to lament that she was afraid, was frightened that Africa was not for her.

On the first day that she set foot on African soil, Mariam Sziszler began to feel worse day by day – and finally became very ill, confined to her bed, which she, alas, never left.

At the last minute, when she was already wrestling with the Angel of Death, she called her husband, Hersh, to her and asked him to read something from his letters to her. He read accompanied by tears – and at that terrible moment, Mariam Sziszler fell into her eternal sleep.

She was beloved and valued in her former home city, Chelm. Mariam Sziszler possessed a noble character and good heart. Her dark fate wanted her to come here to die.

Always remember her good and holy soul. May her memory be blessed!

We will never forget here!

Hersh Sziszler and daughter, Rywka Setcen.

[Page Vuv]

In Memory

Let this be a *matseyve* [headstone] for our father Shimkha Ceber, of blessed memory, who died on the third day of *Khol HaMo'ed Sukkos* [the intervening days of the Feast of Tabernacles] in Chelm, 1932.

We also remember our mother, Chava Ceber, daughter, Bluma, sons, Yitzhak and Haim, and daughter, Shlomoh Ceber, wife Alta and children, Feygele and Moshele "Siedlec," Yehoshua and Feyga Rikhtszrejber and sons, Yitzhak and Haim and daughter, Leah; Shlomoh and Chana Samet; Yehoshua and Keyla Gorn and children, Haim, Yakov Dovid and Zisele.

They all perished at the hands of the Nazi murderers. We tell and teach our children that our fathers, mothers, sisters and brothers were annihilated only because they were Jews.

Remaining in grief:

Shmuel Zalman Ceber;
Yitzhak Ceber and wife and children
Melbourne, Australia

*Malka Kunczicki, may she rest in peace, and child,
martyrs of the Hitler tyranny*

I will always mourn the death of my dear mother, Malka Kunczicki, my dear father, sisters, brothers and their entire families that the Hitler murderers annihilated.

Honor their memory!

Yitzhak Kunczicki
Lod, Israel

To the Holy Memory

Of our large, many branched families in Chelm – the Ribeizen, Feldman and Goldman families that were killed at the hands of the Hitler hordes.

We will remember them forever and mourn them.

Caduk Ribeizen and wife, neé Goldman, in Australia

May their souls be bound in the bond of eternal life.

The memory of my devoted and faithfully loving mother Perl Englender, who was a very pious woman and community worker, will be eternal and unforgettable. She died in Chelm in 1938.

May this also be a *matseyve* for my brother, Leibl Englender, and his wife Rywka and sons Manish and Yitzhak, who were gassed at Sobibor; for my father-in-law, Yakov Grynberg, who died in Poland, and for my sister Etl and her son, Siomke, who perished in Treblinka; for my sister Ruchl Manat, who died in America, and for her daughter, Gitl (Gladys) who perished in Chelm with her husband, Monik Felhendler, my uncle, Shmuel, and aunt, Bluma Rozensztajn, who perished in the slaughter of Chelm.

Sura Englender

Perele Boydek, died in Johannesburg
[continued]

Chava-Sheyndl Handelsman, Yankl Handelsman

May It Be a *Matseyve*

Leizer Handelsman

For my mother, Ester Malka Handelsman, who died in Chelm in 1914; for my father, Wewtshe Handelsman, who died in 1935 in Chelm; for my sister, Yenta-Ruchl and her husband, Yankl Feldboim and their seven children, who perished in Chelm or Sobibor at the hands of the Hitler assassins; for my sister, Sura and her husband, Yisroel Binsztok, and their seven children, victims of the Nazi hangmen who annihilated them in Chelm or Sobibor; for my brother, Leizer Handelsman, and his wife and child, perished in Chelm or Sobibor, for my sister, Chava-Sheyndl, and my aunts, uncles, male and female cousins, relatives and friends, who were all murdered by the Nazi brutes. Their memory is eternally with us.

Hersh Handelsman and family

In Eternal Memory

My childhood friend, Yankl Korb, who fell as a victim of the Austrians in 1915.

There was a strong hunger in Chelm during the German occupation during the First World War. It was eight days before Purim. The occupation regime issued a decree that men and women should report for work and that they would be paid several *krone* a day.

The meeting point was near the postal administrative office. I, and many other Jews, reported for work. We were all led to an open place far outside the city, ordered to take apart the wires from the Russian positions.

When I came home, I met my friend, Yankl Korb, who told me that he would also go to work. He was waiting for me the next morning at dawn.

Again we were all taken to work. We were given the most difficult work, too difficult. The Austrian officers insulted us with the words: Dirty Jews, lazy Jews.

I parted from him late in the dark night, not knowing where he went. He was found dead eight days later.

Hersh Handelsman.

[Page Khes]

In Holy Memory!

Motl Goldman, may he rest in peace, communal worker, chairman of Chelemer Handworkers Union, synagogue warden and ORT-OZE[1] worker – perished as a martyr in Chelm

Yitzhak Garn, Yitzhak Kronzajer, Dobe Waserman (Kronzajer's wife), Ester Waserman (Garn's wife) and their children

Yakov Wajnrib, died in 1942, his wife, Brukhatshe, died in 1938

Nekhame Szwerdszarf, who was felled by a hostile bullet on the border between Poland and Russian

Moshe Rozenblum and wife with their little daughter, whom the Nazi murderers annihilated

Josef Akerman and his wife, who were shot by the German murderers in their home. Honor their memory!

[continued]

Asher Grynboim, tragically perished in the revolt at Sobibor in 1943

Malka and Moshe Geldman, perished in the gas chamber at Sobibor

Silke Nisenboim with her little daughter, who perished tragically at the hands of the Nazi assassins

[Page Tes]

May her soul be bound up in the bond of eternal life!

Leah Palman of Chelm, died in Eretz-Yisroel at the age of 81

In Eternal Memory

We immortalize our dear parents

Moshe and Malka Feldman, who tragically perished in the gas chambers of Sobibor, their sons Leizer, Eidl, Avraham, Ber, Motl and their daughters-in-law and grandchildren.

Feldman

May this be an eternal memorial for my devoted husband

Ben-Tzion

who died in New York and also my fervently loved son, who fell in the Second World War, on the battlefields of France.

Gitl Zemelman and children
(America)

Fell in Battle

Dovid Orensztajn, fell in the fight with the Hitler army

May it be an Eternal Memory to My Wife

Bat-Sheva Palman, of blessed memory

And Also My Brother

[continued]

Yissakhar Palman, who perished at the hands of the Nazis; my sister, Yokheved Gotman, died in Israel; my sister, Sura Palman, died in Israel

Yakov Palman

We will always remember

our father, Moshe Rozenblum; our mother, Freyda; our sisters, Frimet and Pesia, who perished in Chelm at the hands of the Nazi murderers; our brother, Leizer, who fell in the ranks of the Polish army.

Yehezkeil Rozenblum and family

[Page Yud]

Nekha Bakalczuk-Akslrod

Died on the 18th of Sivan, 5713, the 1st of June 1953, in Johannesburg, South Africa

It is very painful to write and simply unbelievable that cruel, merciless death tore you away. You were a bright personality, a teacher of the Jewish people, giving away your best years for the Jewish school, on behalf of the Jewish child, and to raising a healthy, young Jewish generation, inculcating the ideals of the people and their culture in them. You carried the load of school work from the first step with a great deal of idealism and saintliness. You worked with great success and appreciation between the two World Wars – in various schools, also in Melnica (Galicia), Rozyszcze (Wolyn) and 10 years in Chelm.

You, dear and unforgettable Nekha, endured all seven divisions of gehinim [hell] of the Hitlerist inquisition, losing your husband, Berl Alslrod in the Ninth Fort in Kovno, and your children, Devorah and Josele – and your old mother, Ravza – who perished in Auschwitz. In April, 1944, you lost your youngest sister, Tayba.

These torture racks of ghetto and concentration camp life in tragic circumstances devoured and gnawed away your health. Yet, ignoring your weak health, you did not want to disrupt your school work in the Lintz-Bindermichel refugee camp [in Austria] and in the Johannesburg Jewish School.

However, it was as if a ruthless and brutal death lay in wait, conquered you and cut short your ambition and striving for creative educational work.

Your holy, holiest memory is unforgettable for us!

May your memory be blessed!

Malekh Bakalczuk
Shimeon and Josef Tabachowicz

The perished Bakalczuk and Beker and their friends

May it be a *Matseyve* [Headstone]

For our unforgettable parents, Yakov and Ruchl Monczarsz and also my sisters, Rayzl, Beyla and Tziva, who all perished at the hands of the Nazi devils in Chelm.

Hersh-Josef and Rayzl Monczarsz (Monti), and children,
Johannesburg, South Africa.

Yakov Monczarsz and family, perished at the hands of the Nazi assassins, except – Pinkhas (on the right) and Moshe (on the left), who survived

Josef and Ciba Monczarsz and family – perished at the hands of the Hitler murderers

To the Holy Memory

of our devoted parents, Reb Yitzhak Najmark, may he rest in peace and Leah Najmark,

may she rest in peace, of Hrubieszow, perished at the hands of the Nazis.

Gershon, Chana Monti and children

Reb Yitzhak Najmark of Hrubieszow, may he rest in peace

Leah Najmark of Hrubieszow, may she rest in peace

> **In Bright Memory**
>
> of my brother
>
> **Yankele Najmark**
>
> and his wife and child;
>
> of my brother-in-law
>
> **Dovid Goldsztajn**
>
> and his wife and children,
> who all were annihilated by the Hitler devils.
>
> Chana and Gershon Monti and children.

Aizik Najman

This year, on November 5th, Aizik Najman, of blessed memory died suddenly in Israel in the bloom of his years.

The deceased Najman was born in Wlodawa (Poland) and received a religious-traditional upbringing and also studied in famous *yeshivus*. He married Hinda Monczarsz of Chelm, daughter of Yakov and Ruchl, and emigrated to Israel with his wife, although times were hard in the country then. He was active in *Mizrakhi* [religious Zionist] circles in Israel as he had been in the same movement in his birthplace of Wlodawa.

Aizik Najman, of blessed memory

He was religious and, at the same time, a Zionist, who strongly love his people and his country.

When the Hitlerist troops occupied Poland, the deceased's heart was full of protest against the people of the country who remained indifferent to our tragedy and did not try to save the suffering Jews.

After the liberation, when the calamity was revealed as much greater than had been imagined, Aizik Najman, of blessed memory, suffered greatly from it and on November 5th of this year, he breathed out his Jewish soul.

May his memory be holy!

Hersh-Josef Monti

Yankl Monczarsz, of Skerniewice, perished at the hands of the Hitler murderers

[Page Yud-Alef]

An Eternal Light

Berele (Krasnistower) Frajman

Josef Goldhaber, perished at the hands of the Nazis

Leibl Nisenboim, grandson of Reb Dovid Krilewer, Hasidic young man, tragically perished with his entire family

Sholom Kelner, of blessed memory

May this be a memorial for all members of our family who perished in Chelm.

A. Glaben and family

In Memory!

Pola Blas, may she rest in peace, who, while still young, was annihilated by the Hitler murderers. She will always be remembered by her surviving family members: Szekhterson, Fiszbajn, Sziszler, Eizen (Israel)

Pola Blas-Szekhterson

Reb Shlomoh Borukh Danciker of Rajwic, half of whose beard and a piece of his cheek was cut off in 1920 by Halertchikes[2] (as a joke), perished at the hands of the Hitler murderers in Dubienko with many other Jews, who were forced to dance around a fire of burning religious books and Torahs, which the Hitler animals had lit. Danciker died from great pain and heartache that broke the heart of the pious Jew.

May it be a *Matseyve*

Jan Szpajzman

For my only son, Jan Szpajzman, who perished at the hands of the Hitler animals.

I will always remember him.

Moshe Szpajzman.

Memorial

For my mother, Ester Hekhtman, my brother, Avraham Yitzhak, and his wife, Gitele, and their child; my sister, Yentl Szukhmakher, and her two little children; my sister, Golda-Masha, and her husband, Moshe Rozmaryn and child; my sister, Margola; for my uncle Avraham and aunt, Sura Krajdman and their seven children; my dear father-in-law, Ahron Sziszler, sister-in-law, Chana-Doba, Hersh and Liba Mantelmakher; brother-in-law and brother, Itshele Sziszler, who perished at the hands of the Hitler beasts.

We will remember you always and still mourn.

Serl and Leibl Hekherman.

Liba Sziszler (center) tragically perished with her brother, Itshele (left) and cousin, Yosele (right)

Chana-Doba and Hersh Frajnd with their little son, Josele, who fell as martyrs of the Hitler tyranny

In the holy, holiest memory of our Parents, brothers, sisters,
brother-in-law, sisters-in-law,
who also were tragically annihilated
in Chelm by the Nazi-Fascist hangmen.

Leah Sziszler and family
(Johannesburg, S.A.)
Brukha Garn and family
(Canada)

[Page Yud-Beth]

To the Eternal Memory

In the center, Reb Yakov Rozenknopf and his wife, Shprintsa, perished in the Sobibor death camp. The first from the right: Shlomoh Rozenknopf – perished in the Warsaw Ghetto Uprising. The last on the left: Yoel Rozenknopf, perished in the Chelm-Hrubieszow death march. His wife (above on the picture) and their two little children – perished in Sobibor.

An Eternal Light for My Annihilated Family Rozenknopf!

*The family of Gabriel Wert
All perished, except for the man and woman who are standing from right to left*

Honor their memory! They will always be remembered by their children and those close to them.

Fajga and Mordechai (Mordko) Rozenknopf
Photo Courtesy of Shlomit Beck
Not in original book

The family of Gabriel Wert
All perished, except for the man and woman who are standing from right to left

Yizkher
(Prayer said in commemoration of the dead)

I remember and will never forget my father, Menakhem Mendl, of blessed memory, who died on the 20th of Tevet 5683, 1908[3] His grave was desecrated by the Nazi bandits.

In 1920 I said good-bye to my family. To my question: "Why are you crying, Mama, I am going to *Eretz-Yisroel*." She said: "You will say *Kaddish* [memorial prayer for the dead] for me."

I consoled her that she would live to see *Moshiakh* [the Messiah].

In 1939-1945, the Fascist vandals did not exclude my entire family from their murderous orgy. I remained the only one to recite *Kaddish* for my mother, Tartsa Gotlib, my annihilated brothers, sisters, brothers-in-law, sisters-in-law, uncles, aunts, male and female cousins and so on.

[continued]

Tartsa Gotlib

I will not forget that at the hands of Fascism, that carried on a war, a third of the Jewish population perished. I sanctify the words when I say *Kaddish*: fight Fascism in all its forms, fight the inciters of war, who call for a new genocide.

W. Gotlib,[a] Austraila

Toyba Nisnboim with her friends, perished in Chelm

[Page Yud-Gimel]

Reb Shlomoh Rikhter and his family perished. His daughter – Mrs. Kelner and her children – live in South Africa.

Josef Alter, may he rest in peace

Josef Alter, the youngest and most cheerful young man, was ruthlessly torn away in his prime; he died at nearly 20 years of age. Fate wished that he be carried away from his home city of Chelm to South Africa, later to *Eretz-Yisroel*, and again to South Africa, where he became ill. His mother, Rywka, rushed to America when it was necessary, wanting to save him. However, this was not successful. He died in New York.

Honor his memory!

We will not forget our

Parents, sisters, brothers,

Comrades and friends,

Who perished during the time of the Hitler regime, may his name be erased.

Sheva and Meir Eyl and family
(Bolivia)

Let it be An Eternal Light for

Feiwl Argun

and family

H. Monti

Reb Dovid Pinker, may he rest in peace

[continued]

Leah Biderman, may she rest in peace, died in Johannesburg

Picture of relatives of the Zilberman, Beker and Winik families

Winik family: Brother, Avraham and his wife, Ruchl and four children perished; his son, Moshe survived and is in Israel. The brother, Feiwl, died in Russia.

Four Winik brothers

Eternal Memory

Parents, sisters, brothers and family

who perished in Chelm. We will remember you always!

Yisroel Feldman and wife and family
Paris, France

[Page Yud-Daled]

In Memory

Of our husband, father, grandfather,
Great grandfather

Moshe Rajkhbind, of blessed memory

**Who died in deep age
In Johannesburg, South Africa**

May his memory be blessed!

Wife Tsipora; daughter Gitl Zimelman and family (America); daughter Rikl Alter and her husband, Motl and family (Johannesburg, S.A.); daughter Sheva Winik and her husband Nakhum and family (Johannesburg, S.A.); daughter Brukha Handelsman and her husband Hersh and family (Johannesburg, S.A.); daughter Sheyndl Bajdek and her husband Berl and family (Johannesburg, S.A.); son Feiwl Rajkhbind and his wife Bina and family (Johannesburg, S.A.); son Ahron and Masha Rajkhbind and family.

May this be an eternal memorial to our brother and uncle

Leibl Monczarsz

and his wife

Chanatshe and children

Who perished at the hands of the Hitler devils.

Gershon and Hersh Josef
Monczarsz (Monti)

[continued]

Rayzl Monczarsz, perished at the hands of the Hitler murderers

Obituary notice

May it be to the memory of our
Father **Moshe Winik**

Died 20 Elul 5679 (15 September 1919)

Mother **Malka Winik**

Died on 14th of November 1929.

Nakhum and Sheva Winik
Akiva and Musha Winik

May it be An Eternal Light

For our brother

Shraga Feiwl Winik

Who died in Tashkent, during
the time of the Second World War.

For our nephew **Gecl Winik**

Who died in Tomsk.
May his memory be blessed.

Nakhum and Sheva Winik
Akiva and Musha Winik

Eternal Memorial

May it be for our brother

Avraham Najman

And his wife

Ruchl

And children:

Gecl, Temka, Surale

And Hershele

Who perished at the hands of the Hitlerist
assassins and executioners.

Nakhum and Sheva Winik
Akiva and Musha Winik
Moshe Winik

May this be a *matseyve*
For our

**Parents, sisters, brothers,
Relatives**

Who perished at the hands of the Hitler assassins.

Gershon and Perl Feldman
(Paris, France)

Martyrs from Chelm
From the right: Goldberg, Feldhendler, and Netaneil Dermon

To the Eternal Memory

[continued]

All of my dearest and closest, who tragically perished.

I shudder when I think of my mother, whom I see in my imagination.

My brother Berish, the oldest, the first in the family, was the first victim with his dear son, Nota.

My sister Gitele was so good hearted and never forgot the poor, the hungry. The Hitler murderers annihilated her and both of her children.

My dear sister-in-law Feygele was like a sister to me and to my family; everyone loved her. She always wanted to see the good in others. She was among the first victims.

My sister Surale was always suffering from need, never had enough bread. Her house was always clean. Her soul was bright. It hurts me that my dear sister perished so tragically with her children in Lublin.

My family and I will never forget you.

May your memory be blessed.

Itshe Akhtman

As a Memorial

May it be to our

**Parents, brothers, sisters, sisters-in-law, brothers-in-law
Relatives and friends**

Their memory is dear and holy!

Motl and Yakov Alter, and wives
Children and grandchildren.

Translator's footnotes:

1. ORT – the Society for Rehabilitation and Training, promoted training in skilled and agricultural areas among Jews. OZE – "Jewish Health Society" – organization promoted health and good hygiene among Jews.
2. Halertchikes were soldiers under the command of General Jozek Haller during and after the First World War, who were widely reported to be anti-Semitic and perpetrators of violence against Jews.
3. 8th of January; 5683 is actually 1923.

Original footnote:

1. W. Gotlib, of blessed memory, did not live to see the Yizkor book; he died suddenly in Melbourne.

[Pages Gimel- Yud Daled]

Necrology - Chelm, Poland

Prepared by Gloria Berkenstat Freund

Last Name	Maiden Name	First Name	Gender	Father's First Name	Mother's First Name	Spouse's First Name	Relationship to submitter	Notes	Submitter	Profession	Photo	Source Page no.
AKERMAN		Josef and wife	male					Shot by German in their home			Photo	Khes
AKHTMAN		Berish	male				brother of submitter	oldest son	Itshe Akhtman			Yud-Daled
AKHTMAN		Hana	female				sister of submitter		Yisroel-Itsche Akhtman, Montreal, Canada			Daled
AKHTMAN		Hentsha	female				sister of submitter		Yisroel-Itsche Akhtman, Montreal, Canada			Daled
AKHTMAN		Nota	male	Berish			nephew of submitter		Itshe Akhtman			Yud-Daled
AKHTMAN		Rywka	female	Yisroel-Pesakh			mother of submitter		Yisroel-Itsche Akhtman, Montreal, Canada			Daled
AKSLROD		Berl	male			Nekha		perished in the Ninth Fort in Kovno	Melakh Bakalczuk Shimoen and Josef Tabakhowicz			Tes
AKSLROD		Devorah	female	Berl	Nekha				Melakh Bakalczuk Shimoen and Josef Tabakhowicz			Tes
AKSLROD		Josele	male	Berl	Nekha				Melakh Bakalczuk Shimoen and Josef Tabakhowicz		Photo of the perished Bakalczuk and Beker families	Tes
AKSLROD	BAKALCZUK	Nekha	female			Berl		died in Johannesburg, South Africa on 1 June 1953	Melakh Bakalczuk Shimoen and Josef Tabakhowicz			Tes
ALTER		Josef			Rywka			Died at nearly age 20 in New York				Yud-Gimel
ARGUN		Feiwl and family	male						H. Monti			Yud-Gimel
BALACZUK		Rayza	female					perished in Auschwitz	Melakh Bakalczuk Shimoen and Josef Tabakhowicz			Tes
BALACZUK		Tayba	female					Perished in April 1944	Melakh Bakalczuk Shimoen and Josef Tabakhowicz			Tes
BANKIERER		Avrahamele	male				nephew of submitter		A. Trajst, Canada	14 years old		Daled
BANKIERER		Beyla	female				sister of submitter		A. Trajst, Canada			Daled
BAS		Chaya-Hena	female				mother of submitter		Pesa and Ester, Canada			Daled
BAS		Gershon	male				Brother of submitter		Pesa and Ester, Canada			Daled
BAS		young daughter	female				Niece of submitter		Pesa and Ester, Canada			Daled
BAS		Zipa	female				Sister-in-law of submitter		Pesa and Ester, Canada			Daled
BEKER		family						no indication as to who perished			Photo	Yud-Gimel
BERGAIZER		Pesha	female						New York, America 1954			Gimel
BERGAIZER		Pinkhus	male						New York, America 1954			Gimel
BERGER	ELTSTER	Sheva and family	female				sister of submitter		Yitzhak Eltster, Canada			Gimel
BIDERMAN		Leah	female					died in Johannesburg			Photo	Yud-Gimel
BINSZTOK		Moshe	male						New York, America 1954			Gimel
BINSZTOK		Motl	male						New York, America 1954			Gimel
BINSZTOK		Perl	female						New York, America 1954			Gimel
BINSZTOK		Sura	female				brother-in-law of submitter		Hersh Handelsman and family			Vuv
BINSZTOK		Yakov	male						New York, America 1954			Gimel
BINSZTOK		Yisroel	male				sister of submitter		Hersh Handelsman and family			Vuv
BLAS	SZEKHTERSON	Pola	female						Szekhterson, Fiszbajn, Sziszler and Eizen (Israel) families		Photo	Yud-Alef

Last Name	Maiden Name	First Name	Gender	Father's First Name	Mother's First Name	Spouse's First Name	Relationship to submitter	Notes	Submitter	Profession	Photo	Source Page no.
BOIM		Breyndl	female				sister of submitter		Baras Sara & Bare Levin, Montreal, Canada			Gimel
BOIM		Hadassah	female				sister of submitter		Baras Sara & Bare Levin, Montreal, Canada			Gimel
BOIM		Slowa	female				mother of submitter		Baras Sara & Bare Levin, Montreal, Canada			Gimel
BOYDEK		Perele	female					died in Johannesburg			Photo	Vuv
BRAUN		Izrael	male				father of submitter		B. Braun, Canada			Daled
BRAUN		Ruwen	male				brother of submitter		B. Braun, Canada			Daled
BRAUN		Rywka Leah	female				mother of submitter		B. Braun, Canada			Daled
BRAUN		Shimeon	male				brother of submitter		B. Braun, Canada			Daled
BRAUN		Yitzhak	male				brother of submitter		B. Braun, Canada			Daled
BRAYER		Golda	female			Welwel			Mala Brayer-Sztajnberg			Gimel
BRAYER		Haya	female	Welwel	Golda				Mala Brayer-Sztajnberg			Gimel
BRAYER		Leah	female	Welwel	Golda				Mala Brayer-Sztajnberg			Gimel
BRAYER		Welwel	male			Golda	Brother of submitter		Mala Brayer-Sztajnberg			Gimel
BRENER		Avraham	male						New York, America 1954			Gimel
BRENER		Sura	female						New York, America 1954			Gimel
BROYER (BRAYER?)		Basha	female				Sister-in-law of submitter		Mala Brayer-Sztajnberg			Gimel
BROYER (BRAYER?)		Feyga	female		Basha				Mala Brayer-Sztajnberg			Gimel
BROYER (BRAYER?)		Ruchl	female		Basha				Mala Brayer-Sztajnberg			Gimel
CEBER		Alta	female						Shmuel Zalman Ceber, Yitzhak Ceber & wife and children, Melbourne, Australia			Vuv
CEBER		Chava	female		Bluma		mother of submitter		Shmuel Zalman Ceber, Yitzhak Ceber & wife and children, Melbourne, Australia			Vuv
CEBER		Feygele	female	Shlomoh	Alta				Shmuel Zalman Ceber, Yitzhak Ceber & wife and children, Melbourne, Australia			Vuv
CEBER		Haim	male						Shmuel Zalman Ceber, Yitzhak Ceber & wife and children, Melbourne, Australia			Vuv
CEBER		Moshele "Siedlec"	male	Shlomoh	Alta				Shmuel Zalman Ceber, Yitzhak Ceber & wife and children, Melbourne, Australia			Vuv
CEBER		Shimkhah	male				father of submitter	died during the intervening day of Sukkos 1932	Shmuel Zalman Ceber, Yitzhak Ceber & wife and children, Melbourne, Australia			Vuv
CEBER		Shlomoh	male						Shmuel Zalman Ceber, Yitzhak Ceber & wife and children, Melbourne, Australia			Vuv
CEBER		Yitzhak	male						Shmuel Zalman Ceber, Yitzhak Ceber & wife and children, Melbourne, Australia			Vuv
CWERN	BRAYER	Basha-Cwia	female				sister of submitter		Mala Brayer-Sztajnberg			Gimel
CYMERMAN		Chava	female				Brother of submitter		Betzalel Cymerman, Basha Cymerman-Hirsh, Canada			Daled
CYMERMAN		Haim	male				Brother of submitter		Betzalel Cymerman, Basha Cymerman-Hirsh, Canada			Daled
CYMERMAN		Leibush	male			Rywka			Mala Brayer-Sztajnberg			Gimel
CYMERMAN		Mindl	female				mother of submitter		Betzalel Cymerman, Basha Cymerman-Hirsh, Canada			Daled
CYMERMAN		Ruchl	female				Brother of submitter		Betzalel Cymerman, Basha Cymerman-Hirsh, Canada			Daled
CYMERMAN	BRAYER	Rywka	female			Leibush	sister of submitter		Mala Brayer-Sztajnberg			Gimel
CYMERMAN		Sholem	male				father of submitter		Betzalel Cymerman, Basha Cymerman-Hirsh, Canada			Daled
DANCIKER		Shlomoh Borukh	male					of Rajwic				Yud-Alef
DAVIDSON		Josef	male	Shlomoh	Hana				Parents, Shlomoh & Hana Davidson, Canada			Gimel
DAVIDSON		Leibl	male	Shlomoh	Hana				Parents, Shlomoh & Hana Davidson, Canada			Gimel
DAVIDSON		Nusan	male	Shlomoh	Hana				Parents, Shlomoh & Hana Davidson, Canada			Gimel
DAVIDSON		Tatsha	female	Shlomoh	Hana				Parents, Shlomoh & Hana Davidson, Canada			Gimel

Last Name	Maiden Name	First Name	Gender	Father's First Name	Mother's First Name	Spouse's First Name	Relationship to submitter	Notes	Submitter	Profession	Photo	Source Page no.
DERMON		Netaniel	male								Photo	Yud-Daled
DIKER		Beyla	female						New York, America 1954			Gimel
DIKER		Moshe	male						New York, America 1954			Gimel
DIMENT		Basha	female				mother of submitter		Shlomoh & Freyda Diment, Canada			Daled
DIMENT		Ester and her husband and children	female				sister of submitter		Shlomoh & Freyda Diment, Canada			Daled
DIMENT		Mindl and her children	female				sister of submitter		Shlomoh & Freyda Diment, Canada			Daled
DIMENT		Ruchla	female				sister of submitter		Shlomoh & Freyda Diment, Canada			Daled
DIMENT		Sheyndl and her husband and children	female				sister of submitter		Shlomoh & Freyda Diment, Canada			Daled
DIMENT		Yisroel Yakov	male				father of submitter		Shlomoh & Freyda Diment, Canada			Daled
DIMENT		Yitzhak and his wife and children	male				Brother of submitter		Shlomoh & Freyda Diment, Canada			Daled
DUNIEC		Shlomoh	male						New York, America 1954			Gimel
DUNIEC		Temar	female						New York, America 1954			Gimel
DUNIEC		Yitzhak	male						New York, America 1954			Gimel
ENGLENDER		Leibl	male			Rywka	brother of submitter	gassed at Sobibor	Sura Englender			Vuv
ENGLENDER		Manish	male	Leibl	Rywka		nephew of submitter	gassed at Sobibor	Sura Englender			Vuv
ENGLENDER		Perl	female				mother of submitter	died in Chelm in 1938	Sura Englender			Vuv
ENGLENDER		Rywka	female			Leibl	Sister-in-law of submitter	gassed at Sobibor	Sura Englender			Vuv
ENGLENDER		Yitzhak	male	Leibl	Rywka		nephew of submitter	gassed at Sobibor	Sura Englender			Vuv
FAJERTOG		Akiva	male						New York, America 1954			Gimel
FAJERTOG		Feyga	female						New York, America 1954			Gimel
FAJERTOG		Gitl	female						New York, America 1954			Gimel
FAJERTOG		Maryam	female						New York, America 1954			Gimel
FAJERTOG		Ruchl	female						New York, America 1954			Gimel
FAJERTOG		Shimkah	male						New York, America 1954			Gimel
FAJGERMAN		Moshe	male						New York, America 1954			Gimel
FAJL		Ruchl'e	female						New York, America 1954			Gimel
FELDBOIM		Yankl and their seven children	male				sister of submitter		Hersh Handelsman and family			Vuv
FELDBOIM		Yenta-Ruchl	female				father of submitter		Hersh Handelsman and family			Vuv
FELDHENDLER	MANAT	Gitl (Gladys)	female	Ruchl		Monik	Niece of submitter	perished in Chelm	Sura Englender			Vuv
FELDHENDLER		Monik	male			Gitl (Glayds)	nephew (by marriage) of submitter		Sura Englender			Vuv
FELDHENDLER			male								Photo	Yud-Daled
FELDMAN		Avraham	male	Moshe	Malka			Perished in the gas chambers of Sobibor	Feldman			Tes
FELDMAN		Ber	male	Moshe	Malka			Perished in the gas chambers of Sobibor	Feldman			Tes
FELDMAN		Daughters-in-laws and their children						Perished in the gas chambers of Sobibor	Feldman			Tes
FELDMAN		Eidl	male	Moshe	Malka			Perished in the gas chambers of Sobibor	Feldman			Tes
FELDMAN		family							Caduk Ribeizen and wife, ne? Goldman, Australia			Vuv

Last Name	Maiden Name	First Name	Gender	Father's First Name	Mother's First Name	Spouse's First Name	Relationship to submitter	Notes	Submitter	Profession	Photo	Source Page no.
FELDMAN		Leizer	male	Moshe	Malka			Perished in the gas chambers of Sobibor	Feldman			Tes
FELDMAN		Malka	female			Moshe		Perished in the gas chambers of Sobibor	Feldman			Tes
FELDMAN		Moshe	male			Malka		Perished in the gas chambers of Sobibor	Feldman			Tes
FELDMAN		Motl	male	Moshe	Malka			Perished in the gas chambers of Sobibor	Feldman			Tes
FISZELZON		Chana	female						New York, America 1954			Gimel
FISZELZON		Ezriel	male						New York, America 1954			Gimel
FISZELZON		Leah	female						New York, America 1954			Gimel
FISZELZON		Moshe	male						New York, America 1954			Gimel
FLIGELMAN		Feyga	female	Jakov	Tzvia		sister of submitter		Miriam Fligelman-Szteinberg			Gimel
FLIGELMAN		Frimet	female	Jakov	Tzvia		sister of submitter		Miriam Fligelman-Szteinberg			Gimel
FLIGELMAN		Jakov	male				father of submitter		Miriam Fligelman-Szteinberg			Gimel
FLIGELMAN		Josef	male	Jakov	Tzvia		Brother of submitter		Miriam Fligelman-Szteinberg			Gimel
FLIGELMAN		Shmuel-Shimcha	male	Jakov	Tzvia		Brother of submitter		Miriam Fligelman-Szteinberg			Gimel
FLIGELMAN		Tzvia	female				mother of submitter		Miriam Fligelman-Szteinberg			Gimel
FLIK		Heykele	male				nephew of submitter		Berish, Frukhter, Montreal, Canada			Daled
FLIK	FRUKHTER	Pesha-Dwoyra	female				sister of submitter		Berish, Frukhter, Montreal, Canada			Daled
FLIK		Yankele	male				nephew of submitter		Berish, Frukhter, Montreal, Canada			Daled
FRAJMAN		Berele (Krasnistower)	male						A. Glaben and family		Photo	Yud-Alef
FRAJND		Chana-Doba	male			Hersh			Leah Sziszler and family (Johannesburg, S.A.); Brukha Garn and family (Canada)			Yud-Alef
FRAJND	SZISZLER	Chana-Doba and two sons	female			Hersh	sister of submitter		Hersh Sziszler, Johannesburg		Photo	Hey
FRAJND		Hersh	male			Chana-Doba	brother-in-law of submitter		Hersh Sziszler, Johannesburg			Hey
FRAJND		Hersh	female			Chana-Doba			Leah Sziszler and family (Johannesburg, S.A.); Brukha Garn and family (Canada)			Yud-Alef
FRAJND		Josele	male	Hersh	Chana-Doba				Leah Sziszler and family (Johannesburg, S.A.); Brukha Garn and family (Canada)			Yud-Alef
FRAJND		Yosele	male						Zlata, Leizer & Hersh Sziszler, Johannesburg		Photo	Hey
FRISZMAN		Shlomoh	male				Brother of submitter		Zelig Friszman and family, Montreal, Canada			Daled
FRISZMAN		Yeheil	male				Brother of submitter		Zelig Friszman and family, Montreal, Canada			Daled
FRISZMAN		Zlata	female				mother of submitter		Zelig Friszman and family, Montreal, Canada			Daled
FRUKHTER		Beyla-Royza	female				mother of submitter		Berish, Frukhter, Montreal, Canada			Daled
FRUKHTER		Haya-Sura	female				sister of submitter		Berish, Frukhter, Montreal, Canada			Daled
GARN	WASERMAN	Ester and her children	female			Yitzhak					Photo	Khes
GARN		Ytizhak	male			Ester Waserman					Photo	Khes
GELDMAN		Malka	female					perished in gas chamber at Sobibor			Photo	Khes
GELDMAN		Moshe	male					perished in gas chamber at Sobibor			Photo	Khes
GLAIZMAN		Brukha	female						New York, America 1954			Gimel
GOLDBERG		Feyga-Rayzl and parents	female					perished in Sobibor in 1942; survivors in Israel		textile merchants	Photo	Yud-Beth
GOLDBERG		Yakov and parents	male					perished in Sobibor in 1942; survivors in Israel		textile merchants	Photo	Yud-Beth
GOLDBERG			male								Photo	Yud-Daled
GOLDHABER		Josef	male						A. Glaben and family		Photo	Yud-Alef

Last Name	Maiden Name	First Name	Gender	Father's First Name	Mother's First Name	Spouse's First Name	Relationship to submitter	Notes	Submitter	Profession	Photo	Source Page no.
GOLDMAN		family							Caduk Ribeizen and wife, ne? Goldman, Australia			Vuv
GOLDMAN	BRAYER	Gitl	female				sister of submitter		Mala Brayer-Sztajnberg			Gimel
GOLDMAN		Hendl	female		Gitl Brayer Goldman				Mala Brayer-Sztajnberg			Gimel
GOLDMAN		Motl	male					perished in Chelm			Photo	Khes
GOLDSZTAJN		Dovid and his wife and children	male				brother-in-law of submitter		Chana and Gershon Monti and children			Yud
GORN		Haim	male	Yehoshua	Keyla				Shmuel Zalman Ceber, Yitzhak Ceber & wife and children, Melbourne, Australia			Vuv
GORN		Keyla	female						Shmuel Zalman Ceber, Yitzhak Ceber & wife and children, Melbourne, Australia			Vuv
GORN		Yakov Dovid	male	Yehoshua	Keyla				Shmuel Zalman Ceber, Yitzhak Ceber & wife and children, Melbourne, Australia			Vuv
GORN		Yehoshua	male						Shmuel Zalman Ceber, Yitzhak Ceber & wife and children, Melbourne, Australia			Vuv
GORN		Zisele	female	Yehoshua	Keyla				Shmuel Zalman Ceber, Yitzhak Ceber & wife and children, Melbourne, Australia			Vuv
GOTLIB		Menakhem Mendl	male			Tartsa	father of submitter	died on 8 January 1923	W. Gotlib, Austraila			Yud-Beth
GOTLIB		Tartsa	female			Menakhem Mendl	mother of submitter					Yud-Beth
GOTMAN	PALMAN	Yokheved	female				sister of submitter		Yakov Palman		Photo	Tes
GRINSZPAN	ELTSTER	Haya and family	female				sister of submitter		Yitzhak Eltster, Canada			Gimel
GROPEN		Yehezkeil	male						New York, America 1954			Gimel
GROPEN		Zlata	female						New York, America 1954			Gimel
GRYNBERG		Yakov	male				father-in-law of submitter		Sura Englender			Vuv
GRYNBOIM		Asher	male					Perished in revolt at Sobibor in 1943				Khes
HANDELSMAN		Chava-Sheyndl	female				sister of submitter		Hersh Handelsman and family		Photo	Vuv
HANDELSMAN		Ester Malka	female					died in 1914 in Chelm	Hersh Handelsman and family			Vuv
HANDELSMAN		Leizer, his wife and child	male				brother-in-law of submitter		Hersh Handelsman and family			Vuv
HANDELSMAN		Wewtsje	male				mother of submitter	died in 1935 in Chelm	Hersh Handelsman and family			Vuv
HANDELSMAN		Yankl	male						Hersh Handelsman and family		Photo	Vuv
HEKHTMAN		Avraham Yitzhak	male				brother of submitter		Serl and Leibl Hekhtman			Yud-Alef
HEKHTMAN		Ester	female				mother of submitter		Serl and Leibl Hekhtman			Yud-Alef
HEKHTMAN		Gitele and child	female			Avraham Yitzhak	Sister-in-law of submitter		Serl and Leibl Hekhtman			Yud-Alef
HEKHTMAN		Margola	female				sister of submitter		Serl and Leibl Hekhtman			Yud-Alef
HERC		Chana	female	Nukhum	Lipa			born 1891, perished in Chelm November 11, 1942	Yehosha Herc & Sholem Herc of Montreal, Efroim Fishl Herc of Shekhunat Borokhow, Israel			Gimel
HERC		Chaya	female	Lipa	Chana			born 1922, perished in Chelm November 11, 1942	Yehosha Herc & Sholem Herc of Montreal, Efroim Fishl Herc of Shekhunat Borokhow, Israel			Gimel
HERC		Feygl-Leah	female					perished at Sobibor, October 1942	Yehosha Herc & Sholem Herc of Montreal, Efroim Fishl Herc of Shekhunat Borokhow, Israel			Gimel
HERC		Lipa	male	Yehoshua	Chana			born 1891, perished in Chelm 1942-43	Yehosha Herc & Sholem Herc of Montreal, Efroim Fishl Herc of Shekhunat Borokhow, Israel			Gimel
HERC		Ruchl	female						New York, America 1954			Gimel
HERC		Yakov	male						New York, America 1954			Gimel
JORPEST		Eliezer	male					died in Haifa	New York, America 1954			Gimel
JOSHA	BRAYER	Hendl	female			Hersh	sister of submitter		Mala Brayer-Sztajnberg			Gimel
JOSHA		Hersh	male			Hendl			Mala Brayer-Sztajnberg			Gimel

Last Name	Maiden Name	First Name	Gender	Father's First Name	Mother's First Name	Spouse's First Name	Relationship to submitter	Notes	Submitter	Profession	Photo	Source Page no.
KAC		Haya-Sura	female						New York, America 1954			Gimel
KAC		Meir Ber	male						New York, America 1954			Gimel
KAC		Yakov haKohan	male					Kohan	New York, America 1954			Gimel
KAC		Yuta	female						New York, America 1954			Gimel
KELNER		Shlomoh	male						A. Glaben and family		Photo	Yud-Alef
KERSZENBERG	BRAUN	Chana	female				Sister of submitter		B. Braun, Canada			Daled
KORB		Yankl	male				brother of submitter	victim of Austrians in 1915	Hersh Handelsman			Vuv
KRAJDMAN		Avraham	male			Sura	uncle of submitter		Serl and Leibl Hekhtman			Yud-Alef
KRAJDMAN		Sura and seven children	female			Avraham	aunt of submitter		Serl and Leibl Hekhtman			Yud-Alef
KRONZAJER	WASERMAN	Dobe	female			Yitzhak					Photo	Khes
KRONZAJER		Yitzhak	male			Dobe Waserman					Photo	Khes
KUNCZIKCI		Malka, husband, sons and daughters	female						Yitzhak Kunczicki, Lod, Israel		Photo	Vuv
MANAT	ENGLENDER	Ruchl	female				sister of submitter	died in America	Sura Englender			Vuv
MANTELMAKHER		Chana-Doba	female				Sister-in-law of submitter		Serl and Leibl Hekhtman			Yud-Alef
MANTELMAKHER		Hersh	male						Serl and Leibl Hekhtman			Yud-Alef
MANTELMAKHER		Liba	female						Serl and Leibl Hekhtman			Yud-Alef
MARDER		Beril	male						New York, America 1954			Gimel
MARDER		Hana	female						New York, America 1954			Gimel
MICFLIKER		Ezra	male				brother of submitter		Yehudas Micfliker-Zylberman, Canada			Daled
MICFLIKER		Mekhl	male				brother of submitter		Yehudas Micfliker-Zylberman, Canada			Daled
MICFLIKER		Rywka	female	Yisroel			mother of submitter		Yehudas Micfliker-Zylberman, Canada			Daled
MICFLIKER		Shmuel Ben-Tzion	male				father of submitter		Yehudas Micfliker-Zylberman, Canada			Daled
MONCZARSZ		Beyla	female	Yakov	Ruchl			Perished in Chelm	Hersh-Josef and Rayzl Monczarsz (Monti) and children Johannesburg, South Africa		Photo: Yakov Monczarsz and family	Yud
MONCZARSZ		Chanatshe and children	female			Leibl	sister-in-law and aunt of submitters					Yud-Daled
MONCZARSZ		Ciba and family	female			Josef					Photo: Josef Monczrasz and family	Yud
MONCZARSZ		Josef	male			Ciba					Photo: Josef Monczrasz and family	Yud
MONCZARSZ		Leibl	male			Chanatshe	brother and uncle of submitters		Gershon and Hersh Josef Monczarsz (Monti)			Yud-Daled
MONCZARSZ		Rayzl	female	Yakov	Ruchl			Perished in Chelm	Hersh-Josef and Rayzl Monczarsz (Monti) and children Johannesburg, South Africa		Photo: Yakov Monczarsz and family	Yud
MONCZARSZ		Rayzl	female								Photo	Yud-Daled
MONCZARSZ		Ruchl	female			Yakov		Perished in Chelm	Hersh-Josef and Rayzl Monczarsz (Monti) and children Johannesburg, South Africa		Photo: Yakov Monczarsz and family	Yud
MONCZARSZ		Tziva	female	Yakov	Ruchl			Perished in Chelm	Hersh-Josef and Rayzl Monczarsz (Monti) and children Johannesburg, South Africa		Photo: Yakov Monczarsz and family	Yud
MONCZARSZ		Yakov	male			Ruchl		Perished in Chelm	Hersh-Josef and Rayzl Monczarsz (Monti) and children Johannesburg, South Africa		Photo: Yakov Monczarsz and family	Yud
MONCZARSZ		Yankl	male								Photo	Yud
NAJMAN		Aizik	male					November 5th of "this year" in Israel	Hersh-Josef Monti		Photo	Yud
NAJMAN		Avraham	male				brother of submitters		Nakhum and Sheva Winik; Akiva and Musha Winik; Moshe Winik			Yud-Daled
NAJMAN		Gecl	male				nephew of submitters		Nakhum and Sheva Winik; Akiva and Musha Winik; Moshe Winik			Yud-Daled

Last Name	Maiden Name	First Name	Gender	Father's First Name	Mother's First Name	Spouse's First Name	Relationship to submitter	Notes	Submitter	Profession	Photo	Source Page no.
NAJMAN		Hershele	male				nephew of submitters		Nakhum and Sheva Winik; Akiva and Musha Winik; Moshe Winik			Yud-Daled
NAJMAN		Ruchl	female				sister-in-law of submitters		Nakhum and Sheva Winik; Akiva and Musha Winik; Moshe Winik			Yud-Daled
NAJMAN		Surale	female				niece of submitters		Nakhum and Sheva Winik; Akiva and Musha Winik; Moshe Winik			Yud-Daled
NAJMAN		Temka	female				niece of submitters		Nakhum and Sheva Winik; Akiva and Musha Winik; Moshe Winik			Yud-Daled
NAJMARK		Leah	female			Yitzhak	mother of submitter	of Hrubieszow	Gershon, Chana Monti and children		Photo	Yud
NAJMARK		Yankele and his wife and child	male				brother of submitter		Chana and Gershon Monti and children			Yud
NAJMARK		Ytizhak	male			Leah	father of submitter	of Hrubieszow	Gershon, Chana Monti and children		Photo	Yud
NISENBOIM		Leibl	male					Hasid, grandson of Reb Dovid Krilewer, perished with his entire family	A. Glaben and family		Photo	Yud-Alef
NISENBOIM		Silke and her daughter	female								Photo	Khes
NISENBOIM		Yakov and entire family	male				brother-in-law of submitter		Hersh Sziszler, Johannesburg			Hey
NISNBOIM		Toyba	female					Perished in Chelm			Photo; caption:with friends	Yud-Beth
ORENSZTAJN		Dovid	male					Fell in battle			Photo	Tes
PALMAN		Bat-Sheva	female			Yakov	wife of submitter		Yakov Palman		Photo	Tes
PALMAN		Leah	female					died in Eretz-Yisroel at age 81				Tes
PALMAN		Sura	female				sister of submitter		Yakov Palman		Photo	Tes
PALMAN		Yissakhar	male				brother of submitter		Yakov Palman		Photo	Tes
PERLMUTER		Dina	female				sister of submitter		Borukh-Nota Perlmuter, Canada			Daled
PERLMUTER		Ester	female				sister of submitter		Borukh-Nota Perlmuter, Canada			Daled
PERLMUTER		Leibush	male				brother of submitter		Borukh-Nota Perlmuter, Canada			Daled
PERLMUTER		Malka	female				sister of submitter		Borukh-Nota Perlmuter, Canada			Daled
PERLMUTER		Pinkhus	male				brother of submitter		Borukh-Nota Perlmuter, Canada			Daled
PERLMUTER	SZOV	Sura Leah	female	Moshe			mother of submitter		Borukh-Nota Perlmuter, Canada			Daled
PERLMUTER		Yisroel	male	Shabatai Yehuda			father of submitter		Borukh-Nota Perlmuter, Canada			Daled
PINKER		Dovid	male								Photo	Yud-Gimel
RAJKHBIND		Moshe	male					died at very old age in Johannesburg, South Africa	Wife Tsipora; daughter Gitl Zimelman and family (America); daughter Rikl Alter and her husband, Motl and family (Johannesburg, S.A.); daughter Sheva Winik and her husband Nakhum and family (Johannesburg, S.A.); daughter Brukha Handelsman and her husband Hersh and family (Johannesburg, S.A.); daughter Sheyndl Bajdek and her husband Berl and family (Johannesburg, S.A.); son Feiwl Rajkhbind and his wife Bina and family (Johannesburg, S.A.); son Ahron and Masha Rajkhbind and family			Yud-Daled
RIBEIZEN		family							Caduk Ribeizen and wife, ne? Goldman, Australia			Vuv
RIKHTER		Shlomoh and family	male					Daughter, Mrs. Kelner and her children live in South Africa				Yud-Gimel
RIKHTSZREJBER		Feyga	female						Shmuel Zalman Ceber, Yitzhak Ceber & wife and children, Melbourne, Australia			Vuv
RIKHTSZREJBER		Haim	male	Yehoshua	Feyga				Shmuel Zalman Ceber, Yitzhak Ceber & wife and children, Melbourne, Australia			Vuv
RIKHTSZREJBER		Leah	female	Yehoshua	Feyga				Shmuel Zalman Ceber, Yitzhak Ceber & wife and children, Melbourne, Australia			Vuv
RIKHTSZREJBER		Yehoshua	male						Shmuel Zalman Ceber, Yitzhak Ceber & wife and children, Melbourne, Australia			Vuv
RIKHTSZREJBER		Yitzhak	male	Yehoshua	Feyga				Shmuel Zalman Ceber, Yitzhak Ceber & wife and children, Melbourne, Australia			Vuv
ROJHSZER		Dwoyra	female				sister of submitter		Josef Rojhszer, Canada			Daled

Last Name	Maiden Name	First Name	Gender	Father's First Name	Mother's First Name	Spouse's First Name	Relationship to submitter	Notes	Submitter	Profession	Photo	Source Page no.
ROJHSZER		Ester	female				sister of submitter		Josef Rojhszer, Canada			Daled
ROJHSZER		Leah, her husband and children	female				sister of submitter		Feyga Rojhszer-Goldsztajn, Canada			Daled
ROJHSZER		Leizer, his wife and children	male				brother of submitter		Feyga Rojhszer-Goldsztajn, Canada			Daled
ROJHSZER		Rywka	female				sister of submitter		Josef Rojhszer, Canada			Daled
ROJHSZER		Rywka, her husband and children	female				sister of submitter		Feyga Rojhszer-Goldsztajn, Canada			Daled
ROJHSZER		Rywka'la, her husband and children	female				Niece of submitter		Feyga Rojhszer-Goldsztajn, Canada			Daled
ROJSZER		Sura	female				sister of submitter, with husband and children.	Married name not given	Josef Rojhszer, Canada			Daled
ROZENBLUM		Freyda	female			Moshe	mother of submitter	perished in Chelm	Yehezkeil Rozenblum and family			Tes
ROZENBLUM		Frimet	female	Moshe	Freyda		sister of submitter	perished in Chelm	Yehezkeil Rozenblum and family			Tes
ROZENBLUM		Haim Zev	male						New York, America 1954	Scribe		Gimel
ROZENBLUM		Leah	female						New York, America 1954			Gimel
ROZENBLUM		Leizer	male	Moshe	Freyda		brother of submitter	fells in the ranks of the Polish Army	Yehezkeil Rozenblum and family			Tes
ROZENBLUM		Manasha	male						New York, America 1954			Gimel
ROZENBLUM		Moshe	male			Freyda	father of submitter	perished in Chelm	Yehezkeil Rozenblum and family			Tes
ROZENBLUM		Moshe and wife and daughter	male								Photo	Khes
ROZENBLUM		Pesia	female	Moshe	Freyda		sister of submitter	perished in Chelm	Yehezkeil Rozenblum and family			Tes
ROZENBLUM		Rywka	female						New York, America 1954			Gimel
ROZENBLUM		Sura	female						New York, America 1954			Gimel
ROZENBLUM		Yakov	male						New York, America 1954			Gimel
ROZENKNOPF		Shlomoh	male					perished in the Warsaw Ghetto uprising			Photo	Yud-Beth
ROZENKNOPF		Shprintsa	female			Yakov		perished at Sobibor			Photo	Yud-Beth
ROZENKNOPF		Yakov	male			Shprintsa		perished at Sobibor			Photo	Yud-Beth
ROZENKNOPF		Yoal and wife and 2 children	male					Yoal perished in the Chelm-Hrubieszow death march; his wife and children perished at Sobibor			Photo	Yud-Beth
ROZENSZTAJN		Bluma	female			Shmuel	aunt of submitter		Sura Englender			Vuv
ROZENSZTAJN		Shmuel	male			Bluma	uncle of submitter		Sura Englender			Vuv
ROZMARYN		Golda-Masha	female			Moshe	sister of submitter		Serl and Leibl Hekhtman			Yud-Alef
ROZMARYN		Moshe	male			Golda-Masha	brother-in-law of submitter		Serl and Leibl Hekhtman			Yud-Alef
SAMET		Chana	female						Shmuel Zalman Ceber, Yitzhak Ceber & wife and children, Melbourne, Australia			Vuv
SAMET		Shlomoh	male						Shmuel Zalman Ceber, Yitzhak Ceber & wife and children, Melbourne, Australia			Vuv
SZERER		Cipa	female						New York, America 1954			Gimel
SZERER		Moshe	male						New York, America 1954			Gimel
SZERER		Szaja	male						New York, America 1954			Gimel
SZERER		Zisha	?						New York, America 1954			Gimel
SZIFMAN		Moshe	male	Yakov	Yochoved		Brother of submitter		Szifman family			Gimel
SZIFMAN		Rayzl	female	Yakov	Yochoved		sister of submitter		Szifman family			Gimel
SZIFMAN	SZAFRAN	Yakov	male				father of submitter		Szifman family			Gimel

Last Name	Maiden Name	First Name	Gender	Father's First Name	Mother's First Name	Spouse's First Name	Relationship to submitter	Notes	Submitter	Profession	Photo	Source Page no.
SZIFMAN		Yochoved	female				mother of submitter		Szifman family			Gimel
SZISZLER		Ahron	male				father-in-law of submitter		Serl and Leibl Hekhtman			Yud-Alef
SZISZLER		Itshele	male						Zlata, Leizer & Hersh Sziszler, Johannesburg		Photo	Hey
SZISZLER		Itshele	male				brother and brother-in-law of submitters		Serl and Leibl Hekhtman		Photo	Yud-Alef
SZISZLER		Liba	female				sister of submitter		Hersh Sziszler, Johannesburg			Hey
SZISZLER		Liba	female						Leah Sziszler and family (Johannesburg, S.A.); Brukha Garn and family (Canada)		Photo	Yud-Alef
SZISZLER		Malka and husband and children	female				Sister-in-law of submitter		Hersh Sziszler, Johannesburg			Hey
SZISZLER	TENENBOIM	Mariam	female	Pinkhus Tenenboim		Hersh		died in South Africa	Hersh Sziszler and daughter, Rywka Setcen		Photo	Hey
SZISZLER		Reb Ahron	male	Beniamin haLevi			father of submitter		Hersh Sziszler, Johannesburg		Photo	Hey
SZISZLER		Ruchl	female				mother of submitter	Died "on eve of Hitler destruction"	Hersh Sziszler, Johannesburg		Photo	Hey
SZISZLER		Ruchl and husband and children	female				Sister-in-law of submitter		Hersh Sziszler, Johannesburg			Hey
SZISZLER		Sura and husband and children	female				Sister-in-law of submitter		Hersh Sziszler, Johannesburg			Hey
SZISZLER	TENENBOIM	Yehudis and husband and children	female	Meir Gelcze			Sister-in-law of submitter		Hersh Sziszler, Johannesburg			Hey
SZISZLER		Yitzhak'l	male				Brother of submitter	killed at his Bar Mitzvah	Hersh Sziszler, Johannesburg			Hey
SZNOBEL		Haim	male				brother-in-law of submitter		A. Trajst, Canada			Daled
SZNOBEL	TRAJST	Shasha	female				sister of submitter		A. Trajst, Canada			Daled
SZPAJZMAN		Jan	male	Moshe			father of submitter	only son	Moshe Szpajzman			Yud-Alef
SZPORER		Hana-Ita	female						Ruchl Szporer-Braun of Canada			Gimel
SZPORER		Hersh	male						Ruchl Szporer-Braun of Canada			Gimel
SZPORER		Israel Jankl	male	Hersh	Chana-Ita				Ruchl Szporer-Braun of Canada			Gimel
SZTAJN		Aizik	male						New York, America 1954			Gimel
SZTAJN		Basha	female						New York, America 1954			Gimel
SZTAJN		Dovid	male						New York, America 1954			Gimel
SZTAJN		Gedalya	male						New York, America 1954			Gimel
SZTAJN		Gitl	female						New York, America 1954			Gimel
SZTAJN		Heika	?						New York, America 1954			Gimel
SZTAJN		Malka	female						New York, America 1954			Gimel
SZTAJN		Moshe	male						New York, America 1954			Gimel
SZTAJN		Ruwen	male						New York, America 1954			Gimel
SZTAJN		Sura	female						New York, America 1954			Gimel
SZTAJNBERG		Ahron	male						New York, America 1954			Gimel
SZTAJNBERG		Dovid	male						New York, America 1954			Gimel
SZTAJNBERG		Hana	female						New York, America 1954			Gimel
SZTAJNBERG		Masha	female						New York, America 1954			Gimel
SZTAJNBERG		Yachet	female						New York, America 1954			Gimel
SZUKHMAKHER		Yentl and two children	female				sister of submitter		Serl and Leibl Hekhtman			Yud-Alef
SZWERDSZARG		Nekhame	female					felled by bullet on border between Poland and Russia				Khes

Last Name	Maiden Name	First Name	Gender	Father's First Name	Mother's First Name	Spouse's First Name	Relationship to submitter	Notes	Submitter	Profession	Photo	Source Page no.
WAJNRIB		Brukhatshe	female					died in 1938			Photo	Khes
WAJNRIB		Yakov	male				friend of submitter	died in 1942			Photo	Khes
WARMAN		Shlomoh	male					Pilot in American Army	New York, America 1954			Gimel
WEBER		Avigdor	male						New York, America 1954			Gimel
WEBER		Leah	female						New York, America 1954			Gimel
WEBER		Ruchl	female						New York, America 1954			Gimel
WEBER		Yakov	male						New York, America 1954			Gimel
WELCZER		Golda	female				sister of submitter		Bat-sheba Welczer, Canada			Daled
WELCZER		Haim	male				Brother of submitter		Bat-sheba Welczer, Canada			Daled
WELCZER		Josef	male				Brother of submitter		Bat-sheba Welczer, Canada			Daled
WELCZER		Moshe	male				brother of submitter		Bat-sheba Welczer, Canada			Daled
WELCZER		Perl	female				mother of submitter		Bat-sheba Welczer, Canada			Daled
WELCZER		Zlata	female				sister of submitter		Bat-sheba Welczer, Canada			Daled
WERT		family of Gabriel									Photo	Yud-Beth
WINER		Aizik	male						New York, America 1954			Gimel
WINER		Dovid	male						New York, America 1954			Gimel
WINER		Malka	female						New York, America 1954			Gimel
WINIK		Avraham	male			Ruchl						Yud-Gimel
WINIK		family						no indication as to who perished			Photo	Yud-Gimel
WINIK		Feiwl						died in Russia			Photo	Yud-Gimel
WINIK		Gecl	male				nephew of submitters		Nakhum and Sheva Winik; Akiva and Musha Winik			Yud-Daled
WINIK		Malka	female			Moshe	mother of submitter	died 14 November 1929	Nakhum and Sheva Winik; Akiva and Musha Winik			Yud-Daled
WINIK		Moshe	male			Malka	father of submitter	died 15 September 1919	Nakhum and Sheva Winik; Akiva and Musha Winik			Yud-Daled
WINIK		Ruchl and four children	female			Avraham		son, Moshe survived and is in Israel			Photo	Yud-Gimel
WINIK		Shraga Feiwl	male				brother of submitters		Nakhum and Sheva Winik; Akiva and Musha Winik			Yud-Daled
WINIK											Photo; caption: four Winik brothers	Yud-Gimel
ZEMELMAN		Ben-Tzion	male			Gitl		Fell in France during the Second World War	Gitl Zemelman and children (America)			Tes
ZILBERMAN		family						no indication as to who perished			Photo	Yud-Gimel
	ENGLENDER	Etl	female				sister of submitter		Sura Englender			Vuv
	AKHTMAN	Gitele and two children	female				sister of submitter		Itshe Akhtman			Yud-Daled
		Siomke	male	Etl			nephew of submitter		Sura Englender			Vuv
	AKHTMAN	Surale and children	female				sister of submitter	perished in Lublin	Itshe Akhtman			Yud-Daled

NAME INDEX

Note: the Necrology names on pages 587 through 596 are not included in this index

A

Achtman, 126, 145, 383, 528
Adamchyk, 259
Ador, 526
Ahrun, 7, 9, 17
Ailiwicki, 351
Ajzen, 233
Ajzenshtein, 107
Akerman, 102, 554
Akhtman, 168, 169, 172, 173, 174, 414, 418, 422, 526, 528, 541, 586
Aks, 52, 74, 161, 394
Akselrad, 135, 137
Akselrod, 121, 122
Akslrad, 69, 245, 246
Akslrod, 79, 185, 186, 187, 188, 348, 559
Alecheim, 172, 339
Alegant, 414
Aleksandrovich, 305
Alergand, 173
Alias, 158
Alkvit, 353
Alkwit, 472, 516
Alkwut, 280
Alster, 134
Alter, 108, 125, 133, 211, 259, 320, 438, 439, 445, 448, 451, 492, 493, 494, 495, 497, 502, 534, 535, 577, 582, 586
Amindov, 161
Anisfeld, 152, 153
Apelboim, 264
Apelcwajg, 118, 123
Arbuz, 108
Argun, 351, 578
Arlan, 497
Arnsztajn, 38, 158
Arnsztayn, 156
Arnsztejn, 154
Aronovytsh, 10
Asch, 84
Ashendorf, 55
Ashkenazi, 201
Ashkhanazy, 17
Ashkhnazy, 18
Aszendorf, 197
Atlas, 127, 134, 189, 374, 375, 377, 380
Auerbak, 208
Ausubel, 352, 516
Auyerbakh, 17
Aydelsh, 18
Aynbinder, 289
Ayzen, 356

B

Ba'al Shem Tov, 132
Baguszewski, 507
Baigel, 102
Bajdek, 582
Bakalacz, 118
Bakalar, 49, 138
Bakalarz, 105
Bakalczuk, 1, 2, 67, 137, 246, 414, 500, 501, 559
Bakalczyk, 394, 405
Bakaliar, 133, 151
Bakalosz, 522
Bakatshuk, 471
Bakszt, 134
Balaban, 95, 227, 231, 311
Baliar, 269, 270
bal-Shem, 520
Bal-Shem, 479
Balyar, 134
Bankierer, 545
Bankirer, 100, 102, 105, 106, 523
Barenholc, 154
Barg, 69, 114, 124, 179, 347
Barnholc, 383
Bas, 16, 408, 543
Bash, 134, 412
Bashlegers, 319
Bas-Meltser, 408
Bas-Meltzer, 16
Basz, 350
Batashansky, 150
Bauer, 464
Baum, 69, 111, 114, 118, 119, 126, 350
Baumgold, 69
Beck, 81, 479, 521, 531, 573
Beckman, 434
Becks, 518
Beder, 249
Bejrekh, 522
Bek, 168
Beker, 1, 3, 62, 67, 69, 77, 111, 114, 116, 117, 118, 119, 120, 122, 125, 127, 128, 135, 137, 155, 158, 161, 162, 178, 179, 183, 185, 186, 188, 247, 261, 310, 320, 330, 344, 345, 401, 479, 579
Bekerin, 477
Beler, 438
bel-Shem, 201, 473
Bel-Shem, 17
Ben-Ahron, 271, 310, 493
Ben-Shmeuni, 116

Ber, 114, 125, 126, 131, 150, 195, 312, 330, 344, 463, 465, 523, 536, 556
Berele, 97, 98, 252, 350, 360, 383, 385, 564
Bereles, 98
Berenfeld, 126
BERGAJZER, 536
Berger, 106, 438, 445, 448, 493, 540
Bergman, 72, 95, 129, 258
Bergson, 29, 30
Berish, 69, 109, 111, 141, 190, 248, 249, 322, 325, 341, 342, 357, 386, 468, 476, 494, 503, 541, 586
Berl, 31, 33, 48, 58, 69, 79, 108, 121, 122, 135, 137, 145, 147, 161, 167, 177, 185, 186, 187, 188, 190, 191, 194, 245, 246, 319, 342, 351, 376, 413, 487, 535, 582
Berland, 82, 194, 413, 514, 523, 525, 526
Berman, 118, 188
Bernard, 239
Bernfeld, 126, 148, 197, 351
Bernshtayn, 16
Bernshteyn, 465
Bernsztein, 152
Beyle, 317, 320, 333, 353, 354, 383
Bialablacki, 154
Biale, 150, 493
Bialekman, 465
Bialik, 310
Bibel, 118, 123, 134, 135, 413
Bibkowski, 39
Bibl, 186, 346
Biderman, 39, 51, 68, 69, 70, 121, 150, 161, 168, 177, 192, 230, 309, 381, 396, 405, 412, 415, 438, 494, 497, 503, 579
Bielakov, 98
Bieler, 439, 445, 446
Bilen, 123
Bimko, 172
Binshtok, 329
Binsztok, 77, 100, 102, 111, 123, 165, 166, 295, 302, 392, 398, 404, 413, 433, 459, 499, 504, 509, 510, 525, 526, 552
BINSZTOK, 536
Birman, 294, 297
Birnbaum, 295
Blajer, 508, 514
Blas, 568
Blatt, 438
Blekhermakher, 356, 424
Bloch, 140, 384, 386
Blojer, 509
Blok, 154, 185
Blum, 280, 353, 452
Blumenfeld, 152
Blumenschtrauch, 147
Blumenshteyn, 463
Blumenshtrauch, 147
Blumensztok, 247
Blumensztraud, 72
Blumensztrochs, 350
Blumensztrof, 154
Blumshteyn, 465
Bobes, 522
Boguszewski, 131
Bohrman, 440
Boim, 145, 173, 174, 540
Bojdek, 497
Bojm, 99, 100, 106, 133, 141, 186
Bojmgold, 131
Bok, 343
Boksenbaum, 404
Boksnboym, 468
Boldman, 499
Borenshtein, 142
Bornshtein, 134
Bornshteyn, 318
Bornsztajn, 80, 125, 191, 351
Borochov, 112, 114, 115, 121, 124, 125, 344, 346
Borokhov, 195
Borokhow, 228, 274, 538
Bostamki, 41
Botwin, 167, 511, 512
Boyarski, 142, 145, 147
Boydek, 551
Brajtman, 85, 247, 248
Bramiler, 404
Brand, 123, 464
Brandes, 239
Braun, 538, 543
Braunmiller, 55
Brayer, 460, 471, 538, 539
Brayfman, 359
Brejtman, 499
Brekher, 173
BRENER, 536
Breytman, 323
Brik, 118, 123, 128
Brilant, 52
Brod, 11, 18, 32
Brofman, 98
Bron, 508, 509
Bronshteyn, 463
Broyer, 538
Bruker, 87, 88, 161, 374, 375
Brustman, 190, 191, 194, 404, 405, 413, 414, 468
Brustyn, 16
Bubes, 413
Bubis, 468
Bubys, 403, 404, 405
Buchbleter, 69
Bukhna, 179
Bukler, 101, 145, 147
Buksbaum, 125
Buksboim, 135, 136
Buksboym, 346
Bund, 46, 47, 65, 91, 95, 96, 97, 98, 100, 101, 102, 103, 104, 105, 106, 107, 108, 109, 110, 112, 117, 133, 134, 140, 149, 152, 167, 179, 183, 193, 195, 217, 219, 220, 222, 224, 227, 230, 274, 352, 357, 388, 473, 479
Burshtok, 320
Bursztajn, 161, 194
Bursztin, 179
Bursztyn, 69, 191
Butman, 523
Butrymovytsh, 12
Buxenboim, 413
Bysko, 9

C

Ceber, 123, 277, 523, 524, 525, 526, 549
Cederboim, 522, 523
Celeminski, 108
Celnik, 165
Celniker, 494
Chaplin, 31, 33
Chelemer, 2, 3, 4, 21, 28, 32, 33, 38, 41, 42, 45, 47, 51, 52, 53, 62, 64, 65, 70, 85, 86, 87, 88, 89, 95, 112, 113, 114, 115, 116, 124, 128, 150, 157, 159, 162, 165, 166, 167, 168, 169, 170, 180, 181, 183, 189, 191, 192, 193, 196, 198, 199, 202, 207, 208, 209, 210, 213, 214, 215, 217, 227, 228, 229, 231, 232, 233, 234, 245, 247, 248, 249, 250, 251, 252, 253, 255, 258, 261, 262, 264, 265, 271, 272, 274, 275, 276, 279, 294, 296, 301, 302, 305, 309, 310, 311, 314, 315, 321, 341, 348, 349, 350, 352, 360, 373, 374, 375, 378, 379, 386, 392, 393, 395, 396, 397, 398, 399, 400, 401, 403, 408, 459, 465, 467, 468, 469, 470, 472, 473, 474, 477, 479, 483, 491, 492, 493, 494, 495, 496, 497, 498, 499, 500, 501, 502, 503, 504, 505, 506, 507, 508, 509, 510, 511, 512, 513, 514, 515, 516, 517, 518, 519, 520, 521, 523, 524, 525, 526, 527, 528, 529, 530, 532, 533, 534, 535, 537, 547, 554
Chelmo, 131
Chmelnitski, 166
Chmielnicki, 201, 204, 206, 214
Churchill, 221, 224
Ciberman, 451
Cikel, 173, 174
Cikl, 126, 252
Cimerman, 124
Citrin, 58, 112, 197
Cohen, 444, 448, 449, 450
Cozzack, 272
Cuker, 152, 534
Cwern, 538
Cwiling, 383
Cygelman, 82
Cykerman, 272
Cymerman, 190, 295, 351, 514, 522, 538, 542
Cymryn, 403, 404
Cytrin, 477
Czar Nikolai, 165, 265, 266, 301
Czarnecki, 87
Czechowicz, 126
Czesner, 509, 514

D

Dajmowicz, 522
Danciker, 569
Dantsiker, 98
Davidson, 1, 158, 159, 160, 539
Dawidzon, 79
Dech, 403
Delitzsch, 206
Delmedigo, 288
Dembicer, 21
Denkop, 528
Derfer, 414
Derman, 74, 82
Dermon, 585

Dichter, 530
Diker, 126, 172, 250
DIKER, 536
Diment, 111, 528, 544
Dinezon, 133
Dinitc, 69
Distler, 113, 229
Dmowski, 212
Dorman, 470
Dreksler, 69, 99, 100, 102, 111, 126, 142, 147, 148, 162, 197, 250, 323, 351, 492, 509
Dresler, 479
Dreszer, 405
Dreyfus, 239, 521
Drimlcr, 69
Droyanov, 205
Druker, 438, 451, 452
Dua, 111, 147
Dubelman, 275
Duber, 21
Dubkova, 481
Dubkovski, 195, 359
Dubkowska, 123, 126, 137, 250
Dubkowski, 95, 147, 197, 250, 416, 479
Dubkowskis, 350
Dublman, 509
Dubno, 10, 129, 312
Dubnow, 129, 231, 234, 236, 314, 497
Dumkop, 194, 522
DUNIEC, 536
Dunkan, 274
Dvorzshetsky, 20
Dyk, 20
Dyn, 272
Dzehigon, 27

E

Ebri, 162
Edelshtein, 141
Edelsztajn, 118
Eden, 290, 474, 516
Edlsztajn, 528
Eichel, 210
Eichenboim, 205
Eidels, 202
Eidl, 63, 201, 556
Eisen, 424
Eizen, 524, 525, 535, 546, 568
Eizenberg, 157
Eizensztat, 116, 125
Ejzen, 514
Elboim, 152, 167, 511
Elcter, 124, 127
Elster, 118, 119
Eltster, 540
Elye, 102, 106, 320, 321
Elzter, 118
Emdin, 201, 202, 287
Emdyn, 17
Engel, 243, 522
Englender, 484, 551

Eplboim, 521, 522, 523
Erlich, 108
Erlikh, 241, 265, 318, 322, 519
Erlikhs, 321
Ervri, 117
Erwi, 179, 180, 181, 182, 183, 184, 185
Ettinger, 205, 344
Evri, 60, 61, 114, 116, 117, 128, 136, 158
Evris, 147
Evry, 82, 102
Eydlshteyn, 316
Eyl, 577

F

Fainsztok, 460
Fajerman, 494
Fajertog, 514
FAJERTOG, 537
Fajfer, 526
Fajgboim, 516
FAJGERMAN, 537
FAJL, 537
Fartaszne, 350
Fasz, 258
Faygbaum, 402
Feder, 113, 173, 174, 355, 514
Feldboim, 552
Feldhendler, 194, 434, 487, 585
Feldman, 52, 55, 72, 82, 111, 118, 125, 126, 147, 161, 162, 519, 522, 550, 556, 581, 585
Feldmois, 382
Feldmus, 522
Feldsher, 147
Felhandler, 322
Felhendler, 77, 551
Felin, 1, 2
Fensterblau, 47, 101, 103, 104, 105, 106, 130, 357
Festytsh, 9
Feterzajl, 117
Feterzeil, 183
Figlosz, 194
Finkelshtein, 141
Finkelsztajn, 179
Finker, 373
Finklsztajn, 69
Finlsztajn, 69
Firszt, 522, 523
Firt, 439
Fischer, 29, 463
Fisher, 51, 55, 139, 344
Fiszbajn, 123, 568
Fiszboim, 193
Fiszelson, 166, 507
FISZELZON, 537
Fiszer, 45, 123, 402
Fiszlson, 162
Flajsher, 105
Flajszer, 99, 102
Flaksman, 492
Fleg, 239
Fligelman, 539

Flik, 541
Flug, 509
Foyas, 96, 98
Frajberger, 405
Frajman, 382, 383, 384, 386, 564
Frajnd, 522, 546, 547, 548, 571
Frank, 2, 393, 397
Frankel, 405, 411, 412
Frankl, 69
Freederickzs, 307
Freiberger, 438
Frenkel, 102, 131, 396, 414, 415, 438, 440, 444, 445, 446, 448, 450, 451, 452, 460, 461
Frenkl, 118
Freud, 29, 30
Frid, 45, 46, 49, 82, 85, 87, 116, 125, 128, 208, 311, 344, 345
Fridling, 320
Fried, 95, 96, 97, 98, 101, 108, 133, 136, 137, 150
Friedman, 107, 150
Frishman, 150, 345
Friszman, 154, 161, 300, 542
Frucht, 112, 125, 126
Fruchter, 528
Fruchtgartn, 101, 103, 105, 106, 193
Fructgartn, 69, 179
Frukht, 344
Frukhter, 541
Frukhtgartn, 183, 196
Fryd, 67, 95, 196, 252, 253, 273, 274, 383
Frydman, 6, 69, 232
Fryszman, 528
Fuks, 438, 445, 448, 451
Furer, 143
Furman, 341, 342, 343
Furt, 446
Fus, 403
Fybysh, 10

G

Galik, 127
Gamulke, 373
Ganslowski, 435
Gantz, 475
Garn, 554, 571
Gebirtog, 526
Gecele, 299
Geiger, 206
Gelber, 205
Gelbord, 438
Gelcze, 546, 548
Gelczer, 244
Geldman, 555
Gelenter, 97
Geliber, 205
Geltshes, 327
Genik, 56
Gershonson, 27
Gerstajn, 438
Gerszt, 492
Gertner, 137
Getc, 492

Gewant, 374
Gikhman, 342
Gilboa, 521
Gingold, 463, 465
Ginsberg, 21
Glaben, 519, 567
GLAJZMAN, 536
Glas, 321
Glatshteyn, 516
Glatstein, 355
Glatsztajn, 348
Glazman, 125
Glezer, 322, 323, 324
Glincman, 125
Glintsman, 134, 142
Globen, 119, 497, 498
Globn, 249
Globoznik, 2
Gobel, 522
Goebbels, 362
Goerings, 362
Gojwaser, 194
Goldbaum, 77, 126, 128
Goldberg, 69, 72, 82, 85, 95, 147, 161, 196, 211, 239, 249, 343, 400, 401, 479, 585
Goldboim, 351
Goldbojm, 134
Goldfarb, 274
Goldfeder, 522, 530
Goldfeld, 134, 301
Goldgevikht, 193
Goldgewikht, 249
Goldhaber, 87, 126, 145, 147, 197, 249, 476, 565
Goldhar, 124, 264, 265, 322
Goldhocher, 350
Goldman, 52, 82, 89, 161, 194, 196, 351, 373, 374, 403, 424, 468, 469, 471, 514, 526, 538, 550, 554
Goldrajch, 60, 61, 62, 67, 112, 116, 124, 125
Goldrajkh, 87, 188
Goldraykh, 345, 479
Goldreich, 137
Goldrelch, 131
Goldsobel, 519
Goldstajn, 413
Goldsztajn, 68, 351, 545, 562
Gomulka, 137
Gordin, 145, 190
Gordon, 172, 206, 210
Goren, 445, 451
Gorin, 438
Gorky, 343
Gorlovski, 287
Gorn, 63, 320, 549
Gorodetsky, 13
Goron, 438
Gotfarsztajn, 28, 33
Gotlib, 111, 123, 162, 163, 352, 523, 524, 525, 526, 574, 575, 586
Gotlieb, 99
Gotman, 558
Grabaski, 156
Graber, 99

Grabski, 168, 504, 512, 521
Grabskis, 518
Grajdinger, 198
Greber, 145, 147, 248, 249
Gretschus, 434
Grigorevich, 305
Grinbaum, 124
Grinberg, 49, 119, 143, 325
Grinbojm, 102
Grinman, 52, 77
Grinszpan, 399, 540
Gris, 239
Grodzicki, 258
Grofman, 249
Groman, 530
GROPEN, 536
Gros, 150, 349
Groser, 100, 105, 106, 107, 108, 149
Groskop, 392
Gross, 319, 416
Grosser, 45
Grozinski, 131
Grunwald, 382, 386
Grynberg, 193, 271, 551
Grynboim, 229, 555
Grynwald, 194
Gus, 530
Gut, 135, 180, 183, 413
Guterman, 102, 103, 106, 363, 376
Gutfraynd, 154
Gutharc, 514
Gutman, 116, 124, 126, 128, 134
Gyntsburg, 18

H

Haftacz, 94
Haga, 412
Hager, 460
Hakatan, 325, 327
Hakhsztajn, 523
Halevy, 18
Haller, 113, 228, 309, 324, 351, 586
Halperin, 150, 158
Halpern, 154
Handelman, 194
Handelsman, 102, 105, 106, 131, 189, 190, 191, 193, 493, 494, 497, 500, 552, 553, 582
Handlsman, 80, 322
Haranczik, 338, 341
Harkavy, 311
Harsh's, 325
Hausman, 80
Hauzman, 69
Haylperyn, 18
Hecman, 108
Hedfings, 29
Heftman, 101, 103
Heidrich, 2
Heker, 29
Hekherman, 570
Hekhtman, 546, 570

Heldhas, 409
Heler, 152, 153, 299
Helfbajn, 79
Helfenbein, 134, 143
Helfer, 145, 147, 173, 377, 378, 383
Helfman, 70
Helga, 398
Helper, 351
Hendel, 123
Hendl, 197, 319, 538
Hendler, 479
Henes, 216
Her, 16, 104, 144, 246, 262, 263, 317, 318, 320, 321, 322, 338, 363, 364, 367, 404, 416, 420, 549, 586
Herc, 126, 162, 172, 173, 177, 240, 251, 376, 381, 514, 528, 537, 538
HERC, 536
Hercberg, 159, 194
Hercman, 122, 499
Herman, 55, 210, 522
Hersh, 4, 12, 64, 86, 87, 89, 102, 106, 118, 128, 143, 150, 166, 189, 190, 193, 196, 211, 241, 243, 247, 248, 250, 272, 299, 303, 310, 311, 320, 323, 332, 372, 373, 383, 404, 413, 414, 468, 492, 493, 494, 500, 522, 538, 546, 547, 549, 552, 553, 560, 563, 570, 571, 582
Hershom, 108
Herszberg, 377
Herszhorn, 72
Hertc, 508, 509
Herts, 322, 471
Hertz, 129, 139, 142, 145, 147, 239, 323, 351
Herzl, 162, 163, 205, 209, 211, 309
Hilfnbeyn, 287
Hindes, 319, 359
Hipshman, 99, 100, 133, 135
Hipszman, 69, 111, 113, 114, 118, 121, 122, 124, 179, 185, 186, 229, 272
Hirsh, 113, 139, 201, 206, 210, 272, 319, 323, 356, 542
Hirshbein, 145, 172
Hirshben, 294
Hirshbeyn, 323
Hirszfeder, 161
Hirzh, 330
Hitler, 2, 3, 34, 51, 54, 55, 67, 69, 72, 77, 79, 88, 94, 108, 129, 130, 140, 147, 149, 161, 167, 168, 184, 185, 188, 239, 240, 243, 245, 251, 253, 254, 259, 262, 266, 267, 268, 270, 271, 273, 274, 299, 302, 373, 375, 378, 384, 386, 392, 393, 395, 398, 402, 407, 417, 452, 453, 471, 472, 474, 475, 477, 495, 498, 499, 532, 546, 547, 548, 550, 560, 562, 569, 570, 571, 577, 582, 583, 585, 586
Hiz, 398
Hkhahn, 17
Hkhhan, 18
Hochgelernter, 203
Hochgraf, 72
Hochman, 91, 120, 393, 430, 431
Hoizman, 194, 529
Hokhman, 244, 245
Holovetsh, 317
Hopszman, 188, 196
Hoptasz, 350
Horodler, 195, 325

Hos, 424
Housman, 191, 192
Houzman, 191, 193
Huberman, 152
Hull, 516
Humboldin, 204
Huz, 72, 77

I

Icykowicz, 89, 194
Ide, 317, 318, 343
Ilewitski, 145
Ilivitsky, 291
Iliwicki, 121, 122, 186
Ilywicki, 172
Imeretinsky, 207
Itshe, 42, 52, 53, 126, 145, 147, 158, 168, 169, 172, 177, 195, 252, 291, 319, 322, 331, 332, 351, 359, 373, 507, 522, 523, 526, 528, 530, 586
Ivinska, 219
Ivre, 363, 460
Ivri, 318, 322
Izbicer, 183
Izhbitser, 318

J

Jabotinsky, 159, 160
Jaczkowski, 274
Jakubowicz, 529, 530, 532
Janosowicz, 521
Janovski, 192
Jarszin, 492
Jasinowski, 211
Jaworski, 318, 320, 321
Jermus, 69, 72, 194
Jevlogi, 109, 306
Jewlogi, 165, 212
JORPEST, 536
Jòsefowicz, 206

K

Kac, 311, 394
KAC, 536
Kacizne, 125
Kaczergynsky, 14
Kaczergyynski, 237
Kafka, 31, 32
Kaganowski, 521
Kahan, 369
Kaj, 514
Kajfer, 523
Kalb, 110
Kalejev, 305
Kalmanovitch, 233, 234, 236, 237
Kalmanowicz, 79, 82
Kalmans, 317
Kalrnis, 130
Kamanszteper, 194
Kamentz, 411

Kaminska, 145, 149, 351
Kaminski, 101
Kanfer, 46, 47, 101, 111, 130, 133, 178, 253
Kaplan, 30, 99, 105
Karlik, 351
Karp, 77, 116, 119, 191, 192, 193, 425, 509, 528
Kashemakher, 333
Kasriel, 318, 320
Katarinazh, 321
Kats, 465
Katsenelboygen, 18
Katz, 297, 438, 450, 451
Kazimierz the Great, 139, 313
Kejwan, 492
Kelberman, 48, 58, 126, 148, 190, 191, 194, 197, 319, 404, 405, 413, 468
Kelerer, 123
Kelner, 355, 356, 567, 576
Kener, 346
Kerszenberg, 543
Kesler, 319
Kesterman, 439
Kezys, 19
Khaskes, 319
Khelma, 18, 19
Khmelnytsky, 313
King Solomon, 31, 472
King Zygmunt August, 7
Kipnis, 27, 41, 42, 150, 348, 511
Kirer, 332
Kirzhner, 341, 342, 468
Kitei, 147
Klackin, 242
Klajn, 526
Klajner, 131, 156, 197
Klajnman, 514
Klatzkin, 211
Kleinhoiz, 439
Klerer, 34, 50, 126, 148, 197
Kleyner, 322, 325
Klunimus, 289
Koc, 375, 387
Kodnzajer, 123
Kohen, 438
Kohn, 286, 288, 290, 514
Kolodny, 159
Komblit, 134
Kon, 348
Konfer, 125
Kopelman, 118, 121, 186
Korb, 553
Kore, 329
Korengeld, 72
Koricer, 24
Korn, 525, 526
Kornblit, 87, 125, 128, 247, 258, 463
Kornblum, 69, 142
Kornfeld, 127, 186, 193, 382
Kornzajer, 112, 117, 119, 125
Kornzeyer, 348
Korski, 225
Kosman, 294, 297

Kot, 465
Kowal, 398
Koyfman, 134
Kozak, 330, 331
Kozhukh, 438, 448
Kraft, 438, 444, 447, 450, 451
Krajdman, 124, 570
Kramer, 527, 528
Kranc, 312
Kraszinski, 152
Kratka, 69, 80, 82, 191, 192, 193, 253
Kratke, 125, 127, 459, 469, 470
Kratki, 134
Kratko, 142, 194
Krauz, 55
Krieger, 444, 445
Krilewer, 566
Kritnicer, 272
Krokhmal, 207
Kroman, 530
Kronzajer, 554
Krotke, 470
Krotman, 351
Kruger, 438
Kruk, 125, 134, 438, 451
Kuliner, 154
Kunczicki, 550
Kuper, 48, 109, 111, 126, 190, 262, 288, 323, 325, 357, 414, 476, 479, 514, 522
Kupershtok, 316, 343
Kupersztak, 511
Kupersztok, 299, 528
Kuropatkin, 307
Kuszerman, 514
Kuznowicz, 156
Kwitko, 27

L

Laks, 111, 113, 126, 229, 404, 413, 414, 529
Landa, 69, 296
Landau, 97, 325
Landsman, 546
Lang, 69, 103, 144, 158, 350, 351, 487, 522, 533
Langs, 318
Larber, 111, 229
Las, 400, 431, 438
Lauer, 151, 153
Lauwaser, 72
Lazar, 85, 87, 91, 126, 174, 179, 192, 196, 198, 251, 258, 369
Lederer, 206, 207, 310, 505, 520
Lederman, 69, 77, 79, 131, 135, 158, 179, 395, 411, 413, 464
Lehrer, 444, 447, 450, 451
Leiner, 259
Leizerowicz, 209
Lemberger, 7, 18, 19, 41, 131, 322
Lerber, 162
Lerer, 20, 40, 101, 125, 128, 133, 150, 233, 234, 235, 236, 237, 259, 261, 286, 287, 288, 289, 332, 345, 350, 438, 479, 522
Lerman, 145
Levenshteyn, 471, 479
Levenshtyn, 17

Levetover, 319
Levin, 412, 540
Levita, 288
Levkovitsh, 10
Levy, 134
Lew, 72, 436
Lewensztajn, 84, 97, 113, 373, 378, 383, 385, 395
Lewensztein, 208
Lewensztejn, 252
Lewi, 205, 206
Lewin, 74, 77, 82, 147
Lewinsztajn, 351
Lewitska, 147
Leyeles, 355
Lias, 451
Liber, 151, 460, 521
Liberman, 161, 320, 396, 487
Libhober, 404, 405, 407, 408, 468
Libivner, 332, 333
Liebhober, 413, 418
Likhtensztajn, 348
Likhterman, 231
Likhtman, 526
Lilenblum, 210
Linczner, 350
Lindenboim, 99
Lindnboim, 523
Linherz, 272
Lipkowcz, 82
Lipkowicz, 135
Lipman, 101, 149, 151, 152, 203, 534
Lipps, 29
Lipshitz, 142
Lipszic, 69, 82
Lishchen, 147
Litvakov, 144
Loew, 38
Long, 230, 322, 514
Lorber, 113, 456, 514
Loszojnsztejn, 229
Lubartowski, 157
Luksenburg, 145, 147, 162, 172, 250, 252, 291, 351
Luksnburg, 494
Luksnburgs, 350
Lunski, 235
Luri, 322
Luria, 201, 287
Lustiger, 82, 85, 87, 89, 101, 194
Lustiker, 154, 161, 251
Lutzato, 206

M

Maged, 212
Mager, 103, 105, 106, 193, 194
Magier, 124
Mahalewicz, 108
Mahler, 125, 129, 150, 346
Majer, 52
Makhno, 269
Malach, 40, 111, 286
Malier, 295

Manat, 551
Mandel, 3, 258, 409, 521
Mandelbaum, 119, 376, 382
Mandelboim, 162, 212, 213, 514, 523
Mandelbojm, 96
Mandelstam, 210
Mandl, 69
Mandlbaum, 126, 295
Mandlboim, 522
Mantelmakher, 570
Mantszarsz, 120
MARDER, 536
Marglyus, 18, 19
Margolis, 400
Margulius, 205
Markish, 49, 125, 344
Markman, 524, 525, 526
Mastbaum, 49
Maurer, 55
Meches, 142
Medem, 133
Meirson, 152
Meis, 521
Melamed, 41, 150, 271, 294, 315, 325
Meler, 383, 465
Menacham, 294
Mendelbaum, 52, 79
Mendele, 31, 236, 323, 324, 325, 345, 351, 398, 516
Mendelson, 134, 142, 259
Mendlbaum, 109
Mendlzon, 125
Mernsztajn, 119
Metz, 492
Meyer, 96, 98, 99, 100, 102, 108, 139, 144, 145, 147, 259, 327, 343, 411, 438, 445, 446, 448, 451, 452, 465
Micflig, 118
Micfliker, 72, 404, 545
Mickewicz, 351
Mickiewicz, 152
Micpilker, 519
Mietek, 4, 187, 372, 383
Migdal, 438, 450
Milchtajch, 456
Milkhman, 424
Milner, 21, 22, 28, 29, 67, 95, 96, 98, 150, 155, 156, 158, 195, 201, 207, 208, 210, 211, 212, 239, 240, 241, 261, 305, 309, 479, 497, 500, 518, 519, 520, 521
Milsztajn, 126, 190, 522
Mincer, 77, 207, 208
Minkov, 355
Minkus, 147
Mirlas, 101, 105, 151, 229
Mitelman, 499
Mitsfliker, 468
Mitzfliker, 413, 466
Molyer, 323
Monczarsz, 494, 560, 562, 563, 582, 583
Mondelboim, 261
Mondszain, 213, 214
Monshteyn, 479
Montag, 205
Montefiori, 206

Monti, 492, 493, 494, 497, 500, 560, 561, 562, 563, 578, 582
Moraczewski, 167
Mordecai, 315
Morewski, 149
Morgenshtern, 139, 140, 141, 147
Morgenshterns, 139
Morgenstern, 94, 416
Morgenthau, 309
Morgnsztern, 125, 162
Mstyslavysh, 6
Murawicz, 519
Murowiec, 497, 498
Mylner, 19
Myzes, 19

N

Nachtman, 102
Najchaus, 157
Najhaus, 307
Najhojz, 131, 244, 259
Najman, 108, 413, 562, 563, 584
Najmark, 561, 562
Nakhaners, 318
Nakhman, 110, 207, 263, 522, 523
Nankin, 190, 191, 192, 193, 194, 277, 278
Nardou, 239
Natlich, 119
Naturman, 145, 173, 174, 177, 528, 535
Nayhoyz, 19
Nayman, 468
Naymark, 470
Neihaus, 89
Neiman, 404
Neimanowitz, 207
Neiner, 150
Nejdl, 72
Nekhe, 343
Nelkenbaum, 77
Nerlas, 101
Neshchizer, 257
Neszkhizer, 255
Neumann, 433
Nfichalenko, 131
Nfirlas, 103
Nicholas II, 165
Niclich, 124
Nikolai II, 305, 307
Nikolaievitch, 266
Nisbaum, 403, 404
Nisen, 126
Nisenbaum, 21, 34, 50, 53, 54, 55, 57, 58, 59, 60, 394, 395
Nisenboim, 413, 424, 546, 555, 566
Nisnboim, 194, 575
Nisnboym, 468
Nitslach, 135, 150
Nobel, 523
Nodel, 514, 522
Nodelman, 194
Note, 1, 63, 99, 101, 102, 103, 105, 106, 255, 256, 257, 529
Novokovytsh, 9
Noyekhs, 320

Nunison, 264
Nusenkorn, 194
Nutala, 39, 40

O

Oberlander, 439
Ochs, 3
Oder, 202, 460, 524, 525
Oks, 125, 276, 277, 373, 376, 438, 447, 448, 451, 520
Oksman, 402
Olickij, 150
Opatoshu, 47
Orenshtein, 147
Orensztajn, 106, 261, 336, 556
Orgun, 142, 147, 351
Orlean, 518
Ornitz, 263
Ornsztajn, 67
Orzeszkowa, 152
Ostropoler, 41
Ostropolier, 198

P

Paderewski, 309
Padskyi, 43
Paiper, 526
Paks, 133
Palewski, 208, 209, 382
Palievshi, 329
Palman, 99, 105, 106, 107, 494, 495, 497, 500, 555, 557, 558
Papir, 525
Parboek, 519
Parobek, 95, 99, 101, 102, 105, 106, 497, 504
Parobik, 99, 100
Pasternik, 465
Pat, 108
Pawliak, 186
Payas, 154
Perelstajn, 438
Peretz, 3, 27, 41, 49, 96, 98, 99, 104, 125, 145, 149, 150, 164, 168, 169, 170, 171, 172, 195, 196, 205, 206, 207, 236, 293, 294, 295, 296, 298, 300, 302, 303, 304, 315, 323, 344, 345, 349, 351, 473, 479, 508
Perles, 18
Perlmuter, 528, 544
Perlstein, 445
Pesakh, 42, 78, 93, 211, 250, 253, 279, 290, 294, 295, 296, 382, 494, 541
Peterzayl, 134, 346
Peterzeil, 186
Petrovich, 305
Pinchesowicz, 123
Pinieles, 317
Pinker, 578
Pinsker, 41, 204
Pinski, 172
Pitshke, 323, 359
Plioder, 320
Pludermakher, 345
Plus, 154

Podczacki, 159
Pokrivker, 320
Poliak, 492
Pomeranc, 50
Ponczak, 414
Pondrik, 332
Ponsczak, 3, 4, 409
Pontshak, 14
Prilicki, 234
Prilucki, 194, 234, 237
Prilutsky, 20
Pristarowa, 375, 387
Prostak, 81
Prus, 152

R

R'Rappoport, 19
Rabinowicz, 155, 161
Rabinowitz, 21
Rabinzon, 80
Rajchbind, 99
Rajf, 508, 509, 514
Rajfer, 91
Rajkhbind, 494, 582
Rajn, 95, 99, 101, 102, 105, 124
Rajzman, 101, 102, 105, 106
Ralfink, 405
Ralnik, 79
Rapaport, 206
Rapoport, 18
Raschendorf, 402, 404
Rasner, 194
Ravitch, 344
Raytses, 19
Reichman, 133
Reif, 99
Reifman, 206
Reiz, 438
Reizen, 233, 234, 237
Reymont, 152
Reyzen, 308, 345
Ribayzn, 134, 150, 356, 357
Ribeizen, 525, 550
Ribeizn, 126
Rikhszrajber, 260
Rikhter, 187, 576
Rikhtshrayber, 361
Rikhtszrejber, 549
Rikkh, 245, 247
Ringlblum, 346
Riszberg, 306
Robkowska, 111
Rogak, 158
Rohlfing, 55
Rojhszer, 542
Rojszer, 545
Rojtman, 75
Rojznblats, 350
Rokeach, 71
Rolnik, 131, 154, 414, 534
Romanovitsh, 6

Roosevelt, 221, 224, 309
Rosenbaum, 499
Rosenknopf, 531
Roshendorf, 407
Rota, 514
Roter, 438, 445
Rousseau, 207
Roytman, 325
Royzn, 346
Rozen, 79, 104
Rozen Family*, 81
Rozenberg, 325, 465
Rozenblat, 77, 111, 134, 145, 147, 180, 373, 376, 382, 533
Rozenblit, 113, 118
Rozenblum, 118, 229, 241, 554, 558
ROZENBLUM, 537
Rozenboim, 438, 498, 508, 515, 534
Rozenfeld, 112, 195, 228, 508, 509
Rozenknop, 385
Rozenknopf, 531, 532, 572, 573
Rozenkop, 102
Rozensztajn, 551
Rozmaryn, 570
Roznblat, 291
Roznblum, 460
Roznfeld, 149
Rubenshteyn, 343
Rubin, 21, 117
Rubins, 131
Rubinson, 191
Rukhwang, 522
Rutker, 522
Rybajzen, 253, 254

S

Safianleder, 531
Safir, 239
Sajkewycz, 438
Sajkowicz, 161
Sakharmarozhnik, 290
Sakular, 160
Sakuler, 82
Salan, 52, 394
Salon, 382
Salzman, 40
Samet, 101, 141, 146, 260, 261, 262, 549
Schafer, 55
Schiffer, 96
Schildberger, 32
Schlesinger, 55
Schlezinger, 406
Schor, 231
Schteinert, 406
Schwamberger, 427, 428
Schwartz, 315, 323, 410
Segalowicz, 49
Sekuler, 52
Selch, 405
Setcen, 549
Sforim, 31, 236, 516
Shafran, 101, 463, 465

Shaht, 99
Shakher, 320
Shalit, 99, 100
Shapiro, 108, 210
Shargel, 346, 363
Shechterson, 523
Shechterzon, 99, 100, 102, 106, 143
Shein, 438, 440, 448, 451
Shekhterzon, 323
Shelishtshekh, 329
Shelley, 352
Shener, 134
Sher, 102
Sheyfeles, 331, 332
Shifman, 138
Shimel, 99, 100, 106, 142, 147
Shindetski, 317, 318, 320
Shindler, 362, 363
Shishier, 8, 150
Shishler, 243
Shiyes, 98
Shkolnik, 9, 10
Shlakhtman, 469
Shlivke, 147
Shm, 18
Shmelke, 18
Shmeunovitsh, 10
Shnaper, 150
Shnaps, 316
Shnayder, 319, 324, 357
Shneider, 147
Shneiderman, 103
Shnobel, 99, 106
Sholem Aleichem, 30, 37, 65, 138, 145, 164, 177, 178, 199, 284, 345, 355
Shos, 316
Shperling, 95, 99, 101, 102, 104, 105, 106
Shpringer, 446
Shreibman, 139
Shreier, 214, 215
Shroyt, 322
Shtal, 79, 80
Shtam, 310, 320
Shteinberg, 101, 103, 105, 106, 107
Shtekn, 99, 101, 102, 104, 105, 106
Shtern, 49, 479, 485
Shtikendreyer, 320
Shtshupak, 468
Shumakher, 27
Shur, 287
Shuster, 333, 342
Shutkovski, 317
Shwartsman, 134
Shwartzber, 142
Shyper, 13
Siedlec, 211, 212, 549
Sigal, 482, 516
Sikorski, 495, 504
Simon, 1, 27, 213, 236
Sirkish, 311
Skladkowski, 186, 375
Skuler, 125

Slivkin, 237
Slonimski, 204, 207, 287
Slowacki, 152
Smolenskin, 211
Sobel, 58, 413
Sobol, 126, 138, 142, 319, 404, 452, 468
Sochaczewski, 259
Sokolow, 206, 207, 209, 210, 211, 239
Solman, 137
Sonto, 17
Sore, 286, 317, 320, 321, 322, 324, 334
Spajzman, 519
Spenser, 29
Spinoza, 21, 242
Springer, 439, 446
Stahl, 514
Stajn, 509
Stajnwurtzel, 438
Stal, 118, 120, 530
Stam, 276
Starzynski, 219
Staszic, 204
Stav, 325, 442
Staw, 496, 497, 519
Stechirz, 435
Steinwurzel, 445
Stol, 275, 276
Stoler, 269
Stoliar, 50
Stolier, 382
Streicher, 2
Stroj, 514
Strojl, 186
Syrkes, 17
Szacki, 242
Szafran, 110, 262, 263, 264, 487, 539
Szagel, 304
Szajdwaser, 373, 384
Szajer, 522
Szajewicz, 405
Szajn, 82, 186, 383
Szakher, 165
Szalit, 126
Szapira, 118
Szargel, 111, 112, 114, 117, 118, 123, 125, 126, 128, 137, 150, 186, 283, 478, 479, 481
Szczipak, 404
Szczupak, 413, 454, 477
Szebtl, 82
Szechterzon, 118
Szein, 159
Szekhter, 523
Szekhterson, 568
Szener, 158, 188
Szepel, 42
Szepeles, 272
Szer, 523
SZERER, 537
Szifman, 205, 539, 540
Szildkraut, 79
Szimel, 126, 179
Sziper, 112, 114, 168, 227, 228, 229, 230, 231, 479, 520

Sziszler, 64, 86, 87, 89, 128, 194, 310, 311, 489, 493, 494, 497, 500, 517, 535, 546, 547, 548, 549, 568, 570, 571
Szitlowski, 242
Szklacz, 124
Szlajer, 522
Szlechter, 383
Szmaragd, 298, 519
Szmern, 400
Sznajder, 351, 523, 524
Sznejderman, 272
Sznicer, 373, 378, 383
Sznobel, 545
Szocher, 96
Szor, 338
Szov, 544
Szpader, 53
Szpajzman, 570
Szpan, 402, 403
Szpejzman, 497, 498
Szperling, 101, 189, 190, 523
Szporer, 538
Szrajer, 519
Szreiber, 229
Szrojt, 117, 118, 120, 121, 123, 186, 358
Szroyt, 111
Sztajn, 487, 508, 509, 514, 515
SZTAJN, 537
Sztajnberg, 161, 193, 514, 539
SZTAJNBERG, 537
Sztajner, 522
Sztajnworcl, 35
Szteinberg, 539
Sztejn, 499
Sztekn, 190, 195
Szteper, 194
Sztern, 204
Szternberg, 514
Sztiglic, 522
Sztul, 131, 179, 187
Sztywelman, 295, 296, 297, 298, 300
Szuchmacher, 51, 52, 53
Szucmacher, 34
Szufl, 159
Szukhmakher, 570
Szulklaper, 522
Szulman, 123, 518
Szumlan, 514
Szundecki, 36
Szuster, 492
Szwarcblat, 56, 439
Szwarcman, 69, 152, 161, 187
Szwartzblat, 412
Szwarz, 3
Szweber, 97
Szwerdszarf, 554

T

Tabachowicz, 559
Tantshe, 403, 404, 424, 468
Tarbiner, 352
Tenenbaum, 82, 124, 378, 379, 382
Tenenboim, 98, 154, 161, 244, 275, 278, 405, 414, 438, 546
Tenenboum, 548
Tenenboym, 327, 341
Teper, 123
Terfitz, 180
Terner, 463, 464
Theimer, 55
Tikatsinki, 465
Tikatsinski, 463
Tish, 437, 439, 445, 446, 450
Tom, 99, 101, 102, 103, 105, 106, 142
Tomashefsky, 323
Tomaszewski, 186, 401
Tomosz, 201
Torn, 101, 126, 142, 351, 497, 518, 519
Tove, 321
Toymer, 407, 408
Trager, 322
Trajst, 545
Trajzt, 545
Trayst, 383
Traytls, 289
Treger, 289
Treuhaender, 448, 452
Trunk, 27, 150, 315, 348
Tsar Nicholas I, 342
Tseber, 360, 361
Tseichn, 142
Tselnik, 96, 98
Tsheslers, 323
Tshesner, 141, 469, 470
Tsicrelman, 147
Tsimennan, 137
Tsimerman, 96, 469
Tsitron, 319, 468, 471
Tuchman, 96, 98, 101, 103, 106
Tuchsznajder, 63, 119
Tudrus, 259, 351
Tukhman, 425, 509
Tukhshnayder, 316, 320
Turkeltaub, 310
Twerski, 91, 258
Tzale, 414
Tziberman, 438

U

Unger, 71, 245, 255
Urban, 55

V

Valberger, 363
Varman, 318
Varzoger, 320, 322
Vasertreger, 317
Vaynshenkerin, 324
Vayntraub, 320
Velcher, 4
Volf, 17, 18, 438, 445
Volzhin, 306
Vyshnytser, 17

W

Wadzager, 114
Wadzalowski, 158
Wadzilawski, 138
Wahrzorger, 454
Wajc, 126, 351
Wajchert, 126
Wajnrib, 476, 523, 524, 554
Wajnsztajn, 85, 106, 158, 174, 177, 196
Wajnsztok, 374, 375, 376, 377, 378, 380, 387
Wajs, 108
Wajsman, 114, 116, 121, 122, 134
Waksman, 320, 494
Walberger, 82, 197, 251, 376, 401
Walter, 401, 402, 403
Wardi, 511
Warhaftig, 307
Warman, 79, 208, 383
WARMAN, 536
Warszawski, 159, 526
Warzager, 117, 118, 123, 124
Warzoger, 62
Waserman, 59, 112, 118, 123, 125, 128, 275, 499, 528, 529, 554
Wasserman, 33, 125, 139, 142, 150, 228, 262, 314, 315, 320, 322, 344, 388, 479
Weber, 320
WEBER, 536
Weinreich, 233, 234, 237
Weissman, 135
Welberger, 414
Welczer, 372, 373, 383, 542
Weltch, 30
Weltsch, 29, 30, 32
Wert, 572, 574
Wetsztajn, 194
Wierzbicki, 131
Wikusz, 106
Wilder, 241, 242, 295, 296, 297, 298, 301, 302, 383, 522
Wilenka, 82, 122, 154
Wilhelm, 165, 317
Willenka, 161
Wilner, 108
Wilson, 309
Winer, 98, 109, 118, 241, 242, 243, 265, 266, 267, 268, 293, 295, 299, 303, 499, 508, 512, 513
WINER, 536
Winik, 77, 95, 96, 99, 101, 102, 103, 105, 106, 112, 113, 123, 125, 129, 130, 227, 322, 344, 350, 351, 411, 413, 414, 422, 492, 493, 494, 495, 497, 500, 579, 580, 581, 582, 583, 584
Wishnicer, 208
Wispianski, 351
Wlaberger, 382
Wlodower, 271, 378
Wodzilowski, 499
Wolberg, 446
Wolberger, 147, 415, 416, 439
Wolfson, 88, 118, 251, 271, 318
Wormser, 521
Woronowicz, 159
Worzoger, 150, 344, 347
Woslewitsker, 334
Wykusz, 352

Y

Yakubovitsh, 9
Yakubowski, 152, 153
Yankev, 325, 329, 330, 331, 332, 333, 334, 346, 355, 359, 363, 478, 516
Yavorski, 318
Yazefovytsh, 12
Yedvabnik, 523
Yelen, 438, 445, 451
Yermus, 80, 183, 191
Yeshaye, 325
Yitzhakl, 272
Yorfest, 499
Yosefowicz, 201
Yost, 206
Yoviovitsh, 9
Yoykenen, 466
Yozepovitsh, 19

Z

Zagan, 346
Zajdenfeld, 376
Zajdfodim, 127
Zajdradem, 52
Zajsn, 82
Zakhnovytsh, 9
Zaks, 20, 206, 210
Zalc, 514
Zalctreger, 126
Zalmen, 17, 343
Zaltstreger, 137
Zamelman, 508
Zamler, 273
Zaszczekno, 274
Zederboim, 205, 207
Zeidenberg, 167
Zeidfoden, 439
Zeifin, 154
Zeiger, 409, 410
Zeitlin, 27, 41, 150, 315, 516
Zelig, 18, 204, 207, 236, 237, 318, 542
Zemelman, 110, 261, 295, 509, 510, 556
Zerubavel, 183, 187, 188
Zheromski, 152
Zhitlowski, 297
Ziebert, 108
Ziegelboym, 360
Ziegfried, 439
Zigel, 147
Zigelboim, 45, 46, 49, 126, 167, 197, 216, 217, 218, 219, 220, 221, 222, 223, 224, 225, 226, 227, 373, 473, 475, 493, 494, 497, 500, 502, 503, 516, 520, 523
Ziglboim, 126
Ziglboym, 479
Zilber, 158, 161, 310, 400, 413, 468, 528
Zilberman, 108, 118, 438, 579
Zilbersztajn, 69, 487
Zimelman, 582

Zinger, 248, 249, 438
Zinkler, 274
Zisberg, 112, 126
Ziskind, 197
Zitrin, 411, 413, 414
Zonenszajn, 118
Zrubavel, 114, 116, 125

Zrubel, 346
Zygielboim, 145
Zygielbojm, 99, 100, 101, 102, 103, 104, 105, 106, 348, 349, 351
Zylberman, 522, 545
Zyv, 9

www.ingramcontent.com/pod-product-compliance
Lightning Source LLC
Chambersburg PA
CBHW081421160426
42814CB00039B/264